T0074398

Software System Design Methods

The Challenge of Advanced Computing Technology

NATO ASI Series

Advanced Science Institutes Series

A series presenting the results of activities sponsored by the NATO Science Committee, which aims at the dissemination of advanced scientific and technological knowledge, with a view to strengthening links between scientific communities.

The Series is published by an international board of publishers in conjunction with the NATO Scientific Affairs Division

A Life Sciences **B Physics**	Plenum Publishing Corporation London and New York
C Mathematical and Physical Sciences	D. Reidel Publishing Company Dordrecht, Boston and Lancaster
D Behavioural and Social Sciences **E Applied Sciences**	Martinus Nijhoff Publishers Boston, The Hague, Dordecht and Lancaster
F Computer and Systems Sciences **G Ecological Sciences** **H Cell Biology**	Springer-Verlag Berlin Heidelberg New York London Paris Tokyo

Series F: Computer and Systems Sciences Vol. 22

Software System Design Methods

The Challenge of Advanced Computing Technology

Edited by

Jozef K. Skwirzynski

Consultant on Theoretic Aspects, GEC Research Laboratories
Marconi Research Centre, West Hanningfield Road
Great Baddow, Chelmsford, Essex CM2 8HN, United Kingdom

Springer-Verlag
Berlin Heidelberg New York London Paris Tokyo
Published in cooperation with NATO Scientific Affairs Divison

Proceedings of the NATO Advanced Study Institute on The Challenge of Advanced Computing Technology to System Design Methods held at Grey College, University of Durham, U.K., July 29 – August 10, 1985

ISBN-13:978-3-642-82848-5 e-ISBN-13:978-3-642-82846-1
DOI: 10.1007/978-3-642-82846-1

Library of Congress Cataloging in Publication Data. NATO Advanced Study Institute on the Challenge of Advanced Computing Technology to System Design Methods (1985 : Gray College, University of Durham) The challenge of advanced computing technology to system design methods. (NATO ASI series. Series F, Computer and systems sciences ; vol. 22) "Published in cooperation with NATO Scientific Affairs Division." 1. Computer software—Development—Congresses. 2. Computers—Access control—Congresses. 3. System design–Congresses. I. Skwirzynski, J. K. II. North Atlantic Treaty Organization. Scientific Affairs Division. III. Title. IV. Series: NATO ASI series. Series F, Computer and system sciences ; no. 22.
QA76.76.D47N37 1985 005 86-17697
ISBN-13:978-3-642-82848-5 (U.S.)

Softcover reprint of the hardcover 1st edition 1986

2145/3140-543210

Acknowledgement

The editor wishes to express his appreciation to the following members of NATO's Scientific Affairs Division for their support and cooperation, without which the Advanced Study Institute would not have been possible:

Professor Henry Durand
Dr. Mario di Lullo
Dr. Craig Sinclair

The Institute was also supported by:

National Science Foundation – USA

European Research Office of the US Army – UK

European Office of Aerospace Research & Development, US Air Force – UK

GEC Research Laboratories – UK
Special thanks are due to its Managing Director, Dr. J.C. Williams, for granting the Editor permission to undertake the time-consuming organisation of the Institute, and to prepare this volume.

Preface

In this volume we present the full proceedings of a NATO Advanced Study Institute (ASI) on the theme of the challenge of advanced computing technology to system design methods. This is in fact the second ASI organised by myself and my colleagues in the field of systems reliability; the first was about Electronic Systems Effectiveness and Life Cycle Costing, and the proceedings were published by the same publisher in 1983, as "Series F (Computer and System Sciences, No. 3)".

The first part of the present proceedings concentrates on the development of low-fault and fault-tolerant software. In organising this session I was greatly helped by *Mr. John Musa* and *Professor V.R. Basili*. The latter and *Dr. R.W. Selby* open our text with their interesting approach to the problem of data collection and of observation sampling for statistical analysis of software development, software testing strategies and error analysis. The problem of clean-room software development is also considered. Next *Professor B. Randell* discusses recursively structured fault-tolerant distributed computer systems, and bases his approach on a UNIX system example. His aim is to establish that a distributed system should be functionally equivalent to an individual computing system. *Dr. L.F. Pau* considers knowledge engineering techniques applied to fault detection, test generation and maintenance of software. This is illustrated by a variety of examples, such as electronic failure detection, control system testing, analysis of intermittent failures, false alarm reduction and others. Following this *Mr. M. Dyer* discusses software development under statistical quality control, which should provide software management visibility into the development process, and the opportunity to introduce process changes to enhance product quality. This first part of our proceedings is closed with the paper by *Dr. G.G. Weber* on life time distributions for coherent systems, particularly with the help of fault tree analysis, whereby it can be shown that a system's life time distribution can be obtained as a function of the life time distributions of its components.

Then follows an interesting panel discussion on SAFETY ANALYSIS OF COMPUTER PROGRAMS USING FAULT TREES, organised and chaired by *Dr. G.G. Weber*. He begins with an introduction of the Fault Tree Analysis (FTA), showing as well instructive examples how to use it in practice. Then *Professor Nancy Leveson* continues with this matter, advocating as well the use of Petri nets. *Dr. Paul Harter* concentrates on formal methods in software programming, and claims that to know them is to love them. A discussion then ensues on various aspects of these techniques and of meanings of some of its terminology. For instance, many people argue what is meant by "complete" specifications. Next *Mr. Norman Harris* discusses the fundamental concepts of probability, possibility and causality, recalling the work of Boole and others. The remaining discussion is on various aspects of software quality, in particular on the problem of redundancy in coding.

The second part of our studies is concerned with the very relevant issue of the human factor in development and use of software. In the organisation of this session I was greatly helped by *Dr. B. Curtis*, who opens this part of the proceedings with his account of the psychological research on software development. He claims that data on programming productivity collected both in laboratory experiments and on actual projects indicate that individual differences in skills among programmers are still the largest factor affecting productivity in software development. His model psychological study can be condensed into six psychological paradigms: individual differences, group behaviour, organisational behaviour, human factors, cognitive ergonomics, and cognitive science. All these are considered and exemplified. Next, *Professor G. Fischer* discusses the passage from interactive to intelligent systems. His claim is that knowledge-based systems with qualitatively new human-computer communication capabilities are one of the most promising ways to create intelligent systems, and that this can be achieved by dedicating a large fraction of computational power of the machine to sophisticated user support systems. The third paper in this section is by *Dr. T.R.G. Green* who discusses the problem of design and of use of programming languages. He concentrates on the psychological processes of using programming languages, stressing particularly the requirements of language design and of environmental support.

This section of our proceedings closes with a complete, almost 'verbatim' reproduction of panel discussion, chaired by *Dr. B. Curtis*, under the challenging title: WILL ARTIFICIAL INTELLIGENCE MAKE HUMAN FACTORS OBSOLETE? The generally agreed answer to this question was: NO! *Professor G. Fischer* argues that there are two goals for the artificial intelligence research, namely to replace human beings by machines in situations where the latter can do particular things better, and to augment, or amplify, the human intelligence to allow us to do things with the assistance of computers, which we could not do without them. *Dr. T.R.G. Green* considers the present status of design technology of editor and interface details, and finds these poor at present, illustrating this with many interesting examples. He stresses that artificial intelligence cannot replace human creativity, though the latter has many difficult tasks ahead. *Mr. J. Watson* considers inadequacies of our knowledge of cognitive psychology, and relates this to the human tendency of not optimising things, but just trying to make them good enough. He produces details of his work on a task: REDUCING HUMAN ERROR IN PROCESS OPERATION. *Dr. B. Curtis* demonstrates an example of an INTELLIGENT USER INTERFACE MANAGEMENT SYSTEM, used in situations where safety can be assured only if systems take over functions that go below the response time of a human being. Then general discussion ensues, raising such problems as the role of speech recognition with artificial intelligence, difficulties of defining precisely the task of this science, and its goals, and others.

The third and central part of this volume deals with the development and status of empirical/statistical reliability models for software and with their relation to reality. This part of our programme was organised with the help of *Professor Bev Littlewood* and *Mr. John Musa*. The latter presents software reliability models which are based on execution time, using sets of failure data from a varied group of software projects. The main tools in his method are the basic and logarithmic Poisson execution time models, which are compared with a number of other published models. Then *Professor Bev Littlewood* considers the whole problem of predicting reliability of software projects and relates the present status of the situation, where we have now up to forty models, each claiming to be good, and this has resulted in the so-called 'model war'. He points out the way towards more accurate predictions via models which learn from past successes and failures. *Mr. Tony Bendell* utilises exploratory data analysis for assessment and prediction of software reliability. He lays emphasis on searching all the available data for patterns in failure types in order to use these in his time series analysis method. *Dr. Larry Crow*, the specialist on reliability growth models, this time concentrates on software systems and also discusses failure patterns, as they appear, using an elegant analytic technique. Next, *Dr. Harry Ascher* utilises regression techniques for matching models to the real world. He uses the principles of Cox's proportional hazards model to isolate the operational stresses which most affect reliability, and tries to quantify their effects. *Mr. Chris Dale* considers the important problem of measuring and modelling software reliability for systems with high reliability requirements, where its need is motivated by safety considerations. He discusses practical consequences of failures under these conditions and advocates further research in this field. *Ms. Gillian Frewin* discusses the process and design considerations as they affect the number, nature and disclosure of software faults. She offers comparison methods between products, in terms of their faultiness, their disposition to reveal faults as failures, and the likelihood that failures will be traceable and remediable.

At this stage we enlarge our subject, including not just software, but whole computer systems. *Professor Hani Doss* presents a theoretical method for estimating jointly system and component life-length distributions, using the approach of mutual censorship, and testing this method by Monte Carlo techniques. *Professor Ali Riza Kaylan* concentrates on computer systems, rather than on software alone, and offers a methodology for statistical design of experiments to aid a computer performance analyst. He concludes that the work in this important field is still in its infancy. *Dr. Peter Kubat* considers reliability assessment for communication and computer networks. He provides a simple analytic model and demonstrates its application to selected cases.

The last two papers in this section deal with special yet important subjects. Thus *Professor F. L. H. M. Stumpers* gives us an extensive presentation of computers of the fifth generation and of their role in communications. He sets this in a historical context and provides well agreed directions for future development and research. Finally, *Mr. Norman Harris* presents to us an extensive and challenging discussion on the rationale of reliability prediction in a very general context.

The next part of the proceedings concerns another prediction technique, namely that of the cost of software projects. This session was organised with the help of *Dr. Gerry McNichols*. He starts with an account of needs for cost assessment and claims that this should be the first step in a cost-effective design of a computer-based system. His guiding tenets are that to be efficient means that you are "doing things right", and to be effective means that you are "doing right things". The second paper is by *Mr. T. Capers Jones*, who presents a short account of steps towards establishing normal rules for software cost, schedule, and productivity estimating. His argument is that, whereas this predicting technique has been subject to wide variations and large errors, this has been caused by the lack of standard definitions for dealing with main cost-driving factors. He lists these and argues for their acceptance. Then *Mr. Bernard de Neumann* discusses the contrast of impinging economic considerations of life cycle costing and of decision analysis for software reliant products, which include VLSI, VHPIC, etc.

Next follow two panel discussions on this subject. The first was organised by *Dr. Gerry McNichols* and concentrated on COMPARISON OF EVALUATION METHODS OF COST ASSESSMENT IN COMPUTING. The main presentation was by *Mr. Elmer R. Bryan* of the General Electric Company in the USA. He provides us with a thorough discussion of existing methods and with difficulties of collecting data for proper cost evaluation; in fact he proposes several well-defined instruction sets for that purpose. The second panel discussion was organised by the second speaker in this session, namely *Mr. T. Capers Jones*, on techniques and rules for SOFTWARE COST ESTIMATING. In this discussion there was a long argument on the validity of calculating number of lines, of number of function points for predicting the main driving factor to the cost of a project, and a similar argument arose on the nature and definition of the concept of software complexity. Here we have also two similar, yet independently developed structures of software development life cycle, presented by *Major A. L. Lake* and *Mr. Alan Wingrove*. This was the terminal discussion in our Institute, and in it we have interesting general comments on this Institute by *Mr. John Musa* and by *Dr. Bill Curtis*.

Now we come to the last, and very important part of our proceedings, concerned with security, safety, privacy and integrity in developing and using computer communication and computer data storage and retrieval. It was organised by *Professor Rein Turn* who opens this part with his paper on security, privacy, safety and resilience in computing. He claims that, whereas traditional computer system design requirements, such as high performance and reliability, software portability, system interoperability and easy maintainability must be strengthened, new requirements are now necessary, such as system safety, system and data security, privacy protection for private information, and preservation of societal resiliency. His paper reviews the rationale of these new requirements and he discusses approaches taken for their implementation. *Professor Nancy G. Leveson* considers software hazard analysis techniques. First she presents the method for software fault tree analysis, a technique well developed for hardware systems, and only recently expanded for applications to software. Then she describes the use of Petri net models, a new application for testing software. Finally, *Mr. Donald W. Davies* discusses the problem of data security. He first summarises the reasons for threats and vulnerabilities of information systems, and then goes on to a thorough discussion of the present status of encryption techniques, their strengths, weaknesses and their applications.

This part finishes with a panel discussion on HUMAN BEINGS AS THE SOURCE OF PROBLEMS, CONCERNS AND PROTECTION NEEDS, e.g. COMPUTER CRIME, organised by *Professor Rein Turn.* First *Major A.L. Lake* discusses the problems associated with weaknesses of project management in understanding the nature of tasks. Then *Mr. Glenn Karpel* provides a humorous yet valid critique of misunderstandings arising during the specification stage of a project, in communication between a contractor and a producer. *Ms. Sheila Brand* gives us an interesting overview of the 'hacking' situation in the USA, and the lack of understanding of its dangers among managers and lawyers. *Dr. Dennis Heimbinger* relates this situation from the point of view of young and clever computer science students. A lively discussion ensues on relative merits of methods used to understand and to combat this situation in the USA and in the UK.

The proceedings close with a short summary of a panel discussion on WOMEN IN INFORMATION SCIENCE, organised by *Mrs. Eileen Jones*, who has summarised its arguments, since we have not reproduced it in the ususal 'verbatim' fashion at the request of the majority of speakers (!?). Most likely the subject was too controversial.

It is hoped that this volume will be of interest to anyone who wishes to be acquainted with recent trends in computer technology, in the status of artificial intelligence, and other related matters. We may follow this Institute with another one in 1988, concentrating this time on the problem of designing and operating dependable embedded-computer systems, and we shall also have a session on the advances of artificial intelligence in the period 1985–1988.

It took me two years to prepare this Institute, and this could not have been done without the help and advice of my colleagues: Mr. Bernard de Neumann, Mr. John Musa, Professor Bev Littlewood, Dr. Bill Curtis, and Professor Rein Turn. It is my privilege now to thank them for their counsel, which ensured a coherent yet wide subject matter of this Institute.

I would also thank my colleague, Mr. F.P. Coakley, who has organised the on-tape reproduction of our panel discussions, so that I could reproduce them here.

My assistant at this Institute was Mr. Barry Stuart, one of my bridge partners, who did an excellent job manning our office and settling all accounts.

Finally, I wish to thank Dr. John Williams, the Managing Director of our Laboratory, who has allowed me to organise this venture.

Great Baddow, February 1986 *J.K. Skwirzynski*

Table of Contents

Part 1. The Development of Low-Fault and Fault-Tolerant Software
Organised by John Musa and Victor R. Basili

Four Applications of Software Data Collection and Analysis Methodology
Victor R. Basili, Richard W. Selby, Jr. 3

Recursively Structured Fault-Tolerant Distributed Computing Systems
B. Randell 35

Knowledge Engineering Techniques Applied to Fault Detection Test Generation and Maintenance
L.F. Pau 53

Software Development Under Statistical Quality Control
M. Dyer 81

Life Time Distributions for Coherent Systems
G.G. Weber 95

Panel Discussion on Safety Analysis of Computer Programs Using Fault Trees 123

Part 2. Human Factors in Development and Use of Software
Organised by Bill Curtis

Psychological Research on Software Development
Bill Curtis 155

From Interactive to Intelligent System
Gerhard Fischer 185

Design and Use of Programming Languages
T.R.G. Green 213

Panel Discussion on Will Artificial Intelligence Make Human Factors Obsolete? 243

Part 3. The Development and Status of Empirical/Statistical Reliability Models for Software and Their Relation to Reality
Organised by Bev Littlewood and John Musa

Application of Basic and Logarithmic Poisson Execution Time Models in Software Reliability Measurement
John D. Musa, Kazuhira Okumoto 275

Tools for the Analysis of the Accuracy of Software Reliability Predictions
B. Littlewood, A.A. Abdel Ghaly, P.Y. Chan 299

The Use of Exploratory Data Analysis Techniques for Software Reliability Assessment and Prediction
Tony Bendell . . . 337

Failure Patterns and Reliability Growth Potential for Software Systems
Larry H. Crow . . . 353

The Use of Regression Techniques for Matching Reliability Models to the Real World
Harold Ascher . . . 365

The Assessment of Software Reliability for Systems with High Reliability Requirements
Chris Dale . . . 379

Process and Design Considerations as They Affect the Number, Nature and Disclosure of Software Faults
Gillian Frewin . . . 399

Assessing System Reliability Using Censoring Methodology
Hani Doss, Steven Freitag, Frank Proschan . . . 423

Statistical Design of Experiments for Computer Performance Evaluation
Ali Riza Kaylan . . . 439

Reliability Analysis for Integrated Voice/Data Networks
Peter Kubat . . . 463

Computers of the Fifth Generation and Their Role in Communications
F. L. H. M. Stumpers . . . 475

The Rationale of Reliability Prediction
L. N. Harris . . . 491

Part 4. The Economics of Computing and Methods of Cost Assessment

Organised by Gerry McNichols

Needs Assessment: The First Step in a Cost-Effective Design of a Computer-Based System
Gerald R. McNichols, Gary L. Sorrell . . . 539

Steps Toward Establishing Normal Rules for Software Cost, Schedule, and Productivity Estimating
T. Capers Jones . . . 567

The Economics of Software
Bernard de Neumann . . . 577

Panel Discussion on Comparison of Evaluation Methods of Cost Assessment in Computing . . . 587

Panel Discussion on Software Cost Estimating . . . 619

Part 5. Security, Safety, Privacy and Integrity in Developing and in Using Computer Communication and Computer Data Storage and Retrieval

Organised by Rein Turn

Security, Privacy, Safety and Resiliency in Computation
Rein Turn . . . 653

Software Hazard Analysis Techniques
Nancy G. Leveson 681

Data Security
D. W. Davies 701

Panel Discussion on Human Beings as the Source of Problems, Concerns and Protection Needs, e. g. Computer Crime 721

Summary of Panel Discussion on Women in Information Science 739

List of Delegates 743

Part 1

The Development of Low-Fault and Fault-Tolerant Software

Organised by John Musa and Victor R. Basili

FOUR APPLICATIONS OF A SOFTWARE DATA COLLECTION AND ANALYSIS METHODOLOGY

Victor R. Basili [1] and Richard W. Selby, Jr. [2]

[1] Department of Computer Science, University of Maryland, College Park, MD 20742, USA
[2] Department of Information and Computer Science, University of California, Irvine, CA 92717, USA; was with the Department of Computer Science, University of Maryland, College Park, MD 20742, USA

ABSTRACT

The evaluation of software technologies suffers because of the lack of quantitative assessment of their effect on software development and modification. A seven-step data collection and analysis methodology couples software technology evaluation with software measurement. Four in-depth applications of the methodology are presented. The four studies represent each of the general categories of analyses on the software product and development process: 1) blocked subject-project studies, 2) replicated project studies, 3) multi-project variation studies, and 4) single project studies. The four applications are in the areas of, respectively, 1) software testing strategies, 2) Cleanroom software development, 3) characteristic software metric sets, and 4) software error analysis.

1. Introduction

Software management decisions and research need to be based on sound analysis and criteria. However, it seems that many decisions and issues are resolved by inexact means and seasoned judgment, without the support of appropriate data and analysis. Problem formulation coupled with the collection and analysis of appropriate data is pivotal to any management, control, or quality improvement process, and this awareness motivates our investigation of the analysis processes used in software research and management. Our objectives for this work, which updates [14], include 1) structuring the process of analyzing software technologies, 2) investigating particular goals and questions in software development and modification, 3) characterizing

NATO ASI Series, Vol. F22
Software System Design Methods. Edited by J.K. Skwirzynski

the use of quantitative methods in analysis of software, and 4) identifying problem areas of data collection and analysis in software research and management.

Section 2 outlines a seven-step methodology for data collection and analysis. Section 3 discusses coupling the formulation of goals and questions with quantitative analysis methods. The application of the data collection and analysis paradigm in four empirical studies is presented in Section 4. Section 5 identifies several problem areas of data collection and analysis in software research and management. Section 6 presents a summary of this paper.

2. Methodology for Data Collection and Analysis

Several techniques and ideas have been proposed to improve the software development process and the delivered product. There is little hard evidence, however, of which methods actually contribute to quality in software development and modification. As the software field emerges, the need for understanding the important factors in software production continues to grow. The evaluation of software technologies suffers because of the lack of quantitative assessment of their effect on software development and modification.

This work supports the philosophy of coupling methodology with measurement. That is, tying the processes of software methodology use and evaluation together with software measurement. The assessment of factors that affect software development and modification is then grounded in appropriate measurement, data analysis, and result interpretation. This section describes a quantitatively based approach to evaluating software technologies. The formulation of problem statements in terms of goal/question hierarchies is linked with measurable attributes and quantitative analysis methods. These frameworks of goals and questions are intended to outline the potential effect a software technology has on aspects of cost and quality.

The analysis methodology described provides a framework for data collection, analysis, and quantitative evaluation of software technologies. The paradigm identifies the aspects of a well-run analysis and is intended to be applied in different types of problem analysis from a variety of problem domains. The methodology presented serves not only as a problem formulation and analysis paradigm, but also suggests a scheme to characterize analyses of software development and modification. The use of the paradigm highlights several problem areas of data collection and analysis in software research and management.

The methodology described for data collection and analysis has been applied in a variety of problem domains and has been quite useful. The methodology consists of seven steps that are listed below and discussed in detail in the following paragraphs (see also [14, 16]). 1) Formulate the goals of the data collection and analysis. 2) Develop a list of specific questions of interest. 3) Establish appropriate metrics and data categories. 4) Plan the layout of the investigation, experimental design, and statistical analysis. 5) Design and test the data collection forms or automated collection scheme. 6) Perform the investigation concurrently with data collection and validation. 7) Analyze and interpret the data in terms of the goal/question framework.

A first step in a management or research process is to define a set of goals. Each goal is then refined into a set of sub-goals that will contribute to reaching that goal. This refinement process continues until specific research questions and hypotheses have been formulated. Associated with each question are the data categories and particular metrics that will be needed in order to answer that question. The integration of these first three steps in a goal/question/metric hierarchy (see Figure 1) expresses the purpose of an analysis, defines the data that needs to be collected, and provides a context in which to interpret the data.

In order to address these research questions, investigators undertake several types of analyses. Through these analyses, they attempt to substantially increase their knowledge and understanding of the various aspects of the questions. The analysis process is then the basis for resolving the research questions and for pursuing the various goals. Before actually collecting the data, the data analysis techniques to be used are planned. The appropriate analysis methods may require an al-

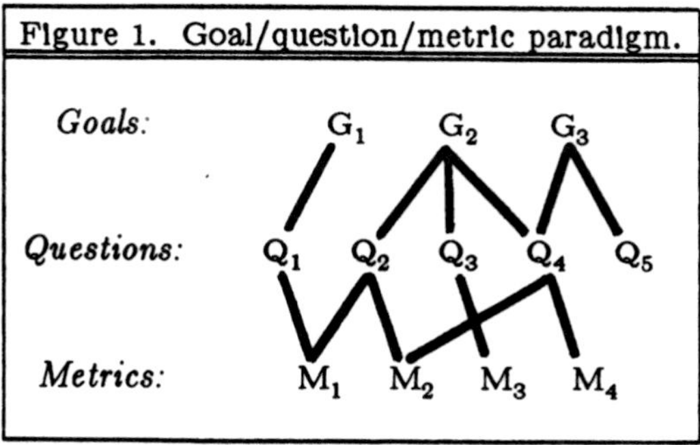

Figure 1. Goal/question/metric paradigm.

ternate layout of the investigation or additional pieces of data to be collected. A well planned investigation facilitates the interpretation of the data and generally increases the usefulness of the results.

Once it is determined which data should be gathered, the investigators design and test the collection method. They determine the information that can be automatically monitored, and customize data collection forms to the particular environment. After all the planning has occurred, the data collection is performed concurrently with the investigation and is accompanied by suitable data validity checks.

As soon as the data have been validated, the investigators do preliminary data analysis and screening using scatter plots and histograms. After fulfilling the proper assumptions, they apply the appropriate statistical and analytical methods. The statistical results are then organized and interpreted with respect to the goal/question framework. More information is gathered as the analysis process continues, with the goals being updated and the whole cycle progressing.

3. Coupling Goals With Analysis Methods

Several of the steps in the above data collection and analysis methodology interrelate with one another. The structure of the goals and questions should be coupled with the methods proposed to analyze the data. The particular questions should be formulated to be easily supported by analysis techniques. In addition, questions should consider attributes that are measurable. Most analyses make some result statement (or set of statements) with a given precision about the effect of a factor over a certain domain of objects. Considering the form of analysis result statements will assist the formation of goals and questions for an investigation, and will make the statistical results more readily correspond to the goals and questions.

3.1. Forms of Result Statements

Consider a question in an investigation phrased as "For objects in the domain **D**, does factor **F** have effect **S**?". The corresponding result statement could be "Analysis **A** showed that for objects in the domain **D**, factor **F** had effect **S** with certainty **P**.". In particular, a question could read "For novice programmers doing unit testing, does functional testing uncover more faults than does structural testing?". An appropriate response from an analysis may then be "In a blocked subject-project study of novice programmers doing unit testing, functional testing uncovered more faults than did structural testing ($\alpha < .05$).".

Result statements on the effects of factors have varying strengths, but usually are either characteristic, evaluative, predictive, or directive. Characteristic statements are the weakest. They describe how the objects in the domain have changed as a result of the factor. E.g., "A blocked subject-project study of novice programmers doing unit testing showed that using code reading detected and removed more logic faults than computation faults ($\alpha < .05$)." Evaluative statements associate the changes in the objects with a value, usually on some scale of goodness or improvement. E.g., "A blocked subject-project study of novice programmers doing unit testing showed that using code reading detected and removed more of the expensive faults to correct than did functional testing ($\alpha < .05$)." Predictive statements are a stronger statement type. They describe how objects in the domain *will* change if subjected to a factor. E.g., "A blocked subject-project study showed that for novice programmers doing unit testing, the use of code reading *will* detect and remove more logic faults than computation faults ($\alpha < .05$)." Directive statements are the strongest type. They foretell the value of the effect of applying a factor to objects in the domain. E.g., "A blocked subject-project study showed that for novice programmers doing unit testing, the use of code reading *will* detect and remove more of the expensive faults to correct than will functional testing ($\alpha < .05$)." The analysis process then consists of an investigative procedure to achieve the result statements of the desired strength and precision after considering the nature of the factors and domains involved.

Given any factor, researchers would like to make as strong a statement of as high a precision about the factor's effect in as large a domain as possible. Unfortunately, as the statement applies to an increasingly large domain, the strength of the statement or the precision with which we can make it may decrease. In order for analyses to produce useful statements about factors in large domains, the particular aspects of a factor and the domains of its application must be well understood and incorporated into the investigative scheme.

3.2. Analysis Categorization

Two important sub-domains that should be considered in the analysis of factors in software development and modification are the individuals applying the technology and what they are applying it to. These two sub-domains will loosely be referred to as the "subjects," a collection of (possibly multi-person) teams engaged in separate development efforts, and the "projects," a collection of separate problems or pieces of software to which a technology is applied. By examining the sizes of these two sub-domains ("scopes of evaluation") considered in an analysis, we obtain a general classification of analyses of software in the literature.

Figure 2 presents the four part analysis categorization scheme. Blocked subject-project studies examine the effect of possibly several technologies as they are applied by a set of subjects on a set of projects. If appropriately configured, this type of study enables comparison within the groups of technologies, subjects, and projects. In replicated project studies, a set of subjects may separately apply a technology (or maybe a set of technologies) to the same project or problem. Analyses of this type allow for comparison within the groups of subjects and technologies (if more than one used). A multi-project variation study examines the effect of one technology (or maybe a set of technologies) as applied by the same subject across several projects. These analyses support the comparison within groups of projects and technologies (if more than one used). A single project analysis involves the examination of one subject applying a technology on a single project. The analysis must partition the aspects within the particular project, technology, or subject for comparison purposes.

Result statements of all four types mentioned above can be derived from all these analysis classes. However, the statements will need to be qualified by the

Figure 2. Categorization of Analyses of Software

#Teams per project	#Projects: one	#Projects: more than one
one	Single project	Multi-project variation
more than one	Replicated project	Blocked subject-project

domain from which they were obtained. Thus as the size of the sampled domain and the degree to which it represents other populations increase, the wider-reaching the conclusion.

The next section cites several software analyses from the literature and classifies them according to this scheme pictured in Figure 2. Segments of four examinations in different analysis categories will then be presented.

3.3. Analysis Classification and Related Work

Several investigators have published studies in the four general areas of blocked subject-project [17, 28, 29, 33, 36, 37, 38, 49, 55, 64, 70, 71], replicated project [4, 10, 21, 25, 34, 43, 44, 45, 46, 47, 52, 56, 60, 62, 63], multi-project variation [1, 3, 8, 11, 12, 18, 20, 22, 24, 66, 67, 68], and single project [2, 5, 9, 13, 15, 19, 32, 35, 54, 57]. Study overviews appear in [23, 51, 59, 61].

4. Application of the Methodology

The following sections briefly describe four different types of studies in which the data collection and analysis methodology described above has been applied. The particular analyses are 1) a blocked subject-project study comparing software testing strategies, 2) a replicated project study characterizing the effect of using the Cleanroom software development approach, 3) a multi-project variation study determining a characteristic set of software cost and quality metrics, and 4) a single project study examining the errors that occurred in a medium-size software development project.

4.1. Software Testing Strategy Comparison

After first giving an overview of the study, this section describes the software testing techniques examined, the investigation goal/question framework, the experimental design, analysis, and major conclusions.

4.1.1. Overview and Major Results

To demonstrate that a particular program actually meets its specifications, professional software developers currently utilize several different testing methods. An empirical study comparing three of the more popular techniques (functional testing, structural testing, and code reading) has been conducted with 32 professional programmers as subjects. In a fractional factorial design, the individuals applied each of the three testing methods to three different programs containing faults. The formal statistical approach enables the distinction among differences in the testing techniques, while allowing for the effects of the different experience levels and programs. The major results from this study of junior, intermediate, and advanced programmers doing unit testing are the following. 1) Code readers detected more faults than did those using the other techniques, while functional testers detected more faults than did structural testers. 2) Code readers had a higher fault detection rate than did those using the other methods, while there was no difference between functional testers and structural testers. 3) The number of faults observed, fault detection rate, and total effort in detection depended on the type of software tested. 4) Subjects of intermediate and junior expertise were not different in number of faults found or fault detection rate, while subjects of advanced expertise found a greater number of faults than did the others, but were not different from the others in fault detection rate. 5) Code readers and functional testers both detected more omission faults and more control faults than did structural testers, while code readers detected more interface faults than did those using the other methods.

4.1.2. Testing Techniques

Figure 3 shows the different capabilities of the three software testing techniques of code reading, functional testing, and structural testing. In functional testing, which is a "black box" approach [41], a programmer constructs test data from the program's specification through methods such as equivalence partitioning and boundary value analysis [53]. The programmer then executes the program and contrasts

Figure 3. Capabilities of the testing methods.

	code reading	functional testing	structural testing
view program specification	X	X	X
view source code	X		X
execute program		X	X

its actual behavior with that indicated in the specification. In structural testing, which is a "white box" approach [40, 42], a programmer inspects the source code and then devises test cases based on the percentage of the program's statements executed (the "test set coverage") [65]. The structural tester then executes the program on the test cases and compares the program's behavior with its specification. In code reading by stepwise abstraction [48, 50], a person identifies prime subprograms in the software, determines their functions, and then composes these functions to determine a function for the entire program. The code reader then compares this derived function and the specifications (the intended function).

4.1.3. Investigation Goals

The goals of this study comprise four different aspects of software testing: fault detection effectiveness, fault detection cost, classes of faults detected, and effect of programmer expertise level. A framework of the goals and specific questions appears in Figure 4.

Figure 4. Structure of goals/subgoals/questions for testing experiment. (Each of these questions should be prefaced by "For junior, intermediate, and advanced programmers doing unit testing, ... ".)

I. Fault detection effectiveness
- A. Which of the testing techniques (code reading, functional testing, or structural testing) detects the greatest number of faults in the programs?
  1. Which of the techniques detects the greatest percentage of faults in the programs (the programs each contain a different number of faults)?
  2. Which of the techniques exposes the greatest number (or percentage) of program faults (faults that are observable but not necessarily reported)?
- B. Is the number (or percentage) of faults observed dependent on the type of software?

II. Fault detection cost
- A. Which of the testing techniques has the highest fault detection rate (number of faults detected per hour)?
- B. Which of the testing techniques requires the least amount of fault detection time?
- C. Is the fault detection rate dependent on the type of software?

III. Classes of faults detected
- A. Do the methods tend to capture different classes of faults?
- B. What classes of faults are observable but go unreported?

IV. Effect of programmer expertise level
- A. Does the performance of junior, intermediate, and advance programmers differ in any of the above goal categories?

4.1.4. Experimental Design

Admittedly, the goals stated here are quite ambitious. It is not implied that this experiment can definitively answer all of these questions. The intention, however, is to gain insights into their answers and into the merit and appropriateness of each of the techniques.

A fractional factorial experimental design was employed in the analysis [27]. There were three testing techniques, three programs containing faults, and three levels of programmer expertise. Each subject used each technique and tested each program, while not testing a given program more than once. The analysis of variance model included the two-way and three-way interactions among the main effects, and nested the random effect of subjects within programmer expertise.

The programs were representative of three different classes of software: a text formatter (also appeared in [52]), an abstract data type, and a database maintainer [38]. The programs had 169, 147, and 365 lines of high-level source code, respectively, and were a realistic size for unit testing. They had nine, seven, and twelve faults, respectively, which were intended to be representative of commonly occurring software faults [69].

The subjects were professional programmers from NASA Goddard and Computer Sciences Corporation, a major NASA contractor. They had an average of 10 years professional experience (SD = 5.7).

For a complete description of the programs, faults, subjects, experimental operation, and analysis see [17, 59].

4.1.5. Data Analysis

Segments of the data analysis and interpretation for two of the goal areas appear in the following sections. Figure 5 displays the number of faults in the programs detected by the techniques.

Figure 5.

Number of faults detected in the programs.

Key: code readers (C), functional testers (F), and structural testers (S).

```
            S
            S
            S
            S
            F
            F
         S  F
         S  F
         S  F     S
         S  F     S
         S  F     S  S
         S  F     F  S
         S  F  S  F  F
         S  F  S  F  F
      S  S  F  F  F  C
      S  S  F  F  F  C
      S  F  F  F  F  C
      S  F  F  F  C  C
   S  S  F  C  F  C  C
   S  S  C  C  C  C  C
   S  F  C  C  C  C  C
S  S  C  C  C  C  C  C
C  F  C  C  C  C  C  C  C
+--+--+--+--+--+--+--+--+--+
0  1  2  3  4  5  6  7  8  9
```

4.1.5.1. Fault Detection Effectiveness

The subjects applying code reading detected an average of 5.09 (SD = 1.92) faults per program, persons using functional testing found 4.47 (SD = 1.34), and those applying structural testing uncovered 3.25 (SD = 1.80); the subjects detected an overall average of 4.27 (SD = 1.86) faults per program. The overall F-test that the techniques detected the same number of faults (Question I.A) was rejected ($\alpha =$ .0001; the probability of Type I error is reported). Subjects using code reading detected 1.24 more faults per program than did subjects using either functional or structural testing ($\alpha<.0001$, 95% confidence interval 0.73 – 1.75). Subjects using functional testing detected 1.11 more faults per program than did those using structural testing ($\alpha<.0007$, 95% c.i. 0.52 – 1.70). Since the programs each had a different number of faults, an alternate interpretation compares the percentage of the programs' faults detected by the techniques (Question I.A.1). The techniques performed in the same order when percentages are compared: subjects applying code reading detected 16.0% more faults per program than did subjects using the other techniques (α<.0001, c.i. 9.9 – 22.1%), and subjects applying functional testing detected 11.2% more faults than did those using structural testing (α<.003, c.i. 4.1 – 18.3%). Thus comparing either the number or percentage of faults detected, individuals using code reading observed the most faults, persons applying functional testing found the second most, and those doing structural testing uncovered the fewest.

4.1.5.2. Fault Detection Cost

The subjects applying code reading detected faults at an average rate of 3.33 (SD = 3.42) faults per hour, persons using functional testing found faults at 1.84 (SD = 1.06) faults per hour, and those applying structural testing uncovered faults at a rate of 1.82 (SD = 1.24) faults per hour; the subjects detected faults at an overall average rate of 2.33 (SD = 2.28) faults per hour. The overall F-test that the techniques detected faults at the same rate (Question II.A) was rejected (α < .0014). Subjects using code reading detected 1.49 more faults per hour than did subjects using either functional or structural testing (α<.0003, c.i. 0.75 – 2.23). Subjects using functional and structural testing were not statistically different in fault detection rate (α>.05). The subjects spent an average of 2.75 (SD = 1.57) hours per program detecting faults. Comparing the total time spent in fault detection, the techniques were not statistically different (α>.05). Thus, subjects using code reading detected faults at a higher rate than did those applying functional or structural testing, while the total fault detection effort was not different among the methods.

4.1.6. Research Summary

The strategies of functional testing, structural testing, and code reading are compared in four different aspects of software testing: fault detection effectiveness, fault detection cost, classes of faults detected, and effect of programmer expertise level. The major results of this study appear in the earlier "Overview and Major Results" section.

Presented in this section are some fundamental features and results of an empirical study. The results given are from a sample of junior, intermediate, and advanced programmers applying the techniques to given programs with particular faults – the direct extrapolation of these findings to other testing environments is not implied. However, valuable insights into improving the effectiveness of software testing have been gained. For a complete presentation of the study, see [17, 59].

4.2. Cleanroom Development Approach Analysis

After first giving an overview of the study, this section describes the Cleanroom software development approach, the investigation goals, a replicated project study applying the Cleanroom approach, the analysis of its effect relative to a more traditional approach, and the conclusions.

4.2.1. Overview and Major Results

The Cleanroom software development approach is intended to produce highly reliable software by integrating formal methods for specification and design, complete off-line development, and statistically-based testing. In an empirical study, fifteen teams developed versions of the same software system (800 - 2300 source lines); ten teams applied Cleanroom, while five applied a more traditional approach. This analysis characterizes the effect of Cleanroom on the delivered product, the software development process, and the developers. The major results from this study of teams of novice and intermediate programmers building a small system are 1) most developers were able to effectively apply the techniques of Cleanroom; 2) the Cleanroom teams' products more completely met system requirements and had a higher percentage of successful test cases; 3) the source code developed using Cleanroom had more comments and less dense complexity; 4) the use of Cleanroom successfully modified development style; and 5) most Cleanroom developers indicated they would use the approach again.

4.2.2. Cleanroom Software Development

The need for highly reliable software and for discipline in the software development process motivates the Cleanroom software development approach. In addition to improving the control during development, this approach is intended to deliver a product that meets several quality aspects: a system that conforms with the requirements, a system with high operational reliability, and source code that is easily readable and modifiable.

The Federal Systems Division of IBM [30, 31] presents the Cleanroom software development method as a technical and organizational approach to developing software with certifiable reliability. The idea is to deny the entry of defects during the development of software, hence the term "Cleanroom." The focus of the method is imposing discipline on the development process by integrating formal methods for specification and design, complete off-line development, and statistically-based testing. With the intention that correctness is "designed" into the software rather then "tested" in, developers are not allowed to test their own programs. They focus on off-line review techniques, such as code reading, inspections, and walkthroughs, to assert the correctness of their system. Independent testers then simulate the operational environment of the product with functional testing, record observed failures, and determine an objective measure of system reliability.

4.2.3. Investigation Goals

Some intriguing aspects of the Cleanroom approach include 1) development without testing and debugging of programs, 2) independent program testing for quality assurance (rather than to find faults or to prove "correctness" [39]), and 3) certification of system reliability before product delivery. In order to understand the effects of Cleanroom, the goals of this investigation are to I) characterize the effect of Cleanroom on the delivered product, II) characterize the effect of Cleanroom on the software development process, and III) characterize the effect of Cleanroom on the developers. An example question under goal I would be "For teams of novice and intermediate programmers building a small system, does Cleanroom deliver a product more completely meeting its requirements than does a traditional development approach?". A complete framework of goals and questions for this study appears in [60].

4.2.4. Empirical Study Using Cleanroom

In order to pursue the above goals, an empirical study was executed comparing team projects developed using Cleanroom with those using a more conventional approach. Fifteen three-person teams each developed an approximately 1200 line electronic mail system over a six week period at the University of Maryland. The subjects had an average of 1.7 years professional experience. Ten three-person teams applied Cleanroom, while five applied a more traditional approach. The other aspects of the development were the same.

4.2.5. Data Analysis

Segments of the analysis and interpretation of the data collected in the study appear in the following sections, organized by the goal areas outlined earlier. The systems developed by the various teams ranged from 824 to 2264 source lines, from 410 to 999 executable statements, and from 18 to 67 procedures.

4.2.5.1. Characterization of the Effect on the Product Developed

Completeness of implementation was examined as one contrast among the operational properties of the systems delivered by the two groups (Question I.A.1). A measure of implementation completeness was calculated by partitioning the required system into sixteen logical functions (e.g., send mail to an individual, read a piece of mail, respond, add yourself to a mailing list, ...). Each function in an implementation was then assigned a value of two if it completely met its requirements, a value of one if it partially met them, or zero if it was inoperable. The total for each system was calculated; a maximum score of 32 was possible. Figure 6 displays this subjective measure of requirement conformance for the systems (Cleanroom teams in upper case; the significance levels for the Mann-Whitney statistics reported are the probability of Type I error in an one-tailed test). A first observation is that six of the ten Cleanroom teams built very close to the entire system. While not all of the Cleanroom teams performed equally well, a majority of them applied the approach effectively enough to develop nearly the whole product. More importantly, the Cleanroom teams met the requirements of the system more completely than did the non-Cleanroom teams.

Figure 6. Requirement conformance of the systems.

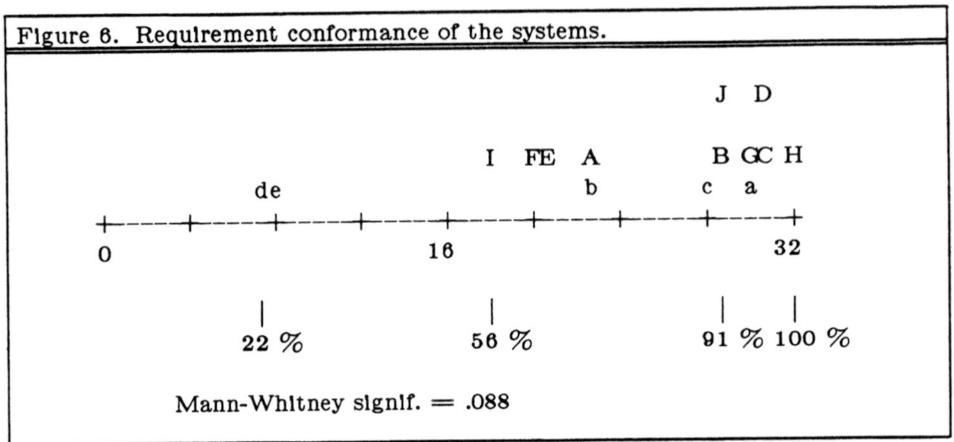

In summary of the effect on the product, Cleanroom developers delivered a product that 1) more completely met system requirements, 2) had a higher percentage of successful operationally-based test cases, and 3) had more comments and less dense complexity.

4.2.5.2. Characterization of the Effect on the Development Process

Schedule slippage continues to be a problem in software development. It would be interesting to see whether the Cleanroom teams demonstrated any more discipline by maintaining their original schedules (Question II.C). All of the teams from both groups planned four releases of their evolving system, except for team 'G' which planned five. At each delivery an independent party would operationally test the functions currently available in the system, according to the team's implementation plan. In Figure 7, we observe that all the teams using Cleanroom kept to their original schedules by making all scheduled deliveries.

Figure 7.
Number of system releases.

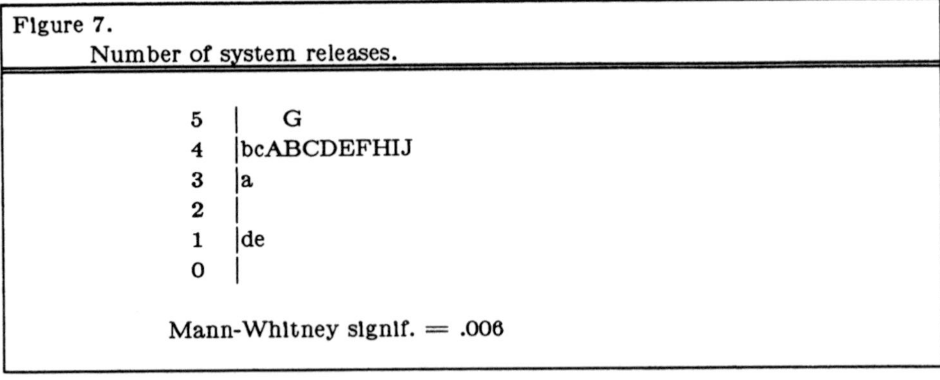

Summarizing the effect on the development process, Cleanroom developers 1) felt they more effectively applied off-line review techniques, while non-Cleanroom teams focused on functional testing; 2) spent less time on-line and used fewer computer resources; and 3) tended to make all their scheduled deliveries.

4.2.5.3. Characterization of the Effect on the Developers

The first question posed in this goal area is whether the individuals using Cleanroom missed the satisfaction of executing their own programs (Question III.A). Figure 8 presents the responses to a question included in the postdevelopment attitude survey on this issue. As might be expected, almost all the individuals missed some aspect of program execution. As might not be expected, however, this missing of program execution had no relation to several product quality measures.

Figure 8.
Breakdown of responses to the attitude survey question, "Did you miss the satisfaction of executing your own programs?".

13 – Yes, I missed the satisfaction of program execution.
11 – I somewhat missed the satisfaction of program execution.
4 – No, I did not miss the satisfaction of program execution.

In summary of the effect on the developers, most Cleanroom developers 1) modified their development style, 2) missed program execution, and 3) indicated they would use the approach again.

4.2.6. Research Summary

This section describes a study of "Cleanroom" software development – an approach intended to produce highly reliable software by integrating formal methods for specification and design, complete off-line development, and statistically-based testing. This is the first investigation known to the authors that applied Cleanroom and characterized its effect relative to a more traditional development approach. The major results of this study appear in the earlier "Overview and Major Results" section.

This empirical study is intended to advance the understanding of the relationship between introducing discipline into the development process (as in Cleanroom) and several aspects of product quality (conformance with requirements, high operational reliability, and easily modifiable source code). A more complete description of the application of the Cleanroom in the study, the data analysis, and the conclusions appears in [59, 60].

4.3. Characteristic Software Metric Set Study

After first giving an overview of the study, this section briefly describes a characteristic software metric set, the investigation goals, empirical study, and data analysis.

4.3.1. Overview

In software development and maintenance, several metrics have been proposed to predict product cost/quality and to capture distinct project aspects. Since both cost/quality goals and production environments differ, this study examines an approach for customizing a characteristic set of software metrics to an environment. The approach is applied in the Software Engineering Laboratory (SEL), a NASA Goddard production environment [6, 7, 26, 58]. The uses examined for a characteristic metric set include forecasting the effort for development, modification, and fault correction of modules based on historical data.

4.3.2. Characteristic Software Metric Sets

A characteristic software metric set is a concise collection of measures that capture distinct factors in a software development/maintenance environment. A characteristic metric set could be used to 1) characterize an environment, 2) compare an environment with others, 3) monitor current project status, or 4) forecast project outcome relative to past projects, when metrics in the set are available early in development.

4.3.3. Investigation Goals

The goals for this investigation are to I) develop an approach for customizing a set of measures to particular cost/quality goals in a particular environment, II) calculate the metric set for the NASA/S.E.L. environment, and III) examine the usability of the approach as a management tool. An example question under Goal III would be "In the NASA/S.E.L. environment of projects and programmers, does determining a characteristic metric set and using historical data enable one to predict which modules will be difficult to change?". A goal/question framework appears in [18, 59].

4.3.4. Empirical Study

A proposed approach for calculating a characteristic set consists of three steps: 1) formulate the goals and questions that represent cost/quality factors in an environment, 2) list all measures that capture information relating to the goals, and 3) condense the measures into a set capturing distinct factors (e.g., by using factor analysis). This approach has been applied to six projects from the NASA/S.E.L. environment consisting of 652 newly developed modules. The projects range from 51,000 to 112,000 lines of FORTRAN and from 6900 to 22,300 person-hours of development.

4.3.5. Data Analysis

The particular goals chosen for the NASA/S.E.L. environment are to analyze system development effort, system faults, and system modifications. A total of 49 candidate process and product metrics were examined. The use of principal factor analysis isolated the characteristic metric set for the NASA/S.E.L. environment: {source lines, fault correction effort per executable statement, design effort, code effort, number of I/O parameters, number of versions}.

4.3.6. Research Summary

This study investigates an approach for customizing a set of software metrics to an environment. A characteristic software metric set is intended to help support the effective management of software development and maintenance. The approach examined for building a characteristic metric set will be adaptable to different cost/quality goals and different environments. A more complete presentation of this study appears in [18].

4.4. Software Error Analysis

This section first gives an overview of the software error study, then describes the error classification schemes, investigation goals, software project examined, data analysis, and conclusions.

4.4.1. Overview and Major Results

Insights into the characterization and improvement of software development can be gained through analysis of the types of errors made during software projects. This study analyzes various relationships involving the errors occurring in one project from the NASA/SEL production environment. The major results from this study of a team of intermediate and advanced programmers building a medium-scale system are the following. 1) A majority of the errors were due to incorrect or misinterpreted functional specifications or requirements. 2) The larger a module was, the less error-prone it tended to be. 3) Errors contained in modified modules required more effort to correct than did those in new modules. 4) Although both new and modified modules had a high percentage of interface errors, new modules had a higher percentage of control errors, while modified modules had a higher percentage of data and initialization errors. 5) The error data reflects that the developers were involved in a new application with changing requirements.

4.4.2. Error Classification

Several classification and distribution schemes were applied to the errors observed during the project. Two abstract classification schemes characterize the types of software errors. One error categorization method separates errors of omission from errors of commission. A second error categorization scheme partitions software errors into the six classes of 1) initialization, 2) computation, 3) control, 4) interface, 5) data, and 6) cosmetic. A third approach distinguishes among errors based on the source of the error during development, e.g., incorrect or misinterpreted requirements, design error involving several modules, misunderstanding of the external environment, etc. An explanation of these classification schemes appears in [13]. These classification schemes are intended to distinguish among different reasons that programmers make errors in software development.

4.4.3. Investigation Goals

There are three goal areas in this investigation. I.) Characterize the frequency and distribution of errors that occurred during development. An example question would be "What are the sources of the errors that occur?". II.) Analyze the relationships between the frequency and distribution of errors and various environmental factors. An example question here would be "How does the reuse of existing design and code relate to the effort required for error correction?". III.) Interpret the results of the analysis relative to other software error studies. "Are the distributions of error types in this project similar to errors in projects from the same (SEL) environment?" would be an example question under this goal area. Each of the above questions should be prefaced by "When a team of intermediate and advanced programmers builds a medium-size software project, ... ".

4.4.4. Empirical Study

The software project analyzed in the study was developed in the Software Engineering Laboratory (SEL), a NASA Goddard production environment. The system developed was a general-purpose program for satellite planning studies and was approximately 90,000 lines of FORTRAN. The error data was collected over a period of 33 months, including the development phases of coding, testing, acceptance, and maintenance. The system represents a new application for the developers, even though it uses several algorithms similar to those in other SEL projects. Consequently, the system requirements kept growing and changing more than would be expected in a typical ground-support software project.

4.4.5. Data Analysis

Segments of the analysis and interpretation of the data collected in the study appear in the following sections, organized by the goal areas outlined earlier.

4.4.5.1. Characterize the Frequency and Distribution of Errors

In the system of 370 modules, there were a total of 215 errors found during the development, which were contained in 96 (26%) of the modules. Of the modules found to contain errors, 51% were newly developed modules and 49% were modified from previous projects. Figure 9 presents a distribution of the errors based on their source. Sixty five percent of the errors was attributed to incorrect or misinterpreted functional specifications or requirements. Two thirds of the functional specification errors were in modules modified from systems with different applications. Therefore, although these modules had the desired basic function, it appears that they were not well-enough specified to be reused under slightly different circumstances.

Figure 9. Distribution of Project Errors by Source.	
Error Source	%Total
Requirements incorrect or misinterpreted	16
Functional specification incorrect or misinterpreted	49
Design error involving several modules	5
Error in design or implementation of a single module	30
Misunderstanding of external environment	0
Error in the use of the programming language or compiler	0

4.4.5.2. Analyze the Relationships Between Errors and Environmental Factors

Although modifying modules from previous systems may reduce the amount of coding effort, developers need to consider the effort required to correct any errors in the modified modules. Figure 10 displays the distribution of effort required for error correction in both new and modified modules. Forty five percent of the errors required at least one day to correct. Of the errors needing at least one day to correct, a higher percentage were in modified modules (27% of total) as opposed to newly developed modules (18% of total). In general, errors occurring in newly developed modules needed less effort to correct than did those in modified modules.

4.4.5.3. Interpretation of the Errors Relative to Other Projects

Figure 11 compares the distribution of error sources in this project with another project developed in the SEL environment [69]. The other project shown is a typical SEL ground-support software project with a representative distribution of faults.

Figure 10. Distribution of Error Correction Effort for New and Modified Modules.			
Correction Effort	%New	%Modified	%Total
1 hour or less	21	15	36
1 hour to 1 day	11	8	19
1 day to 3 days	3	15	18
more than 3 days	15	12	27

The overall distributions of errors sources are not very similar. In the typical SEL project, the project requirements tend to be stable and the appropriate high-level designs are pretty well understood. Hence, the majority of errors are localized within single modules. In the current project examined, the frequent change of the system requirements is reflected in a higher proportion of errors associated with incorrect or misinterpreted requirements.

4.4.6. Research Summary

This section describes an analysis of the errors found during a medium-scale software project. The study is intended to increase the understanding of relationships among types of errors, environmental factors, and project characteristics. A more complete presentation of the error analysis in this software project appears in [13].

5. Problem Areas

From the use of the data collection and analysis methodology, we identify several problem areas in data collection and analysis in software research and management. 1) The process of formulating intuitive problems into precisely stated goals is a nontrivial task. The inherent difficulty in goal writing reflects the uncertainty of all aspects of quality in the software product and development process. 2)

Figure 11. Comparison of Error Source Distributions.

Error Source	Current Project (%)	Another SEL Project (%)
Requirements incorrect or misinterpreted	16	5
Functional specification incorrect or misinterpreted	49	3
Design error involving several modules	5	10
Error in design or implementation of a single module	30	72
Misunderstanding of external environment	0	1
Error in the use of the programming language or compiler	0	8
Other	0	1

Numerous software metrics have been proposed to measure distinct attributes of software. These metrics need to be validated to determine whether they actually capture what is intended. 3) The process of collecting accurate data is a continuing challenge. While there is increasing potential in automated collection schemes, the more common data collection forms are subject to incompleteness, inconsistency, and human error. 4) There have been a growing number of controlled experiments done to determine which factors contribute to software quality. In order for the results of these studies to apply to other environments, the samples (of programmers, programs, ...) must be of sufficient size and be representative of production environments. 5) These controlled studies are expensive to conduct. Both industry and academia must help support these efforts; e.g., academic researchers using subjects from industry. 6) There seems to be an interdependency among several factors that contribute to product and process quality. The use of several techniques together may be effective as a "critical mass," making the isolation of their individual effects difficult. 7) The methods of analysis must account for the high variation in individual performance. Without careful planning, the many-to-one differential among humans can taint experimental results. 8) Researchers have rarely been able to reproduce results across environments. In addition to the lack of consistent use of measures, every software development or modification environment seems to differ.

6. Summary

Problem formulation coupled with the collection and analysis of appropriate data is pivotal to any quality improvement process. This work investigates various problem analysis approaches that are relevant to software research and management. A seven-step data collection and analysis methodology was described that has been feasible and useful in a variety of problem domains. Aspects of the approach include the use of the goal/question/metric paradigm, and the need to couple proposed goals and questions with measurable attributes and appropriate analysis methods. We presented the goal structure, analysis, and preliminary conclusions for segments of four different types of studies in which the analysis methodology is applied: a blocked subject-project study comparing software testing strategies, a replicated project study characterizing the effect of using the Cleanroom software development approach, a multi-project variation study determining a characteristic set of software cost and quality metrics, and a single project study examining the errors that occurred in a medium-size software development project. In addition to exhibiting a research methodology and a spectrum of software analyses, these empirical studies are intended to advance the understanding of 1) the contribution of various software testing strategies to the software development process and to one another; 2) the relationship between introducing discipline into the development process and several aspects of product quality (conformance with requirements, high operational reliability, and easily modifiable source code); 3) the use of software metrics to characterize environments and predict project cost/quality outcome; and 4) the relationships between software error types and various aspects of development. Finally, we identified several problem areas in data collection and analysis in software research and management.

7. Acknowledgement

Research supported in part by the Air Force Office of Scientific Research Contract AFOSR-F49620-80-C-001 and the National Aeronautics and Space Administration Grant NSG-5123 to the University of Maryland. Computer support provided in part by the Computer Science Center at the University of Maryland.

8. References

[1] E. N. Adams, Optimizing Preventive Service of Software Products, *IBM Journal of Research and Development* **28**, 1, pp. 2-14, Jan. 84.

[2] J.-L. Albin and R. Ferreol, Collecte et analyse de mesures de logiciel (Collection and Analysis of Software Data), *Technique et Science Informatiques* **1**, 4, pp. 297-313, 1982. (Ralro ISSN 0752-4072)

[3] J. W. Bailey and V. R. Basili, A Meta-Model for Software Development Resource Expenditures, *Proc. Fifth Int. Conf. Software Engr.*, San Diego, CA, pp. 107-116, 1981.

[4] J. W. Bailey, Teaching Ada: A Comparison of Two Approaches, Dept. Com. Sci., Univ. Maryland, College Park, MD, working paper, 1984.

[5] F. T. Baker, System Quality Through Structured Programming, *AFIPS Proc. 1972 Fall Joint Computer Conf.* **41**, pp. 339-343, 1972.

[6] V. R. Basili, M. V. Zelkowitz, F. E. McGarry, R. W. Reiter, Jr., W. F. Truszkowski, and D. L. Weiss, The Software Engineering Laboratory, Software Eng. Lab., NASA/Goddard Space Flight Center, Greenbelt, MD, Rep. SEL-77-001, May 1977.

[7] V. R. Basili and M. V. Zelkowitz, Analyzing Medium-Scale Software Developments, *Proc. Third Int. Conf. Software Engr.*, Atlanta, GA, pp. 116-123, May 1978.

[8] V. R. Basili and K. Freburger, Programming Measurement and Estimation in the Software Engineering Laboratory, *Journal of Systems and Software* **2**, pp. 47-57, 1981.

[9] V. R. Basili and D. M. Weiss, Evaluation of a Software Requirements Document By Analysis of Change Data, *Proc. Fifth Int. Conf. Software Engr.*, San Diego, CA, pp. 314-323, March 9-12, 1981.

[10] V. R. Basili and R. W. Reiter, A Controlled Experiment Quantitatively Comparing Software Development Approaches, *IEEE Trans. Software Engr.* **SE-7**, May 1981.

[11] V. R. Basili and C. Doerflinger, Monitoring Software Development Through Dynamic Variables, *Proc. COMPSAC*, Chicago, IL, 1983.

[12] V. R. Basili, R. W. Selby, Jr., and T. Y. Phillips, Metric Analysis and Data Validation Across FORTRAN Projects, *IEEE Trans. Software Engr.* **SE-9**, 6, pp. 652-663, Nov. 1983.

[13] V. R. Basili and B. T. Perricone, Software Errors and Complexity: An Empirical Investigation, *Communications of the ACM* **27**, 1, pp. 42-52, Jan. 1984.

[14] V. R. Basili and R. W. Selby, Jr., Data Collection and Analysis in Software Research and Management, *Proceedings of the American Statistical Association and Biometric Society Joint Statistical Meetings*, Philadelphia, PA, August 13-16, 1984.

[15] V. R. Basili and J. R. Ramsey, Structural Coverage of Functional Testing, Dept. Com. Sci., Univ. Maryland, College Park, Tech. Rep. TR-1442, Sept. 1984.

[16] V. R. Basili and D. M. Weiss, A Methodology for Collecting Valid Software Engineering Data*, *Trans. Software Engr.* **SE-10**, 6, pp. 728-738, Nov. 1984.

[17] V. R. Basili and R. W. Selby, Jr., Comparing the Effectiveness of Software Testing Strategies, Dept. Com. Sci., Univ. Maryland, College Park, Tech. Rep., 1985. (submitted to the *IEEE Trans. Software Engr.*)

[18] V. R. Basili and R. W. Selby, Jr., Calculation and Use of an Environment's Characteristic Software Metric Set, *Proc. Eighth Int. Conf. Software Engr.*, London, August 28-30, 1985.

[19] V. R. Basili, E. E. Katz, N. M. Panlilio-Yap, C. L. Ramsey, and S. Chang, A Quantitative Characterization and Evaluation of a Software Development in Ada, *IEEE Computer*, September 1985.

[20] B. W. Boehm, *Software Engineering Economics,* Prentice-Hall, Englewood Cliffs, NJ, 1981.

[21] B. W. Boehm, T. E. Gray, and T. Seewaldt, Prototyping Versus Specifying: A Multiproject Experiment, *IEEE Trans. Software Engr.* **SE-10**, 3, pp. 290-303, May 1984.

[22] J. Bowen, Estimation of Residual Faults and Testing Effectiveness, *Seventh Minnowbrook Workshop on Software Performance Evaluation,* Blue Mountain Lake, NY, July 24-27, 1984.

[23] R. E. Brooks, Studying Programmer Behavior: The Problem of Proper Methodology, *Communications of the ACM* **23**, 4, pp. 207-213, 1980.

[24] W. D. Brooks, Software Technology Payoff: Some Statistical Evidence, *J. Systems and Software* **2**, pp. 3-9, 1981.

[25] F. O. Buck, Indicators of Quality Inspections, IBM Systems Products Division, Kingston, NY, Tech. Rep. 21.802, Sept. 1981.

[26] D. N. Card, F. E. McGarry, J. Page, S. Eslinger, and V. R. Basili, The Software Engineering Laboratory, Software Eng. Lab., NASA/Goddard Space Flight Center, Greenbelt, MD Rep. SEL-81-104, Feb. 1982.

[27] W. G. Cochran and G. M. Cox, *Experimental Designs,* John Wiley & Sons, New York, 1950.

[28] B. Curtis, S. B. Sheppard, P. Milliman, M. A. Borst, and T. Love, Measuring the Psychological Complexity of Software Maintenance Tasks with the Halstead and McCabe Metrics, *IEEE Trans. Software Engr.*, pp. 96-104, March 1979.

[29] B. Curtis, S. B. Sheppard, and P. M. Milliman, Third Time Charm: Stronger Replication of the Ability of Software Complexity Metrics to Predict Programmer Performance, *Proc. Fourth Int. Conf. Software Engr.*, pp. 356-360, Sept. 1979.

[30] M. Dyer and H. D. Mills, Developing Electronic Systems with Certifiable Reliability, *Proc. NATO Conf.*, Summer, 1982.

[31] M. Dyer, Cleanroom Software Development Method, IBM Federal Systems Division, Bethesda, MD, October 14, 1982.

[32] A. Endres, An Analysis of Errors and their Causes in Systems Programs, *IEEE Trans. Software Engr.*, pp. 140-149, June 1975.

[33] J. D. Gannon and J. J. Horning, The Impact of Language Design on the Production of Reliable Software, *Trans. Software Engr.* **SE-1**, pp. 179-191, 1975.

[34] J. D. Gannon, An Experimental Evaluation of Data Type Conventions, *Communications of the ACM* **20**, 8, pp. 584-595, 1977.

[35] J. D. Gannon, E. E. Katz, and V. R. Basili, Characterizing Ada Programs: Packages, *The Measurement of Computer Software Performance*, Los Alamos National Laboratory, Aug. 1983.

[36] J. D. Gould and P. Drongowski, An Exploratory Study of Computer Program Debugging, *Human Factors* **16**, 3, pp. 258-277, 1974.

[37] J. D. Gould, Some Psychological Evidence on How People Debug Computer Programs, *International Journal of Man-Machine Studies* **7**, pp. 151-182, 1975.

[38] W. C. Hetzel, An Expermental Analysis of Program Verification Methods, Ph.D. Thesis, Univ. of North Carolina, Chapel Hill, 1976.

[39] W. E. Howden, Reliability of the Path Analysis Testing Strategy, *IEEE Trans. Software Engr.* **SE-2**, 3, Sept. 1976.

[40] W. E. Howden, Algebraic Program Testing, *Acta Informatica* **10**, 1978.

[41] W. E. Howden, Functional Program Testing, *IEEE Trans. Software Engr.* **SE-6**, pp. 162-169, Mar. 1980.

[42] W. E. Howden, A Survey of Dynamic Analysis Methods, pp. 209-231 in *Tutorial: Software Testing & Validation Techniques, 2nd Ed.*, ed. E. Miller and W. E. Howden, 1981.

[43] D. H. Hutchens and V. R. Basili, System Structure Analysis: Clustering With Data Bindings, Dept. Com. Sci., Univ. Maryland, College Park, Tech. Rep. TR-1310, August 1983.

[44] S-S. V. Hwang, An Empirical Study in Functional Testing, Structural Testing, and Code Reading/Inspection*, Dept. Com. Sci., Univ. of Maryland, College Park, Scholarly Paper 362, Dec. 1981.

[45] W. L. Johnson, S. Draper, and E. Soloway, An Effective Bug Classification Scheme Must Take the Programmer into Account, *Proc. Workshop High-Level Debugging*, Palo Alto, CA, 1983.

[46] J. P. J. Kelly, Specification of Fault-Tolerant Multi-Version Software: Experimental Studies of a Design Diversity Approach, UCLA Ph.D. Thesis, 1982.

[47] J. Knight, A Large Scale Experiment in N-Version Programming, *Proc. of the Ninth Annual Software Engineering Workshop*, NASA/GSFC, Greenbelt, MD, Nov. 1984.

[48] R. C. Linger, H. D. Mills, and B. I. Witt, *Structured Programming: Theory and Practice,* Addison-Wesley, Reading, MA, 1979.

[49] R. J. Miara, J. A. Musselman, J. A. Navarro, and B. Shneiderman, Program Indentation and Comprehensibility, *Communications of the ACM* **26**, 11, pp. 861-867, Nov. 1983.

[50] H. D. Mills, Mathematical Foundations for Structural Programming, IBM Report FSL 72-6021, 1972.

[51] T. Moher and G. M. Schneider, Methodology and Experimental Research in Software Engineering, *International Journal of Man-Machine Studies* **16**, 1, pp. 65-87, 1982.

[52] G. J. Myers, A Controlled Experiment in Program Testing and Code Walkthroughs/Inspections, *Communications of the ACM,* pp. 760-768, Sept. 1978.

[53] G. J. Myers, *The Art of Software Testing,* John Wiley & Sons, New York, 1979.

[54] T. J. Ostrand and E. J. Weyuker, Collecting and Categorizing Software Error Data in an Industrial Environment, Dept. Com. Sci., Courant Inst. Math. Sci., New York Univ., NY, Tech. Rep. 47, August 1982 (Revised May 1983).

[55] D. J. Panzl, Experience with Automatic Program Testing, *Proc. NBS Trends and Applications,* Nat. Bureau Stds., Gaithersburg, MD, pp. 25-28, May, 28 1981.

[56] D. L. Parnas, Some Conclusions from an Experiment in Software Engineering Techniques, *AFIPS Proc. 1972 Fall Joint Computer Conf.* **41**, pp. 325-329, 1972.

[57] J. Ramsey, Structural Coverage of Functional Testing, *Seventh Minnowbrook Workshop on Software Performance Evaluation,* Blue Mountain Lake, NY, July 24-27, 1984.

[58] Annotated Bibliography of Software Engineering Laboratory (SEL) Literature, Software Eng. Lab., NASA/Goddard Space Flight Center, Greenbelt, MD Rep. SEL-82-006, Nov. 1982.

[59] R. W. Selby, Jr., Evaluations of Software Technologies: Testing, CLEANROOM, and Metrics, Dept. Com. Sci., Univ. Maryland, College Park, Ph. D. Dissertation, 1985.

[60] R. W. Selby, Jr., V. R. Basili, and F. T. Baker, CLEANROOM Software Development: An Empirical Evaluation, Dept. Com. Sci., Univ. Maryland, College Park, Tech. Rep. TR-1415, February 1985. (submitted to the *IEEE Trans. Software Engr.*)

[61] B. A. Sheil, The Psychological Study of Programming, *Computing Surveys* **13**, pp. 101-120, March 1981.

[62] B. Shneiderman, R. E. Mayer, D. McKay, and P. Heller, Experimental Investigations of the Utility of Detailed Flowcharts in Programming, *Communications of the ACM* **20**, 6, pp. 373-381, 1977.

[63] E. Soloway, You Can Observe a Lot by Just Watching How Designers Design, *Proc. Eight Ann. Software Engr. Workshop*, NASA/GSFC, Greenbelt, MD, Nov. 1983.

[64] E. Soloway and K. Ehrlich, Empirical Studies of Programming Knowledge, *Trans. Software Engr.* **SE-10**, 5, pp. 595-609, Sept. 1984.

[65] L. G. Stucki, New Directions in Automated Tools for Improving Software Quality, in *Current Trends in Programming Methodology*, ed. R. T. Yeh, Prentice Hall, Englewood Cliffs, NJ, 1977.

[66] I. Vessey and R. Weber, Some Factors Affecting Program Repair Maintenance: An Empirical Study, *Communications of the ACM* **26**, 2, pp. 128-134, Feb. 1983.

[67] J. Vosburgh, B. Curtis, R. Wolverton, B. Albert, H. Malec, S. Hoben, and Y. Liu, Productivity Factors and Programming Environments, *Proc. Seventh Int. Conf. Software Engr.*, Orlando, FL, pp. 143-152, 1984.

[68] C. E. Walston and C. P. Felix, A Method of Programming Measurement and Estimation, *IBM Systems J.* **16**, 1, pp. 54-73, 1977.

[69] D. M. Weiss and V. R. Basili, Evaluating Software Development by Analysis of Changes: Some Data from the Software Engineering Laboratory, *IEEE Trans. Software Engr.* **SE-11**, 2, pp. 157-168, February 1985.

[70] L. Weissman, Psychological Complexity of Computer Programs: An Experimental Methodology, *SIGPLAN Notices* **9**, 6, pp. 25 - 36, June 1974.

[71] S. N. Woodfield, H. E. Dunsmore, and V. Y. Shen, The Effect of Modularization and Comments on Program Comprehension, Dept. Com. Sci., Arizona St. Univ., Tempe, AZ, working paper, 1981.

RECURSIVELY STRUCTURED FAULT-TOLERANT DISTRIBUTED COMPUTING SYSTEMS

B. Randell

Computing Laboratory,
University of Newcastle upon Tyne

ABSTRACT

Two design rules which aid the construction of distributed computing systems and the provision of fault tolerance are described, namely that:

(i) a distributed computing system should be functionally equivalent to the individual computing systems of which it is composed, and

(ii) fault tolerant systems should be constructed from generalised fault tolerant components.

The reasoning behind these two "recursive structuring principles", and the consequences of attempting to adhere to them, are discussed. Where appropriate this discussion is illustrated by reference to a distributed system based on UNIX† that is now operational at Newcastle and numerous other locations. This system has been implemented by adding a software subsystem, known as the Newcastle Connection, to each of a set of UNIX systems. By this means we have constructed a distributed system which is functionally equivalent at both the user and the program level to a conventional uni-processor UNIX system.

(Based on the paper "Recursively Structured Distributed Computing Systems" by B. Randell appearing in IEEE 1983 PROCEEDINGS OF THE THIRD SYMPOSIUM ON RELIABILITY IN DISTRIBUTED SOFTWARE AND DATABASE SYSTEMS, October 17-19, 1983, Clearwater Beach, FL, pp. 3-11. Copyright C 1983 IEEE.)

1. INTRODUCTION

The purpose of this paper is to describe a particular approach to the design and implementation of distributed computing systems. This approach is aimed at achieving logical separation between a number of design issues. The design issues in question are those related to the presence of multiple interacting computers, and to the provision of various forms of fault tolerance. The intent of such logical separation is to simplify the overall system design, and hence to facilitate its implementation,

† UNIX is a trademark of AT&T Bell Laboratories.

NATO ASI Series, Vol. F22
Software System Design Methods. Edited by J.K. Skwirzynski

validation and modification.

The approach underlies recent work at Newcastle which has resulted in the implementation of yet another distributed system based on UNIX. This has involved the development of a software sub-system (called the Newcastle Connection) which can be added to each of a set of physically connected UNIX or UNIX-lookalike systems in order to combine them into a distributed system. (For the purposes of this paper such a distributed system will be called a UNIX United system.) The first UNIX United system was constructed at Newcastle in 1982, using a set of PDP11s running UNIX Version 7, and connected by a Cambridge Ring; since this date the connection has been used to construct distributed systems based on various other computers and versions of UNIX, both at Newcastle and elsewhere.

Many of the techniques involved in the design of the UNIX United system are not particularly novel. In combination, however, they constitute an interesting example of the exploitation of two very illuminating design rules for the structuring of distributed computing systems. In this paper we concentrate on these design rules and their consequences, illustrating our discussion with references to the design of UNIX United. However no attempt is made to give a full account or evaluation of UNIX United, or of the various related systems developed elsewhere, since such material is to be found in Brownbridge et al[1] (Randell[2] provides a somewhat updated version of this paper.)

Both the design rules are in fact concerned with issues of what we term recursive structuring, and are formulated in Sections 2 and 4 below, perhaps rather grandiloquently, as two "recursive structuring principles".

2. THE PRINCIPLE OF RECURSIVE TRANSPARENCY

The first design rule can be stated quite simply:

> A distributed system should be functionally equivalent to the individual systems of which it is composed.

We refer to this rule, for reasons which are discussed below, as the "principle of recursive transparency". We first learnt of this principle, though not under this name, from a paper by W. Wilner.[3] In this paper Wilner, influenced by earlier work by Barton, advocates that VLSI computer architectures should be recursive. The idea is to design a basic processor architecture and its geometrical layout so that a design which occupies a complete chip can be directly replaced by a small number of interconnected reduced size copies of the original design. This requires the actual layout to have a geometrically recursive structure. More significantly, it also requires the architecture to be functionally recursive. Given such recursiveness, increased integration levels can be used to provide greater performance and perhaps storage capacity, without in any way changing the functionality of the chip. By such means, it is claimed, one can get away from the apparently inexorable progression of incompatible microprocessor architectures, with ever bigger word lengths and instruction sets, that have accompanied the evolution of VLSI technology.

Such recursive structuring is however of relevance at various architectural levels, and especially at what can loosely be called the operating system level. In particular, it is basic to the design of UNIX United.

Thus UNIX United is a distributed system which is functionally equivalent to a conventional UNIX system running on a single processor. All the standard UNIX facilities, e.g. for protecting, naming and accessing files and devices, for input/output re-direction, for inter-process communication, etc., are applicable without apparent change to the system as a whole. It follows, therefore, that all issues of inter-processor communication, network protocols, etc., are completely hidden from users and their programs.

The first recursive structuring principle thus implies the use of network transparency - in fact a very particular form of network transparency. Many systems exist which provide network transparency, to a greater or lesser degree, but this is usually what might be described as a flat (as opposed to a recursive) transparency, and often applies merely to file and device access. With flat transparency it is not possible to repeat the construction process, and build a further, larger, distributed system using several first level distributed systems as though they were basic components. (Even though it is likely to be possible to add further individual computers to the system, this is a fundamentally different, and more limited process.) With recursive transparency, on the other hand, exactly the same construction process can readily be repeated - in the resulting larger distributed system, the first level distributed systems will retain their separate identities.

A distributed system which is recursively structured in this way is - by definition - indefinitely extensible, at least in theory. Indeed UNIX United has been designed with the intention of constructing very large distributed systems, involving both wide and local area networks. It thus can be contrasted with a number of other UNIX-based distributed systems which are designed to provide network transparency for a comparatively small number of machines, interconnected over a single particular type of local area network. This is not to say that such limitations are inevitable unless one uses recursive structuring - rather that adherence to the recursive transparency principle leads naturally to a design which avoids these limitations.

A major implication of the recursive transparency principle is that the component computers must possess characteristics that are appropriate for the distributed system as a whole. If the distributed system is to provide facilities for parallel processing, the component computers must also provide (at least the appearance of) parallel processing facilities. A conventional UNIX system is suitable in this regard, because of its ability to allow users and their programs to initiate asynchronous processes. The second required characteristic relates to issues of naming. A system's naming facilities (i.e. the means it provides for identifying its various constituent objects, such as devices, files, programs, etc.) must be independent of whether the system is in fact a complete one, or merely a component of some larger system.

This characteristic is not common in the world of computing systems, despite the fact that it is well known elsewhere, for example in telephone systems. (The telephone numbers used in a company's internal telephone system need not be affected if the system becomes part of a national telephone system. National telephone numbers need not be changed if the country becomes part of the international telephone system, etc.)

Specifically, the component computer systems need to support a general "contextual naming" scheme for their various objects. In order for a system to be extensible, it should have means for introducing and entering (and leaving) new naming contexts. Such facilities are reasonably common. What is not so common is a system in which *all* names are context-relative. This is a characteristic that UNIX possesses by virtue of its very simple yet general scheme for naming files, devices and commands, in which directories serve as the required contexts.

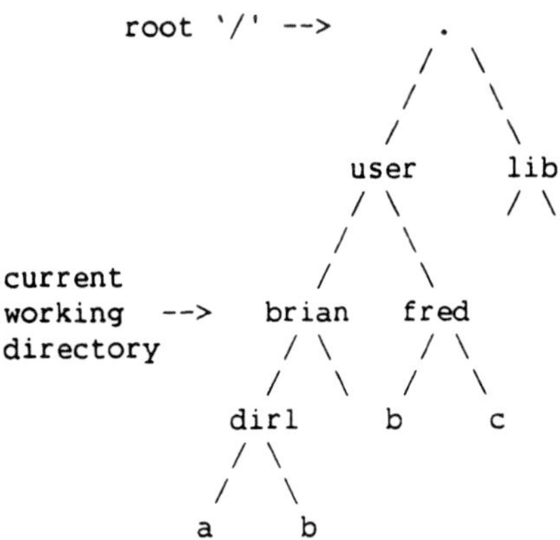

Figure 1: A Typical UNIX Name Space

Figure 1 shows part of a typical UNIX naming hierarchy. Files, directories, etc., can only be named relative to some implied "location" in the tree. It so happens that UNIX provides two such locations, namely the directory which is designated as being the "current working directory" and that which is designated as the "root directory". Thus in the figure "/user/brian/dirl/a" and "dirl/a" identify the same file, the convention being that a name starting with "/" is relative to the root directory. Objects outside a context can be named relative to that context using the convention that ".." indicates the parent directory. (Note that this avoids having to know the name by which the context is known in its surrounding context.) The names "/user/fred/b" and "../fred/b" therefore identify the same file, the second form being a name given relative to the current working directory rather than the root directory.

The root directory is normally positioned at the base of the tree, as shown in the figure, but this does not have to be the case. Rather, like the current working directory, it can also be re-positioned at some other node in the naming tree, *but this position must be specified by a context-relative name*. Thus all naming is completely context-relative - there is no means of specifying an absolute name, relative to the base of the tree, say. (The base directory can itself be recognised only by the convention that it is its own parent.) Moreover *all other means* provided for identifying any of the various kinds of objects that UNIX deals with, e.g. users, processes, open files, etc., are related back to its hierarchical naming scheme. It is for these reasons that UNIX, in contrast to most operating systems, can be said to support a contextual naming scheme.

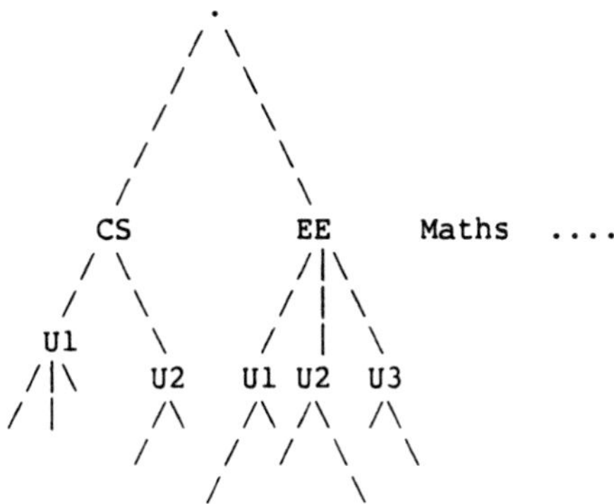

Figure 2: A University-Wide UNIX United System

This simple and elegant scheme of context-relative naming has been taken advantage of in UNIX United by identifying individual component UNIX systems with directories in a larger name space, covering the UNIX United system as a whole. In actual fact, it is not necessarily one specific hardware system that is associated with a particular directory. Rather it is a "virtual UNIX machine", which could in principle be moved on occasion from one set of hardware to another, or even implemented on replicated sets of hardware. (This latter possibility is discussed further in Section 4.) In Figure 2 we show how a UNIX United system spanning an entire university might be created from the machines in various university departments, using a naming structure which matches the departmental structure. (This naming strucure need bear no relationship to the actual topology of the underlying communications networks. Indeed this exact naming structure could be set up on a single conventional UNIX system.)

The figure implies that from within the Computing Science Department's U1 machine, files on its U2 machine will normally have names starting "/../U2" and files on the machine that the Electrical Engineering Department has also chosen to call "U2" will need to be identified with names starting "/../../EE/U2". Indeed U2 and the directory structure beneath it might not be associated with a single machine. Rather it might be a UNIX United system, itself containing an arbitrary number of other UNIX United systems, unknown to U1 in CS.

One can contrast this naming scheme, in which in fact <u>any</u> directory can be associated with a separate UNIX system, with the sort of scheme that provides only flat transparency. Typical of such schemes are those which group all the UNIX system names together into a single global context, perhaps even using some additional special syntax (e.g. an exclamation mark) to differentiate system names from local names.

In summary, the recursive transparency principle has a profound (and highly beneficial) effect on the usability of a distributed system. It also provides a number of valuable guidelines as to how to tackle the various implementation issues. These include the provision of fault tolerance and also the construction of a coherent system from a collection of heterogeneous components, topics which form the subjects of Sections 4 and 5 below.

3. IMPLEMENTATION OF RECURSIVE TRANSPARENCY

The recursive transparency principle leads one to regard "distributedness" (i.e. the fact that a system incorporates a set of autonomous yet interacting computers) as a separable design issue. Thus we view it as one which could and should be treated independently of many other aspects of the design of (possibly distributed) systems.

We have accordingly tried to identify the minimum set of facilities that are needed for the provision of distributedness (in a recursively structured system) and to implement them in a clearly separate mechanism. UNIX United has in fact been implemented merely by inserting the Newcastle Connection sub-system, in the form of a software layer, into an otherwise unchanged UNIX system.

The positioning of the Connection layer is governed by the structure of UNIX itself. In UNIX all user processes and many operating system facilities (such as the 'shell' command language interpreter) are run as separate time-shared processes. These are able to interact with each other, and the outside world, only by means of 'system calls' - effectively procedure calls on the resident nucleus of the operating system, the UNIX kernel. The Connection is a transparent layer that is inserted between the kernel and the processes. It is transparent in the sense that from above it is functionally indistinguishable from the kernel and from below it appears to be a set of normal user processes. It filters out system calls that have to be re-directed to another UNIX system (for example, because they concern files or devices on that system), and accepts calls that have been re-directed to it from other systems. Thus processes on different UNIX machines can interact in exactly the same way as do processes on a single machine.

Since system calls act like procedure calls, communication between the Connection layers on the various machines is based on the use of a remote procedure call protocol,[4] which is shown schematically below.

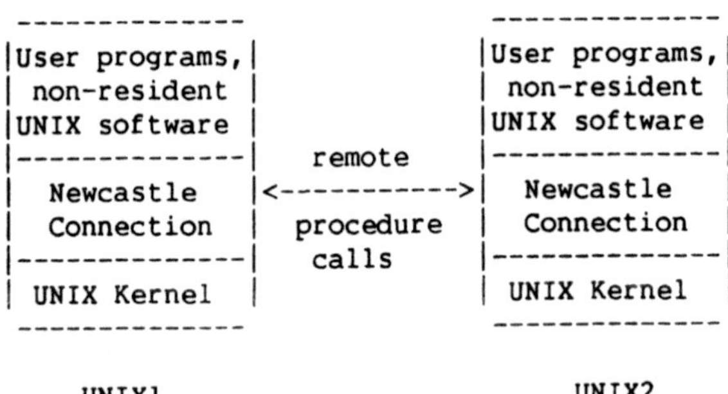

Figure 3: The Position of the Connection Layer

A slightly more detailed picture of the structure of the system would (perforce) reveal that communications actually occur at the hardware level, and that the kernel includes means for handling low level communications protocols. However all such issues are hidden from the user of UNIX United, as indeed is the remote procedure call protocol itself.

It is of course still left to each UNIX programmer to choose to implement a given algorithm in the form of a single process, or alternatively as a set of interacting processes. This latter approach takes advantage of the quasi-parallelism in UNIX, and perhaps real parallelism in UNIX United. Thus the existence of the Newcastle Connection still leaves open the question of whether a centralised or decentralised implementation of, say, a data base manager is most appropriate in given circumstances - neither implementation need deal explicitly with issues of distributedness.

3.1. Names and Addresses

In a recursively structured system each component computer possesses what appears to be a complete name space, but which in fact is just part of the overall name space. Thus one of the consequences of distributedness is the requirement for some means of combining these component name spaces.

The technique that we have evolved for this purpose in UNIX United is as follows. Each component UNIX system stores just a part of the overall naming structure. Firstly, each system stores the representation of the section of the naming tree associated with the system's own files and devices. Secondly, each system also stores a copy of those parts of the overall naming structure that relate it to its "name neighbours". These are the other UNIX systems with which it is directly connected in naming terms (i.e. which can be reached via a traversal of the naming tree without passing through a node representing another UNIX system).

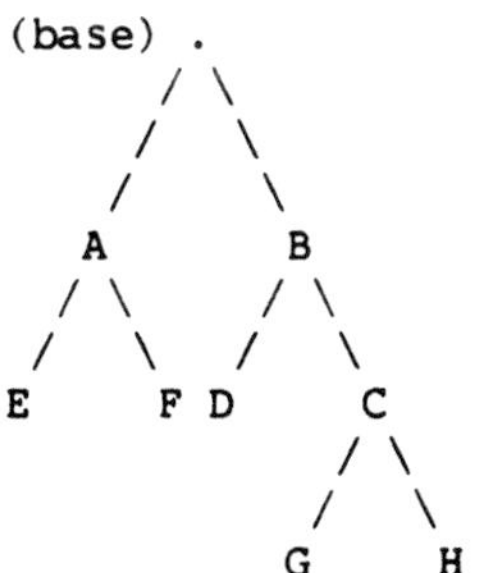

Figure 4(a): A UNIX United Name Space

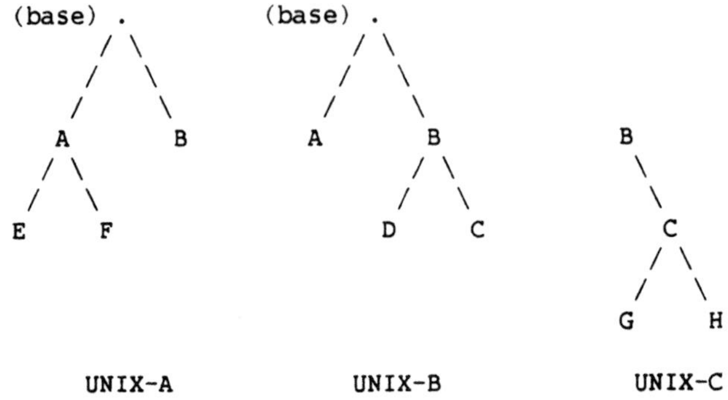

Figure 4(b): Representation of the Name Space

In Figure 4(a), if "directories" A, B and C are associated with separate UNIX systems, the parts of the tree representation stored in each system are as shown in Figure 4(b), namely:

UNIX-A: A,B,E,F,(base)

UNIX-B: A,B,C,D,(base)

UNIX-C: B,C,G,H

It is assumed that shared parts of the naming tree are agreed to by the administrators of each of the systems involved, and do not require frequent modification - a major modification of the UNIX United naming structure can be as disruptive as a major modification of the naming structure inside a single UNIX system. This is because names stored in files or incorporated in programs (or even just known to users) may be invalidated. (Again one can draw a useful analogy to the telephone system. Changes to international and area codes would be highly disruptive, and are avoided as far as possible. For example, they are not changed merely because the underlying physical network has to be modified.)

The names we have been discussing so far concern objects that form part of the distributed computing system itself. There is also the question of how the system identifies its users, i.e. what names they use in order to log into the system. We would argue that user names also need to be context-dependent, since we do not wish to assume that the distributed system is part of an environment which itself is organised centrally.

Thus in UNIX United it is possible to connect together a number of component UNIX systems, allowing users to retain their existing login names. In consequence, the name by which a user identifies him or herself to a UNIX United system may well depend on which component system he logs into. A single login however suffices for him or her to be able to make use of the whole UNIX United system, subject of course to access permissions. The administrator of each component system is therefore responsible for maintaining tables not only of authorized local users, but also of authorized non-local users and of the local names by which they will be known inside his/her system.

It is interesting to compare the approach to name management described above with that based on the concept of a name server.[5] The basic function of a name server is to provide a central repository for information regarding the physical addresses of the various other components of the distributed system, information that can then be used to enable these components to be accessed directly.

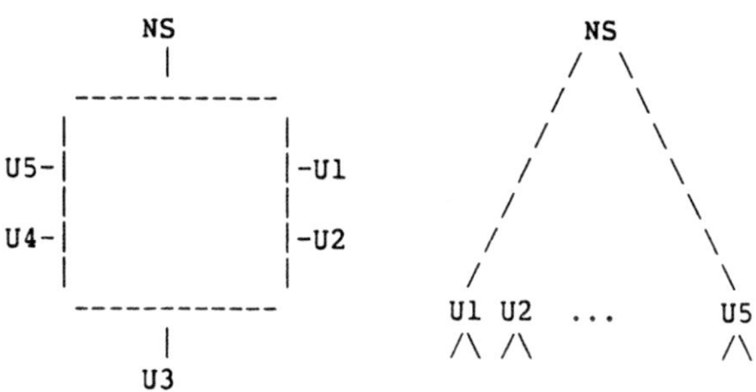

Figure 5: A Name Server

A UNIX United system can in fact easily be set up, using a Ring network, say, to work in just this way, as is illustrated in Figure 5. Here all but one of the component UNIX systems are made subservient, in terms of the global naming tree, to the remaining system, labelled NS in the diagrams. This system will contain hardware addresses (ring station numbers) for all of the other systems, each of which will hold the hardware address of just the NS system. If U1, say, needs to access a file on U2 it can 'open' the file using a name which starts "/../U2". The 'open' system call will have to access NS in order to check permissions, but will in due course return the station number of U2 so that thereafter reads and writes to the file will go directly to U2, and not involve NS.

We thus view the name server approach as just a specialised usage of a more general name management scheme. It can be contrasted with another specialised usage, in which no constituent UNIX systems are made subservient to any others. In such circumstances every system contains the address of all other systems. Neither of these extremes is appropriate for a very large distributed system - indeed neither fits well with the concept of recursive structuring, for which it would appear that a more general approach such as that which we have described is necessary.

4. FAULT TOLERANCE ISSUES AND RECURSIVE CONSTRUCTION

System structuring techniques play a very large role in the provision of effective fault tolerance, as is discussed by Anderson and Lee.[6] This book describes our approach to the construction of fault tolerant systems based on the concept of what might be termed a "generalized fault tolerant component". Each such component contains and carefully delineates such facilities as are thought appropriate for trying to tolerate:

(i) faults in underlying components that are reported to it,

(ii) its own faults, and

(iii) faulty invocation of the component by its environment, i.e. the enclosing component, or a co-existing component with which it is interacting.

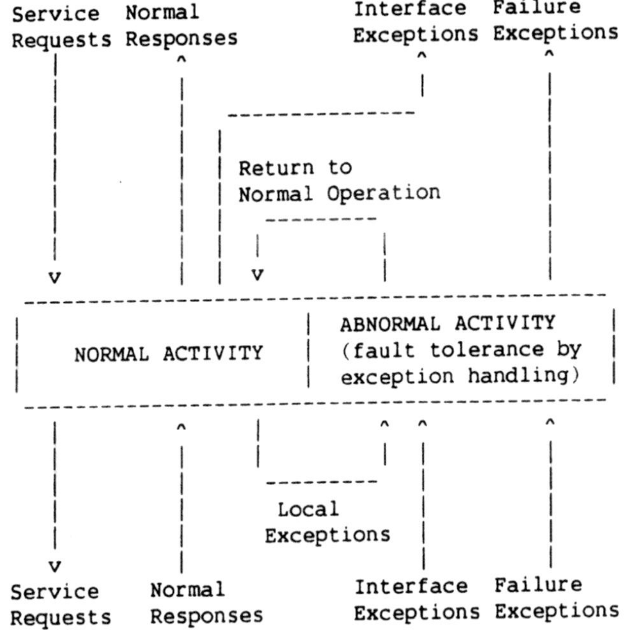

Figure 6: A Generalized Fault Tolerant Component

These notions are expressed pictorially in Figure 6. They are intended to apply to both hardware and software, though they are described in programming language terms.

This concept of a generalized fault tolerant component directly implies a second design rule, again relating to recursive structuring. Thus we have a "principle of recursive construction" which states that:

Fault tolerant systems should be constructed out of generalized fault tolerant component systems.

This seems almost like a truism. In fact it expresses both the need to identify, at each level of system construction, the various different faults that might arise and the fault tolerance mechanisms that have been provided for them, and also a scheme for categorizing these faults and mechanisms. In particular, it implies a simple (albeit strict) discipline of exception handling, based on the so-called "termination model".[7] In the figure, failure exceptions, local exceptions and interface exceptions are the respective means by which the three types of fault listed above are reported. Ideally a component that receives one of these exceptions handles it successfully, and returns to normal operation - if not it in turn is supposed to signal a failure exception to its environment. (A detailed discussion and justification of these points can be found in [6].) Here we wish to concentrate on the application of the principle to distributed systems, especially in conjunction with the principle of recursive transparency.

This latter principle has immediate relevance to fault tolerance since the functional equivalence between a distributed system and its component computing systems which the principle demands must apply to exceptional, as well as to any normal, system behaviour. Thus combining the two principles it seems reasonable to require that a fault tolerant distributed system should be functionally equivalent to the generalized fault tolerant component computing systems of which it is composed.

In UNIX United, the Connection layer reports by means of failure or interface exceptions any errors that it cannot recover from in terms similar to those used by the UNIX kernel. For example, it reports merely that a file cannot be opened, rather than that the communications line to the machine containing the file is not operational. (In practice, facilities to aid fault location and repair may well be needed, but we regard this as an issue which is separate from that of exception reporting for purposes of fault tolerance.)

Compared to a centralized system, a distributed system provides (i) new opportunities for the provision of high reliability by means of fault tolerance, and (ii) new types of fault that could impair reliability unless properly tolerated. These are different issues and should be treated as such. Moreover they are also separable from any opportunities or requirements for fault tolerance that would exist in an equivalent non-distributed system. The recursive structuring principles facilitate such separation of logical concerns not just during design discussions, but also in the form of the resulting distributed system.

Thus UNIX United is structured so that the only reliability problems which are treated within the Connection layer are those which arise specifically from the fact that the system is distributed. The Connection layer uses a remote procedure call protocol which addresses the problems caused by breakdowns ("crashes") of the component computers and communication links, and by the occasional loss of messages across the links. These faults will either be discovered by the Connection layer, so causing a local exception to be raised, or will be reported to it by failure exceptions. In either case the layer attempts to handle the exception so as to mask the fault. In doing so it tries to avoid accidental repetition of a remote procedure call - i.e. it aims to conform to an "exactly once" semantics.[8]

There remain the problems due to a computer which is trying to make a (perhaps related) series of remote procedure calls itself crashing on occasion, or of the Connection layer, despite its best efforts, being unable to achieve all the requested calls. These problems can arise from faults in the underlying hardware, from user error or from contention for shared objects in a centralized (multiprogramming or time-sharing) system. As such, they are not regarded as the province of the Connection layer, but instead as problems to be dealt with by separate mechanisms - this point is treated in greater detail in papers relating to the remote procedure call protocol.[9,10]

One form of fault tolerance that is often provided in a distributed system is that of support for transactions or, more generally, recoverable atomic actions. Such support "guarantees" that a process in effect performs a sequence of operations on shared objects either in its entirety and without interference from or to other processes, or not at all. Support for atomic actions *per se* is not regarded as part of UNIX United, since it would augment the functionality of UNIX itself and is in any case of equal relevance to a multiprogramming system as to a distributed system. However we are developing further software which will provide UNIX, and hence UNIX United, with atomic actions which are recoverable, at least with respect to file usage. It is based on the Distributed Recoverable File System[11] developed earlier at Newcastle for UNIX. In essence it will just provide three additional system calls:

(i) Establish Recovery Point (i.e. start state-saving, and locking files),

(ii) Discard Recovery Point (i.e. discard saved state, and unlock relevant files), and

(iii) Restore Recovery Point (i.e. go back to latest uncommitted recovery point).

This additional software is being implemented in the first instance as a separate layer, which will be interposed between the Connection layer and the kernel, as shown in Figure 7 below. However the layer is to all intents and purposes an extension of, and could be incorporated into, the kernel. In either case, the Connection layer will have to be augmented to deal with the three additional system calls. (In the case of the Discard Recovery Point call, it might well be thought necessary to incorporate a simplified form of "two-phase commit protocol",[12] which would involve the provision of another system call "Prepare to Discard Recovery Point" by the Atomic Action layer. This should minimise the risk of having some but not all the component UNIX systems complete their Discard Recovery Point calls. In fact virtually all the mechanisms required within the Connection layer for two-phase commit already exist, being needed to support some existing UNIX system calls.)

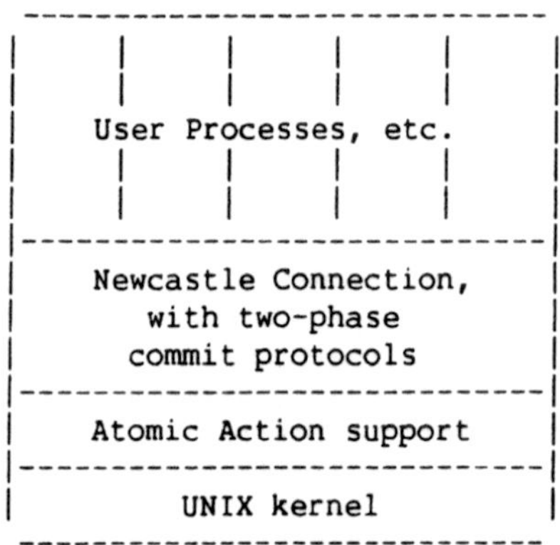

Figure 7 : Provision of Atomic Actions

The effects of hardware crashes or malfunctions can often be masked using another well known form of fault tolerance, that of replication and majority voting. A prototype extension to UNIX United has already been constructed which uses this approach. It has involved adding an additional transparent software sub-system (the Triple Modular Redundancy layer) to each of a number of UNIX machines on top of their Connection layers, as shown in Figure 8. The TMR layer goes on top of the Connection layer because it can then rely on the latter to handle all problems relating to the physical distribution of processes, files, etc. Copies of a conventional application program and its files can then be loaded onto each of three machines and run so that file accesses are synchronized and voted upon. Any malfunctioning computer so identified by the voting is automatically switched out and in due course another switched in to replace it.

This of course is not a new idea. The point is that the technique is very simple to implement when it is separated from issues of distributedness. Needless to say, given that the Triple Modular Redundancy layer is transparent, one can envisage using both it and the Atomic Action layer together, the latter having the task of trying to cope with situations where the problem is not a hardware fault, but one arising, say, from erroneous input data.

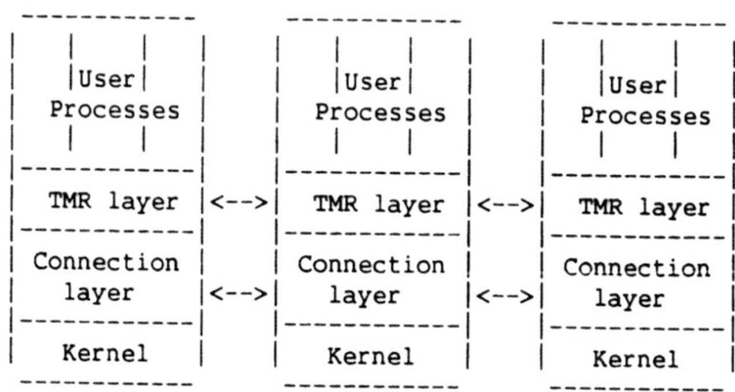

Figure 8: Hardware Fault Masking

The simplicity, generality and mutual independence that these various mechanisms possess by virtue of their design adhering to the recursive structuring principles are, we believe, considerable. After all, complexity is one of the major impediments to reliability. Complicated and needlessly interdependent fault tolerance mechanisms are more likely to reduce than to improve reliability, because of the danger of situations arising, particularly during error recovery and system reconfiguration, that have not been catered for properly.

5. HETEROGENEITY

Our pair of structuring principles is also relevant to the task of constructing a system out of a somewhat heterogeneous collection of components of various specialised types. This is because we can, when appropriate, achieve the functional equivalence called for by the first principle merely by means of the interface exception signals that result from the use of the second principle.

One can thus incorporate into a UNIX United system a component that is capable of performing only a subset of the UNIX system calls, as long as it responds with appropriate interface exception messages to any other types of call that are diverted to it by other computers. By this means one might, for example, interconnect UNIX systems which are functioning just as file servers with others that serve as personal workstations, to form what appears to be a complete conventional UNIX system. This idea is not novel.[13] It is just that it is particularly simple to design and implement such a system when the overall system structure is based on the notion of recursive transparency.

Naturally, specialised components in a UNIX United system do not actually have to be based on UNIX - they just have to interact properly with other component computers, by adhering to the general format of the inter-machine system call protocol used by the Newcastle Connection, even if most types of call are responded to by interface exception reports.

Thus the syntax and semantics of this protocol assume a considerable significance, since it can be used as the unifying factor in a very general yet extremely simple scheme for building sophisticated distributed systems out of a variety of size and type of component - an analogy we like to make is that the protocol operates like the scheme of standard-size dimples that allow a variety of shapes of LEGO* children's building blocks to be connected together into a coherent whole.

In fact one example of the use of specialised components was mentioned earlier, namely the name server. Although the name server was discussed as though it was a standard UNIX system (perhaps even with its own files and processing activities) this does not have to be the case. Rather, if it is functioning solely as a name server it could well make sense for it to have been implemented specially.

Another specialised component that is being investigated at Newcastle is a terminal concentrator. The concentrator is designed to serve as part of an existing campus network, incorporating various host computing systems, and is in no way related to UNIX. However the concentrator is now being extended so as to have a (very limited) remote UNIX system call interface. This is so that it can be linked to a UNIX United system, from which it will appear to be a conventional UNIX system whose naming tree contains just terminals. This will enable some special (and complex) terminal handling and networking software in one of the computers forming our UNIX United system to be completely discarded.

A further development that is currently being pursued at Newcastle is that of providing a limited remote UNIX system call interface on a totally different operating system. Initially just the basic system calls concerned with file accessing would be supported, and mapped into equivalent facilities within this other system. The simplicity and extensibility of this approach contrast favourably with the more conventional current approach of having each operating system support a general file transfer protocol, particularly since it enables a remote file to be accessed and updated

LEGO is a Registered Trademark of LEGO Systems A/S.

selectively.

In summary, what we are suggesting is that a coherent distributed system can be constructed, using the recursive structuring principles, by providing any non-standard component with a more-or-less complete standard facade, supplemented by the use of interface exception messages when inadequacies of the facade obtrude. The practicability of this approach in the UNIX United context rests on the suitability of the UNIX system call interface as an interface onto which all inter-computer requests have to be mapped. Our confidence in the approach is based on its relative simplicity and generality, and on the rapidity with which it is becoming available on an ever-growing variety of different hardware.

Nevertheless, this approach has its limitations - in practice, different component computers may achieve only approximate functional equivalence with each other due to differing instruction and data representations, variant implementations of UNIX system calls, etc. Some differences can be dealt with by the Connection layer. Unfortunately it cannot in general perform mapping between data representations. This is because UNIX does not maintain information about the types of the various items held in its files, treating them instead all as sequences of bytes. However in many situations this suffices, and where this is not the case one could adopt or define a specific application-dependent mapping protocol.

6. CONCLUSIONS

The structuring principles that we have attempted to describe and justify here are, in retrospect, fairly obvious. As mentioned much earlier, they are potentially applicable at virtually any level of system architecture. Clearly, the lower the level (i.e. the smaller the basic component) the more difficult it will be to ensure that performance overheads remain acceptable. However as applied at the operating system level they are just a modest generalisation and extension of various current approaches to the design and implementation of distributed and/or fault tolerant computing systems. Nevertheless, the principles provide a surprisingly effective and constructive methodology for the design of such systems.

Certainly our experience with UNIX United provides what we regard as strong evidence for the merits of this methodology. As reported in,[1] a very useful distributed system, enabling full remote file and device access, was constructed within about a month of starting implementation of the Connection layer. Needless to say, the fact that - due to the transparency of the Newcastle Connection - it was not necessary to modify or in most cases even understand any existing operating system or user program source code was a great help! In only a few months this system had been extended to cover remote execution, multiple sets of users, etc. Moreover two prototype extensions of the system, for multi-level security and hardware fault tolerance, had been successfully demonstrated, and the design of others commenced. However we have barely begun to explore all the many possible ramifications of the scheme, and of course there are many evaluation exercises and engineering improvements to be investigated.

Incidentally, the work on military-type multi-level security takes advantage of the fact that the principle of recursive transparency can be viewed as a means of subdividing a system, perhaps repeatedly, as well as a means for combining systems. Attempts to implement (and certify the trustworthiness of) multi-level security mechanisms within a general purpose time-sharing system have not met with great success. An alternative approach has been advocated by several groups. This is to construct a multi-level secure distributed system, each of whose constituent computers operates at a single security level. Very strict controls on information flow between these computers can then be enforced by comparatively simple mechanisms, typically involving the use of encryption. This approach fits in well with the idea of recursive transparency, since the constituent computers can be used as a single computer which contains hidden mechanisms for enforcing multiple security partitions. A project to build a complete multi-level secure UNIX United system based on these ideas is described by Rushby and Randell.[14]

What has been presented here as a discussion of structuring principles for the design of distributed computing systems could equally well be viewed as a rationale for the design of UNIX United. It would be gratifying to be able to report that the process of designing UNIX United had been guided, at all times, by explicit recognition of these principles. In practice the above account is in some ways as much a rationalisation of, as it is a rationale for, the design of UNIX United. The various structuring ideas, in particular those on fault tolerant components and on recursive architectures, had already been a subject of much study at Newcastle. Nevertheless the work that led to the specification and detailed design of the Newcastle Connection has contributed to, as well as greatly benefitted from, our understanding of these system structuring issues. Equally it owes much to the external form (if not internal design) of the UNIX kernel - the only operating system we know of which is at all close to being an ideal component of a recursively structured distributed computing system. However we would not wish to give the impression that UNIX is perfect, and that these structuring ideas are relevant only to UNIX and UNIX-like systems. Rather, we believe that they are of considerable generality. We can but hope that the fact that we have found it convenient to draw so heavily on UNIX (and UNIX United) to illustrate our arguments will not obscure this point.

7. ACKNOWLEDGEMENTS

The discussion of structuring issues presented in this paper owes much to the work of the author's many colleagues, at Newcastle and elsewhere, over a number of years. Recent work specifically on the Newcastle Connection and the Remote Procedure Call Protocol, however, has been mainly in close collaboration with Lindsay Marshall, Dave Brownbridge, Fabio Panzieri, Santosh Shrivastava and Jay Black. The work on multi-level security has been largely carried out with John Rushby, and that on hardware fault tolerance with Li-Yi Lu. Research on distributed computing systems at Newcastle is sponsored by the U.K. Science and Engineering Research Council and the Royal Signals and Radar Research Establishment.

References

1. D.R. Brownbridge, L.F. Marshall, and B. Randell, "The Newcastle Connection - or UNIXes of the World Unite," Software Practice and Experience, vol. 12, no. 12, pp. 1147-1162, December 1982.

2. B. Randell, "The Newcastle Connection: A Software Subsystem for Constructing Distributed UNIX Systems," Technical Report TR194, Computing Laboratory, University of Newcastle upon Tyne, September, 1984.

3. W. Wilner, "Recursive Machines," Internal Report, Xerox Corporation, 1980. Also: In 'VLSI: Machine Architecture and Very High Level Language', Ed. P.C. Treleaven, ACM Computer Architecture News 8(7) December 1980 pp. 27-38 (Technical Report 156 University of Newcastle upon Tyne).

4. F. Panzieri and S. K. Shrivastava, "Reliable Remote Calls for Distributed UNIX: An implementation study," in Proc. Second Symp. on Reliability in Distributed Software and Database Systems, pp. 127-133, IEEE, Pittsburg, July 1982.

5. R. M. Needham and A. J. Herbert, The Cambridge Distributed Computing System, Addison-Wesley, 1982.

6. T. Anderson and P.A. Lee, Fault Tolerance: Principles and Practice, Prentice-Hall, Englewood Cliffs, N.J., 1981.

7. B.H. Liskov and A. Snyder, "Exception Handling in CLU," IEEE Transactions on Software Engineering, vol. SE-5, no. 6, pp. 546-558, November 1979.

8. B. J. Nelson, Remote Procedure Call, Ph.D. Thesis, Computer Science Dept., Carnegie-Mellon Univ., Pittsburg, Pa., 1981.

9. S. K. Shrivastava, "Structuring Distributed Systems for Reliability and Crash Resistance," IEEE Trans. Software Eng., vol. SE-7, no. 4, pp. 436-447, July 1981.

10. S. K. Shrivastava and F. Panzieri, "The Design of a Reliable Remote Procedure Call Mechanism," IEEE Trans. on Computers, vol. C-31, no. 7, pp. 692-697, July 1982.

11. M. Jegado, "Recoverability Aspects of a Distributed File System," Software Practice and Experience, vol. 13, no. 1, pp. 33-44, Jan. 1983.

12. J.N. Gray, "Notes on Data Base Operating Systems," in Lecture Notes in Computer Science 60, ed. R. Bayer, R. M. Graham and G. Seegmueller, pp. 393-481, Springer-Verlag, New York, N.Y., 1978.

13. G.W.R. Luderer, H. Che, J.P. Haggerty, P.A. Kirslis, and W.T. Marshall, "A Distributed Unix System Based on a Virtual Circuit Switch," Proc. 8th Symp. Operating System Principles, pp. 160-168, ACM, Pacific Grove, California., December 1981. Also in: ACM Special Interest Group on Operating Systems - Operating Systems Review, Vol.

15(5) (December 1981).

14. J. M. Rushby and B. Randell, "A Distributed Secure System," Computer, vol. 16, no. 7, IEEE, July 1983.

KNOWLEDGE ENGINEERING TECHNIQUES APPLIED TO FAULT DETECTION TEST GENERATION, AND MAINTENANCE

L.F. Pau, Battelle Memorial Institute,
7, route de Drize, CH 1227 Carouge, Switzerland

Abstract: The use of knowledge engineering in diagnostic systems, is aiming primarily at exploiting procedural knowledge (about: systems operations, configuration, observations, calibration, maintenance), in connection with failure detection and test generation tasks. Next, the goal is to devise knowledge representation schemes whereby the failure events can be analyzed by merging highly diverse sources of information: analog/digital signals, logical variables and test outcomes, text from verbal reports, and inspection images. The final goal, is to ease the operator workload when interfacing with the system under test and/or the test equipment, or with reliability assessment software packages.

The paper will present key notions, methods and tools from: knowledge representation, inference procedures, pattern analysis. This will be illustrated by mentions to a number of current and potential applications for e.g.: electronics failure detection, control systems testing, analysis of intermittent failures, false alarm reduction, test generation, maintenance trainers.

Notation:

AI	:	Artificial intelligence
ATPG	:	Automatic test program
BIT	:	Built-in test
KB	:	Knowledge base
KBS	:	Knowledge based system/Expert system
KR	:	Knowledge representation
LRU	:	Least repairable unit
SIT	:	System integrated test

NATO ASI Series, Vol. F22
Software System Design Methods. Edited by J.K. Skwirzynski

1. INTRODUCTION

1.1 KNOWLEDGE BASED SYSTEMS

To improve the computerizing of failure detection, testing and maintenance, artificial intelligence and knowledge based techniques are currently being explored (7, 8, 21, 22, 28). Knowledge based systems (KBS) are software programs supplemented with man-machine interfaces, which use knowledge and reasoning to perform complex tasks at a level of performance usually associated with an expert either of these three domains.

An expert system essentially consists of a knowledge base containing facts, rules, heuristics, and procedural knowledge, and an inference engine which consists of reasoning or problem solving strategies on how to use knowledge to make decisions (7, 28). It also consists of a user interface with the user in either natural language, via interactive graphics, or through voice input. The explanation generator in the expert system provides answers to queries made by the user. The knowledge base is developed by a small group of knowledge engineers who query the domain expert(s). As an aid to getting knowledge into the knowledge base, a knowledge acquisition tool is used (either by the domain expert or knowledge engineer).

1.2 APPLICATIONS TO FAILURE DETECTION, TESTING AND MAINTENANCE

Failure detection, testing and maintenance are knowledge intensive and experience-based tasks (7, 8, 21). Although test procedures and maintenance manuals contain recommended detection, localization, testing, maintenance and repair actions, their use alone does not assure successfull completion of troubleshooting and repair in a timely manner. Skilled maintenance staff, apart from using test procedures and maintenance manuals, use heuristics and an understanding of how the system works to solve problems. It is this "beyond procedures" type of knowledge that enables them to perform at an exceptional level. Based on years of experience, a highly skilled test/maintenance technician develops the following traits:

- a familiarity with procedures and documented maintenance manuals
- an understanding of LRU and symptoms interactions
- an understanding of the relationships between symptoms and failed LRU's
- an intuitive understanding of how the system works
- an intuitive understanding of how the system will behave when certain subsystems or LRU's fail.

The high level of performance of experts suggests that, confronted with a problem, they analyze the problem in a structured manner rather than randomly trying all possible alternatives. Experience with medical diagnosticians, in particular, suggests that expert diagnosticians have their diagnostic knowledge organized in powerful hierarchical structures that enables them to quickly reason from given symptoms to specific system level problems to LRU level problems using various testing procedures wherever appropriate.

Problems with e.g. an aircraft are typically reported through pilot squawks (21). Pilot squawks contain information on lost capabilities of aircraft functions. Based on the reported problem, the pilot is debriefed for more specific information, during which the test/maintenance specialist tries to narrow the list of possible malfunctioned LRU's. Sometimes the malfunctioned LRU can be identified based on the debriefing session. During the debriefing session the specialist is "Interpreting" the symptons and "Diagnosing" the problem by asking more specific data. Often at the end of the debriefing, the specialist will have limited the malfunctions to a few LRU's. The specialist will then "troubleshoot" the problem by following the specified procedures.

If the failed LRU is identified, then the appropriate "replacement/repair" action will be taken. After the repair action is complete, the system is retested and the response "monitored" to assure that the problem is removed.

Sometimes the problem cannot be easily diagnosed. In such situations the historical database of the specific aircraft and the fleetwide database are consulted in order to obtain a clue (21). Failing this, the test/maintenance specialist has to use his "deep understanding" (i.e., the knowledge on how the system works) to diagnose the problem and sometimes "design" new tests to test for unusual conditions. Finally, the logical and structural coherence of symptoms, tests, and maintenance actions must be checked for final detection decisions, test selection, and repair. This decision level involves quite often pattern recognition techniques, as discussed in (21). Because this process is time consuming, special considerations may be required under wartime conditions. Due to the constraints of limited resources (available technicians, their skill level, available spare parts, and testing equipment) and available time for aircraft repair, the tests to be performed, and the repair actions to be taken are "scheduled" in order to effect a short turn-around time.

In designing a KBS that will perform the above mentioned tasks, several types of tasks will need to be modeled. Identifying these tasks and associated reasoning processes distincly, and modelling them as independent modules is extremely important to achieving a high degree of performance and modularity for future expansion and modification of the system. Some of the tasks identified in the above discussion are interpretation, diagnosis, troubleshooting, repair, design, planning and scheduling, monitoring, reasoning with functional models, and metarules (21,22,24).

2. EXAMPLES OF KNOWLEDGE-BASED FAULT DETECTION, TEST GENERATION, AND MAINTENANCE KBS

Several KBS systems exist that address some of the problems relevant to the detection/test/diagnosis/maintenance task. A review of the capabilities and limitations of some of these KBS is presented to identify methods and techniques that can be used. Other KBS exist or are under development, but cannot be mentioned here for lack of space and/or published open descriptions. KBS characteristics used here are defined in later Sections.

2.1 MYCIN is one of the earliest KBS which diagnoses bacterial infections in blood samples. MYCIN was designed as an experimental system using a production systems approach. It uses backward chaining inferencing and has a modest size knowledge base. MYCIN contains around 700 rules. MYCIN solves only one type of problem-solving type: diagnosis. MYCIN can combine confidence factors associated with individual rules to obtain an overall confidence factor for the decision made. MYCIN's query facility is rather simple. It can inform the user why it is asking for certain data and how a certain decision was made. Designers of MYCIN have now decided to implement a similar system using a distributed problem solving approach (27). MYCIN has under various names found its way into KBS shells, e.g. EMYCIN, several of which have been tested for diagnostics. GUIDON is a MYCIN-like program for teaching diagnosis (7), and STEAMER (18) another one.

2.2 Failure detection schemes using pattern recognition techniques, and corresponding learning information, have been developed e.g. for aircraft/missile engine monitoring, rotating machinery, guidance systems (21, 24, 26). Detection performances, as well as diagnostic results have often been excellent, provided failure modes could be characterized well enough from measurements and observations. None, however, includes explicitely symbolic knowledge, apart from implicit knowledge in the form of measurement data organization and logic conditions applicable to a hierarchical tree organization of the classification rules.

2.3 DELTA/CATS-1(7) is a production system type expert system that performs trouble-shooting for locomotive engines. This expert system is a feasibility type demonstration system. The system was initially designed with 50 rules, and at last report has 530 such rules. Future plans are to expand the knowledge base. Like MYCIN this system solves a single type of problem: diagnosis.

2.4 MDX is distributed problem solving type KBS based on the notion of a society of specialists organized in a strictly hierarchical structure (13). Apart from the "diagnosis" part, MDX also consists of other KBS called PATREC and RADEX. The diagnosis portion interacts with these two auxiliary expert systems to obtain and interpret historical and lab data.

2.5 AUTOMECH is a KBS written in the CSRL language which diagnoses automobile fuel systems (7). It is patterned after MDX (13).

2.6 DART is diagnostic expert system that uses functional models of the components instead of diagnostic rules to diagnose a problem. DART is one of the earlier systems to use deep functional knowledge in designing expert systems (16). (14) has reported the use of deep knowledge in terms of system structure and behavior for diagnosing computers.

2.7 ISIS is a distributed problem solving type expert system designed to perform a job shop scheduling task in a manufacturing plant. In order to do job shop scheduling, ISIS has to take into account various types of constraints. Constraints considered by ISIS are: organizational constraints to assure profitability, physical constraints to check the capability of a machine, gating constraints to check if a particular machine or tool can be used and preference constraints to enable the shop supervisor to override the expert program (15). ISIS is a feasibility type demonstration system. It is still under development.

2.8 A diagnostic and test selection KBS shell has been developed and used for integrated circuit testing, datacommunications monitoring, avionics maintenance training, and EW systems (7, 23). It uses nested list frame representations per LRU, similar to failure-mode effect analysis. The inference is by truth maintenance, with propagated constraints, and a set of domain independent diagnostic metarules. The detection/test selection/failure mode recognition is by a subsequent domain dependent pattern recognition procedure (21).

2.9 IN-ATE (ARC) a model-basic probabilistic rule-based KBS for electronics troubleshooting has been written (7) which produces automatically a binary pass/fail decision tree of testpoints to be checked. The search is by the gamma miniaverage tree search (21). This KBS does not use explicit symbolic knowledge.

2.10 ARBY/NDS is using a LISP based forward-and-backward logic inference scheme (DUCK) for avionics or communications networks troubleshooting (7). The hypothesis refinement algorithm can be quite cumbersome, and all failure modes must be known in advance.

2.11 ACE is a KBS for preventive maintenance of telephone cable, by selecting equipments for said maintenance (7). The knowledge base is a database containing repair activity records. ACE is in regular use.

2.12 LES is a production rule based KBS for electronic

maintenance (7), the various LRU are described by frames, to which about 50 rules are applied.

2.13 SMART BIT is a KBS to incorporate false alarm filters, fault recording in built-in-test systems.

2.14 STAMP is an avionics box failure detection KBS, with test sequences organized by failure history, and dynamic modification of the fault tree.

2.15 IDT (10).

2.16 CRIB (11).

Our review shows that most earlier KBS are simple, solve only one type of problem, have a modest size knowledge base, have a rather simple uncertainty handling capability, and used rules as the primary means of knowledge representation. It is also seen that some of the early researchers now prefer the distributed problem solving approach over the production systems approach. KBS are now focussing on using knowledge other than heuristics. Using metarules (4, 23) makes these systems more robust decision aids.

3. KNOWLEDGE BASE DESIGN AND KNOWLEDGE REPRESENTATION

The fault detection/test/maintenance knowledge base will consist of several knowledge bases (KB) each dedicated to an independent source of knowledge such as:

- signals
- LRU and system structure (layout, causality structure)

- images
- observation reports
- FMEA analysis
- action lists
- maintenance manual
- historic maintenance and performance data
- experimental knowledge of maintenance staff
- time, location

Each of these specialized KBs appears as a node in the global KB (Figure 1).

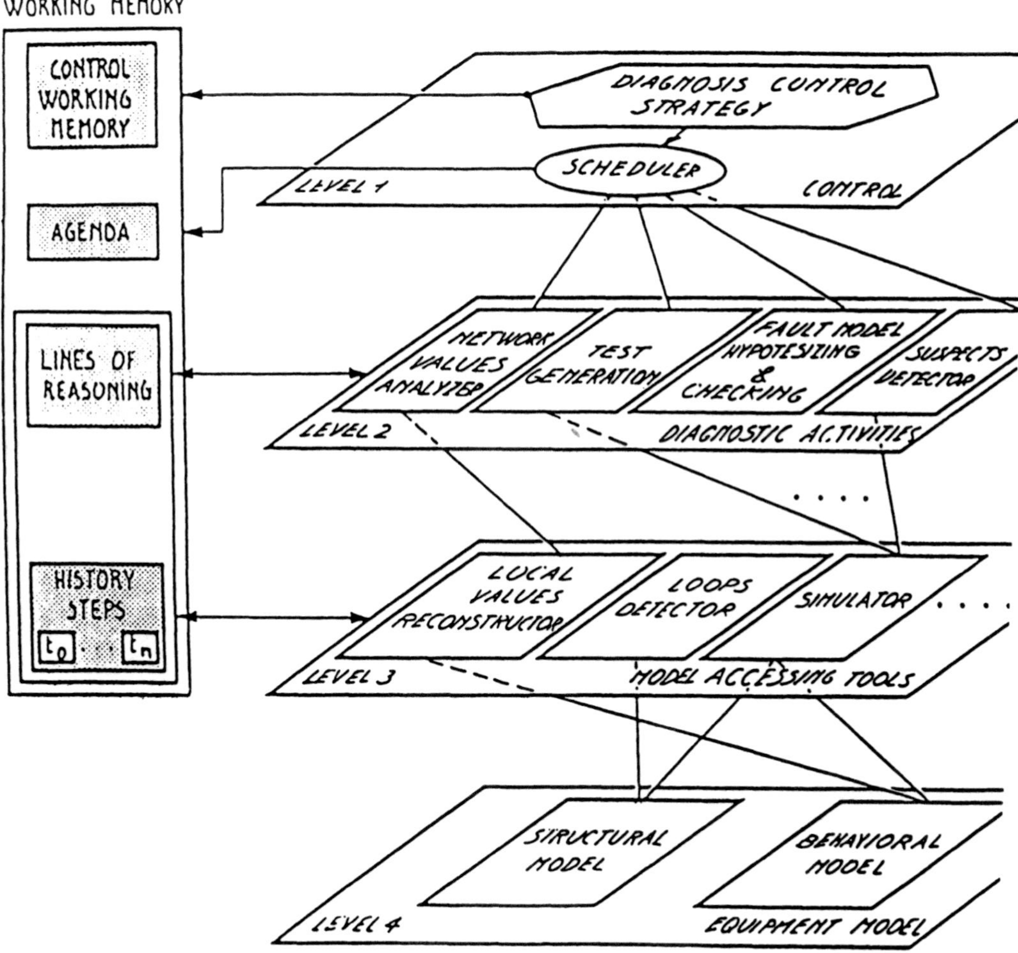

Figure 1: Layered Knowledge base for failure detection/ test/maintenance.

3.1 KNOWLEDGE REPRESENTATION

Knowledge representation refers to the task of modelling real world knowledge in terms of computer data structures. The basic task is to identify knowledge primitives and to define a system to combine the primitives to represent higher level knowledge.

The problem of representation is closely related to the problem of how the knowledge is used. In KBS, knowledge is used to solve problems, i.e., determine new facts based upon what is already known. The knowledge should be efficiently usable and easily expandable. Knowledge, therefore, has to be represented for quick and easy retrieval, for adequately expressing the various similarities and distinctions, for high computational efficiency, for ease in further expansion and modification, for use in reasoning or solving a specific problem, and for efficient storage.

In order to satisfy the various requirements for the knowledge representation, different techniques have to be used for different types of knowledge (28). Selecting appropriate knowledge representation schemes is important because AI research has shown that the problem solving strategy heavily depends upon the representation (20). Selecting an appropriate representation has the impact of either rendering the system successful or a failure. The knowledge representation scheme can effectively limit what the system can perceive, know, or understand (6).

The basic knowledge representation techniques are: symbols, fact lists, semantic networks, logic predicates, rules or production systems, frames, and knowledge objects. These basic representation entities are used to construct representation schemes with desired characteristics for the particular applications. To provide powerful expressiveness, conciseness, and easy modifiability by domain experts, the representation schemes evolve into stand-alone, high-level programming languages.

Representation schemes are evaluated on the basis of:

- Expressiveness: Does the representation scheme make all of the important distinctions between the concepts being represented (6)

- Structural Representation: Can it support different specialized forms of representation? (12)

- Computational Efficiency: Does the representation scheme allow for efficient computation of various inferences required for the task (6)

- Modifiability: Is the representation scheme easily modifiable?

- Conciseness: Is the representation scheme compact, clear, and at the right level of abstraction? (6)

- Representation Uniformity: Can different types of knowledge be expressed with the same general knowledge representation scheme? (12)

- Logical Consistency: Are the different knowledge units mutually and logically consistent? (12)

- Easy Retrieval and Access: Is the representation scheme such that the desired knowledge can be easily accessed? (12)

- Multiple Level Representation of Knowledge: Does the

representation scheme allow the representation of the same concept at different levels of abstraction? (4, 12)

Figure 2 presents a comparison of four popular representation languages or schemes based upon a discussion in (12). Because of its flexibility in representing different types of real world knowledge and because very little commitment is required to any one representation technique, our preferred choice is a frame based representation scheme.

For large knowledge bases that need to evolve with time and may require frequent updating, both production systems and frame type representations are adequate. Requirements for computational efficiency, expressiveness, conciseness, and easy software maintenance dictate frames over production systems.

The representation schemes will be identified based upon the detailed analysis of the desired characteristics of various knowledge sources such as situation databases, historical database, maintenance manuals, expert maintenance technician experience, and the functional knowledge pertinent to maintenance task.

Frame type representations can be extended to inheritance mechanisms for sharing information to achieve conciseness; another inheritance scheme used in (23, 25) is the LRU-Block-Module-Subsystem hierarchy, applicable both to structural descriptors, observations, and interfaces between objects.

Features	Frames	Semantic Networks	Predicate Calculus	Production System
Expressiveness	10	10	2	2
Structural Representation	8	10	2	2
Computational Efficiency	10	5	3	3
Modifiability	10	1	1	1
Conciseness	10	2	2	2
Representational Uniformity	8	5	10	10
Logical Consistency	5	5	10	5
Easy Retrieval and Access	10	5	5	5
Multiple Level of Representation	10	10	4	4

Figure 2: Comparison of Knowledge Representation Schemes.

Failure detection/test/maintenance KBS are required to be able to interface with maintenance personnel with different levels of skill. This requires representing the knowledge at various levels of abstraction. This involves designing mapping mechanisms from primitives to higher levels of representation. Development tools are available that provide this type of layered KB capability.

4. REASONING TECHNIQUES

The failure detection/testing/maintenance KBS is implemented on a processor to assist the reasoning process of maintenance personnel or test equipments. For each specialist knowledge base node, a specialist reasoning process is designed; this process will also use general inference procedures inherited from the general inference engine of the entire KBS.

4.1 COMMUNICATION BETWEEN KB NODES

Communication problems arise because of unrestricted crosstalk between the nodes. The proposed approach to this problem is to build in hierachical communication between the problem solving specialist nodes (17). Since most of the specialist nodes have to access intelligent database nodes, this cross communication is handled through a blackboard mechanism (29). In the blackboard mechanism, all KB nodes read data from a blackboard and write their results on the blackboard. Nodes not in direct hierarchical link, exchange information through the blackboard without being explicitly aware of each other. This approach mixes the power of direct hierachical communication whenever possible, and avoids the drawback of cross-talk through the use of blackboards.

4.2 CONTROL STRUCTURE

KBS need to have a highly efficient control structure. The purpose of a control structure is to determine which subtask should be done next, i.e., what KB node to access next. In simpler KBS, a common approach is to use production systems type of control where a list of condition match and act rules is evaluated repeatedly. For large KBS consisting of several KB nodes, the issue of control and communication are inter-related. Where possible, a node hierarchy is constructed and the hierarchy inherently determines the next KB node to be accessed. When not possible, blackboard communication is used. In this case the KB nodes invariably interact only with the blackboard.

Apart from having a control structure at the KB node level, there is also a need for an overall global control. Global control determines when to start the detection/test/diagnosis process, and when the process is complete.

4.3 INFERENCE ENGINE

The inference engine uses knowledge in the knowledge base to solve a specific problem by emulating the reasoning process of a human expert. The AI approach to solving a problem essentially consists of searching a solution from a search space. In AI terminology, the set of all possible solutions is known as the search space. The inference engine essentially consists of problem solving strategies that use knowledge in the knowledge base to search for a solution.

The problem solved by the failure detection/test/maintenance KBS is to determine the correct maintenance actions based on the symptoms, repair history and maintenance (21). The KBS will consist of several search spaces: the set of possible symptoms, the set of all component malfunctions, the set of all possible tests that can be conducted, and the set of all possible repair actions. The historical database is also a kind of search space.

The search space can be finite and small, it can be finite but quite large, or even practically infinite. The search space can be structured or unstructured. For structured search spaces, the search strategy and the criteria for selecting a solution are both algorithmic. In unstructured search spaces, the search strategy cannot be prespecified in an algorithmic way. Expert knowledge in terms of heuristics and trial and error techniques are generally used to search through such spaces. Additional problems arise when the search space is large. Not only is there a problem of time to evaluate each possible solution, but also there is a problem of focusing the problem solving strategy. That is, which nodes should be evaluated and in which order. Human experts are known to successfully perform under these conditions. In expert systems search and focusing problems are solved by the inference engine.

The experience knowledge used by an expert to solve a problem is rarely precise. It generally consists of less-than-certain facts, heuristics from other domains, assumptions which are made unless a contradiction is reached, solutions which are proposed and tested, and some rules and facts which are not used because of constraints or relevancy considerations. To handle various kinds of search spaces and to use imprecise knowledge to search for a solution, AI research has developed many approaches. Some of the important inference mechanisms are:

1. Heuristic search. In many domains and in particular, in failure detection and maintenance, some personnel can diagnose problems more quickly and effectively than others.

When this ability is due to special, domain specific knowledge, acquired as a result of experience, then that knowledge is known as heuristics or rules-of-thumb. This is the type of knowledge that gives expert systems their power because it permits rapid search. For example, in repairing an auto, if the car won't start, the battery is examined for failure before the starter is examined. If the battery is faulty, the starter is never examined, unless there are multiple problems.

2. Generate/test In this case, the search space is not built a priori, but is built as needed. In effect, possible solutions are generated as the system procedes, and are evaluated shortly thereafter.

3. Forward chaining/backward chaining. In some problems, it is desirable to determine the hypothesis supported by the given data. Such problems can be solved using either forward or backward chaining. In forward chaining the reasoning procedes from data or symptoms to hypotheses, i.e., given data, preconditions for the truth of certain hypothesis are tested. This process is similar to pruning a decision tree. In backward chaining the reasoning procedes from hypothesis to data, i.e., the inference engine first selects a hypothesis to be tested and then seeks for data required to test the hypothesis. If a certain hypothesis turns out to be false, the system can undo all conclusions that preceded or followed the false hypothesis.

4. Recognize/act. In some problems, the occurrence of certain data in terms of features and symptoms necessitate certain actions. The actions are specified by IF (features pattern) THEN (take action) types of rules. The most thoroughly researched and validated approach is to determine/recognize the pattern of features by discriminant analysis, nearest neighbor rules, syntax driven statistical classifiers

(24, 21, 23, 25). For symbolic feature information only, the inference mechanism then matches the IF part of the rule against the available data and takes action specified by the THEN part of the rule.

5. Constraint Directed. This approach is usually used in design because it is based on the existence of predefined plans, or plans which can be generically defined. Usually, a skeleton of the overall plan is known and subportions of the plan are specialized or completed in a predefined manner, if they satisfy the certain constraints.

6. Metarules (4): These are in this instance basic blocks of IF-THEN rules, or hypothesis refinement procedures (such as 1., 3., 4.) which rely on exhaustive mapping of causality relations and basic actions in the three dimensional space of (physical/functional layout, observed features, failure propagation/search strategy) (22, 23). They allow for KBS to be developed that can be applied to many projects.

The purpose of the global control structure is to coordinate and control the interactions between the node KBS and provide a friendly interface with the user. The global control performs e.g. the preliminary analysis of the conditions of tl aircraft reported in pilot squawks and determines if the maintenance is needed. It takes into account the time constraints on turn-around time and determines how the problem solving should proceed. The role of the global control system can be compared to that of a maintenance supervisor. The design of the global control is based upon principles similar to the inference engine design.

5. KBS ARCHITECTURE

5.1 REQUIREMENTS

Standard requirements put on failure detection/testing/maintenance KBS are (24):

- Minimum non-detection probability
- Minimum false alarm probability
- Minimum detection/test selection/maintenance action selection time, especially in interactive usage mode
- Knowledge Integration: To enable effective use of procedural heuristic knowledge, specific historical data, fleet data, and a deep knowledge of the functional understanding of the system (incl. CAE data) (21)

- Types of Problems Solved: Most KBS solve a single type of problem in a narrowly defined area of expertise. The KBS will be required to solve several types of problems in order to perform different tasks.

- Resource and Constraint conformance: The KBS should be capable of exploiting inherent redundancy in the system and should take into account the limitations of a particular maintenance squadron in fault isolation and in recommending repair actions. Some of the constraints are time available for repair, personnel/test equipment availability, skill level, and available spare parts.

- Expandability and Maintenance: The knowledge base should be easily expandable to accommodate the addition of new knowledge or changes in the current knowledge. The requirement of easy maintenance is critical for large systems.

- Capable of Using Meta-Knowledge: In order to handle unforseen situations, the KBS should possess detailed knowledge on how the system works, on general failure modes propagation, what happens in case of LRU failures, and what will happen if certain repair actions are taken. Simulation models are to be included in this class of knowledge (21).

- Capable of Handling Uncertainties: In knowledge base systems, uncertainty arises from three sources: lack of complete data, incomplete pertinent knowledge, and uncertainty inherent in the process. The KBS will have to resolve such uncertainty using redundant knowledge from other knowledge sources or through statistical means.

- Explanation Generation and Query Capability: For the KBS to be usable by the maintenance technicians with different levels of skill. It is essential to have sophisticated explanation capability. It must be capable of explaining its line of reasoning and justify the advice it gives to the user. It should also allow the user to query its knowledge base in order to debug or to gain a better understanding about the maintenance task.

5.2 KBS ARCHITECTURES

There are three basic KBS architectures: production systems, structured production systems, distributed reasoning (28). These architectures must be specified, both for the total KBS, and the specialized node KBS.

5.2.1 Production systems (Figure 3) use a single inference engine and a single knowledge base. The inference engine consists of problem independent control strategies which determine which rules should be executed next and executes the actions specified by the rules. The knowledge base consists of a list of production rules (IF -features- THEN -decisions-). All the rules in the list are checked repeatedly untill the designed result is achieved. If the number of rules is small then production systems are ideal. However, for even moderately sized knowledge bases, the execution time is very large. For applications that need to have non-delay interactive execution or almost real time execution, this aspects is major a drawback.

5.2.2 Structured production systems (Figure 4) divide the knowledge base into knowledge chunks and use meta-rules to determine which knowledge chunk should be accessed next. Since only a selected number of rules are checked for a given set of date, structured production systems are usually capable of near real-time execution.

5.2.3 Distributed reasoning (Figure 5) is based on the notion of specialized KB cooperatively solving a specific inference. Each specialized KBS may be a production or structured production system; the corresponding KB are organized in a hierarchical structure. A blackboard allows all specialist nodes with a structured common area to access information.

5.3 COMPARISON

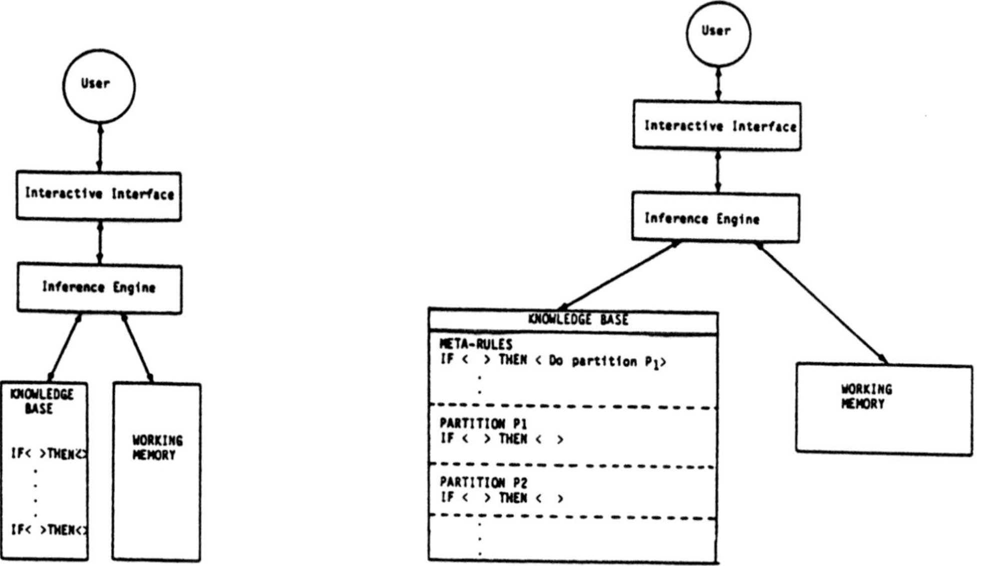

Figure 3: A Production System Structure.

Figure 4: A Structured Production System Structure.

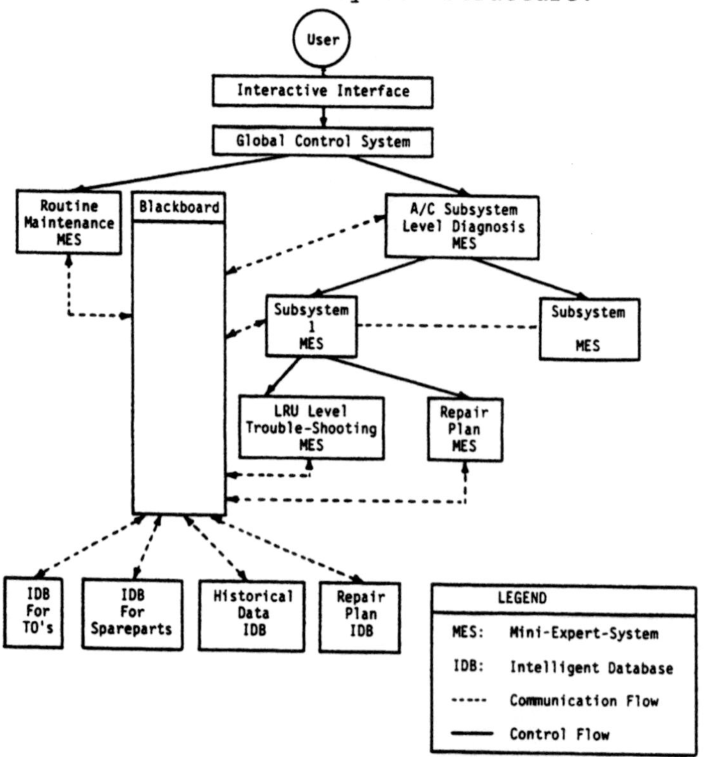

Figure 5: Distributed Problem Solving Structure.

For potentially complex detection/test generation/maintenance systems, distributed reasoning has several advantages (22):

- for a given problem of specified KB size, the execution time is the least (19)
- specialized KB limit the search required, and render execution times relatively independent of KB size
- easy updates.

In order to handle unforseen failures, the KBS has to possess some functional knowledge about the system. This requires representation schemes different from the simple IF-THEN constructs. Although in principle any type of knowledge can be represented as IF-THEN rules, it is more efficient to represent knowledge in its natural form. This is important because knowledge and how it is used are two different things. Commitment to an IF-THEN structure forces one type of use. For example, knowledge about facts (x is the name of an aircraft), knowledge about system structure (system consists of actuators, flight computers, and sensors), knowledge about processes (To repair electromechanical servo valves follow step 3.4.2 in the TO number 34), knowledge about events (during a sudden takeoff the computers failed), knowledge about causal relationships (failure of computer will cause following malfunctions), knowledge about goals (the purpose of mission is to monitor area Z), knowledge about time, and knowledge about actions, do not easily fit a simple IF-THEN type representation.

Production and strutured production systems do not allow the use of more sophisticated knowledge representation techniques. In distributed reasoning each specialist node can have its own unique knowledge representation which is better suited for its particular problem. This feature enables incorporating meta-rules and functional knowledge into the KBS. A similar problem arises in trying to use situational databases and historical databases in the KBS. Each of these databases will have different structures for these databases, a feature only provided by the distributed reasoning approach.

6. POTENTIAL APPLICATIONS

Five major improvement areas can be considered to have a potential for application, with the use of knowledge engineering techniques (7, 8, 2, 3, 5):

i self improving diagnostics: functional test sequences can be cost effectively improved, and automated learning through metarules is a promising area (21)

ii more effective fault detection and isolation, thru built-in-test KBS (22, 24)

iii discrimination between false alarms and intermittent faults

iv reduction of skills required for test and maintenance

v integrated diagnostics (21)

These improvements are considered likely to go into 8 generic failure detection/testing/maintenance systems (8):

a. computer aided preliminary design for testability: testability KBS available during preliminary design phases (1, 9)

b. smart built-in-test (Smart BIT) to identify intermittent faults and reduce false alarms, and carry out recalibration

c. smart system integrated test (Smart SiT) for system level testing while in operations

d. box maintenance KBS to provide offline test management with self improvement of functional tests

e. system maintenance KBS

f. automatic-test program generation (ATPG) (2, 23)

g. smart bench which is a maintenance KBS developed for use with bench test equipment controlled by an engineering workstation.

Finally, it should be stressed that sensor fusion, which consists in applying distributed reasoning to different information sources (e.g. analog/digital signals, test outcomes, text from verbal reports, inspection images), may lead to novel micro-electronic sensors implementing in hardware some of the corresponding knowledge representation schemes (25).

REFERENCES

1. P.W. Horstman, Design for testability using logic programming, Proc. IEEE 1983 Int. Test Conf., 706-713

2. A.J. Kunert, ATE-applications of AI, Proc IEEE 1982 Autotestcon, 153-

3. T.G. Freund, Applying knowledge engineering to TPS development, Proc. IEEE 1983 Autotestcon, 318 - 321

4. A. Barr, Metaknowledge and cognition, Proc 6th IJCAI, August 1979, 31 - 33

5. G.C. Sumner, Knowledge based systems maintenance applications, Proc IEEE 1982 Autotestcon, 472 - 473

6. W.A. Woods, What's important about knowledge representation, IEEE Computer, oct. 1983

7. Proc-Artificial intelligence in maintenance, AFHL, USAF Systems Command, T.R. AFHRL-TR-84-25, June 1984

8. Artificial intelligence applications to testability, RADC, USAF Systems Command, T.R. RADC-TR-84-203, October 1984

9. Computer aided testability and design analysis, T.R. RADC-TR-83-257, 1983

10. H. Shubin et al, IDT: an intelligent diagnostic tool, Proc. AAAI, August 1982, 156-

11. R.T. Hartley, CRIB: computer fault finding through knowledge engineering, IEEE Computer, March 1984.

12. D.G. BOBROW, Panel discussion on AI, Proc. IJCAI, 1977

13. B. Chandrasekaran, S. Mittal, J. Smith, Reasoning with uncertain knowledge: the MDX approach, Proc. 1st Conf. American Medical informatics ass., 1982

14. R. Davis, H. Shrobe, Representing structure and behaviour of digital hardware, IEEE Computer, Oct. 1983, 75 - 82

15. M.S. Fox, G. Strohm, Job-shop scheduling: an investigation in constraint directed reasoning, Proc. AAAI, August 1982

16. M.R. Genesereth, Diagnosis using hierarchical design methods, Proc. AAAI, August 1982, 178 - 183

17. F. Gomez, Knowledge organization and distribution for diagnosis, IEEE Trans., Vol SMC, Jan. 1979

18. J.D. Hollan et al, STEAMER: an interactive inspectable simulation-based training system, AI Magazine, summer 1984

19. Kiyoshi Niwa et al, An experimental comparison of knowledge representation schemes, AI Magazine, summer 1984

20. A. Newell, H. Simon, Human problem solving, Prentice Hall, N.J., 1972

21. L.F. Pau, Failure diagnosis and performance monitoring, Marcel Dekker, NY, 1981

22. L.F. Pau, Failure diagnosis systems, Acta IMEKO 1982, North Holland, Amsterdam, 1982

23. L.F. Pau, Failure diagnosis by an expert system and pattern classification, Pattern recognition letters, Vol 2,

Dec. 1984, 419 - 425

24. L.F. Pau, Applications of pattern resognition to failure analysis and diagnosis, in J. Rasmussen, W.B. Rouse (Ed), Human detection and diagnosis of system failures, Plenum Press, NY, 1981; 429 - 446

25. L.F. Pau, Integrated testing and algorithms for visual inspection of integrated circuits, IEEE Trans., Vol PAMI-5, no 6, Nov. 1983, 602 - 608

26. L.F. Pau., An adaptive signal classification procedure: application to aircraft engine monitoring, Pattern recognition, Vol 9, 1977, 121 - 130

27. W.J. Clancey et al, NEOMYCIN, Proc. IJCAI, 1982.

28. P.H. Winston, Artificial intelligence, Addison-Wesley. Publ., 1983

29. L.D. Earman et al, Hearsay-II, Computing surveys, Vol 12, no 2, 1980.

SOFTWARE DEVELOPMENT UNDER STATISTICAL QUALITY CONTROL

M. Dyer
IBM Corporation
Federal Systems Division
Bethesda, MD 20817/USA

ABSTRACT

Recent software initiatives identify a practical approach to putting software development under statistical control, that provides software management visibility into the development process and the opportunity to introduce process changes to enhance product quality. Two underlying principles to the approach are that product development should be performed with no unit debugging and product testing should be based on user representative statistical samples. Current experience with the approach and the use of process controls for product quality are discussed.

INTRODUCTION

Recent software engineering initiatives identify a practical approach to putting software development under statistical quality control. Similar to modern manufacturing practice, software outputs are continuously sampled, statistical measures taken, and corrections fed back to the development process. The approach gives software management visibility into the development process and an opportunity to introduce process changes to enhance product quality.

Recognizing that software engineering has been practiced for a relatively short period, essentially starting in the 1950's, there is considerable potential for change and growth. As with any young technology, future software practice can be expected to be surprisingly different from current practice.

The notion of putting software development under statistical quality control, which is the focus of the cleanroom development method, is one such departure from current practice. As the term implies,

NATO ASI Series, Vol. F22
Software System Design Methods. Edited by J.K. Skwirzynski

cleanroom attempts to incorporate error prevention into the software process, which is quite different from the current view that software errors are always present and error detection is the critical consideration. It recognizes as impractical the placing of a trial and error software development process under statistical control. No meaningful statistics would be obtained from any attempted execution of such software because of its high error content and unpredictable execution characteristics.

To apply statistical quality control, a statistical basis for evaluating the software product is needed. Unlike manufacturing, the basis can not be found in the large numbers of similar products that are produced, since software is a logical one of a kind product. Rather it has to be in the testing of the software product, which must be a statistical rather than selective process and performed on the total product rather than its parts. With hardware, physical dimensions and the statistical tolerances on physical parts are additive components and can be combined for considering the statistical quality of a product. With software, the combination of parts is a more complicated question, with no practical rules for collecting part failures into product failures because of the deep and complex logical interactions between parts.

Two underlying principles for developing software under statistical quality control come out of these considerations — product development should be performed with no unit debugging and product testing should be based on user representative statistical samples. It is generally recognized that unit debugging leads to idiosyncratic product designs (which errors fixed in which order) and, more importantly from our perspective, interferes with the statistical testing of original designs. It is also recognized that the most thoughtful and thorough selective testing can provide nothing but anecdotal evidence about software quality. There is no scientific basis for extrapolating testing results to operational environments as provided with statistical testing.

Software engineering design practice currently exists to support the generation of software products with sufficient quality to forego unit debugging. Rigorous software verification both by the software originator and independent inspectors ensure the delivery of correct software prior to any execution. Software testing is instead used to assess product quality and operating reliability. Testing is defined as a statistical process which uses randomly selected samples of product inputs, selected on the basis of their expected operational usage.

This paper describes a method for obtaining quality and reliability measurements which can then be used in controlling the development process. Software verification and statistical testing methods defined for the cleanroom process are discussed and the results from their use in recent product developments are illustrated.

QUALITY CONTROL PROCESS

The cleanroom software development method represents a first practical approach to placing software development under statistical quality control. The method was developed at the IBM Federal Systems Division (FSD) as an extension to the FSD software engineering program (1).

In contrast to current development approaches, the cleanroom method embeds software development and testing within a formal statistical design. Software engineering methods support the creation of software designs with sufficient quality to forego unit debugging so that software testing is used to make statistical inference about the software reliability. This systematic process of assessing and controlling software quality during development permits the certification of product reliability at delivery. Certification in this sense attests to a public record of defect discovery and repair and to a measured level of operating reliability.

The ingredients for cleanroom are a new software development life cycle and independent quality assessment through statistical testing. The development life cycle starts with a product specification, referred to as a Structured Specification, and is organized about the release of executable product increments. The Structured Specification identifies functional requirements but additionally establishes a nested sequence of function subsets that will be developed and tested as increments and also quantifies the operational usage statistics for the product function.

Selective testing (stressing boundaries, etc.) is generally considered faster and more effective at finding software errors than statistical testing. However, statistical testing may have more capability than currently thought, if the variability in the failure rate of different errors is considered. Recent evidence with IBM products (2) indicates that this variability is significant, with as much as four orders of magnitude difference in the failure rates of the existing errors. When failure rates are considered, statistical testing is more efficient in finding the errors with high failure rates and, consequently, those which most impact the product reliability. Selective testing on the other hand may find more errors, but not necessarily provide a similar improvement in reliability.

Cleanroom Software Development

Cleanroom development uses software engineering methods (3) to produce provably correct software designs. Rigorous software verification by both the designer and independent inspectors accounts for the increased product quality and provides a confirmation of software readiness for release from development

The software engineering methods are organized about a mathematically based design practice (1) which promotes intellectual control of design complexity, and uses modules, programs, and data as underlying design objects. Software is viewed as a hierarchy of components or subsystems whose designs are defined by modules and programs, which themselves may also be organized into component levels of modules and programs. Design is considered a repetitive refinement or decomposition of software specifications into design objects. A mathematical rule, the Axiom of Replacement, supports replacing program parts by functionally equivalent components and has been extended to cover the replacement of data objects and modules.

Stepwise refinement guarantees that design function is unchanged when functionally equivalent elaborations are substituted. Design verification checks that the substitution hypothesis is satisfied and demonstrates the equivalence between the original and substituted parts, using both formal (requiring documented analysis) and informal (satisfied through correctness questions) methods. This distinction in formality is not one of verification rigor, since the same correctness arguments are considered and resolved in each instance.

It should be noted that the basis for correctness does not rely on the infallibility of the software designer, his being more careful, or working harder. It stems rather from the recognition of programs as mathematical objects, subject to logic and reasoning, with defined rules for their orderly combination, based on structured programming principles.

Process Controls

Statistical quality control in any process requires measurement, feedback, and corrective action as needed. The cleanroom development life cycle with structured specifications and product development as executable increments supports such interaction and provides the controls for addressing software quality during product development. Two new measurements that are unique to the cleanroom method for process control are the verification of provably correct designs and the statistical projection of product reliability.

Quality Control Through Rigorous Verification

Formal inspections (4) in current software practice serve the primary purpose of detecting defects in the material being inspected. A software product (its design and code), the product documentation, and testing material for product validation are all subject to inspection. In this context product quality is defined in terms of the numbers of defects that are uncovered.

However, these counts tend to be ineffective for establishing an absolute measure of product quality since, regardless of the number of defects found, there is no certainty about how many remain. Because there is no basis for deciding whether these numbers should be high or low, they really have only academic interest. When the number is high, the defect removal process may be working or the number of real defects may be high. When the number is low, it is similarly not clear whether the defect removal process has broken down or there are, in fact, few defects to find.

Verification on the other hand offers an effective quality measure since it strives to certify software correctness in an absolute sense. The outcome of verification is not an enumeration of product defects but the confirmation that a design is or is not correct. Unlike inspections where there can be uncertainty on the need for design rework based on the number of uncovered defects, if a design can not be verified then it must be reworked. Thus verification provides an effective process control which triggers design rework without any ambiguity.

Since provable correctness is an objective measure the introduction of verification should also enhance the prospects for quality software development. The verification rules are embodied in software engineering practice and can be equally effective in originating as well as checking designs. If designers anticipate an independent verification of their work prior to its release, they are more likely to consider design correctness to insure passing the independent check.

Quality Control Through Reliability Measurements

Software MTTF (mean time to failure) predictions provide a second approach to process control. Unlike counts of software defects, the times between successive software failures are numbers of direct user interest particularly when available during development with representative statistical testing. In very simple terms, the higher these interfail times are, the more user satisfaction can be expected. Increasing interfail times indicates progress towards a reliable product unlike increasing defect discovery which may be more symptomatic of an unreliable product.

Software reliability can be certified at product release from a public record of failure detection, the measurement of interfail times, and the calculation of product MTTF based on this execution record. In this sense, certification is the guarantee that all failure data has been correctly recorded and that product MTTF has been calculated in a prescribed manner.

As the executable increments of a product are delivered and tested, the product reliability can be projected from the testing experience with the functions in each increment. While the initial projections will depend on the functions in the earlier increments, the functions in later increments can be expected to behave and mature in the same way, since all the software is developed under a uniform process. The projections at each incremental release permit the assessment of product reliability and its growth in order to trigger any corrective action to the process. Subsequent projections verify whether the actions had the intended effect or whether additional process correction is required to insure that development is carried out under good control.

In addition to monitoring product reliability, MTTF predictions at the component level are also useful for understanding the make up and direction of the product reliability. The behavior of the specific functions within a product should also be tracked to understand their effect (positive or negative) on the product reliability. Specific product defects have different effects on the seriousness of product failures so that reliability projections by failure severity are also useful measures. Detailed analyses of functions and defects are particularly helpful in isolating the source and severity of product unreliability, in order to plan corrective process actions.

QUALITY CONTROL EXPERIENCE

The cleanroom method has been used for the development of several software products, so that experience exists with both the verification and reliability controls. Rigorous verification of product designs has proved sufficiently effective to forego unit debugging without jeopardizing established quality and productivity standards. In the cases where verification was performed to full design detail, significant quality strides (order of magnitude improvements in defect rates) were experienced.

Reliability projections have also been made in the product developments but their use for process control has been limited until some experience in the interpretation and quantification of software MTTF can be gained. Timing data from statistical testing has been recorded and used in various analyses which are providing the necessary insight into the potential uses of software reliability measurements.

The cleanroom method has also been demonstrated at the University of Maryland in an advanced course in software engineering. In this course, a controlled experiment was conducted in team software development of a sizable class project with some classes using cleanroom methods and some not. The results (5) not only demonstrate the feasibility of foregoing unit debugging with good software engineering process, but that, even with student teams, cleanroom performance equals or betters performance with traditional methods.

Software Verification Practice

Software verification is a systematic method for demonstrating the correctness of a design against its intended specifications, which should be carried out to the same degree of rigor, as embodied in the design. The verification reasoning is based on a correctness proof which identifies the necessary proof steps and provides the mathematical justification for the proof arguments. These rules embody a functional approach to software verification in which a program is described in terms of its behavior as a computation on a set of inputs to produce a set of outputs.

A four-part proof must be applied at each decomposition step in a design hierarchy. The proof entails (1) the specification of the intended function for the given design level, (2) the identification of the design objects at the next decomposition level, (3) the demonstration of functional equivalence between the design objects and the intended function, and (4) the confirmation of the result. Specific proofs are organized for each design construct used in the software engineering design methodology (ifthenelse, case, etc.) and are fully described in reference 3. Table 1 shows the proof steps for the ifthenelse construct where two correctness questions must be considered for any alternation logic in a design.

TABLE 1

CORRECTNESS PROOF EXAMPLE FOR THE IFTHENELSE CONSTRUCT

[Z:=Max(X,Y)]	States the intended function
IF	
X > Y	
THEN	
Z: = X	First correctness consideration is that 'For the case X > Y Does Z:=X satisfy Z:=Max(X,Y)'
ELSE	
Z: = Y	Second correctness consideration is that 'For the case of X⩽Y Does Z:=Y satisfy Z:=Max(X,Y)'
FI	

Verification Experience

The principal conclusion from current cleanroom experience is that complete verification to full design detail is practical and compatible with good productivity. That means that every correctness condition for every design construct in a software system can be verified without any negative impact on product schedules and cost. Moveover, complete verification results in software error rates which are an order of magnitude smaller than currently realized with other technologies.

These dramatic results stem from the crucial distinction between formally verifying software correctness and finding defects through inspections. When the focus is on uncovering defects, the inspector tends to mentally execute the program using different input sequences. Generally he must remember different pieces of data as he runs through these executions, which requires non-local reasoning. Since the number of potential input sequences is large (usually infinite) for programs of any significance and there is no way of knowing the number of product defects, inspections can be viewed as an unbounded activity.

Rigorous verification on the other hand depends only on the structure of the design to be reviewed as defined by the number and type of design constructs that are used. Therefore verification, while a significant activity, at least has a finite bound. Moreover, since verification is performed on one design construct at a time and is concerned only with the data used in that construct it requires only local reasoning.

The second significant result from rigorous verification is an emphasis on design simplicity since this is key to making design verification a doable human activity. The volume of design data to be considered in verification must be kept to manageable proportions and can be best achieved by using data abstraction to reduce the number of data objects and by eliminating complexity in control predicates. Complexity creeps into a design when convoluted control logic and unchecked numbers of data variables are introduced which obscure the design and make its implementation, verification, and maintenance both difficult and error prone. Design simplicity on the other hand fosters conservative designs which are both implementable and verifiable.

Reliability Certification

In the cleanroom process software reliability is independently certified during development. Verification replaces unit debugging as the development method for demonstrating correctness so that all product execution occurs during certification and focuses on demonstrating reliable operation in user operating environments. Statistical methods are introduced to create realistic environments through user representative input samples and to generate product reliability projections. A standard reliability measure of software MTTF is computed based on test executions in the representative user environments.

Software reliability predictions are made with statistical models using the times between successive failures of test case executions. Model predictions are made for the functions in each of the executable product increments as increments are delivered for certification. The product MTTF is not projected directly by the statistical models but is separately computed as the weighted sum of the increment MTTF's. The product MTTF is computed continuously as increments are released. At product delivery, the product MTTF can be certified or guaranteed based on all product failures being recorded during development and the history of reliability projections.

Reliability Experience

To show the use of software reliability measurements for process control, data from a recent cleanroom software product development is used. The particular product contained some 30,000 HOL statements and was incrementally developed in five discrete increments. The first four increments delivered new function to the product, whereas the fifth increment was used to clean up defects and obtain a releasable form of the product. The product was composed of ten unique subfunctions which were released according to the following schedule:

- Increment one contained subfunctions 1 and 2
- Increment two contained subfunctions 3, 4, 5, and 6
- Increment three contained subfunctions 7, 8, and 9
- Increment four contained subfunction 10

The releases contained about 10,000 HOL statements for each of the first three increments with the residual code in the fourth increment.

Several analyses were performed on the product data to demonstrate process control potentials. Statistical modelling was used to project the increment MTTF's as described in reference 6, and product MTTF was separately calculated from the increment MTTF's. The certification model, developed for the cleanroom method as described in reference 7, showed reasonable fit with all the recorded data and was used exclusively in the analyses to simplify computations. It should be noted that no separate model projections were made for subfunctions 9 and 10 because only a few failures were recorded in each case.

Product Analysis

For statistical quality control the first use of reliability measurements is tracking the product reliability during development to ensure that reliability growth does occur. Product reliability is computed from the increment MTTF projections or more exactly the reciprocal failure rates which are additive quantities. Table 2 shows the general form of this calculation where the coefficients (C_{ij}'s) provide the increment contributions to total product function and bridge the test and operating environments.

TABLE 2

PRODUCT MTTF CALCULATION

$$MTTF_i = 1/R_i$$

where

$R_1 = C_{11}\ R_{11}$	after increment 1 release
$R_2 = C_{12}\ R_{12} + C_{22}\ R_{22}$	after increment 2 release
•	•
•	•
•	•
$R_n = C_{1n}\ R_{1n} + C_{2n}\ R_{2n} + \cdots + C_{nn}\ R_{nn}$	after increment n release.

For the particular product, reliability calculations were made across five releases, as shown in Table 3. Reliability growth was exhibited by each increment and consequently would be expected in the product as it passed through certification testing. The projections for the increment 1 functions are of particular interest since at release 3 the MTTF projection was larger than ever realized, as exhibited in Figure 1, but seemed reasonable with the growth trend at that point. The subsequent dropoff in MTTF should be examined in more detail (see next section) to pinpoint the cause of the MTTF change and focus where process changes should be applied to reverse the trend. It should also be noted that the number of increment 4 failures was too small for modelling so that the MTTF estimates were calculated by simple averaging of the recorded interfail times, which gave conservative results.

TABLE 3

Product Reliability Calculation When All Failures are Considered.

at release 1 $R_1 = C_{11}(1/\ 6451)$

at release 2 $R_2 = C_{12}(1/\ 8760) + C_{22}(1/4449)$

at release 3 $R_3 = C_{13}(1/10044) + C_{23}(1/4498) + C_{33}(1/2444)$

at release 4 $R_4 = C_{14}(1/\ 8315) + C_{24}(1/5387) + C_{34}(1/3709) + C_{44}(1/1443)$

at release 5 $R_5 = C_{15}(1/\ 7691) + C_{25}(1/6039) + C_{35}(1/3837) + C_{45}(1/1594)$

Function Analysis

Examining the component reliabilities of product functions is particularly useful for localizing the causes of changes in product MTTF and for identifying effective process controls. Generally product MTTF changes can be traced to the failure characteristics of component functions as was the case with the increment 1 MTTF dropoff. Specifically the increment 1 function analysis shown in Figure 1 indicated a significant drop in subfunction 2 MTTF from release 3 testing onward. This plot uses a relative defect scale of where specific function defects occurred in relation to all defects that occurred during the increment testing.

The drop in subfunction 2 MTTF was traced to the introduction of additional equipment into the test laboratory which resulted in the first time testing of a subfunction 2 interface. A basic processing defect which had gone unnoticed was then uncovered and required code modifications. The subfunction 2 MTTF drop seems to have bottomed out so that subsequent MTTF growth can be expected. For this case, the function analysis was useful in isolating the cause of the increment MTTF problem which was due to incompletely verified interface code which had not previously been tested. Possible process changes would be a reverification of the interface logic and a reexecution of all subfunction 2 cases in the upgraded laboratory configuration.

An examination of increment 2 subfunctions gives some different insight into MTTF growth as shown in Figure 2. With the initial release, there was no apparent MTTF growth since defects were uncovered at a fairly uniform rate. Test results from subsequent releases show the start of steady MTTF growth for all functions except subfunctions 3 and 5. These MTTF plots remain flat and indicate a need for more detailed analysis to determine the causes for no growth. Areas to be considered would include the development personnel, the stability of the subfunction requirements, the thoroughness of the subfunction design verification, etc.

The examination of increment 3 subfunctions indicates a similar situation as found with increment 2. Figure 3 shows a relatively flat initial increment MTTF followed by the start of some growth. One function, subfunction 7, shows no growth and should be analyzed further to uncover the causes. As in the increment 2 case, various process changes should be considered to obtain subfunction MTTF growth.

Failure Analysis

A third perspective from which to consider reliability analysis is the seriousness or significance of the failures that were encountered during test. Failure severity classification is a standard testing practice, which usually uses only a small number of classification levels. When software is basically inoperable, its severity is classified at the one level. When software is operable but one of its major subfunctions is inoperable, then the severity is classified at the two level. All other problems are considered less serious and classified into some number (usually three) of additional levels.

A user would be particularly interested in determining product reliability when only the more serious failures (severity 1 and 2) were considered since these would impact mission performance. Generally the user can continue to perform his function or accomplish his mission when the less severe failures occur.

For the particular product, the product reliability recomputed for the severity 1 and 2 case is as shown in table 4. There is an obvious dramatic difference in the MTTF projections for each increment and consequently in the product reliability. Again the increment 4 MTTF's were obtained by simple averaging of the few interfail times and result in conservative estimates.

TABLE 4

Product Reliability Calculation When Only Severity 1 and 2 Failures are Considered

at release 1 $R_1 = C_{11}(1/11405)$

at release 2 $R_2 = C_{12}(1/18869) + C_{22}(1/8021)$

at release 3 $R_3 = C_{13}(1/18291) + C_{23}(1/9187) + C_{33}(1/23320)$

at release 4 $R_4 = C_{14}(1/22930) + C_{24}(1/12945) + C_{34}(1/61356) + C_{44}(1/2886)$

at release 5 $R_5 = C_{15}(1/24591) + C_{25}(1/15409) + C_{35}(1/66496) + C_{45}(1/2391)$

Figures 4, 5, and 6 plot the MTTF projections for each increment when only severe failures are considered. They point out that the severe errors tend to occur early in the increment testing but drop off dramatically as testing proceeds. This is probably attributable to the randomized testing approach which is particularly adept at finding errors in the order of their seriousness to product operation, as suggested by the Adams study (2). Figure 7 which plots defects against cumulative interfail time, highlights this point since each curve is initially flat followed by a very steep rise.

From a process control perspective, overall MTTF growth is obvious but two further analyses might be particularly useful. From Figure 4 it would appear that the late appearing subfunction 2 failures were not particularly severe. They do not pull down the increment reliability as sharply as when all classes of failures were considered (Figure 1). This additional analysis should influence the timing and implementation of process changes since the seriousness of the problem has diminished. Figures 5 and 6 similarly indicate that the flatness of the subfunctions 3 and 7 MTTF curves may not be caused by severe failures so that there could be less urgency in implementing process changes.

A second process study might consider the flatness of the increment 2 MTTF curve for the severe failure case, which indicates that the errors are occurring at a relatively uniform rate. While this did not persist, it might be of interest to understand why it occurred for the particular increment and what process changes could have avoided the situation.

REFERENCES

(1) M. Dyer, R. C. Linger, H. D. Mills, D. O'Neill, and R. E. Quinnan, "The Management of Software Engineering," *IBM Systems Journal*, Vol. 19, No. 4, 1980.

(2) E. N. Adams, "Optimizing Preventive Service of Software Products" *IBM Journal of Research and Development*, Vol. 28, No. 1, January 1984.

(3) R. C. Linger, H. D. Mills, and B. I. Witt, *Structured Programming: Theory and Practice*, Addison-Wesley Publishing Co., Inc. (1979).

(4) M. E. Fagan, "Design and Code Inspections to Reduce Errors in Program Development," *IBM Systems Journal*, Vol. 15, No. 3, 1976.

(5) F. T. Baker, V. R. Basili, and R. W. Selby, Jr., "Cleanroom Software Development: An Empirical Evaluation," University of Maryland TR #1415, February 1985.

(6) M. Dyer, "Software Designs of Certified Reliability": to be given at the Reliability '85 conference, July 1985.

(7) P. A. Currit, M. Dyer, and H. D. Mills, "Certifying the Reliability of Software," In Preparation.

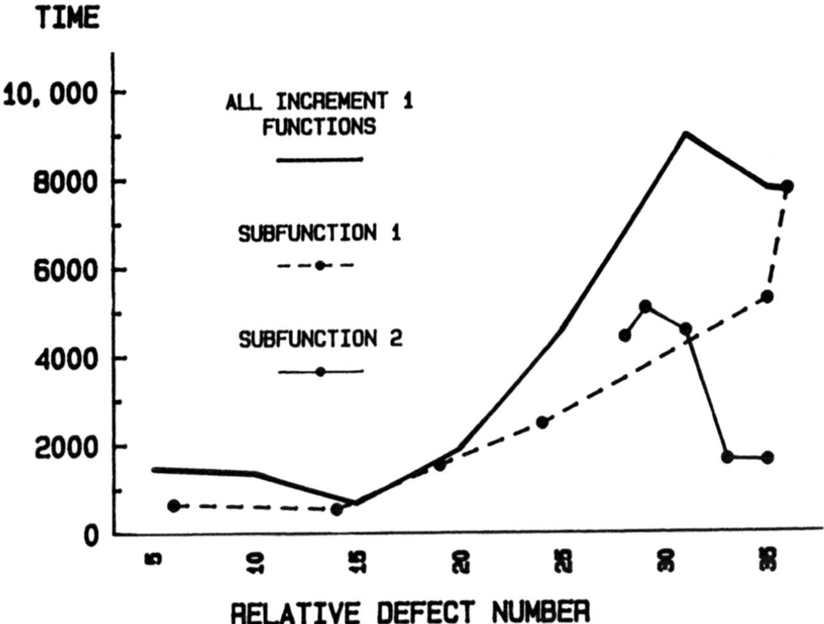

Figure 1. Increment 1 MTTF Comparison

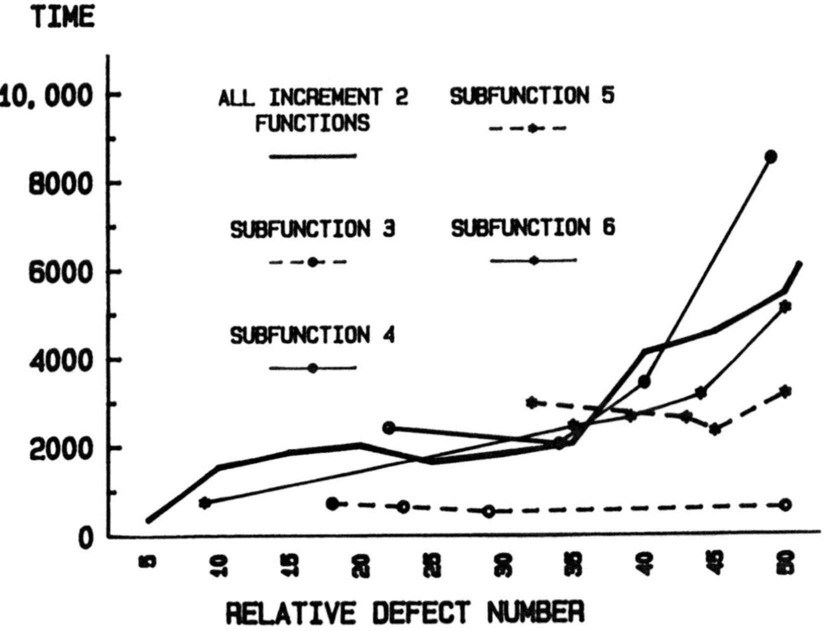

Figure 2. Increment 2 MTTF Comparison

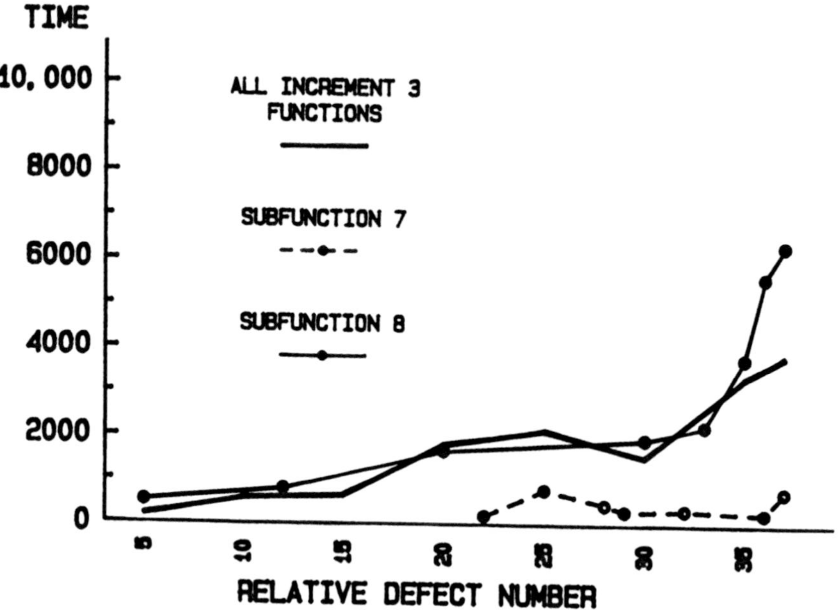

Figure 3. Increment 3 MTTF Comparison

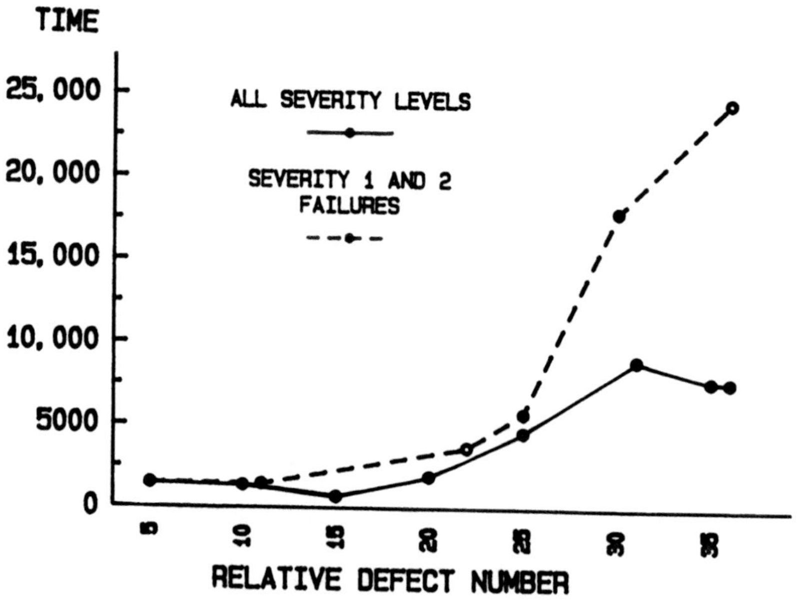

Figure 4. Comparison of Increment 1 MTTF's
By Failure Severity Levels

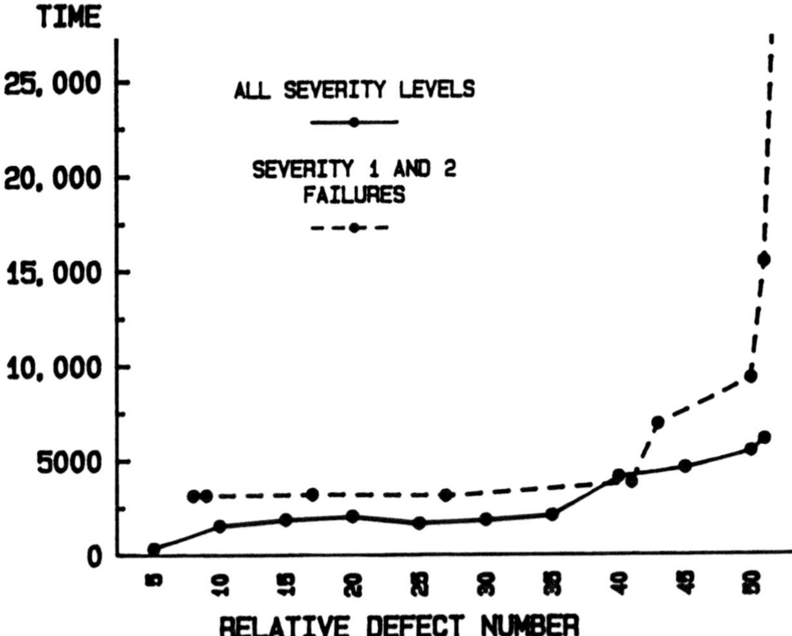

Figure 5. Comparison of Increment 2 MTTF's By Failure Severity Levels

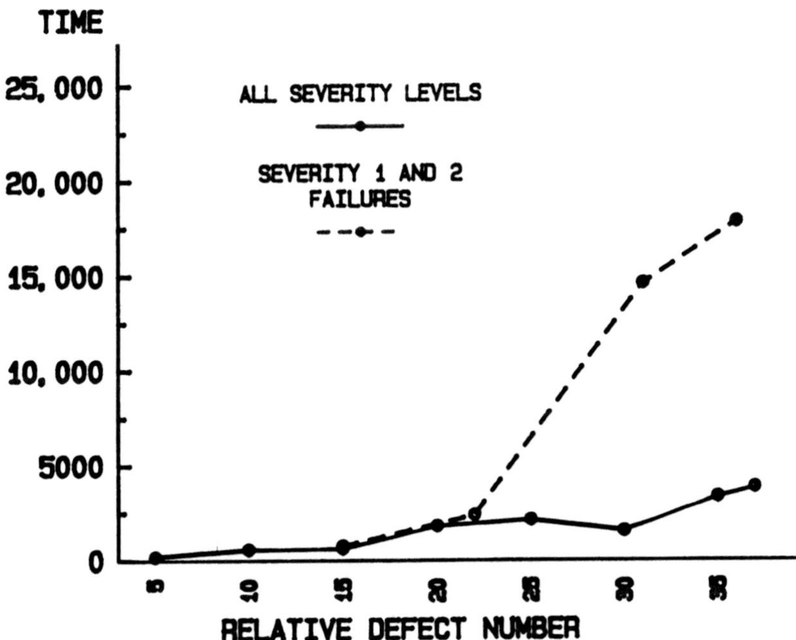

Figure 6. Comparison of Increment 3 MTTF's By Failure Severity Levels

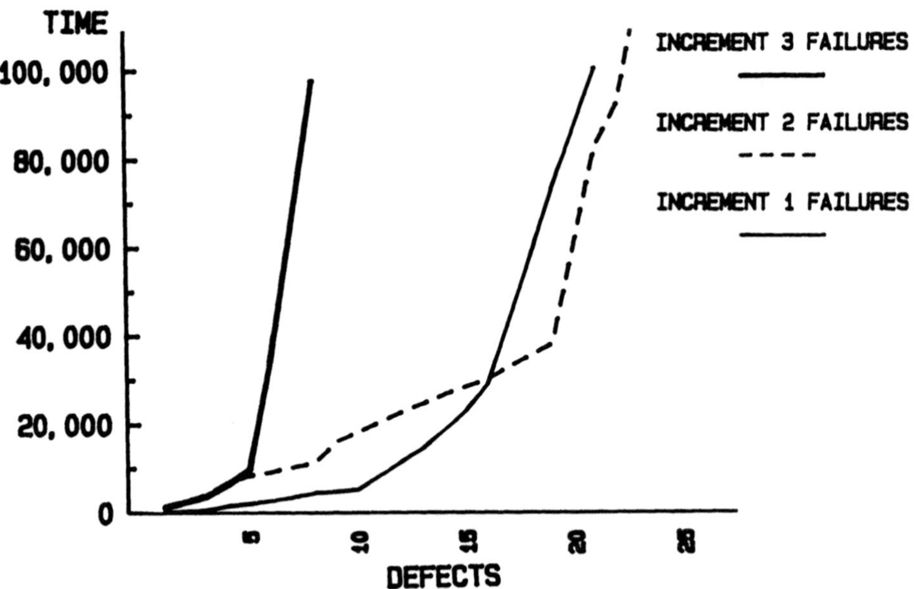

Figure 7. Cumulative Interfail Times For Severity 1 and 2 Failures

LIFE TIME DISTRIBUTIONS FOR COHERENT SYSTEMS

G.G. Weber
Kernforschungszentrum Karlsruhe GmbH
Institut für Datenverarbeitung in der Technik

Postfach 3640, D-7500 Karlsruhe

Abstract

Fault tree analysis is a well known technique used for problems of system reliability. A short introduction to basic concepts and techniques of fault tree analysis will be given. It is possible to use these techniques to evaluate system unavailability and the corresponding expected number of failures. In the present paper it will be shown how the system's life time distribution can be obtained as a function of the life time distributions for its components.

For this relation some additional concepts are required. First, the phase type distribution (PH-distribution) is defined. It is a distribution of the time until absorption in a finite Markov process. Also, the representation and some properties of PH-distributions will be discussed. For coherent systems there exists a closure property of PH-distributions (related to AND- and OR-gates of a fault tree). Moreover, the life time distribution of the system can be given explicitly by a suitable combination of representations of PH-distributions, using stochastic and matrix theoretic techniques. This type of representation seems to be the main result of our contribution. But also relations to stopping times and point processes are indicated.

1. A Few Basic Concepts of Fault Trees

1.1 Definition and Representation of a Fault Tree

Although the term 'fault tree' is often used in a rather wide sense it seems preferable to us to use the following definition:

Definition

A fault tree is a finite directed graph without (directed) circuits. Each vertex may be in one of several states. For each vertex a function is given which specifies its state in terms of the states of its predecessors. The states of those vertices without predecessors are considered the independent variables of the fault tree /1/, /2/.

Some general properties of a fault tree:

1. The vertices without predecessors are the inputs to the fault tree, representing the components. We are interested in the state of every other vertex, but in particular with the state of one vertex without successors, an output vertex which we identify with the state of the system as a whole. The graphical term 'vertex' here is roughly synonymous with 'item' and generally denotes any level in the system, whether a component, sub-system or the whole system.

NATO ASI Series, Vol. F22
Software System Design Methods. Edited by J.K. Skwirzynski

2. We mostly specialize to only two states per vertex. This makes all of the functions Boolean functions. We call one of the two states 'functioning', 'false' or 0, and the other 'failed', 'true' or 1.

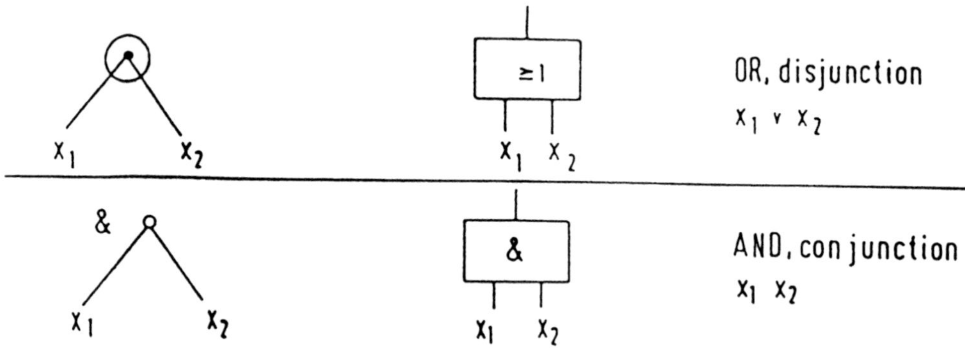

Fig. 1 Gates of a Fault Tree

3. The no-circuit condition in the graph is equivalent to the condition that the current output of a switching circuit is entirely determined by current inputs, without memory of previous inputs or internal states.

4. Also the more general case of manyvalued logic and logic trees is included in this definition.

Representation

For a fault tree and a combinational circuit standard components, called gates can be used. E.G. AND, OR, NOT are such gates.

1.2 Boolean Approach

Structure function

We introduce the concept of structure function which is of central importance to fault tree analysis. It can be seen that it is closely related to the concept of switching function. We assume a system S, which has n components which can be in two states (functioning, failed). Also the system S can be in two states, either functioning or failed. The components are the vertices without predecessors of our fault tree definition. The function which specifies the state of a vertex in terms of its predecessors is a Boolean function (AND, OR, NOT). The states of the top vertex can be given by a structure function /2/.

Definition of structure function

Let $x_1, x_2, \ldots, x_n$ be Boolean variables which can assume the values 0,1, where

$$x_i = \begin{cases} 0 \text{ if component } i \text{ is functioning} \\ 1 \text{ if component } i \text{ is failed.} \end{cases} \qquad (1.2\text{-}1)$$

The assumption that 1 corresponds to failure is used throughout this paper and is useful for fault tree analysis. The Boolean variable x_i indicates the state of component i, whereas the state vector $\underline{x} = (x_1, x_2, \ldots, x_n)$ indicates the state of the system. The Boolean function $\Phi(x_1, x_2, \ldots, x_n)$ is called structure function and determines completely the state of a system S in terms of the state-vectors:

$$\Phi(x_1, x_2, \ldots, x_n) = \begin{cases} 0 \text{ if system S is functioning} \\ 1 \text{ if system S is failed.} \end{cases} \qquad (1.2\text{-}2)$$

Remark: The structure function is equivalent to a switching function representing a combinational circuit.

Definition of Coherence

A system S represented by a structure function Φ is called coherent iff the following conditions hold:

(1) If $\underline{x} < \underline{y}$ then $\phi(\underline{x}) \leq \phi(\underline{y})$ where $\underline{x} < \underline{y}$ means $x_i \leq y_i$ for every i, and $x_i < y_i$ for at least one i.

(2) $\Phi(\underline{1}) = 1$ and $\Phi(\underline{0}) = 0$.

Note: An informal rephrasing of (1), (2) is:

(1) If a system S is functioning no transition of a component from a failed state to functioning can cause a system failure.

(2) If all components of S are failed (functioning) the system is failed (functioning).

Minimal Cuts

Let $M = \{K_1, K_2, \ldots, K_l\}$ be a set of components of a coherent system S. A subset $\mathcal{C}$ of M such that S is failed if all components K_i belonging to $\mathcal{C}$ are failed is called a cut. A cut is minimal if it has no proper subsets which are also cuts. It is called minimal cut $\mathcal{C}_j$.

Representation of coherent systems: Every irredundant sop representation of a structure function is a union of prime implicants. If the structure function is coherent, the representation by prime implicants greatly simplifies. We quote a theorem which leads to this simplification.

Theorem: A coherent structure function $\Phi(\underline{x})$ can be represented as a sum

$$\Phi(\underline{x}) = \sum_{j=1}^{l} p_j \qquad (1.2\text{-}3)$$

with prime implicants p_j, where this representation is unique and can be written using the concept of min cuts

$$\Phi(\underline{x}) = \sum_{j=1}^{l} \prod_{K_i \in \mathcal{C}_j} x_i \qquad (1.2\text{-}4)$$

where $K_i \in \mathcal{C}_j$ are the components belonging to $\mathcal{C}_j$, x_i the Boolean variables describing the states (functioning, failed) of the components.

Minimal Paths: The dual to minimal Cut is Minimal Path, (see /6/).

Remark:

Note, that there is only one (minimal) cover, and there are only 'essential' prime implicants which may not be replaced by any other prime implicants.

The concept of coherence may be generalized to cases where more than two states are possible. Even then the coherent structure functions give a considerable simplification as has been shown in /5/.

2. Probabilistic Evaluation

2.1 Basic Concepts and Notations

We describe the behavior of a component which can be in a finite number of states, preferably in two states: up (functioning) or down (failed).

We describe the states by indicator variables. There is a one-one-relation between indicator variables and Boolean variables (see e.g. Barlow /2/).

Thus we get for an indicator variable $x_i^!(t)$ the following realizations:

$$x_i^!(t) = \begin{matrix} 1 \\ 0 \end{matrix} \text{ if component } i \text{ is } \begin{matrix} \text{down} \\ \text{up} \end{matrix} \text{ at time } t \qquad (2.1\text{-}1)$$

We describe the behavior of a repairable component by an alternating renewal process. Later on, it will be shown, how a system, given by a structure function, can also be represented using alternating renewal processes for components.

Availability and Reliability

We introduce a few basic quantities for reliability.

Life time distribution

Assume a component which may be modeled by a life time distribution F(t):

$$F(t) = P\{T \leq t\}, \qquad (2.1\text{-}2)$$

where the r.v. T is the component's life time.

Reliability

We introduce the reliability of a component R(t) as

$$R(t) = 1 - F(t) \qquad (2.1\text{-}3)$$

Note:

- For $t = o$, a component is up with probability 1.
- For $t = \infty$, a component is down with probability 1.

It is sometimes convenient to use an interval reliability.

Availability

We introduce the availability of a component A(t)

$$A(t) = P\{x'(t) = 0\}, \qquad (2.1\text{-}4)$$

i.e. the probability that a component is up at time t.

Unavailability

$$\bar{A}(t) = P\{x'(t) = 1\}, \qquad (2.1\text{-}5)$$

i.e. the probability that a component is down at time t. Clearly

$$A(t) + \bar{A}(t) = 1$$

To obtain non-trivial statements on availability and other quantities related a few concepts of renewal theory are required.

2.2 Alternating Renewal Processes

We consider a component which can be in one of two states, up and down, but is no longer repaired instantaneously /2/, /6/, /7/,/8/. Thus we have this realization:

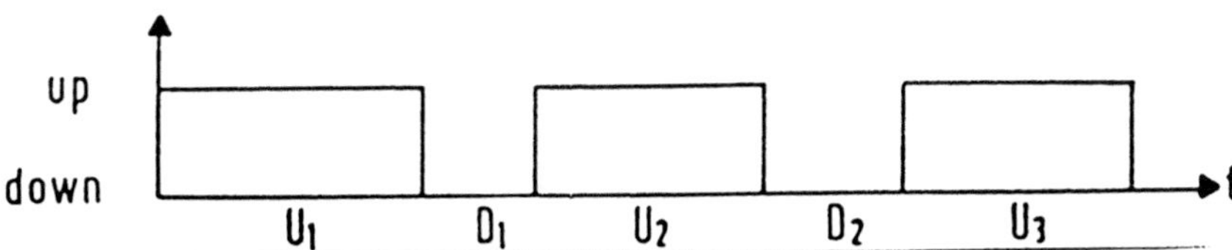

Initially it is up and remains for a time U_1, then it goes down and remains down for a time D_1 etc.

The time intervals

$$T_i \equiv (U_i + D_i) \qquad i = 1,2,3,... \qquad (2.3.\text{-}1)$$

are assumed to be mutually independent.

Let $U_i (i = 1,2,3,...)$ be distributed with F(t),
let $D_i (i = 1,2,3,...)$ be distributed with G(t), and
let $T_i \equiv (U_i + D_i)$ $(i = 1,2,3,...)$ be distributed with $F_T(t)$ $(i = 1,2,3,...)$.

Then the sequence of r.v. $\{T_i;\ i \geq 1\}$ defines an <u>alternating renewal process</u>, where

$$F_T(t) = P\{T_i \leq t\} = \int_0^t f(x)\, G(t-x)dx \qquad (2.2\text{-}2)$$

A few concepts related to alternating renewal processes

1. Ordinary renewal process: The definition already refers to the ordinary process.

2. Mean values (u, d):

$$\begin{aligned} &(a) \quad u = E(U_i) \\ &(b) \quad d = E(D_i) \qquad (i = 1,2,\ldots) \\ &(c) \quad u+d = E(T_i) \end{aligned} \qquad (2.2\text{-}3)$$

3. Renewal function: We get for the mean number of failures H(t) assuming an up state for t=0 (where * refers to the Laplace transform):

$$H^*(s) = \frac{F^*(s)}{1-f^*(s)\, g^*(s)} \qquad (2.2\text{-}4)$$

Relation to Point Processes

It is interesting to note that the abovementioned renewal processes are special cases of point processes. A <u>point process</u> over the half line $[0,\infty)$ can be viewed as follows:

(a) as a sequence of nonnegative r.v.: $T_o, T_1, T_2, \ldots$.

(b) as an associated counting process N_t where

$$N_t = \begin{cases} n & \text{if} \quad t \in [T_n, T_{n+1}) \\ \infty & \text{if} \quad t = \lim T_n = \infty . \end{cases} \qquad (2.2\text{-}5)$$

The Poisson process is a well known example for a point process. The counting process N_t, is related to the intensity λ and the martingale M_t (see Brémaud /10/ and section 4).

Availability of a Component

We now obtain a few relations of Availability and alternating renewal processes. Assume a component which is in an up state for t=0. The time U_1 to the first failure is distributed as $F_A(t) = 1-\bar{F}_A(t)$. The times U_i (i>1) (referring to operation) are distributed as $F(t) = 1-\bar{F}(t)$ and the times D_i are all distributed as G(t) (see (2.2-1)). Then we obtain for the availability A(t) the following formulas:

$$A(t) = \bar{F}_A(t) + \int_0^t \bar{F}(t-x)dH(x) \qquad (2.3\text{-}6)$$

Example: For an alternating renewal process where up and down times are exponentially distributed, we get

$$A(t) = \frac{\rho}{\lambda+\rho} + \frac{\rho}{\lambda+\rho} e^{-(\lambda+\rho)t}$$

Asymptotic behavior

As applications of the key renewal theorem we get the following relations (see / 7 /):

$$\text{(a)} \lim_{t\to\infty} \frac{H(t)}{t} = \lim_{t\to\infty} h(t) = \frac{1}{u+d} \tag{2.2-7}$$

(The same holds for $\tilde{H}(t)$, $\tilde{h}(t)$).

$$\text{(b)} \lim_{t\to\infty} (H(t+x) - H(t)) = \frac{x}{u+d} \text{ for all } x > 0 \tag{2.2-8}$$

$$\text{(c)} \lim_{t\to\infty} A(t) = \frac{u}{u+d} \tag{2.2-9}$$

An interpretation of renewal function and density

For the application of renewal function and density to fault tree evaluation the following notation is convenient. It is possible to understand the expected number of failures of a component i of a system as follows:

$$W_i^{01}(t) = E \text{ (Number of failures in } (0,t) \text{ for component i)} \tag{2.2-10}$$

corresponding to H(t). Moreover:

$$w_i^{01}(t)dt = P\{\text{component i fails in } (t, t+dt)\} \tag{2.2-11}$$

where $w_i^{01}(t)$ is the failure intensity. Similarly it is also possible to introduce repair intensities $w_i^{10}(t)$ /6/.

However, $w_s^{01}(t)$ is the failure intensity of the system.

Note

1. The failure intensity-notation replaces for the rest for this representation the usual h(t).

2. The failure intensity may be easily generalized to a transition rate for a finite number of states /5/.

3. Assume that up times and down times are exponentially distributed. Then we get

$$w_i^{01}(t) = \lambda_i A_i(t) \tag{2.2-12}$$

where λ_i, is the failure rate of i.

2.3 Stochastic Modeling of a System

Based on 2.1-2.2 we now introduce concepts which are useful for reliability evaluations of systems. We assume a coherent system (C,ϕ) with n components /6/, /8/.

Alternating renewal process

1. Component i is replaced at failure (not instantaneously) thus generating an alternating renewal process, where renewal densities are $w_i^{01}(t)$, $w_i^{10}(t)$ $(i = 1,2,\dots,n)$.

2. For a stationary process we have (2.2-9):

$$w_i^{01} = w_i^{10} = A_i/u_i = 1/(u_i + d_i) \qquad (2.3\text{-}1)$$

By a few assumptions, it is possible to exclude that two failures or one failure and one repair occur at 'the same time' /6/.

3. Of course, a coherent system will in general not follow a renewal process.

Unavailability

The state $X_s'(t)$ of the system can be expressed in terms of component states, $X_1'(t),\dots,X_n'(t)$:

$$X_s'(t) = \Phi(X_1'(t),\dots,X_n'(t)) \qquad (2.3\text{-}2)$$

It follows that unavailability $\bar{A}_s(t)$ of the system at time t is given as

$$\bar{A}_s(t) = E(X_s'(t)) = h(\bar{A}_1(t),\dots,\bar{A}_n(t)) \qquad (2.3\text{-}3)$$

where h is the 'reliability function' of system (C,Φ), i.e. the (point-) unavailability at time t /2/.

Limiting unavailability

Let U_{ji} represent the i th up time for component j with distribution F_j (mean u_j), and D_{ji} represent the i th down time for component j with distribution G_j (mean d_j), for $j = 1,2,\dots,n$, $i = 1,2,3,\dots$.

Since h is multilinear in its arguments, the stationary unavailability $\bar{A}_s$ is, for nonlattice distributions of F_j, G_j,

$$\bar{A}_s = h\left(\frac{d_1}{u_1+d_1},\dots,\frac{d_n}{u_n+d_n}\right) \qquad (2.3\text{-}4)$$

For AND and OR-gates we get as unavailability:

1. AND-gate

$$\bar{A}_s(t) = P\{X_1'(t) \cdot X_2'(t) = 1\} = \bar{A}_1(t)\,\bar{A}_2(t) \qquad (2.3\text{-}5)$$

$$\bar{A}_s = d_1/(u_1+d_1) \cdot d_2/(u_2+d_2) \qquad (2.3\text{-}6)$$

2. OR-gate

$$\bar{A}_s(t) = P\{1-(1-X_1'(t))(1-X_2'(t)) = 1\} = 1-(1-\bar{A}_1(t))(1-\bar{A}_2(t)) \qquad (2.3\text{-}7)$$

$$\bar{A}_s = 1 - u_1/(u_1+d_1) \cdot u_2/(u_2+d_2) \qquad (2.3\text{-}8)$$

Failure intensity

The evaluation of failure intensity of a system is related to a few assumptions /6/.

Theorem

If a system is coherent, we get

$$w_s^{01}(t) = \sum_{i=1}^{n_c} I_i(t)\, w_i^{01}(t) \qquad (2.3\text{-}9)$$

where $I_i(t) = \dfrac{\partial h(\underline{\bar{A}}(t))}{\partial \bar{A}_i(t)}$,

and the summation has to be taken over all states i ($1 \le i \le n_c$) in which the failure of a component is critical(see also /97/). This theorem shows a fundamental relation between the failure intensity of a system and its components.

Examples

1. AND-gate
Note, that for an AND-gate components i = 1,2 are critical. They are also predecessors of this gate.

$$w_s^{01}(t) = \bar{A}_2(t)\, w_1^{01}(t) + \bar{A}_1(t)\, w_2^{01}(t) \qquad (2.3\text{-}10)$$

2. OR-gate

Note, that for an OR-gate components i = 1,2 are critical.

$$w_s^{01}(t) = (1 - \bar{A}_2(t))\, w_1^{01}(t) + (1 - \bar{A}_1(t))\, w_2^{01}(t) \qquad (2.3\text{-}11)$$

3. Evaluation with Min Cuts and Min Paths

3.1 Basic Concepts

Consider a coherent system which can be represented using, min cuts $\mathcal{C}_j$ or min paths $\mathcal{T}_k$. We denote by $x_i^!$ an indicator variable (see (2.1-1) and use the notations:

<u>Product:</u>
$$\prod_{i=1}^{n} x_i^! \tag{3.1-1}$$

<u>Coproduct:</u>
$$\coprod_{i=1}^{n} x_i^! = 1 - \prod_{i=1} (1-x_i^!) \tag{3.1-2}$$

(3.1-1) and (3.1-2) is related to Boolean products and Boolean sum respectively. For the reliability function $h(\underline{p})$ we may write:

$$E(\prod_{k=1}^{m} \coprod_{i\varepsilon\mathcal{T}_k} x_i^!) = h(\underline{p}) = E(\coprod_{j=1}^{l} \prod_{i\varepsilon\mathcal{C}_j} x_i^!) \tag{3.1-3}$$

where $\mathcal{T}_k$, ($\mathcal{C}_j$) refers to min paths (min cuts).

Note that this is related to two major forms for a Boolean expressions: The sum of products form (r.h.s.) and the product of sums form (l.h.s.) which are equivalent.

If there is a coherent structure, we get in general the following bounds

$$\prod_{k=1}^{m} \coprod_{i\varepsilon\mathcal{T}_k} p_i \leq h(\underline{p}) \leq \coprod_{j=1}^{l} \prod_{i\varepsilon\mathcal{C}_j} p_i \tag{3.1-4}$$

However, for noncoherent structures, the bounds will not hold in general /2/.

<u>The time to failure for a Coherent System</u>

Let t_i be the time to failure of the i-th component (i=1,2...,n), and $\tau_\phi(t)$ the time to failure of a coherent system (C,ϕ) with structure function ϕ.

We give now a result which is related to (3.1-3) but not based on Boolean variables.

<u>Theorem:</u> If (C,ϕ) is a coherent system with minimal paths $\mathcal{T}_k$ (k=1,2,...,m) and minimal cuts $\mathcal{C}_j$ (j=1,2,...,l).

Then

$$\max_{1\leq k\leq m} \min_{i\varepsilon\mathcal{T}_k} t_i = \tau_\phi(t) = \min_{1\leq j\leq l} \max_{i\varepsilon\mathcal{C}_j} t_i \tag{3.1-5}$$

Proof: A coherent system fails when the first minimal cut $\mathcal{C}_j$ fails. A parallel structure fails when the last component i of this cut $\mathcal{C}_j$ fails. (A similar argument holds for minimal paths).

(3.1-5) is of interest for methodological considerations (see section 4.1 on systems evolution).

3.2 Inclusion - Exclusion - Principle

It is convenient to have a procedure to evaluate complex fault trees, where (3.1-3) would be impractical. In general, an exact evaluation is not feasible. But it is possible to obtain bounds for unavailability, failure intensity etc.

Now the inclusion-exclusion-principle (Poincaré's theorem) will be given.
In a discrete probability space (i.e. with countable elementary events) we get the following theorem:

Theorem: Let $A_1, A_2, \ldots, A_n$ be events. Then we get

$$P\{\bigcup_{i=1}^{n} A_i\} = \sum_{i=1}^{n} P\{A_i\} - \sum_{i<j} P\{A_i A_j\} + \ldots + (-1)^{n-1} P\{A_1 A_2 \ldots A_n\} . \tag{3.2-1}$$

This is a theorem which applies to events contained in a discrete probability space. Then it also applies to indicator variables and to events such as 'min cut failed'. Moreover, Poincaré's theorem can be restated for expectations $E(\bigcup_{i=1}^{n} A_i)$. If is possible to obtain upper (lower) bounds for $P\{\bigcup_{i=1}^{n} A_j\}$ from (3.2-1) /6/,/8/.

3.3 Evaluation with Bounds

Usually, the exact formula of inclusion exclusion needs a large amount of computation. Therefore, bounds are required. This will be demonstrated for a fault tree represented by min cuts, where all components are repairable. The usefulness of bounds and/or approximations will be discussed.

Theorem

We assume a coherent fault tree with min cut representation. Let the K_i be independent and let C_j be the event 'the min cut $\mathcal{C}_j$ is down '($j = 1,\ldots,m$). Upper bounds for unavailability $\bar{A}_s(t)$ are:

$$\text{(a)} \quad \bar{A}_s(t) \le \sum_{j=1}^{m} P\{C_j\} \tag{3.3-1}$$

Let K_i be independent and in a stationary state.
Upper bounds for failure intensity w_s^{01} are:

$$\text{(a)} \quad w_s^{01} \le \sum_{j=1}^{m} P\{C_j\} \sum_{i\in\mathcal{C}_j} \frac{1}{d_i} \tag{3.3-2}$$

Expected number of failures

In the stationary state, we get for the expected number of failures in the interval (0,t)

$$W_s^{01}(t) = \int_0^t w_s^{01} dt' = t \cdot w_s^{01} \qquad (3.3\text{-}3)$$

This is

$$W_s^{01}(t) \leq t \sum_{j=1}^{m} P\{C_j\} \sum_{i \in \mathcal{C}_j} \frac{1}{d_i} \qquad (3.3\text{-}4)$$

4. Evolution of a Coherent System

The question is as follows: If a coherent system has alternating renewal processes at the component level, what can be said regarding the evolution of the system? Evidently the following holds:

- Unavailability and failure intensity can be evaluated.
- The alternating renewal processes are a special type of point processes and of Markov renewal processes (see also /18/).

Three approaches are possible: use of stopping times, distributions of phase type, Markov renewal processes. We are not discussing other approaches (see /Ross /19/ and Barlow /2/).

4.1 Times to failure and stopping times

The basic idea is very simple: Consider two components in series with random life times T_1, T_2. Then this system fails at the time

$$T_* = \inf(T_1, T_2). \qquad (4.1\text{-}1)$$

Consider also two components in parallel with random life times T_1, T_2. Then this system fails at the time

$$T^* = \sup(T_1, T_2) \qquad (4.1\text{-}2)$$

It is evidently possible to use the relations (4.1-1), (4.1-2) to obtain statements for a coherent system (C, ϕ).

As a stochastic concept, the stopping time T is required. The stopping time is based on the understanding that at time $t \geq 0$ it is known whether an event (component failure) occurred or not.

Def. Let F_t be a collection of events, representing the known information at time t. (F_t is also called a σ-field of events).

F_t is typically the collection of events generated by one or more stochastic processes up to time t. Now let $\{F_t, t \geq 0\}$ be a family of such information collections. We shall always assume that $\{F_t\}$ is increasing, i.e. that no forgetting is allowed:

$$s \leq t \quad \Rightarrow F_s \subseteq F_t \qquad (4.1\text{-}3)$$

here $\{F_t, t \geq 0\}$ is called a <u>history</u>.

With this concept we may define the stopping time.

<u>Def.</u> Let $\{F_t\}$ be a history and T be a possible random variable. Then T is called a F_t-<u>stopping time</u> iff the event $\{T \leq t\}$ can be characterized by

$$\{T \leq t\} \in F_t \ , \quad t \geq 0 \tag{4.1-4}$$

i.e. it is known at time t whether or not T has occurred.

<u>A few properties of stopping times</u>

A process X_t is called "adapted" to $\{F_t, t \leq 0\}$ if for every t, X_t is completely determined by F_t.

1. <u>Theorem</u>: Let X_t be a right-continuous $\mathbb{R}$-valued process adapted to F_t, and c a given real number. Define T as follows:

$$T = \begin{cases} \inf\{t \mid X_t \geq c\} \\ +\infty \text{ if this set is empty} \end{cases} \tag{4.1-5}$$

Then T is a F_t - stopping time.

Proof: See Brémaud /10/. We note that T under conditions (4.1-5) is a "first passage time". An important special case of a first passage time will be used in sect. 4.2 (phase type distributions).

2. <u>Relation of two stopping times:</u> If T_1, T_2 are F_t - stopping times, then

$$\begin{aligned} T_1 \wedge T_2 &:= \inf (T_1, T_2) \\ T_1 \vee T_2 &:= \sup (T_1, T_2) \end{aligned} \tag{4.1-6}$$

are <u>also</u> F_t - stopping times.

Note that $\wedge$ ($\vee$) is here <u>not</u> the conjunction (disjunction) but a useful symbol for inf(sup), corresponding to series (parallel) systems life times.

Combining these relations we obtain the following theorem:

<u>Theorem:</u> Let (C,ϕ) be a coherent structure where $T_1,\ldots,T_n$ are stopping times (life times). Then T_ϕ,

$$T_\phi = \inf_{1 \leq j \leq l} \sup_{i \in \mathcal{C}_j} T_i \tag{4.1-7}$$

is also a stopping time.

Here $\mathcal{C}_j$ is a minimal cut and l is the number of minimal cuts of (C,ϕ). This theorem follows from formulas (4.1-6) and from equation (3.1-5). (See also Greenwood /11/).

Thus our question regarding the time to system failure has been answered. It is interesting to know also the kind of stochastic process which describes this system.

Point Processes

It is possible to define point processes as a sequence of stopping times. We can make with (4.1-7) the following statement.

If on the component level we have point processes (renewal processes are a special type of point processes) then on the system level we have also a point process (for a coherent system (C,Ø)). This has been shown in (4.1-7).

Relation to Martingales

It is important to draw attention to the relation between point processes and martingale dynamics (Brêmaud /10/). Using the martingale approach, the notion of stochastic intensity λ_s receives a rigorous mathematical definition, and, more importantly, the martingale definition of intensity is the basis on which a martingale calculus can be developed which has for point processes a comparable power as Ito calculus for diffusion processes.

Let F_t be a history of a point process N_t. The locally integrable F_t - progressive process λ_t is called the F_t - intensity of N_t if

$$M_t = N_t - \int_0^t \lambda_s \, ds \qquad (4.1\text{-}8)$$

is a martingale.

Here $\int_0^t \lambda_s \, ds$ is called compensator (integral of the intensity).

Note: If X_t is an E-valued process adapted to F_t (and underlying some conditions regarding topology and continuity), then X_t is progressive.

Example: If $\lambda(t)$ is a deterministic function, N_t is a Poisson-process with intensity $\lambda(t)$. For λ = const., we have

$$M_t = N_t - \lambda t$$

Further considerations are due to Arjas /27/ and Greenwood /26/. But this is not the place to discuss this in detail.

A few remarks on point processes

1. Based on the decomposition which has been sketched (see (4.1-8)) it is possible to do some considerations which come very close to the IFRA-properties of systems (see also closure property for cohernt systems with IFRA /2/).

2. Using a "marked point process" we can formalize the considerations we already mentioned referring to a coherent system (Greenwood /11/). Note that the point process approach uses classical methods such as imbedded Markow chains, imbedded Markow processes and semi-Markow processes (see König, Stoyan /13/, Cox and Miller /14/). It is sometimes perferable to use

methods which are specific to point processes.

3. It has been shown by various anthors (Arndt, Franken /15/, Jansen /16/) that point processes can be applied for repair. This analysis has been generalized to dependent components but without associated variables. It is important to note that these considerations are strongly related to queuing theory and that they can cover a wide region where fault tree analysis alone is no longer useful.

4. We will learn more about certain closure properties of distributions in the next section.

4.2 Phase type distribution

There is also a second method which can be related to system reliability. This is an algorithmic approach and can be referred to

- computational probability
- matrix geometric methods and to
- phase type distributions (PH-distributions).

It is due to M. Neuts /17/ and his school.

For instance, it could be shown that PH-distributions are very useful for many problems in queuing theory /17/. We only recall that queuing processes are a special type of point processes and Markow renewal processes. They may be used for a number of problems in reliability, e.g. related to repairmen and to computers.

General properties

It has been shown (see Neuts /17/) that the class of PH-distributions is closed under some operations, e.g. under

- finite mixtures of PH-distributions
- convolutions
- formation of maxima and minima
- construction of coherent systems.

Clearly, under these operations with PH-distributions, the resulting distributions are still of phase type, and moreover, it is possible to construct representations of PH-distributions. This is a very interesting development in the region of applied and computational probability. Let us note a few basic concepts.

Definition and some basic properties

We consider a Markow process

$$\{X_t,\ 0 \leq t < \infty\} \tag{4.2-1}$$

with a finite number of states labeled 1,...,m+1. We have

$$p_{ij}(s,t) = P\{X_t(w) = j \,|\, X_s(w) = i\} \tag{4.2-2}$$

We may write with (4.2-2) a special case of the Chapman-Kolmogorow-equation characterizing a Markow process. A stochastic process is said to have stationary transition probabilities if for each pair ij the transition probability $p_{ij}(s,t)$ depents only on t-s. This is sufficient for the following discussion. We may write the Chapman-Kolmogorow equation:

$$p_{ik}(t) = \sum_j p_{ij}(s)p_{jk}(t-s) \tag{4.2-3}$$

with

$$p_{ij}(t) \geq 0, \sum_j p_{ij}(t) = 1 \tag{4.2-4}$$

With suitable continuity assumptions we have:

$$\lim_{t\to 0} p_{ij}(t) = \begin{cases} 1 & \text{for } i=j \\ 0 & \text{for } i\neq j \end{cases} \tag{4.2-5}$$

Assuming that $p_{ij}(t)$ has a derivative $p_{ij}'(t)$ for all $t \geq 0$ and that (4.2-5) holds we may obtain the following relations:

$$q_i = \lim_{t\to 0} \frac{1-p_{ii}(t)}{t} = -p_{ii}'(0) \tag{4.2-6}$$

$$q_{ij} = \lim_{t\to 0} \frac{p_{ij}(t)}{t} = p_{ij}'(0) \tag{4.2-7}$$

These relations can be used to define the "infinitesimal generators" q_i, q_{ij} of a Markow process.
Let Q be the matrix $[q_{ij}]$, where we use $q_{ii} := -q_i$ as diagonal elements. From (4.2-3) we obtain the backward equation

$$p_{ik}'(t) = \sum_j q_{ij}p_{jk}(t) \tag{4.2-8}$$

The q_{ij} determine the $p_{ij}(t)$ uniquely.
This system may be also written in matrix form

$$P'(t) = Q\,P(t) \tag{4.2-8}$$

where Q is the infinitesimal generator.
Then we can write a solution

$$P(t) = \exp(Qt) \tag{4.2-8}$$

where

$$\exp(Qt) = \sum_{r=0}^{\infty} Q^r \frac{t^n}{r!} \tag{4.2-9}$$

Remark: It can be shown that if the eigenvalues of Q are all distinct, we obtain (for(4.2-8)):

$$P(t) = B\begin{pmatrix} e^{\lambda_1 t} & & \\ & \ddots & \\ & & e^{\lambda_r t} \end{pmatrix} C' \tag{4.2-10}$$

where $BC' = I$ (4.2-11)

with I identity matrix. (see Cox, Miller /14/).

Infinitesimal generators

We consider a Markow process with the states {1,2,..., m+1} and the infinitesimal generator

$$\underline{Q} = \begin{pmatrix} \underline{A} & \underline{A}^o \\ \underline{0} & 0 \end{pmatrix} \tag{4.2-12}$$

where the mxm - matrix $\underline{A}$ satisfies

$$\begin{aligned} \lambda_{ii} &< 0 \\ \lambda_{ij} &\geq 0 \end{aligned} \qquad \text{for } 1 \leq i \leq m$$

we also have this relation:

$$\underline{A}\ \underline{e} + \underline{A}^o = \underline{0} \tag{4.2-13}$$

where e is a unit vector. Moreover, for t = 0 we have

$(p_1(0),\dots,p_m(0),p_{m+1}(0)) = (\underline{\alpha},\alpha_{m+1})$

and

$$\underline{\alpha}\ \underline{e} + \alpha_{m+1} = 1 \tag{4.2-14}$$

which is equivalent to (4.2-4).

We assume that all states 1,..,m are transient and that state m+1 is absorbing.

Theorem The probability distribution F of the time until absorption in the state m+1 corresponding to the initial probability vector $(\underline{\alpha}.\alpha_{m+1})$ is given by

$$F(x) = 1 - \underline{\alpha}\exp(\underline{A}x)\cdot\underline{e} \tag{4.2-15}$$

where $\underline{A}$ is the submatrix of the generator $\underline{Q}$ (4.2-12).

Scetch of a proof: We refer to (4.2-8). With initial conditions

$$(p_1(0),\dots, P_m(0)) = \underline{\alpha}$$

we obtain (due to (4.2-4)) the relation (4.2-15).

Definition: A probability distribution F on $[0,\infty)$ is a distribution of phase type (PH-distribution) iff it is the distribution of the time until absorption in a finite Markow process of the type defined in (4.2-12) (infinitesimal generators). The pair $(\underline{\alpha},\underline{A})$ is called representation of F.

A few properties of PH-distributions

1. These distributions have a jump of height α_{m+1} at x = 0
2. The Laplace-Stieltjes transform F*(s) of F(x) is

$$F^*(s) = \alpha_{m+1} + \underline{\alpha}(s\underline{I} - \underline{A})^{-1}\underline{A}^o \tag{4.2-16}$$

3. The noncentral moments μ_i' of F(x) are given by

$$\mu_i' = (-1)^i i! (\underline{\alpha}\ \underline{A}^{-i} \underline{e}) \qquad (4.2\text{-}17)$$

Example: The Erlang distribution of order m (pdf) is:
(pdf) is:

$$f(x) = \frac{\lambda(\lambda x)^{m-1}\ e^{-\lambda x}}{(m-1)!} \qquad (4.2\text{-}18)$$

and has the following representation

$$(\underline{\alpha}, \underline{A}) \qquad (4.2\text{-}19)$$

with

$$\underline{\alpha} = (1,0,\ldots,0)$$

$$\underline{A} = \begin{pmatrix} -\lambda & \lambda & & & \\ & -\lambda & \lambda & & \\ & & \cdots & & \\ & & & -\lambda & \lambda \\ & & & & -\lambda \end{pmatrix}$$

where $\underline{A}$ is a mxm-matrix.

Closure properties

It has been indicated that PH-distributions are closed under certain operations. We discuss here:

- convolution and
- construction of coherent systems.

Convolution

Convolution may be used for addition of life lengths. If a failed component is replaced by a spare, the total accumulated life time is obtained by the addition of two life lengths. To express the distribution of the sum of two independent life times (where T_1 has distribution F_1, T_2 distribution F_2) and T_1+T_2 distribution F) we use the convolution

$$F(t) = \int_0^t F_1(t-x) d\, F_2(x) \qquad (4.2\text{-}20)$$

Notation: If A^o is an m-vector (4.2-13) and β an n-vector, we denote by $\underline{A}_1{}^o\overline{\underline{B}}{}^o$, the mxn matrix $\underline{A}_1^o\ \underline{\beta}$, with elements $A_{1i}^o\ \beta_j$, $1 \leq i \leq m$, $1 \leq j \leq n$.

Theorem:

If F(x) and G(x) are both continuons PH-distributions with representations

$$(\underline{\alpha}, \underline{A}_1)\ ,\ (\underline{\beta}, \underline{A}_2)$$

of orders m and n respectively,

then their convolution F*G(x) (see also (4.2-20)) is a PH-distribution with representation $(\underline{\gamma}, \underline{L})$ given by

$$\underline{\gamma} = (\underline{\alpha},\ \underline{\alpha}_{m+1} \cdot \underline{\beta})$$

$$\underline{L} = \begin{pmatrix} \underline{A_1} & \underline{A_1}^{o}\ \underline{B}^{o} \\ 0 & \underline{A_2} \end{pmatrix} \qquad (4.2\text{-}21)$$

Proof: See Neuts /17/. It can be shown, using the Laplace-Stieltjes-transform of F and G (4.2-16) and the product corresponding to a convolution that (4.2-21) holds.

Example: Convolution of Erlang distributions (both of degree 2), but with different failure rates $\lambda_i (i=1,2)$ and $\lambda_j (j = 1,2)$.
(see (4.2-18)).

F*G(x)

For F(x) we have representation

$$(\underline{\alpha}, \underline{A}_1)$$

with $$\underline{A}_1 = \begin{pmatrix} -\lambda_1 & \lambda_1 \\ 0 & -\lambda_2 \end{pmatrix}$$

and $$\begin{pmatrix} \underline{A}_1 & \underline{A}_1^{o} \\ 0 & 0 \end{pmatrix} = \begin{pmatrix} -\lambda_1 & \lambda_1 & 0 \\ 0 & -\lambda_2 & \lambda_2 \\ 0 & 0 & -0 \end{pmatrix} .$$

For G(x) we have representation $(\underline{\beta}, \underline{A}_2)$.

Thus F*G is represented by

$$(\underline{\gamma}, \underline{L})$$

with $$\underline{\gamma} = (\underline{\alpha},\ \alpha_{m+1}\underline{\beta})$$

$$\underline{L} = \begin{pmatrix} \underline{A}_1 & \underline{A}_1^{o}\ \underline{B}^{o} \\ & \\ 0 & \underline{A}_2 \end{pmatrix} = \begin{matrix} \underline{A}_1 & \underline{A}_1^{o}\ \underline{B}^{o} \\ \begin{pmatrix} -\lambda_1 & \lambda_1 & 0 & 0 \\ 0 & -\lambda_2 & \lambda_2 & 0 \\ & & -\lambda_3 & \lambda_3 \\ & & 0 & -\lambda_4 \end{pmatrix} \end{matrix} \}\underline{A}_2$$

(4.2-22)

By a representation (see (4.2-20)) and by use of the convolution property of Erlang distributions we can indeed obtain the same matrix $\underline{L}$ (given in (4.2-22)).

Repairable components

The convolution theorem (4.2-21) may be also applied for a repairable component. We have the following structure for the generator of a Markow process:

$$\underline{M} = \begin{pmatrix} \underline{A}_1 & \underline{A}_1^o \; \underline{B}^o \\ \\ \underline{A}_2^o \; \underline{A}^o & \underline{A}_2 \end{pmatrix} \qquad (4.2\text{-}23)$$

Without loss of generality, we may assume $\alpha_{m+1} = \beta_{n+1} = 0$. If at time t the Markow process is in the set of states $\{1,2,\ldots,m\}$, the point is covered by an interval with distribution F. A similar consideration holds for sojourns in the set $\{m+1,\ldots,m+n\}$. Transitions between these sets are called renewals. We obtain an alternating renewal process.

Construction of coherent systems

It is sufficient to consider for PH-distributions of life times T_1, T_2 the distribution of min (T_1,T_2) and max (T_1,T_2) (see also (4.1-17)).

Kronecker Product

If $\underline{L}$ and $\underline{M}$ are rectangular matrices of dimensions k_1k_2 and $k_1'k_2'$, their Kronecker product $\underline{L} \otimes \underline{M}$ is defined as the matrix of dimensions $k_1k_1'.k_2k_2'$ written as follows:

$$\underline{L} \otimes \underline{M} = \begin{pmatrix} L_{11}\underline{M} & L_{12}\underline{M} & \ldots & L_{1k_2}\underline{M} \\ \cdot & & & \\ \cdot & & & \\ \cdot & & & \\ \cdot & & & \\ L_{k_11}\underline{M} & L_{k_12}\underline{M} & \ldots & L_{k_1k_2}\underline{M} \end{pmatrix} \qquad (4.2\text{-}24)$$

Note that the r.h.s of (4.2-24) is written as a matrix of submatrices (in block partitioned form).

Now, for independent r.v. T_1, T_2 with PH-distributions a theorem will be statet. Let

$$F_{max}(t) = F_1(t)\, F_2(t), \text{ and}$$

$$F_{min}(t) = 1 - \left[1-F_1(t)\right]\left[1-F_2(t)\right] \qquad (4.2\text{-}25)$$

be distributions, corresponding to $\max(T_1,T_2)$ and $\min(T_1,T_2)$ respectively.

Theorem

Let $F_1(t)$ and $F_2(T)$ have representations $(\underline{\alpha},\underline{A})$ and $(\underline{\beta},\underline{B})$ of orders m and n respectively.

(a) Then $F_{max}(t)$ (4.2-25) has the representation $(\underline{\alpha},\underline{L})$ of order mn + m + n, given by

$$\underline{\gamma} = (\underline{\alpha} \otimes \underline{\beta},\ \beta_{n+1}\underline{\alpha},\ \alpha_{m+1}\underline{\beta}),$$

$$\underline{L} = \begin{pmatrix} \underline{A} \otimes \underline{E} + \underline{E} \otimes \underline{B} & \underline{E} \otimes \underline{B}^{\circ} & \underline{A}^{\circ} \otimes \underline{E} \\ 0 & \underline{A} & 0 \\ 0 & 0 & \underline{B} \end{pmatrix} \qquad (4.2\text{-}26)$$

where $\underline{E}$ is the unit matrix.

(b) Similarly, $F_{min}(t)$ (4.2-25) has the representation $(\underline{\delta},\underline{M})$ given by

$$\underline{\delta} = (\underline{\alpha} \otimes \underline{\beta})$$

$$\underline{M} = \underline{A} \otimes \underline{E} + \underline{E} \otimes \underline{B} \qquad (4.2\text{-}27)$$

Remarks

We will not go into the details of a proof. But let us note this: For a Markow matrix which is decomposable, a Kronecker product of two Markow matrices represents this decomposition. For a proof of this theorem see Neuts /17/. The main step is there to show that $\underline{A} \otimes \underline{E} + \underline{E} \otimes \underline{B}$ cannot be singular. The infinitesimal generators $\underline{A},\underline{B}$ (see (4.2-12)) are nonsingular matrices.

Examples:

Let us consider the two basic elements of a coherent system. We assume systems with two components where the life times are exponentially distributed, with λ_1,λ_2.

(a) Series system

For min (T_1,T_2) we obtain

$$F_{min}(t) = 1 - (1-F_1(t))(1-F_2(t))$$
$$= 1 - e^{-(\lambda_1+\lambda_2)t}$$

For a PH-distribution we obtain the following representation (see (4.2-27)):

$$\underline{A} \otimes \underline{E} + \underline{E} \otimes \underline{B} = \lambda_1 + \lambda_2$$

(b) Parallel system

For max (T_1, T_2) we obtain

$F_{max}(t) = F_1(t)\, F_2(t) = (1-e^{-\lambda_1 t})(1-e^{-\lambda_2 t})$

With (4.2-26) we obtain as representation $(\underline{\gamma}, \underline{L})$, where

$$\underline{L} = \begin{pmatrix} \underline{A} \otimes \underline{E} + \underline{E} \otimes \underline{B} & \underline{E} \otimes \underline{B}^{o} & \underline{A}^{o} \otimes \underline{E} \\ 0 & \underline{A} & 0 \\ 0 & 0 & \underline{B} \end{pmatrix}$$

With (4.2-13) we obtain

$$\underline{A} \cdot \underline{e} + \underline{A}^{o} = 0, \quad \underline{B}\, \underline{e} + \underline{B}^{o} = 0$$

For exponential distributions, we have

$$-\lambda_i \cdot 1 + \lambda_i = 0 \qquad (i = 1,2)$$

The representation is of order $mn + m + n = 1 \cdot 1 + 1 + 1 = 3$. Finally

$$\underline{L} = \begin{pmatrix} -(\lambda_1+\lambda_2) & \lambda_1 & \lambda_2 \\ 0 & -\lambda_2 & 0 \\ 0 & 0 & -\lambda_1 \end{pmatrix}$$

The same result may be also obtained by a transition matrix and a transition diagram. This transition matrix is closely related to system reliability.

4.3 Representation of a Life Time Distribution

It is possible to represent the life time distribution for a coherent system if its components have life times which are PH-distributed. This is based on (4.1-7) (stopping time property of T_ϕ) and on (4.2-26), (4.2-27) (closure property with regard to a coherent system). To write this distribution explicity, a new concept is useful:

Kronecker Sum

Let A be a n·n-matrix and B be a m·m-matrix. Then the Kronecker sum of A and B is

$$\underline{A} \oplus \underline{B} = \underline{A} \otimes \underline{E}_m + \underline{E}_n \otimes \underline{B} \qquad (4.3\text{-}1)$$

where $\underline{E}_k$ is the unit matrix of order k.

Examples:

1. The representation for $F_{max}(x)$ (see(4.2-26)) can be written using a Kronecker sum:

$$\underline{L} = \begin{pmatrix} \underline{A} \oplus \underline{B} & \underline{E} \otimes \underline{B}^{\circ} & \underline{A}^{\circ} \otimes \underline{E} \\ 0 & \underline{A} & 0 \\ 0 & 0 & \underline{B} \end{pmatrix} \qquad (4.3\text{-}2)$$

2. For $F_{min}(t)$ (see(4.2-27)) the representation is:

$$\underline{M}_s = \underline{A} \oplus \underline{B} \qquad (4.3\text{-}3)$$

Of course the expressions for $\underline{\gamma}, \underline{\delta}$ remain (see 4.2-26).

Generalization

1. It is (due to some properties of the Kronecker product /20/) possible to generalize also the Kronecker sum. Let $\underline{A}, \underline{B}, \underline{C}$ be three matrices of order m each. Then we obtain:

$$\underline{A} \oplus \underline{B} \oplus \underline{C} = (\underline{A} \otimes \underline{E}_m + E_m \otimes \underline{B}) \otimes \underline{E}_m + \underline{E}_{m^2} \otimes \underline{C}$$

where $\underline{E}_m, \underline{E}_{m^2}$ are unit matrices of order m and m^2 respectively.

2. It is also possible to define the Kronecker sum of n matrices A_i recursively:

$$\bigoplus_{i=1}^{n} \underline{A}_i = \left(\bigoplus_{i=1}^{n-1} \underline{A}_i\right) \otimes \underline{E}_m + \underline{E}_{m^{n-1}} \otimes \underline{A}_n \qquad (4.3\text{-}4)$$

where $\underline{E}_m$, $\underline{E}_{m^{n-1}}$ are unit matrices of order m and m^{n-1} respectively.

Note: + refers to a matrix sum and $\oplus$ to a Kronecker sum.

Notation

For the following discussion it is possible to write instead of $\underline{A}^{\circ}$ the term $-\underline{A}\,\underline{e}$. This holds due to the relation

$$\underline{A}\,\underline{e} + \underline{A}^{\circ} = 0 \qquad (4.2\text{-}13)$$

A Represenatation for min $(T_1, T_2, \ldots, T_n)$

Discussion

Let the distributions for T_1, T_2, T_3 be represented by $(\underline{\alpha}_1, \underline{A})$, $(\underline{\alpha}_2, \underline{B})$, $(\underline{\alpha}_3, \underline{C})$, where all three matrices are of order 2. Then we find the representation for min (T_1, T_2, T_3).

Then we obtain

$$\underline{M}_s = \underline{A} \oplus \underline{B} \oplus \underline{C} \tag{4.3-5}$$

$$= \begin{pmatrix} (a_{11}+b_{11})\underline{E}+\underline{C} & b_{12}\underline{E} & a_{12}\underline{E} & 0 \\ b_{21}\underline{E} & (a_{11}+b_{22})\underline{E}+\underline{C} & 0 & a_{12}\underline{E} \\ a_{21}\underline{E} & 0 & (a_{22}+b_{11})\underline{E}+\underline{C} & b_{12}\underline{E} \\ 0 & a_{21}\underline{E} & b_{21}\underline{E} & (a_{22}+b_{22})\underline{E}+\underline{C} \end{pmatrix}$$

where a_{ij}, b_{ij} are elements of $\underline{A},\underline{B}$ and $\underline{E}$ is a unit matrix of order 2.

Note that for evaluation of $\underline{M}_s$ to obtain the distribution for min (T_1,T_2,T_3) a Gauss elimination procedure is useful. If we have Erlang-distributions represented by $\underline{A},\underline{B},\underline{C}$, the matrix $\underline{M}_s$ reduces to a triangular matrix.

Result

For $\min(T_1,T_2,\dots,T_n)$ we obtain as representation

$$\underline{M}_s = \bigoplus_{i=1}^{n} \underline{A}_i \tag{4.3-6}$$

$$\underline{\alpha}_s = (\alpha_1 \otimes \alpha_2 \otimes \cdots \otimes \underline{\alpha}_n)$$

(see also (4.2-27)).

The life time distribution for this series system is (see also (4.2-15)):

$$F_s(x) = 1 - \underline{\alpha}_s \exp(\underline{M}_s x)\underline{e} \tag{4.3-7}$$

A Representation for max $(T_1,T_2,\dots,T_n)$

Discussion

Let the distributions for T_1,T_2,T_3 be represented by $(\underline{\alpha}_1,\underline{A}_1)$, $(\underline{\alpha}_2,\underline{A}_2)$, $(\underline{\alpha}_3,\underline{A}_3)$ where all three matrices are of the same order (e.g. 3). Then we may find the representation for $\max(T_1,T_2,T_3)$ recursively (see also (4.2-26)) as the matrix $M_p^{(3)}$ (where (3) refers to 3 components, p refers to a system where all components are in parallel).

$$\underline{M}_p^{(3)} = \begin{pmatrix} \underline{M}^{(2)} \oplus \underline{A}_3 & -\underline{E} \otimes \underline{A}_3 e & -\underline{M}^{(2)}\underline{e} \otimes \underline{E} \\ 0 & \underline{M}^{(2)} & 0 \\ 0 & 0 & \underline{A}_3 \end{pmatrix} \tag{4.3-8}$$

where

$$\underline{M}^{(2)} = \begin{pmatrix} \underline{A}_1 \oplus \underline{A}_2 & -\underline{E} \otimes \underline{A}_2\underline{e} & -\underline{A}_1\underline{e} \otimes \underline{E} \\ 0 & \underline{A}_1 & 0 \\ 0 & 0 & \underline{A}_2 \end{pmatrix}$$

We also obtain

$$\underline{\gamma}^{(3)} = (\underline{\gamma}^{(2)} \otimes \underline{\alpha}_3,\ \alpha_{3,m+1}\ \underline{\gamma}^{(2)},\ \gamma^{(2)}_{m'+1}\ \underline{\alpha}_3) \qquad (4.3\text{-}9)$$

where

$$\underline{\gamma}^{(2)} = (\underline{\alpha}, \otimes\ \underline{\alpha}_2,\ \alpha_{2,m+1}\ \underline{\alpha}_1,\ \alpha_{1,m+1}\ \underline{\alpha}_2) \qquad (4.2\text{-}26)$$

With this representation, $(\underline{\gamma}^{(3)}, \underline{M}_p^{(3)})$ the life time distribution can be given:

$$F_p(x) = 1 - \underline{\gamma}^{(3)} \exp(\underline{M}_p^{(3)} x)\underline{e} \qquad (4.3\text{-}10)$$

<u>Result</u>

For Max $(T_1, T_2, \ldots, T_n)$ we obtain as representation

$$\underline{M}_p^{(n)} = \begin{pmatrix} \underline{M}^{(n-1)} \oplus \underline{A}_n & -\underline{E} \otimes \underline{A}_n\underline{e} & -\underline{M}^{(n-1)}\underline{e} \otimes \underline{E} \\ 0 & \underline{M}^{(n-1)} & 0 \\ 0 & 0 & \underline{A}_n \end{pmatrix} \qquad (4.3\text{-}11)$$

and

$$\underline{\gamma}^{(n)} = (\underline{\gamma}^{(n-1)} \otimes \underline{\alpha}_n,\ \alpha_{n,m-1}\ \underline{\gamma}^{(n-1)},\ \gamma^{(n-1)}_{m'+1}\ \underline{\alpha}_n) \qquad (4.3\text{-}12)$$

Now the representation for a complete coherent system will be given. This is represented by minimal cuts $\mathcal{C}_j (j=1,\ldots,l)$.

We obtain for a minimal cut $\mathcal{C}_j$ using (4.3-11) the matrix $\underline{M}^{(nj)}_{\mathcal{C}_j}$.

<u>A Representation for a Coherent System</u>

For a coherent system (C,ϕ) we get with (4.3-6) as representation:

$$\underline{M}_\phi = \bigoplus_{j=1}^{l} \underline{M}^{(nj)}_{\mathcal{C}_j} \qquad (4.3\text{-}13)$$

$\underline{M}^{(nj)}_{\mathcal{C}_j}$ represents minimal cuts (see(4.3-12).

$\underline{\gamma}_\phi$ has to be calculated as follows:

$$\underline{\gamma}_\phi = (\underline{\gamma}_1^{(n_1)} \otimes \underline{\gamma}_2^{(n_2)} \otimes \cdots \otimes \underline{\gamma}_l^{(n_l)}) \qquad (4.3\text{-}14)$$

where $\underline{\gamma}_j^{(nj)}$ is defined by (4.3-8) and (4.3-12). The PH-distribution of the coherent system (see also (4.2-15) and (4.3-7)) is

$$F_\phi(x) = 1-\underline{\gamma}_\phi \exp(\underline{M}_\phi x)\underline{e} \qquad (4.3\text{-}15)$$

($\underline{\gamma}_\phi$, $\underline{M}_\phi$) as given in (4.3-13), (4.3-14) is the <u>representation for the phase type distribution (PH-distribution) of the system's life time for a coherent system</u> where all components have PH-distributed life times and where a search for all minimal cuts $\mathcal{C}_j$ (j=1,2,...,l) has been completed.

<u>Evaluation and Applications</u>

1. The evaluation of (4.3-13) goes over the eigenvalues of $\underline{M}_\phi$ (see also (4.2-10)). It is useful to make this with a block Gauss-Seidel iteration (Neuts /2/).

2. This evaluation clearly depends on the structure of $\underline{M}_\phi$. Again, for some distributions e.g. for generalized Erlang distributions the procedure greatly simplifies (see also (4.3-5)).

3. It has been shown (Neuts /21/) that the method of PH-distributions can also be applied to systems with repairable components and with standby. Here the procedure of evaluation may strongly increase in complexity even for 3 components.

4. Also the relation to systems which have statistically dependent components can be treated with a similar method (Amoia et al. /22/).

4.4 <u>Markow renewal process (MRP)</u>

The Markow renewal process is a generalization of Markow processes and of renewal processes. It is one of the best known processes with non-Markowian behavior. This will not be discussed here.

It is possible to evaluate for a system suitable measures of effectiveness (reliability, maintainability) using MRP. This can be done with techniques known partly from Markow processes. There exist relations to fault tree analysis and stopping times and techniques for evaluation are available. But also problems which are not suitable for fault tree analysis can be dealt with MRP (see /18/).

<u>References</u>

/1/ MURCHLAND, J.D., WEBER, G.
A Moment Method for the Calculation of a Confidence Interval for the Failure Probability of a System, Proceedings 1972 Annual Symposium on Reliability, San Francisco, pp. 565, 1972

/2/ BARLOW, R.E., PROSCHAN, F.
Statistical Theory of Reliability and Life Testing, Probability Models, Holt, Rinehart and Winston, New York, 1975

/3/ CHU, T.L., APOSTOLAKIS, G.
Methods for Probabilistic Analysis of Noncoherent Fault Trees, IEEE Trans. Reliability, Vol. R.29, pp. 354-360, 1980

/4/ KOHAVI, Z.
Switching and Finite Automata Theory (2nd Ed.), Mc Graw Hill Book Company, New York, 1978

/5/ BARLOW, R.E., FUSSELL, J., SINGPURWALLA, N. (Ed.)
Reliability and Fault Tree Analysis, SIAM, Philadelphia, PA, 1978

/6/ WEBER, G.
Complex system modelling with faut trees and stochastic processes. Conf. 'Electronic Systems Effectiveness and Life Cycle Costing', Norwich, GB, July 19-31, 1982

/7/ COX, D.R.
Renewal Theory, Methuen & Co. Ltd., London 1962

/8/ HÖFELE-ISPHORDING, U.
Zuverlässigkeitsrechnung, Einführung in ihre Methoden, Springer Verlag, Berlin, 1978

/9/ JOKELA, S.
The Availability and Reliability of Complex Systems, Electrical Engineering Laboratory, Report 15, Espoo, Finland, 1976

/10/ BRÉMAUD, P.,
Point Processes and Queues: Martingale Dynamics, Springer Verlag, New York, 1981

/11/ GREENWOOD, P.
Point Processes and System Lifetimes in "Stochastic Differential Systems" (Proc. of 3rd IFIP-WG7/1 Working Conference Sept. 1980), Lecture Notes in Contr. and Inform. Scienees No 36, Springer Verlag, Berlin, S. 56-60, 1981

/12/ ARJAS, E.
The Failure and Hazard Processes in Multivariable Reliability Systems, Math. of Operations Research 6, pp. 551-562, 1981

/13/ KÖNIG, D., STOYAN, D.
Methoden der Bedienungstheorie, Akademie-Verlag, Berlin, 1976 (Vieweg-Braunschweig 1976)

/14/ COX, D.R., MILLER, H.D.
Stochastic Processes, Chapman & Hall, London, 1972

/15/ ARNDT, K., FRANKEN, P.
Random Point Processes Applied to Availability Analysis of Redundant Systems with Repair, IEEE Trans. Reliability R-22, 1977, pp. 266-269

/16/ JANSEN, U.
Stationäre Verfügbarkeit und Unempfindlichkeit der Zustandswahrscheinlichkeiten - Formeln für die Zuverlässigkeitstheorie, Elektronische Informationsverarbeitung und Kybernetik (Journal of Information Processing and Cybernetics) Vol. 16, No 10/12, Berlin 1980

/17/ NEUTS, M.
Matrix-Geometric Solutions in Stochastic Models, An Algorithmic Approach, Johns Hopkins University Press, Baltimore and London, 1981

/18/ WEBER, G.
Methods of fault tree analysis and their limits.
The Institute of Physics, Conf. on Reliabilty Aspects, Brunel University, Egham, GB, September 11-12, KfK-3824 (Dezember 84)

/19/ ROSS, S.M.
On the Calculation of Asymptotic System Reliability Characteristics in /5/, pp. 331-350

/20/ BELLMAN, R.
Introduction to Matrix Analysis Mc Graw Hill Book Company, New York, 1970

/21/ NEUTS, M.F., MEIER, K.S.
On the Use of Phase Type Distributions in Reliability Modelling of Systems with Two Components
OR Spectrum 2, 227-234 (1981) (Springer Verlag 1981)

/22/ AMOIA, V., DE MICHELI, G., SANTOMAURO, M.
Computer-Oriented Formulation of Transition-Rate Matrices via Kronecker Algebra, IEEE Trans. Reliability, Vol. R-30, 123-132, 1981

PANEL DISCUSSION

ON

SAFETY ANALYSIS OF COMPUTER PROGRAMS USING FAULT TREES

Tuesday, 6th of August, 1985 at 9.00 hours

Chairman and Organiser: Dr. G.G. Weber, Kernforschungszentrum, Karlsruhe, FGR.

Panel Memmbers: Prof. N.G. Leveson, Univ. of California, Irvine, U.S.A.
Dr. P.K. Harter, Univ. of Colorado, U.S.A.
Mr. N. Harris, British Aerospace, U.K.

Contributors: Mr. J. Milewski, Warsaw University, Poland
Mr. M.A. Gordon, GEC Avionics Ltd., U.K.
Mr. J. Musa, AT&T Bell Laboratories, U.S.A.
Mr. T.C. Jones, SPR Inc., U.S.A.
Mr. A.A. Wingrove, RAE, Farnborough, U.K.
Mr. C. Dale, UKAEA, U.K.
Mr. B. de Neumann, GEC Research Lab., U.K.
Major A.L. Lake, Royal Artillery, U.K.
Dr. D. Hutchens, Clemson Univ., U.S.A.
Mr. P. Mellor, City Univ., London, U.K.

Dr. Weber. This panel discussion will be about the safety analysis of computer programs, using fault-trees. For safety-critical computer programs various methods are used to obtain reliable software. Some of these methods have been discussed already in previous lectures of this Institute. Let us hope that this panel discussion will become here a desired great event, and not an undesired great event.

Fault Tree Analysis

I will now say a few words about the fault-tree analysis (FTA). It is a well known technique which has been used for problems of system reliability and safety. The subject of this presentation is two-fold: basic concepts and methods will be discussed. The application of FTA with its use to analyse some of the logic of computer programs, and the use of software FTA's for computer programs has been shown to be an efficient approach. Let me say a few words about the purposes of the FTA. These are:

(a) systematic identification and classification of possible causes which lead to an undesired event (e.g. system failure);

(b) generation of clear and systematic documentation of

NATO ASI Series, Vol. F22
Software System Design Methods. Edited by J.K. Skwirzynski

failure modes;

(c) definition of criteria for reliable systems. (For instance, you can find a number of weak spots, which are also called minimal cuts; you do quantitative analysis to evaluate failure probability, unavailability, expected number of failures, and other reliability quantities).

Please note here that for software FTA there is no quantitative analysis, and we shall concentrate on points (a) and (b) above for qualitative evaluation.

Switching Algebra and Failure Diagnosis

Now a few words on switching algebra which is closely related to the FTA. The theory deals with binary variables, so let us consider some fundamental concepts.

We denote the binary variables by x_i. A combinational switching function is a mapping

$$f : B^n \rightarrow B$$

where $B = \{0,1\}$ and B^n denotes the set of the 2^n binary n-tuples. Every switching function is a Boolean function. A switching function can be specified for every input combination

$$(x_1, x_2, \ldots, x_n).$$

A physical realisation of a switching function is called a combinational circuit. For a combinational circuit, standard components, called gates, can be used, e.g. AND, OR, NOT are such gates, and their meaning and significance are illustrated in Fig.1.

We shall next define the meaning of Boolean polynomials and of prime implicants. A switching function f "covers" another function g if f assumes the value 1 whenever g does. A prime implicant p of a function f is a monomial which is covered by f. However, if any variable is deleted from p, the monomial is no longer covered by f.

Any irredundant polynomial which is equivalent to a switching function f(x) may be written:

$$f(x) = \sum_{i=1}^{\ell} p_i$$

All prime implicants may be found by algorithms. It is also possible to find a single irredundant polynomial by an algorithm.

Next we consider adjacent monomials, another concept for switching algebra. Let p_i be a prime implicant. Then every monomial which differs in exactly one variable from p_j will be called an adjacent monomial p^*_{jk}.

Name	Circuit symbol	Truth table	Equation
AND	x_1, x_2, z	x_1 x_2 z 0 0 0 0 1 0 1 0 0 1 1 1	$z = x_1 x_2$ or $z = x_1 \wedge x_2$
OR	x_1, x_2, z	x_1 x_2 z 0 0 0 0 1 1 1 0 1 1 1 1	$z = x_1 + x_2$ or $z = x_1 \vee x_2$
NOT	x, z	x z 0 1 1 0	$z = \bar{x}$
NAND	x_1, x_2, z	x_1 x_2 z 0 0 1 0 1 1 1 0 1 1 1 0	$z = \overline{x_1 x_2}$
NOR	x_1, x_2, z	x_1 x_2 z 0 0 1 0 1 0 1 0 0 1 1 0	$z = \overline{x_1 + x_2}$
EXCLUSIVE-OR	x_1, x_2, z	x_1 x_2 z 0 0 0 0 1 1 1 0 1 1 1 0	$z = x_1 \oplus x_2$

Fig 1 The major gate types

Example: $p_j = x_1 x_2$ gives $p^*_{j1} = \bar{x}_1 x_2$, $p^*_{j2} = x_1 \bar{x}_2$.

It is useful to take a binary representation for tables with p^*_{jk}.

A typical representation is shown in Fig.2. Adjacent monomials are needed to describe certain faults in circuits. They may be found by algorithms. Further concepts will be introduced when appropriate.

Now let us turn to the failure diagnosis, by considering first the fundamental concepts. We assume a combinational circuit, consisting of AND-, OR-, NOT- gates and of wires. The circuit is characterised by a switching function (Boolean function). The following faults are considered:

- static 0 faults (s-a-0)
- static 1 faults (s-a-1).

Other faults, e.g. intermittent faults, bridge faults, etc. are not taken into account.

<u>Some FTA - Concepts</u>

The fundamental concepts of the FTA are as follows:

With a fault tree analysis it is possible to get the causes for a previously specified event (e.g. system failure)

- a systematic identification of possible failure combinations, and
- an evaluation of safety relevant characteristics (e.g. unavailability, expected number of failures).

Now we define a fault tree: A <u>fault tree</u> is a finite directed graph without (directed) circuits. Each vertex may be in one of several states. For each vertex a function is given which specifies its state in terms of the states of its predecessors. The states of those vertices without predecessors are considered the independent variables of the fault tree.

Please note that we assume two states for each vertex, and so we obtain Boolean expressions. This definition of a fault tree corresponds to a combinational circuit. A typical, quite simple fault tree is shown in Fig.3.

This is equivalent to a structure function. Here a Boolean function is introduced which describes the fault tree. Evidently this function is closely related to a switching function. This Boolean function specifies the states of each vertex in terms of its predecessors. A structure function may be used for all fault trees, e.g. consisting of AND-, OR-, NOT- gates. However, for sequential systems the structure function cannot be used.

Frequently a system S is coherent, i.e. the following conditions (a) and (b) hold:

(a) If S is functioning, no transition of a component from failure to the non-failed state can cause system failure (positivity of the structure function).

(b) If all components are functioning, the system is

- Switching function

  $f(\underline{x}) = x_1 x_2 + x_3 x_4$

- KARNAUGH - MAP

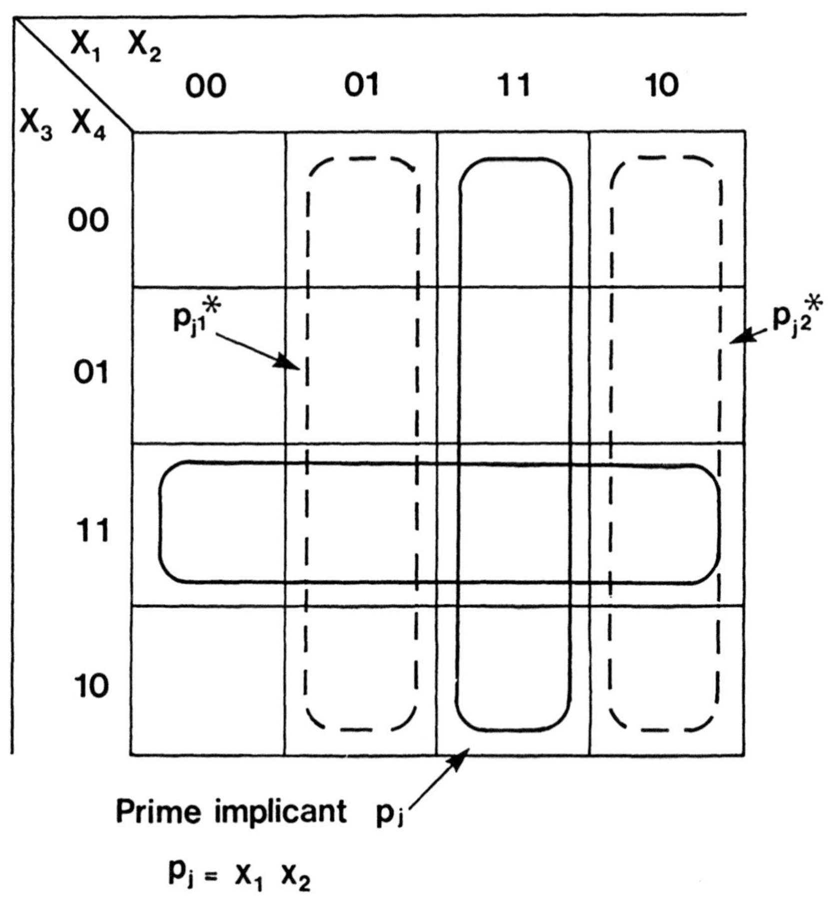

$p_j = x_1 \; x_2$

adjacent monomial to p_j

$p_{j1}^* = \bar{x}_1 \; x_2$

$p_{j2}^* = x_1 \; \bar{x}_2$

Fig 2

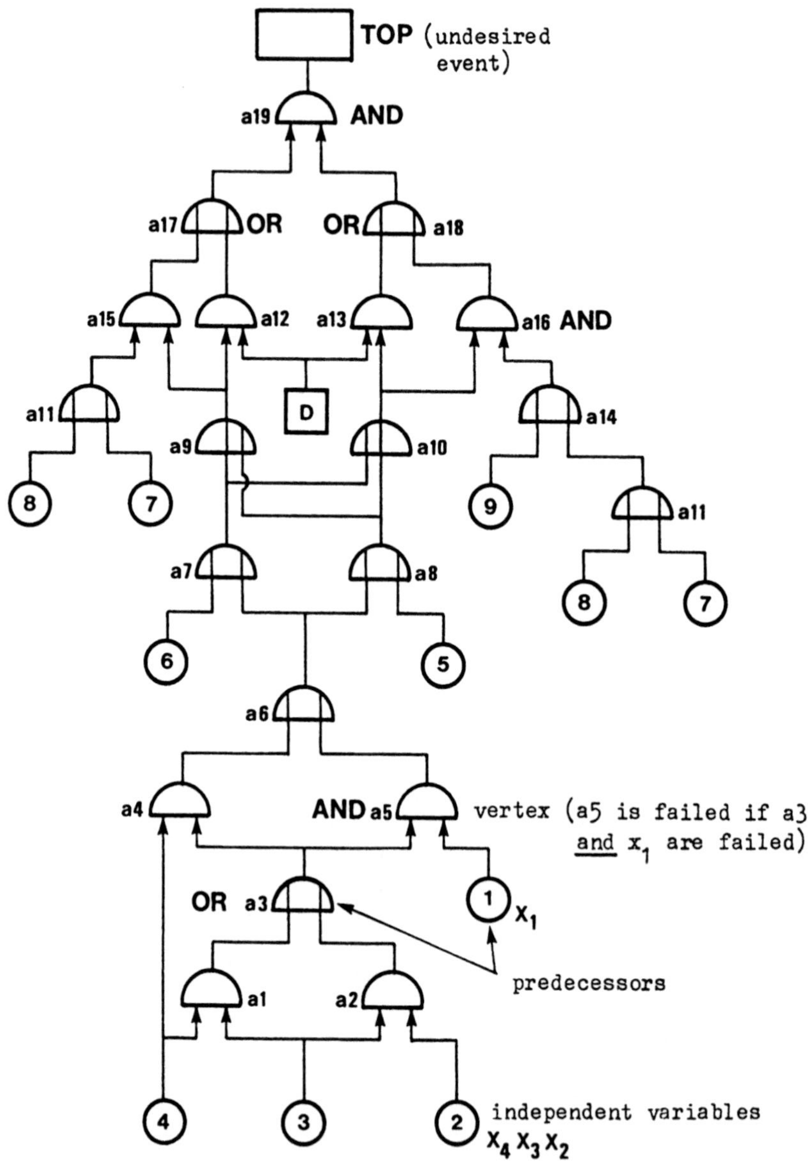
TOP (undesired event)
a19
AND
a17
OR
OR
a18
a15
a12
a13
a16 AND
D
a11
a9
a10
a14
8
7
9
a11
a7
a8
8
7
6
5
a6
a4
AND a5
vertex (a5 is failed if a3 and x1 are failed)
OR a3
1
X1
predecessors
a1
a2
4
3
2
independent variables
X4 X3 X2

Fig 3

functioning, and if all componenets are failed, the system is failed.

If the system may be represented by AND and OR, but without complements, then the structure is coherent. For coherent systems exactly one irredundant polynomial exists which is also minimal (minimal cut representation).

Failure Daignosis Procedures related to FTA.

Now we come to the actual diagnosis procedures, starting with fundamental concepts. We want to apply methods from failure diagnosis of combinational circuits to systems represented by fault trees. We assume that for relevant components failure symptoms are automatically detectable. This detection should be possible for operating and for failed systems. It is beyond the scope of this discussion to consider the implementation of detection. This method should skip redundant signals, decrease false alarms, and be applicable to realistic systems.

For detection of causes for system failure we have two procedures:

Procedure a. This procedure leads to failure disgnosis on the component level of a failed system as follows:

1. Representation of system S by structure function.
2. Search for min cut p_j with value 1.
3. Search for a minterm a_j covered by p_j.

Procedure b. This procedure leads to the detection of states adjacent to system failure. It detects these states as follows:

1. Representation of system S by structure function.
2. Search for min cuts and adjacent monomials p^*_{jk}.
3. Search for a minterm b_{jk} covered by p^*_{jk}.

We should note that both procedures are applicable to non-coherent systems. While procedure (a) increases availability, procedure (b) increases safety of a system. Relations of these procedures to tests for s-a-0 and s-a-1 are apparent.

We shall now show a simple example of FTA for a hardware system. Consider a communication network shown here Note the relation to Procedure a (Fig.4).

Which units have to fail to interrupt communication from A to B? Clearly these are: (1,2), (3,4), (1,4,5), (2,3,5).

This can be given as a fault tree (fig.5).

The structure function is:

$$F(x) = x_1x_2 + x_3x_4 + x_1x_4x_5 + x_2x_3x_5$$

At this stage I will hand over the discussion to Nancy Leveson.

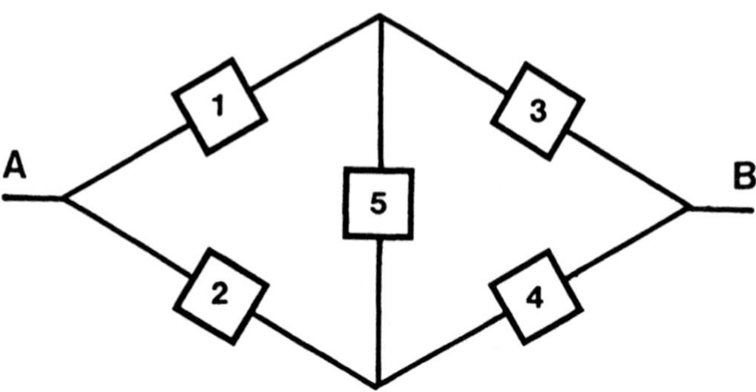

Fig 4

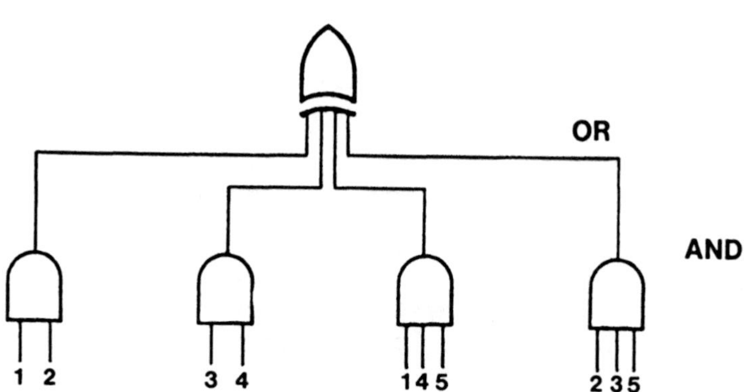

Fig 5

Professor Leveson. Let me review quickly a few points I made in my lecture (1). Dr. Weber has been telling you about the principles of FTA. When I first started looking into this, I discovered that the people using FTA could get no further than to show a box which essentially said the "software failed". We have been examining how to continue the FTA into software logic.

The difference between FTA and formal correctness is important to understand. Essentially, the output space can be divided into into two regions: correct and incorrect. Verification of correctness attempts to show that the output always is correct. In the proof of safety, we are really only interested that the system does not reach unsafe states (which are a subset of the incorrect states). The software may produce incorrect results and the system still be safe. Proof of safety using fault trees involves proof of contradiction: we assume that the software produces an unsafe result and then shows that this leads to a contradiction.

To provide a little more detail about how this is done, let us now look at the "IF THEN ELSE" statement, and let us assume that the event occured in this statement. Either the condition was TRUE, then the THEN part must have caused the event, or the condition was FALSE and the ELSE part has caused the event (see Fig.5). If the THEN part was TRUE, then 1) the condition was true prior to the IF THEN ELSE and 2) the THEN part has caused the event. It might be claimed that there should be another branch saying that the Boolean condition caused the event. This can only happen if the evaluation of the Boolean expression has a side-effect and changes the state of the computer (i.e. global variables). We assume that the hardware is working correctly.

Mr. Milewski. A side-effect free function could go into an infinite recursion and produce no result.

Professor Leveson. You are right. We could remedy this by adding another condition.

Mr. Gordon. Perhaps what we are thinking of is a case statement without a catch-all condition, in which case it sits there because it cannot go anywhere.

Professor Leveson. No. This is not a case statement.

To continue, the WHILE statement can cause the event either by not being executed or the execution of the WHILE statement causes the event. If the WHILE is executed n times, then the condition was TRUE prior to the WHILE (see Fig.6) and the n-th iteration caused the event. This is where the FTA analysis starts getting difficult and becomes non-automatable. The analyst must come up with a loop invariant. This is not a trivial task. We can automate a part of the FTA process and provide a semi-automatic tool.

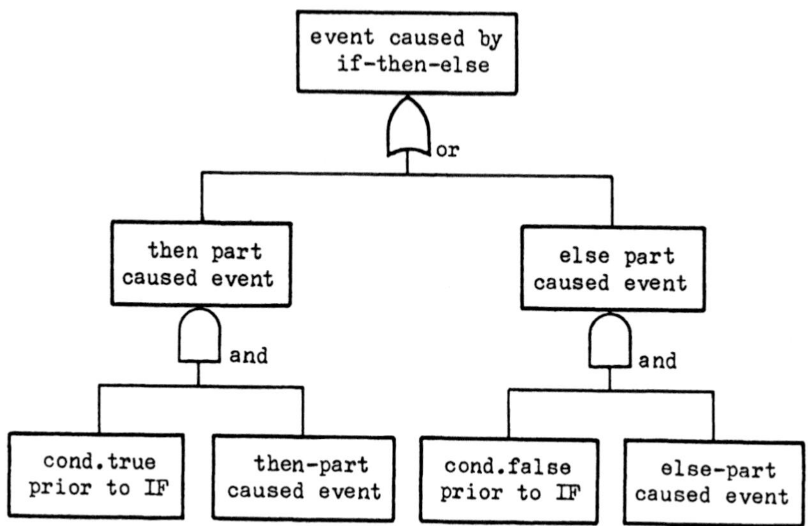

Fig 6 Fault Tree for IF THEN ELSE - Statement

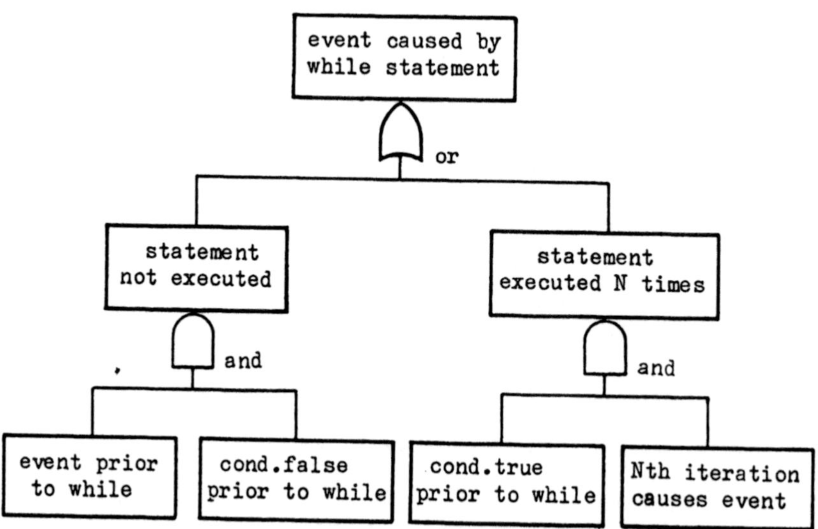

Fig 7 Fault Tree for WHILE - Statement

Heuristics can help to determine the invariant.

For those of you who are familiar with formal axiomatic verification methods, software FTA is equivalent to weakest pre-condition methods. As one goes through the software FTA process, if a contradiction is reached, then it has been shown that at least the logic of the software cannot cause the event. The other thing that can happen is that the FTA can run out of the software and back into the environment. If the latter happens, then there is a path through the software which could cause the event and it is necessary to make some changes to ensure that this cannot happen. This may involve changes in the software or in other parts of the system.

Software FTA can be a very tedious process and difficult to complete for a large program. However, important information is still obtained from a partially complete analysis. For example, as soon as the software interface is reached in the FTA process, the software safety requirements have been specified. And partially complete trees can be used to determine what types of run-time checks must be made to detect unsafe states and recover. So it is possible for this type of analysis to be useful even if all the code is not examined in detail. As an example of the time it takes to do this type of analysis, it took us two days to analyze a 1200 line assembly language program for one hazard. Of course, we were figuring out how to do a software FTA as we went along. The process may be more practical then a complete proof of correctness since:

1) the examination of a path stops as soon as a contradiction is found,

2) it is only necessary to examine part of the code.

We can now handle concurrency with the fault trees, at least in the form of ADA rendezvous. Timing is a problem and that is one of the reasons for looking at Time Petri nets (1). We think that the Petri net analysis can provide us with information which will assist with the FTA. Also, so far we have concentrated on software logic problems. We are now starting to look at a lower level (i.e. at assembler) and to examine the effects of computer hardware failures on software. It may be possible to determine particular credible hardware failures which would affect software in an unsafe way and to redesign the software to make it impervious to these types of failures. For example, it may be possible to design the software so that a harware failure cannot cause an accidental branch into a hazardous routine.

Mr. Musa. This is really a special case of a software fault tolerance study, is it not?

Professor Leveson. Yes it is.

Dr. Weber was talking to us about measurement and I would like to say something about the quantitative analysis of fault trees. Hardware FTA has been used quantitatively, but

I do not see how you could do this for the software. I am a little suspicious of the things that are done in real life using numbers in hardware FTA; often the data is very uncertain; they are from very small samples, and common cause failures are often ignored. FTA is very good in a qualitative sense, and we can find problems that we might not have found otherwise. The FTA can help to give us run-time failure analysis which will hopefully give more information about how to build run-time cheks in.

At this stage, I will pass over the microphone to Dr. Paul Harter.

Dr. Harter. It seems to me that one of the things that have been happening during this Institute is that Formal Methods in general have been getting a little bad rap; in spite of the fact that statistics and probability are also in their own way formal, maybe, with some probability! So I am going to talk a little bit today about Formal Systems. To know them is to love them.

First of all, look at the programming process, from the time someone comes up with an idea to the time that we actually have some executable code, there are a number of phases that are gone through. Somebody has an idea, and based on that idea a specification is drawn up. There are some number of design phases, maybe some high-level designs, some intermediate level designs, and some low level designs. Eventually someone sits down and writes some code and nowadays almost everyone stops at coding in some high level language. Twenty years ago people went all the way down to the machine code, and you will notice that as we go down this process, we have decreasing abstraction and corresponding increase in complexity. The idea for a program in the beginning was very small and concise; the specification was probably twenty pages, the high level design was probably a book, and there maybe a two-foot stack of program listings in the final implementation.

So at some point we are going to find out that human beings are uncapable of dealing with the complexity. People realised this and one of the first steps that were taken was to come up with some ways to manage the complexity a little bit better. The first thing that people did (thirty years ago) was to manage the complexity at the bottom level, where it was worse at first. Other methods have come up; using data abstractions and procedural abstractions have helped to manage the complexity at the level between the high level code and the low level design, and we have some methods of design such as stepwise refinement, which try to concentrate our attention on small pieces at a time, so that it is not necessary to be able to match all the complexity at once. For the top two levels nobody has anything that has been widely accepted to my knowledge, but it seems that this is something that is going to happen eventually.

Mr. Jones. Toshiba in Japan has a library of specifications, called "Blueprints", for common application types. When they want to deliver a product to a customer, instead of starting with an idea and a specification, they search through the "Blueprints" until they select a specification which resembles what the client wants, and then, since they have many of the modules and the standard specification, all they have actually to code are the pieces that are exceptions, where they do not match the standard blueprint or the standard code, and they are able to deliver software systems with over a quarter million lines of source code at a rate of about 27000 lines of code per man/year. That is because they have all these standard pieces.

Dr. Harter. Well, I was not aware of that particular library, and this will probably apply to at least the first time that something is implemented.

Generally, if we start at the top, we have an idea, and somebody wants to build something. The idea is abstract, and also somewhat loose; it might be ambiguous. By the time we get down to the bottom, we have the machine code which, if the hardware functions correctly, is completely unambiguous, and does exactly the same thing every time it runs, and if we want to know anything about the way the program behaves, we can presumably find that out by looking at the program. So at some point, on the way from the top to the bottom, we introduce formalism. What I mean by formalism is that we have got a complete and unambiguous specification of the desired observable behaviour. That is what I mean by a formal specification of the behaviour of the program. Now, when I say desired and observable behaviour, I mean the behaviour which the original inventor had in mind when he had the idea of a program. Observable applies to just those things which are externally observable, so there are all kinds of factors which come into the way a program behaves, which I am not interested in, and I claim I can have a perfectly formal specification of what we want, without specifying all the extra garbage. Furthermore, at the point where we introduce the formalism, the transition from informal to formal is handled by humans. Once we have formal specification machines, they will be capable of doing something, and I claim that the higher up we can make this transition, then with less detail and less complexity the human has to deal with, and the better are our chances for getting a good product.

When do we get formal? The last resort is when we hand it over to the computer, and the longer we wait the more detail we want in this transition, and we can use machines once we have a formalism. That is: "SOONER = BETTER".

Mr. Wingrove. Surely, these definitions are difficult to apply to real time computer systems, when the machine state at any instant might not be entirely determinable.

Dr. Harter. Well, generally in real time systems, in process control, etc., we can still have a formal specification in terms of reaction time to stimulus - how long it is from when you read a sensor to the time the program takes some action. I do not really care what the internal state of the machine is before, during, or after that reaction. What I am concerned about in a real time system is the response time.

Mr. Dale. I am still a little confused by the use of the word "complete" for a specification. If a specification is lacking in detail, in what sense is it complete?

Dr. Harter. It is complete in the sense that if I say to you: "What should it do in such-and-such case?", then you should be able to answer this from the specification. If I say to you: "How many variables are necessary to implement that function?", then you should not be able to answer that question.

So it is complete at the level you care about. That is you should be able to answer the questions you want to answer, without being able to answer deep questions which you don't care about. It is a question of choosing the level at which you decide to look at it. It is not a terribly precise notion.

Mr. Jones. For many years I have been counting specifications to see how big they have to be before they are complete. For a million line system, which is normal for a major operating system, or a big commercial application, it takes in general around thirty English words for every line of source code of a system in order to specify it. But by working backwards from the listings, I discovered that those specifications were less than half complete. Thus even for thirty English words for every source code line, over half of the functions were not even listed. A practical problem then is that a system specification for one million lines of code produces sixty thousand pages of text. If you were to specify fully a million line system in any formal way, I submit that the quantity of English text would probably be more bulky, like 60-70 words/line of code. So you are probably talking of specifications which approach a quarter million pages; beyond the life-time reading of any normal human being. How can you apply formal methods to these large systems?

Dr. Harter. Thank you very much. English is not a very good language for writing formal specifications.

Mr. Gordon. Surely what you mean is completeness of what a system is to do, rather than completeness of how it is to do it? And that defines it completely, does it not?

Dr. Harter. I thought that this is what I have just said.

Professor Leveson. There is another answer to what Mr. Jones has just told us, and that is that some formal specifications are shorter: one formal specification line can produce twenty lines of code automatically.

Mr. Jones. The smallest ones I have seen are five-to-one expressions; one statement of specification generates about five lines of code. I have heard of twenty-to-one ratios, but I have never seen these.

Dr. Harter. Well, I have promised you a slightly more formal view, and what I am going to talk a little now is what I mean by a formal system in the logical sense. We have some language in which we express statements or facts, and get some set of deduction rules which may be empty depending on the system. And we can look at a formal specification, not necessarily the top level specification, but if we stop anywhere in the hierarchy and treat that as a formal specification in our formal language, then using the deduction rule we can prove some set of theorems which are true facts, and which must hold for anything which satisfies the specification. On the other hand, if we look at an implementation of what we have got, then we come up with another set and this is much larger set in referred to in mathematical logic, as the theory of the object. The theory of the object is the set of true statements which one could make about the object, and some of them may be provable, and most of them are not. Most of you have heard of Goedel's incompleteness result.

For a formal system that is giving a specification for a program product, we have to expect to have some behaviour which we can derive from our specification, and when we observe the implementation, there may be a lot of other stuff that is not necessarily true. What is important that the containment shown here goes on (Fig.8). When design phase takes place, and based on the design, there are some more facts which we can claim to be true about the implementation, and these again are not derivable from our specification, but one thing that we have to worry about is that it is giving from the original specifications to the design phase , that we keep within two facts about the design, and all these things are derivable from the specifications.

What can we do about it? Well, the way that has been used in the past was to take the advantage of complexity management technique, such as stepwise refinement. We take a specification and change it locally in small ways and in ways which we hope will be preserved by the correctness of our specifications, so that we can continue to get the containment. On the other hand we can look at program verification. Program verification involves logical system and a model. A model in the sense of program verification is an idealised view of the system. The formal system that we

Formal System = Language + Deduction Rules

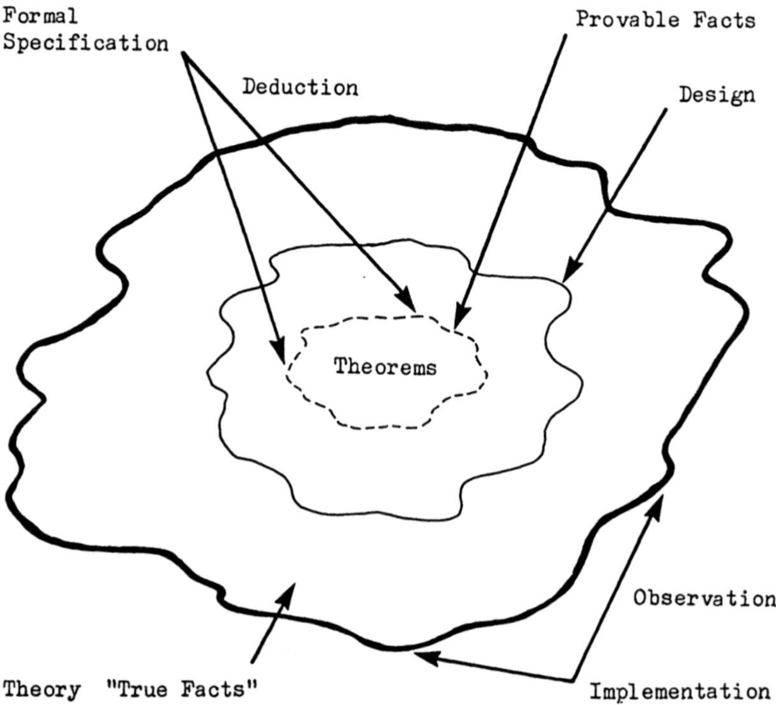

Fig 8 A Formal View

have got allows us to make true statements about the model, corresponding directly to the true statements about the system and finally the model is equivalent to giving the semantics of the system as a whole. Semantic models which are accepted today, are broken down into two major classes. The functional models which treat all the objects, variables, programs and functions, and give the semantics in terms of the ways that functions are modified. And there are state-base models which are more familiar to most of you, which are described by Hoare's axioms (2), Dijkstra's weakest precondition functions (3), and this is also the system on which temporal logics are based.

I will very briefly look at some of Hoare's axioms (2). We have a set of predicates P, Q and R, and these predicates describe a set of program states which are assigned to values of variables. If I execute a program, it begins in one state and halts with the system into another state which has variables with other values. We can describe the overall behaviour of the program by describing the initial state and the final state. With this system we can prove theorems of the form (called Hoare's triplets):

$$P\ (S)\ Q,$$

which says that if the program or statement S begins an execution in state P, satisfying P, then if and when it halts, the final state satisfies Q. So we are talking about what does S do. Here are two more examples:

To prove $P\ (S_1;\ S_2)\ Q$,

find R such that

$$P\ (S_1)\ R$$

and

$$R\ (S_2)\ Q$$

To prove $P\ (\text{if } B_1 \text{ then } S_1 \text{ else } S_2)\ Q$,

show that

$$P \wedge B_1\ (S_1)\ Q$$

and

$$P \sim B_2\ (S_2)\ Q.$$

This the formal basis of software fault tree analysis.

In the last section, I will mention temporal logic. Temporal logic is a logical system related to modal logics, and I think that Mr. Harris is going to mention this. It fills a gap which was left by Hoares's system. Hoare's system is very good for talking about programs which start in one state and end in another state, because you can characterise these states by using two different predicates. On the other hand, if we look at operating systems, communication protocols, process control systems, program operating elevators, etc., all these things are slightly difficult. What we have to specify then is some ongoing behaviour, some response to a given stimulus, you are going to be lucky, for they never halt.

Mr. Milewski. That is exactly the point which I have made when Professor Leveson was lecturing to us. Perhaps one difference between hardware failure analysis and software failure analysis is that in hardware are here essentially two-valued logic; it works, or it does not. In software perhaps there are three-valued logic, which would be better because it can give good results, wrong results, or nothing at all. I think that two-valued software fault trees which was mentioned by Professor Leveson, corresponds to a partial correctness proof, without considering the stop condition, and if you use three-valued software tree analysis, perhaps you could deal with the stopping condition.

Dr. Weber. In hardware in some cases we have components which have to be modelled for with a three-valued logic. Now a switch may be closed when it should be open, and open when it should be closed, and it may be normal.

Dr. Harter. So the gap is that, as I have mentioned, we cannot describe behaviours in the Hoare's system or in the Dijkstra's system. In temporal logic we add a few new operators, and different people use different symbols here. I use the following:

$\Box P$ - P is always true of execution

$\Box \sim P$ - P is never true

$\Diamond P$ - P must be true sometime

$P \mathcal{U} Q$ - P must be true until Q is true.

So we can describe the priority of service using $\mathcal{U}$. What do we get from this? Well, let us just take a look at the applications. First of all, the studying of formal semantics and formal systems for programming verification has allowed us for some programmer insight. The use of the notion of current state of a system, the notion of invariance of loops, etc. allow programmers to write a better code, just by having a new way of looking at things. Formal methods have been adapted to the development of large systems with stepwise refinement applying truth rules at increasing higher level of the development hierarchy, and

Mr. Dyer has told us about this (4). That is something that has been developed directly from formal systems. Some work has been done on automatic synthesis of synchronisation skeletons. A synchronisation skeleton is a program without normal assignment statements, just showing the synchronisation of the program, particularly for communication protocols. Based on a decision procedure for propositional temporal logic, it has been applied to finite state systems.

We have software FTA based on Hoare's logic and on Dijkstra's systems. Let us look ahead a little bit. What can we expect in the future? It is possible that we can have some automatically supervised program development, where the programming system would allow you to apply some predefined transform atoms to your program, and these could guarantee the preserving of correctness. The system would monitor your activity. We are nearly at the boundary to being able to do this.

Let us think big. It may be possible at some point to have some intelligent interaction system where you just sit down and deal with a software system. The system manages the formalism all the time, and the interface with a user is through a formal language at a high enough level for the programmer to make a sense of it. I have no idea when something like this might be possible, but I think that if it is going to happen, it will increase the productivity enormously, and if it is possible at all, it will come from the work on formal systems.

Lastly, I would like to talk to Mr. De Neumann; I am glad he is here among us. He is the second to the Fast Fourier Transform for wide use, and in matrix multiplier. Numerical analysts and algorithm people have been devoting life-times to increase the speed of these operations. The naive algorithm requires n-cubed time to do matrix multiplication, but very fancy algorithms have been developed to get this down to n raised to the binary log of 2.57, or something like that, but we are still not at the bottom of the theoretical absolute lower bound. So we may expect a wild dream in the future that the newspaper "Guardian" will announce "Computer Invents (n squared) Multiply!!"

Mr. De Neumann. I do not read the Guardian newspaper.

Dr. Harter. Then read the "Sun" newspaper.

Mr. De Neumann. The software of the models in the "Sun" newspaper are very intersting.

Dr. Harter. Allright, this ends my peroration.

Mr. Harris. One of the advantages of being last is that most of the difficult stuff has been said. One of the disadvantages of being last is that you have got to think of something different to say.

In a conference held in London in 1983 the spectrum of considerations of how computing might go is described in the table below:

SPECTRUM OF CONSIDERATIONS		
Programming language	Program organisation	Machine organisation
Conventional	Control flow	Centralised
Single assignment	Data flow	Packet communication
Applicative	Reduction	Expression manipulation
Object-oriented	Actor	?
Predicate logic	Logic	?

PROGRAMMING LANGUAGES	
Conventional	- BASIC, FORTRAN, COBOL
Single assignment	- ID, VAL, VALID
Applicative	- PURE LISP, FP, SASL
Object-oriented	- SMALLTALK
Predicative logic	- PROLOG

Quite clearly the computer has revolutionised much that is done in engineering, in Academia and much in how NATO holds its conferences. My concern is with the real-time systems, and that is my background, and in consequence over the last year or so I have been trying to fit these things together, and one has come to the conclusion that essentially there are four concepts that we need to understand: probability, causality, time, and I will put the whole amorphous area called mathematical logic under logic. Not only do we need to understand these, we need also to understand what are the relationships between them. I have argued quite strongly that probability in conjunction with causality leads to causal propensity that was the subject of my lecture (5). Probability + Logic has to lead to the developemnt of Boolean Logic. Probability + Time involves the concept of of Entropy, or in a more formal system that of Modal Logic. Logic + Time is Temporal Logic, and I just do not know yet what Probability + Time is, but one would suspect that it has something to do with the stochastic theory, but stochastic theory is not in it. So who was the first person who took this holistic view of the thing? In actual fact it was George Boole and here are his ideas:

THE LAWS OF THOUGHT (George Boole) 1854		
A	=	Necessary and Sufficient Conditions → Algebra of Logic
B	=	Cause → Logic of Cause
C	=	Probability → Factual and Logical Probability
D	=	Judgement → Subjective Probability
A + B + C + D → Scientific Method		

The approach he took was to consider algebra of logic, the logic of cause, the logic of probability and the logic of judgement. Interestingly, for the statistical fraternity, he had acknowledged that probability could be both factual and logical, and he was very well aware of the deductive interpretators. When he put these together, he described what he termed the scientific method.

Boole developed his ideas from the John Stuart Mills method of, what I call, the experimental cases, and I think we have talked here a little bit about the necessary conditions of a cause, and have associated that with the contingent necessary conditions. This can be formulated as follows:

NECESSARY CONDITION
An event C is a cause of an event E if and only if C and E are actual and all other things being equal C is necessary for E

We should also refer to the sufficient condition:

SUFFICIENT CONDITION
An event C is a cause of an event E if and only if C and E are actual and all other things being equal C is a sufficient condition of E

The basic problem is that Boolean logic does not handle what

I refer to as the INUS conditions, defined here:

INSUFFICIENT BUT NONE REDUNDANT PARTS OF UNNECESSARY BUT SUFFICIENT CONDITIONS (INUS)

If an event C is a cause of an event E (on certain occasions), C is a condition which ususally combines with other conditions to cause E. C is itself unnecessary but exclusively sufficient for E (on that occasion)

These are sometimes referred to as weakly sufficient conditions. The reason it did not handle it very well was that we had to wait for C.I. Lewis to come onto the scene and devise what we call today the modal logic. Dr. Harter has already referred to the temporal logic, and I have tried to find an example of what we mean by possibility.

If we take the development of probability, it splits into two parts

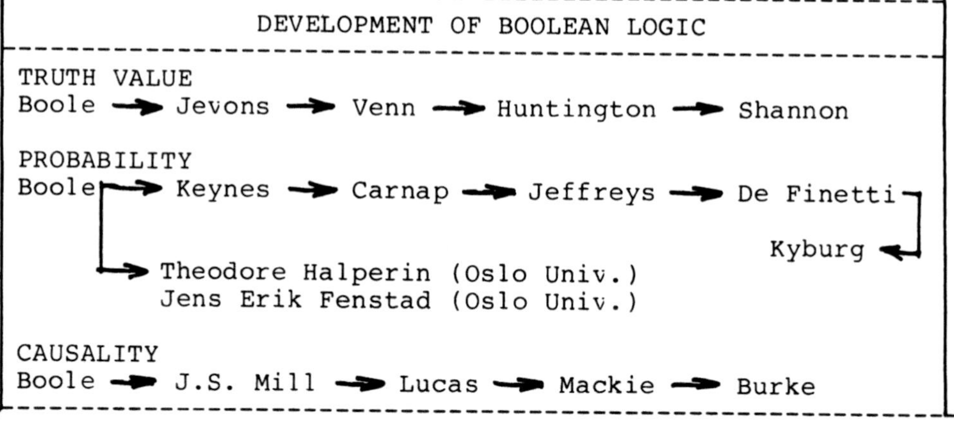

DEVELOPMENT OF BOOLEAN LOGIC
TRUTH VALUE
Boole → Jevons → Venn → Huntington → Shannon
PROBABILITY
Boole → Keynes → Carnap → Jeffreys → De Finetti
Kyburg
→ Theodore Halperin (Oslo Univ.)
Jens Erik Fenstad (Oslo Univ.)
CAUSALITY
Boole → J.S. Mill → Lucas → Mackie → Burke

Kyburg wrote a book on the formal approach and Halperin & Fenstad had a breakthrough in defining probability and randomness in terms of recursive theory. If that is not formalism, then I do not know what it is.

To get back to the modal logic, I had a great difficulty in coming up with an example to convey to you what one means by possibility; I could not find a pictorial example, so I have to do with an oral one: For instance, if Prince Charles was to make a statement "If I was king", then in language the mood is active, and in calculus this would be probability. If I was to make the statement "If I were king", the mood would be subjunctive, and in calculus this would be a possibility. The reason for this is that in any factual interpretation there is a measurable notion of reality that Prince Charles at some time in the future could or would become a king. If I was to say it, there is not a measurable reality, and in actual fact I stand a dog's chance of becoming king, but this is not a totally unrealistic thing to say. Certain things could happen, there could be a revolution, and the whole point about this is that this is not an impossibility. So when one talks about a possibility, one conveys a notion that it could happen, given the right circumstances. When one talks about probability, there is an expectation of it happening. When one talks about probability and about possibility, one can break these notions down as is shown here:

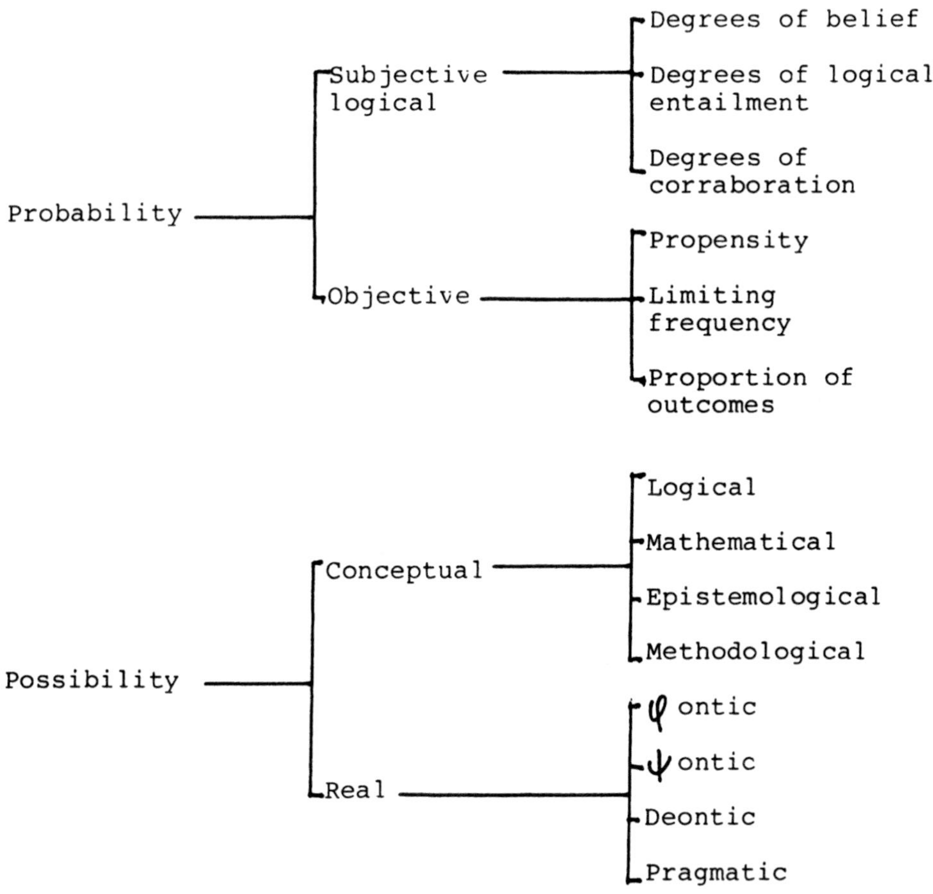

Let us consider in more detail the notion of conceptual possibility (de dicto), for it is within the modal logic where its major developments have been. Unfortunately, when one comes to talk about the real world, it has not had great advances.

CONCEPTUAL POSSIBILITY (de dicto)

(I) P is logically possible to A
A does not entail P

(II) P is mathematically possible relative to K
There is a model M in K such that P is realisable in M

(III) P is epistemologically possible relative to K
P and K are mutually compatible (i.e. P contradicts no memeber of K)

(IV) P is methodologically possible relative to K
There is a model M in K such that test runs within M do not disconfirm P relative to K

P is conceptually possible relative to K

P is either logically
mathematically
epistamologically
methodologically possible relative to K

Those people who argue that formalism provides a way of progressing software are right I think. But the next step is that this has to be interpreted into everyday language, and I do not think that much opportunity exists for engineers to learn logic. We find it very difficult to get the engineers to convey ideas behind statistics, or ideas behind probability. It needs to be simplified. What you normally do in a logical system is to construct the language and to use normal symbols. If you look at the logic language itself, you can break down arguments and apply very formal proving systems to find whether a statement is true or false. That is all I wish to say. Thank you.

Dr. Weber. Thank you very much. Now the floor is open to all.

Mr. Musa. I would like to strongly support what Mr. Harris has just said concerning making formal methods clear enough to understand. Engineers have many things to learn. We researchers must structure our findings as simply as possible, so that they can be acquired rapidly. It is a question of return on investment. If you have to spend several months or a year learning an approach that increases your efficiency, say 10%, that approach will stagnate. You are never going to sell it and you are never going to persuade people to use it. That is one criticism I have of formal methods. If they are ever going to be accepted, it is certainly necessary to make them simple and to convince people of their value.

Mr. Harris. I think the whole education system is facing a problem if you have a look at the growth of knowledge. Knowledge at the moment is doubling every five years, and by the end of this century it will double every thirteen months. How do you teach people? We may have to teach people to learn and give them access to literature and information. There is going to be a revolution in the way we educate and train engineers.

Major Lake. Can I follow the statement of Mr. Harris? I have just finished designing a course whose objective is to teach people to learn. You are absolutely right, but can you say how to do this?

Mr. Harris. I think it is very important to teach people concepts and how to understand concepts, and then to relate concepts to concepts, and not concentrating upon the implementation of these concepts. I think that for instance if you are called an engineer, you are, in principle, supposed to be able to do electronics one day, possibly hydraulics the next day, etc. If you begin to look at these engineering structures, you find they have much in common. Concepts at the higher level are ismorphic, they are generalisations. The education system has got to adopt to teaching people generalisations, teaching people concepts, and maybe when they get into industry, when they have to earn a living, they should then be trained in particular implementations of these concepts.

Mr. Musa. In the absence of somebody else I will be the gadfly on formal methods. Consider a specification for a program. It will have some amount of information, in the sense of Shannon's Information Theory. If you look at the implementation of the program, you obviously have a lot more volume, but you may or may not have more information. It seems to me that if formal methods really work, then essentially what you are saying is that you have to be able to go from the specification to the implementation automatically, without adding any information. That means that all the information in the final program must be there in the specification for formal methods to work. If that is the case, then what we are saying is that a program is a storehouse of redundancy. That is the only thing that can explain the great expansion. Are we saying that this is what these methods contribute? I am a little sceptical that there is that much redundancy in our programs.

Dr. Harter. There are a couple of points I wish to mention. The first one is that there is a fair amount of redundancy in programs, and that is what allows machines to process them the way they are written down today. The other point is one which I was discussing with Mr. De Neumann the other evening, namely that people looking at formal methods should appreciate that there is one-to-one correspondence or equivalence in the amount of information in a specification and in a program. There is not necessarily a one-to-one mapping between the specification and the program. There is not in an absolute sense an equivalent amount of information. At least not in the way I understand it.

Professor Leveson. I agree, but I think that there is also another aspect. To equate formal methods with essentially automatic programming and generation of code is a mistake. I think there is a lot of reason for using formal methods, yet I am sceptical whether we ever get to automatic programming. If you have a hundred people working on a project, and if you have some kind of specification, what you really need is communication. I do not believe that using an ambigous language for communication is going to have any effect other than to cause ambiguity and inconsistency. So, what I mean by formal is: There is an unambigous definition for the language.

Mr. Musa. In the definition of formal Dr. Harter used the term "complete". Now "complete" means to me: "Containing all of the information - information in the Shannon sense - that will be in the program". If that is not what it means, what do you mean by "complete"?

Dr. Harter. What I mean is that a specification should be complete in the sense that it should be possible to answer any question about the behaviour of the thing.

Mr. Musa. That is exactly what I am talking about.

Dr. Harter. But there is a lot of information involved in the program that is not part of specification.

Mr. Musa. Then that is redundant information.

Dr. Harter. With regard to the function it is not redundant.

Mr. Harris. Clarity of language is one thing that one ought to look at the notion of formal, in the same sense as David Hilbert set out a program for mathematics to make it understandable. What you have to do is to introduce a clarity of notions, and to do it in such a way that you can show theorems to be consistent with axioms. The problem is that English is ambigous, and what the formal methods set out to do is to introduce clarity at each stage of the operation. The notion of formal methods is not a single notion; it conveys many. It does not only apply at a system specification level, but runs all the way down.

Professor Leveson. Let me look at completeness now, but in a different sense. When I write a formal specification, it is somewhat of a pain. One reason is that I have to be really clear about what I want. I tend also to have to be complete about what I mean. It is very easy in English to gloss over all the hard parts of the problem. When you write formally, this sometimes makes you aware where the difficult parts are.

Dr. Hutchens. I would like to give an example of what I think is meant by this completeness idea. Suppose I had a system which was written entirely in FORTRAN and was running. Would you say that FORTRAN code gives a complete description of what the thing does?

Mr. Musa. With redundancy.

Dr. Hutchens. Now here is the question. At a particular point in the program, is the value of variable X in register 3? The answer is not determined from the FORTRAN code; it is a decision that is made by the computer. So there are different levels of completeness.

Mr. Musa. The compiler has essentially added zero information here in the Shannon sense.

Dr. Hutchens. That is not true. There are questions which cannot be answered from the FORTRAN code, but which can be answered from the machine code.

Mr. Harris. A further notion of what formal methods is about comes from the electronics industry. It was rapidly realised that circuits had to be described in something other than English, and circuit diagrams evolved to symbolise electronics.

Professor Leveson. I am not sure that I would agree that circuit diagrams are equivalent to circuits.

Mr. Mellor. It is a pity we were not shown few examples of bugs. I had a nice one the other day. A single line of PASCAL contained an error which depended upon the compiler not reporting an integer overflow and also doing the calculation in a certain order. It made me think about formal methods generally. Unless these formal methods take into account actual physical constraints, in other words how large a number has to be before you get overflow, you can never show that a given program is not going to fail in practice.

Professor Leveson. I agree, but that is not what we are

trying to show. First of all the bug was in the compiler.

Mr. Mellor. It was both in the compiler and in the program.

Professor Leveson. But your program is depending on the compiler working correctly. A formal proof of the program itself examines the logic of that program. We are making certain assumptions about the environment. This is true of any model, you always make assumptions, and then you have to verify them independently.

Mr. Mellor. I would think that a lot of errors would actually lie in these assumptions, outside of the formal proof.

Professor Leveson. That is why we have to know the assumptions, and why the formal methods people will tell you that they are not going to fly on a plane where the software was "proved" correct. Nobody is that silly! We know that we are only verifying a part of it. Nobody is saying that everything in the world has been verified.

Mr. Jones. I want to support the formalism concept in commercial software. One company is producing executable COBOL application direct from the formal specification without doing any coding. This is so successful that they do maintenance in the same fashion. They have not hired any new programmers in seven years and now have a surplus.

Mr. De Neumann. Can I just say that I feel most honoured that this panel should devote so much time to my formal education. I have learned something this morning, but I still feel a little bit bothered about formal methods. The real problem is (and I can see the reasons for the difference of opinions that we had earlier on) trying actually to encode what you want, using a formal specification. As I see it now, from what you are telling me, the language in which you write this formal specification forms the basis of a set of axioms which you then use to prove theorems about the program. You try and obtain a model of the software which you want to construct within that framework, so it is like a set of constraints. The problem with formal methods and formal systems is trying to prove actually that your axioms are consistent, and you can make theorems about the software in the first place.

Dr. Harter. You seem to be saying that it is our fault, that we are doing something wrong, because we cannot solve the consistency of a specification problem. In fact if you write all your specifications in English, you could not solve the consistency problem because English is ambigous.

Mr. De Neumann. I agree. All I am saying is that there is a

problem of proving that you have actually got what you want, and this is not the same as proving that this is the same as your specification.

Professor Leveson. You may be expecting too much.

Mr. De Neumann. I have a suspicion that I am expecting too little!

Dr. Weber. The time has now come to close this very interesting discussion, and now I thank our panelists and contributors, and close the discussion.

REFERENCES

(1) Software Hazard Analysis Techniques, Prof. Nancy G. Leveson (in this volume)
(2) Prof. C.R. Hoare: An Axiomatic Basis for Computer Programming, Comm. ACM, Vol.12, Oct. 1969, pp.576-580.
(3) Prof. E.W. Dijkstra: A Discipline of Programming, Prentice-Hall, Inc., Englewood Cliffs, N.J., 1976.
(4) Software Development under Statistical Quality Control, Mr. Mike Dyer (in this volume)
(5) The Rationale of Reliability Prediction, by Mr. Norman Harris (in this volume)

Part 2

Human Factors in Development and Use of Software

Organised by Bill Curtis

PSYCHOLOGICAL RESEARCH ON SOFTWARE DEVELOPMENT

Bill Curtis
MCC
9430 Research Blvd.
Austin, Texas 78759

PSYCHOLOGICAL PARADIGMS IN SOFTWARE ENGINEERING

Every psychological study portrays a paradigm, a model of what the investigator believes is really important in human behavior. When the choice of paradigms is unconscious, investigators are often faced with attempting to defend their hypotheses with data which do not bear on the argument. The motley body of psychological studies on programming has been guided by six psychological paradigms:

1) individual differences,
2) group behavior,
3) organizational behavior,
4) human factors,
5) cognitive ergonomics, and
6) cognitive science.

However, in many cases it is difficult to establish that investigators were aware of the paradigms underlying their studies. Nevertheless, these paradigms are important because they represent different ways of looking at human beings.

These six paradigms differ in the aspects of human behavior on which they focus. The difference is often whether they present a static or dynamic view of a particular factor which influences human behavior. In a static view of a factor, all relevant phenomena are treated as not differing across individuals or situations. Thus, a paradigm does not provide explanations for those influences on behavior. However, research is designed to investigate those factors which the paradigm treats dynamically.

Table 1 presents an analysis of how the six paradigms used in studying the psychology of programming treat various aspects of human behavior. The major influences on human behavior which differentiate the focus of the six paradigms are individual differences among people, cognitive phenomena, the individual's immediate personal environment, the group environment, and the larger organizational environment. For example, the human factors

NATO ASI Series, Vol. F22
Software System Design Methods. Edited by J.K. Skwirzynski

and cognitive ergonomics paradigms differ in their treatment of cognitive events, cognitive ergonomics choosing to treat them dynamically.

TABLE 1

Explanatory Focus of Six Paradigms

Paradigm	Individual differences	Cognition	Environmental factors		
			Personal	Group	Organization
Individual differences	dynamic	static	static	static	static
Group behavior	static	static	static	dynamic	static
Organizational behavior	static	static	static	dynamic	dynamic
Human factors	static	static	dynamic	static	static
Cognitive ergonomics	static	dynamic	dynamic	static	static
Cognitive science	dynamic	dynamic	dynamic	static	static

Each of the six paradigms allows for the sophisticated analysis of a factor influencing human behavior. Yet, each paradigm is limited in its explanatory power. Integration of results from studies using different paradigms has been sufficiently difficult to retard the development of a body of explanatory theory for the psychological aspects of programming. Even post hoc explanations of results often ramble aimlessly in search of a helpful frameword.

In this paper I will review research from the human factors, cognitive ergonomics, and cognitive science paradigms on software development.

HUMAN FACTORS AND COGNITIVE ERGONOMICS

The term most frequently associated with behavioral research on computer systems is 'human fators'. Human factors work has traditionally been thought of as fitting knobs, displays, and workstation layouts to the idiosyncracies of the human anatomy. The human factors paradigm seeks to determine relationships between the stimuli presented to individuals and the response they make to them. These stimuli might be software tools, information displays, documentation, terminal devices, etc. The human factors perspective does not care how people think about these stimuli, just how they respond to them. This paradigm produces principles of behavior without references to cognitive process; a decorticated model of people.

However, with the advent of computerized information processing and display; problem solving, information analysis, and procedural skills have become critical research topics. This latter type of research has come to be called 'cognitive ergonomics'. Cognitive ergonomics reflects the application of findings emerging from cognitive psychological research to the human factors questions of information display and analysis and human-computer interaction. Cognitive ergonomics is a more appropriate paradigm where the task under study primarily involves mental rather than physical effort.

The distinction between whether researchers are using a human factors or cognitive ergonomics paradigm is whether they resort to cognitive events to explain how a stimuli is expected to influence behavior. These paradigms have been most in evidence in the study of design problem solving, specification formats, and programming languages. Contributions to these three areas will be reviewed in this section.

Design problem solving. Most problem solving research has been performed on well defined problems with finite solution states. In problems such as the Towers of Hanoi, there is an optimal path to the solution. The path to a successful solution in chess is not so clearly defined. Nevertheless, in chess there are a finite number of moves which can be chosen at any time and a well defined solution state. In a semantically rich domain such as programming, neither are the options from which one can choose limited nor is there a clearly defined solution state. Therefore, studying problem solving in programming is a qualitatively different task than most of those used in problem solving research.

Carroll, Thomas, and Malhotra (1980) argued that solving unstructured problems could not be explained with existing theory. They began their investigations of the design process by studying how analysts and clients interacted in establishing the requirements for a system. Carroll, Thomas, and Malhotra (1979) observed that client/analyst requirements sessions were broken into cycles which represented the decomposition of the problem. However, these cycles did not decompose the problem in a top-down fashion as recommended by structured programming practices. Rather, these cycles represented a linear or sequential decomposition of the problem in which the subproblem to be attacked in the next cycle was cued by the results of the last cycle. The only a priori structure placed on the content of these client/analyst cycles was determined by the initial goal structure of the client.

The problem in moving from the idea for a system to its final implementation is in transforming a linearly derived sequence of desired components into a hierarchical arrangement of functions or data transformations. Once the requirements have been delineated, they must be organized so that the inherent structure of the problem becomes visible. The next step is to construct a solution structure which matches the problem structure. To the extent that these structures are logically organized and matched, the system will possess a structural integrity which can expedite its implementation.

A series of studies by Carroll and his associates at IBM's Watson Research Center identified several factors which impact the effectiveness of designing a solution. First, they demonstrated differences in problem analysis based on differences in the application attempted. It has been consistently found in problem solving research that people do not transfer solution structures across problem isomorphs. Isomorphs are problems with the same structural characteristics, but whose cover stories (or subject areas) differ. Previous problem solving research has established that there is poor transfer of previously learned problem solutions across isomorphs. The structure of the cover story affects the difficulty people experience in reaching a solution.

Carroll et al. (1980) observed that people had more difficulty solving a problem that involved temporal realtions (designing a manufacturing process) than an isomorph which involved spatial relations (arranging an office layout). The difference arose in part because the spatial problem lends itself to graphical representation. However, the temporal isomorph does not present spatial cues and participants had difficulty representing it to themselves. Many retreated to a verbal description of the problem, and several were totally unable to solve it. When a graphical aid was provided for solving the temporal problem, it appeared to make the problem easier to understand. The spatial aid did not make the problem easier to solve, however, since the same number of participants were unable to solve it.

The structuring of the requirements also seems to have an impact on the characteristics of the problem solution. Presenting the requirements in clusters based on their inherent structure assisted participants in designing solutions which better reflected the problem structure and were more stable when new requirements were added (Carroll, Thomas, Miller, & Friedman, 1980). Greater structure in the original problem statement seems to reduce the amount of iteration through design cycles. Thus, a critically important focus of the structured programming movement should be on methods of structuring the statement of requirements. Far less attention has been paid this problem than to areas, such as coding, that have less impact on system integrity and costs.

Hoc (1981) studied the results of designing a program from the data structure versus the results structure. He suggested that a choice of design method is often made prematurely, prior to understanding the relation between the data and results structures and the processing which transformed the former into the latter. He felt that the choice of design method was better made after this problem analysis stage.

The conceptual integrity of the program design is critical to the success of a programming project. No level of management talent can sustain high productivity and quality on a project which fails to achieve it. A most critical area for programming research, then, is requirements and design techniques. The current level of behavioral research on these topics is only a start in what needs to be a major thrust.

Specification formats. Research on specification formats in software engineering emerged in response to the debate over the use of flowcharts. Much of this debate had less to do with the actual format of flowcharts than with the difficulty of modifying them manually or the fact that they were often developed in the same unstructured manner as the code they documented. These problems are more related to the semantic content of what is documented in flowcharts than with the syntactic problem of how this information is organized and presented.

Four seminal studies on non-programming tasks were performed in the mid-1970's comparing flowcharts to other formats for presenting decision-aiding information. In the first of these studies, Wright and Reid (1973) found short phrases, decision tables, and tree charts to be more effective than prose descriptions for presenting information about simple (i.e., two conditional decisions) time, cost, distance, and mode of transportation decisions. For problems involving four conditional decisions fewer errors were made with tree charts than with any other presentation format. Blaiwes (1974) and Kammann (1975) obtained similar results.

Mayer (1976) varied both the presentation format and the types of conditionals used in expressing information. He found interesting interactions which led him to conclude that diagrams help to locate relevant information primarily when it was difficult to locate in verbal form. However, Mayer concluded that diagrams were not as effective as well structured verbal material. He also concluded that the representational format does not influence the reasoning process separate from its effect on quickly identifying relevant information.

The initial provocative study suggesting that flowcharts were of little use in a number of programming tasks was published by Shneiderman, Mayer, McKay, and Heller (1977). In five experiments on the composition, comprehension, debugging, and modification of programs, they found little benefit from flowcharts if listings of the code were available. Similarly, Ramsey, Atwood, and Van Doren (1983) found no differences in the effectiveness of producing code from specifications presented i in either a program design language (PDL) or a flowchart. However, they found that designs expressed in PDL were more detailed and complete than those expressed in flowcharts.

Sheppard, Kruesi, and Curtis (1981) distinguished between the spatial arrangement of a specification and the symbology used to express information within it. The following categories were used, shown with examples of each.

Spatial arrangement	Symbology
Sequential - listing	Ideograms - flowchart symbols
Branching - flowchart	Constructed language - PDL
Hierarchical - tree chart	Natural language - prose

The spatial arrangement dimension varies on the extent to which spatial dispersion is used to indicate the flow of control in the program. The symbology dimension varies on the conciseness of symbols required to express information.

The results obtained by the GE team (Sheppard et al., 1981; Sheppard & Kruesi, 1981) indicated that natural language is a poor medium for expressing procedural information. On tasks where control flow information was important for obtaining a solution, branching arrangements were found to enhance performance. Generally, however, a constrained language was found to be as effective as any other format for expressing procedural specifications, confirming the results of Ramsey et al. (1978).

Brooke and Duncan (1980a & b) found results similar to those of Sheppard and her associates for the benefits of flowcharts. After three debugging studies they concluded that flowcharts provided little assistance in finding program defects. However, flowcharts seemed to help, especially novices, follow the decision structure of the program. The contribution of flowcharts to the debugging process was in helping programmers to eliminate irrelevant questions in designing tests, but they did not help eliminate characteristic debugging mistakes among programmers. The advantages of flowcharts diminished as one moved from tracing control flow to comprehending relationships among separate procedures.

In their research on specification formats, Brooke and Duncan (1980a & b) observed that a common problem in fault diagnosis was conducting a test whose results had already been logically determined by the outcomes of previous tests. For instance, one path in a control flow diagram of a program had already been eliminated as the location of a procedural fault, but the programmer continues to exercise it on subsequent tests. Brooke and Duncan found that flowcharts helped avoid retesting paths which had already been eliminated. However, flowcharts did not eliminate certain other characteristic mistakes in fault detection, such as not distinguishing between calling and called procedures or attempting to localize a fault without having logically eliminated other parts of a program.

Rather than continue to study control flow, Shneiderman (1981) investigated the effectiveness of documenting the data structure. He found that data structure documentation contributed significantly to comprehension even when the input specification and PDL were also provided. In fact, data structure information contributed more to performance than control structure information, regardless of whether it was presented in a textual or graphic format. Table 4 presents the number of right answers to the 14 comprehension questions Shneiderman used as his criterion.

TABLE 4

Number of Comprehension Questions Answered Correctly

Document content	Textual	Graphic
Control flow	4.5	3.9
Data structure	7.8	8.4

Fitter and Green (1979) argued that the primary problems in specification formats are the tractability and visibility of structure. Useful notations contained not only symbolic information, but also perceptual cues. For instance, the following list describes the perceptual cues used with certain types of diagrams:

<u>Type</u>	<u>Cue</u>
Maps	- spatial location
Histograms	- size variation
Flowcharts	- connectedness
Venn diagrams	- insidedness
Traffic lights	- color

Fitter and Green listed five characteristics of a good notational scheme. These characteristics are:

1) Relevance - the notation is valuable only if it highlights information or relationships useful to the reader,
2) Restriction - the syntax of a notation should prohibit

the construction of unallowable expressions,

3) Redundant recoding - both the perceptual and the symbolic aspects should present and highlight the same information,
4) Revelation - the notation should perceptually mimic the solution stucture or the manipulation performed, and
5) Revisability - the notation should be easily revised when changes are made to the solution.

Two important themes have emerged from the research on specification formats. First, although flowcharts have been shown to be effective in aiding a decision making task, they have not been shown to be as useful as other forms of specification formats (such as constrained languages) for programming tasks. The results of research on software specifications generally confirm Mayer's contention that diagrammatic notations are not as effective as well structured verbal material. Further, a branching or hierarchical arrangement appears to contribute to comprehension only when control flow information is integral to the task (Fitter & Green, 1979). Yet, the frequency of these situations is not so ubiquitous as the flood of control flow documentation would suggest.

Second, as will be further elaborated in the language section, data structure seems to be more important than control flow in imparting information about a program. The reader must be cautioned, however, that control flow information may become increasingly important as real-time applications become a larger portion of the programs that one is reading or writing. Most of the research has been performed on small batch-like systems, rather than on the large, interrupt driven, embedded systems programming in which control flow is much more complex.

Programming languages. One way of classifying programming language is based on the extent to which they force one to write in machine level procedures versus natural language. This continuum runs all the way from machine languages and assemblers through high level programming languages through qeury languages to natural language. As one progresses up to this continuum the languages hide more and more of the details of integrating the software with the hardware. Languages at the upper end of this scale make computers accessible to more people because they are not forced to understand the intricacies of the hardware in order to interact with the machine. However, these higher level languages usually make working at the machine level, as in real-time microprocessor-based porgramming, extremely difficult or impossible.

The Whorfian hypothesis suggests that our ability to think is limited by the language we use to represent our thoughts. Recent research suggests that it may be more accurate to say that the way we think constrains the way we use language. In either case, there is a strong interaction between language and thought. On the one hand, the structures a language presents for manipulating words and the vocabulary available for representing ideas constrain the thoughts that can be easily and accurately represented. At the same time, the structures and patterns that characterize an individual's thought process affect how he is able to use the facilities provided by a language.

An early program of research on languages was initiated by Lance Miller and his associates at IBM's Watson Research Center. Miller studied the use of natural language commands by people who were not familiar with a computer language. Miller (1974) found that 'or' problems were more difficult to handle than 'and' problems, and that negation increased the difficulty of a problem. In a second study Miller (1981) investigated how non-programmers expressed procedural specifications in English. He observed that people used a characteristic personal approach to solving different problems, even when the structure of the problem was inappropriate for the approach. People also had difficulty being explicit about procedures and assumed that variable references were clear from the context of their paragraph.

One of Miller's most important observations in this study was that people used a limited vocabulary in developing their specifications. Only 610 unique words were used in the 84 protocols he collected. The size of this vocabulary could be reduced even further when redundancies and synonyms were removed or replaced. He believed that a vocabulary of 100 words would have been sufficient to express the specifications developed in his study. This finding was similar to the determination by Kelly and Chapanis (1977) that a vocabulary of 300 words was sufficient for a computer-aided problem solving task.

Miller (1981) observed that people spent much more time describing data manipulations than control flow. This is an important point since programming languages provide for the development of massive control structures with embedded data manipulations. Yet, the natural human tendency seems to start with data manipulations and add control flow as an afterthought, a qualification to the action. Miller concluded that natural language was not adequate for procedural specifications, but that a limited and structured subset of natural language might be more effective.

Interest in the design of specific language structures began when Dijkstra assailed the GO TO statement in 1968. He argued that having the control paths created by the structure of the program's logic wander throughout the program, as it often did with the GO TO conditional structure, made fprograms difficult to develop correctly and even more difficult to understand. This argument is psycholinguistic in that it is predicated on the interaction between human problem solving and language structure. Over the next few years the structured programming movement emerged calling for greater discipline in developing program logic by limiting the nature of the conditional structures allowed in the program.

Early studies on structured control constructs were conducted ducted by Weissman (1974) and Lucas and Kaplan (1974). These experiments were some of the first behavioral studies on programming languages. The first program of research on language structures was initiated by Max Sime, Thomas Green, and their associates at the University of Sheffield (Sime, Green, & Guest, 1973; Sime, Green, & Arblaster, 1977; Green, 1977; Green, 1980; Green, Sime, & Fitter, 1980). Their research represents the entry of cognitive ergonomics into programming. Through research publications that have spanned a decade, the Sheffield group has demonstrated:

- o the superiority of IF THEN ELSE (a structured conditional) over the GO TO conditional,
- o possible advantages of using scope markers to delineate the boundaries of the code governed by a conditional espression,
- o how the benefits of a programming technique may vary with the nature of the programming task, and

o a standard (perhaps automated) procedure for generating the syntax of a conditional statement can improve coding speed and accuracy.

Subsequent research by Sheppard, Curtis, Milliman, and Love (1979) at GE suggested that it was the discipline of a top down flow of control that was important, rather than the specific conditionals employed. They found that Dijkstra's rigid prescriptions for structured code could be violated in ways that made the control flow more natural for the language being used (i.e., Fortran), without damaging the comprehensibility of the program. The empirical evidence favoring structured control flow has been consistent, although discussion still continues on the most appropriate forms for control constructs. In fact, Gannon (1976) found that while changes in language structures could eliminate specific problems related to the particular structures, an overall decrease in error occurance may not necessarily result.

Gannon and Dunsmore (Gannon, 1977; Dunsmore & Gannon, 1979) have gone further than control structures and investigated how data affects programming. In studying a statically typed versus a typeless language, Gannon (1977) found little evidence that the compile-time checking of data types in the statically typed language aided the performance of experienced programmers. Rather, the value of the statically typed language stemmed from the increased power it received from supporting a broader range of data types. These additional data types freed a programmer from worrying about machine level representations of data. This finding resembled Miller's observations that people prefer to think about manipulating data structures en masse.

In a further investigation of data referencing, Dunsmore and Gannon (1979) found that programs in which the programmer had kept only a moderate number of variables 'live' at any given point in the program were easier to produce. A variable was 'live' from its first to its last reference in a procedure. A moderate level of variable referencing was found to be between 0.57 and 2.06 live variables per statement.

Two primary themes have emerged in research on language structures. First, structuring the control flow assists programmers in understanding a program. Rather than geographically dispersing the statements governed by a control construct, structured control flow organizes these control episodes into groups. This organization allows these segments of code to be fused more easily into a recognizable chunk. Atwood and Ramsey (1978) would describe this as the development of a macro-proposition from several elementary micro-propositions.

Structured control flow also allows programmers to direct more of their cognitive resources to the semantic content of the program. They are able to do this because structuring allows them to develop expectations about the control flow, rather than having to actively track its direction. Cognitive resources are freed when expectations about flow are cued by the language structure, rather than existing as a phenomena separate from the design of the language.

The second theme emerging from this research is the importance of the data structure. Gannon found that the advantage of strongly typed languages was in the enhanced data structures they supported. Miller argued that people tend to think in terms of data manipulations rather than control structures. The area of data structures has only been lightly considered in behavioral research. In one of the few such studies, Durding, Becker, and Gould (1977) demonstrated that people are quite capable of organizing data into structures which maintain the relations inherent among the elements. Additional research on data structure and control flow may provide a better integration of programming tools and procedures with the structure of human cognition.

There are a number of important issues which have not been addressed in a systematic program of research on language design and use. Some of these are:

- o the size and versatility of a language versus its learnability and ease of use,
- o the tradeoff to be made in programming with data structures versus control structures,
- o the use of procedural versus non-procedural languages,
- o the effect of the structure of the first language learned on the learning and use of other types of languages (see Du Boulay & O'Shea, 1981; Wexelblat, 1981; Coombs, Gibson, & Alty, 1982), and
- o the design of requirements and specification languages.

Conclusions. The human factors and cognitive ergonomics paradigms have been helpful in determining the characteristics of programming languages and specifications which impact performance. However, these paradigms were not designed to study how knowledge structures grow and are organized. The cognitive ergonomics paradigm uses cognitive explanations, but takes a static view of mental organization. As such Brooks (1980), Sheil (1981), and Moher and Schneider (1981) have criticised research performed under this paradigm because of the enormous size of the individual differences variation observed in the experiments. For instance, Sheppard, Kruesi, and Curtis (1981) determined that over half of the variance in comprehension performance in their experiment on documentation formats was related to individual differences among participants. In order to better describe programming performance a paradigm must be employed which lets us account for these individual differences.

COGNITIVE SCIENCE

The paradigm of cognitive science seeks to understand how knowledge is developed, represented, and structured in memory. It provides a dynamic view of knowledge acquisition and use. The interaction of cognitive science and computer science has led to the emergence of artifical intelligence, the attempt to make computers process information in ways similar to those used by humans. It is the role of cognitive science to delineate human thought processes.

There are several different levels at which researchers have modelled cognitive processes in programming. The differences in the models presented here are primarily in the levels of explanation. Cognitive theories of programming have not been elaborated to the extent that they present alternative explanations of programmer performance. In fact, on the surface many of the theories are interesting applications of psychological principles to programming, but they have not been sufficiently elaborated for consistent practical application at a technical level. Nevertheless, the models presented here are promising approaches to understanding how programmers develop programs.

Most cognitive models of programming begin with the distinction between short and long term memory. Short term memory is a limited capacity workspace which holds and processes those items of information currently under our attention. The capacity of short term memory was originally characterized by Miller (1956) as holding 7 $\pm$ 2 items. An item is a single piece of information, although there is no requirement that it be an elementary piece resulting from the decomposition of a larger body of information.

Currently many cognitive theorists portray short term memory as allocating the scarce resources of the cognitive processor, rather than as possessing a limited number of mental slots for information. Nevertheless, this limited capacity information buffer provides one of the greatest limitations to our ability to develop large scale computer systems. That is, we simply cannot think of enough things simultaneously to keep track of the interwoven pieces of a large system.

A process called 'chunking' expands the capacity of our short term mental workspace. In chunking, several items with similar or related attributes are bound together conceptually to form a unique item. For instance, through experience and training programmers are able to build increasingly larger chunks based on solution patterns which emerge frequently in solving problems. The lines of code in the program listing:

```
      SUM = 0
      DO 10 I = 1,N
      SUM = SUM + X(I)
   10 CONTINUE
```

would be fused by an experienced programmer into the chunk "calculate the sum of array X" The programmer can now think about working with an array sum, a single entity, rather than the six unique operators and seven unique operands in the four program statements above. When it is necessary to deal with the procedural implementation, the programmer can call these four statements from long term memory as underlying the chunk "array sum".

Much of a programmer's maturation involves observing more patterns and building larger chunks. The scope of the concepts that programmers have been able to build into chunks provides one indication of their programming ability. The particular elements chunked together have important implications for educating programmers. Educational materials and exercises should be presented in a way which maximize the likelihood of building useful chunks.

Long term memory is usually treated as having limitless capacity for storing information. An important concern with long term memory is how the information stored there is interrelated and indexed such that:

1) items in short term memory can quickly cue the recall of appropriate chunks of information from long term memory,
2) items in short term memory can be linked into and transferred quickly to long term memory for retention, and
3) information retrieved from long term memory can cue the retrieval of additional chunks of information when appropriate.

The effects of both experience and education are on the knowledge base they construct in long term memory. The construction of this base is not merely one of accumulating facts, but of organizing them into a rich network of semantic material.

Schneiderman and Mayer (1979) have characterized the structure of knowledge in long term memory into a syntactic/semantic model. In their model, syntactic and semantic knowledge are organized separately in memory. Semantic knowledge concerns general programming concepts of relationships in the applications domain which are independent of the programming language in which they will be executed. Syntactic knowledge involves the procedural idiosyncracies of a given programming language.

An important implication of the Shneiderman and Mayer model is that the development of programming skill requires the integration of knowledge from several different knowledge domains (Brooks 1983). For instance, the programming of an onboard aircraft guidance system may require knowledge of:

1) aeronautical engineering
2) radar and sensors technology
3) mathematical algorithms
4) the design of the onboard processor
5) the development machine and tools
6) a high level programming language
7) an assembly language

Each of these is separate field of knowledge, some of which require years of training and experience to master. Thus, programming skill is specific to the application being considered. One can be a talented avionics programmer, and still be a novice at programming simultaneous multi-user business databases.

Several efforts have been made to model the structure of programming knowledge at a level deeper than that of Shneiderman and Mayer. Brooks (1977) used Newell and Simon's (1972) production system approach to model the rules a programmer would use in writing the code for a program. These rules are of the type, "If the following conditions are statisfied, then produce the following action". Based on analysis of a verbal protocol, Brooks identified 73 rules which were needed to model the coding process of a single, and relatively simple, problem solution. Brooks estimated that the number of porduction rules needed to model the performance of an expert programmer was in the tens to hundreds of thousands.

Atwood, Turner, Ramsey, and Hooper (1978) modelled a programmer's understanding of a program using Kintsch's (1974) model of text comprehension. Their approach treats a program as a text base composed of propositions.

Comprehension occurs as elementary or micro-propositions fused into macro-propositions which summarize their meaning or content. This process is similar to chunking. The result of this process is a hierarchy of macro-propositions built from the micro-propositions at the bottom of the tree. A micro-proposition is a simple statement composed of a relational operator and one or more arguments (operands).

Atwood et al. (1979) demonstrated that a program design could be broken into a hierarchical structure of propositions. They observed that after studying the design, more experienced programmers were able to recall propositions at a greater depth in the hierarchy than novices. The more experienced programmers had a more elaborate structure in long term memory for use in encoding such designs. Thus, they were able to retain propositions at greater depth because:

1) the higher level macro-propositions in the design did not represent new information, and thus could be referenced by existing knowledge structures, and
2) the propositions representing new information could be linked into the existing knowledge structures of experienced programmers and shifted into long term memory.

This propositional hierarchy is one representation of how knowledge is structured in long term memory. To understand how these knowledge structures develop, cognitive scientists have studied differences between expert and novice programmers.

Expert-novice differences. The study of expert-novice differences in programming knowledge base is developed. Both Adelson (1981) and Shertz and Weiser (1981) demonstrated that novices comprehend a program based on its surface structure that is, the particular applications area of the program such as banking or avionics. Experts, however, analyze a program based its deep structure, the solution or algorithmic structure of the program. Similarly, McKeithan, Reitman, Rueter, and Hirtle (1981) observed that experts are able to remember language commands based on their position in the structure of the language. Novices, not having an adequate mental representation of the language structure, often use mnemonic tricks to remember command names.

Results of the expert-novice differences research in programming agree with the results of similar research on other subject areas (e.g., thermodynamics, physics, and chess) conducted by Herbert Simon and his associates at Carnegie-Mellon. They have determined that experts are not necessarily better at operational thinking than novices. Rather, experts are better at encoding new information than novices. The broader knowledge base of experts guides them to quickly cue in on the most important aspects of new information, analyze them, and relate them to appropriate schema in long term memory.

Developing technical skill is not merely a matter of learning a long list of facts. Rather, developing technical skill is an effort to learn the underlying structure of the knowledge base. McKeithan et al. found that the knowledge structures developed by experts were much more similar to each other than were those of intermediates or novices. Thus, programmers tend to gravitate toward a similar understanding of the language structure with experience. The development of this structure enhances the ability of experienced programmers to assimilate new information.

In a psychological study of the program design process, Jefferies, Turner, Polson, and Atwood (1981) noted that programmers with greater experience decomposed a problem more richly into minimally interacting parts. The design knowledge of novices did not appear sufficient to provide for a full decomposition. In particular, more experienced programmers spend greater time evaluating the problem structure prior to beginning the design process. Observations similar to these were also made by Nichols (1981).

Jeffries et al. hypothesized that there is the equivalent of a mental design executive. This executive attempt to recuraltively decompose the problem statement and relate the components emerging from the decomposition to patterns in the programming knowledge base in long term memory. The shallowness of the novices' decomposition reflects the shallowness of the knowledge base against which they attempt to compare pieces of the problem statement. The richer knowledge base of experts allows them a fuller decomposition of the problem statement. The criterion used by experts for terminating the decomposition process for a particular aspect of the problem is when it has been decomposed to a level for which the programmer can retrieve a solution pattern.

At least part of this process of developing an organized knowledge structure is the abstraction of rules from the myriad patterns and facts that programmers know or can recognize. Whereas an expert programmer may be able to recognize 50,000 patterns, the number of rules which govern the structure of these patterns is substantially less, perhaps 1000 to 3000. (Brooks estimated many more rules, but he may have been refering to the recognizable paterns from which these rules are drawn). Rule-based knowledge in programming has been studied most frequently in the detection of procedural faults.

The detection of procedural faults. One of the most critical and time consuming tasks in programming is the detection and correction of faults (bugs). While debugging has been used as an experimental task for studies on specifications or language features, relatively little behavioral research has been directed toward understanding the debugging process.

John Seely Brown and his associates (Brown & Burton, 1978; Brown & Van Lehn, 1980) have laid some theoretical groundwork for modeling the generation of bugs in procedural tasks. They treat bugs not as random occurences, but as systematic and predictable outcomes of the imcomplete or incorrect application of the rules underlying a procedural skill. Their explanation entails four component:

1) the first component is that an individual acquire a formal representation of a procedural skill. Such a representation would be a set of rules which guide the development of procedures for solving a problem.
2) the second component of their model is a set of principles for determining which rules can be deleted from the formal representation to simulate the incomplete or incorrect learning of rules or the forgetting of rules.
3) the third component is a set of repair heuristics used by the individual to patch over gaps in the formal representation. The heuristics generate bugs by creating inappropriate procedures for completing procedural solutions.
4) the final component is a set of mechanisms for screening out some of the heuristics which generate blatantly incorrect procedures.

This type of model is currently being applied to programming by Elliot Soloway and his associates at Yale (Soloway, Bonar, & Erlich, in press; Soloway, Erlich, & Bonar, 1982) in studying how novices learn to program. Kahney and Eisenstadt (1982) are using a similar model to analyze the difficulty novices have in solving recursive problems.

Youngs (1974) reported some descriptive data on the types of errors typically made by programmers. His data were similar to several databases collected on large system development projects by the Information Sciences Program at Rome Air Development Center. The most frequent category of faults was logic errors, especially for experienced programmers. Syntactic errors occurred relatively infrequently. This observation reinforces the importance of providing useful control constructs in programming languages. The results also indicate that novices and professionals make different kinds of errors.

During the early 1970s John Gould and his associates at IBM's Watson Research Center made several studies of program debugging. In the first study, Gould and Drongowski (1974) found that providing debugging aids to programmers did not necessarily make fault detection faster. Programmers adopted debugging strategies based on the types of information they were presented about the program and the problem. This strategy included attempts to localize the section of code likely to contain the error, and employed a hierarchical search in which the most complex sections were left for last. In a further study, Gould (1975) identified that this hierarchical search was for:

1) syntactic faults,
2) grammatical faults not caught by the compiler, and
3) substantive faults.

Sheppard, Curtis, Milliman, and Love (1979) observed several different search strategies among programmers. Some programmers felt they had to understand the entire program before they could begin searching for the fault. The more effective strategy, however, was to identify that portion of the output which was in error and quickly trace back from the print statement for that variable to locate the area in which the fault was likely to have occurred. This technique is similar to the program slicing strategy studied by Weiser (1982).

One of the most extensive programs of research on fault diagnosis has been conducted by William and Sandra Rouse now at Georgia Tech. They have made an important distinction between perceptual complexity and problem solving complexity (Rouse & Rouse, 1979). They suggest that the latter is more affected by individual differences, especially those related to understanding a problem. Brooke and Duncan (1981) demonstrated that factors which primarily impact perceptual complexity, such as the display format, can affect problem solving effectiveness. Subsequently, Rouse, Rouse, and Pelligrino (1980) have developed a rule-based model of fault diagnosis that agrees at a global level with the actual performance of people on a similar task.

<u>Learning to program</u>. There are two primary ways in which the rules which govern programming can be learned. They can be abstracted from the developing knowledge base as the programmer can increase in experience. This, of course, is a lengthy process. On the other hand, rules can be taught in organized training programs. Training not only develops the knowledge base more quickly than experiential learning, but it is also likely to be more thorough and accurate. However, experiential learning is

often the primary method for acquiring the contextual information used in interpreting the appropriateness of various rules for programming.

Mayer (1976, 1981) described several training techniques grounded in psychological theory and research which can be used successfully in training novice programmers. Mayer (1976) stressed the importance of 'advanced organizers' to help structure new material as it is learned. These advanced organizers help build a preliminary model or outline of the new information so that later input can be more easily assimilated into an appropriate knowledge structure. Mayer emphasized that one of the more effective advanced organizers is a concrete model of the machine which is manipulated by instructions coded in a computer language. Mayer argued that students benefit from being forced to elaborate these models in their own words.

DuBoulay, O'Shea, and Monk (1981) extended Mayer's concept of a concrete model of the machine. They discussed a 'notational machine' which is a simplified machine whose facilities are only those which are implemented by the available commands in the programming language. They also stressed the importance of a student's gaining visibility into the processes occurring inside the abstract notional machine. They have built several training systems based on this concept.

Coombs, Gibson, and Alty (1982) have identified two learning styles which characterize the different ways novices learn to program: comprehension learning and operational learning. Comprehension learners acquire an overall layout of the information under study, but may not understand the rules which allow them to operate with and on the information. Operational learners grasp the rules for operating on information, but they do not acquire a complete picture of the knowledge domain. Comprehension learners are primarily interested in understanding, while operational learners are primarily interested in doing something. These characterizations represent idealized students, whereas most people will fall on a continuum in between, displaying varying degrees of both styles.

Coombs et al. concluded from their data that operational learners were better able to learn a programming language. Their learning strategy was characterized by attention to the details of the language structures, the abstraction of critical language features, and an orientation towards representing important structural relations in rules. The major learning activity for operational learners was in practice sessions, whereas for comprehension learners this occurred in lectures.

Lemos (1979) investigated the benefits of structured walk-throughs as a classroom learning exercise. This approach seemed to have advantages in allowing novices to compare alternative approaches to the problem and gain immediate feedback on their strategy. Shneiderman (1980) has used a similar feedback mechanism with experienced programmers and found benefits in terms of learning new approaches to a problem.

Conclusions. I have argued elsewhere (Curtis, 1981a, b) that individual differences accounted for the largest source of variation in project performance. However, the individual differences paradigm only allows us to characterize and predict these differences, but not explain how they develop and change over time. Cognitive science has provided a representation of knowledge organization and development which presents and explanation of the basis for these differences. Therefore, cognitive science is a paradigm which offers the best opportunity to study and gain control over the largest source of influence of project performance.

Cognitive science presents an opportunity for psychologists to get on the leading edge of programming technology, rather than sweeping up behind the directions already set by computer scientists. As a driving force in artificial intelligence programming, cognitive science provides a vehicle for analyzing the most appropriate ways to automate more of the programming process in ways that are helpful to those who must develop large systems.

The following points describe some of the important points emerging from cognitive science research on software engineering:

- The development of expertise involves building a massive knowledge base of recognizable patterns (perhaps 50,000) and abstracting a set of rules (perhaps 1000 to 3000) which govern their behavior.
- Expertise is specific to different knowledge domains. A programmer can be expert in one domain and a novice in another.

- o Rule-based models of programming need to be expanded far beyond their current use, primarily in fault diagnosis. Rule-based models hold substantial promise for automating programming tasks.
- o Rather than teaching isolated commands, educators should liberally model abstract machines for teaching the structure of a programming language.
- o Learning styles will play an important role in how quickly, accurately, and thoroughly an individual learns to program.
- o Cognitive science is the easiest way for a psychologist to communicate with a computer scientist.

REFERENCES

Adelson, B. Problem solving and the development of abstract categories in programming languages. Memory and Cognition, 1981, 9(4), 422-433.

Arblaster, A. Human factors in the design and use of computer languages. International Journal of Man-Machine Studies, 1982, 17, 211-224.

Atwood, M.E. & Ramsey, H.R. Cognitive structures in the comprehension and memory of computer programs: An investigation of computer program debugging (Tech. Rep. TR-78-A21). Alexandria, VA: Army Research Institute, 1978.

Atwood, M.E., Turner, A.A., Ramsey, H.R., & Hooper, J.N. An exploratory study of the cognitive structures underlying the comprehension of software design problems (Tech. Rep. 392). Alexandria, VA: Army Research Institute, 1979.

Blaiwes, A.S. Formats for representing procedural instructions. Journal of Applied Psychology, 1974, 59, 683-686.

Boysen, J.P. & Keller, R.F. Measuring computer program comprehension. Proceedings of the National Computer Conference. New York: ACM, 1980, 92-100.

Brooke, J.B. & Duncan, K.D. An experimental study of flowcharts as an aid to identification of procedural faults. Ergonomics, 1980, 23(4), 387-399.a

Brooke, J.B. & Duncan, K.D. Experimental studies of flowchart use at different stages of program debugging. Ergonomics, 1980, 23(11), 1057-1091. b

Brooks, R. Towards a theory of cognitive processes in computer programming. International Journal of Man-Machine Studies, 1977, 9, 737-751.

Brooks, R. Studying programmer behavior experimentally: The problems of proper methodology. Communications of ACM, 1980, 23(4), 207-213.

Brooks, R. Towards a theoretical model of the comprehension of computer programs. International Journal of Man-Machine Studies, 1983.

Brown, J.S. & Burton, R.R. Diagnostic models for procedural bugs in basic mathematics skills. Cognitive Science, 1978, 2, 155-192.

Brown, J.S. & VanLehn, K. Repair theory: A generation theory of bugs in procedural skills. Cognitive Science, 1980, 4, 379-426.

Carroll, J.M., Thomas, J.C., & Malhotra, A. Clinical-experimental analysis of design problem solving. Design Studies, 1979, 1(2), 84-92.

Carroll, J.M., Thomas, J.C., & Malhotra, A. Presentation and representation in design problem solving. British Journal of Psychology, 1980, 71, 143-153.

Carroll, J.M., Thomas, J.C., Miller, L.A., & Friedman, H.P. Aspects of solution structure in design problem solving. American Journal of Psychology, 1980, 93(2), 269-284.

Coombs, M.J., Gibson, R., & Alty, J.L. Learning a first computer language: strategies for making sense. International Journal of Man-Machine Studies, 1982,16, 449-486.

Curtis, B. Measurement and experimentation in software engineering. Proceedings of the IEEE, 1980, 68(9), 1144-1157.

Curtis, B. Human Factors in Software Development. Silver Spring MD: IEEE, 1981, a

Curtis, B. Substantiating programmer variability. Proceedings of the IEEE, 1981, 69(7), 846.b

Dijkstra, E. GO TO considered harmful. Communications of the ACM, 1968, 11(3) 147-148.

Du Boulay, B. & O'Shea, T. Teaching novices programming. In M.J. Coombs & J.L. Alty (eds.), Computer Skills and the User Interface. London: Academic, 1981, 147-200.

Du Boulay, B., O'Shea, T., & Monk, J. The black box inside the glass box: presenting computer concepts to novices. International Journal of Man-Machine Studies, 1981, 14, 237.249.

Dunsmore, H.E. & Gannon, J.D. Data referencing: An empirical investigation. Computer, 1979, 12(2), 50-59.

Durding, B.M., Becker, C.A., & Gould, J.D. Data organization. Human Factors, 1977, 19(1), 1-14.

Fitter, M. & Green, T.R.G. When do diagrams make good computer languages? International Journal of Man-Machine Studies, 1979, 11, 235-261.

Gannon, J.D. An experiment for the evaluation of language features. International Journal of Man-Machine Studies, 1976, 8, 61-73.

Gannon, J.D. An experimental evaluation of data type conventions, Communications of the ACM, 1977, 20(8), 584-595.

Gould, J.D. Some psychological evidence on how people debug computer programs. International Journal of Man-Machine Studies, 1975, 7, 151-182.

Gould, J.D. & Drongowski, P. An exploratory study of computer program debugging. Human Factors, 1974, 16(3), 258-277.

Green, T.R.G. Conditional program statements and their comprehensibility to professional programmers. Journal of Occupational Psychology, 1977, 50, 93-109.

Green, T.R.G. Programming as a cognitive activity. In H.T. Smith & T.R.G. Green (Eds.), Human Interaction with Computers. London: Academic, 1980.

Green, T.R.G, Sime, M.E., & Fritter, M.J. The problem the programmaer faces. Ergonomics, 1980, 23(9), 893-907.

Hoc, J.M. Role of representation in learning a computer language. International Journal of Man-Machine Studies, 1977, 9, 87-105.

Hoc, J.M. Planning and direction of problem solving in structured programming; And empirical comparison between two methods. International Journal of Man-Machine Studies, 1981, 15, 363-383.

Jefferies, R., Turner, A.A., Polson, P.G., & Atwood, M.E. The processes involved in designing software. In J.R. Anderson (Ed.), Congitive Skills and Their Acquistion. Hillsdale, N.J.: Erlbaum, 1981, 255-283.

Kahney, H. & Eisenstedt, M. Programmers' mental models of their programming tasks: The interaction of real world knowledge and programming knowledge. Proceedings of the Fourth Annual Conference of the Cognitive Science Society.

Kammann, R. The comprehension of printed instructions and the flowchart alternative. Human Factors, 1975, 17, 183-191.

Kelly, M.J. & Chapanis, A. Limited vocabulary natural language dialogue. International Journal of Man-Machine Studies, 1977, 9, 479-501.

Kintsch, W. The Representation of Meaning in Memory. Hillsdale, NJ: Erlbaum, 1974.

Lemos, R.S. An implementation of structured walkthroughs in teaching Cobol programming. Communications of the ACM, 1979, 22(6), 335-340.

Lucas, H.C. & Kaplan, R.B. A structured programming experiment. The Computer Journal, 1974, 19(2), 136-138.

Mayer, R.E. Comprehension as affected by the structure of the problem representation. Memory & Cognition, 1976, 4(3), 249-255. a

Mayer, R.E. Some conditions for meaningful learning in computer programming: Advance organizers and subject control of frame order. Journal of Educational Psychology, 1976, 68, 143-150.b

Mayer, R.E. The psychology of how novices learn computer programming. ACM Computing Surveys, 1981, 12(1), 121-141.

McKeithen, K.B., Reitman, J.S., Rueter, H.H., & Hirtle, S.C. Knowledge organization and skill differences in computer programmers. cognitive Psychology, 1981, 13, 307-325.

Miller, G. A. The magical number seven plus or minus two: Some limits on our capacity to process information. Psychology Review, 1956, 63, 81-97.

Miller, L. A. Programming by non-programmers. International Journal of Man-Machine Studies, 1974, 6, 237-260.

Miller, L. A. Natural language programming: Styles, strategies, and contrasts. IBM Systems Journal, 1981, 20(2), 184-215.

Moher, T. & Schneider, G.M. Methods for improving controlled experimentation in software engineering. Proceedings of the Fifth International Conference on Software Engineering. Silver Spring, MD: IEEE Computer Society, 1981, 224-233.

Myers, G.J. A controlled experiment in program testing and code walkthroughs/inspections. Communications of the ACM, 1978, 21(9), 760-768.

Newell, A. & Simon, H.A. Human Problem Solving. Englewood Cliffs, NJ: Prentice-Hall, 1972.

Nichols, J.A. Problem solving strategies and organization of information in computer programming. Dissertation Abstracts International, 1981.

Ramsey, H.R., Atwood, M.E., & Van Doren, J.R. Flowcharts vs. program design languages: An experimental comparison. Communications of the ACM, 1983, 26(7).

Rouse, W.B. & rouse, S.H. Measures of complexity of fault diagnosis tasks. IEEE Transactions on Systems, Man, and Cybernetics, 1989, 9(11), 720-727.

Rouse, W.B., Rouse, S.H., & Pelligrino, S.J. A rule-based model of human problem solving performance in fault diagnosis tasks. IEEE Transactions on Systems, Man, and Cybernetics, 1980, 10(7), 366-376.

Sheil, B.A. The psychological study of programming. ACM Computing Surveys, 1981, 13(1), 101-120.

Sheppard, S.B., Curtis, B., Milliman, P., & Love, T. Modern coding practices and programmer performance. Computer, 1979, 12(12), 41-49.

Sheppard, S.B. & Kruesi, E. The effects of the symbology and spatial arrangement of software specifications in a coding task. Trends and Applications 1981: Advances in Software Technology. Silver Spring, MD: IEEE Computer Society, 1981, 7-13.

Sheppard, S.B., Kruesi, E., & Curtis, B. The effects of symbology and spatial arrangement on the comprehension of software specifications. Proceedings of the Fifth International Conference on Software Engineering. Silver Spring, MD. IEEE Computer Society, 1981, 207-214.

Shertz, J. & Weiser, M. A Study of programming problem representation in novice programmers. Proceedings of the Nineteenth Conference on Computer Personnel Research. New York: ACM, 1981, 302-322.

Shneiderman, B. Software Psychology: Human Factors in Computer and Information Systems. Cambridge, Ma: Winthrop, 1980.

Shneiderman, B. Control flow and data structure documentation: Two experiments. Communications of the ACM, 1982, 25(1), 55-63.

Shneiderman, B. & Mayer, R.E. Syntactic/semantic interactions in programmer behavior: A model and experimental results. International Journal of Computer and Information Sciences, 1979, 8, 219-238.

Shneiderman, B., Mayer, R., McKay, D. & Heller, P. Experimental investigations of the utility of detailed flowcharts in programming. Communications of the ACM, 1977, 20(6), 373-381.

Sime, M.E., Arblaster, A.T., & Green, T.R.G. Structuring the programmer's task. Journal of Occupational Psychology, 1977, 50, 205-216.

Sime, M.E., Green, T.R.G., & Guest, D.G. Psychological evaluation of two conditional constructions used in computer languages. International Journal of Man-Machine Studies, 1973, 5, 105-113.

Soloway, E., Bonar, J., & Ehrlich, K. Cognitive strategies and looping constructs: An empirical study. Communications of the ACM, in press.

Soloway, E., Ehrlich, K., & Bonar, J. Tapping into tacit programming knowledge. Proceedings of Human Factors in Computer Systems. New York: ACM, 1982, 52-27.

Weinberg, G.M. The Psychology of Computer Programming. New York: Van Nostrand Reinhold, 1971.

Weiser, M. Programmers use slices when debugging. Communications of the ACM, 1982, 25(7), 446-452.

Weissman, L. Psychological complexity of computer programs: An experimental methodology. Sigplan Notices, 1974, 9(6), 25-36.

Wexelblat, R.L. The consequences of one's first programming language. Software-Practice and Experience, 1981, 11, 733-740.

Wright, P. & Reid, F. Written information: Some alternatives to prose for expressing the outcome of complex contingencies. Journal of Applied Psychology, 1973, 57, 160-166.

Youngs, E.A. Human errors in programming. International Journal of Man-Machine Studies, 1974, 6, 361-376.

From Interactive to Intelligent Systems

Gerhard Fischer
Department of Computer Science
University of Colorado
Boulder, CO 80309 USA

Abstract

Feature-rich software systems of today are the result of the continuous increase in computational power and growing requirements for broad functionality; these systems have to be mastered by casual or untrained users. This leads to operability problems (systems are too complicated), ineffective use, erroneous behavior and frustration. Careful empirical studies indicate that even in current systems only *a small percentage* of the available functionality is actually used. The availability of more computational power in the future will be of little value in constructing more usable systems, unless we open up new access paths to enable the user to take advantage of this increased functionality.

We claim that knowledge-based systems with qualitatively new human-computer communication capabilities are one of the most promising ways to create *intelligent systems*. We propose to extend the comprehensibility of systems by dedicating a large fraction of the computational power of the machine to sophisticated user support systems.

1. Introduction

The overall goal of this paper is to illustrate how to move on from interactive to intelligent systems. Two research areas are crucial for this transition: *knowledge-based systems* and *human-computer communication*. General principles for the design of intelligent systems will be postulated and a variety of system components will be described which we have designed and implemented over the last few years. The role of ergonomics research in relationship to intelligent ssytems will be discussed. Despite the fact that progress has been made towards the goal of making intelligent systems more a reality, many challenges remain which will be briefly described in the last section.

NATO ASI Series, Vol. F22
Software System Design Methods. Edited by J.K. Skwirzynski

2. Why Do We Need Intelligent Systems?

The microelectronics revolution of the 1970s made computer systems cheaper and more compact, with a greatly increased range of capabilities. Computing moved directly into the workplace and the home to the fingertips of a large number of people. Much of this power is wasted, however, if users have difficulties in understanding and using the full potential of their new systems. Too much attention has been given in the past to technical aspects which have provided inadequate technical solutions to real world problems, have imposed unnecessary constraints on users and have been too rigid to respond to changing needs. More *intelligent* software is needed which has knowledge about the user, the tasks being carried out and the nature of the communication process.

The increased functionality of modern computer systems, driven by the many different tasks that a user wants to do, will lead to increased complexity. Empirical investigations show that on the average only a small fraction of the functionality of complex systems is used. Figure 2-1 summarizes empirical investigations and careful observations of persons using systems like UNIX, EMACS, SCRIBE, LISP etc. in our environment. It also describes different levels of system usage which typically can be found within many complex systems.

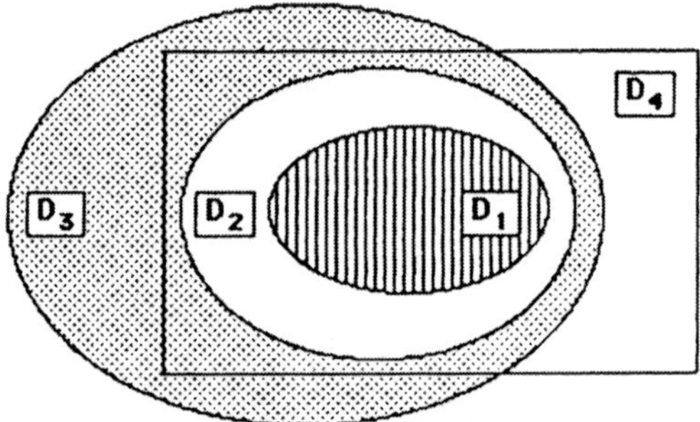

Figure 2-1: Different Levels of System Usage

The different domains correspond to the following:

D_1: The subset of concepts (and their associated commands) that the users know and use without any problems.

D_2: The subset of concepts which they use only occasionally. They do not know details about them and they are not too sure about their effects. Description of commands (e.g. in the form of property sheets), explanations, illustrations and safeguards (e.g. UNDOs) are important so that the user can gradually master this domain.

D_3: The mental model [Norman 82; Fischer 84] of the user, i.e. the set of concepts which she/he thinks exist in the system. A *passive help system* (see section 5.2.1) is necessary for the user to communicate her/his plans and intentions to the system.

D_4: Represents the actual system. Passive help systems are of little use for the subset of D_4 which is not contained in D_3, because the user does not know about the existence of these system features. *Active help systems* and *Critics* (see sections 5.2.2 and 5.3) which advise and guide a user similar to a knowledgeable colleague or assistant are required so that the user can incrementally extend her/his knowledge to cover D_4.

The only way to master complex systems is through incremental learning approaches. A partial knowledge of a system can lead to the following situation (see Figure 2-2): a user (based on her/his knowledge) makes a typing mistake which is interpreted (as an existing command) within the complete system and the user will be dumped in an area which is unfamiliar to her/him.

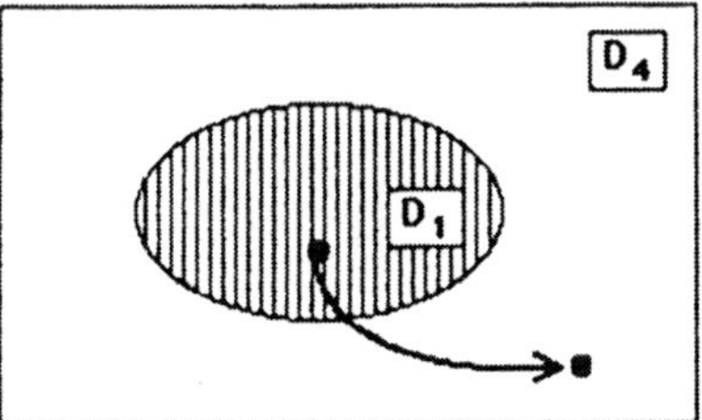

Figure 2-2: Protective Shields

Protective shields (based on the system's model of the user) are needed to avoid problems of this sort. These protective shields must not be so restrictive that they prohibit the exploration of additional system features by the user.

3. From Interactive to Intelligent Systems

Everyone today will agree that we do not want to operate computing systems in a batch mode any more. Interactive computing systems have made a major contribution to the widespread use of computers. Some of the most advanced interactive systems have been built as programming environments by Artificial Intelligence researchers [Barstow, Shrobe, Sandewall 84; Sheil 83] and around the SMALLTALK system [Goldberg 84].

3.1 The Architecture of Intelligent Systems

The next step will be to move on from interactive to intelligent systems. In intelligent systems a substantial part of the computational power will be used to document, explain and justify their expertise to others. They will provide insight, help and useful criticism so that a novice can slowly become an expert. They will augment human intelligence by providing visualization tools. Figure 3-1 describes our vision of the architecture of an intelligent system. It is important to note that the outer circle of system components in Figure 3-1 are not "add-ons" to existing systems, but should be an integral part of the system design right from the beginning.

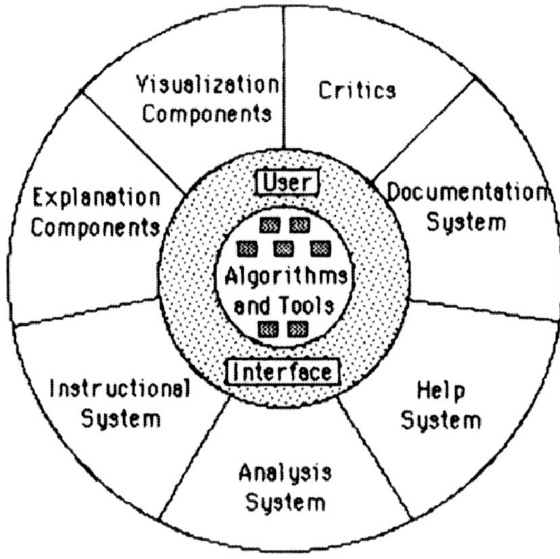

Figure 3-1: From Interactive to Intelligent Systems

Intelligent systems will contain many more tools than the functionally rich environments which are available to us today (e.g. the UNIX operating system, powerful AI programming environments). Empirical findings indicate that the following problems occur which prevent many people from successfully exploiting the potential of the systems available to us today:

- users do not know about the existence of tools,
- users do not know how to access tools,
- users do not know when to use these tools,
- users do not understand the results which tools produce for them,
- users cannot combine, adapt and modify a tool to their specific needs.

Unless we are able to solve these problems, users will "reinvent the wheel" constantly instead of taking advantage of already existing tools.

3.2 Human-Computer Communication (HCC)

Human communication and cooperation can serve as a model for how computing systems should be. What can humans do that most current computer systems cannot do? Human communication partners

- do not have the literalness of mind which implies that not all communication has to be explicit; they can supply and deduce additional information which was not explicitly mentioned and they can correct simple mistakes; empirical evidence shows that in any but the simplest human communication a substantial portion of the communicated message is not explicit;
- can apply their problem solving power to fill in details if we give statements of objectives in broad functional terms;
- can articulate their misunderstanding and the limitations of their knowledge;
- can provide explanations to others of how they reached a conclusion or why they behaved in a particular way;
- can solve problems by taking imaginative leaps, for example by conceiving of an analogous situation of similar characteristics with which they are more familiar.

Traditionally the relationship between the user and the computer was sufficiently remote that it was more like a literary correspondence than a conversational dialogue. Today the user is coupled directly with the computer which causes the following changes:

- interaction with computers is emerging as a human activity;
- the prior styles of interaction have been all extremely restricted (e.g. comparable to the driver of an automobile or the secretary using a typewriter); there was a limited range of tasks to be accomplished and a narrow range of means (e.g. like having a control stick in video games); the user was just an operator;
- the increased availability, the decreased cost and the greatly improved hardware allow that an increasing amount of computational resources can be spent on human-computer communication, rather than on purely computational tasks (see Figure 3-1);
- system designers tend to concentrate on the commands of the computer systems (just look at the documentation for almost any system, which is usually a catalogue of commands); yet it is how, when and why the commands are used that is most important to the user;
- there is a growing understanding that guidelines and classifications of the appropriate ergonomic dimensions for human-computer communication are less clear cut. Detailed prescriptions or check-lists cannot be provided to cover all aspects of human-computer communication because so much is dependent on human *cognitive* abilities - how people behave, think and perceive the world. Such subjective factors cannot be measured and predicted with the same precision that is possible with elements in a physical environment (see chapter 6).

Human-computer communication is more than drawing nice pictures on the screen. The viewers on the display screen are important, but they are of little use if there are no interesting knowledge structures behind them.

3.3 Knowledge-based Systems (KBS)

Knowledge-based systems are the most promising approach to qualitatively improve human-computer communication. Based on the above analysis of communication processes among humans the model in Figure 3-2 is suited to fulfill the stated requirements. It contains a knowledge base which can be accessed by both communication partners; this implies that the necessity to exchange all information explicitly between user and system does not exist any more.

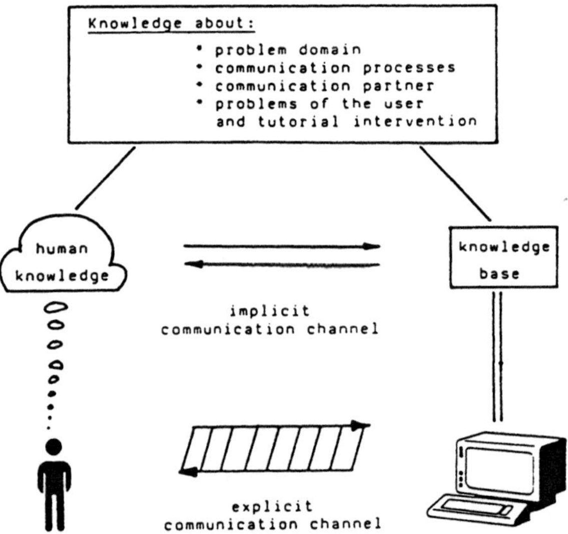

Figure 3-2: Architecture for Knowledge-Based Human-Computer Communication

This system architecture has the following advantages compared to current architectures:

1. the *explicit communication channel* is widened. The interfaces use windows with associated menus, pointing devices, color and iconic representations; the screen is used as a design space which can be manipulated directly.

2. information can be exchanged over the *implicit communication channel*. Both communication partners have knowledge which eliminates the necessity that all information has to be exchanged explicitly.

The four domains of knowledge shown in Figure 3-2 have the following relevance:

1. **Knowledge of the problem domain:** Intelligent behavior builds upon large amounts of

knowledge about specific domains. This knowledge imposes constraints on the number of possible actions and describes reasonable goals and operations. If, for example, in UNIX a user needs more disk space it is in general not adequate help to advise him to use the command **"rm *"** (the command will delete all files in the current directory; [Wilensky et al. 84]) although it would perfectly serve her/his explicitly stated goal. The user's goals and intentions can be inferred if we understand the correspondence between the system's primitive operations and the concepts of the task domain.

2. **Knowledge about communication processes:** The information structures which control the communication should be made explicit, so the user can manipulate them.

3. **Knowledge about the communication partner:** *The* user of a system does not exist; there are many different kinds of users, and the requirements of an individual user grow with experience. To pay attention to individual differences the following knowledge structures have to be represented:

   - The user's conceptual understanding of a system (e.g. in an editor, text may be represented as a sequence of characters separated by linefeeds which implies that a linefeed can be inserted and deleted like any other character).
   - The user's individual set of tasks for which she/he uses the system (a text editor may be used for such different tasks as writing books and preparing command scripts for an operating system).
   - The user's way of accomplishing domain specific tasks (e.g. does she/he take full advantage of the systems functionality?).
   - The pieces of advice given and whether the user remembered and accepted them.
   - The situations in which the user asked for help.

   A prerequisite for knowledge-based human-computer communication is to monitor the user's behavior and reason about her/his goals. Sources for this information are: the user's actions including illegal operations. This is based on the hypothesis that *a user does not make arbitrary errors; all operations are iterations towards a goal* [Norman 82].

4. **Knowledge about the most common problems which users have in using a system and about instructional strategies:** This kind of knowledge is required if someone wants to be a good coach or teacher and not only an expert; a user support system should know when to interrupt a user. It must incorporate instructional strategies which are based on pedagogical theories, exploiting the knowledge contained in the system's model of the user. Strategies embodied in our systems [Fischer 81] include:

   - *Take the initiative* when weaknesses of the user become obvious. Not every recognized suboptimal action should lead to an intervention.
   - *Be non-intrusive.* Only frequent suboptimal behavior without the user being aware of it should trigger an action of the system.
   - *Give additional information* which was not explicitly asked for but which is likely to be needed in the near future.
   - Assist the user in the *stepwise extension* of her/his view of the system. Be sure that basic concepts are well understood. Don't introduce too many new features at once.

The main issues in building knowledge-based systems (which are actively pursued in Artificial Intelligence research) are:

1. **knowledge acquisition:** how is knowledge acquired most efficiently from human experts

and from data gathered by instruments? Can the experts themselves directly manipulate the knowledge base or do they need a knowledge engineer?

2. **knowledge representation:** how can the needed knowledge for complex problem solving processes be represented to be effective for the inference engine and to be understandable for the human?

3. **knowledge utilization:** how can we retrieve the relevant knowledge needed in specific situations? Does the knowledge base help us in finding the relevant knowledge? Does it support browsing techniques to navigate through a knowledge space whose structure and content is unknown to the user in advance?

We will briefly describe our work on knowledge representation which has led to the development of *ObjTalk* [Laubsch, Rathke 83; Rathke, Lemke 85; Lemke 85], an object-oriented knowledge representation language and programming environment in which most of our software is implemented.

3.4 Object-Oriented Knowledge Representation

A major strength of object-oriented knowledge representations is their ability to provide the designer for many problems with a concise and and intuitively appealing means of expression. The claim of intuitive appeal is based on our experience that object-oriented styles of description often closely match our understanding of the domain being modeled and therefore lessens the burden of reformulation in developing and understanding a formal description. The implementation of our window, menu and icon systems [Boecker, Lemke, Fabian 85] serves as a convincing example for this claim.

ObjTalk is an object-oriented programming language as well as a general formalism for knowledge representation. *ObjTalk* as a programming environment includes the following features:

- *message-passing* as the basic model for computation;
- *class-instance* relationship; instances of a class are specified by filling the "slots" described in their class with specific values; their class also provides a description of the messages that they understand and how to respond to them; these descriptions are called *methods*;
- *class-inheritance* framework (with multiple superclasses); it supports the methodology of "programming by specialization"; the *method* of a class may be extended or replaced by a *method* with the same name contained in one of the subclasses of the class.

There are a variety of features that make *ObjTalk* an interesting formalism for knowledge representation; among them are the following:

- *if-set, if-changed, if-needed* and *if-forget* demons (which are triggered automatically when the corresponding operations are carried out);
- Rules (as in rule-based expert systems) which may be associated with classes; they may be used to automatically update relationships among the slots of (an instance of) a class.

As mentioned above, a major application of *ObjTalk* is our window system (see for example Figures 5-3 and 5-4 in section 5.4 for two applications using the window system and Figure 3-3 for the inheritance network underlying the window system).

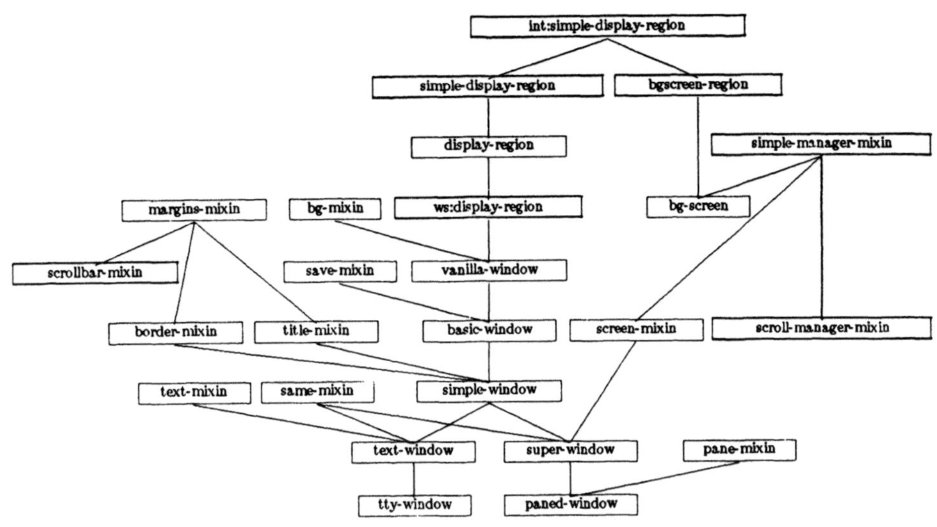

Figure 3-3: The *ObjTalk* Inheritance Hierarchy of our Window System

The facilities of *ObjTalk* allowed for the highly modular and flexible structure of the window system and they led to an open architecture providing high level interfaces to applications and at the same time keeping lower level parts of the system accessible for situations where nonstandard extensions are needed.

4. Design Considerations for Intelligent Systems

In this chapter we summarize major principles that have emerged from our work. They are based on a growing understanding of human information processing capabilities and on our prescriptive goals about system design. These principles provide a basis for developing and assessing some aspects of intelligent systems.

4.1 Design Considerations Based on the Human Information Processing System

Users of computer systems are humans and the human information processing system has strengths and weaknesses. Examples of the human mental processing limits are the limited short term memory and our tendency to make errors (for a great variety of reasons). Examples of the strength is the great power of our visual system which is slowly taken more into account in the new two-dimensional interfaces, using iconic and spatial information as well as color.

We postulate a few principles which provide the most important design criteria derived from the human information processing system:

1. *The limited resource in human information processing is human attention and comprehension, not the quantity of information available.* Modern communication and information technologies have dramatically increased the amount of information available to individuals. Most persons will have access to more information than they can deal with. An important function of future computing systems is to allow for the selection of the information we actually want and need and presentation of it in the most appropriate way.

2. *In complex situations, the search for an optimal solution is a waste of time.* There are limits to the extent to which people can apply rational analyses and judgements to solving complex, unpredictable problems. It is insufficient to ask people to "Think more clearly" without providing new tools such as knowledge-based systems, which help extend the boundaries of human rationality. The aim is to achieve the most satisfactory solution (i.e. we have to "satisfice" instead of "optimize", see [Simon 81]) given current knowledge, accepting that better solutions will emerge as a result of experience and enhanced knowledge and understanding.

3. *The nature of human memory mechanisms are important design considerations.* The limitations and structure of human memory must be taken into account in system design. People have limited short term memories. Dialogues should, therefore, be constructed which do not expect the user to remember everything and which reinforce, prompt and remind the user of necessary information in a supportive but unobtrusive way. Recognition memory and recall memory are two memory structures with different access mechanisms which are relevant to judge the advantages and limitations of function-key versus menu-based systems.

4. *The efficient visual processing capabilities of people must be utilized fully.* New technologies (like raster displays) have opened ways to exploit human visual perception more fully, e.g. through the use of windows, color, graphics, icons and mice. These technologies support an interaction technique like "direct manipulation" which is an important alternative in human-computer communication to be further explored in future systems.

5. *The structure of a computer system must be understandable by people using it rather than requiring the user to learn by rote the functions that can be performed.* An adequate understanding of how a system works gives users the knowledge and confidence to explore the full potential of a system, which can have a vast range of different options. Learning by rote may train the user to operate a limited number of functions but makes it difficult for the user to cope with unexpected occurrences and inhibits their exploration of the full potential of the system.

4.2 Design Considerations Based on our Prescriptive Goals for Intelligent Systems

Our systems have to be flexible enough to support the variety of behavior occasioned by the unpredictable details of particular situations. The design of hard- and software and human-computer communication capabilities must be responsive to the knowledge worker's amorphous responsibilities. We must base our theories, methodologies and tools on an understanding of what users are doing. The work of the users we want to support can be characterized along the following dimensions:

- to deal with fuzzy problems, with instabilities in specifications and uncertainties; the existence of partial solutions incrementally increases the user's understanding of the problems to be solved and allows her/him to analyze a prototypical situation instead of anticipating it;
- formal approaches (e.g. methods from operations research) fail in most cases, because we do not understand the problems well enough;
- the space of possibilities is unlimited; choosing is not always good enough, in many situations it is necessary to generate new solutions; this requires the exploration of unknown situations and not the application of habitual means;
- in complex decision making there are always too many things which are not articulated; therefore in many situations, tasks can not be delegated because they cannot be described well enough for an assistant to do them.

Based on this brief description we postulate additional principles which can serve as further guidelines to design intelligent systems:

1. *There is no such thing as <u>the</u> user of a system; there are many different kind of users and the requirements of an individual user grows with experience.* Computer systems must adaptively grow with the experience of the user. The heterogeneity of the user community and the growing experience of one user working with a system over a long period of time requires an adaptive behavior based on a system model of the user's abilities for a specific task.

2. *The "intelligence" of a complex tool must contribute to its easy use.* Truly intelligent and knowledgeable human communication partners, such as good teachers, use a substantial part of their knowledge to explain their expertise to others. In the same way, the "intelligence" of a computer system should be used to provide effective communication.

3. *The user interface in a computer system is more than just an additional component; it is an integral and important part of the whole system.* The traditional design process, proceeding from the "inside" to the "outside", has to be reversed as much as possible. The design, development and evaluation of new information systems should start with an understanding of the overall social and technical environment in which any particular new technology is embedded (see Figure 4-1).

5. Components of Intelligent Systems

Over the last several years we have designed and implemented the following prototypical components of intelligent systems (see Figure 3-1):

- documentation systems,
- passive and active help systems,

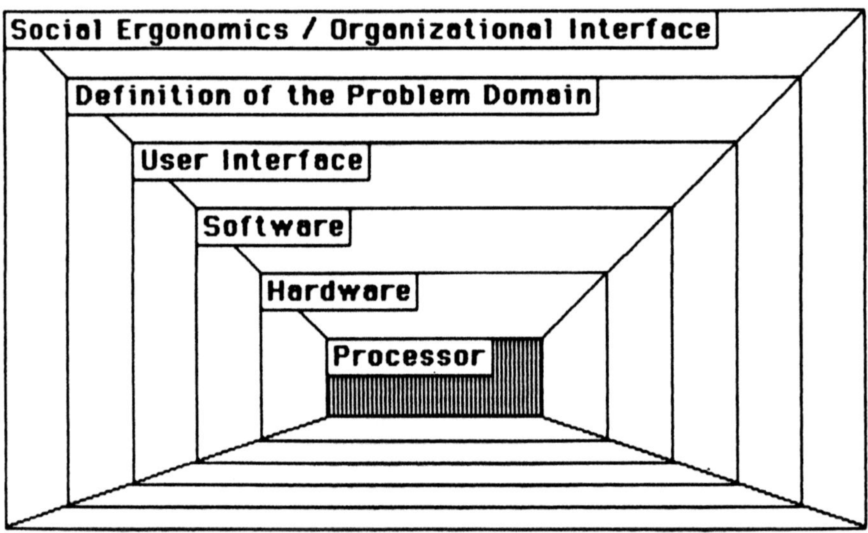

Figure 4-1: Different Levels in a System Development Process

- critics,
- visualization tools.

These components will be briefly described in the next sections. Most of them are of equal importance to the system designer and the system user.

5.1 Documentation Systems

A program documentation system should be a part of a software engineering environment. Its importance stems from the large range of different tasks documentation is used for:

- to serve as a communication medium between different people (clients, designers and users),
- to enhance the designers understanding of the problem to be solved and to assist them in improving the problem specifications,
- to support the designers during the implementation of their solution,
- to enable programmers to reuse a program and to extend existing systems to tool kits,
- to maintain a programming system,
- to make a program portable and sharable in a larger community.

In our design and implementation [Lemke, Schwab 83; Fischer, Schneider 84] a program documentation system is a knowledge base containing all of the available knowledge about a system combined with a set of tools useful for *acquiring, storing, maintaining* and *using* this knowledge.

The knowledge base is

- in part interpreted by the computer to maintain the consistency of the acquired knowledge about structural properties; it supports the users in debugging and maintaining their programs;
- in part only useful for the user, i.e. not directly interpretable by the machine. In this case the machine serves as a medium for structured communication between the different users. The computer can support the user to maintain the non-interpretable information in the knowledge base and do user-guided changes of information.

A documentation system should support the entire design and programming process. Valid and consistent documentation is of crucial importance during the programming process itself. The information structures that are accumulated around a program can be used to drive an evolutionary and incremental design process.

In the traditional view documentation is created at the end of the programming process; in our model documentation serves as the communication medium for all people involved with a software product. Documentation is useful throughout the entire process and serves as a starting point for new solutions of the problem. The purpose of documentation in this view is comparable to that of a proof in mathematics: a crystallization point for new ideas.

We gain the full benefit of a program documentation system only, if it is an *integral* part of a programming environment. Program documentation produced as a separate document by a word processing system has the following disadvantages:

- it is impossible to provide pieces of information automatically,
- it is impossible to maintain consistency between the program and its documentation automatically (or at least semi-automatically),
- it is impossible to generate different external views dynamically from one complex internal structure (e.g. to read a documentation either as a primer or as a reference manual),
- it is impossible to create links between the static description and the dynamic behavior.

Program documentation for whom? Program documentation has to serve different groups who try to perform different tasks. Therefore the amount and quality of information offered to these groups of people has to be different. We distinguish the following groups and their tasks:

- the *designers* of a system during the programming process. They have to have access to their design decisions and the different versions of the system. They also need information about the state of their work during the whole design process.
- the *programmers* who are trying to reuse or modify a program that they do not know yet. They want to understand the purpose and algorithms of the program to decide which parts of it have to be changed to fit their needs. They need information about design decisions (in order to avoid known pitfalls) as well as a thorough documentation of the existing code.
- the *clients* who are trying to find out whether the implemented system solves their problem. They want to improve their own understanding by working with a prototypical version of the system and are therefore not interested in any programming details but in design decisions.
- the *users* want to see a description in terms of "What does it do? How can I achieve my goals?"; for end-users the documentation has to offer different views of the system: a primer-like description for the beginner and manual-type explanations for the expert.

Knowledge acquisition and updating. The information structures which are used in our system come from two sources:

- a program analysis system provides information about the structural properties (cross references, side effects) of a program. The users do not have to provide information that can be created automatically, so they are free to concentrate on the creative aspects of their work.
- the programmers have to provide semantic information about the different parts of the program, information about the internal (semantic) structure of their systems, descriptions of the algorithms used etc..

Most of the analysis done by the system is done at read-time. This means that we have to do the analysis after each alternation of the program code. The system knows about possible dependencies between knowledge units and, if necessary, reanalyzes the units in question. It informs the programmer about possible inconsistencies in the knowledge base. These techniques help us to maintain the consistency between different representations of the information.

The way the system decides if a knowledge unit has to be updated is the following:

- the system knows that it has to change certain structural information (e.g. "calls" and "is-called-by" relations) automatically. The system is able to alter information by using its cross-reference knowledge. This knowledge can also be used to guide the users to places where they possibly want to change information.
- for each unit users can provide a list of other knowledge units they want to inspect and possibly alter if a unit has been updated.

Using the available knowledge. A knowledge-based program documentation system is only useful if the relevant information can be easily obtained. The following two requirements must be supported:

- *availability:* the knowledge about the system (incorporating the consequences of all changes) must be available at any time.
- *views of reduced complexity:* the structures in our knowledge base are too complex to be used directly. A filter mechanism where the filters can be defined by the user [Lemke, Schwab 83] allows the generation of views of reduced complexity showing only the information which is relevant for a specific user at a specific time.

5.2 Help Systems

The following system descriptions [Fischer, Lemke, Schwab 84; Fischer, Lemke, Schwab 85] are based on preliminary investigations for a passive and an active help system for a screen-oriented editor. *Passive* help systems are needed if the users know their goals but cannot communicate them to the system. *Active* help systems assist users when they are not aware that the system offers better ways to achieve a task (see Figure 2-1).

5.2.1 *Passivist*: A Passive Help System

The first step in the design of *Passivist*, a natural language based help system, was to get an idea of the real needs of the user. In several informal experiments a human expert simulated the help system in editing sessions with users of different expertise. The results indicated a fairly diverse set of problems ranging from finding keys on the keyboard to complex formatting tasks.

Passivist provides help to requests such as:

- *How can I get to the end of the line?*
- *I want to delete the next word.*

Passivist uses a help strategy in which each step of the solution is presented and explained to the user who then executes this step and immediately sees the resulting effects. Help is given as text generated from sentence patterns according to the goal structure of the problem solving process and key sequences and subgoals are displayed graphically.

Passivist is implemented in OPS5 [Forgy 81]. Flexible parsing using OPS5 is achieved by a rule-based bottom-up method. The consistent structure of the system as a set of productions and a common working memory allows the use of the same knowledge in several stages of the solution process. For example, knowledge about the state of the editor is not only used to select a possible solution for the user's problem but also to disambiguate the user's utterance. In the phrase *the last line* with the cursor being at the beginning of the editing buffer it is clear that the user refers to the last line of the buffer (and not to the previous one).

The following rule (an English-like transcription of the corresponding OPS5 rule) represents the systems knowledge about deleting the end of a line:

```
IF   the goal is to delete a string
       AND  the string is the end of the current line
       AND  the cursor is not at the end of the current line

THEN remove the goal from the working memory
       AND  create a new goal to propose the command "rubout-line-right"
```

5.2.2 *Activist*: An Active Help System

Activist, an active help system for a screen-oriented editor, is implemented in *FranzLisp* and *ObjTalk* (see section 3.4).

Activist deals with two different kinds of suboptimal behavior:

1. the user does not know a complex command and uses suboptimal commands to reach a goal (e.g. she/he deletes a string character by character instead of word by word).
2. the user knows the complex command but does not use the minimal key sequence to issue the command (e.g. she/he types the command name instead of hitting the corresponding function key).

Similar to a human observer, *Activist* handles the following tasks (for details see [Fischer, Lemke, Schwab 84] and [Fischer, Lemke, Schwab 85]):

- to *recognize* what the user is doing or wants to do,
- to *evaluate* how the user tries to achieve her/his goal,
- to *construct a model of the user* based on the results of the evaluation task,
- to decide (dependent on the information in the model) *when* and *how* to interrupt (tutorial intervention).

In *Activist* the recognition and evaluation task is delegated to 20 different *plan specialists*. Each one recognizes and evaluates one possible plan of the problem domain. Such plans are for example *"deletion of the next word"*, *"position at the end of line"*, etc..

A plan specialist consists of:

- A transition network (TN), which matches all the different ways to achieve the plan using the functionality of the editor. Each TN in the system is independent. The results of a match are the *used editor commands* and the *used keys* to trigger these commands.
- An expert which knows the optimal plan including the *best editor commands* and the *minimal key sequence* for these commands.

Figure 5-1 displays the user model that *Activist* has built up. For each plan there is a pane which shows the performance of a specific user concerning this plan. Panes with black background indicate that the corresponding plan is currently not monitored by the active help system.

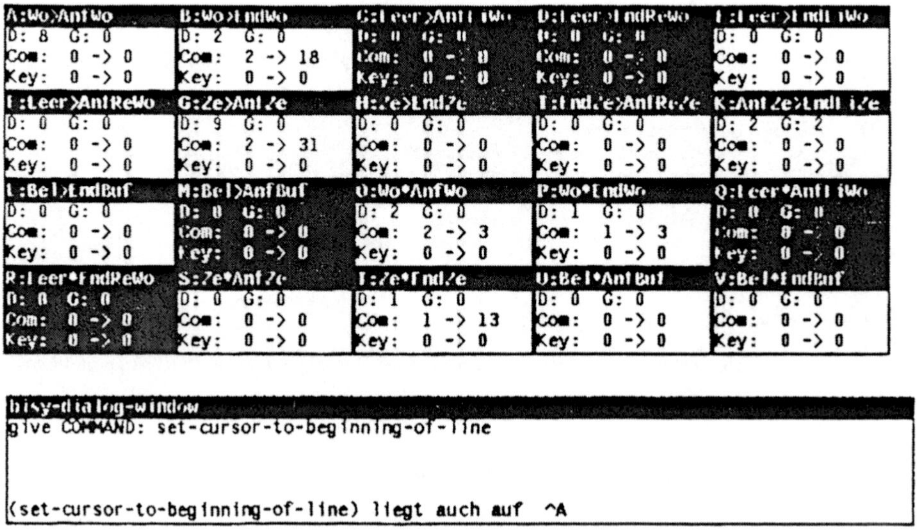

Figure 5-1: The User Model of *Activist*

The dialogue window at the bottom displays a help message given to the user. She/he has executed the command *set-cursor-to-beginning-of-line* by typing in the command name. *Activist* gives the hint, that this command is also bound to the key *CTRL-A*.

Figure 5-2 relates to the monitoring of the plan *"delete-the-left-part-of-the-current-word"*. The window shows one pane of Figure 5-1 in more detail: the proposed command (with the optimal keys) for this plan and the state of the plan recognition.

The user has executed the command *rubout-character-left* with the DEL-key three times. After these actions the cursor is located to the right of the first character of the word. If the user once again invokes *rubout-character-left* the plan will be recognized. Then the evaluation will begin: the commands used will be compared with the optimal commands for this plan and *Activist* will recognize the first kind of suboptimal behavior (as described above). Based on the instructional strategies chosen *Activist* may then decide to interrupt the user and describe how to use the *"delete-the-left-part-of-the-current-word"* command.

```
DELETE left part of word
USER   MODEL

plan executed:                 1
good done:                     0
wrong command used:            1
with unnescessary keys:        6
command with wrong keys used:  0
with unnescessary keys:        0
messages sent to user:         0

INTERNAL   INFORMATION

proposed commands:  rubout-word-left
optimal keys:       ESC h

commands: rubout-character-left rubout-character-left rubout-character-left
keys:( DEL )( DEL )( DEL )
automaton in state: Start
```

Figure 5-2: Monitoring the Recognition Task

5.3 Critics

In our current work we extend the work on active help systems in order to develop systems which can serve as *critics*. This is done primarily by representing more elaborate knowledge structures in the computer. The following four information structures are prerequisites to support systems which can serve as *Critics:*

- *Characteristics of the User:* General knowledge of the user's abilities in the subject domain independent of the current problem. This knowledge can be viewed as an abstraction from individual problem solving attempts.
- *The User's Problem Solving Approach:* The system's idea of the problem solving path chosen by the user. This may be an explicit hierarchical model of the design choices which led to the code produced by the user where the user explicitly indicates in which way she/he wants to

attack the problem. Plan recognition strategies attempt to infer the user's plan through observation of her/his steps performed in solving a task. For these systems the plan essentially *is* the user model.

- *Task Model:* The system's understanding of which problem the user currently wants to solve. In tutorial systems this knowledge can be built into a system in advance. In systems which can serve as critics (i.e. they have to support the users in their own doing) we need methods to infer the current task.
- *Domain Knowledge:* User independent expert knowledge of the selected domain of competence of the system.

Given this detailed model of the user and the task domain, the following actions of the system become possible (e.g. to support learning strategies like *learning on demand*):

- *Select appropriate actions with respect to the user:* If the comparison of the user model and the system's expert knowledge reveals weaknesses in a specific area, the system should only become active if this area is adjacent to already known areas and does not require too many other areas unknown to the user.
- *Select examples from the domain the user is familiar with:* By using an executable form of representation it is possible to generate illustrations out of areas which the user already understands and thus reduce the cognitive distance that has to be bridged.
- *Present only the missing pieces of knowledge:* In dialogues a large amount of time is spent to find out what each communication partner knows and does not know about the subject area. With a detailed user model, the system can concentrate on the very points where the user needs help.
- *Better understanding of the user:* Using knowledge about the user's understanding of a problem domain makes it much easier to find out about her/his real problem. We encountered many cases where a user had a problem which originated in a wrong decomposition of a higher level problem. Using knowledge about the user it is possible to trace a problem back to its real roots.

The Code-Improver System. Our currently existing system, called *Code-Improver*, is used to get ideas on how to improve *Lisp* code. Improvements may be in either of two directions (which can be chosen by the user):

- to make the code more *cognitively* efficient (e.g. more readable or concise) or
- to make the code more *machine* efficient (e.g. smaller or faster); this improvements include those that can be found in optimizing compilers.

The system is in regular use by different groups for slightly different reasons:

- by intermediates who want to learn how to produce better *Lisp* code; we are currently testing the usefulness of the tool by gathering empirical, statistical data using advanced undergraduate students of an introductory *Lisp*-course as subjects;
- by experienced users who want their code to be "straightened out"; instead of doing that by hand (which these users in principle would be able to), they use the system to carefully reconsider the code they have written. The system is used to detect optimizations and simplifications that can be done to the code. The system has proven especially useful with code that is incrementally developed, i.e. gets changed and modified continuously.

The system operates by using a set of ($>$ 200) transformation rules that describe how to transform 'bad' code into better one. The user's code is matched against these rules and the transformations suggested by the rules are given to the user; the code is not modified automatically. It is important to note, that the system is *not* restricted to a specific class of *Lisp* functions or application domain. It accepts whatever *Lisp*-code is given to it. However, there is a trade-off: since the system does not have any knowledge of specific application areas or algorithms it is naturally limited in the kind of improvements that derive from its more general knowledge about programming. The improvements suggested by the system are of the following kind:

- suggesting the use of macros (e.g. `(setq a (cons b a))` may be replaced by `(push b a)`);
- replacing compound calls of *Lisp* functions by simple calls to more powerful functions (e.g. `(not (evenp a))` may be replaced by `(oddp a)`);
- specializing functions (e.g. replacing `equal` by `eq`);
- using integer arithmetic wherever possible;
- finding alternative (simpler or faster) forms of conditional or arithmetic expressions;
- eliminating common subexpressions;
- replacing 'garbage' generating expressions by non-copying expressions (e.g. `(append (explode word) chars)` may be replaced by `(nconc (explode word) chars)`);
- finding and eliminating 'dead' code (as in `(cond (...) (t ...) (dead code))`);
- (partial) evaluation of expressions (e.g. `(sum a 3 b 4)` may be simplified to `(sum a b 7)`).

The current version of the *Code-Improver* system runs in batch mode. Like the "writers-workbench" UNIX tools, *diction* and *explain*, it is given a file containing *Lisp* code and comes back with suggestions on how to "improve" that code.

The problem of knowledge acquisition for the system's model of the user is solved using program code written by the user. Our current techniques will be extended from recognizing pieces of code which can be improved to both recognizing the goals of a piece of code as well as existing and missing concepts which led to its generation. Since only in very few cases a definitive assumption about the knowledge of the user can be made, it is important to have many clues which allow to make uncertain inferences when no specific evidence is available.

5.4 Visualization Tools

Many communication problems between humans and computers are due to the fact that the strongest information processing subsystem of the human brain, the *visual system*, is hardly utilized by current software systems. Most systems present the result of computational processes in textual and symbolic ways that are not suited to the human information processing capabilities. Over the last several years we have actively pursued the goal of constructing a *software oscilloscope* whose visualization techniques enhance the communication process (see [Boecker, Nieper 85; Boecker, Fischer, Nieper 85]) by broadening the explicit communication channel between computer and machine (see Figure 3-2).

5.4.1 Visualization of Data Structures: The *Kaestle* System

The most important data structure of *Lisp* is the *list*. With *Kaestle* [Boecker, Nieper 85] the graphic representation of a list structure is generated automatically and can be edited directly with a pointing device. By editing we do not only mean changing the structure itself but changing the graphic representation, the layout, of the structure. *Kaestle* is integrated into a window system and multiple *Kaestle*-windows may be used at the same time. The *user interface* is menu-based (see Figure 5-3) and the *program interface* is realized through *ObjTalk* methods which can be triggered by sending messages to a *Kaestle*-window.

Kaestle provides the following *functionality*:

1. generating a graphic display (multiple independent structures may be displayed at a desired position);
2. changing the graphic representation (additional display of structures which are truncated in the current display, deleting parts of the structure from the screen and moving parts of the structure on the screen);
3. changing the structure (the manipulation (insertion of atoms or pointers) of the graphic representation immediately changes the underlying structure);
4. controlling the layout planning in advance (selecting the maximum depth and length of lists to be displayed, selecting the maximum length of atom names to be displayed, selecting a planning algorithm (car-first or cdr-first algorithm) and selecting the font to be used);
5. general undo and redo mechanisms.

The user of *Kaestle* can take one of the following roles:

1. an *active* role: A graphic representation can be generated from whatever the user types in and the user is encouraged to an exploratory style of learning.
2. a *passive* role: An inexperienced user does not know which structures and which operations on them lead to interesting effects. To display prestored examples or examples taken from the actual context, *Kaestle* can be used through a program interface, i.e. programs can be written which generate graphic representations in a movie-like manner.

We will combine *Kaestle* with the documentation, help and critic tools described in the previous sections. *Kaestle* is a tool which will be used by the *Code-Improver* to illustrate explanations given by the system to answer questions like:

- What is the difference between several list creation functions (e.g. `cons` and `list`)?
- What is the difference between `equal` and `eq`?
- What is the difference between non-destructive and destructive functions (e.g. `append` and `nconc`)?
- Why is it possible to transform `(append (explode word) chars)` to `(nconc (explode word) chars)`?
- Why is it wrong to transform `(append chars (explode word))` to `(nconc chars (explode word))`?
- How is a stack implemented in *Lisp*? What are `push` and `pop` doing?

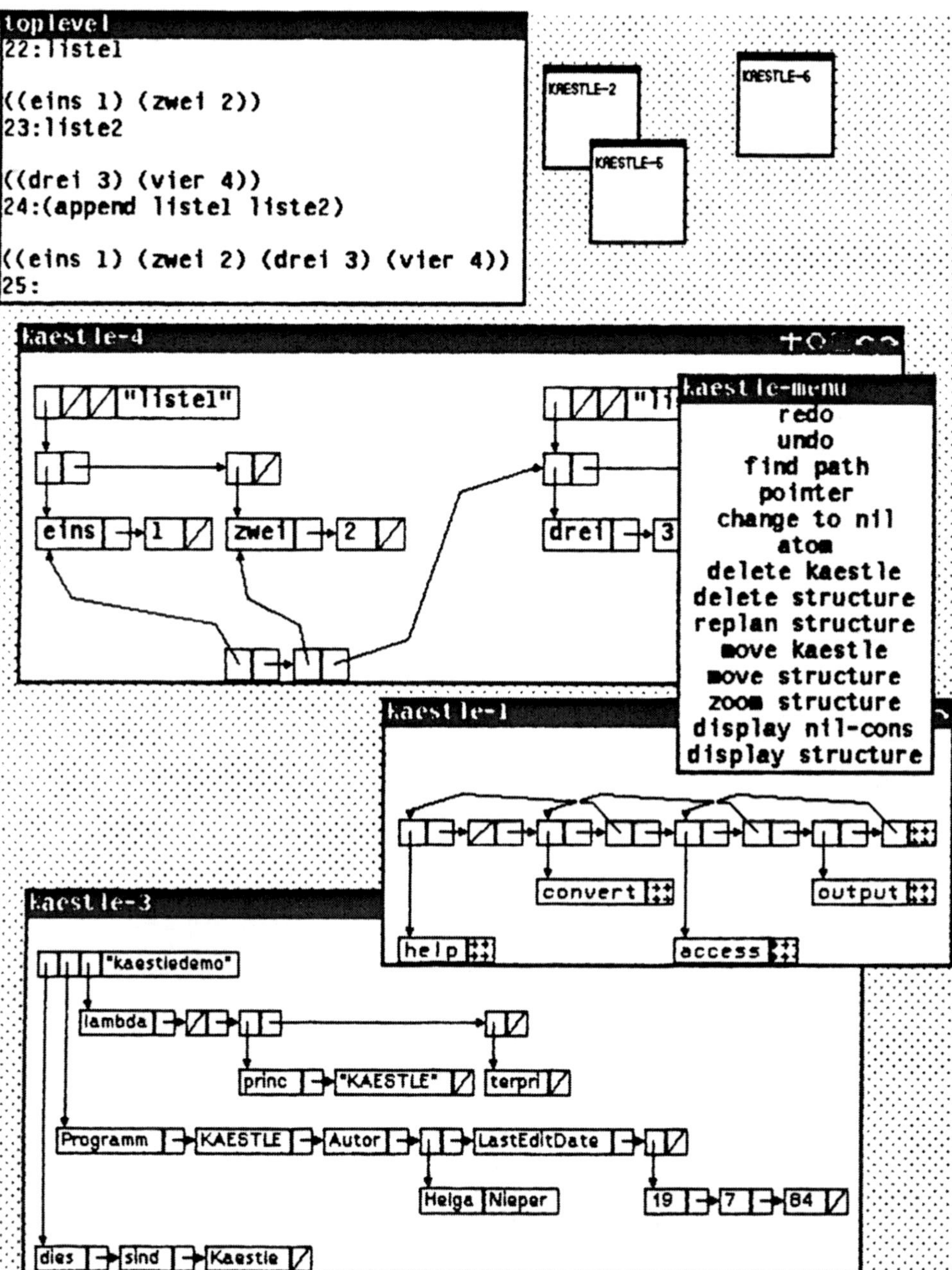

Figure 5-3: *Kaestle*: Visualization of Data Structures

5.4.2 Visualization of Control Structures: The *FooScape* System

One of the most helpful tools for understanding programs which are composed of a large set of procedures is a *program tree* that displays the hierarchical calling structure (see Figure 5-4, "Dynamic Calling Tree"). In reality however, most programs are more appropriately described as a *network of functions* rather than a tree (see Figure 5-4, "FooScape"). In *FooScape* functions are displayed as ellipses and an arrow connects ellipses *a* and *b* if function *a* calls function *b*.

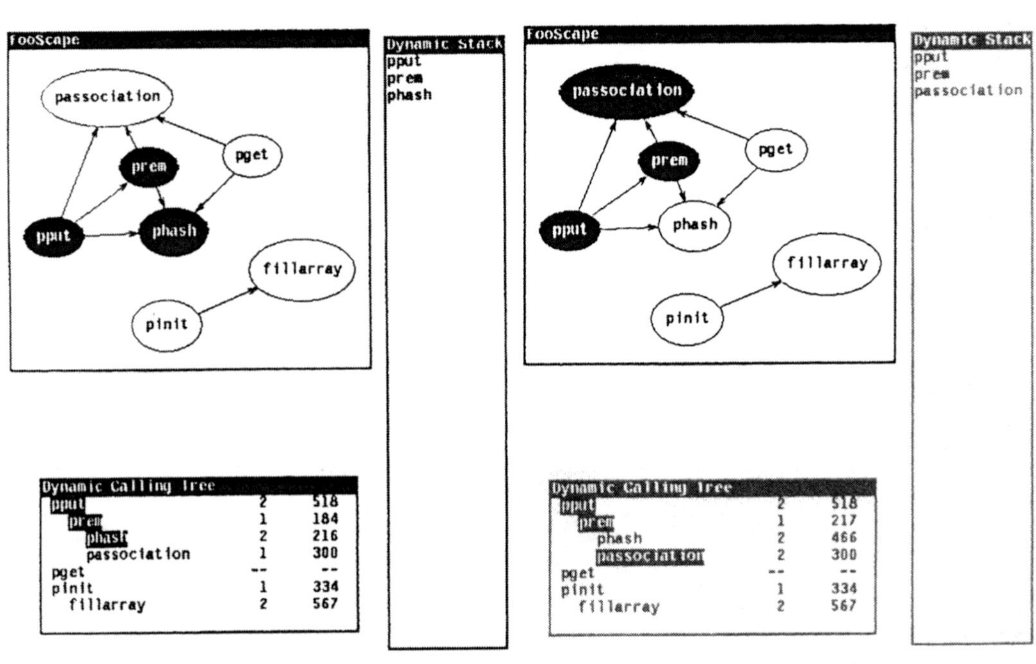

Figure 5-4: *FooScape*: Showing the Dynamic Behavior of a Program

The planning of the layout (placement of the ellipses and arrows) is done automatically. However, because the "beauty" of the solution sometimes is not acceptable we allow the user to modify the layout interactively by moving "bubbles" around or by altering the set of functions included in the display. The interaction style is similar to the one of the *Kaestle* system.

FooScape can be used to display the dynamic behavior of programs. Figure 5-4 shows two snapshots. A function name is highlighted - i.e. flips from white to black - whenever the function is active. *FooScape* can be augmented by a tool that displays the current stack of function calls. Traditional techniques for monitoring the *dynamic behavior* of programs (eg. breakpoints, dumps) capture just one state of the data and too often generate a huge amount of data. The animated *FooScape* system tries to avoid these disadvantages, while, on the other hand, trying to preserve the dynamics of the processes being monitored.

6. The Role of Ergonomics Research in Intelligent Systems

Ergonomics analyzes the consequences of technology to the learning and working environment of a human. It is dominated by the goal to create environments which support the human and do not require that the human has to put up with inadequate technical solutions.

In the past properties of systems were investigated which could be measured with methods from physics (e.g. according to the size of an average hand, what is the optimal distance between the keys on a keyboard). This approach is insufficient for the design and evaluation of human-computer communication and knowledge-based systems.

Design conflicts. The first thing a designer is confronted with is that *there are no optimal solutions -- only tradeoffs.* One has to cope with conflicting design issues; some of the major ones are:

- cognitive efficiency versus machine efficiency of a system,
- simplicity of a tool (to be easily handled by a large community) versus power (to be used in the construction of a large variety of different and complex systems),
- the necessity to remain compatible with existing systems (e.g. timesharing computers) versus exploiting the power of new media (e.g. networks of personal machines),
- ease for novice users (like mnemonic names in editors or menu-driven systems) versus convenience for experienced users (like a terse command language),
- tight integration between different subsystems versus flexible, reconfigurable modules or tool kits.

Costs of ignoring ergonomics. Without a great concern for ergonomics (especially software ergonomics) computing systems may prove detrimental to the people who have to work with them. Once a computer system has been installed, it is difficult to avoid the assumption that the things it can deal with are the most relevant things (e.g. text-processing systems do not support graphics, therefore papers get written without graphics). Introducing a system whose functioning is incompletely understood may cause unintended transfers of power and obscured responsibilities. Designs which ignore the fact that computing systems are embedded systems (see Figure 4-1) may lead to systems where satisfying work procedures are subdivided in meaningless parts and intellectual assembly line work is created. Contrary to that, good systems have the potential to reduce stress (by being forgiving towards errors from the user; e.g. by providing an UNDO command for every operation) and to augment human capabilities. Ergonomics research should indicate wrong developments in an early state; this requires that evaluation of a system should start at the beginning of the development process and should not be restricted to acceptance testing. The use of computer systems as tools is a complex skill which is acquired over long periods of time and it is very costly to untrain people after they have become familiar with one way of doing something.

Ergonomics research faces one critical problem: technology has progressed so fast that some of the questions which were too closely tied to a certain technology became obsolete before the studies were completed. A detailed understanding of the optimal design of a keypunch is of little value today, because keypunches are dying out anyway. The question whether a terminal or a printer should support small *and* capital letters is not discussed any more, because all products which do not are driven out of the market.

When is ergonomics research most important? Applying criteria from ergonomics and psychology to the *acceptance testing* of a given system is definitely easier than applying evaluation criteria to the *design* of systems. In acceptance testing, the system is given; all of its parts and properties are specified. In design, the system is still largely hypothetical; it is a class of systems. But there is much more leverage in evaluation of the system design than in acceptance testing of the finished product. The long ranging goal is that the designer of a complex computer system has a design handbook (similar to the handbooks which are available to the civil engineer today) which gives him access to the important design criteria. Unfortunately this is not the case. We are lacking cognitive theories which are prescriptive enough to be used as design criteria and of planning and a detailed understanding of the specific task structure. In addition, productivity gains inherent in new technology cannot be realized simply by carrying out existing operations at a faster pace; a careful analysis of work procedures is crucial for a substantial improvement.

Why not just ask the user? There is no doubt that the user community should play an active part in the design of a system (shared system design among users and designers) -- but unfortunately most potential user communities can not articulate in enough detail the characteristics of the systems which they would like to have. Therefore it is important that there are research places where users can explore and criticize new system designs in a prototypical development stage.

7. Problems and Challenges for Research in Intelligent Systems

What can we do without complete specifications? System design belongs to the "Sciences of the Artificial" [Simon 81]. Contrary to natural scientists who are given a universe and seek to discover the laws, the system designer makes "laws" in the form of programs and the computer brings a new universe to life. Many interesting problem areas (especially the domain of intelligent systems) contain mostly ill-structured problems. The main difficulty in these domains is not to have a "correct" implementation with respect to given specifications, but to develop specifications which lead to effective solutions which correspond to real needs. Correctness of the specifications is in general no meaningful question because it would require a precise specification of intent, and such a specification is seldom available.

We have to accept the empirical truth that for many tasks system requirements cannot be stated fully in advance - in many cases not even in principle because neither the user nor anyone else knows them in advance.

The development process itself changes the user's and designer's perceptions of what is possible, increases their insights into the application environment, and indeed often changes the environment itself.

The following (not mutually exclusive) possibilities exist to cope with this situation:

1. Development of *experimental programming systems which support the coevolution of specifications and implementations.* Prototypical implementations allow us to replace anticipation (i.e. how will the system behave) with analysis (i.e. how does it actually behave), which is in most cases much easier. Most of the major computing systems (operating systems, editors, expert systems, software development systems) have been developed with extensive feedback (based on their actual use) which continually contributed to improvements as a response to discrepancies between a system's actual and desired state.
2. *Heavy user involvement and participation in all phases of the development process.* The user should be able to play with the preliminary system and to discuss the design rational behind it. An existing prototype makes this cooperation between designer and user much more productive, because the users are not restricted to reviewing written specifications to see whether or not the system will satisfy their needs with respect to functionality and ease of use.
3. *Let the end-users develop the systems.* This would eliminate the communication gap altogether. They are the persons who know most about the specific problems to be solved and by giving them the opportunity to change the system there is no longer a necessity to anticipate all possible future interactions between user and system. *User tailorability* is a first step towards *convivial systems* [Fischer 83] which give the users the capability to carry out a constrained design process within the boundaries of the knowledge area modeled. A strong test for the intelligence of a system is not how well its features conform to anticipated needs but how well it performs when one wants to do something the designer did not foresee.
4. Accept changing requirements as a fact of life and do not condemn them as a product of sloppy thinking; we need *methodologies and tools to make change a coordinated, computer-supported process.*

Understanding the limitations of systems. A critical problem can be that the users do not have a clear understanding of the limitations of a system. This is an important problem for natural language interfaces where users are often seduced to believe that they can talk to these systems like to their colleagues. Users will be especially disappointed if the projected illusion is that of intelligence but the reality falls far short (the ELIZA system may serve as a good example). Despite progress in the area of intelligent systems, it is still the user who is more intelligent and can be directed into a particular context. Giving the user the appropriate cues is one of the essences of human-computer communication. Windows, menus, spreadsheets, documentation, help, explanations, critics and visualization provide a context that allows the user's intelligence to keep choosing the appropriate next step.

Towards Human-ProblemDomain Communication. Despite the fact that we have used the term Human-Computer Communication throughout this paper, we believe that the goal to achieve is Human-ProblemDomain Communication, where the users can deal with descriptions within their world of expertise. Knowledge-based systems are one important step towards this goal and allow users to deal with content instead of form or low-level mechanisms.

Human-oriented computer systems. There is no difficulty in getting people to use computers provided the computer and its application are genuinely useful. The goal of intelligent systems has to be to create human-oriented computer systems where the users have control and can achieve *their* goals in *their* way. These systems should eliminate the necessity that the human has to become a computer-oriented person (see Figure 7-1).

Figure 7-1: Human-centered and computer-centered system
Design of Peter Hajnozcky, Zuerich

References

[Barstow, Shrobe, Sandewall 84]
D. Barstow, H. Shrobe, E. Sandewall.
Interactive Programming Environments.
McGrawHill, New York, 1984.

[Boecker, Fischer, Nieper 85]
H.-D. Boecker, G. Fischer, H. Nieper.
The Enhancement of Understanding through Visual Representations.
Technical Report, University of Colorado, Boulder, 1985.

[Boecker, Lemke, Fabian 85]
H.-D. Boecker, A.C. Lemke, F. Fabian, Jr.
WLisp: A Window Based Programming Environment for FranzLisp.
In *Proceedings of the First Pan Pacific Computer Conference.* The Australian Computer Society, Melbourne, Australia, September, 1985.

[Boecker, Nieper 85]
H.-D. Boecker, H. Nieper.
Making the Invisible Visible: Tools for Exploratory Programming.
In *Proceedings of the First Pan Pacific Computer Conference.* The Australian Computer Society, Melbourne, Australia, September, 1985.

[Fischer 81]
G. Fischer.
Computational Models of Skill Acquisition Processes.
In R. Lewis, D. Tagg (editor), *Computers in Education,* pages 477-481. 3rd World Conference on Computers and Education, Lausanne, Switzerland, July, 1981.

[Fischer 83]
G. Fischer.
Symbiotic, Knowledge-Based Computer Support Systems.
Automatica 19(6):627-637, November, 1983.

[Fischer 84] G. Fischer.
Formen und Funktionen von Modellen in der Mensch-Computer Kommunikation.
In M.J. Tauber (editor), *Psychologie der Computernutzung*. Oldenbourg Verlag, Wien - Muenchen, 1984.
Schriftenreihe der Oesterreichischen Computergesellschaft.

[Fischer, Lemke, Schwab 84]
G. Fischer, A. Lemke, T. Schwab.
Active Help Systems.
In T.Green, M.Tauber, G.van der Veer (editor), *Proceedings of Second European Conference on Cognitive Ergonomics - Mind and Computers, Gmunden, Austria*. Springer Verlag, Heidelberg - Berlin - New York, September, 1984.

[Fischer, Lemke, Schwab 85]
G. Fischer, A. Lemke, T. Schwab.
Knowledge-Based Help Systems.
In *Human Factors in Computing Systems*. CHI-85 Conference Proceedings, 1985.

[Fischer, Schneider 84]
G. Fischer, M. Schneider.
Knowledge-Based Communication Processes in Software Engineering.
In *Proceedings of the 7th International Conference on Software Engineering*, pages 358-368. Orlando, Florida, March, 1984.

[Forgy 81] C.L. Forgy.
OPS5 User's Manual.
Technical Report CS-81-135, CMU, 1981.

[Goldberg 84] A. Goldberg.
SMALLTALK-80, The Interactive Programming Environment.
Addison-Wesley, Reading, Ma., 1984.

[Laubsch, Rathke 83]
J. Laubsch, C. Rathke.
OBJTALK: Eine Erweiterung von LISP zum objektorientierten Programmieren.
In H.Stoyan, H.Wedekind (editor), *Objektorientierte Software- und Hardwarearchitekturen*, pages 60-75. Teubner Verlag, Stuttgart, 1983.

[Lemke 85] A. Lemke.
ObjTalk84 Reference Manual.
Technical Report CU-CS-291-85, University of Colorado, Boulder, 1985.

[Lemke, Schwab 83]
A. Lemke, T. Schwab.
DOXY: Computergestuetzte Dokumentationssysteme.
1983.
Studienarbeit Nr. 338, Institut fuer Informatik, Universitaet Stuttgart.

[Norman 82] D. Norman.
Some Observations on Mental Models.
In D. Gentner, A. Stevens (eds.) (editor), *Mental Models*. Erlbaum, Hillsdale, N.J., 1982.

[Rathke, Lemke 85]
Ch. Rathke, A. C. Lemke.
ObjTalk Primer.
Technical Report CU-CS-290-85, University of Colorado, Boulder, February, 1985.
Translated by V. Patten and C. Morel.

[Sheil 83] B.A. Sheil.
Power Tools for Programmers.
Datamation , February, 1983.

[Simon 81] H.A. Simon.
The Sciences of the Artificial.
MIT Press, Cambridge, Ma., 1981.

[Wilensky et al. 84]
R. Wilensky, Y. Arens, D. Chin.
Talking to UNIX in English: An Overview of UC.
Communications of the ACM 27(6):574-593, June, 1984.

Design and Use of Programming Languages

T R G Green

MRC Applied Psychology Unit
15 Chaucer Road, Cambridge CB2 2EF, UK

ABSTRACT: The methods and techniques of computer science have been greatly advanced by the doctrines of structured programming. However, the psychological component of structured programming, which relies on simplistic cognitive models of top-down planning and comprehension, does not include many of the phenomena revealed by recent research. The ability to decompose problems into satisfactory hierarchic strctures apparently requires a learent repertoire of <u>plans</u> and a learnt ability to interleave these plans into standard hierarchic forms. Conversely, comprehending programs may requiree the plan structure to be inferred from the code. Notational aids to these procedures are described.

Advancement of applied disciplines combines ad hoc creation with partial theoretical understanding, and the successful generalisation and exploitation of new ad hoc creations is impossible if prevailing beliefs cannot explain why the creation is effective. It is argued that it is time for the prevailing orthodoxy to be modernised. Examples are given of recent advances that fit into the newer models. At the same time it must be acknowleged that some important issues remain unresolved.

Introduction

Effective software development requires many different conditions to be met, but of all the many ways in which software development environments could be improved, I shall concentrate on psychological aspects. Clarifying the psychological processes of using programming languages will, I believe, clarify the requirements of language design and of environmental support.

This paper can be read as an acknowledgement that computer science has stridden forward by using, and using thoroughly, very simple models of human reasoning; and as a call for adopting less simple models in the future.

In fact, it is gratifying to realise that computer scientists are now basing their evaluations of languages much more openly on the attributes, real or supposed, of human information processing. Hoare (1981) insists that the language Ada is too big, both

NATO ASI Series, Vol. F22
Software System Design Methods. Edited by J.K. Skwirzynski

technically, for implementors (which as a psychologist I cannot comment on), and cognitively, for users (which in this paper definitely is our concern). Ichbaiah, Ada's principal creator, replies (1984, p. 933) that

> "The human mind has an incredible ability to understand structures. Provided it understands the major lines of a structure, it will make inferences and immediately see the consequences. When you judge something, the complexity is not in the details but in whether or not it is easy to infer details from the major structural lines. From this point of view I consider Ada to be very simple."

It is gratifying to hear first-rank computer scientists arguing cognitive psychology; but it is sad that they should do so with no acknowledgement that empirical studies might well answer their questions, or that others beside themselves take an interest in the human mind.

The first section of the paper describes some empirical studies bearing on the psychological models underlying structured programming's doctrines, applied both to the comprehension and the creation of programs. The second section presents examples of research aimed at elucidating the mental representation of programs and programming knowledge, in terms of algorithmic plans and sub-plans. This is followed by examples of research dealing with the language itself: how far we succeed in "inferring details from the major structural lines", and some of the determinants of readability. The final section sketches implications, by considering some recent instances of software engineering or linguistic design in the light of the previous remarks.

STRUCTURED PROGRAMMING AS A PSYCHOLOGICAL HYPOTHESIS

In the dawn of programming, the need to save instruction cycles on slow, expensive machines led to ingenious dodges and thence to the display of ingenuity for its own sake. Comprehensibility was little regarded, and programs were debugged with midnight oil and crossed fingers. This state of affairs was remedied by the rise of 'structured programming', associated with the names of Dijkstra, Wirth, and Hoare. It was shown that programs constructed by more disciplined means were in some cases provably correct; it was claimed, very convincingly, that by concealing unwanted information, more complex structures could be managed; and it was claimed that the method of divide-and-rule ('stepwise refinement') was the suitable way to attack programming. A number of programming methodologies sprang up to promulgate systematic techniques of structured programming, and great successes were claimed.

Subsequently, the movement has led to the development of axiomatisation systems for programming languages, to the development of applicative or functional languages in which side-effects are limited or impossible, and to the development of advanced mechanisms for information concealment, using data abstraction techniques.

I would be prepared to defend the thesis that over the last two decades, there have been few examples of applied cognitive psychology - that is, technological advance founded on principles about cognition - as impressive as the development of structured programming methodologies. Nevertheless, psychologists have had mixed feelings about the structured programming school. Some of the developments lie outside psychology, of course, such as the work on program proofs and program transformation techniques. Other parts include claims that appear to be correct, claims that appear to be wrong, and claims that appear to be correct for the wrong reason. The problem is that the principles about cognition have too often resembled dogma; and dogmatisms, as everyone knows, lie beyond the reach of empirical assessment and reality testing.

The argument that programs should be written by stepwise refinement leads to the assertion that control structures should be hierarchical: thus conditional structures should be nested, rather than allowed to use arbitrary branching. In this way, successive layers of detail can be added to the program plan. Moreover the comprehension of hierarchically constructed programs will be easier, since they can be understood by a reverse process - understand the outer layer, then the inner layers, etc. And finally these programs will be easy to modify because the inter-relations between parts will be simple. Thus the argument starts from the intuitively appealing premise that simple parts, simply connected, will be easy to use, and leads to quite fierce conclusions about program design. Considerations of formal simplicity lead to the same conclusion.

Program Comprehension

An area where structured programming claims have now been well researched is in the design of control structures, especially conditionals. Many experiments, in a series started by Sime, Green and Guest (1973; 1977) have now investigated the ability of novice and expert subjects to recode short, declaratively-presented conditional structures into procedural terms. The result which is most commonly quoted (eg. Shneiderman, 1980; Sheil, 1981) is that Jump-style (GOTO) conditionals are harder to use than Nested ones, contrary to what one might expect on the basis of natural language studies. Mayer (1976) obtained results similar to Sime et al.'s with a different experimental technique. Other studies have extended the comparisons to diagrammatic notations (Sheppard et al. 1981) with similar results. Van der Veer and van de Wolde (1983) have shown that for novices, the results are influenced by cognitive style. Vesey and Webber (1984) have shown that controlling for coding effects may alter the pattern of results.

Many of these interpretations can best be described as atheoretical, as noted by Pennington (1982). They address themselves almost exclusively to the evaluation of current programming practice. But a much more interesting question is, Can we elucidate the underlying psychological principles, to allow us to generalise our results to other classes of information structure in programming?

Here is one hypothesis: if one language is better than another, it is <u>always</u> better, whatever the context. For instance, Mayer (1976) suggests that his four types of language might be "points on a continuum of structural integration; our results are consistent with the idea that the four, respectively, allow subjects to process increasing amounts of complexity." This line is developed further by Shneiderman and Mayer (1979).

Here is a second hypothesis with different implications: every notation highlights some types of information at the expense of others; the better notation, for a given task, is the one that highlights the information the given task needs. More generally, the comprehensibility of a notation may depend on the number and complexity of 'mental operations' required to extract needed information. A closer look at the details of studies by Sime et al. (1977) and Green (1977) suggests this hypothesis may be correct. Certainly, some subjects in the Sime et al. study got themselves severely tangled up in their own GOTOs in the Jump conditions, and - exactly as the structured programming platform predicts - these subjects fared badly, presumably because they could not comprehend their own programs and therefore easily lost track. But in the study by Green, subjects (all experienced programmers) had to answer questions about programs that were well-structured but were written in Jump or in two varieties of Nest, thus eliminating the problem of tangled GOTOs. In this study, questions about circumstantial information ("Under what circumstances will this program perform this action?") were answered fastest from the language called 'Nest-INE' (for If-Not-End), and slowest from the Jump style (see Figure 1). On the other hand, questions about sequential information ("Given these circumstances, what will this program do first?") were answered in similar time for all languages. This result was predicted from the finding by Sime et al. that subjects debugged their programs in far fewer attempts when using Nest-INE.

Clearly, these results support the second hypothesis better than the first; and they are not predicted by the arguments of the structured programming school, which are based exclusively on the presence or absence of good structure.

Statement of Problem

Fry: everything which is juicy but not hard
Boil: everything which is hard
Chop and roast: everything which is neither hard nor juicy

Solutions in three different micro-languages

Jump

```
     if hard goto L1
     if juicy goto L2
     chop roast stop
L2:  fry stop
L1:  boil stop
```

Nest-BE

```
if hard then
   begin boil end
else
   begin
   if juicy then
      begin fry end
   else
      begin chop roast end
end
```

Nest-INE

```
if hard: boil
not hard:
   if juicy: fry
   not juicy: chop roast
   end juicy
end hard
```

Figure 1. An easy problem, with solutions in three micro-languages. Naive subjects found Nest-INE easiest for programming (Sime et al. 1977) and professional programmers answered questions fastest from it (Green, 1977).

Gilmore and Green (1984) attempted to push these arguments one stage further. (They also used more complex programs, containing loops as well as conditionals.) The advantage of Nest-INE over its nearest rival, Nest-BE, appeared to be that although the notation was essentially procedural, and therefore biassed towards sequential information, it included cues to circumstantial information. Gilmore and Green reasoned that by comparing question-answering using both circumstantial and sequential questions, and both procedural and declarative languages, it should be possible to demonstrate a cross-over effect, in which the procedural language was the better for sequential questions, and the declarative language the better for circumstantial questions. They called this the 'Match-Mismatch' hypothesis: performance would be good when the language paradigm matched the task. Moreover, they also reasoned that mismatches could be alleviated by cues. The cues introduced into Nested languages had made Nest-INE better than Nest-BE for answering circumstantial questions: could cues reduce the effects of Mismatch conditions when the language paradigm was declarative?

Their results, while clearly supportive, seem to indicate that some cues work much better than others. Their subjects answered questions about programs first from the printed text, then from recall of the text after it was unexpectedly taken away from them. As expected, subjects performed best on 'matched pairs' of tasks and languages. With the 'unmatched pairs', both types of cue improved performance during the second stage of the experiment, when subjects were answering from recall of the text, but during the first part it was the perceptual cues that had the greatest effect.

It would appear from this result that the underlying psychological model of comprehension, as propounded by the structured programming doctrine, is not wrong, but seriously incomplete. At least in our sample, programmers were not simply decoding the programming structure, top-down, into some undescribed mental representation. They were reworking one structure into another. The difficulty of answering questions depended not only on the source structure but also on the relation between source and target structures. (One might also observe in passing that this result appears to raise insuperable difficulties for those simple-minded computer scientists who attempt to measure the 'psychological complexity' of a program by means of a single number, such as McCabe, 1976.)

Program Creation

The conclusion from the psychological literature is that the stepwise-refinement psychological model used by the structured programming school does not lead to adequate predictions of the effects reported for program comprehension. What about writing programs? The great mass of amateur domestic programmers have gone for Basic: is that just because Basic is there, or have they voted massively with their feet - a vote of No Confidence in languages like Pascal which prevent 'hacking' and evolutionary development?

An interesting study in this area, by Hoc (1983), reports on the performnce of students being taught structured programming techniques, using the LCP method. This method, a top-down approach, requires five steps: the structure of the output is described; the structure of the input is described; the program structure is 'deduced' from the previous two steps; the structure is flowcharted; and the flowchart is coded. Studying performance on simple business problems, Hoc found that, even at the end of training,

- only 40 to 70 percent of the subjects showed structural compatibility between the input file and the program structure (which, as Hoc put it, "contradicts the author's idea of a deduction" of the latter from the former);
- only 50 to 70 percent of the subjects preserved the program structure, 'deduced' in step 3, in their flowchart version, even though it is supposed to be isomorphic;
- and that is because only 40 to 50 percent of the subjects present correct first descriptions of the input and output files, and these errors are frequently corrected when the flowchart is written.

Hoc suggests that top-down design fails because it runs counter to two clearly apparent characteristics of novice performance. First, the beginner cannot readily describe procedures except in terms of their execution: a static analysis of structure is difficult for novices. Second, the strategies and algorithms known to beginners are learnt in non-computer contexts, and they are not always well adapted to a computing context; but this fact does not become apparent during top-down design until part of the program has already been designed.

However, the first of Hoc's explanatory suggestions, the difficulty experienced by beginners in creating static structural descriptions, raises deeper issues. A recent study by Ratcliff and Siddiqi (1985) shows this very clearly. These authors used a problem which could be decomposed into two different structures, which we shall call D1 and D2. In their first study, carried out over 129 subjects from a variety of educational backgrounds at which they were studying computer science as a major subject, they found that over 90 percent favoured one structure. Why should one structure be so overwhelmingly preferred, especially as, in the authors' opinion, it was less satisfactory in terms of modularity than D2, the alternative? In their second experiment they timed 20 computer science students, trained in stepwise refinement, in the task of inserting elementary actions into a skeleton. The elementary actions were the 'content' of the program, while the skeleton indicated the program's control structure (Figure 2). Subjects who received the skeleton for D2 took over 50 percent longer than the D1 group to find the solution (median times 15 minutes for D1, 23 for D2).

Closer examination of performance, and the results of a third study, led the authors not only to concur with Hoc's suggestion that their subjects appeared to conceive a program via its execution path, but also to conclude that the process of program development, despite their training, was still rudimentary: "Basically, the first stage involves isolating familiar subgoals which lead immediately or eventually to one or more of the processing requirements being fulfilled. A partial solution steered by the separate achievement of each subgoal is then developed and the remainder of the design subsequently made to conform. We apply the term 'incremental design' to such goal-driven strategy; its somewhat bottom-up character can be summed up by the phrase 'do what you can and make the rest fit around it'." (p. 86).

In short, it is extremely difficult for even computer science students to obey the precepts of stepwise refinement to their full extent. Perhaps one could retort that of course it's difficult, that programming is difficult, and that's why training is needed. But before dismissing the difficulties of students it would be wise to look more closely at what students are really doing, instead of what a normative theory says they should be doing. This is the topic of the next section.

PROGRAMS AS PLAN STRUCTURES

A very different view of a program is that it is a vehicle to express the composition of 'plans'. Each plan contains knowledge about how to achieve a certain goal within the medium of the programming language. Adelson (1981) showed that, after reading a program whose lines had been scrambled, experts attempted to impose an organisation on it when they recalled it, while novices did not do so; experts were apparently seeking plans within the program. This line of analysis, associated with the work of Soloway and his colleagues, leads to rather different conclusions about desirable properties of languages and support environments.

Descriptions of Plans

Waters (1982) showed that real-life programs could be successfully analysed into a set of producer-consumer components, which he called PBMs (program building methods). The very simple program in Figure 3A would be analysed as shown in Figure 3B. Each PBM can supply data to another, or it can receive data from another, but it has no other form of influence over it.

The underlying hypothesis of Waters was that the PBM was the unit of programming knowledge. One of the difficulties of programming, if that is true, will be the fact that in the program code, parts of PBMs are not contiguous but are interleaved with parts of other PBMs.

Although Waters had visions of a Programmer's Apprentice which could supply and integrate PBMs as required, the PBM has also become the basis of the descriptions of program plans developed by Soloway et al. (1983) and by Rist (1985). Rist distinguished between several types of plan, of which the most basic is the Pplan.

3A. A program fragment before analysis:

```
      x := 0;
      j := 1;
loop: if a[j] < 0 then x := x + a[j];
      j := j + 1;
      if j < n then goto loop
```

3B. Analysis by 'temporal abstraction' into PBMS:

```
A. Counting:
      j := 1
      j := j + 1
B. Termination:
      loop: ...
      if j < n then goto loop
C. Filter:
      if a[j] < 0 then ...
D. Augmentation:
      x := 0
      x := x + a[j]
```

Figure 3. Program analysis, following Waters (1982). The aim is to produce fragments which only interact in the fashion of producer and consumer: A -> B -> C -> D.

A typical Pplan expresses knowledge about how to find an occurrence of something - say a word in a dictionary, a value in an array, a record in a file. Rist describes this plan in the form shown in Figure 4; this is a much more complex knowledge unit than the PBM. Rist writes, "The plan links three levels of abstraction. The goal, which is usually the result of the plan, links the plan to the specification and design process. The goal itself is used as an index into the plan and forms an abstract label. The plan is used in plan translation and simulation. The code is used to implement the plan and contains the links to the goal within the program code. It expresses how the goal is integrated into the plan. Note that the plan can be, and often is, used when the goal itself (?X) is still poorly specified. In that case, it provides a powerful method of refining the goal from the problem specification into a form that can be used within the plan.

"Other including or included plans package the plan within its usual plan environment. The 'found' plan makes no sense, nor is it ever used, outside the context of a loop or sequence that presents examples of the category of ?X. ... A third type of link indicates the optional plans that often occur with the plan."

Rist notes also that the links contain a large amount of redundant information, which is an important advantage of the approach. When one plan is identified, there are strong guides to further development of the design or comprehension processes that inform and constrain search.

```
Goal: find an occurrence of ?x
                    CODE                              PLAN TERMS
Plan:       ?found := false;                   initialise to 'not found'
            [loop through category of ?x]
               if ?x then ?found := true;      set to true when found
               ... := ?x;                       use it when found

Variations:
         i) loop using ?found as an end test
        ii) loop using ?found within the loop
       iii) a marker to be used outside the loop

Included plans: none
Optional plans: store ?x instance when found
```

Figure 4. Description of a 'Pplan' for finding instances of objects (Rist, 1985).

How are Pplans used? Rist suggests that they are combined into common packages called complex Pplans or CPplans, as shown in Figure 5, containing indices to subsidiary Pplans and indicating their role in the CPplan, and also containing the extra code needed to calculate the average. Further plan types distinguished by Rist include Abstract plans, derived from different ways of satisfying the same goal, such as a 'loop' Aplan which indexes different looping constructs available in a language; Specific plans, which are more complex and are designed for a specific goal, such as a particular sort algorithm; and Global plans, very general schemata that are abstracted over many different plans. Although global plans remain rather under-specified in the present state of this theory, the existence of similar high-level schemata is postulated by many other cognitive theorists.

Support for this type of analysis of programming knowledge comes both from studies of Pascal programmers and from its general consistency with other attempts to characterise knowledge acquisition and use. Rist's record of the verbalisation of a novice programmer finding a way to check for prime numbers sounds very familiar: "I have the number 2, that's in the array already, I have the number 3 and I need to check it. I need to check it with all those that are in there already, hold onto that thought ... a[1] to a[k] incrementing k when I find one ... I've got i and k numbers to compare it with ... WHILE a[j] <> 0." Compare that to the equivalent record from an expert in Rist's studies: "..and yes, there's a classic kind of loop test, get what we want or we don't have any more to look at".

Goal: calculate the average of all ?x

	CODE	PLAN TERMS
Plan:	sum plan	find the sum of ?x
	count plan	find the number of ?x
	[zero error test]	
	?average := ?sum / ?count	calculate the average
	... := ?average	use average

Notes: ?average must be type REAL

Figure 5. Description of a 'CPplan' for computing an average (Rist, 1985).

Rist's studies were very small scale: few programmers, and limited to Pascal. Taking his results at their face value, however, it appears that his novices characteristically made a cursory analysis of the problem at hand to identify the problems needed, and then coded the program 'from the front'. New plans were added and existing ones modified as they went. Experts, in contrast, explored the program more, by tracing back through the requirements of the goals to identify the plans and storage needed at a fairly detailed level. Only then would they start writing pseudo-code or program modules, and they would proceed by expanding goals, starting from a 'focal line' in the process part of a module, rather than by using top-down process and control refinement.

It might be argued, of course, that Rist's experts should have used top-down refinement. But their methods seem to be typical of experts in other fields, in that they used what has been called backward chaining of goals, as demonstrated in the reasoning of physics experts, for instance (Larkin, 1981).

Role-expressiveness

The outcome of the programmer's effort is an information structure in which each part has some role vis-a-vis the original intention of the programmer. One can point to any part and ask, "What does that do? Why did you need it? How is it related to the other parts of this structure?". Easy program comprehension requires role-expressiveness in the notation, which in turn requires:

1. rapid chunking into components;
2. visible or easily inferred purposes for each components part (intensional semantics);

3. and visible or easily inferred relationships between each part and the larger structure (extensional semantics).

Following the arguments presented in the context of the studies of sequential and circumstantial information, the particular components to be sought will vary with the user's task. If Rist and Soloway are correct, the components are frequently plans rather than individual statements.

In a recent lab study at this Unit, Gilmore tested some of these ideas by asking computer science students to search for errors in short programs, from half a page to one page long, written in either Pascal or Basic. The programs exemplified simple plans, such as averages and totals. Four categories of error were deliberately introduced:

- surface errors, such as undeclared variables, minus instead of plus, or missing quote signs;
- control structure errors, such as missing begin-end, or wrong construct used;
- plan errors, such as a missing increment, inadequate guard, or wrong initialisation;
- structural interaction errors, with a plan structure interacting with a control structure - eg, initialisation in wrong place, or read-process-read errors.

Three program styles were used, the first being for warm up. Two errors were introduced for each presentation of each program, although subjects were not aware of this, and each error type was used 5 times in the latter two programs. The subjects' task was to find and describe these errors.

It was expected that the reader's access to structures, and thus to the errors, could be improved by introducing perceptual cues. Control structures were cued by indenting, plan structures by colour highlighting (Figure 6), and all four combinations of no cueing, one type of cueing, or both types were compared. The predictions, and their outcomes, were as follows:

- surface errors, which were not cued, should not be affected by the different cueing conditions; and the results showed no significant effects.
- plan errors should be, and were, located significantly more often in the conditions in which they were cued (an average of 73% located when cued, as against 38% when not cued).
- control errors should be located significantly more often in the conditions where they were cued. This effect was present but weaker.
- interaction errors should be located significantly more frequently in the condition where both types of cueing were present; this prediction was <u>not</u> supported, possibly because the colour cues dominated the indentation cue when both were used simultaneously.

Curiously enough, this promising result was by no means supported by the parallel results for the equivalent Basic programs. No significant differences emerged! At the same time, the Basic subjects also described the errors they found in very different terms from the Pascal subjects, very frequently not attempting to describe the nature of the error at all and instead giving a program patch. For instance, instead of a description such as "The division by N, to get the mean, has no guard against the case when N is zero", which the Pascal subjects might give, the Basic subjects might report that "The program needs IF N=0 GOTO ... inserted". One is forced to conclude that they thought in terms of roles and plans a great deal less than the Pascal subjects used either by Rist or by Gilmore, although whether the difference is purely due to the notation or is also due to the characteristics of the subject sample cannot be decided at present.

To summarise the current status of plan structures as studied by Rist and by Gilmore, interpretations have been found that combine the elements of computing science, drawn from Waters's work, and cognitive science. These interpretations (such as Rist's Pplans) have worked well in Pascal in two very different paradigms, but they failed when Basic was used. At present the work in this area of program knowledge representation is very limited: too few experiments with too few subjects, so that it is difficult to be completely confident of the results at present. The idea of role-expressiveness, put forward here as a partial explanation of the differences between Pascal and Basic, needs further investigation.

THE PROGRAMMING LANGUAGE

Up to here we have mainly concentrated upon the methods of programming. Now we turn to the raw material, the language itself, because here it seems that received views tend to under-estimate human abilities in some directions and over-estimate them in others.

Linguistic Consistency

It is well known among computer scientists that certain languages are 'consistent' in their design. To some degree, consistency can be interpreted semantically: the attributes of classes of objects are inherited by subclasses. Another important requirement, however, is consistency of syntactic form.

The classic form in which to describe a computer language is Backus-Naur Form, a type of context-free phrase structure grammar. It is this form, I suspect, that dominates the thinking of some computer scientists: a language is 'big' if its BNF grammar contains many rules. Yet, as we saw in the Introduction, it is claimed that "the human mind has an incredible ability to understand structures", as Ichbaiah puts it - structures which are not visible in a BNF representation. And without doubt, in many areas of human performance it has been repeatedly demonstrated that performance and learning are improved when a visible organisation can be imposed on the material.

Green (1983) suggested that the van Wijngaarden two-level grammar might be a better model than BNF of the internal representation of syntax. In a two-level grammar, one level contains meta-rules. These generate ordinary rules, which constitute the second level. Two-level grammars were originally proposed for their interesting ability to create a unified representation of the syntactic and semantic features of a language, but their interest as potential psychological models lay in their ability to represent family resemblances between rules. A simple illustration can be given.

Suppose we have three ordinary production rules:

declaration sequence ::= declaration | declaration sequence + declaration

statement sequence ::= statement | statement sequence + statement

letter sequence ::= letter | letter sequence + letter

Because of their family resemblance, all those rules can be replaced by a single meta-rule:

SEQ-ITEM sequence :: SEQ-ITEM | SEQ-ITEM sequence + SEQ-ITEM,

where SEQ-ITEM is defined as one of declaration, statement, or letter. The three original production rules can then be derived by substituting back.

Following this line, Green and Payne (1984) described the idea of a 'set-grammar' representation of linguistic knowledge, based on the postulates that:

production rules operate on sets of objects, not on individuals;

the output of a production rule can be used as a new production rule;

choice of elements from sets is governed by "selection rules";

elements within sets are both syntactically and semantically similar.

A typical selection rule would be that identical members of sets were to be chosen (this would follow the van Wijngaarden approach), or that corresponding members of different sets were to be chosen, etc.

Although this may seem no more than the introduction of a notational convenience in describing a language, as a psychological hypothesis it confers far more power on the human representation of syntax than does the corresponding, single-level, hypothesis underlying BNF, when taken as a psychological model. In particular it predicts that having learnt some parts of a language, others could be deduced by generalisation, in exactly the manner proposed by Ichbaiah. Experiments in the learning of abstract, meaningless syntactic structures have consistently supported this analysis. In particular, a study by Payne (1985; summary in Payne, 1984) showed that of two experimental languages, the easier one to learn was the one that could be described by fewest meta-rules - even though its description in a single-level BNF grammar required more rules than the description of its counterpart. If the human representation of syntax used single-level rules, therefore, the opposite result should have been obtained.

Subsequent work by Payne (1985) has extended both the notation, and the underlying theory. Payne's approach has been based on the analysis of command language use. He advocates the Task-Action Grammar, TAG, as a theory of the user's knowledge of the command language. In a TAG representation, the user knowledge of the task structure is represented by distinctive semantic features of 'simple tasks'. A typical simple task, such as moving the cursor of a text editor, might have features describing the direction and size of movement. The tasks are mapped into the required actions by a two-level feature grammar.

The experiments reported by Payne have lain in the field of interactiye computing, rather than of true programming. For instance, in an experiment requiring subjects to receive, remember, and forward a variety of messages, it was shown that when message syntax varied with semantic role, performance was better than when the syntax variations cut across semantic roles. Nevertheless, when applied to programming the analysis fits extremely well with the plan-level analysis of Soloway and Rist, described above, and puts a further constraint on syntax. Not only should the notation indicate the roles of program components, as required by our notion of 'role-expressiveness' above, but also similar roles should be indicated by similar syntax.

Reading the Notation

Too little attention may have been paid to low level details of programming notations, in the apparent belief that anyone can get used to anything. Many examples offer themselves of notational details that one would wish otherwise: for instance, Green (1980) pointed to the frequent use of the 'significant omission' in language designs, where the absence of a symbol has meaning. The Pascal parameter declaration is one such, where the absence of the keyword 'var' indicates call by value. Programmers who intended call by reference but forgot the 'var' may find the behaviour of their program puzzling, since - as I at least know to my cost - without a physically present sign, one can readily assume that the procedure in question is using call by reference, simply because one meant it to do so and there is nothing to gainsay this assumption. Result: slow debugging. Significant omissions are presumably introduced to reduce typing time, but I wonder how many notation designers have thought about the overall effect of their decision, weighing time saved typing against time lost debugging.

Although few such notational details have been systematically investigated outside the armchair, one issue on which at least some evidence now bears is the readability of functional languages which use heavy doses of parentheses. It is a common enough observation that balancing Lisp parentheses is difficult, and customisable editors like EMACS are often tailored for automatic balancing. This observation is not, however, commonly generalised, nor examined to discover the limits of its applicability.

Schneider et al. (1984) evaluated various delimiter choices, and although they worked in the context of command languages their results may quite likely extend to programming languages. They found that their subjects (professional programmers) could more easily identify different syntactic fields - verb, operand, and option - when the language used 'two-level hierarchical delimiters', space and comma:

```
PUT  BILL,DOG,KENNEL  OPEN,BIG
```

than when only a single delimiter was used, space:

```
PUT  BILL  DOG  KENNEL  OPEN  SMALL
```

A somewhat similar result was reported earlier by Green (1979), who showed that miniature artificial language with no referential meaning were learnt much more quickly when the syntax contained markers to the phrase structure. These results are perhaps not surprising. Yet it must not be overlooked that in some important ways, the grammar of Schneider et al.'s two-level case is more complex than that of the second, and the grammar of my miniature languages with markers was more complex than that of the ones with markers absent or reduced. The moral is that a naive parsing algorithm, such as top-down left-to-right (ie. recursive descent), is not always a good model for human parsing, which appears to use a mixed strategy at least for natural language (King, 1983) and probably, therefore, in other contexts too.

Lisp, as we all know, is full of parentheses. These results suggest that if there were a way to differentiate between at least some levels, readability might go up: but although one could readily enough introduce a greater variety of styles of parenthesis, say round, square, angled, and curly, sooner or later the supply would be exhausted; and in any case, that approach might confuse more than it clarified.

An alternative approach has been investigated by Gilmore (1985), who tried mapping functional language syntax into a two-dimensional tree-like layout (Figure 7). Novices were able to evaluate programs expressed in the tree layouts faster and more accurately than programs in the conventional form of indented layout. Gilmore also tested their ability to write programs; for this, he supplied the subjects with a list of primitive actions from which they could pick with a pointer, the actions then automatically being built onscreen into either the indented form or else the tree form. Once again, speed and accuracy improved in the tree form.

Gilmore's result is one of many that illustrate the importance of perceptual cues. Put at its bluntest, humans are not so good at discerning the structure of a string of arbitrary symbols, but they are pretty hot at differentiating shapes, thicknesses, spatial positions, and other perceptual factors. As Fitter and Green (1979) argued, with particular reference to diagrammatic notations, when relevant information, already present in a string of symbols, is redundantly recoded in a perceptual dimension, it will more easily be comprehended. It would be extremely interesting to see how far these perceptual effects extended into the performance of highly skilled programmers working with real programs.

The present position on notational details might be put thus. Recent work is making it possible to find more adequate means to express those regularities that humans perceive readily, using such devices as feature grammars, and experimental work is supporting the inferences drawn from these developments. This area is beginning to look a good deal more tidy. At lower levels, we have more of a hodge-podge of occasional results, such as those cited on delimiters and on perceptual cues, badly in need of a unifying framework.

IMPLICATIONS

The overall message of this paper has been, as stated, a call for more complex models of human cognition to be incorporated into the practice of computer science. Such messages are worthless unless they can be cashed in specific terms. In this last section I shall address some specific issues. One must beware of seeming to be engaged in amateur software engineering, so let me stress the important fact that these remarks are no more than attempts to communicate between cultures, to show how ideas born of the lab study or of the highly abstract cognitive theory might relate to some recent developments or continuing problems. Certainly they are not intended to teach professionals their business!

Syntax Design Should Use Perceptual Cues

A well-known syntactic ambiguity was the 'dangling else' in the first proposed version of Algol:

```
if A then
      if B then X
else Y
```

Does the else-arm attach to 'if A' or to 'if B'? The problem is to find an unambiguous construction that meets linguistic and psychological criteria.

The solution adopted in Algol 60 was to forbid the construction altogether, creating a more complex grammar by insisting that statements nested inside the if-arm (as opposed to the else-arm) must either be of a type that could not create an ambiguous else-clause, or else be surrounded by statement delimiters. Not all users realised that the reason why a nested for-statement needed delimiters was that a for-statement could govern an if-statement, thereby potentially creating a dangle. Moreover the resulting rules are specialised to conditionals: mastering the conditional structure does not give insight into other structures, nor vice versa, so that the consistency criterion sketched above is not met. Green (1980) argued that the user's perception of the grammar of Algol 60 conditionals probably included exception rules, since the BNF form was so complicated and, to many users, arbitrarily so.

Other languages have found other solutions: for instance, every 'else' can be attached to the most recent 'if' (Pascal), so that the else-arm above attaches to 'if B', unless delimiters are introduced to change the scoping. Or a 'fi' can be compulsorily attached to the end of the statement to terminate its scope (Algol 68):

```
if A then
        if B then X fi
        else Y fi
```

These solutions all modify the <u>syntax</u>. The solution adopted in BBC Basic, on the contrary, modifies the <u>semantics</u>. When an 'if' arm fails, the interpreter looks for the first 'else' it can find, and proceeds from there. Thus if A is false, Y is executed; and Y is also executed if A is true but B is false. The meaning of the syntax depends on the truth values. Ho hum.

All these solutions appear to have disadvantages. The Algol 60 solution creates a difficult syntax, which is also inconsistent with other Algol 60 constructs; both that and the Algol 68 solution create forgettable scope markers (forgetting 'fi' or 'end' is a common error). The Pascal solution can be misread, and can also cause trouble when modifications are required: given

```
if A then X
else Y
```

the user who discovers that 'X' should be guarded by say 'if B then X' must now apply a special test to the surrounding context: "Is the conditional I have just introduced followed by an 'else'? If so - and <u>only</u> if so - then scope markers will be compulsory." Better to make scope markers compulsory in the first place, some say; but then the closing scope marker can be forgotten ... The BBC Basic solution is the most hideous of all, of course.

Certain recent languages (B; Occam) have pioneered the use of indentation as a direct indication of scope, so that the form

```
if A then
        if B then X
        else Y
```

attaches the else-arm unambiguously to 'if B'. Although no empirical tests have been reported this solution should be highly successful. The syntax is simple, the cues are highly salient to a human reader, and there are no forgettable scope markers.

The virtues of the B/Occam solution may be more apparent than real. But they agree with the Gilmore results on tree layouts, described above; and if real, they should be taken to heart as principles for language design in other contexts. Perhaps the real question is, Why did it take so long to find that solution?

Syntax Should be Role-Expressive

Arguments presented above led to the conclusion that the design of the syntax should allow readers of programs to discern the functional role of each program components without undue difficulty. Many programming languages are not, in fact, particularly role-expressive. An extreme example is Micro-Prolog, a CP/M version of standard Prolog.

In Prolog many clauses can be interpreted as declarative role-expressions of constraints. There is no syntactic differentiation between 'input parameters' and 'output parameters', as there is in most languages; instead, Prolog seeks to satisfy each clause by finding appropriate bindings for any unbound variables in any of the arguments to that clause. This means that we can express Lisp-like list construction very simply:

```
cons(x, y, [x|y]) :-   .
```

This clause means EITHER "cons of x and y produces the list [x|y]" OR "given the list [x|y] you can split it into the (head) component x and the (tail) component y". In the second meaning, cons is essentially being used in the reverse sense: what was an 'output parameter' has now become an 'input parameter'. While this certainly has its uses, my point is that reading that clause will give the reader no clues as to how 'cons' is to be used; whereas reading a conventional Lisp definition, in which the arguments are clearly differentiated from the result, will tell the reader more about the role of that definition in the given program.

The Micro-Prolog dialect adds to the reader's troubles by restricting identifiers to the exceedingly abstract forms x0-x9, y0-y9, and z0-z9. Moreover, the syntactic clues are further reduced by using round brackets, rather than square, for list structures; and the overall 'chunkability' is reduced by using more bracket-pairs than in Standard Prolog. The equivalent definition becomes:

```
((cons, x, y, (x|y)))
```

Thus Micro-Prolog is weak on all three of the role-expressiveness requirements listed above.

One might hazard the guess here that role-expressiveness tends to detract from the re-usability of program fragments. When a program fragments makes its role and purpose very clear, it is probably not easy to transport it unchanged to a new environment, because its role may be slightly but significantly different. However, I have no data on this conjecture.

Syntax Should Map Roles Consistently

Lisp is another language in which the syntax is weak on role-expressiveness. Even worse, it is inconsistent in its mapping from role to surface syntax. A recent experiment by Domingue (1985) displays this aspect of Lisp very clearly. Domingue's purpose was to gain data for an automated programming advisor, for which it was useful to him to observe that many of the errors could be trapped with a cliche library or else by some simple checks. What would, of course, be still more useful would be to predict at least some of these language hotspots from theoretical grounds, without needing expensive experimental testing. Successful predictive ability would allow designers to improve the original notational design (although that might be a bit late for Lisp!) or else to foresee what facilities an automated programming advisor might usefully be able to provide.

Domingue recorded all interactions by nine experienced Cobol programmers while they learnt Lisp from a standard text, and then classified their errors. Many of their errors were standard Lisp errors, too familiar for comfort to anyone who has learnt or taught the language; for instance, putting extra brackets around atoms in some contexts, or omitting them in others. This problem, so frequently observed, could be remedied by reworking Lisp syntax so that the different contexts could be visibly differentiated. When we observe that over 60% of his errors were notational problems of that sort, it is clear that the syntax creates trouble for novices.

Many of these hotspots appear to involve inconsistency in the mapping from role to syntax. An example is the method of indicating formal arguments in Lisp. A simple function might begin

```
(DEF F (X)
     (G X) (H X) ...)
```

Here, occurrence of argument X is bracketed in one context but not in others. While there are good structural reasons for this, they are not appreciated by novices, and the difficulties novices experience in knowing when to bracket are very well-known. This is not surprising; there are very large numbers of 'mal-rules' - rules which describe part of Lisp but not all of it - that novices can form while learning. One way to reduce the inconsistency might be by this slight change:

(DEF F (ARGLIST X) ...)

Other well-known syntactic inconsistencies can be found in the Pascal use of semicolons and begin-end delimiters. These too are frequent sources of problems for novices.

Choice of Program Paradigm

The early programming languages all used the procedural paradigm; Hobson's Choice. But that has been joined by many others: object-oriented, declarative, logic programming, data-flow, applicative, ... Quite a choice problem. I mention it to indicate that psychologists do not have all the answers! Virtually no work has been reported on the comparison of paradigms, and indeed almost all reported studies on the psychological aspects of programming have been limited to the old work-horse of procedural programming.

The Programming Medium and the Development Cycle

The reign of the VDU as unsurpassed medium of input may be drawing to a close. It is interesting to speculate on the effect of the input medium on the design and use of the programming language. A speech input programming system has recently been described by Crookes et al. (1985), working in a modified form of Pascal. The program words and symbols are spoken one by one and are recognised by a sophisticated isolated-utterance recognition device. The vocabulary size of this device is quite small, of the order of 100 utterances; and quite apart from this upper bound fixed by the hardware, performance of such devices usually drops quickly (both in speed and accuracy) as the vocabulary size increases, because each target is compared linearly to each stored vocabulary item, looking for the best match.

For effective recognition performance, the team have therefore used the highly constrained nature of Pascal to narrow the number of candidate utterances to be considered, taking advantage of both syntactic and semantic constraints. A syntactically correct program is guaranteed by this process. Programs are edited using a structure editor in order to preserve the guarantee of syntactic correctness, since the entire constrained recognition method would be fouled up if the program were ever allowed to become ungrammatical.

No criticism is intended of the experiment, but brief experience with it prompts one to consider how voice input would become fully integrated into program development. The seed that prompted Crookes et al.'s experimental system was consideration of handicapped people unable to write or type their programs. Pascal was adopted because it allowed contemporary voice recognisers to be used, taking advantage of the syntactic constraints, but the choice of Pascal with a structure based editor also means that a program has to be almost fully prepared before it can be dictated to the computer. Pascal syntax does not allow forward commitments to be postponed: identifiers must be declared before use, arrays must be dimensioned early, procedures cannot be mentioned before they are defined, etc. Where the input system relies on a structure based editor which enforces all such syntactic constraints, one would expect that the program developoment cycle would include a substantial paper-and-pencil stage during which the initial plan is elaborated into a fully-formed program. It might be difficult for handicapped persons, unable to write and therefore unable to elaborate their plans on paper, to dictate Pascal.

More generally, this extremely interesting experiment has highlighted the way in which structured program development alters the development cycle. Incremental program development, much favoured by the Lisp community, is replaced by the attempt to get the program right first time; exploration at the VDU is tarred with the same brush as uncontrolled hacking. The stage of program elaboration, whether or not it proceeds by the stepwise refinement method, is squeezed out of the VDU medium and onto the paper medium.

If new media are to be introduced, we shall have to reconsider. The program development cycle must be taken as a whole; when one part is changed, we must look at the effects on the other parts.

Comprehension Aids

Programmers use a variety of tools, such as tracers, filters, and analysers, to help them to understand programs. Recent developments show indications of supplying more of the types of information that, according to our analysis, they will need.

Take, for instance, tracers. The earliest tracers, which of course worked with procedural languages, gave sequence information, in the form of a 'footprint trace' showing the path taken by the program. According to our analysis, such information would be less useful in procedural languages than in declarative languages, because procedural languages already display the sequence information reasonably well; it is circumstantial information that is obscured.

On the other hand, the footprint trace of a program written in a declarative notation should be a highly effective addition to the programmer's armoury. An interesting example here is the Prolog Trace Package, PTP (Eisenstadt, 1985). Being primarily a declarative language, but with some degree of procedural content, Prolog can be a hard language for debugging. Programs consist of clauses which assert that a given relation can be taken as true if some other set of relations can be taken as true; where arguments occur in clauses, they must be unified - ie. an interpretation must be found in which the same argument has the same interpretation throughout a clause. Prolog seeks this interpretation by depth-first search with mildly constrained backtracking. Each clause to be proved becomes a goal which may generate subgoals.

The standard Prolog interface tells the user that an assertion could, or could not, be proved, but gives little other information. Eisenstadt's trace package operates by recording the Prolog program's operation in complete detail, and then offering the user a retrospective view, with the ability to zoom in on different parts of the goal-subgoal tree in any detail desired. By distinguishing visibly between different reasons for failing to prove a clause, the programmer is given much helpful information.

Moreover, the PTP tracer can also offer clues to the likely source of certain bugs. Searching the trace, it can identify clusters of symptoms which suggest errors. Some of these clusters can be identified on the basis of the trace alone; others need also a 'cursory inspection of the users' source code', as Eisenstadt puts it. Examples of the type of symptom that can be detected include 'Subgoal-fails-after-all-resolving-heads-tried-and-failed', and 'Cut-used-as-protector-of-earlier-subgoals-accidentally-fails-parent'. Unfortunately explanation of these symptoms depends critically on technical aspects of Prolog and would be out of place here.

It is clear that Eisenstadt's trace package, although it was in fact an ad hoc creation, can be analysed as a solution to a mismatch problem: Prolog programmers need sequential information from a declarative language. Indeed, it goes farther, and the search for symptom clusters offers guidance at the plan level.

Another impressive ad hoc creation which can be analysed in our terms is the DOXY system of Fischer and Schneider (1984), which helps Lisp programmers to comprehend the structure and purpose of large programs. DOXY maintains a knowledge base, partly provided automatically by static analysis techniques (yielding knowledge of the call graph, side effects of functions, etc), and partly provided by the programmer (descriptions of the algorithm used, etc). This information is held in structured frames. During the evolution of a program the system attempts to maintain its knowledge, both by recomputing the parts provided automatically and by inviting the user to update the user-provided parts when touched.

Program documentation, Fischer and Schneider point out, has to serve different purposes for different consumers. They distinguish the needs of designers, programmers, clients, and users. A variety of tools are provided to enhance DOXY for their differing needs, amongst which are browsing tools and filters. These filters can be defined by the user, to supply particular views of the program and to hide complexity irrelevant to the user's purpose. The filters are perhaps the most striking aspects of the system, helping to overcome the problems highlighted above of mismatch between the user's needs and the notation's properties.

One final example of a comprehension aid is the system for interactive program verification being developed by Back and Hietala (1984), with which users can move through their program text (written in a simple but by no means trivial language) testing whether particular verification conditionals are true at particular points. Users can offer assumptions to help the background system achieve a proof, using an advanced windowing display. Informal observation of users at all experience levels reveals that at times they perform activities very much like verifying that particular assertions hold at particular points in the program, so here again we have an example of a tool well fitted to the user's needs. Verification techniques, however, are closely related to the doctrines of structured programming, and indeed they supplied the initial impetus; so I am happy to close by acknowledging the enormous and continuing impact of those doctrines, and repeating that what we need is to extend them, not discard them.

CONCLUSIONS

The advancement of applied technique, such as programming, marries prevailing beliefs at the theoretical level with inspired but ad hoc creations. Frequently these creations, being uninterpretable at the theoretical level, cannot be generalised. They remain bound to the particular areas where they were conceived, and lead to no parallel developments in related areas.

The set of beliefs about cognition that underlay structured programming allowed impressive advances in the technique of programming. The argument of this paper is that it is time for these beliefs to be modernised. Laboratory based research has revealed phenomena that cannot be accommodated into the older model: the representation of programs as plan structures, the importance of alleviating mismatches between the programmer's task and the information structure, and the probablity that certain notational 'hotspots' can be predicted from the language design. At least some of the interesting contemporary developments in programmer support can be fitted into the newer views. Doing so, I claim, increases the likelihood that these developments can be made more fruitful.

At the same time it would be silly to suggest that every aspect of, say, Fischer and Schneider's DOXY or Eisenstadt's PTP can be given a theoretical underpinning. In fact, on some questions, like the choice between different programming language paradigms, theory has as yet very little to say. Inspired, but ad hoc, creations will continue to be a major source of innovation.

ACKNOWLEDGEMENTS. - I am grateful to David Gilmore, Jean-Michel Hoc and Rachel Bellamy for their helpful comments on an earlier version of this paper.

REFERENCES

Adelson, B. (1981) Problem solving and the development of abstract categories in programming languages. Memory and Cognition, 9, 422-433.

Back, R.J.R. and Hietala, P. (1984) A simple user interface for interactive program verification. Proc. INTERACT 84, 1st IFIP Conf. Computer-Human Factors.

Crookes, D., Murray, E., Smith, F.J. and Spence, I.T.A. (1985) A voice input programming system. Unpub. MS, Queen's University, Belfast.

Domingue, J. (1985) Towards an automated programming advisor. Tech. Report 16, Human Cognition Research Laboratory, Open University, Milton Keynes.

Eisenstadt, M. (1985) Retrospective zooming: a knowledge based tracing and debugging methodology for logic programming. Int. Joint. Conf. Artificial Intelligence, 1985.

Fischer, G. and Schneider, M. (1984) Computer supported program documentation systems. Proc. INTERACT 84, 1st IFIP Conf. Computer-Human Factors.

Fitter, M.J. and Green, T.R.G. (1979) When do diagrams make good computer languages? Int. J. Man-Machine Studies, 11, 235-261.

Gilmore, D.J. Unpublished Ph.D. thesis, University of Sheffield, Sheffield, UK.

Gilmore, D.J. and Green, T.R.G. (1984) Comprehension and recall of miniature programs. Int. J. Man-Machine Studies, 21, 31-48.

Green T.R.G. (1977) Conditional program statements and their comprehensibility to professional programmers. J. Occupational Psychology, 50, 93-109.

Green, T.R.G. (1979) The necessity of syntax: two experiments with artificial languages. J. Verbal Language and Verbal Behavior, 18, 481-496.

Green, T.R.G. (1980) Programming as a cognitive activity. In H.T. Smith and T.R.G. Green (eds.) Human Interaction with Computers. London: Academic Press.

Green T.R.G. (1983) Learning big and little programming languages. In A.C. Wilkinson (ed.), Classroom Computers and Cognitive Science. New York: Academic Press.

Green, T.R.G. and Payne, S.J. (1984) Organisation and learnability in computer languages. Int. J. Man-Machine Studies, 21, 7-18.

Hoare, C.A.R. (1981) The emperor's old clothes. Comm. ACM, 24, 75-83.

Hoc, J-M. (1983) Analysis of beginner's problem-solving strategies. In T.R.G. Green, S.J. Payne, and G.C. van der Veer (eds.) The Psychology of Computer Use. London: Academic Press.

Ichbaiah, J. (1984) Ada: past, present, future. An interview with Jean Ichbaiah. Comm. ACM, 27, 990-997.

King, M. (1983) Parsing Natural Language. London: Academic Press.

Larkin, J. H. (1981) Enriching formal knowledge: a model for learning to solve textbook physics problems. In J.R. Anderson (ed.), Cognitive Skills and their Acquisition. Erlbaum.

Mayer, R.E. (1976) Comprehension as affected by structure of problem representation. Memory and Cognition, 4, 249-255.

McCabe, T.J. (1976) A complexity measure. IEEE Trans. Software Engineering, 2, 308-320.

Payne, S.J. (1984) Task-action grammars. Proc. INTERACT 84, 1st IFIP Conf. on Computer-Human Factors.

Payne, S.J. (1985) Unpublished PhD thesis, University of Sheffield.

Pennington, N. (1982) Cognitive components of expertise in computer programming: a review of the literature. Tech. Report. 46, Cognitive Science Dept., University of Michigan.

Ratcliff, B. and Siddiqi, J.I.A. (1985) An empirical investigation into problem decomposition strategies used in program design. Int. J. Man-Machine Studies, 22, 77-90.

Rist, R.S. (1985) Program plans and the development of expertise. Unpublished MS., Dept of Computer Science, Yale Univ.

Schneider, M.L., Hirsh-Pasek, K. and Nudelman, S. (1984) An experimental evaluation of delimiters in a command language syntax. Int. J. Man-Machine Studies, 20, 521-535.

Sheil, B.A. (1981) The psychological study of programming. Computing Surveys, 13, 101-120.

Sheppard, S.B., Kruesi, E. and Curtis, B. (1981) The effects of symbology and spatial arrangement on the comprehension of software specifications. Proc. 5th Int. Conf. Software Engineering, 207-214.

Shneiderman, B. (1980) Software Psychology. Cambridge, Mass.: Winthrop.

Shneiderman, B. and Mayer, R.E. (1979) Syntactic/semantic interactions in programmer behaviour: a model and some experimental results. Int. J. Computer and Information Sciences, 8, 219-238.

Sime, M.E., Green, T.R.G. and Guest, D.J. (1973) Psychological evaluation of two conditional constructions used in computer languages. Int. J. Man-Machine Studies, 5, 105-113.

Sime, M.E., Green, T.R.G. and Guest, D.J. (1977) Scope marking in computer conditionals: a psychological evaluation. Int. J. Man-Machine Studies, 9, 107-118.

Soloway, E. and Ehrlich, K. (1983) Empirical studies of programming knowledge. IEEE Trans. Software Eng., SE-10, 595-609.

Van der Veer, G.C. and van de Wolde, G.J.E. (1983) Individual differences and aspects of control flow notation. In T.R.G. Green, S.J. Payne, and G.C. van der Veer (eds.), The Psychology of Computer Use. London: Academic Press.

Waters, R.C. (1982) The programmer's apprentice: knowledge based editing. IEEE TRans. Software Eng., 8.

Vesey, I. and Weber, R. (1984) Conditional statements and program coding: an experimental evaluation. Int. J. Man-Machine Studies, 21, 161-190.

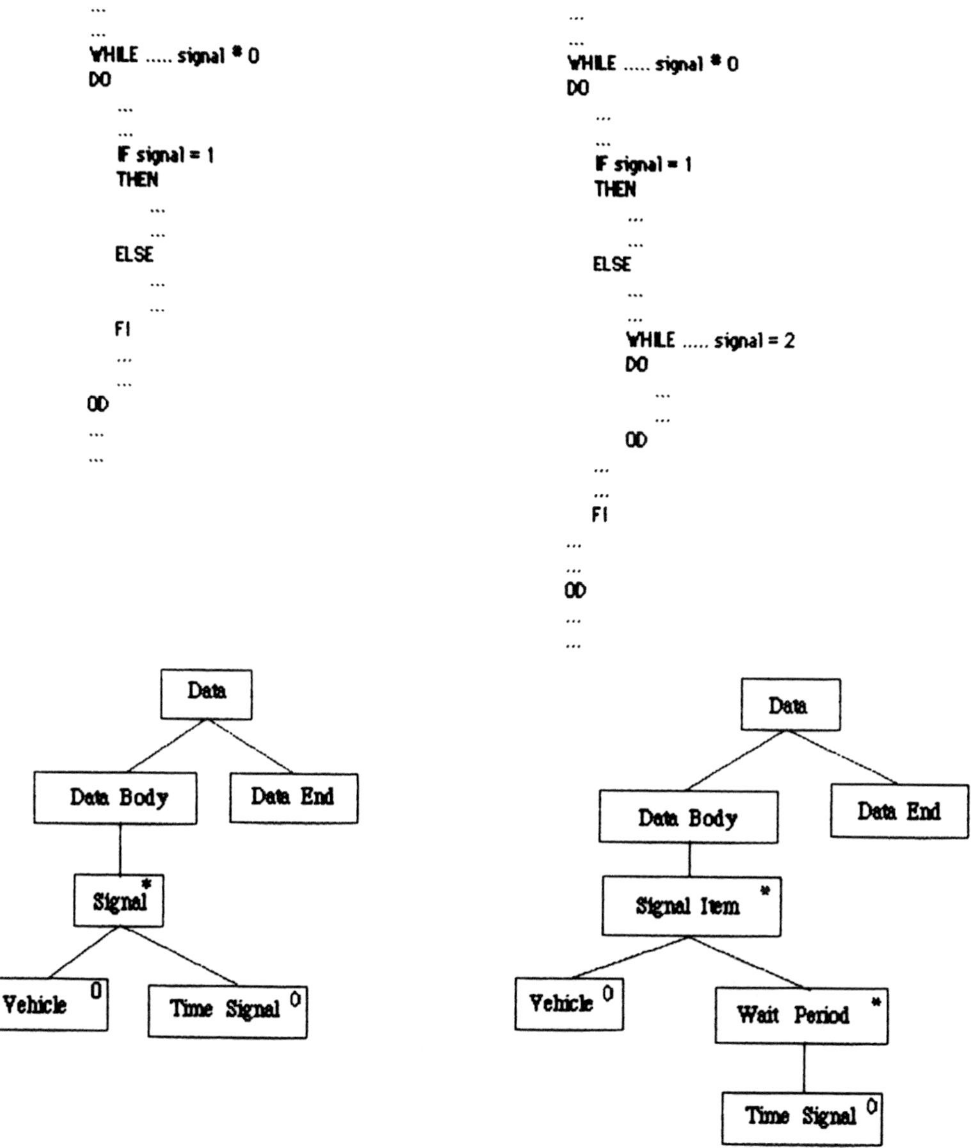

Figure 2: Decomposition strategies used by Ratcliffe and Siddiqi (1985). Above, the skeletal forms presented to subjects; below, the corresponding Jackson diagrams.

```
10   program prob25;
20   var totalrain, days, rainfall : integer;
30       averain : real;
40   begin
50       totalrain := 0;
60       days := 0;
70       wetdays := 0;
80       repeat
90               writeln('Noah, please enter todays rainfall - ');
100              readln(rainfall);
110              while rainfall < 0 do
120              begin
130                 writeln('Rainfall cannot be negative, Noah!!');
140                 writeln('Please enter today's rainfall - ');
150                 readln(rainfall)
160              end;
170           if rainfall > 0 then
180           begin
190              wetdays := wetdays + 1;
200              totalrain := totalrain + rainfall
210           end;
220      until wetdays = 40;
230      averain := totalrain / days;
240      writeln('Average rainfall was ', averain);
250      writeln('Number of dry days was ', days - wetdays);
260  end.
```

Figure 6. Sample program from Gilmore's experiment. Control highlighted by indenting, plan structure by coloured background, shown here by shading. This program contains a surface error ('wetdays' not declar and a plan error ('days' not incremented).

The highlighted plans link (a) lines 50-60-200-230-240;
(b) lines 70-200-250;
(c) lines 100 to 160.

```
IF ( greater ( length ( [a b c] ), length ( [2 3] ) ),

     IF ( islist ( letterlist (2) ),

          length ( [1 2 3] ),

          length ( [d f] ) ),

     length ( [a e i 4 3] ) ) = ?
```

(a) Indented ('prettyprinted') text

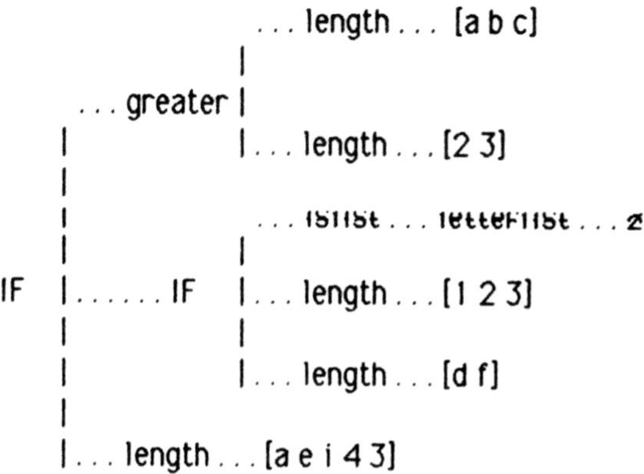

(b) Tree diagram

Figure 7. Alternative layout styles (Gilmore 1985). Performance was better with the tree diagram. Read as "If the length of [a b c] is greater than the length of [2 3], then the answer is ...
if the letterlist of 2 is a list, then the length of [1 2 3],
otherwise the length of [d f]
otherwise (ie. length of [a b c] not greater than that of [2 3]), the answer is the length of [a e i 4 3]."

PANEL DISCUSSION

ON

WILL ARTIFICIAL INTELLIGENCE MAKE HUMAN FACTORS OBSOLETE?

Wednesday 7th of August, 1985 at 15.30 hours.

Chairman and organiser:	Dr. Bill Curtis	MCC, Austin, U.S.A.
Panel Members:		
	Professor G.Fischer	Univ. of Colorado, U.S.A.
	Dr. T. Green	MRC APU, Cambridge, U.K.
	Mr. A.I. Watson	UKAEA, U.K.
Contributors:		
	Major A.L.Lake	Royal Artillery, U.K.
	Prof. N.G.Leveson	Univ. of California, Irvine, U.S.A.
	Mr. J.Musa	AT&T, Bell Laboratories, U.S.A.
	Dr. E.Bedrosian	The Rand Corp., U.S.A.
	Mr. P.Mellor	City Univ., U.K.
	Ms. J. Clapp	The MITRE Corp., U.S.A.
	Mr. E.R.Branyan	General Electric Co., U.S.A.
	Dr. R.W. Selby Jr.	Univ. of Maryland, U.S.A.

Dr. Curtis. The topic we are going to discuss has several interpretations. We shall start by trying to distinguish among three fields, those of human factors, of cognitive psychology, and of cognitive science. In classical human factors we have inputs to a human and his outputs, i.e. what this human does. Processes occuring in-between are treated as irrelevant. We do not care if there is anything inside the head; it is treated as a black box. Something comes in and you behave in a certain way - that is all. Traditionally human factors were a part of behaviourism where you study behaviour and do not care about cognitive issues.

Cognitive psychology assumes that if we understand the human information processing that occurs inside the head, we can better understand how people solve problems. For instance, we can predict more accurately what the effects of different kinds of displays, or of information presentations, are going to be.

NATO ASI Series, Vol. F22
Software System Design Methods. Edited by J.K. Skwirzynski

Cognitive science has several definitions, but for this panel I am concerned with its attempts to make human cognition computable. It tries to construct a theory of how human information processing works, and how to abstract this into a program that can instruct a machine. Then we wish to see if the machine behaves in the same way as a human behaves in the same circumstances. This approach links cognitive psychology to artificial intelligence (AI). There are several definitions of AI. One involves the attempt to make machines do things that people currently do better. There are several ways of stating this, the one quoted here appears in a popular AI textbook by Elaine Rich (5).

These fields represent different views on what the psychologists do. Some of them pay attention to the ways we think, others do not care about it. The question of whether artificial intelligence will replace human factors depends on how you define human factors.

We are now building extremely complex systems that people have to deal with; adding more intelligence to the system and taking some of the control decisions away from the operator. One important issue that arises is how much control should an operator have over a system? This will depend on how intelligent the system is , and under what conditions we want to take away certain decisions from people and put them into machines, assuming that machines can have available the necessary knowledge and can work with it faster.

The first speaker today is Professor Gerhard Fischer from the University of Colorado, who gave here a lecture on bringing intelligent knowledge-based systems into the human-computer interface (1).

Major Lake. I have a question. What is the relation of human factors to the man-machine interface problem?

Dr. Curtis. The man-machine interface problem is an application of the human factors theory. There are several interpretations here. Some people say that in analyzing man-machine interactions, we should only worry about inputs and outputs, others worry about human information processing.

Professor Fischer. If I have an answer to the question in the title of the panel, then my answer is: NO! AI will definitely not make Human Factors obsolete. However, it will and can make a major contribution to the research on Human Factors, and some problems which AI tries to solve will require a major effort in Human Factors.

I believe that there are two goals for AI research: the first one is to replace human beings and the second one is to augment human intelligence, to amplify it and to allow humans to do things with the assistance of computers which they could not do without them.

Let me now state that I strongly believe in the second goal and our research has focused on it. Human and machines should form some kind of symbiotic system. This is not only my view, but you can find the same view in the book by Feigenbaum and McCorduck (2) on fifth generation systems. They claim that most knowledge-based systems are intended to be of assistance to humans. They are almost never intended to be autonomous agents. If we believe in this, then a human-computer interaction subsystem is a necessity. Therefore the research on Human Factors is of critical importance.

Examples of symbiotic AI systems are: advisory systems, decision support systems, or intelligent user support systems. I discussed these kinds of systems in my lecture (1) and so did Dr. Green (3).

Dr. Curtis told us briefly what Human Factors research is. My view is a little bit different, at least it uses different words. Human Factors research started originally with hardware ergonomics. A result of this research is that we have now flat keyboards to avoid the problem that there is an angle between hands and arms when we are typing. Hardware ergonomics studied questions related to the sensor and motor system. Examples are: how to design a screen which is flicker-free; what is the right angle to look at a screen; what is an adequate background colour? Another typical problem is: how do we deal with systems which have a mouse? We cannot expect to breed humans with three hands, two on the keyboard and one on the mouse. Therefore we must organise the interaction in a way that the number of required switches between keyboard and mouse is minimised.

The new challenge in Human Factors is software ergonomics. Dr. Curtis has told us that we cannot regard the human information processing system as a "black box". If we wish to understand software ergonomics, we have to look into information processing issues like memory, problem solving, decision making and knowledge representation.

There is another level which Human Factors research has to be concerned with social ergonomics. Many computer systems are not isolated systems but they are embedded systems. For example in computer-supported office automation there is the need for an organisational interface which incorporates computer systems in the larger socio-technical structure of an office.

In this panel the participants should have different opinions. Let me try to make a statement where Dr. Green, who speaks next, might have a different opinion. What do we believe are the most crucial problems in Human Factors research?. Is the most important problem in the area of system demonstration? This view assumes that there is a large number of systems (e.g. programming language number 1 to 255) around and we have to find out which is the best one. Or is the most important problem in the area of system development, where we assume that real progress can be achieved by constructing new kinds of systems which overcome the limitations of the current ones?

I believe that many of the approaches in the Human Factors research have been at a too low level. These approaches are tied too closely with the actual level of system development and they study too many transient properties of technology. In the early 70-ies there was a big debate and a large number of papers about interactive vesus batch-oriented use of computer systems. Most papers came to the conclusion that interactive use of computers is bad, because it makes you sloppy in your thinking, due to the fact that it is too easy to do something. Batch systems forced the user to "think harder", because they imposed a big penalty for doing something wrong. Contrary to the results of these studies, almost nobody uses punched cards any more today.

My personal opinion is that we should put emphasis on system development and come up with new ideas how to do things. As an illustration, let me go back to an example of my lecture. In the UNIX system changing a directory in a large file tree (see Fig.1) requires that the user has to type long lines as shown in this Figure. If I mistype just one character I either have to retype the whole line or learn a strange editor. There are some advanced UNIX commands (e.g. POPD, PUSHD) which allow the user to establish a stack of directories and which make it easier for him/her to switch between directories. Human Factors research could study this problem and improve it within the given context. Another approach would reconceptualise the problem and come up with a totally different representation of a directory, namely a two-dimensional tree displayed on the screen. The user could move to a new directory by clicking it with the mouse. Dr. Green (3) has mentioned the EMACS system where some of the commands are difficult to remember. We have integrated a mouse into our EMACS system which reduced the number of necessary commands drastically and made it much easier and less error-prone to deal with EMACS.

These are examples of my claim that there is a need to reconceptualise a problem in a fundamental way and develop a new solution. This is as important (especially in a fast moving field like information processig) as finding out which is the best system in a given class of systems.

I would like to see that the main impact of Human Factors is not restricted to acceptance testing. When humans have to deal with a system after it has been built, they have to learn to adapt themselves to that system, including its insufficient technical solutions. Human Factors specialists should become part of the design teams and they should be involved in the early parts of the design process. Early evaluation should serve as a driving force towards further system construction.

How do we make progress in Human Factors research? The following possibilities exist:

1. Proceed empirically: we built systems and then let people find out what is wrong with them. These systems can be prototypes or mock-ups which illustrate important points of design.

An Example:

Changing Directories in UNIX

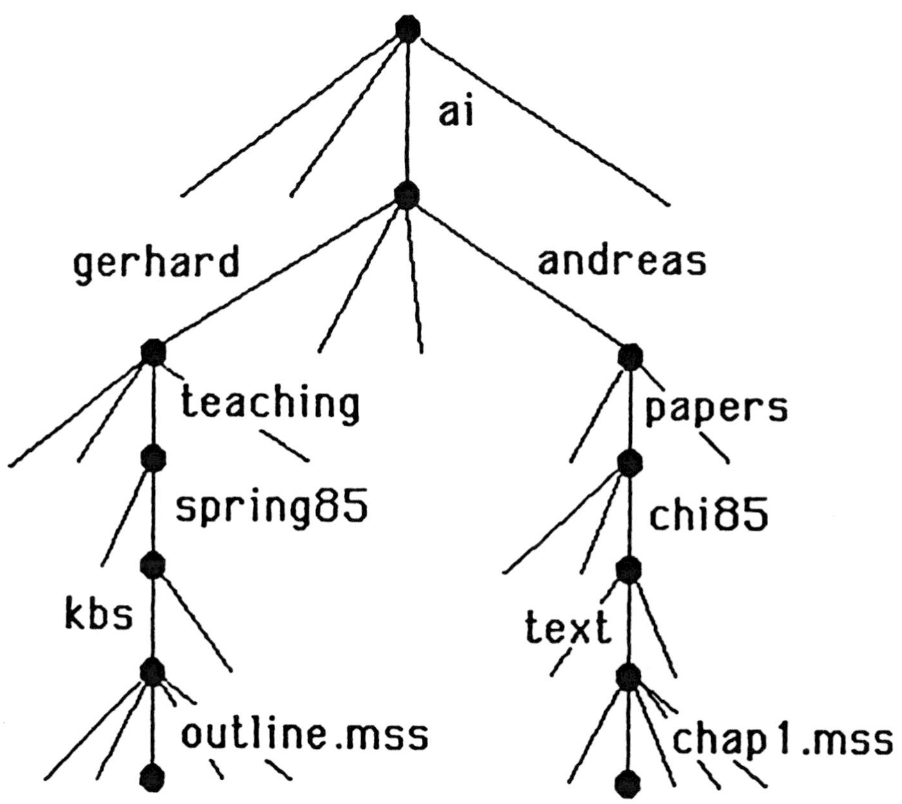

% cd /ai/gerhard/teaching/spring85/kbs/outline.mss

% cd /ai/andreas/papers/chi85/text/chap1.mss

Fig: 1

2. Develop quantitative rules which can be used for prediction: this is the approach taken by Card, Moran and Newell in their book "The Psychology of Human-Computer Interaction" (4) and by Kieras and Polson in their work on "An Approach to the Formal Analysis of User Complexity" (4a). Their models (e.g. the 'key-stroke' model) try to predict, the behaviour of a system before it has been built. These approaches do not expand the design space and they have so far been applied to very low-level skills (e.g. typing).

3. Exploit the potential of new technologies: this may result in new designs but it may lead us into territory where we do not want to be.

4. Study success of models: look at extremely successful developments, e.g. the class of "spread-sheet" programs which are now widely used and try to understand, why these programs are so successfull. What can we learn from such programs? Another very interesting program is the "Pinball Construction Set" by Bill Burge (marketed by Electronic Arts, San Mateo, Calif., U.S.A.) which shows the power of the direct manipulation paradigm in constructing software systems. We have tried to understand success models (see Fischer (6)) and developed a general framework for understanding them.

5. Create interesting visions: a good example for this approach is the idea of DYNABOOK developed by Alan Kay (7) in the late 60-ies, which has led to the developemnt of personal workstations and object-oriented programming. An even earlier vision of a similar kind was a device called MEMEX envisioned by Bush in 1945 (8). Both devices were intended to serve as a general personal, portable and easy-to-use device which would fulfill all the information needs of their users.

Let me articulate a few challenges for Human Factor research:

1. Today (and even more in the future) we have large amounts of computational resources available (despite the fact that many of us still feel a need for more hardware). I was recently invited to a presentation by Texas Instruments and they told us that they will have a LISP machine available in a shoebox, within the next five years. So the important question is: if we have all this computational power available, what will we do with it? New technologies (e.g. modern raster displays, windows, menus, icons, mice, etc. comapred to 24X80 line character terminal) create huge design spaces and there is very little knowledge around to exploit these to the benefit of their users.

2. How can we develop techniques which do not just throw information at us but which take into account that the scarce resource is human attention.

3. This Institute is concerned with reliability. I think we can enhance reliability not only with formal techniques (like program verification, assertions, etc.) but with visualisation techniques which provide insight and understanding into complex structures and processes.

4. One of the goals of Human Factors research is to minimise cognitive effects. This can be achieved by moving from human-computer communication to <u>human-problem domain communication</u> where the domain specific abstractions are represented within a knowledge-based system. This allows the domain expert to deal with a world she/he is familiar with.

Let me conclude: AI can make major contributions to Human Factors research by developing new interesting knowledge-based systems. Human Factors research can enhance AI by providing guidelines to user-centered system design. There is no confrontation between the two disciplines but fruitful cooperation.

<u>Dr. Curtis</u>. The next speaker is Dr. Thomas Green from the Applied Psychology Unit of Cambridge University, U.K., who gave us a lecture on the structure of programming languages (3).

<u>Dr. Green</u>. Dr. Curtis opened by asking what Human Factors research means. One response to the title of this panel is this: if Human Factors means low-level research into how to make truly unpleasant systems slightly less unpleasant, by polishing their details, then the sooner that progress makes it obsolete the better! We cannot go on having systems that anybody's grandmother could improve!

Consider the editor that comes with UNIX, already mentioned. It turns out that your commands make frequent use of the slash symbol, / (see Fig.1). If you then want to edit something which involves that same symbol, which is not at all unlikely in UNIX, you must use something to 'escape' it. What do you find you have to use? You use the back slash, . This means that fairly soon you will have strings of these and other special symbols building up, like this:

s/\/\.\\/.\\\// (change "/.\" to "\./")

I will give you now a Human Factors result. David Olson some years ago compared the discriminability of various pairs of symbols:

/\ [] () | - etc.

Which of these pairs is by far the hardest? You guessed. Anyone could have told them.

That is just one example; in general, the Human Factors aspects of design technology is quite appalling! However, I think that market forces are killing off the most awful systems fairly fast. That kind of really classical mistake will soon go away. And I think that the present emphasis on low-level details in Human Factors research will lessen. Once the need to sort out the really grim designs has gone, we shall see more systematic work with a better theoretical base than it has at present.

Thus the question remains, what will happen in the future? What contribution will AI make at the stage when simple common sense and a few obvious results are no longer enough to improve designs?

I think that the role of studies that involve people (which is what I choose to mean by Human Factors) is going to increase, not decrease. It seems to me that systems now being designed are certain to have more communication problems, as was already pointed out by Professor Fischer. However, I am not sure he brought out fully the problems of ambiguity that can be important in a dialogue like this:

A: Fetch me my file.
B: Which file?
A: You know.
B: No, I don't.
A: Yes, you do.
B: Oh! THAT file!

We have such conversations frequently with people, but it is hard to imagine a machine acting as B until our understanding of inference and reference in discourse has advanced considerably.

We need, in fact, to know a lot more about how person-to-person communication works, how certain messages are sent - such as "I need a clarification please", a message frequently indicated by body language - which at present cannot easily be read by a terminal. Until we incorporate body language, then the natural methods of saying "Look, I'm terribly sorry, but I really cannot understand what you are saying!" are going to be difficult to get into a machine. So one part of my message is: the increasing possibilities being opened by AI will increase the need for a good understanding of human behaviour. Far from making Human Factors obsolete, we shall need more of it.

Another problem is to make sure that we are using the technology in the appropriate way. For instance, we need to make sure that the machine is working with the same class of objects as we humans are. Take for instance some functions of a typical text editor - in particular, suppose I want to change a word. I know that for a single change, I can now use a mouse as a pointer; but if I have spelled Jozef Skwirzynski wrongly, as it is easy to do, and I have misspelt it say 400 times in one document, I don't want to use a mouse, I want a global 'search and replace' facility. All too often, I am now in trouble. Search and replace uses a simpe form of pattern matching programming language, and all too often I am forced to specify the patterns character by character using some version of a regular expression language, which makes it really difficult for me: unless I take special care, the text editor will be unable to match the target phrase with a near version that contains an extra space.

Or if I discover that I have mistaken the gender and I wish to change "hers" to "his" throughout , I may find that the words "feathers" come out as "feathis". And there is absolutely no way to specify that everything that looks pretty much like Skzyrinski should be changed to the correct form. Very frequently what users would really like, especially for words like Skzyrzinski or manaoevre, is something that would go through and change all near misses (Szkyrzinski, Skrizinski, etc.) to the correct form.

Problems like this can easily be solved by existing technology - there is no need to introduce AI techniques. But it takes more than technology to solve them, it takes the attitude of mind that says "Users are having problems. Let's get our there and fix them". So here is the second part of my message: even though we are going to be able to construct far more intelligent interfaces with AI tecniques, making interfaces that are usable as well as intelligent needs user-centered design.

Another kind of problem is going to be the market response, or the social response. Professor Fischer has used the phrase 'social ergonomics'; I am not sure exactly what he meant by this, but it's certainly clear that the introduction of word-processors has caused a certain amount of reshuffling of job roles. In fact you have to design some of these devices so they look like jobs for managers, rather than jobs for secretaries, and design others the other way round - even if the underlying machines are very similar. We do not yet understand much about the social psychology of the workplace, but we are beginning to find out. I certainly class the problems of social impact under Human Factors, so the third part of my message is if the machines we are creating are to be absorbed gracefully by society, then AI technology needs to be supplemented by a great deal of 'social ergonomics'.

Now I want to pick up the argument that Human Factors research is always out of date, because technological advances are unpredictable and full of the unexpected. Professor Fischer has told us how he can now use a mouse to edit the UNIX directory. Instead of those mind-bending commands,

```
cp/usr/thos/programs/stats/ttest/usr/fred/analyses/expt3
```

and the like, he displays the directory and moves programs around by directly manipulating their images on the VDU screen. This is splendid news. Does it invalidate the work of Human Factors? It might seem to, because recently there have been various papers published about sources of difficulty in command languages such as UNIX. But this time round, technological advance is well behind Human Factors research. We already know (and indeed it's fairly obvious) that direct manipulation will reduce certain aspects of the mental load, reduce typing time and errors, increase visual search time, etc. We know what will happen when Fischer's splendid system is available, we do not even have to try it.

So I think we should beware of the argumant that Human Factors research is always going out of date. Topical studies limited to one system do date quickly, of course. But a good deal of research is intended to elucidate general principles of human preformance. This work is essentially future-proof. Human Factors research, taken in the broad sense of including all behavioural science, is not going to be left behind by technology: it is well ahead of technology.

However, neither Human Factors knowledge nor technological know-how is going to replace creativity. To invent Fischer's system, what was necessary was not far-seeing Human Factors research, but someone clever enough and creative enough to think of doing what he did, to find a way to fill a need.

Where I think we should be looking for a contribution from AI to interface design is in understanding more deeply the human cognitive processes and finding ways to support them or simplify the task demands. For instance, in my lecture (3) I gave a description of psychological 'plans' in programming. These plans are interleaved in the final program and are probably not usable by the simplest AI models of planning, only by rather powerful ones such as Sacerdoti's NOAH (9). The art of creating an environment suitable for evolutionary incremental programming seems to me to depend on the ability to produce a programming environment with 'minimal commitment to the future', where programmer can add one step to a program without having to make loads of mental notes about what has to be done next, and where you can also delay decisions until you know what to do. In short, an environment where your plans can be separated out.

This would be an environment which would fulfil the needs of the masses who buy machines to run BASIC and who never want to learn how to design programs - because, like BASIC, it would be a hacking environment. At the same time, it would preserve the tractability and shapeliness of a well-designed program, because it would be high-level hacking - hacking at the plan level, not at the code level. In order to do this we need to understand the process of planning much more deeply than we do at present, and this is an input that is probably going to come from AI.

To sum up:

- the increasing technological possibilities of AI increase the need for understanding human behaviour, and hence increase the need for Human Factors rather than reduce it;
- the route to useable interfaces demands a commitment to user-centered design, not just technical wizardry;
- to design systems appropriate to our social system requires 'social ergonomics', a certain type of Human Factors research;
- at present, we already know a great deal about some areas of Human Factors, and can predict the usability of many suggested systems - but we cannot mechanically design an innovatory system, we cannot replace creativity;

- and finally, I see the most important advances coming from a partnership between AI and Human Factors, in which cognitive processes are understood more deeply and effective ways are found to support them.

Dr. Curtis. Our next speaker is Mr. Ian Watson, who is the head of Systems Reliability Service at the United Kingdom Atomic Energy Authority.

Mr. Watson. Dr. Curtis has instructed me to talk just for ten minutes, and several things I wanted to say were already mentioned by my predecessors. What I want to suggest is that there are considerable differences between AI and Human Factors (HF), (see Fig.2) and, unlike Professor Fischer, I believe that ergonomics is not much concerned with AI. What it is concerned with, at least in industry, is physiology and environment study, and plant safety. Robotics is more concerned with AI, so is man-machine interaction. There is a lot of work in this country in the chemical and process industry about man-computer interaction.

Other issues concerning AI and HF are decision support, intelligence (which relates to human intelligence), and finally sensory perception.

I do agree with Professor Fischer that AI and all its manifestations will not replace human beings. What we need is to augment human potential and activities. Non-humans will not replace us; how can they replace our political, moral and ethical appreciations?

Dr. Curtis has said already that there are a lot of parallel issues in both AI and in HF. One is the cognitive science, which is concerned with knowing, but at its fringe there is yet another issue, namely the meaning. Also cognitive psychology emphasises this. It is concerned with humans as constructive beings, and not just black boxes, in terms of their behaviour. It is interesting that both AI and HF draw very heavily from the ideas of computer science, particularly in the areas I have already mentioned.

It is our experience that humans do not tend to optimise; in complex situations they just try to make things good enough. This is something well worth understanding. I am aware of this, for as an engineer, I am concerned with assessment of designs of systems.

There are certain inadequacies in cognitive psychology, which I will list:

- it analogises BRAIN FUNCTIONING, that is thinking, with COMPUTERISED INFORMATION PROCESSING,
- but science has no explanation of BRAIN FUNCTIONING above the neuron and synapse level operation:
- We do not know how useful is the analogy mentioned above, since it is not a description of REALITY; at least we do not know that it is;
- what sort of description of mental processes do we need for human error assessment?

Q.

WILL A I MAKE H F OBSOLETE ?

1) APPLES V PEARS / ROCKS ?

A I	H F
	ERGONOMICS { PHYSIOLOGY / ENVIRONMENT }
	PLANT SAFETY
ROBOTICS	
M M I (H C I)	M M I
DECISION SUPPORT	D S
PROJ. INTELLIGENCE	HUMAN INTELLIGENCE
SENSORY PERCEPTION	PERCEPTION

Fig: 2

I agree with Dr. Green, when he mentioned the inadequacy of application of known ergonomic information. This, by the way, has severe effects on the safety and reliability of industrial plants.

What we have done at our SAFETY AND RELIABILITY DIRECTORSTE (SRD), in connection with the HUMAN FACTOR AND RELIABILITY GROUP, of which I am now the chairman, is to produce a GUIDE TO REDUCING HUMAN ERROR IN PROCESS OPERATION (6). The contents of this guide include:

- OPERATOR/PROCESS INTERFACE (Display and Control Channels - Paged VDU Displays - Operator's Information - Instrument of Plant Failure - Actions and Effects - Indicators and Codes - Instrument Layout)
- PROCEDURES (Concise Procedures - Mandatory Procedures - Supporting Procedures - Correct Operational Procedures)
- WORK PLACE AND WORKING ENVIRONMENT (Posture and Movement - Environmental Conditions)
- TRAINING (Training Requirements - Training Methods)
- TASK DESIGN AND JOB ORGANISATION (Operator Performance - Operator Assistance - Optimum Operator Activity - Team Responsibility - Operator's Individual Responsibilities - Incident Follow-up). demands.

Personally I think that this is a crucial area from the assessment point of view. In the first issue of this document, there are about 70 questions which designers of systems, including people like yourselves, working in computer engineering should ask themselves in order to ensure that they do relevant things regarding the man-machine interface design.

Now we are in the process of producing a second version of it to augment the data base, since at the moment the data base is widely scattered and it is not collected conveniently for engineers or assessors. What we are trying is to put all this together.

An issue which I do not think that AI can deal particularly well is the issue of management. Good management is very important to plant safety and reliability. There is a good evidence to show this, although in a rather gross form. It is available to the HEALTH AND SAFETY EXECUTIVE (HSE) in the U.K., to the NUCLEAR INSTALLATION INSPECTORATE (NII), and to the CIVIL AVAIATION AUTHORITY (CAA). The famous examples of poor management in the field of application of HF are well known to some of you. They are the Flixborough chemical plant accident, the recent Bhoopal chemical plant disaster, and the Three Mile Island incident.

The management are responsible for task structuring, task supervision, personnel selection and of course the R & D policy. Task structure and supervision are crucial areas regarding reliability. They would have to tackled in a structured understanding of management relationship to technical tasks. This illustrates an area where HF just cannot say much to us at the moment.

In the field of aviation flight simulator training has been a very fruitful HF area, and a lot of useful work has been done. Pilots are now being trained in management, because flying a large modern aeroplane is really a management job. So in very sophisticated simulators, which are now in operation, pilots can now be certified on a simulator, without ever flying an aeroplane. The 767 is an example of this. Is anyone worried about this? (Laughter) In fact, one 767 disaster was not a crash - it was a glide to a successful crash landing - one pilot knew how to glide, he was a glider pilot! The aircraft had a classic common cause failure, when the two engines failed at the same time. The other pilot knew where a race track was based on a disused runway. Thus, between them, they glided to this race track and no one was killed.

Dr. Curtis. The HF issue in this case was that they ran out of the gas, because in 767 fuel is computed in litres and not in gallons. The service crew had made a serious mistake in computing the amount of fuel needed to cross Canada in this new aircraft.

Mr. Watson. This is an example of important issue with HF, namely the recovery from errors. AI has no meaning to the system itself. That is why in my opinion AI can only augment that activity and not replace it.

My conclusion regarding the question raised at this panel is that AI is still at a primitive level, and all that was said up to now supports this statement. HF is useful mainly for issues concerning routine system operations, and AI is now applied to automate routine processes, to improve reliability and to remove drudgery. Dr. Curtis has told me that I am a practical person, so I will show you what we are trying to do in reliability and risk assessment. Here we have a procedure which we call the SYSTEMATIC HUMAN ACTION RELIABILITY PROCEDURE (10). It encapsulates what human reliability assessors, and system reliability assessors are trying to do. This is particularly applicable to the assessment of reliability of nuclear power plants (Fig.3). Here the STEP 1 (Definition) is the production of fault trees to identify where human errors are likely to occur. The next step is screening this fault tree for likely human errors; following that (in STEP 3) we screen the fault tree for significant human errors. This is not just a total error, but rather an error with probability of one. If there are no significant human errors, we go to the end (STEP 7). Otherwise we proceed with the human reliability modelling (STEP 4). I am not going to discuss this in detail, because at the moment I am totally dissatisfied with this situation; we have very few adequate human reliability models to do a good reliability assessmant. I suppose that they are just sufficient in most cases, but often we end up with making rather coarse judgements.

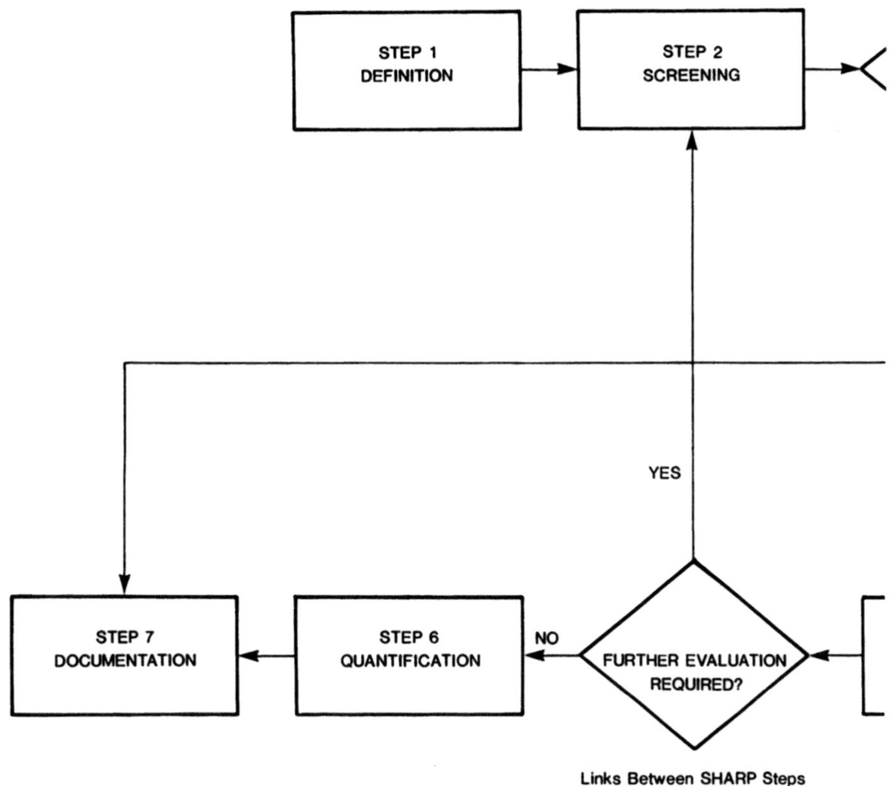

Fig: 3. Systematic Human Action Reliability F

Finally, to take up one point mentioned by Dr. Green, I do believe that more work should be done in this area. There are many reasons that we have problems here, but one of them is that between the specialist researchers and industry there are considerable differences of perspective as to what should be done. The researchers still deal with matters at a fundamental level. I believe that one new thing we should do is to appreciate intentionality and the importance of understanding that is required to uderstand tasks. This can be divided into four parts:

1. Assuming the MENTAL ASPECTS OF A TASK is important, then understanding the intentions and mental models of people involved is also important.
2. The INTENTIONS, and to a lesser extent, the mental models are best appreciated by those having similar experience.
3. The role of engineers in assessing TECHNICAL TASKS, e.g. plant operation, is therefore important.
4. To what extent has the role of INTENTIONALITY been included in HF assessment techniques?

That is the end of my peroration. Thank you.

Dr. Curtis. Before I open the panel to questions from the audience, I would like to make a couple of points. One aim of HF research is to provide better systems to people. One thing we hope to accomplish at MCC is to create better interfaces to complex systems. That means (see Fig.4) that we want to put between a user and an application package, an 'intelligent user interface management system' which allows a specialist, who is a dialogue engineer or interface engineer, to design better interfaces. His special task is to interpret what the person wishes to do and to inform him what the application package can do. We know that 40% or more of the code in many application programs implements the user interface. So the task of this specialist is to do 'dialogue engineering'. He is to provide tools that will create good communication between the user and the application. One HF problem is that frequently we make systems easy for novices, and this is not what experts want. We want to provide a natural language interface to a system, so that people who know little about it can have a natural way to communicate with it. But, as they learn more and more, they do not want this natural language baggage. Rather, they want a more succint form of interaction. As people go from a novice level to expertise, the way they want to interact with a system changes. The question is how do we get the system to recognise what level of expertise a user has, and how does a system have to change to adapt to a user?

To a novice the UNIX is the 'seventh ring of Hell'. To a very sophisticated programmer it is marvellous; everything is available there. They recognise that this system has power and they try to use it. We argue sometimes that there is no inherent difference between the ease of learning and the ease of using, but in practice we see this difference.

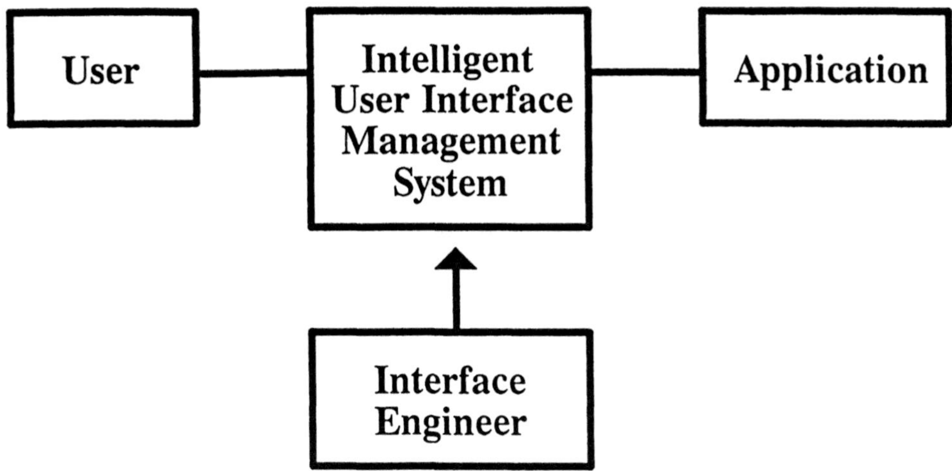

Fig: 4. Intelligent User Interface Management System

What a novice wants is to get a mental model of a system - to understand how does this crazy thing work. What an experienced user wants is a great deal of power available to him - he does not care how it is organised, as long as he can get to it quickly. People change as they operate a system. AI might possibly offer us a method for recognising a user's level of skill, and then to alter the interface to meet his needs.

Another question that typically creates debates is how much you want the system to take over functions of the operator. This is where AI might have a dramatic impact. Thus, we need not worry about HF, for humans are not included in that loop. For instance, do we want the system to take over functions that go below the response time of a human being? This is an important issue in some areas of flight. In a lot of high performance jet fighters the biggest limitation that the pilot cannot respond fast enough to handle some of the new technology.

If you have a situation when somebody has to respond in less than 1/10 of a second to correct a problem that might cause the destruction of a system; you are getting below the response capability of a human being. If at the same time he has to do some cognitive processing, there is no way that he can respond quickly enough. We see this already in automatic pilots. There was a case recently of a 767 aeroplane which has three engines on it, going from Dallas to San Diego.

One of the engines fell off the plane when it was struck by a piece of debris. This is supposed to happen, for engines designed to fall off if something hits them. The automatic pilot knew that, so it immediately corrected for flight with two engines. The human pilot did not know the engine has fallen off, only someone sitting in the back seat saw it. The FAA regulations say that the pilot should then land at the next airfield (Phoenix). He actually flew to San Diego not knowing he was missing an engine.The engine did what it was supposed to do, the automatic pilot immediately picked this up and adjusted itself. There was no need for the pilot to be in the decision loop. However, the pilot might have appreciated a message that he had lost an engine.

There are occasions when we may want to take decision away from a human being beacause he cannot think fast enough or know enough to solve a problem in a safe amount of time. This is a very sensitive question. How do we cue people to critical information in dangerous situations they might meet? Professor Fischer has told us that AI will augment HF; the question is do we want to augment, and when do we want to take it away?

Now I open the forum to the audience

Professor Leveson . Concerning Mr. Watson's comment about the Three Mile Island story, operators there followed to the letter the rules and procedures that were given to them. The problem was that they should not have. It is not quite clear that the computer would have not followed these rules and procedures. What happened was something that nobody thought was possible. There was another case in a nuclear power plant, where a computer did what it was programmed to do, but this turned out to be an error. The only way that a disaster was avoided was that a human operator stepped in. So we have two sides to your panel question: Should we take the decision from the human (when, say the jet engine falls off), or should we give the human pilot the information he needs to make decisions in a critical emergency. If an operator has to take responsibility, then he should be able to have enough information to build a cognitive model, so he knows what is going on and is not thrown into a critical situation without any information or context to make decisions.

Dr. Green. There was a recently published a report, called the Hoogovens report, which raised these very issues. My collegues Max Sime and Mike Fitter have discussed this report (10a) and pointed out that the allocation of responsibility to people and to machines can lead to interesting problems in law. When something goes wrong, who is responsible? The consequences,as seen by society, might dependend on the nature of the job. Consider a charge-hand at a steel works, whose job is to produce a particular mix of steel.

At a Sheffield steel mill my collegues studied, there was a system for computer assistance which helped the operator to mix the required grade of steel. This is often quite difficult - you may go past the required grade, by adding too much of one ingredient, and then you may have to make this steel for a different batch on the order book. An error under such conditions may cost the company a large amount of money. If the charge-hand does not do what the computer advises, then he is in a very different position from a hospital consultant who disagrees with a computer diagnosis, even though the logical grounds may be the same. The social positions of a charge-hand and of a consultant are so different that such questions of responsibility are no longer in the domain of technology or of AI.

Mr. Musa. There is another realm of that I would like to bring into discussion. Dr. Green inadvertedly raised this in my mind when he mentioned 'high-level hacking'. Perhaps high-level hacking is something that managers are doing with projects. This brings up the issue of program evolution. Rapid changes in specifications can be a problem. How is HF involved in this, and how can AI help in this?

Professor Fischer. I have tried to understand the evolution for quite a while and I am convinced that this is an important topic for the future. We just cannot assume that complex systems will not change after they were originally developed. Our systems have to fit an environment of needs which is in almost all cases not completely defined in the specifications for the original system development.

There are problems with evolutionary models. One of them is that they are myopic. After we have reached a local maximum, then wherever we go from there, we have to go downhill. The QWERTY arrangement on typewriters came into existence, because typing had to be slowed down to avoid jamming keys. This is not a design requirement any more, but people who tried develop other keyboards have not been too successful. What is neccessary to overcome shortsighted solutions is to sit back, take a broader view and do small scale experiments. Before a system is released we should test it in a small context, because if humans have spent a large effort in learning something, then there is a lot of resistance to unlearn it.

There was a panel in 1974 during the IFIP world congress in Stockholm, where a question was asked: "Will there be a FORTRAN in 1980?" Most of the computer scientists on this panel answered the question negatively. In 1985, we can claim that they were wrong. They did not understand that after people and organisations have made a large investment in something, there will be a large resistance against change and a few new features in a programming language are not important enough to FORTRAN users to abandon their known territory.

Mr. Watson. I think I can take this analogy a bit further to answer Mr. Musa's question. One technique of optimisation is hill climbing using triangular mapping. You just keep moving a triangle about, looking at values at its vertices. You can change the size of it and possibly find another local maximum. It is the manager's job to expand this triangle sometimes and see if we can find something better.

Mr. Musa. If I uderstood the panel correctly, you are saying that managers should be encouraged in high-level hacking. Many people at lower levels of a project find this a great problem in motivation, when parts of project are cancelled.

Mr. Watson. A good manager has to know when to do that, and often he may have reasons for not doing this.

Dr. Green. My comments on high-level hacking were concerned with an individual making a plan, rather than with a team relationship. The point that Professor Fischer has made about social resistance to change and about inertia were rather interesting. My opinion is that it would be desirable to have an environment where an easily changed structure was the one in which you were ready to think.

Dr. Curtis. How do we manage to get a product that sells well? Some person creates one utility, then another person creates another utility, and so on. Then somebody sees the possibility of combining these utilities and says:'Hey! We have a product here - we must get it on to the market!' Often there is no consistency between different parts of a system when we are all hacked together and customers complain. This is a part of HF.

The problem in such cases is that there is no consistency of thought - for people who have programmed the pieces were mostly building something for themselves, and were not worried whether anybody else could possibly understand how to use it. We see this in products of very large companies. That is the reason why we want to establish an intelligent user interface management system, to create a class of engineers who can build consistent interfaces to a broad range of computer applications.

Dr. Bedrosian. How will speech recognition work out with AI?

Dr. Green. Dr. Crookes of Belfast (10b) has recently produced a speech-driven PASCAL machine. I was very impressed with it, you can just seat there and dictate PASCAL to his machine and it is very good at recognising what you are saying. But if you consider this method of program development as a complete system, then it is less convincing. The system was designed for someone who had developed arthritis in the fingers and could no longer easily use a pen or a keyboard.

Yet he would not be able to use this machine effectively, because it is very difficult to dictate PASCAL from scratch without working it out on paper first.

So the answer to how speech recognition is going to help us is that it will depend on he circumstances. In speech you have to rely on your own short-term memory, so if you put speech recognition into an interface you have to design your system so that you do not overload your short-term memory.

Dr. Curtis. Using speech recognition is going to require associated developments in natural language processing. We can now use speech recognition for isolated words, or single commands to computers, but we cannot present a sentence to it, and have it easily parsed into component words. Even if we could parse a sentence, it would have to be readily unerstood.

Mr. Mellor. I could not help noticing here that hard-line enthusiasts of AI are not evident on this panel. I can recall seeing a TV programme, when an American expert, I think it was Dr. Feigenbaum, was interviewed. His opinion was that computers were developing in power so much, that very soon they would not need us humans. He gave as an example the fact that we have recently learned to communicate with apes. They were taught a few words of American sign language and everyone was keen to learn what the apes would tell us. Unfortunately all that they were interested in was where the next banana was coming from! He thought that computers of the future will be like that. They will be on a higher mental plane and not interested in our lowly thought processes, though they might occasionally condescend to play games with us, throw us the odd banana, so to speak. Nobody here even gave a hint of that view. Do I take it that the AI community now regards the 'hard line' AI position, as exemplified by this man, with the contempt it deserves ?

Professor Fischer. I think the relevance of your story depends greatly who the interviewed person was. Was it a scientist or a science fiction writer?

Mr. Mellor. He was definitely introduced as a computer specialist, and not a science fiction writer.

Professor Fischer. Some of the problems AI is concerned with have not made too much progress over the last twenty years. Concerning the question raised by Dr. Bedrosian, understanding spoken language is far away from the goal of understanding a general conversation. Most of the AI researchers are aware of these limitations and a number of AI problems to remain to be solved in the future is very large.

I am not worried (despite the fact that I consider myself working in AI) about the picture which Mr. Mellor has illustrated: here are clever computers and there are the dumb humans, and we will become second class objects because we are not smart enough.

Mr. Watson. Another analogy is that the operation of modern aircraft does not make birds obsolete.

Dr. Curtis. There was an article published recently on the gradual encroachment by AI (11). This is exactly what we have observed with computer languages. Mr. Capers Jones claims in his book (12) that 60% to 80% of all programs are still written in COBOL, even with the introduction of newer languages. The issue of knowledge acquisition is still a massive task. Ruven Brooks estimates that it takes one and half times as much time to produce an expert system, as it is to produce an original expert. So the acquisition of knowledge is going to be a very gradual process. We are not going to be replaced by computers anytime soon.

Mr. Mellor. Yet some researchers of AI seem to take the view that computers can actually possess consciousness, intelligence and intentionality of their own.

Dr. Curtis. If you look right now at most cognitive models, they are based on von Neumann's notion of 'one in - one out' processing. We are in the infancy of developing a model of how people think that involves how our brain operates in parallel. Until we understand how we operate, we cannot expect to implement human intelligence into machines.

Mr. Mellor. We are not finite-state machines, while computers, even though they have parallel processing facilities and variable interconnectivity, are. Finite-state machines can be described by Turing's mathematical model.

Ms. Clapp. I am concerned that we still do not know what the goal is in AI research and in some areas of the HF research. I see two goals that both sets of specialists ought to have in common. One is to understand the functions of human understanding, and the other is how to employ your research to solve some problems. I think that it is very important to decide on your research goals, because you might be doing research for its own sake, when you intend to be useful.

I can give you some examples of useful goals. People talk of knowledge acquisition - this should be applied to the process of developing systems. If we use what is considered as conventional software engineering, we still have to understand requirements; this is the process we need to go through. We have heard here that we are not doing it well. I think that HF researchers should tell us why we are not doing it well, or what means we can use to communicate better. For example, we could do something interesting with graphic notation, which is useful for system designs.

I will give you one more example concerning the study of factors in the selection of programmers. You need to understand what really affects productivity. TRW is spending a lot of money preparing a proper environment for programmers. They have designed rooms with user's work stations, where programmers have their own computers, program storage, access to larger computers, and tools to help. After a year, TRW asked their people: 'Are you more productive?'. They answered positively and were asked 'Why?' Their answer was: 'Because each one of us has his own room now, and we have good access to computers and we have documentation tools'. No mention was made of other tools. If you look at cost, documentation is about 20% of the effort. Yet you concentrate on coding skills. There are surely other parts of the process that need looking into. So my question is, do you realy look at what is happening in the large, and pick a major problem to solve, rather than getting wrapped up in minutiae?

Dr. Green. The sort of problems for us psychologists is that a classical PhD in experimental psychology starts up by saying that there exists a really large problem and there are five theories, each of which, if accepted, would have an enormous impact on the future of society for the next thousand years. Five pages later you find the author discussing whether it's easier to learn a list of words if you present some of them in red. You cannot do experiments in the 'grand' - you have to do them in the 'small'. You have to base experiments on attempts to create principles that can then be applied much more widely.

What we need is to regard communication between person-to-person or person-to-machine in a more systematic way. The questions that you raised about documentation, specification languages and graphics notations should be referrable to psychology of notation which recognises that different classes of user will have different needs. It would be nice to point to general principles by which to design a particular piece of documentation. You should make your point about avoiding minitiae quite often, and insist on it. I am on your side.

Dr. Curtis. Academia is not close to applied problems, so they worry about general principles. They tend to select those problems which they can study close at hand. In industry they worry how to make a particular problem go away, and we also tend to be under time pressure, so we do not publish much. You infrequently see the results of studies made widely accross industry.

Where I am now, at the MCC, we are in a sort of half-house between these two. A number of companies do not want us to do a basic theoretical research; they want us to do technology research, which they interpret in terms of products.

I think there is going to be more of that sort of thing, where somebody has to sit in-between and say that there is an important theoretical technological issue we have got to wrestle with, and get a result that somebody can apply. This type of research often goes no further than to pick an application area and give a demonstration of the solution. It is not that this does not happen; it is just not so visible in theoretical journals, because people solving this have no time to write.

Mr. Watson. I would like to answer this. I have already indicated here earlier that from the reliability point of view, generally speaking, we are basically tackling the wrong problems. It is possible that under the heading HF we have the wrong subject. One of the issues I have mentioned was with management, the other issue was the proper structuring of a task, to use the jargon of industry. It has been well known in industry for over hundred years, that people are highly variable and that there are all sorts of personal problems. What the management has to do is to encompass that. What we should be looking for indeed is the proper designof a task. Then we need to look at different problems.

Mr. Branyan. I would like just to say that there is a group in the U.S.A., at the Carnegie-Mellon University, who are not naming as AI the things you are talking about. What you are talking about is the operational research. Their Department of Operational Research have been doing this work, using dynamic programming, for the last thirty years, since computers have come about. The decision making process has been going for a long time and we never referred to it as AI. The rule-based system has been referred to there as the 'Rule-Based Forward Looking Dictionnary'. When we deal with atomic energy plants we use this method to analyse all the possible classes of failures that can come up. Mechanical engineers have been doing this 'rule-based' system for a hundred of years, and again they never referred to it as AI. I do not think that we have even attacked the problem of really understanding the cognitive process. At Carnegie-Mellon they insist in trying to separate these things.

There is a lot of aircraft which cannot fly if they do not have a computer on board; they would literally fail, especially the high-performance weapon systems. It has been proven with a simulator, that if the computer was not there doing algorithmic decisions, these aircraft, or the Shuttle, would fail.

My challenge is not that I am attacking the notion what AI has to do with the cognitive process. We are talking here about AI and about HF, and I agree with things you talking about HF, about keyboards and interfaces. These are things which we tackle with the normal human process ; none of them have anything to do with AI. I challenge you to say that you have drawn no connection between HF (which is a good stuff) and AI.

Dr. Curtis. The systems you are talking about have complete control structure already built-in, and this indeed has nothing to do with AI. What about systems where that control structure does not exist, and you have to go through some inference or reasoning process to come up with an answer in a critical situation?

Mr. Branyan. You did not talk about that. You talked about straightforward 'forward looking dictionnary'.

Dr. Curtis. We are talking about what we should tell an operator. Too often you just flash lots of light in front of him and leave him alone to deduce a critical decision. I am talking about situations in which we want to provide an automated assistant. In some of these situations decisions may have to be reached faster than the human operator can make them. Many of these situations may not have been anticipated by the original designers or programmers. It is under these conditions that the inferencing procedures available in AI may become relevant. An important issue in such situations concerns how much control the machine should wrest from the human operator and when. Another issue concerns how to search through a knowledge base in a machine to determine the most relevant and succint information to present to a human operator.

Professor Fischer. I would support in part what Mr. Branyan has said. There is no fixed boundary between things which are AI and not-AI. During my last year at the University of Colorado, there were many occasions when someone came to my office and told me that they have a linear programming model to solve a problem in Operations Research. Yet there are many situations where we cannot optimise and all we can expect is to "satisfice" (a concept introduced by Simon in his book "The Sciences of the Artificial" (9a)). With more research in Operations Research, researchers in this area may be able to solve a few more problems. It would obviously be stupid to restrict ourselves to satisfaction in areas where we can optimise. The example which I use in my classes to illustrate the limitations of optimising is getting married. A person intending to get married only knows a very small percentage of potential candidates, i.e. there is no way to go for the best solution. All we can say from an objective view is: "Well, this person is good enough" - hopefully in our subjective view we believe that we have found the optimal solution.

Operations Research relies on the fact that we must be able to optimise. AI is able to cope with situations where heuristic search can find a satisfying solution.

AI is considered by some people as a losing discipline, because after we understand a problem more clearly, we may be able to tackle it with more algorithmic techniques (instead of heuristic ones). An example for this is symbolic differentiation and integration which was done mostly using heuristics in the 60-ies, whereas today we can rely on much more algorithmic solutions. These examples provide evidence that the borderline of AI is not sharply defined.

Dr. Curtis. The other problem is that AI covers several fields that are not necessarily related. Also, everybody now talks of AI because research in it is readily founded (Laughter). Some people call it 'Sophisticated Software Engineering', others call it AI.

Professor Fischer. The AI started in the mid 50-ies. Some of today success stories (like the R1 program, developed by McDermott at Carnegie Mellon University to configure VAXes) are built on research work of 30 years. Newell and Simon have begun AI work at Carnegie Mellon University 30 years ago by seeing a computer not as a number cruncher but as a symbolic information processing engine. Studying human information processing has led to many promising research areas in AI and this research has been absorbed by computer science in general (e.g. general dynamic memory structures). Nobody calls this AI research any more, but these ideas were first developed within AI.

Dr. Green. I should like to rebutt the criticism that the panel has not addressed itself to AI. I will try to make three points:

Firstly, as machines get more like people, through the advance of AI, we shall need to improve our understanding of communication between partners, whether they are people or machines.

Secondly, when we consider what AI can bring us, we need to consider the development of system as a whole. The example I used was that as we improve our ability to handle spoken language in real time, which is clearly anAI project, we need to consider what kinds of development systems this can be fitted into.

Thirdly, I have pointed to promising areas for partnership between AI and HF, where AI can bring increased understanding of cognitive processes and thereby help us to simplify tasks and offer support tools. My example here was the 'high level hacking' environment.

Professor Leveson. I received a master's degree in AI a long time ago and then I never quite knew what it was, and now I cannot figure out at all what it is. It seems to contain everything: human intelligence, artificial intelligence, human psychology and a lot more. I remember then being told that we shall make machines like humans; later the argument went that we shall not be able to do that, we can just make them to do the same things as we humans do. I guess that this argument is still going on. I would like to ask what is the definition of AI?

Dr. Curtis. It seems that even somebody sitting in the middle of AI cannot come up with a more precise definition. It means also that AI covers a broad collection of fields. First you need to describe these fields separately from global statements about AI.

Professor Leveson. Would you say that AI is about problems rather than techniques?

Dr. Curtis. Some people who are tring to provide robots with vision, a perceptual problem, and believe that this is AI. Others do not. This is based on their approach to AI, and their belief about how to cathegorize the fields contributing to machine pattern recognition.

Professor Fischer. There are many definitions for AI; one of them is to be (or at least contribute to) a science of intelligence. If there is intelligent behaviour in this world, then there should be a science for it which tries to explain it. For a long time we could observe birds flying. Then we tried to built airplanes and eventually succeeded. These efforts contributed towards a science of aerodynamics. And the science of aerodynamics explains the flying of birds as well as airplanes, even though these objects are quite different. We hope that a science of intelligence may eventually give us a deeper understanding of human intelligence by trying to achieve some intelligence in machines.

Dr. Curtis. In my own mind I distinguish between the understanding of human behaviour and the contents of AI. The machines we try to work with are quite different from a human brain. I do not include cognitive psychology in AI. In trying to understand human behaviour, we almost act as detectives - we do not have specifications for this study. We are not allowed to go about sticking probes into people's heads. We must gather what is going in the human mind from bits and pieces of evidence. In AI we are interested in generating interesting behaviour from a machine, not just explaining it.

Mr. Watson. I think one of the reasons of this confusion is that the cognitive psychology is not using enough analogy with computer science. Whether such use would lead very far, I do not know, but this could be one of the reasons for this confusing definition.

Dr. Selby. Could someone please summarise this discussion in terms of purposes of this panel?

Professor Fischer. I would summarise it answering the question of the panel: I do not believe that AI makes Human Factors obsolete, but that AI can contribute a lot towards Human Factors.

Dr. Selby. Is this good enough?

Professor Fischer. I also said that as systems become more and more complex, we need software which is more intelligent and more responsive to the user than our current systems.

Mr. Watson. I agree with that, but would add that the purpose of AI is to improve system reliability.

Dr. Curtis. There is an almost universal agreement on this panel, that one of our best aims is to develop techniques to be able to make decisions under uncertainty. If we believe we can improves expert systems, or any other systems, to help us make decisions in a very short period of time when facing complex and dangerous situations, this should be investigated. There are tough issues to be resolved when we think what sort of technology we should create, for there are political and social problems to be considered when we try to apply new technologies.

Unfortunately now is the time to close this discussion. I thank you all.

REFERENCES

(1) Professor G. Fischer: 'From Interactive to Intelligent Systems' (in this volume).

(2) E.A. Feigenbaum, P. McCorduck: 'The Fifth Generation. Artificial Intelligence and Japan's Computer Challenge to the World', Addison-Wesley, Reading, Ma., 1983.

(3) Dr. T.R.G. Green: 'Design and Use of Computer Languages' (in this volume)

(4) S.K. Card, T.P. Moran, A. Newell: 'The Psychology of Human-Computer Interaction', Lawrence Erlbaum Associates, Hillside, N.J., 1983.

(4a) D.E. Kieras, Peter G. Polson: 'An Approach to the Formal Analysis of User Complexity', Working paper 2. University of Arizona and University of Colorado, October 1982.

(5) E. Rich: 'Artificial Intelligence', McGraw-Hill, 1983

(6) G. Fischer: 'Computational Models of Skill Acquisition Processes'. In R. Lewis, D. Tagg (editors): 'Computers in Education', pp. 477-481. 3rd World Conference on Computers and Education, Lausanne, Switzerland, North-Holland Publishing Company, July 1981.

(7) A.Kay: 'Microelectronics and the Personal Computer', Scientific American, pp.231-244, 1977.

(8) V. Bush: 'As we may think', Atlantic monthly, 176 (7); pp.101-108, 1945.

(9) E.D.Sacerdoti: 'A Structure for Plans and Behaviour', Elsevier, New York, 1975.

(9a) H. Simon: 'The Sciences of the Artificial', 2nd Edition, MIT Press, Cambridge, MA., 1981.
(10) Systematic Human Action Reliability Procedure, UKAEA.
(10a) M.J. Fitter and M.E. Sime: 'Creating responsive computers: responsibility and shared decision making'. In H.T. Smith and T.R.G. Green (eds.): 'Human Interaction with Computers', Lonodn, Academic Press, 1980.
(10b) D. Crookes, E. Murray, F.J. Smith and I.T.A. Spence: 'A voice input programming system'. In P. Johnoson and S. Cook (eds.): Proc. Brit. Comp. Soc. Human Computer Interaction Specialist Group, BCS Workshop Series: 'People and Computers: Designing the Interface', 1985.
(11) E. Rich: 'The Gradual Encroachment of AI', IEEE Computer, 1984.
(12) C.T. Jones: 'Programming Productivity', McGraw-Hill, 1984.

Part 3

The Development and Status of Empirical/Statistical Reliability Models for Software and their Relation to Reality

Organised by Bev Littlewood and John Musa

Application of Basic and Logarithmic Poisson Execution Time Models in Software Reliability Measurement

John D. Musa
Kazuhira Okumoto

AT&T Bell Laboratories
Whippany, NJ 07981

ABSTRACT

Two software reliability models that share the advantageous property of being based on execution time are presented. They are compared with a number of other published models. Predictive validity is established using sets of failure data from a varied group of software projects and two different parameter estimation methods. The characteristics and advantages and disadvantages of the two with respect to each other are discussed.

1. BASIC CONCEPTS

Software reliability is defined as the probability that a program will operate without failure for a specified time in a specified environment. It is a function of the inputs to and use of the system as well as the existence of faults in the software. A *failure* is an unacceptable departure of program output from requirements. It is distinguished from a *fault* or the software defect that causes a failure. The foregoing definition of software reliability is an *operational* one; it offers the greatest utility to software engineers and managers, since it directly measures the impact on the user of a system.

NATO ASI Series, Vol. F22
Software System Design Methods. Edited by J.K. Skwirzynski

The term "unacceptable" implies that the user must determine what is considered to be a failure; this usually depends on the effect of the particular behavior of the system in question on the user's operation, costs, etc. In fact, the situation is often more complex than "acceptable" or "unacceptable": the user may wish to establish several classes of failures of differing severities and define reliability requirements for each class.

There are two alternative ways of expressing software reliability. The *failure intensity* is the expected number of failures per unit time. The *mean time to failure (MTTF)*, if it exists, is defined as the expected value of the failure interval.

Measurement of software reliability involves estimation of software reliability or its alternate quantities from failure data. The term software reliability *prediction* is defined [1] as the process of computing software reliability parameters from program characteristics (*not* failure data). Typically, software reliability prediction takes into account factors such as the size and complexity of a program, and it is normally performed during a program phase prior to test.

The principal objective of a software reliability model is to forecast failure behavior that will be experienced when the program is operational. This expected behavior changes rapidly and can be tracked during the period in which the program is tested. Reliability or MTTF generally increases as a function of execution time.

2. TWO SELECTED SOFTWARE RELIABILITY MODELS

The first work in software reliability dates to about 1967. Since then, a number of different models have been developed (see [2] for history and survey). Two models will be presented here: the basic execution time model of Musa [3] and the logarithmic Poisson model of Musa and Okumoto [4]. The reasons for the concentration on these two models will become clear after they are compared with a number of other models.

Both the basic and logarithmic Poisson execution time models are based on the premise that execution time (the actual processor time used in executing the program) is the best time domain for expressing reliability. Execution time is the most practical measure of the failure-inducing stress being placed on a program. The foregoing premise has been verified in [5,6]. Both models consist of two components: an execution time component and a calendar time component. The former component characterizes reliability behavior as a function of execution time τ. The latter component relates execution time τ to calendar time t, which is more useful for managers and engineers in expressing when a specified reliability goal is expected to be reached.

2.1 Execution Time Component

The execution time components of these models are defined in terms of a random process $\{M(\tau), \tau \geqslant 0\}$ that represents the number of failures experienced by execution time τ. The process is characterized by specifying the distribution of $M(\tau)$, including either the mean value function

$$\mu(\tau) = \mathrm{E}[M(\tau)] \tag{1}$$

or the failure intensity function

$$\lambda(\tau) = \frac{d\mu(\tau)}{d\tau} . \tag{2}$$

Both models are assumed to be nonhomogeneous Poisson processes*, but they have different failure intensity functions. The basic execution time model has a failure intensity function which decays exponentially with execution time τ, i.e.,

$$\lambda(\tau) = \lambda_0 \exp(-\phi\tau) , \tag{3}$$

where λ_0 is the initial failure intensity and ϕ is the rate of decrease per unit time. The logarithmic Poisson model has a failure intensity function which decays exponentially with respect to the mean value function, i.e.,

$$\lambda(\tau) = \lambda_0 \exp[-\theta\mu(\tau)] , \tag{4}$$

where θ is the rate of decrease per failure. For the basic execution time model, the initial failure intensity λ_0 is given by

$$\lambda_0 = \nu_0\phi . \tag{5}$$

* The basic execution time model was not at first described as a nonhomogeneous Poisson process.

The parameter ν_0 is the expected number of failures in infinite time (note that it is usually finite). The parameter ϕ may be viewed as the (constant) hazard rate that characterizes any individual failure. The failure intensity for the basic model is readily expressed in terms of μ by integration of (3) and some manipulation:

$$\lambda(\mu) = \phi(\nu_0 - \mu) . \tag{6}$$

We obtain a similar result for the logarithmic Poisson model directly from (4):

$$\lambda(\mu) = \lambda_0[\exp(-\theta)]^{\mu} . \tag{7}$$

It will be seen from (6) and (7) that the rate of change of failure intensity with respect to failures experienced is constant for the basic execution time model but decreases exponentially with failures experienced for the logarithmic Poisson model. The latter model can account for nonuniform operational profiles, where some functions are executed more frequently than others. In this case, frequently occurring failures tend to be experienced first. Early repairs therefore have the largest effects in reducing failure rate.

The expressions for expected failures for the two models are, respectively.

$$\mu(\tau) = \nu_0[1-\exp(-\phi\tau)] \tag{8}$$

and

$$\mu(\tau) = \frac{1}{\theta} \ln(\lambda_0\theta\tau + 1) . \tag{9}$$

The name "logarithmic Poisson model" is derived from the form of (9). Plots of expected failures and failure intensity are provided for both models in Figs. 1 and 2, respectively.

The reliability $R(\tau'|\tau)$ for either model at a time τ' measured from time τ is given by [7]

$$R(\tau'|\tau) = \exp\{-[\mu(\tau+\tau') - \mu(\tau)]\} . \tag{10}$$

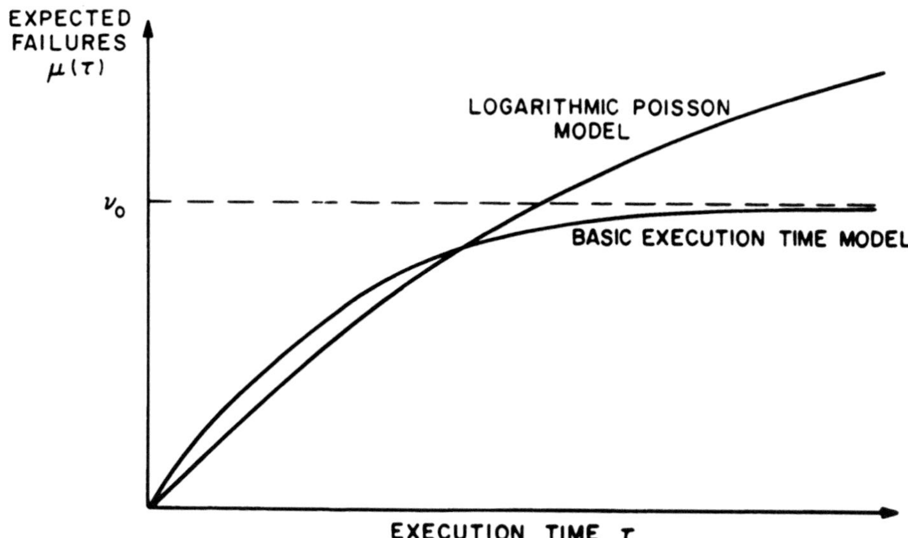

Fig. 1. Expected failures vs. execution time.

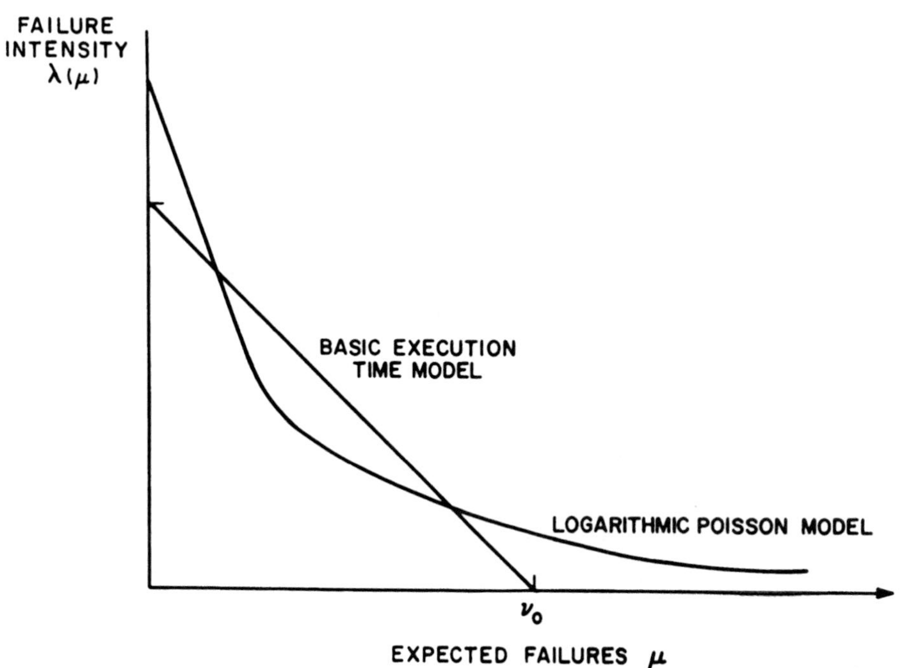

Fig. 2. Failure intensity vs. expected failures.

Expressions for several useful quantities can be derived from (3), (4), (6), (7), and (9), including the additional execution time $\Delta\tau$ and additional expected failures $\Delta\mu$ to be experienced to reach a failure intensity goal of λ_F, given a present failure intensity λ_P. For the basic execution time model we have

$$\Delta\tau = \frac{1}{\phi} \ln \frac{\lambda_P}{\lambda_F}, \tag{11}$$

$$\Delta\mu = \frac{1}{\phi} (\lambda_P - \lambda_F) . \tag{12}$$

For the logarithmic Poisson model

$$\Delta\tau = \frac{1}{\theta} \left[\frac{1}{\lambda_F} - \frac{1}{\lambda_P} \right], \tag{13}$$

$$\Delta\mu = \frac{1}{\theta} \ln \frac{\lambda_P}{\lambda_F} . \tag{14}$$

2.2 Calendar Time Component

The calendar time component relates execution time to calendar time based on resources available to a project. That is, the rate of testing is constrained by the failure identification or test team personnel, the failure correction or debugging personnel, and the computer time available. The quantities of these resources available to a project may be more or less established in its early stages, but increases are generally not feasible during the system test phase because of the long lead times required for training and computer procurement. At any point in testing, one of these resources will be limiting and will be determining the rate at which execution time can be spent per unit calendar time. The test phase may consist of from one to three periods, each characterized by a different limiting resource.

The following is a common scenario. At the start of testing one identifies a large number of failures separated by short time intervals. Testing must be stopped from time to time in order to let the people who are fixing the faults keep up with the load.

As testing progresses, the intervals between failures become longer and longer and the failure correction personnel are no longer fully loaded. The test team becomes the bottleneck. The effect required to run tests and analyze the results is occupying all their time. Finally, at even longer intervals, the capacity of the computing facilities becomes limiting.

The calendar time component of the model is derived by assuming that the quantities of the resources available are constant for the remainder of the test period and that the rates of resource expenditure $\frac{d\chi_k}{d\tau}$ for resource k ($k = C$ for computer time, $k = I$ for failure identification personnel, and $k = F$ for failure correction personnel) can be approximated by

$$\frac{d\chi_k}{d\tau} = \theta_k + \mu_k \frac{d\mu(t)}{d\tau}, \qquad (15)$$

where θ_k is an execution time coefficient of resource expenditure and μ_k is a failure coefficient of resource expenditure.

For both models we find that

$$\frac{dt}{d\tau} = \max_k \left\{ \frac{1}{P_k \rho_k} \frac{d\chi_k}{d\tau} \right\}, \quad k = C,I,F, \qquad (16)$$

where P_k is the resource quantity available and ρ_k the utilization for resource k.

For the basic execution time model we have

$$\frac{d\chi_k}{d\tau} = \theta_k + \mu_k \lambda_0 \exp(-\phi\tau) \qquad (17)$$

and for the logarithmic Poisson

$$\frac{d\chi_k}{d\tau} = \theta_k + \mu_k \frac{\lambda_0}{\lambda_0 \theta\tau + 1}. \qquad (18)$$

The foregoing quantities are plotted in Fig. 3. Note that the difference is due solely to the difference in the failure intensity curves.

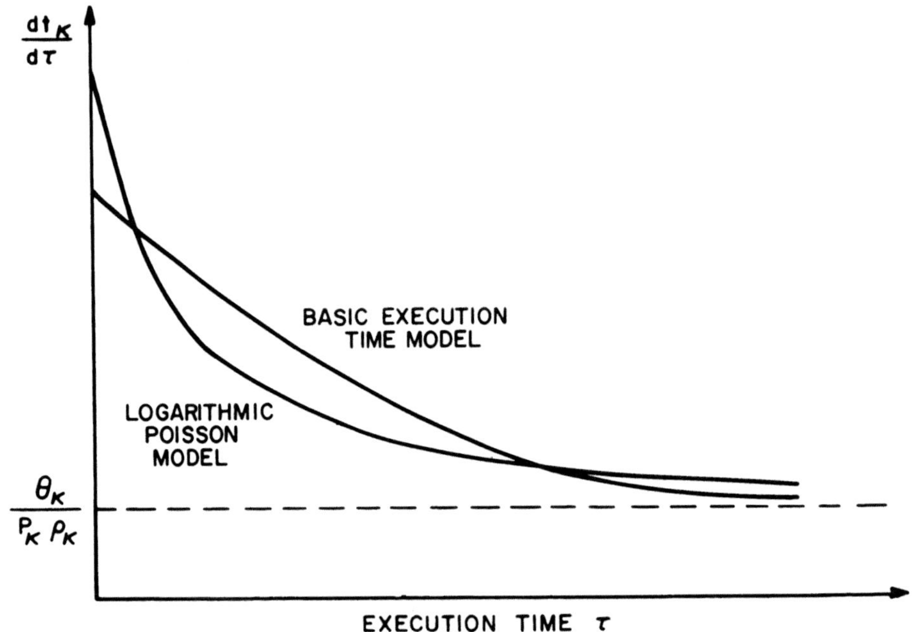

Fig. 3. Instantaneous calendar time to execution time ratio.

2.3 Determination of Model Parameters

In the case of the two models described above, two parameters must be estimated for the execution time components: initial failure intensity λ_0 in both cases, total failures experienced ν_0 for the basic execution time model, and the rate of reduction in the failure intensity per failure θ for the logarithmic Poisson model. Once failure data is available in terms of execution time, these these parameters may be estimated, using a statistical inference method (e.g., maximum likelihood estimation). The accuracy with which they are known generally increases with the size of the sample of failures. The accuracy may be characterized by constructing confidence intervals.

Procedures for predicting the values of the execution time component parameters before failure data is available are presently developed just for the basic execution time model.

The parameter ν_0 may be estimated, prior to test, from the number of inherent faults υ_0 and the fault reduction factor B, since

$$\nu_0 = \frac{\upsilon_0}{B}. \tag{19}$$

The number of inherent faults is dependent on the size of the program. Some data has been taken on average faults per instruction. A range of 3.36 to 7.98 faults/1000 delivered executable source instructions for assembly language programs at the start of system test has been reported [3]. It may be that measures of program complexity can improve the prediction of ν_0; this is an active current research area.

The parameter λ_0 may be predicted from

$$\lambda_0 = fK\nu_0 , \tag{20}$$

where f is the linear execution frequency of the program or the average instruction execution rate divided by the number of object instructions in the program and K is a fault exposure ratio which relates failures to "fault velocity". The fault velocity is the rate at which faults in the program would pass by if the program were executed linearly. It accounts for the following facts:

a. programs are not generally executed in "straight line" fashion, but have many loops and branches, and

b. the machine state varies and hence the fault associated with an instruction may or may not be exposed at one particular execution of the instruction.

It may be that the range of values of K over different software systems is small. This could be due to program dynamic structure averaging out in some fashion for programs of any size. Thus it may be possible to determine a value for K, perhaps as a function of some program characteristic.

There are two categories of parameters that must be established for the calendar time components of the two models; the parameters are the same and have the same values for both models. The categories are planned and resource usage. The planned parameters are established by project objectives and available resources. The resource usage parameters relate to the resources required for failure identification and correction. It is hoped that ultimately values of these parameters can be determined for all software projects or for large classes of projects. The values of the resource usage parameters may be related to such factors as batch debugging versus interactive debugging, debugging aids available, computer used, language used, administrative and documentation overhead associated with corrections, etc.

3. COMPARISON OF MODELS

It is assumed that comparison should be done with relation to a variety of software systems; it does not appear likely that the evaluation of the models will be application-dependent but one must watch for this possibility. It is expected that comparisons will cause some models to be rejected because they meet few of the criteria that we will discuss. On the other hand, there may or may not be a clear choice between the more acceptable models. The relative weight to be placed on the different criteria may depend upon the context in which the model is being applied. However, the criteria have been ranked in approximate order of importance. When comparing two models, all criteria should be considered simultaneously (i.e., models should not be eliminated by one criterion before other criteria are considered).

3.1 Comparison Criteria

The comparison criteria that are described below represent an approximate consensus among a number of researchers in the field [8]. They are:

a. predictive validity,

b. capability,

c. quality of assumptions,

d. applicability, and

e. simplicity.

3.1.1 Predictive Validity Predictive validity is the ability of the model to determine future failure behavior during either the test or the operational phases from present and past failure behavior in the respective phase. Note that "predictive validity" does not carry the connotation of "prediction" in referring to determination from program characteristics. In comparing predictive validity of models, one must keep in mind that differences should be larger than other sources of error (especially measured error) before any advantage can be attributed to one model over another.

We will evaluate predictive validity by attempting to predict number of failures that will be experienced by the end of the period of execution over which data has been collected and compare this with actuals. It is an excellent but not necessarily the only possible approach.

In this approach, the failure random process is described by $\{M(t), t \geq 0\}$, representing the number of failures experienced by time t. Such a counting process is characterized by specifying the distribution of $M(t)$, including the mean value function $\mu(t)$.

Assume that q failures have been observed by the end of test time t_q. The failure data up to time t_e ($\leq t_q$) is used to estimate the parameters of $\mu(t)$. Then, the number of failures by t_q can be predicted by substituting the estimates of the parameters in the mean value function to obtain $\hat{\mu}(t_q)$, which is compared with the actually observed number q. This will be repeated for various values of t_e.

The predictive validity can be checked visually by plotting the normalized relative error $\{\hat{\mu}(t_q)-q)/q\}$ against the normalized time t_e/t_q (Fig. 4). The error will approach zero as t_e approaches t_q. If the points are positive (negative), the model tends to overestimate (underestimate). Numbers closer to zero imply more accurate prediction and hence the better model.

The use of normalization enables one to overlay relative error curves obtained from different failure data sets. For an overall conclusion as to the relative predictive validity of models, we may compare plots of the medians (taken with respect to the various data sets). The model which yields the curve that is the closest to zero will be considered superior.

Note that predictive validity *may* be a function of both the model and the inference procedure.

3.1.2 Capability Capability refers to the ability of the model to estimate with satisfactory accuracy quantities needed by software managers, engineers, and users in planning and managing software development projects or controlling change in operational software systems. The degree of capability must be gauged by looking at the relative importance as well as number of quantities estimated. The quantities, in approximate order of importance, as denoted by the letters, are:

a. present reliability, MTTF, or failure intensity,

b. expected date of reaching a specified reliability, MTTF, or failure intensity goal (it is assumed that the goal is variable and that dates can be computed for a number of goals, if desired. If a date cannot be computed and the goal achievement can be described only in terms of additional execution time or failures experienced, this limited facility is preferable to no facility, although it is very definitely inferior),

c. resource and cost requirements related to achievement of the foregoing goal(s).

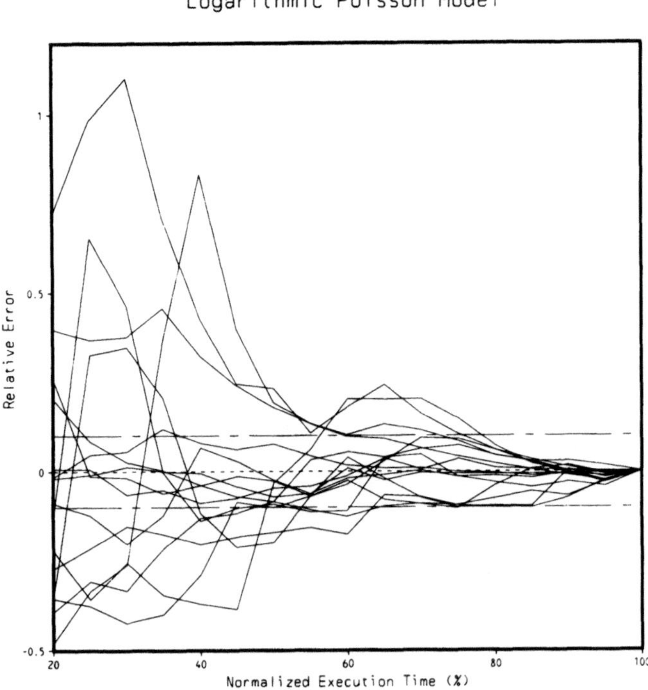

Fig. 4. Relative error curves for a model applied to 15 failure data sets.

Any capability of a model for prediction of software reliability in the system design and early development phases would be extremely valuable because of the resultant value for system engineering and planning purposes. It appears that these predictions must be made through measurable characteristics of the software (size, complexity, structure, etc.), the software development environment, and the operational environment.

3.1.3 Quality of Assumptions The following considerations of quality should be applied to each assumption in turn. If it is possible to test an assumption, the degree to which it is supported by actual data is an important consideration. This is especially true of assumptions that may be common to an entire class of models. If it is not possible to test the assumption, its *plausibility* from the viewpoint of logical consistency and software engineering experience should be evaluated. Finally, the clarity and explicitness of an assumption should be judged; these characteristics are often necessary to determine whether a model applies to particular circumstances.

3.1.4 Applicability Another important characteristic of a model is its applicability. A model should be judged on its degree of applicability across different software products (size, structure, function, etc.), different development environments, different operational environments, and different life cycle phases. However, if a particular model gives outstanding results for just a narrow range of products or development environments, it should not necessarily be eliminated.

There are at least five situations that are encountered commonly enough in practice that a model should either be capable of dealing with them directly or should be compatible with procedures that can deal with them. There are:

a. phased integration of a program during test (i.e., testing starts before the entire program is integrated, with the result that some failure data is associated with a partial program),

b. design and requirements changes to the program,

c. classification of severity of failures into different categories,

d. ability to handle incomplete failure data or data with measurement uncertainties (although not without loss of predictive validity),

e. Operation of same program on computers of different performance.

Finally, it is desirable that a model be robust with respect to departures from its assumptions, errors in the data or parameters it employs, and unusual conditions.

3.1.5 Simplicity A model should be simple in three aspects. The most important consideration is that it must be simple and inexpensive to collect the data that is required to particularize the model. If the foregoing is not the case, the model will not be used. Second, the model should be simple in concept. Software engineers without extensive mathematical background should be able to understand the nature of the model and its assumptions, so they can determine when it is applicable and the extent to which the model may diverge from reality in an application. Parameters should have readily understood interpretations that relate to characteristics of the program, the development environment, or the execution environment. This property makes it more feasible for software engineers to estimate the values of the parameters where data is not available. Finally, a model must be readily implementable as a program that is a practical management and engineering tool. This means that the program must run rapidly and inexpensively with no manual intervention required other than the initial input.

3.2 Classification of Models

Some models share common characteristics, particularly predictive validity. Hence it is efficient to classify models for the purpose of making comparisons. We will base our classification on five attributes [9]:

a. time domain - calendar time or execution (CPU or processor) time,

b. category - the expected number of failures that can be experienced in infinite time is *finite* or *infinite*,

c. type - the failure quantity distribution,

d. class (finite failures category only) - functional form of the failure intensity in terms of time,

e. family (infinite failures category only) - functional form of the failure intensity in terms of the expected value of failures experienced.

Table I illustrates the classification scheme with respect to the last four attributes (it is identical for both kinds of time) and notes where most of the published models fit in it. Table II summarizes the functional relationships of the failure intensity of various models with respect to (execution) time and the expected number of failures experienced (see [6] for detailed derivations).

Table I. Software reliability model classification scheme.

• Finite Failures Category Models

Class	Type		
	Poisson	Binomial	OtherTypes
Exponential	Musa execution time [3] Goel-Okumoto NHPP [7] Moranda geometric Poisson [10] Schneidewind [11]	Jelinski/Moranda [12] Shooman [13]	Littlewood-Verrall general with rational $\psi(i)$ suggested by Musa [2] Keiller-Littlewood [17] Goel-Okumoto imperfect debugging [18]
Weibull		Wagoner [14] Schick/Wolverton [15]	
Pareto		Littlewood differential [16]	

• Infinite Failures Category Models

Family	Type			
	T1	T2	T3	Poisson
Geometric	Moranda geometric De-eutophication [10]			Musa-Okumoto [4]
Inverse Linear		Littlewood/Verrall general with $\psi(i)$ linear [19]		
Inverse Polynomial (2nd degree)			Littlewood-Verrall general with $\psi(i)$ polynomial [19]	
Power				Crow [20]

Table II. Functional relationships for failure intensity with respect to time t and expected number of failures experienced $\mu(\omega_0,\omega_1,\omega_2,\omega_3,\phi_0,\phi_1,\phi_2$ are real).

• Finite Failures Category (All Types)

Class	$\lambda(t)$	$\lambda(\mu)$
Exponential	$\omega_0 e^{-\omega_1 t}$	$\phi_0(\phi_1-\mu)$
Weibull	$\omega_0 t^{\omega_2-1} e^{-\omega_1 t^{\omega_2}}$	$\phi_0\{-\ln(1-\mu/\phi_1)\}^{\phi_2}(\phi_1-\mu)$
Pareto	$\omega_0(\omega_1+t)^{-\omega_2}$	$\phi_0(\phi_1-\mu)^{\phi_2}$

- Infinite Failures Category (All Types)

Family	$\lambda(t)$	$\lambda(\mu)$
Geometric	$\omega_0(\omega_1+t)^{-1}$	$\phi_0\phi_1^{\mu}$
Inverse Linear	$\omega_0(\omega_1+t)^{-1/2}$	$1/(\phi_0+\phi_1\mu)$
Inverse Polynomial (2nd Degree)	$\frac{\omega_0}{\sqrt{t^2+\omega_1}}\left\{\sqrt[3]{t+\sqrt{t^2+\omega_2}}+\sqrt[3]{t-\sqrt{t^2+\omega_1}}\right\}$	$1/(\phi_0+\phi_1\mu^2)$
Power	$\omega_0\omega_1 t^{\omega_1-1}$	$\phi_0\mu^{\phi_1}$

3.3 Comparison of Predictive Validity

We will make comparison using the following seven model groups (classes or families), which include most published models: exponential class, Weibull class, Pareto class, geometric family, inverse linear family, inverse polynomial (2nd degree only) family, and power family. As can be seen from (7), the logarithmic Poisson model is a member of the geometric family. We do not consider different types because the mean value functions of the models are independent of type, and the mean values function is the primary determinant of the model's predictive validity characteristics. The approach previously described for evaluating predictive validity will be employed.

The failure data used is composed of 15 sets of data on a variety of software systems (such as real time command and control, real time commercial, military, and space systems) with system sizes ranging from small (5.7 K object instructions) to large (2.4 M object instructions). The data sets were all taken during system test (except for one taken during subsystem test). Consult [6] for detailed descriptions of the data source and system characteristics.

Note that failure data is used to estimate the parameters of the failure intensity function that represents the model group. We will utilize two different inference methods, maximum likelihood and least squares, to see if inference method has any substantial effect on predictive validity. Since most models are associated with particular inference procedures, we may not be precisely representing them in some cases; the difference will be significant only if different inference procedures yield substantially different results in regard to predictive validity.

3.3.1 Maximum Likelihood Estimation An evaluation of predictive validity for the case of inference by maximum likelihood estimation is shown in Fig. 5. (See [4] for a detailed discussion on the inference method.) This plot represents a summary of the data from the system test periods of about 15 different software systems. Plots of the median (over the 15 systems) error curves for the model groups are shown. The geometric family yields the best prediction at most points in time, followed closely by the inverse polynomial family. Note that the exponential group is inferior for small values of time, but not markedly so past 60% of the period in question. In fact, the prediction error is well under 10% after this point.

3.3.2 Least Squares Estimation We will now repeat the comparison among model groups for predictive validity, using inference by least squares estimation.

The failure intensity is first estimated based on groups of failures. The functional relationship $\lambda(\mu)$ of the failure intensity with respect to the mean value function (Table II) is then used to estimate the model parameters by fitting the function to the estimated failure intensity data.

Assume that the failure data is available in the form of m successive failure intervals, denoted by τ_i', $i = 1,...,m$. Then, the cumulative time to the i-th failure is given by $\tau_i = \sum_{l=1}^{i} \tau_l'$.

The observation interval $(0, \tau_m]$ is partioned at every k-th failure occurrence time so that there are p (the largest integer of m/k) disjoint subintervals. Then, the failure intensity for the j-th subinterval $(\tau_{k(j-1)}, \tau_{kj}]$ may be estimated by

$$y_j = \begin{cases} \dfrac{k}{\tau_{kj} - \tau_{k(j-1)}}, & j = 1,...,p-1 \\[2ex] \dfrac{m - k\,(p-1)}{\tau_m - \tau_{k(j-1)}}, & j = p \end{cases} \tag{21}$$

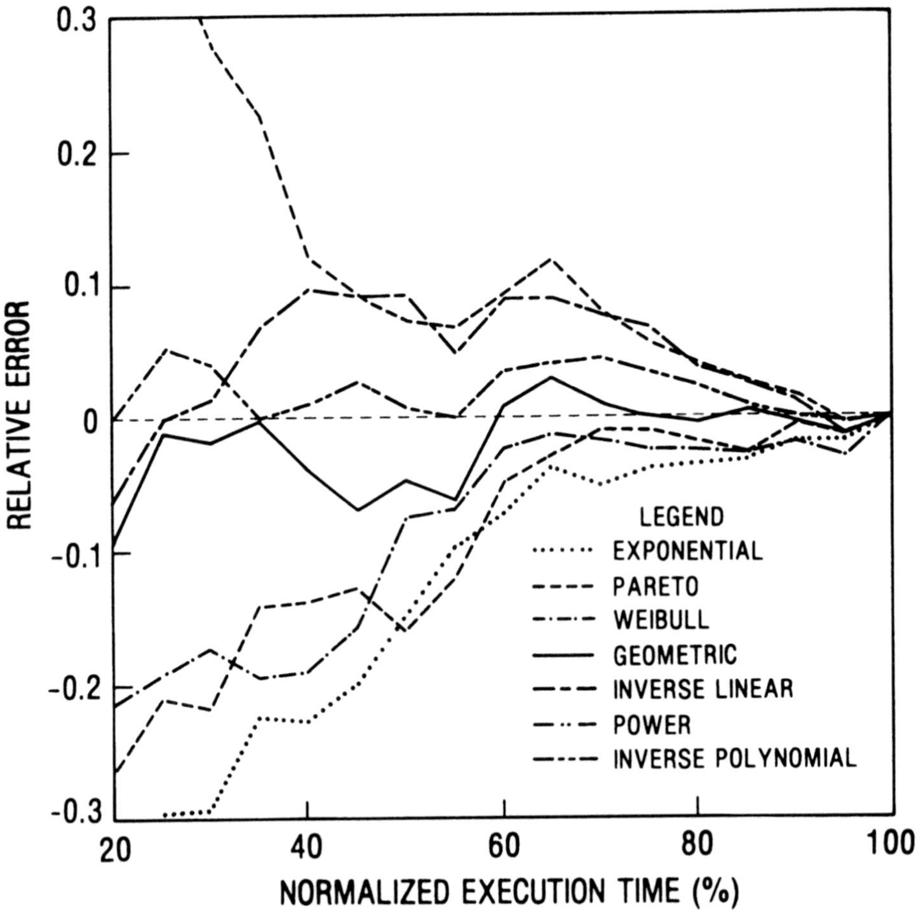

Fig. 5. Median curves of relative error for seven model groups, maximum likelihood estimation.

The corresponding estimate of the mean value function for the j-th subinterval is

$$x_j = k\,(j-1), \quad j = 1,\ldots,p\,. \tag{22}$$

Note that grouping a small number of failures (a small value of k) will result in large variations in the estimated failure intensity while grouping a large number of failures (a large value of k) will result in too much smoothing. A group of five failures (i.e., $k = 5$) has been selected as a reasonable compromise in the following analysis. Although some information may be lost due to grouping of failures, an advantage of the foregoing approach is that no specific model or distribution is assumed.

The method of least squares is used to estimate the model parameters by fitting the functional relationship $\lambda(\mu)$ to the estimated failure intensity data $((x_j, y_j), j = 1,\ldots,p)$. Let ϵ_j represent the logarithm of the ratio of the j-th data point to the model. Then, we have

$$\ln y_j = \ln\lambda(x_j) + \epsilon_j\,. \tag{23}$$

The estimates of the model parameters can be found so that the sum of the squares of ϵ_j's is minimized. In the case of the logarithmic Poisson model, if we denote by $S(\lambda_0, \theta)$ the sum of the squares of ϵ_j's from (7) and (23) we have

$$S(\lambda_0, \theta) = \sum_{j=1}^{p} \epsilon_j^2$$

$$= \sum_{j=1}^{p} \left\{ \ln y_j - \ln\lambda_0 + \theta x_j \right\}^2 , \tag{24}$$

which is to be minimized. Results from a simple linear regression yield the least squares estimates of λ_0 and θ. Consult Okumoto [21] for a detailed description of the foregoing approach. It should be pointed out that the least squares estimate of λ_0 based on the mid-point, i.e., $x_j = k(j-1) + k/2$ was found to be biased.

Although the above method is attractive due to its simplicity and practicability, if the fitted mean value function is used to predict the number of failures in some additional execution time, it is not certain that the additional number of failures is always greater than or equal to zero. Since in this paper the number of failures predicted by a model is used to evaluate predictive validity, the above method is modified so that the fitted mean value function passes through a point (τ_m, m), i.e.,

$$\mu(\tau_m) = m\,. \tag{25}$$

In other words, the model parameters are estimated so as to minimize the sum of the squares of ϵ_j's under the condition given by (25). Because of the nonlinear constraints, we cannot find an analytical solution but must obtain it numerically.

The predictive validity is now evaluated once more for the different model groups, using the same procedure as before but with the parameters found by least squares estimation. The results are shown in Fig. 6.

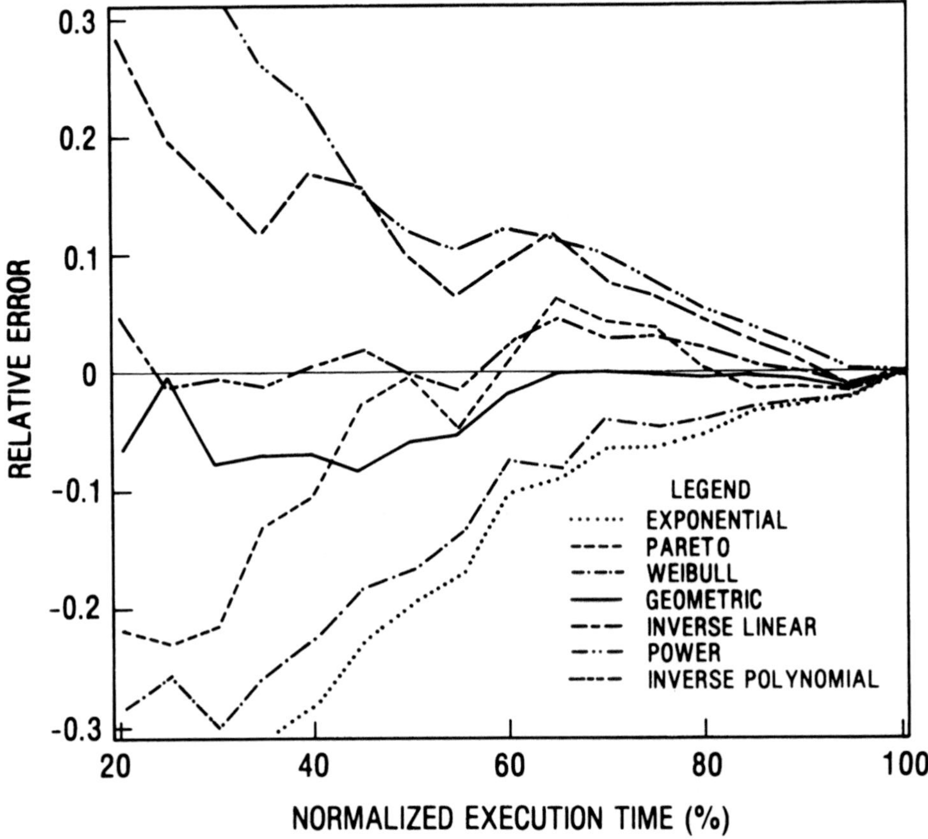

Fig. 6. Median curves of relative error for seven model groups, least squares estimation.

It will be seen that the results, both relatively and in absolute terms, are very similar to those for the case of maximum likelihood estimation. Thus, it does not appear likely that different methods of estimation will have a substantial effect on predictive validity of the models with which they are associated.

3.4 Evaluation of Other Criteria

The capabilities of both the basic and logarithmic Poisson models are superior to those of other published models. Currently, they are the only two models that perform reliability modeling in execution time *and* then employ calendar time components to convert execution time quantities to calendar time. They readily yield present failure intensity. They also provide expected date of reaching a specified failure intensity and the associated resource and cost requirements. To the best of the authors' knowledge, the latter capability is unique.

The basic model has parameters that can be related to the characteristics of the software and the development process (although not with high accuracy at present). Thus it possesses prediction capability or the ability to project software reliability prior to execution. This capability does not appear to exist at present for models outside the exponential class of the finite failures category. Although models such as Jelinski-Moranda, Shooman, and Goel-Okumoto share this property with the basic execution time model, the latter is used because it incorporates some of the concepts involved in the former models.

There has not been a general evaluation of all the assumptions on which the published models are based; hence it would be difficult to draw any conclusions in regard to their relative merits on this criterion.

In general, the published models seem to be widely applicable to most types of software products under various conditions. If the operational profile (set of input states experienced and associated probabilities) is highly nonuniform, then the decrement in failure intensity per failure experienced will tend to be nonuniform. In this situation, models of class or family other than exponential may tend to fit better and yield better predictive validity. On the other hand, the published models are generally developed for programs that are stable in size, while most programs change as the result of the phasing of integration, design changes, etc. A method of compensating for changing size has been developed [22], but it is dependent on being able to relate model parameters to program characteristics, particularly size. Hence only the basic execution time model can be used at present for the large class of programs that are changing in size.

In point of fact, the basic execution time model is the one that has been most widely applied to actual projects, as development was proceeding. Hence, a lot of information and lore is available concerning its use [23-27] and convenient programs have been developed and refined to do the calculations [28,29].

Both the basic and logarithmic Poisson execution time models are simple in concept.

Both have execution time components that are based on only two parameters. These parameters are readily interpretable as physical quantities, especially in the case of the basic model. Models of the Weibull and Pareto types have three parameters, and their physical significance is not as readily apparent. The Littlewood general model uses Bayesian inference. Most engineers find this a difficult approach to comprehend. The analysis is frequently very complex. The computer programs that implement the Littlewood model are substantially more difficult to develop and debug, and the run times are sometimes several order of magnitude greater than those of the two execution time models with maximum likelihood estimation. It should be noted that Kremer [30] presents an interesting analysis of the fault repair process that gives general conceptual insight into the nature of finite failure models (the results do not favor any particular model, however).

4. CONCLUSIONS

After considering all of the foregoing evaluations, it will be seen that the basic execution model is generally superior in capability and applicability to the other published models. It and the logarithmic Poisson are superior in simplicity. The logarithmic Poisson is second in capability to the basic model, but superior to the others. The logarithmic Poisson is superior in predictive validity; the basic model is not, although the deficit is not significant after about 60% of the way through the test period. Thus the foregoing appear to be the two models of choice. One possible approach is to use the basic model for pretest studies and estimates and for periods of phased integration. You would switch to the logarithmic Poisson model when integration is complete and the program is stable. However, the additional complexity of this approach must be considered against the possibly limited improvement in predictive validity.

5. ACKNOWLEDGMENTS

The authors are indebted to John Greene and Wilhelm Kremer for their helpful comments and suggestions.

REFERENCES

[1] H. Hecht, "Measurement, estimation, and prediction of software reliability," in *Software Engineering Technology - Volume 2,* Maidenhead. Berkshire, England, Infotech International 1977, pp. 209-224.

[2] J. D. Musa, "The measurement and management of software reliability," *IEEE Proceedings*, 68(9), Sept. 1980, pp. 1131-1143.

[3] J. D. Musa, "A theory of software reliability and its application," *IEEE Trans. Software Eng.* SE-1(3), Sept. 1975, pp.312-327.

[4] J. D. Musa, K. Okumoto, "A logarithmic Poisson execution time model for software reliability measurement," *Proc. 7th International Conference on Software Engineering,* Orlando, Florida, March 26-29, 1984, pp. 230-238.

[5] H. Hecht, "Allocation of resources for software reliability," *Proc. COMPCON Fall 1981,* pp. 74-82.

[6] J. D. Musa, K. Okumoto, "A comparison of time domains for software reliability models," *Journal of Systems and Software,* 4(4), Nov. 1984, pp. 277-287.

[7] A. L. Goel, K. Okumoto, "Time-dependent error detection rate model for software reliability and other performance measures," *IEEE Trans. Rel.,* R-28(3), August 1979, pp. 206-211.

[8] A. Iannino, B. Littlewood, J. D. Musa, K. Okumoto, "Criteria for software reliability model comparisons," *IEEE Trans. Soft. Eng.,* SE-10(6), Nov. 1984, pp. 687-691.

[9] J. D. Musa, K. Okumoto, "Software reliability models; concepts, classification, comparisons, and practice," *Proc. Electronic Systems Effectiveness and Life Cycle Costing Conference,* Norwich, U. K., July 19-31, 1982, *NATO ASI Series,* Vol. F3, (Ed: J. W. Skwirzynski) Springer-Verlag, Heidelberg, 1983, pp. 395-424.

[10] P. Moranda, "Predictions of software reliability during debugging," *Proc. Ann. Reliability and Maintainability Symposium,* Washington, D. C., January 1975, pp. 327-332.

[11] N. F. Schneidewind, "Analysis of error processes in computer software," *Proc. 1975 International Conference Reliable Software*, Los Angeles, April 21-23, 1975, pp. 337-346.

[12] Z. Jelinski, P. B. Moranda, "Software reliability research," *Statistical Computer Performance Evaluation.* W. Freiberger, Ed., New York: Academic, 1972, pp. 465-484.

[13] M. Shooman, "Probabilistic models for software reliability prediction," *Statistical Computer Performance Evaluation*, see [12], pp. 485-502.

[14] W. L. Wagoner, *The Final Report of Software Reliability Measurement Study*, Aerospace Report No. TOR-0074(4112-1), August 1973.

[15] G. J. Schick, R. W. Wolverton, "Assessment of software reliability," *Proc. Operations Research*, Physica-Verlag, Wurzburg-Wien, 1973, pp. 395-422.

[16] B. Littlewood, "Software reliability-growth; a model for fault-removal in computer-programs and hardware-design," *IEEE Trans. Reliability*, R-30(4), Oct, 1981, pp. 313-320.

[17] P. A. Keiller, et al., "On the quality of software reliability production, "*Proceedings of NATO Advanced Study Institute on Electronic Systems Effectiveness and Life Cycle Costing*, Norwich, U. K., July 19-31, 1982, *NATO ASI Series*, Vol. F3, (Ed: J. W. Skwirzynski) Springer-Verlag, Heidelberg, 1983, pp. 441-460.

[18] A. L. Goel, K. Okumoto, "An analysis of recurrent software errors in a real-time control system," *Proc. ACM Conference*, 1978, pp. 496-501.

[19] B. Littlewood, J. L. Verrall, "A Bayesian reliability growth model for computer software," *1973 IEEE Symp. Computer Software Reliability*, New York, N.Y., Apr. 30 - May 2, 1973, pp. 70-77.

[20] L. H. Crow, "Reliability analysis for complex, repairable system," *Reliability and Biometry,* Edited by F. Proshan and R. J. Serfling, SIAM, Philadelphia, PA, 1974, pp. 379-410.

[21] K. Okumoto, "A statistical method for software quality control," to appear in *IEEE Transactions on Software Engineering.*

[22] J. D. Musa, A. Iannino, "Software reliability modeling-accounting for program size variation due to integration or design changes," *ACM SIGMETRICS Performance Evaluation Review*, 10(2), pp. 16-25.

[23] J. D. Musa, A. Iannino, K. Okumoto, *Software Reliability: Measurement, Prediction, Application*, scheduled for publication by McGraw-Hill, 1986.

[24] J. D. Musa, "Software reliability measurement," *Journal of Systems and Software*, 1(3), 1980, pp. 223-241.

[25] J. D. Musa, "Software reliability measures applied to system engineering," *1979 NCC Proceedings,* New York, N.Y., June 4-7, 1979, pp. 941-946.

[26] J. D. Musa, "The use of software reliability measures in project management," *Proc. COMPSAC 78*, Chicago, Illinois, November 14-16, 1978, pp. 493-498.

[27] P. A. Hamilton, J. D. Musa, "Measuring reliability of computation center software," *Proc. 3rd. Int. Conf. Soft. Eng.,* Atlanta, Ga., May 10-12, 1978, pp. 29-36.

[28] J. D. Musa, "Program for Software Reliability and System Test Schedule Estimation-User's Guide," available from author.

[29] J. D. Musa, P. A. Hamilton, "Program for Software Reliability and System Test Schedule Estimation - Program Documentation," available from author.

[30] W. Kremer, "Birth-death and bug counting," *IEEE Transactions on Reliability*, R-32(1), April 1983, pp. 37-47.

TOOLS FOR THE ANALYSIS OF THE ACCURACY OF SOFTWARE RELIABILITY PREDICTIONS

B. Littlewood, A. A. Abdel Ghaly and P. Y. Chan
Centre for Software Reliability
The City University
Northampton Square
London. EC1V 0HB

Abstract

Different software reliability models can produce very different answers when called upon to predict future reliability in a reliability growth context. Users need to know which, if any, of the competing predictions are trustworthy. Some techniques are presented which form the basis of a partial solution to this problem. In addition, it is shown that this approach can point the way towards more accurate prediction via models which learn from past behaviour.

1. Introduction

Software reliability models first appeared in the literature almost fifteen years ago [1 - 4], and according to a recent survey some forty now exist [5]. There was an initial feeling that a process of refinement would eventually produce definitive models which could be unreservedly recommended to potential users. Unfortunately this has not happened. Recent studies suggest that the accuracy of the models is very variable [6], and that no single model can be trusted to perform well in all contexts. More importantly, it does not seem possible to analyse the particular context in which reliability measurement is to take place so as to decide a priori which model is likely to be trustworthy.

Faced with these problems, our own research has recently turned to the provision of tools to assist the user of software reliability models. The basic device we use is an analysis of the predictive quality of a model. If a user can be confident that past predictions emanating from a model have been in close accord with actual behaviour for a particular data set then he/she would have confidence in future predictions for the same data.

We shall describe several ways of analysing predictive quality. The techniques will be illustrated using several models to analyse several data sets. Our intention, however, is not to act as advocates for particular models, although some models do seem to perform noticeably more badly than others. Rather, we hope to provide the beginnings of a framework which will

NATO ASI Series, Vol. F22
Software System Design Methods. Edited by J.K. Skwirzynski

allow a user to have confidence in reliability predictions calculated on an everyday basis.

An important by-product of our ability to analyse predictive quality will be methods of improving the accuracy of predictions. We shall show some remarkably effective techniques for obtaining better predictions than those coming from 'raw' models, and suggest ways in which other 'meta' predictors might be constructed.

2. The software reliability growth problem

The theme of this paper is prediction: how to predict and how to know that predictions are trustworthy.

We shall restrict ourselves, for convenience, to the continuous time reliability growth problem. Tables 1, 2, 3 show typical data of this kind. In each case the times between successive failures are recorded. Growth in reliability occurs as a result of attempts to fix faults, which are revealed by their manifestation as failures. A detailed conceptual model of this stochastic process, together with an analysis of the nature of the unpredictability, can be found elsewhere [7, 8].

Different models differ considerably in the ways they embody these conceptual assumptions in detailed mathematical structure. However, the basic problem can be summarised in Figure 1.

The raw data available to the user will be a sequence of execution times t_1, t_2, ... t_{i-1} between successive failures. These observed times can be regarded as realisations of random variables T_1, T_2, ... T_{i-1}. The objective is to use the data, observations on the past, to predict the future unobserved T_i, T_{i+1}, ... It is important to notice that even the simplest problem concerning measurement of current reliability is a prediction: it involves the future via the unobserved random variable T_i .

It is this characterisation of the problem as a prediction problem which will underlie all our work reported in this paper. We contend that the only important issue for a user is whether he/she can accurately predict future behaviour. Other metrics, such as estimates of the number of faults left in a program, are of interest only inasmuch as they contribute to this overall aim of predicting with accuracy. Indeed, a recent study [9] of several large IBM systems suggests that this particular metric can be very misleading: systems with very many faults can have acceptably high reliability since each fault occurs very infrequently.

Informally, the prediction problem is solved if we can accurately

3.	30.	113.	81.	115.
9.	2.	91.	112.	15.
138.	50.	77.	24.	108.
88.	670.	120.	26.	114.
325.	55.	242.	68.	422.
180.	10.	1146.	600.	15.
36.	4.	0.	8.	227.
65.	176.	58.	457.	300.
97.	263.	452.	255.	197.
193.	6.	79.	816.	1351.
148.	21.	233.	134.	357.
193.	236.	31.	369.	748.
0.	232.	330.	365.	1222.
543.	10.	16.	529.	379.
44.	129.	810.	290.	300.
529.	281.	160.	828.	1011.
445.	296.	1755.	1064.	1783.
860.	983.	707.	33.	868.
724.	2323.	2930.	1461.	843.
12.	261.	1300.	865.	1435.
30.	143.	108.	0.	3110.
1247.	943.	700.	875.	245.
729.	1897.	447.	386.	446.
122.	990.	948.	1082.	- 22.
75.	482.	5509.	100.	10.
1071.	371.	790.	6150.	3321.
1045.	648.	5485.	1160.	1864.
4116.				

Table 1 Execution times in seconds between successive failures [35]. Read left to right in rows.

479.	266.	277.	554.	1034.
949.	693.	597.	117.	170.
117.	1274.	469.	1174.	693.
1908.	135.	277.	596.	757.
437.	2230.	437.	340.	405.
575.	277.	363.	522.	613.
277.	1300.	821.	213.	1620.
1601.	298.	874.	618.	2640.
5.	149.	1034.	2441.	460.
565.	1119.	437.	927.	4462.
714.	181.	1485.	757.	3154.
2115.	884.	2037.	1481.	559.
490.	593.	1769.	85.	2836.
213.	1366.	490.	1487.	4322.
1418.	1023.	5490.	1520.	3281.
2716.	2175.	3505.	725.	1963.
3979.	1090.	245.	1194.	994.
3902.				

Table 2 Execution times in hundreths of seconds between successive failures.

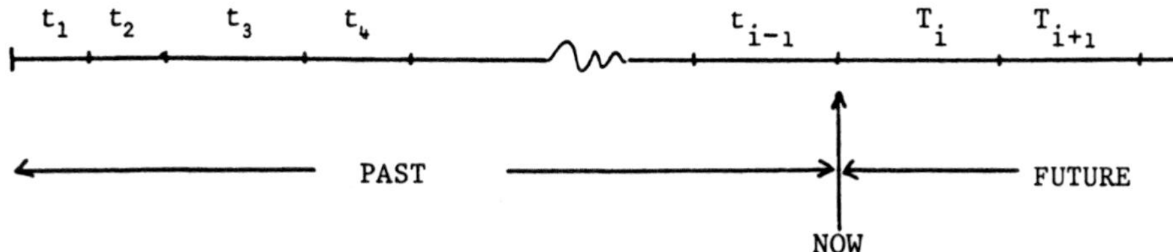

Figure 1 The problem is to make predictions now about the future using only data collected in the past.

39.	10.	4.	36.	4.
5.	4.	91.	49.	1.
25.	1.	4.	30.	42.
9.	49.	44.	32.	3.
78.	1.	30.	205.	5.
129.	103.	224.	186.	53.
14.	9.	2.	10.	1.
34.	170.	129.	4.	4.
35.	5.	5.	22.	36.
35.	121.	23.	35.	48.
32.	21.	4.	23.	9.
13.	165.	14.	22.	41.
12.	138.	95.	49.	62.
2.	35.	89.	90.	69.
22.	15.	19.	42.	14.
11.	41.	210.	16.	30.
37.	66.	9.	16.	14.
24.	12.	159.	89.	118.
29.	21.	18.	2.	114.
37.	46.	17.	1.	150.
382.	160.	66.	206.	9.
26.	62.	239.	13.	4.
85.	85.	240.	178.	34.
102.	9.	146.	59.	48.
25.	25.	111.	5.	31.
51.	6.	193.	27.	25.
96.	26.	50.	30.	17.
320.	78.	39.	13.	13.
19.	128.	34.	84.	40.
177.	349.	274.	82.	58.
31.	114.	59.	88.	84.
232.	108.	38.	86.	7.
22.	80.	239.	3.	39.
63.	152.	63.	80.	245.
196.	46.	152.	102.	9.
228.	220.	208.	78.	3.
83.	6.	212.	91.	3.
10.	172.	21.	175.	371.
40.	48.	126.	90.	149.
30.	317.	500.	673.	432.
66.	168.	66.	66.	129.
49.	332.			

Table 3 Operating times between successive failures. This data relates to a system experiencing failures due to software faults and hardware design faults.

estimate the joint distribution of any finite subset of T_i, T_{i+1}, ... This statement begs the question of what we mean by 'accurately', and it is this issue which forms the central question of our work.

In practice, of course, a user will be satisfied with much less than a complete description of all future uncertainty. In many cases, for example, it will be sufficient to know the current reliability of the software under examination. This could be presented in many different forms: the reliability function, $P(T_i < t)$; the current rate of occurrence of failures (ROCOF), [10]; the mean (or median) time to next failure (mttf). Alternatively, a user may wish to predict when a target reliability, perhaps used as a criterion for test termination, will be achieved.

If we accept that prediction is our goal, it can be seen that the usual discussion of competing software reliability growth models is misleading. We should, instead, be comparing the relative merits of prediction systems. A prediction system which will allow us to predict the future (T_i, T_{i+1}, ...) from the past (t_1, t_2, ... t_{i-1}) comprises:

(i) the probabilistic model which specifies the distribution of any subset of the T_j's conditional on a (unknown) parameter $\underset{\sim}{\alpha}$;

(ii) a statistical inference procedure for $\underset{\sim}{\alpha}$ involving use of available data (realisations of T_j's);

(iii) a prediction procedure combining (i) and (ii) to allow us to make probability statements about future T_j's.

Of course, the model is an important part of this triad and it seems unlikely that good predictions can be obtained if the model is not 'close to reality'. However, a good model is not sufficient: stages (ii) and (iii) are vital components of the prediction system. In fact disaster can strike at any of the three stages.

In principle, it ought to be possible to analyse each of the three stages separately so as to gain trust in (or to mistrust) the predictions. Unfortunately, it is our experience that this is not possible. There are several reasons.

In the first place, the models are usually too complicated for a traditional 'goodness-of-fit' approach to be attempted. Even the simplest exponential order statistic model [1, 2, 4] does not allow this kind of analysis. This should not surprise us: the goodness-of-fit problem for independent identically distributed random variables is hard in the presence of unknown parameters. The reliability growth context is much worse because of non-stationarity.

Secondly, properties of the estimators of unknown parameters in these models are usually not available. For example, several models assume that the software contains only a finite number of faults. There is thus an upper bound on the number of observable T_j's. This implies that, for example, we cannot even trust the usual asymptotic theory for maximum likelihood (ML) estimators. Their small sample properties are invariably impossibly hard to obtain.

Bayesians will no doubt argue that there is a 'correct' way to build a prediction system for a particular model. It involves posterior distributions of the parameters of stage (ii) and Bayesian predictive distributions for (iii). A good account of this approach in the conventional statistical context is contained in the book by Aitchison and Dunsmore [11]. Whilst we agree that this is the best way forward in principle, and will use some Bayesian prediction systems in a later section, it is impractical for most of the proposed models. It is interesting that the classical statistical literature has neglected the prediction problem: 'statistics' has usually come to mean only stage (ii) of our triad.

Finally, it could be argued that there are models which are 'obviously' better than others because of the greater plausibility of their underlying assumptions. We find this a rather dubious proposition. Certainly, the assumptions of some models seem overly naive and it might be reasonable to discount them. However, this still leaves many others which cannot be rejected _a priori_. It is our belief that understanding of the processes of software engineering is so imperfect that we cannot even choose an appropriate model when we have an intimate knowledge of the software under study. At some future time it may be possible to match a reliability model to a program via the characteristics of that program: for example, complexity metrics. This is not currently the case.

Where does this leave a user, who merely wants to obtain trustworthy reliability metrics for his/her current software project? Our view is that there is no alternative to a direct examination and comparison of the quality of the predictions emanating from different complete prediction systems. The intention in this paper is to present the beginnings of a set of tools to assist this examination and comparison. Although we shall show examples of these tools applied to the predictions from several prediction systems using real software reliability data, our intention is _not_ to recommend particular ways of predicting. Rather, it is our experience that no prediction system can be trusted to be always superior to others. Our advice to users, then, is to be eclectic: try many prediction systems and use the reliability metrics which are the best _for the data under consideration_.

We would not claim that the tools described here are complete. Indeed, we shall suggest potentially fruitful areas for future research. We do believe strongly, however, that now is an appropriate time to devote less effort to the proliferation of models and more to studies of this kind.

3. An example

The simplest question a user can ask is: how reliable is my program now? As debugging proceeds, and more inter-failure time data is collected, this question is likely to be repeated. It is hoped that the succession of reliability estimates will show a steady improvement due to the removal of faults.

Let us assume our user has simple requirements, and will be satisfied with an accurate estimate of the median time to next failure at each stage. He decides he will make predictions from two prediction systems: Jelinski-Moranda (JM) described in reference [1], and Littlewood-Verrall (LV) described in reference [3]. Notice that JM is essentially identical to the approaches advocated by Musa [4] and Shooman [2].

Figure 2 shows the results he would get if he were using the data shown in Table 1. At each stage, for a particular prediction system, the point plotted is the predicted median of the time to next failure, T_i, based on the available data t_1, t_2, ... t_{i-1}. Such plots are thus a simple way of tracking progress in terms of estimated achieved reliability.

Our user would, we believe, be alarmed at the results. Whilst the models agree that reliability growth is present, they disagree profoundly about the nature and extent of that growth. The JM predictions are much more optimistic than those of LV: at any particular stage JM suggests that the reliability is greater than LV would suggest.

In addition, the JM predictions are more 'noisy' than those of LV. The latter suggests that there is a steady reliability growth with no significant reversals. JM suggests that important set-backs are occurring.

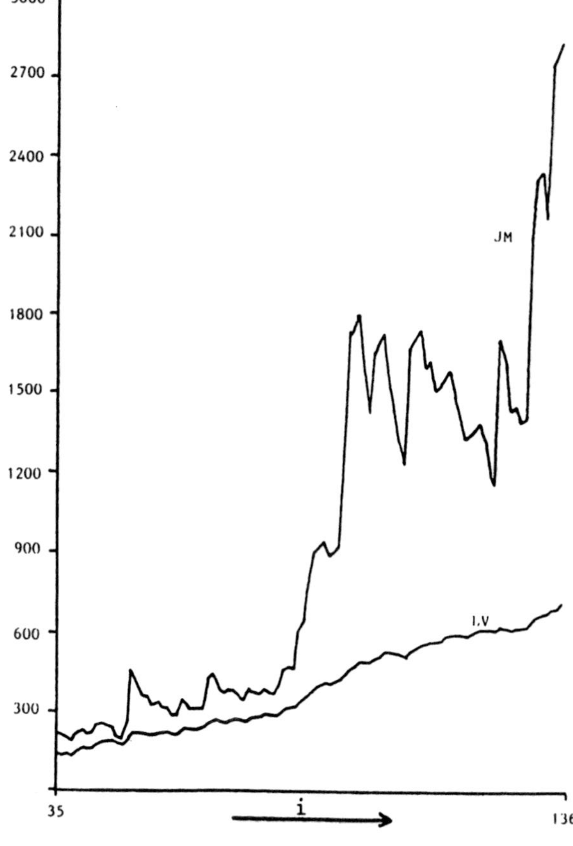

Figure 2 Median plots for JM and LV, data from Table 1. Plotted are predicted median of T_i (based on t_1, t_2, ... t_{i-1}) against i .

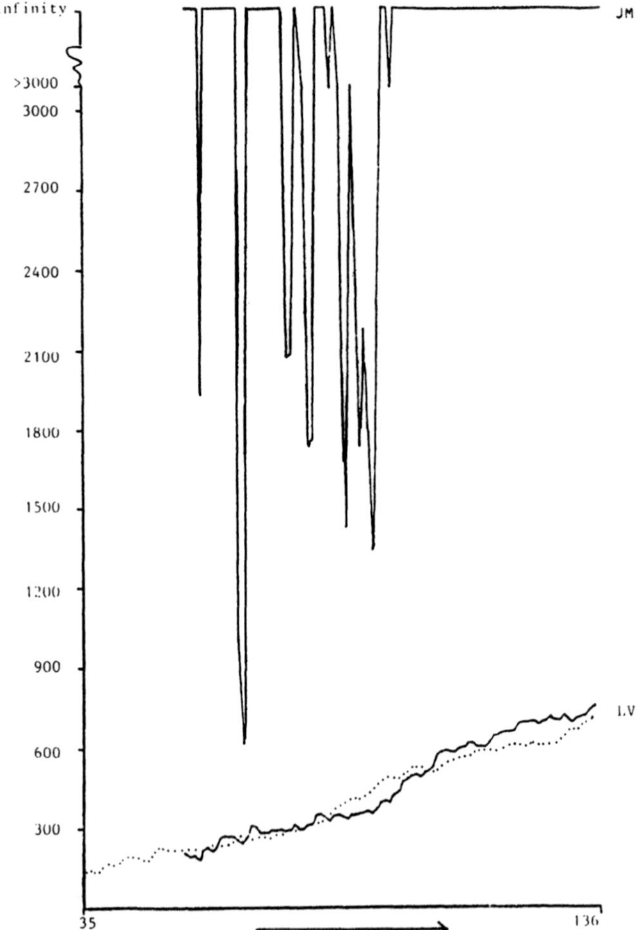

Figure 3 Median predictions 20 steps ahead for JM, LV using data of Table 1. JM makes many excursions to infinity, because it frequently estimates the number of remaining faults to be less than 20! The LV predictions 20 steps ahead are in close agreement with the (later) 1 step ahead median prediction (shown dotted). This is a useful 'self-consistency' property: a prediction system ought to have the property that a prediction from T_i based on $t_1, \ldots t_{i-20}$ is 'close' to a later one based on $t_1, \ldots t_{i-1}$. Clearly JM does not have this property: compare with Figure 2.

What should the user do? There might be a temptation to try yet more prediction systems, and hope to arrive somehow at consensus. The likelihood is that this would merely increase the confusion.

The important point is that there is no guide as to which, if any, of the available predictions is close to the truth. Is the true reliability as high as suggested by JM in Figure 2? Or are the more conservative estimates of LV nearer to reality? Perhaps as important: are the apparent decreases in reliability indicated by JM real (bad fixes?), or artifacts of the statistical procedures? (The JM model does not, in fact, allow for the possibility of bad fixes, so these reversals must be due to stages (ii) and (iii) of the prediction system.)

If our user wished to predict further ahead than the next time to failure, he/she would find the picture even bleaker. Figure 3 shows how JM and LV perform when required to predict a median 20 steps ahead. That is, a prediction is made of the median of T_i at stage i-20, using observations $t_1, t_2, \ldots t_{i-20}$. It is obvious in this case that JM is performing very badly. Its excursions to infinity are caused by its tendency to suggest that at stage i-20 there are less than 20 faults left in the program, so that the estimated median of T_i is infinite. At least LV does not behave in this absurd fashion. In addition it seems reasonably 'self-consistent' in that the prediction of the median of T_i made 20 steps before (based on $t_1, \ldots t_{i-20}$) is usually in good agreement with the later 'current median' estimate (based on $t_1, \ldots t_{i-1}$). Even such self-consistency, though, is no guarantee that these predictions are close to the truth.

These kinds of disagreement between different solutions to the prediction problem are very common. Until recently users had no way of deciding which, if any, reliability metrics could be trusted. All that was available was a great deal of special pleading from advocates of particular models: 'trust my model and you can trust the predictions'. This is not good enough. No model is totally convincing on *a priori* grounds. More importantly, a 'good' model is only one of the three components needed for good predictions.

In the next section we describe some ways in which a user of reliability models can obtain insight into their performance on his/her data.

4. Analysis of predictive quality

We shall concentrate, for convenience, upon the simplest prediction of all concerning current reliability. Most of these techniques can be adapted easily to some problems of longer-term prediction, but there are also novel difficulties arising from these problems. We shall return to this question later.

Having observed $t_1, t_2, \ldots t_{i-1}$ we want to predict the random variable T_i. More precisely, we want a good estimate of

$$F_i(t) \equiv P(T_i < t) \tag{1}$$

or, equivalently, of the reliability function

$$R_i(t) = 1 - F_i(t) \quad . \tag{2}$$

From a particular prediction system we can calculate a predictor

$$\tilde{F}_i(t) \quad . \tag{3}$$

A user is interested in the 'closeness' of $\tilde{F}_i(t)$ to the unknown true $F_i(t)$. In fact, he/she may be only interested in summary statistics such as mean (or median) time to failure, ROCOF, etc. However, the quality of these summarised predictions will depend upon the quality of $\tilde{F}_i(t)$, so we shall concentrate on the latter.

Clearly, the difficulty of analysing the closeness of $\tilde{F}_i(t)$ to $F_i(t)$ arises from our never knowing, even at a later stage, the true $F_i(t)$. If this were available (for example, if we simulated the reliability growth data from a sequence of known distributions) it would be possible to use measures of closeness based upon entropy and information [23], or distance measures such as those due to Kolmogorov or Cramer-von Mises [24].

In fact, the only information we shall obtain will be a single realisation of the random variable T_i when the software next fails. That is, after making the prediction $\tilde{F}_i(t)$ based upon $t_1, t_2, \ldots t_{i-1}$, we shall eventually observe t_i, which is a sample of size one from the true distribution $F_i(t)$. We must base all our analysis of the quality of the predictions upon these pairs $\{\tilde{F}_i(t), t_i\}$.

Our method will be an emulation of how a user would informally respond to a sequence of predictions and outcomes. He/she would inspect the pairs $\{\tilde{F}_i(t), t_i\}$ to see whether there is any evidence to suggest that the t_i's are not realisations of random variables from the $F_i(t)$'s. If such evidence were found, it would suggest that there are significant differences between $\tilde{F}_i(t)$ and $F_i(t)$, i.e. that the predictions are not in accord with actual behaviour. The 20-step ahead predictions of JM shown in Figure 3 are an example of strong evidence of disagreement between prediction and outcome: the predictions are often of infinite time to failure (program fault-free, so $\tilde{F}_i(t) = 0$ for all t), but the program always subsequently fails in finite time.

Consider the following sequence of transformations:

$$u_i = \tilde{F}_i(t_i) \quad . \tag{4}$$

Each is a probability integral transform of the observed t_i using the previously calculated predictor $\tilde{F}_i$ based upon $t_1, t_2, \ldots t_{i-1}$. Now, if each $\tilde{F}_i$ were identical to the true F_i, it is easy to see that the u_i would be realisations of independent uniform U(0, 1) random variables [25, 26]. Consequently we can reduce the problem of examining the closeness of $\tilde{F}_i$ to F_i (for some range of values of i) to the question of whether the sequence $\{u_i\}$ 'looks like' a random sample from U(0, 1). Readers interested in the more formal statistical aspects of these issues should read the recent work of Dawid [26, 27].

We consider now some ways in which the $\{u_i\}$ sequence can be examined.

4.1 The u-plot

Since the u_i's should look like a random sample from U(0, 1) if the prediction system is working well, the first thing to examine is whether they appear uniformly distributed. We do this by plotting the sample cumulant distribution function (cdf) of the u_i's and comparing it with the cdf of U(0, 1), which is the line of unit slope through the origin. Figure 4 shows how such a u-plot is drawn. The 'distance' between them can be summarised in various ways. We shall use the Kolmogorov distance, which is the maximum absolute vertical difference.

In Figure 5 are shown the u-plots for LV and JM predictions for the data of Table 1. The predictions here are $\tilde{F}_{36}(t)$ through $\tilde{F}_{135}(t)$. The Kolmogorov distances are 0.190 (JM) and 0.144 (LV). In tables of the Kolmogorov distribution the JM result is significant at the 1% level, LV only at the 5% level.

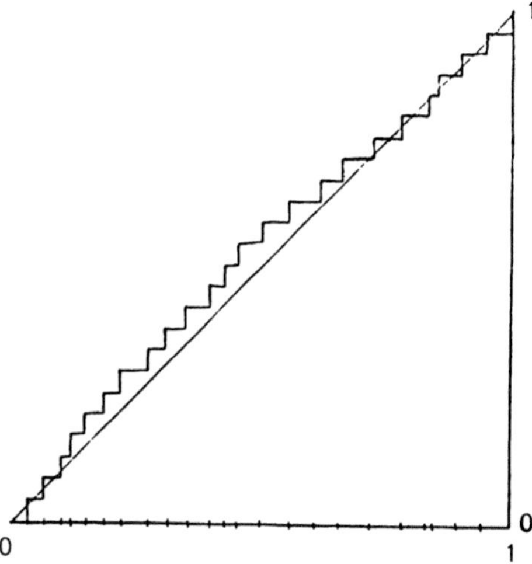

Figure 4 How to draw a u-plot. Each of the n u_i's, with a value between 0 and 1, is placed on the horizontal axis. The step function increases by $\frac{1}{n+1}$ at each of these points.

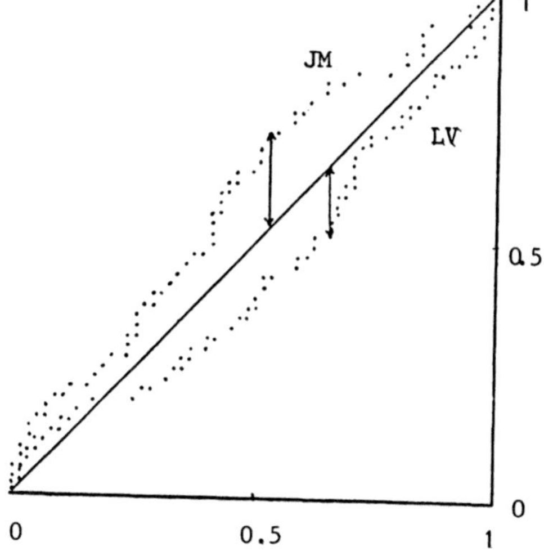

Figure 5 LV, JM u-plots, data of Table 1. Steps omitted for clarity. Note that these are reproduced from line-printer plots and do not correspond exactly to true plot.

From this analysis it appears that neither set of predictions is very good, but that JM is significantly worse than LV.

In fact the detailed plots tell us more than this. The JM plot is everywhere above the line of unit slope (the U(0, 1) cdf), the LV plot almost everywhere below it. This means that the u_i's from JM tend to be too small and those from LV too large. But u_i represents the predicted probability that T_i will be less than t_i, so consistently too small u_i's suggest that the predictions are underestimating the change of small t's. That is, the JM plot tells us that the predictions are too optimistic, the LV plot that these predictions are too pessimistic (although to a less pronounced degree).

There is evidence from this simple analysis, then, that the truth might lie somewhere between the predictions from JM and LV, but probably closer to LV. In particular, the true median plot probably lies between the two plots of Figure 2. We shall return to this idea in a later section, where further evidence will be given for our belief that the two prediction systems bound the truth for this data set.

At this stage, then, a user might take an analysis of this kind to help him make further predictions. He might, for example, adopt a conservative position and decide to use LV for his next prediction, and be reasonably confident that he would not over estimate the reliability of the product.

4.2 The y-plot, and scatter plot of u's

The u-plot treats one type of departure of the predictors from reality. There are other departures which cannot be detected by the u-plot. For example, in one of our investigations we found a data set for which a particular prediction system had the property of optimism in the early predictions and pessimism in the later predictions. These deviations were averaged out in the u-plot, in which the temporal ordering of the u_i's disappears, so that a small Kolmogorov distance was observed. It is necessary, then, to examine the u_i's for trend.

Figure 6 shows one way in which this can be done. First of all, it should be obvious that, since each u_i is defined on (0, 1), the sequence u_i (Stage 1 in Figure 6) will look super-regular. The transformation $x_i = -\ell n(1 - u_i)$ will produce a realisation of iid unit exponential random variables if the $\{u_i\}$ sequence really are a realisation of iid U(0, 1) random variables. That is, Stage 2 of Figure 6 should look like a realisation of a homogenous Poisson process; the alternative hypothesis (that there is trend in the u_i's) will show itself as a non-constant rate for this process. One simple test is to normalise the Stage 2 process onto (0, 1), as in Stage 3 of Figure 6, and plot as in the previous section [28].

Other procedures could be adopted, for example the Laplace test [10, 28], but we think that the plots are more informative. For example, see Figure 7 where this y-plot procedure is applied to the LV and JM predictions of the

Table 1 data. The Kolmogorov distances are 0.120 (JM) and 0.110 (LV), neither of which are significant at the 10% level. More interestingly, a close examination of the JM y-plot suggests that it is very close to linearity in the early stages (until about i=90: see broken line).

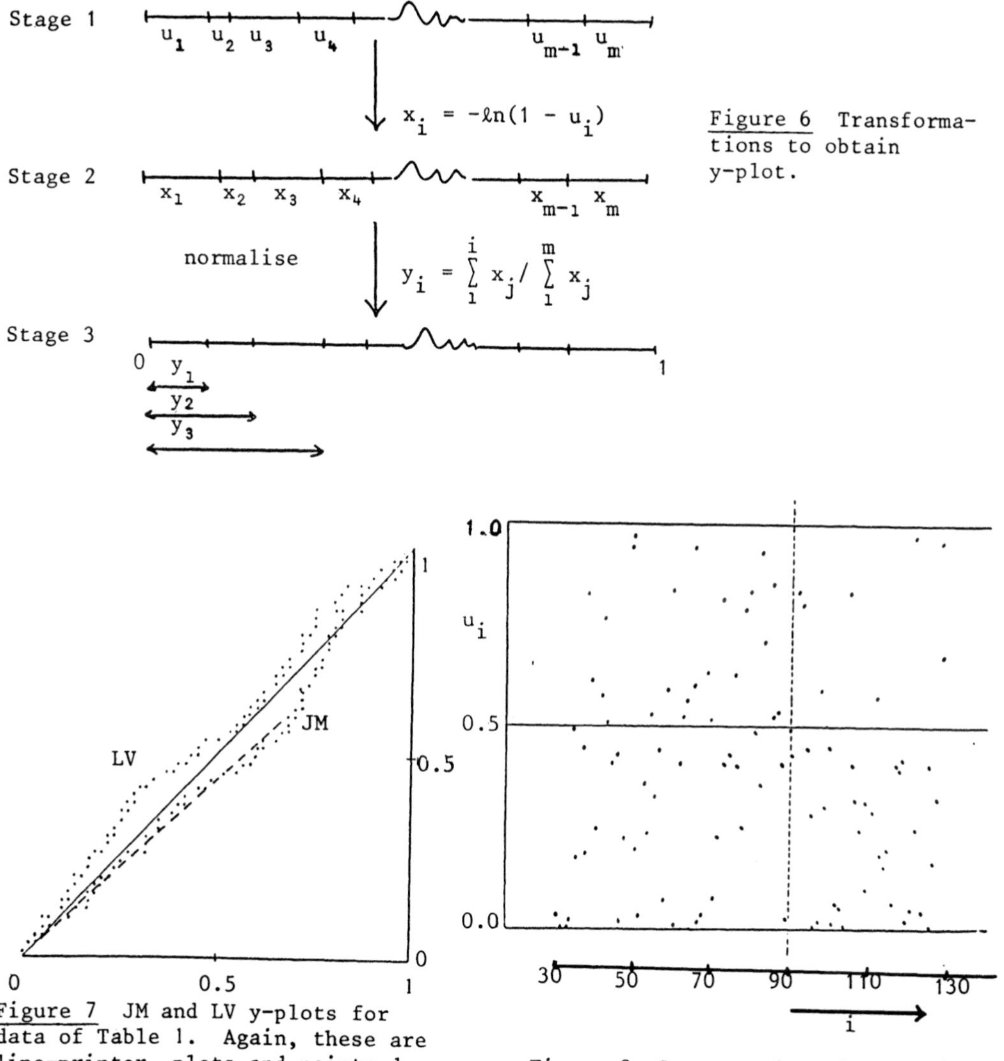

Figure 6 Transformations to obtain y-plot.

Figure 7 JM and LV y-plots for data of Table 1. Again, these are line-printer plots and points do not correspond exactly to true points.

Figure 8 Scatter plot of u_i against i for JM predictions from Table 1 data. There are 'too many' small u's to the right of the dotted line.

This observation is confirmed by a scatter plot of u_i against i: Figure 8. After i = 90 there are only 8 out of 39 u_i's greater than 0.5.

The implication is that the too optimistic predictions from JM are occurring mainly after i = 90. That is, the poor performance arises chiefly from the later predictions. Since these are based upon larger amounts of data, it is unlikely that stages (ii) and (iii) of the prediction system are responsible.

The effect can be seen quite clearly in the median plots (Figure 2). We can now have reasonable confidence that the sudden increase in the median plot of JM, at about $i = 90$, is not a true reflection of the reliability of the software under study. It is noticeable that this effect does not occur in the LV predictions.

4.3 Measures of 'noise'

It is instructive at this stage to digress a little and consider briefly the estimation problem in classical statistics. There we have a random sample (independent, identically distributed random variables) from a population with an unknown parameter, θ. If we assume, for simplicity, that θ is scalar, it is usual to seek an estimator for θ, say $\tilde{\theta}$, which has small mean square error:

$$\text{mse}(\tilde{\theta}) \equiv E\{(\tilde{\theta} - \theta)^2\} \tag{5}$$

$$= \text{Var}(\tilde{\theta}) + [\text{bias } (\tilde{\theta})]^2 \quad . \tag{6}$$

There is thus a trade-off between variance of the estimator and its bias. It is not obvious, without adopting extra criteria, how one would choose among estimators with the same mse but different variances and biases.

In our prediction problem the situation is much more complicated: we wish at each stage to estimate a function, $F_i(t)$, rather than a scalar; and the context is non-stationary since the $F_i(t)$'s are changing with i. However, the analogy with the classical case has some value. We can think of the u-plot as similar to an investigation of bias. Indeed, it is easy to show that, if $E\{\tilde{F}_i(t)\} = F_i(t)$ for all i, the expected value of the u-plot is the line of unit slope. Thus a systematic deviation between $E\{\tilde{F}_i(t)\}$ and $F_i(t)$ will be detected by the u-plot. We shall return to this question when we look at adaptive procedures in a later section.

The fact that we are making a sequence of predictions in a non-stationary context complicates matters. Thus a prediction system could be biased in one direction for early predictions and in the other direction for later predictions (and, of course, more complicated deviations from reality are possible). The y-plot is a (crude) attempt to detect such a situation.

The u-plot and y-plot procedures, then, are simple analyses of something analogous to bias. Can we similarly analyse 'variability' in our more complicated situation?

The median plot of Figure 2, for example, shows JM to be more variable than LV. This suggests that the $\{\tilde{F}_i(t)\}$ sequence for JM is more variable than that for LV. The important question is whether this extra variability of JM is an accurate reflection of what happens to the true $\{F_i(t)\}$. Is $\{\tilde{F}_i(t)\}$ fluctuating rapidly in order to track the truly fluctuating $\{F_i(t)\}$, or is it exhibiting random sampling fluctuations about a slowly changing $\{F_i(t)\}$ sequence?

If we had the true $\{F_i(t)\}$ sequence available, it would be relatively easy to obtain measures akin to variance. We could, for example, average the Cramer-von Mises distances between $\tilde{F}_i(t)$ and $F_i(t)$ over some range of i. Unfortunately, the $\{F_i(t)\}$ sequence is not known. We have been unsuccessful in attempts to obtain good measures of the variability between $\{\tilde{F}_i(t)\}$ and $\{F_i(t)\}$. There follow some quite crude measures of variability. In section 5.4 we shall consider a global measure which incorporates both 'bias' and 'noise': loosely analogous to mse in the iid case.

4.3.1 Braun statistic

Braun has proposed, on obvious intuitive grounds, the statistic

$$\frac{\sum_i \{t_i - \tilde{E}(T_i)\}^2}{\sum_i \{t_i - \bar{t}\}^2} \cdot \frac{n-1}{n-2} \tag{7}$$

where $\tilde{E}(T_i)$ is the estimated mean of T_i, i.e. the expectation of the predictor distribution, $\tilde{F}_i(t)$, and n is the number of terms in the sums. The normalising denominator is not strictly necessary here, since it will be the same for all prediction systems and we shall only be <u>comparing</u> values of this statistic for different systems on the same data: there are no obvious ways of carrying out formal tests to see whether a particular realisation of the statistic is objectively 'too large'.

4.3.2 Median variability

A comparison of

$$\sum_i \left| \frac{m_i - m_{i-1}}{m_{i-1}} \right| \tag{8}$$

where m_i is the predicted median of T_i, between different prediction systems can indicate objectively which is producing the most variable predictions. For example, the greater variability of the JM medians in Figure 2 is indicated by a value of 9.57 against LV's 2.96. Of course, this does not tell us whether the extra JM variability reflects true variability of the actual reliability.

4.3.3 Rate variability

A similar comparison can be based on the ROCOF sequence, r_i, calculated immediately after a fix:

$$\sum_i \left| \frac{r_i - r_{i-1}}{r_{i-1}} \right| \quad . \tag{9}$$

The JM value for the predictions of Table 1 data is 8.37, for LV 3.18.

For both (8) and (9) we can only compare prediction systems on the same data.

4.4 Prequential likelihood

In a series of important recent papers [26, 27, 29, 30], A. P. Dawid has treated theoretical issues concerned with the validity of forecasting systems. Dawid's discussion of the notion of calibration is relevant to the software reliability prediction problem. Here we shall confine ourselves to the prequential likelihood (PL) function and, in particular, the prequential likelihood ratio (PLR). We shall use PLR as an investigative tool to decide on the relative plausibility of the predictions emanating from two models.

The PL is defined as follows. The predictive distribution $\tilde{F}_i(t)$ for T_i based on $t_1, t_2, \ldots t_{i-1}$ will be assumed to have a pdf

$$\tilde{f}_i(t) = \frac{d}{dt} \tilde{F}_i(t) \quad . \tag{10}$$

For predictions of $T_{j+1}, T_{j+2}, \ldots T_{j+n}$ the prequential likelihood is

$$PL_n = \prod_{i=j+1}^{j+n} \tilde{f}_i(t_i) \quad . \tag{11}$$

A comparison of two prediction systems, A and B, can be made via their prequential likelihood ratio

$$PLR_n = \frac{\prod_{i=j+1}^{j+n} \tilde{f}_i^{A}(t_i)}{\prod_{i=j+1}^{j+n} \tilde{f}_i^{B}(t_i)} \quad . \tag{12}$$

Dawid [26] shows that if $PLR_n \to \infty$ as $n \to \infty$, prediction system B is discredited in favour of A.

To get an intuitive feel for the behaviour of the prequential likelihood, consider Figure 9. Here we consider for simplicity the problem of predicting a sequence of identically distributed random variables, i.e. $F_i(t) = F(t)$, $f_i(t) = f(t)$ for all i. The extension to our non-stationary case is trivial.

In Figure 9(a) the sequence of predictor densities are 'biased' to the left of the true distribution. Observations, which will tend to fall in the body of the true distribution, will tend to be in the (right hand) tails of the predictor densities. Thus the prequential likelihood will tend to be small.

In Figure 9(b) the predictions are very 'noisy', but have an expectation close to the true distribution (low 'bias'). There is a tendency, again, for the body of the true distribution to correspond to a tail of the predictor (here either left or right tail). Thus the likely observations (from the body of the true distribution) will have low predictive probability, and the prequential likelihood will tend to be small again.

Notice that this last argument extends to our non-stationary case. Consider the case where the true distributions fluctuate for different values of i, corresponding to occasional bad fixes, for example. If the predictor sequence were 'too smooth', perhaps as a result of smoothing from an inference

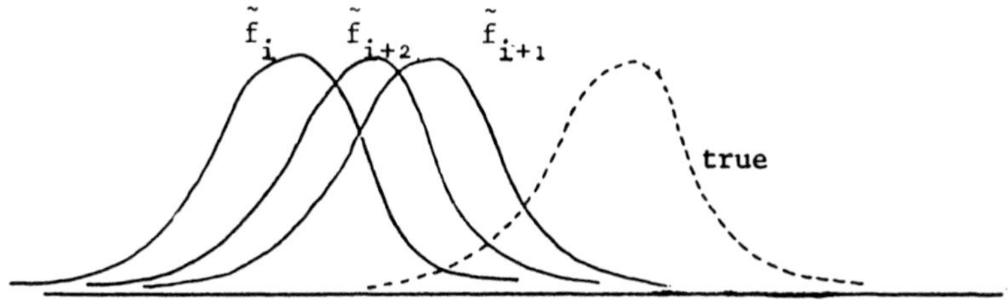

Figure 9(a) These predictions have high 'bias' and low 'noise'.

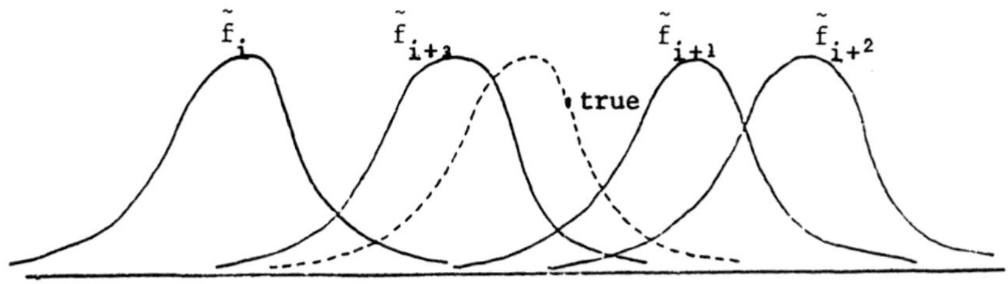

Figure 9(b) These predictions have high 'noise' and low 'bias'.

procedure, this would be detected. The observations would tend to fall in the bodies of the (noisy) true distributions, and hence in the tails of the predictors, giving a small prequential likelihood.

Thus the prequential likelihood can in principle detect predictors which are too noisy (when the true distributions are not variable) and predictors which are too smooth (when the true distributions are variable). This contrasts with the measures of variability proposed in section 4.3: here we could detect noise in a predictor, but could not tell whether it reflected actual noise in the reliability.

The prequential likelihood, then, should allow us to detect both consistent deviations between predictions and reality ('bias'), and large variability in the distance between prediction and reality ('noise'). In this sense it is somewhat analagous to mse in parameter estimation (5, 6).

In fact it is possible to construct predictors which are (almost) exactly unbiased, but are useless in practice because of their great noisiness. An example is suggested by Miller [31]. He proposed, as a counter-example to the efficacy of the u-plot procedure, an estimator based only upon the previous one or two observations. His idea was to assume that the $\{T_i\}$ sequence was of exponential random variables, and estimate the mean of T_{i-1} by using t_{i-1} or by using $\frac{t_{i-1} + t_{i-2}}{2}$. In each case he contrived to obtain a predictor for T_{i-1}, $\tilde{F}_{i-1}(t)$, which was unbiased:

$$E\{\tilde{F}_{i-1}(t)\} = F_i(t) \quad . \tag{13}$$

An extra assumption, that $\tilde{F}_i(t)$ was close to $\tilde{F}_{i-1}(t)$, allowed the latter to be used as an approximate predictor for the unobserved T_i. Miller's intention was to produce an estimator which had a good u-plot ('unbiased') but which was clearly useless. A measure of his success can be seen by calculating the u-plot and y-plot Kolmogorov distances for his predictor (based on the previous two observations) on the data of Table 1. These are 0.078 and 0.069 respectively, which are not significant at the 10% level. These are much better than LV (0.14, 0.11) and JM (0.19, 0.12).

Could the prequential likelihood detect the (incorrect) noisiness of such a prediction system? Table 4 gives the PLR for JM versus Miller and LV versus Miller. In both cases we think it is obvious that the Miller predictions are being discredited.

Of course, this is not a stringent test of the usefulness of PLR for discriminating between realistic good and bad prediction systems. In Table 5 is shown the PLR of LV against JM. There is clear evidence to reject JM in favour of LV. More importantly, there is again strong evidence that JM is doing particularly badly from about i = 95 (n = 60) onwards. Prior to this, the relative fortunes of the two prediction systems fluctuate and it is briefly the case that JM is preferred.

One interpretation of the PLR, when A and B are Bayesian prediction systems [11], is as an approximation to the posterior odds of model A against model B. Suppose that the user believes that either model A is true, with prior probability p(A), or model B is true with prior probability p(B) (= 1 - p(A)). He now observes the failure behaviour of the system; in particular, he makes predictions from the two prediction systems and compares them with actual behaviour via the PLR. Thus, when he has made predictions for $T_{j+1}, T_{j+2}, \ldots T_{j+n}$ the PLR is

$$PLR_n = \prod_{i=j+1}^{j+n} \tilde{f}_i^A(t_i) \Big/ \prod_{i=j+1}^{j+n} \tilde{f}_i^B(t_i) = \frac{p(t_{j+n}, \ldots t_{j+1} | t_j, \ldots t_1, A)}{p(t_{j+n}, \ldots t_{j+1} | t_j, \ldots t_1, B)} \quad (14)$$

in an obvious notation. Using Bayes' Theorem this is

$$\frac{\dfrac{p(A|t_{j+n}, \ldots t_1)\, p(t_{j+n}, \ldots t_{j+1}|t_j, \ldots t_1)}{p(A|t_j, \ldots t_1)}}{\dfrac{p(B|t_{j+n}, \ldots t_1)\, p(t_{j+n}, \ldots t_{j+1}|t_j, \ldots t_1)}{p(B|t_j, \ldots t_1)}}$$

$$= \frac{p(A|t_{j+n}, \ldots t_1)}{p(B|t_{j+n}, \ldots t_1)} \cdot \frac{p(B|t_1, \ldots t_j)}{p(A|t_1, \ldots t_j)} \quad . \quad (15)$$

If the initial predictions were based only on prior belief (j = 0), the second term in (15) is merely the prior odds ratio. If the user is indifferent between A and B at this stage, this takes the value 1 since p(A) = p(B) = ½. Thus (15) becomes

$$\frac{w_A}{1 - w_A} \quad , \quad (16)$$

the posterior odds ratio, with w_A representing his posterior belief that A is true after seeing the data (i.e. after making predictions and comparing them with actual outcomes).

Of course, not all prediction systems are Bayesian ones. It is more usual to estimate the parameters via ML and use the 'plug-in' rule for prediction. Dawid, however, shows [26] that this procedure and the Bayesian predictive approach are asymptotically equivalent.

It is, in addition, not usual to allow j = 0 in practice. Although Bayesians can predict via prior belief without data, non-Bayesians usually insist that predictions are based on actual evidence. In practice though, the

n	JM PLR_n	LV PLR_n
10	4.00	3.26
20	30.8	82.1
30	158.	517.
40	8.92×10^4	7.18×10^5
50	9.32×10^5	1.01×10^6
60	4.91×10^6	5.72×10^5
70	2.48×10^6	2.53×10^7
80	6.01×10^5	2.63×10^8
90	3.67×10^6	3.97×10^{10}
100	6.34×10^8	3.96×10^{11}

Table 4 This table shows the ability of PLR to reject an unbiased model which is very noisy. The Miller model predicts using only the last two observations. Here we show PLR values, at 10-step intervals, for JM versus Miller and LV versus Miller. Clearly, Miller is being discredited by each of the other prediction systems: even JM, which is known to be bad.

n	PLR_n
10	1.19
20	0.318
30	0.252
40	0.096
50	0.745
60	6.50
70	0.088
80	0.00177
90	0.0000813
100	0.00119

Table 5 PLR of JM versus LV, data of Table 1. Clearly LV discredits JM overall, but less obvious for earlier predictions.

value of j may be quite small.

With these reservations, we think that (16) can be used as an intuitive interpretation of PLR. We shall use this idea, with some caution, in later sections.

5. Examples of predictive analysis

In this section we shall use the devices of the previous section to analyse the predictive quality of several prediction systems on the three data sets of Tables 1, 2 and 3. We emphasise that our primary intention is not to pick a 'universally best' prediction system. Rather, we hope to show how a fairly informal analysis can help a user to select, for a particular data source, reliability predictions in which he/she can have trust. Our own analyses suggest that one should approach a new data source without preconceptions as to which prediction system is likely to be best: such preconceptions are likely to be wrong.

The prediction systems we use here are: Jelinski-Moranda (JM), [1], Littlewood-Verrall (LV), [3], Littlewood (L), [17], Weibull order statistic (W), [18], Keiller-Littlewood (KL), [6], Duane non-homogeneous Poisson process (D), [21, 22], Bayesian Jelinski-Moranda (BJM), [16], Bayesian Littlewood (BL), [18] Goel-Okumoto (GO), [37], Littlewood non-homogeneous Poisson process (LNHPP), [18].

Consider first the data of Table 1. Table 6 summarises our results concerning the quality of performance of the various prediction systems on this data.

In Table 6, it can be seen that LNHPP comes first on the PL ranks, followed by L, then BL, LV, KL and W. The Braun statistic rankings closely follow the PL ranks.

Model	$\sum \left\| \frac{m_i - m_{i-1}}{m_{i-1}} \right\|$ (rank)	$\sum \left\| \frac{r_i - r_{i-1}}{r_{i-1}} \right\|$ (rank)	Braun statistic (rank)	u-plot KS distance (sig. level)	y-plot KS distance (sig. level)	$-\log_e$ (PL) (ranks)
JM	9.57 (8)	8.37 (10)	1.31 (10)	.190 (1%)	.120 (NS)	770.3 (9)
BJM		7.21 (8)	1.11 (9)	.170 (1%)	.116 (NS)	770.7 (10)
L[(1)]	6.82 (5)	6.23 (6)	0.86 (3)	.109 (NS)	.069 (NS)	762.4 (2)
BL		3.72 (4)	0.83 (2)	.119 (NS)	.075 (NS)	763.0 (3)
LV	2.96 (2)	3.18 (2)	0.90 (7)	.144 (5%)	.110 (NS)	764.9 (6)
KL	2.79 (1)	3.26 (3)	0.88 (5)	.138 (5%)	.109 (NS)	764.7 (5)
D	3.11 (3)	2.92 (1)	0.89 (6)	.159 (2%)	.093 (NS)	765.3 (7)
GO	8.62 (7)	7.34 (9)	1.11 (8)	.153 (2%)	.125 (10%)	768.6 (8)
LNHPP	4.16 (4)	3.84 (5)	0.82 (1)	.081 (NS)	.064 (NS)	761.4 (1)
W	7.38 (6)	6.61 (7)	0.86 (4)	.075 (NS)	.075 (NS)	763.0 (3)

Table 6 Analysis of data of Table 1 using the prediction systems described in the paper. In this, and the following tables, the instantaneous mean time to failure (IMTTF) is used instead of the predicted mean in the calculating of the Braun statistic for BJM, BL, D, GO, LNHPP, W. This is because the mean does not exist, or is hard to calculate. The IMTTF is defined to be the reciprocal of the current ROCOF.

Note [(1)] that for L the ML routine does not always terminate normally, so we are not certain that true ML estimates are being used. It is possible that we could get better L predictors by allowing the ML search routine to run longer.

Both L and LNHPP have non significant u-plot and y-plot distances, although LNHPP has a smaller u-plot distance. This might suggest that LNHPP is slightly better on the 'bias' criterion. For noise, each of these prediction systems has similar rankings on the median and rate statistics, but in each case the value for LNHPP is smaller than that for L.

In fact, the predictions from L and LNHPP are very similar. Figure 10(a) shows their median predictions along with those of JM and LV shown earlier in Figure 2. Notice that these predictions are less pessimistic than LV, less optimistic than JM, but are closer to LV: this adds weight to our analysis of the LV and JM predictions in section 4. The slightly worse PL value for L compared with LNHPP is probably accounted for by its extra noise, as shown by the median plot and the median and rate difference statistics.

Of the high PL-ranking predictions, that leaves BL, KL and W. Unfortunately, it is not easy to calculate medians for BL, so these are not shown on Figure 10(b) KL gives results which are very similar to LV: significantly too pessimistic on the u-plot. W is non significant on both u- and y-plots but (as for L) is noisier on both the statistics and the plot. Since u- and y-plot distances are so small, this noisiness probably explains its relatively poor performance on the PL.

If we take the best six prediction systems (L, BL, LV, KL, LNHPP and W) and discount BL (because we cannot compute the medians), LV and KL (because they exhibit significant 'bias' as evidenced by the u-plot) we are left with L, LNHPP and W. The agreement between their median predictions is striking (see Figure 10).

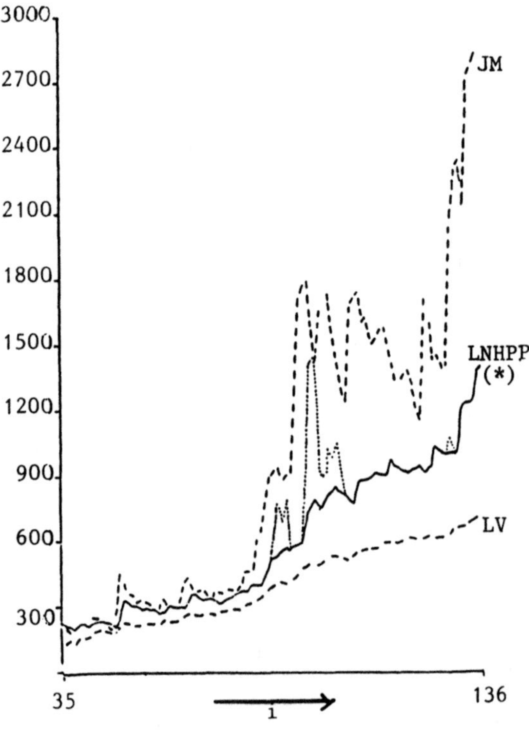

Figure 10(a) Median predictions from L, NHPP, LV, JM for data of Table 1. L and LNHPP are virtually indistinguishable for many predictions. The (dotted) excursions of L could be 'spurious', resulting from non-convergence of the ML optimisation algorithm.

(*) L shown dotted

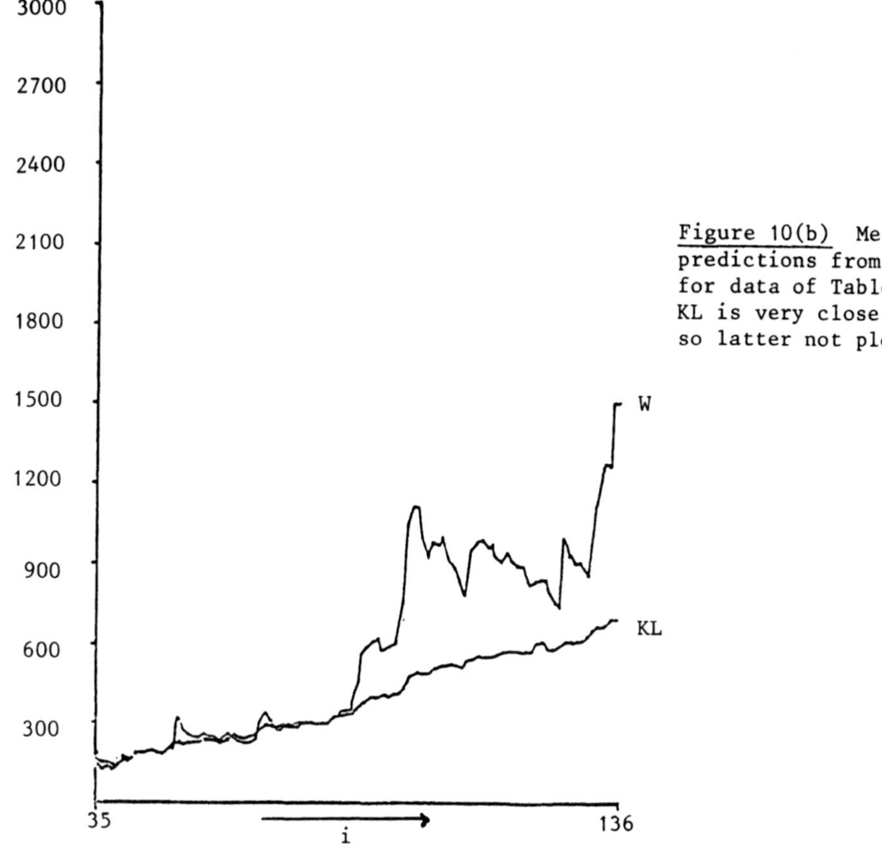

Figure 10(b) Median predictions from W and KL for data of Table 1. KL is very close to LV, so latter not plotted.

What conclusions could a user draw from all this? We assume that he/she wishes to make predictions about the future and has available the data of Table 1 upon which our analysis is based. We also assume that he/she is prepared to trust for future predictions a prediction system whose past predictions have been shown to be close to actual observation (roughly this means that the future development of the software is similar to the past: there is no discontinuity between past and future). In that case we would suggest that, for this data source, a user makes a future prediction using LNHPP.

Notice that it is possible for the 'preferred prediction system' to change as the data vector gets larger. For example, based on the whole of the Table 1 data LV is preferable to JM; on the first 60 observations JM is better than LV (see Table 5). Thus, our advice to a user to use LNHPP is strictly only applicable for the next prediction. In principle this analysis should be repeated at each step. In practice this is sometimes not necessary: we have found that changes usually take place fairly slowly so that relatively infrequent checks on predictive quality are sufficient. However, these analyses are not computationally onerous when compared with the numerical optimisations needed for the ML estimation at each step.

Table 7 shows a similar analysis of the data of Table 2. The prequential likelihood suggests that L, BL, LV and KL perform best. A more detailed study shows an interesting trade-off between 'bias' and 'noise'. The KL and LV u-plot distances are significant and the plots are both below the line of unit slope, indicating that the predictions are <u>too pessimistic</u>. The noise statistics based on medians and rates show that L is more noisy than LV and KL. Since they give similar PL values we can conclude that L is <u>objectively</u> too noisy. We thus have an interpretation of the behaviour of the plots of Figure 11.

Model	$\sum \left\lvert \frac{m_i - m_{i-1}}{m_{i-1}} \right\rvert$ (rank)	$\sum \left\lvert \frac{r_i - r_{i-1}}{r_{i-1}} \right\rvert$ (rank)	Braun statistic (rank)	u-plot KS distance (sig. level)	y-plot KS distance (sig. level)	$-\log_e$ (PL) (ranks)
JM	4.23 (6)	3.81 (8)	1.11 (8)	.121 (NS)	.115 (NS)	466.22 (6)
BJM		3.27 (7)	1.04 (5)	.110 (NS)	.077 (NS)	466.64 (7)
L[(1)]	5.27 (7)	4.66 (9)	1.07 (7)	.123 (NS)	.091 (NS)	465.49 (2)
BL		2.82 (6)	.96 (1)	.138 (NS)	.068 (NS)	465.18 (1)
LV[(1)]	2.33 (3)	2.18 (4)	.97 (3)	.167 (10%)	.051 (NS)	465.52 (3)
KL	2.33 (3)	2.17 (3)	.96 (1)	.170 (10%)	.051 (NS)	465.81 (4)
D	1.96 (2)	1.84 (2)	1.04 (5)	.209 (2%)	.052 (NS)	467.78 (9)
GO	1.06 (1)	1.03 (1)	1.21 (10)	.271 (1%)	.085 (NS)	473.87 (10)
LNHPP	3.05 (5)	2.76 (5)	.97 (3)	.169 (10%)	.082 (NS)	465.85 (5)
W	6.16 (8)	5.48 (10)	1.17 (9)	.100 (NS)	.111 (NS)	466.89 (8)

<u>Table 7</u> Analysis of data of Table 2. Here[(1)] the ML routine did not terminate normally in a high proportion of cases for L and LV. The extreme closeness of LV and KL predictions (the latter always terminating normally) suggests that the LV values are close to optimal. This is not obvious for L, which may be able to give better results.

A user is faced with an interesting choice between L and KL or LV, and the analysis helps him to exercise it intelligently. If he prefers to be conservative, and consistently so, he should use LV or KL. If he prefers to be closer to the true reliability <u>on average</u> (but with fluctuating errors) he should choose L. This is similar to the situation faced by the statistician, with a choice between two estimators having the same mse but different variances and bias (see (6)).

There is evidence here that KL and LV are 'merely' biased. They are therefore good candidates for the adaptive ideas of the next section. There is some evidence that the predictions of KL and LV are almost identical for this data.

Table 8 shows the analysis of Table 3 data. Here BL seems to be giving the best results. It is, however, surprising that so many models do well on this data set. This may have something to do with the way the data was collected. The interfailure times refer to total operating time for a <u>population</u> of copies of the system. When a failure is observed, a fix (i.e. software fix or hardware design change) is introduced into all copies.

There are three successive very large observations near the end of the data set (each is larger than any previous observation in a data set with fairly slow reliability growth). Table 8 shows the PLR for <u>all</u> predictions, and for predictions which exclude these large observations. BL is best in both cases, but others change ranks dramatically. LV, for example does well on the smaller set of predictions, but poorly on the full set. This suggests that LV is assigning low probability density to the large observations (i.e.

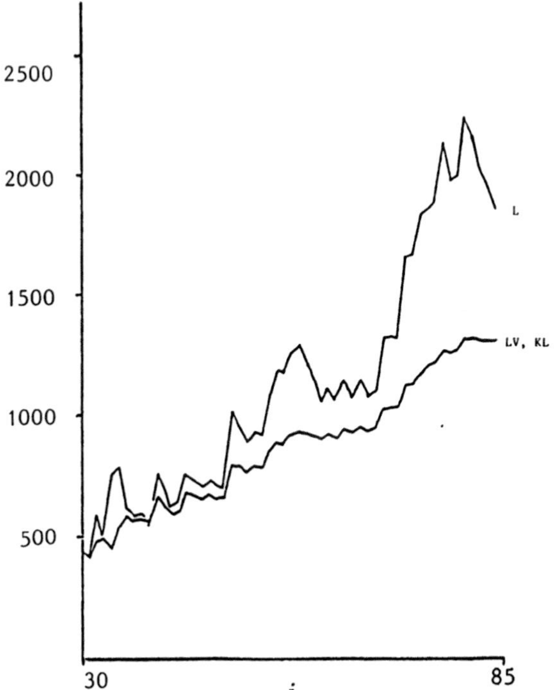

<u>Figure 11</u> Median predictions from KL, LV and L for data of Table 2. KL and LV are identical to within the resolution of this table: less than 2% difference in medians.

they lie in the tails of the predictive distributions). BJM, on the other hand, improves its rank equally dramatically by including the large observations.

If nothing else, this shows the importance of careful data collection. Here, we cannot know whether these large observations should be discounted or not.

Model	$\Sigma \left\lvert \frac{m_i - m_{i-1}}{m_{i-1}} \right\rvert$ (rank)	$\Sigma \left\lvert \frac{r_i - r_{i-1}}{r_{i-1}} \right\rvert$ (rank)	Braun statistic (rank)	u-plot KS distance (sig. level)	y-plot KS distance (sig. level)	$-\log_e$ (PL), rank[3]
JM	4.77 (7)	4.52 (9)	.941 (4)	.083 (NS)	.073 (NS)	711.0, 4 [637.2, 9]
BJM[2]		4.38 (7)	.954 (9)	.084 (NS)	.071 (NS)	710.9, 2 [637.5, 10]
L[1]	4.98 (8)	4.74 (10)	.943 (5)	.079 (NS)	.069 (NS)	711.1, 6 [637.0, 7]
BL		3.11 (4)	.935 (1)	.064 (NS)	.056 (NS)	710.4, 1 [635.9, 1]
LV	2.64 (2)	2.75 (2)	.949 (7)	.087 (NS)	.065 (NS)	711.8, 8 [636.3, 3]
KL	2.76 (3)	2.89 (3)	.953 (8)	.102 (NS)	.066 (NS)	712.6, 9 [636.8, 6]
D	1.98 (1)	1.92 (1)	.994 (10)	.117 (10%)	.074 (NS)	714.5, 10 [636.7, 5]
GO	4.58 (5)	4.30 (6)	.937 (2)	.075 (NS)	.075 (NS)	711.0, 4 [637.1, 8]
LNHPP	3.30 (4)	3.14 (5)	.939 (3)	.072 (NS)	.058 (NS)	710.9, 2 [636.1, 2]
W	4.67 (6)	4.43 (8)	.945 (6)	.064 (NS)	.057 (NS)	711.3, 7 [636.7, 4]

Table 8 Analysis of data of Table 3. Again, ML terminated abnormally for many L predictions [1]. BJM[2] calculations involved overflow on some predictions. Both these predictors may be able to give better results. The second set[3] of [$-\log_e$ (PL), rank] ignores the last ten predictions. There are three very large observations at the end (larger than any experienced before): the switches in rank indicate the effect these observations have upon predictive quality.

6. Adapting and combining predictions; future directions

In several data sets we have found that certain prediction systems seem to be 'only' biased: an example is LV for the data of Table 2. In cases like this, where the relationship between prediction and reality is approximately stationary, we can attempt to estimate this relationship and use the estimate to improve future predictions. Formally, we have $F_i(t) = G_i[\tilde{F}_i(t)]$ where G_i does not depend upon i. Since $\tilde{F}_i(t)$ is a function of data observed so far, the sequence $\{G_i\}$ can be thought of as a random sequence of functions. The stationarity of the sequence is the key idea. If we are assured of this stationarity, we might reasonably attempt to find a 'best' estimate of the function, G_i^* say, to obtain an adapted predictor:

$$\tilde{F}_i^*(t) = G_i^*[\tilde{F}_i(t)] \quad . \tag{17}$$

Of course, this stationarity is a very strong condition and it would be unreasonable to expect it to hold exactly in practice. It may hold approximately. At the very least, it will be necessary to check that previous predictions have given a good y-plot. Better tests for approximate stationarity are needed and are being investigated.

Given that we believe there is approximate stationarity in the relationship between $\{\tilde{F}_i\}$ and $\{F_i\}$, there are various ways we might approach the problem of finding a 'best' G_i^*. One of the simplest is to use the u-plot, as shown in Figure 12.

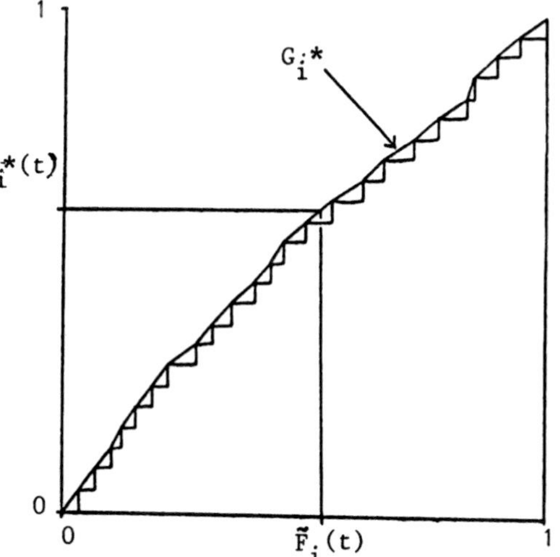

Figure 12 Method of calculating an adapted prediction. G_i^* is the 'joined-up' u-plot based on predictions made prior to observing the random variable T_i. $\tilde{F}_i(t)$ is the raw prediction we would make from the basic prediction system at this stage, $\tilde{F}_i^*(t)$ is the modification of this which learns from the quality of previous predictions.

The procedure is then as follows:

Stage 1: Check that y-plot is good (based on $t_1, t_2, \ldots t_{i-1}$).

Stage 2: Find u-plot for predictions made before T_i (i.e. based on subsets of $t_1, t_2, \ldots t_{i-1}$).

Stage 3: Use the prediction system to make a 'raw' prediction, $\tilde{F}_i(t)$.

Stage 4: Transform the raw prediction via the u-plot to obtain the adapted prediction, $\tilde{F}_i^*(t)$.

It is important to emphasise that this is a genuine prediction system again. At each stage we are obtaining $\tilde{F}_i^*(t)$ by using only information observed earlier. Thus we can use some of the devices of section 4 to examine the quality of the new prediction system.

Figure 13 shows the median of the adapted LV and adapted JM predictions for the data of Table 1. In each case it is obvious that the adapted version is better than the raw version: adapted LV is less pessimistic that the known pessimistic LV, adapted JM is less optimistic than the known optimistic JM. It is clear that the noise of these median plots remains more or less unchanged. This is not surprising, since the $\{G_i{*}\}$ sequence is 'slowly changing': successive $G_i{*}$ differ by the addition of one point to the u-plot.

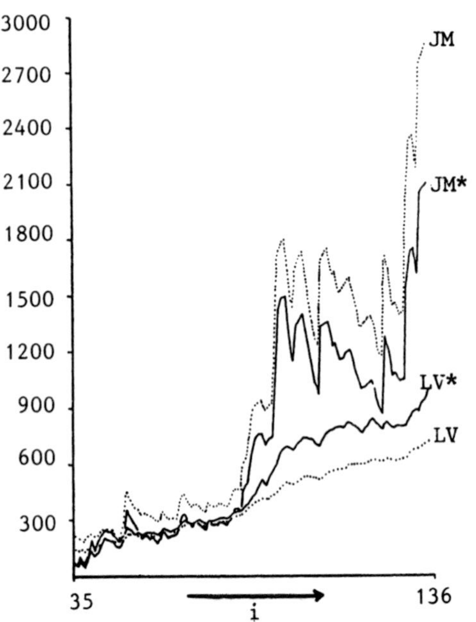

Figure 13 Median predictions for JM, LV, JM*, LV* on data of Table 1. Notice how the adaptive procedure involves a shift from the JM values without an obvious change in noisiness. There is some evidence that LV* is slightly more noisy than LV.

JM* is less optimistic than the known over-optimistic JM, LV* is less pessimistic than the known over-pessimistic LV.

The $\{\tilde{F}_i{*}(t)\}$ sequence can be used to generate

$$u_i{*} = \tilde{F}_i{*}(t_i) \tag{18}$$

as before, since t_i (the realisation of T_i) is observed after $\tilde{F}_i{*}$ is calculated. We can thus form u*-plots and y*-plots in the usual way. In this case the adapted LV has KS distances of 0.084 (u*-plot) and 0.078 (y*-plot) compared with 0.144 and 0.110. Adapted JM gives 0.104 and 0.108 compared with 0.190 and 0.120 for the raw JM. Not only are these an improvement in both cases, but now all four distances are non-significant.

It is surprising that in this case the y*-plots are better than the y-plots. The procedure is only designed to improve 'bias'. This seems to be a common result of using the adaptive procedure. We have used it on several data sets with several different prediction procedures [34]. In no case is the u*-plot significantly worse than the u-plot, and it is usually better. In only one case out of the 30 examined was the y*-plot significantly worse than the y-plot, and again it was usually better.

Figure 14 shows the effect of applying the adaptive procedure to the LV analysis of the data of Table 2. As we detected in section 5, LV is slightly too pessimistic (significant u-plot KS distance, but only at 10% level). The adapted predictions are more optimistic, particularly near the end of the data.

Figure 15 shows raw and adaptive LV and JM on the data of Table 3. Again, the adapted versions are in closer agreement, and differ from the raw predictions in the right way (as indicated by the u-plots).

We have here, then, a very simple procedure which can be used with any prediction system and will usually produce a better prediction system. Computational requirements are light, even for the step-by-step modifications of G_i^* used here.

There does not seem to be any price paid for the improvements which come from 'learning' from past behaviour. However, the timid user has available some of the devices of section 4 to check the quality of the adapted predictions.

Unfortunately, the prequential likelihood cannot be used here. Since the

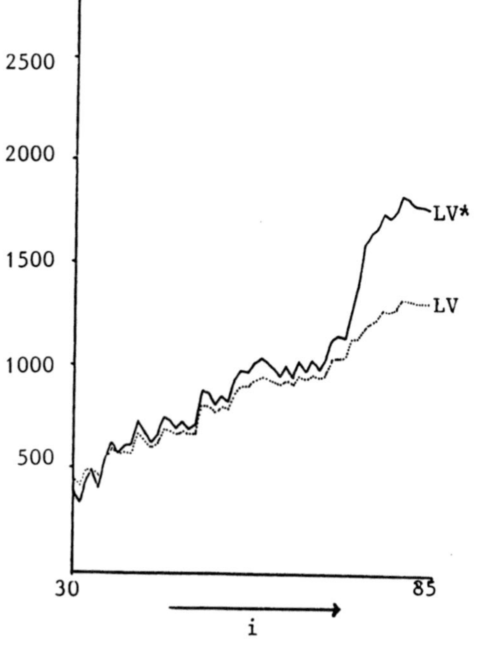

Figure 14 Median predictions for LV and LV* on data of Table 2.

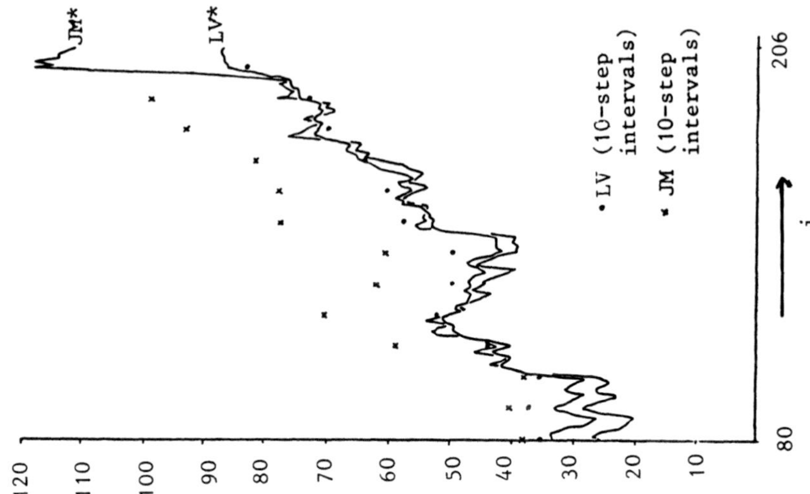

Figure 15 Median predictions for JM, LV, JM*, LV* on data of Table 3 (LV, JM only at 10-step intervals for clarity, JM* broken where it crosses the (unbroken) LV*).
Adaptive predictions are in very close agreement, except at very end. JM* noisier than LV*.

PL depends on predictive *probability densities*, it uses the slopes of the $\{G_i^*\}$ functions. Although we would expect the G_i^* functions to change slowly with i, the slopes (probability density function) for a particular G_i^* are highly variable. Thus a use of PLR to compare $\{\tilde{F}_i^*\}$ with $\{\tilde{F}_i\}$ would 'unfairly' discriminate against $\tilde{F}_i^*$.

There are some interesting unresolved issues here. Most users would be happy to be able to make accurate *probability* statements about future behaviour. PLR, as we have used it, requires accurate prediction of probability *density*. There is a sense, then, in which it is too strong as a criterion for comparing prediction systems.

One way forward might be to construct prequential *probability* ratios. It is not obvious, though, how to choose appropriate intervals on the time axis about which to make predictions.

A more promising approach would be to try to construct sequences $\{G_i^*\}$ where each member is smoother than the ones considered above which use 'joined-up' u-plots. We are currently investigating the use of splines to obtain such sequences from the u_i's.

Another approach is to assume that $G_i^* \in \mathcal{G}$, some suitable parametric family, for example Beta distributions. This raises the interesting possibility of using PL as a means of estimating the transforming function, G_i^*, in the cases where this is differentiable. Since

$$\tilde{F}_i^*(t) = G_i^*[\tilde{F}_i(t)]$$

we have predictive densities

$$\tilde{f}_i^*(t) = g_i^*[\tilde{F}_i(t)].\tilde{f}_i(t) \qquad (19)$$

where g_i^* is the derivative of G_i^* and $\tilde{f}_i(t)$ is the raw predictive density. Consider now the problem of modifying the raw predictor for T_{j+n+1} in the light of the performance of the prediction system in predicting T_{j+1}, T_{j+2}, ... T_{j+n}. It seems sensible to choose our G_{j+n+1}^* to be the member of G which maximises the PL over the observed history from j + 1 to j + n:

$$\max_{G} \prod_{j+1}^{j+n} \tilde{f}_i^*(t_i) \equiv \max_{G} \prod_{j+1}^{j+n} \{g[\tilde{F}_i(t_i)]\} \tilde{f}_i(t_i)$$

$$\equiv \prod_{j+1}^{j+n} \tilde{f}_i(t_i) \cdot \max_{G} \prod_{j+1}^{j+n} g(u_i) \quad . \qquad (20)$$

That is, a procedure based on optimising prequential likelihood over previous predictions is equivalent to using maximum likelihood to estimate the (assumed common) distribution of the $\{U_i\}$ sequence based on u_{j+1}, ... u_{j+n}. This very interesting observation throws light upon the adaptive procedure. It shows, for example, that our strong stationarity assumption has been transformed into an assumption that $\{U_i\}$ have a common distribution: the problem then is simply one of estimating this distribution given some observations, u_i.

Further investigation of some of these ideas looks promising and is being carried out by the authors.

Another way in which we can learn from past behaviour to improve future predictions is to combine the predictions arising from different systems. Given prediction systems A and B, we might consider a predictor

$$\tilde{F}_{j+n+1}^{(A+B)}(t) = w_A \tilde{F}_{j+n+1}^A(t) + w_B \tilde{F}_{j+n+1}^B(t) \qquad (21)$$

where w_A (= 1 - w_B) would be chosen in some optimal way in the light of experience of previous predictions emanating from A and B.

We have tried two ways of combining predictors. The first method is motivated by how we would behave if we were in a pure Bayesian context. If $\{F_i^A\}$ and $\{F_i^B\}$ were Bayesian predictive distributions, we would form the 'meta' Bayesian predictor, (21), by letting w_A, w_B be the posterior probabilities of models A and B.

Of course, it is rare to have two Bayesian prediction systems. We shall therefore appeal to the argument of section 4.4 which showed that the PLR can be interpreted as the approximate posterior odds of A against B (see (16)). Thus at stage j+n+1 in (21) we shall use the value of w_A obtained from

$$PLR = \frac{w_A}{1 - w_A} \tag{22}$$

where PLR is based on predictions j + 1 through j + n. We shall call this meta procedure $(A + B)_1$. It was suggested by Ian Goudie [34].

An alternative approach is to choose that value of w_A to use in (21) which would have maximised the PL for $\{\tilde{F}_i^{(A+B)}, i = j + 1, \ldots j + n\}$. We shall refer to this prediction system as $(A + B)_2$.

We emphasise again that these procedures are proper prediction systems. They rely only upon data collected in the past, which is used dynamically to change the weights w_A, w_B at each stage. Once again, a user does not need to believe a priori that $(A + B)_1$ or $(A + B)_2$ are good: their predictive performance can be monitored, using the techniques of section 4, just like any other prediction system.

Figure 16 shows median plots for $(LV + JM)_1$ and $(LV + JM)_2$ predictions of the data of Table 1. There is a tendency for $(LV + JM)_1$ to give very

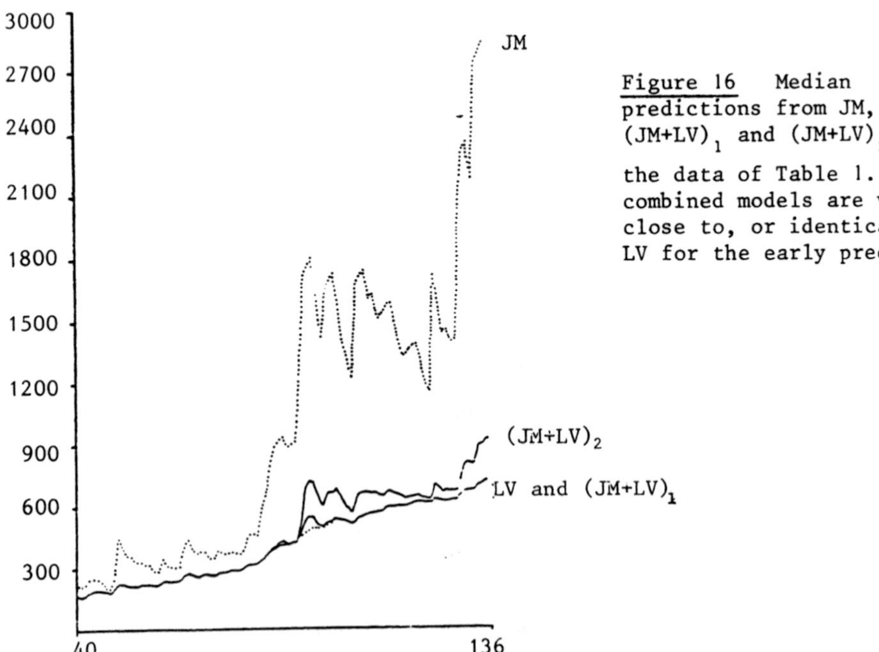

Figure 16 Median predictions from JM, LV, $(JM+LV)_1$ and $(JM+LV)_2$ for the data of Table 1. Both combined models are very close to, or identical to, LV for the early predictions.

small weights to JM throughout the range of predictions. This is reflected in the median plots, where $(LV + JM)_1$ and LV are almost identical. As for $(LV + JM)_2$, this gives weight 0 exactly to JM for predictions 40 through 84.

The PL for the four prediction systems suggests that $(LV + JM)_2$ is significantly better than the other three. The u- and y-plot KS distances are given in Table 9. It can be seen that $(LV + JM)_2$ is best on each.

An analysis of this data using $(L + JM)_2$ is interesting. Here $w_{JM} = 0$ for all predictions, i.e. the 'combined' prediction totally rejects JM. This is plausible since both L and JM are optimistic, but L is less so; also L is less noisy than JM. Thus, for both 'bias' and 'noise' criteria, L is better than JM, and there is no benefit to be gained by incorporating the JM predictions. This contrasts with LV and JM, where we know that one is pessimistic, the other optimistic (particularly for later predictions). There is therefore benefit in using a weighted average, since the truth is known to lie between the two raw predictions.

Both the adaptive and combined predictions described here seem attractive candidates for further study. It would be easy to combine more than two predictions, using either of our two criteria. In fact we can think of generalisations to super meta prediction systems. For example, we could adapt all models first and then combine the adapted models.

Model	KS distances	
	u-plot	y-plot
JM	.189	.126
LV	.145	.107
$(LV+JM)_1$	.145	.105
$(LV+JM)_2$	.134	.076

Table 9 KS distances for u- and y-plots of JM, LV and combined predictions, data of Table 1. Notice that these refer to a slightly different range of i, so the results do not correspond exactly to those of Table 6.

In this paper we have concentrated upon prediction of the next time to failure. Clearly, some of the techniques described here can be used for longer term prediction. We could, for example, predict T_{i+20}, based on data t_1, t_2, ... t_{i-1} and analyse these predictions using the ideas of section 4.

It is fairly obvious that a prediction system which performs well for short-term prediction cannot be guaranteed to perform well for longer-term prediction. In Figure 3, for example, JM does dramatically worse for 20-step ahead predictions than it does for 1-step ahead. This suggests a 'horses for courses' approach: a user should be sure that a prediction system is performing well for the type of prediction of interest.

Clearly, there are certain types of prediction which are not obviously amenable to the analysis described in section 4. For example, it is commonly desired to predict the time to achieve a specified target reliability (perhaps the reliability which must be achieved before the product can be shipped). It is not clear how predictions of this (random variable) time can be analysed directly. They could be examined indirectly via an analysis of predictions of T_i, T_{i+1}, ... based on t_1, ... t_{i-1}, but this may not be adequate. Problems of this kind require further study.

7. Summary and Conclusions

Our theme in this paper has been that predictive quality is the only consideration for a user of software reliability models. We have shown that a good 'model' is not sufficient to produce good predictions, and that there is no universal 'best buy' among the competing methods. Prediction systems perform with varying adequacy on different data sources. Users, therefore, need to be able to select, from a plethora of prediction systems, one (or more) which gives trustworthy predictions for the software being studied. Our aim in this work has been to provide some tools to assist this selection. We do not claim that these are complete; indeed, we hope that other workers will be stimulated to find different techniques. In the meantime, we believe that the work reported here can be used by anyone wishing to predict the reliability of software.

If workers in the community can agree on suitable criteria for quality of prediction, there arise possibilities for new approaches via adaptive and learning techniques. We believe, from our experience with rudimentary adaptive modelling, that these ideas show great promise. Not merely do they allow current models to be improved in very general ways, but they also point the way forward to new methods with weak underlying assumptions.

Acknowledgements

P. Y. Chan's work was supported by ICL plc through a Research Fellowship at the Centre for Software Reliability, City University. B. Littlewood was partially supported by National Aeronautics and Space Administration, and partially by ICL plc.

This work has been helped over the past couple of years by the kind provision of data by several individuals. We have also benefitted greatly from discussions with many people. We would particularly like to single out Tom Anderson, Phil Dawid, Mike Dyer, Ian Goudie, Norman Harris, Earle Migneault and Doug Miller.

Our thanks to Grace Palmer, who typed this and corrected (some of) our mistakes.

References

[1] Z. Jelinski and P. B. Moranda, 'Software reliability research', in Statistical Computer Performance Evaluation (W. Freiberger, ed.). New York: Academic Press, 1972, pp. 465-484.

[2] M. Shooman, 'Operational testing and software reliability during program development', in Record. 1973 IEEE Symp. Computer Software Reliability (New York, NY, 1973, April 30 - May 2) pp. 51-57.

[3] B. Littlewood and J. L. Verrall, 'A Bayesian reliability growth model for computer software', J. Royal Statist. Soc., C (Applied Statistics), 22, 1973, pp. 332-346.

[4] J. D. Musa, 'A theory of software reliability and its application', IEEE Trans. Software Engineering, Vol SE-1, 1975 Sept, pp. 312-327.

[5] C. J. Dale, 'Software Reliability Evaluation Methods', British Aerospace Dynamics Group, ST-26750, 1982.

[6] P. A. Keiller, B. Littlewood, D. R. Miller and A. Sofer, 'Comparison of software reliability predictions', Digest FTCS 13 (13th International Symposium on Fault-Tolerant Computing) pp. 128-134, 1983.

[7] B. Littlewood, 'How to measure software reliability and how not to', IEEE Trans. Reliability, Vol R-28, 1979, June, pp. 103-110.

[8] J. C. Laprie, 'Dependability evaluation of software systems in operation' IEEE Trans. Software Engineering, 1984, December.

[9] E. N. Adams, 'Optimizing preventive service of software products', IBM Journal of Research and Development, Vol 28, No. 1, 1984.

[10] H. Ascher and H. Feingold, Repairable Systems Reliability, Lecture Notes in Statistics, No. 7, Marcel Dekker, New York, 1984.

[11] J. Aitchison and I. R. Dunsmore, Statistical Prediction Analysis, Cambridge University Press, Cambridge, 1975.

[12] P. M. Nagel and J. A. Skrivan, 'Software reliability: repetitive run experimentation and modelling', BCS-40399, Boeing Computer Services Company, Seattle, Washington, 1981, December.

[13] E. H. Forman and N. D. Singpurwalla, 'An empirical stopping rule for debugging and testing computer software', J. Amer. Statist. Assoc., Vol. 72, 1977, Dec., pp. 750-757.

[14] B. Littlewood and J. L. Verrall, 'On the likelihood function of a debugging model for computer software reliability', IEEE Trans. Reliability, Vol. R-30, 1981 June, pp. 145-148.

[15] H. Joe and N. Reid, 'Estimating the number of faults in a system', J. Amer. Statist. Assoc., Vol. 80, 1985 March, pp. 222-226.

[16] B. Littlewood and A. Sofer, 'A Bayesian modification to the Jelinski-Moranda software reliability growth model', available from first author.

[17] B. Littlewood, 'Stochastic reliability growth: a model for fault-removal in computer programs and hardware designs', IEEE Trans. Reliability, Vol. R-30, 4, Oct. 1981, pp. 313-320.

[18] A. A. Abdel Ghaly, Ph.D. Thesis, City University, London, in preparation.

[19] P. A. Keiller, B. Littlewood, D. R. Miller and A. Sofer, 'On the quality of software reliability predictions', Proc. NATO ASI on Electronic Systems Effectiveness and Life Cycle Costing (Norwich, UK, 1982), Springer, 1983, pp. 441-460.

[20] D. R. Miller, 'Exponential order statistic models of software reliability growth', Tech. Report, T-496/84, George Washington University, Washington DC, 1984.

[21] J. T. Duane, 'Learning curve approach to reliability monitoring', IEEE Trans. Aerospace, 2, 1964, pp. 563-566.

[22] L. H. Crow, 'Confidence interval procedures for reliability growth analysis', Tech. Report No. 197, US Army Material Systems Analysis Activity, Aberdeen, Md., 1977.

[23] H. Akaike, 'Prediction and Entropy', MRC Technical Summary Report, Mathematics Research Center, University of Wisconsin-Madison, June, 1982.

[24] M. G. Kendall and A. Stuart, The Advanced Theory of Statistics, Griffin, London, 1961.

[25] M. Rosenblatt, 'Remarks on a multivariate transformation', Ann. Math. Statist., 23, pp. 470-472, 1952.

[26] A. P. Dawid, 'Statistical theory: the prequential approach', J. Royal Statist. Soc., A (1984), 147, pp. 278-292.

[27] A. P. Dawid, 'Calibration-based empirical probability', Res. Report 36, Department of Statistical Science, University College, London, 1984.

[28] D. R. Cox and P. A. W. Lewis, Statistical Analysis of Series of Events, Methuen, London, 1966.

[29] A. P. Dawid, 'The well-calibrated Bayesian', (with discussion) J. Amer. Statist. Assoc., 77, pp. 605-613, 1982.

[30] A. P. Dawid, 'Probability Forecasting', Encyclopedia of Statistical Sciences, Vol. 6 (S. Kotz, N. L. Johnson and C. B. Read, eds.), Wiley-Interscience (to appear).

[31] D. R. Miller, private communication, 1983.

[32] H. Braun and J. M. Paine, 'A comparative study of models for reliability growth', Tech. Report, No. 126, Series 2, Department of Statistics, Princeton University, 1977.

[33] B. Littlewood and P. A. Keiller, 'Adaptive software reliability modelling', Digest FTCS-14 (14th International Conference on Fault-Tolerant Computing), pp. 108-113, 1984.

[34] I. Goudie, private communication, 1984.

[35] J. D. Musa, 'Software reliability data', report available from Data and Analysis Center for Software, Rome Air Development Center, Rome, NY.

[36] N. Langberg and N. D. Singpurwalla, 'A unification of some software reliability models via the Bayesian approach', Tech. Report, TM-66571, The George Washington University, Washington DC, 1981.

[37] A. L. Goel and K. Okumoto, 'Time-dependent error-detection rate model for software reliability and other performance measures', IEEE Trans. Reliability, Vol. R-28, pp. 206-211, 1979.

THE USE OF EXPLORATORY DATA ANALYSIS TECHNIQUES FOR SOFTWARE RELIABILITY ASSESSMENT AND PREDICTION

Tony Bendell
Head of Dept. of Mathematics,
Statistics and Operational Research,
Trent Polytechnic,
Burton Street,
Nottingham NG1 4BU

and Senior Consultant, Services Ltd.

Abstract

As is still largely the case with hardware, much of current software reliability prediction is based upon established models which are largely black-box in nature. The structure of these models reflect supposed scientific observation of the physical processes of software failure, together with the conventional desire for modelling brevity. It is, unfortunately, the case that such models, if automatically applied, may neglect important but unknown structure in the failure data, and may squeeze out of the data much of its information content. For this reason such model validation as may subsequently be used, may not be effective.

In this paper the author introduces the nature of exploratory data analysis (e.d.a.), and discusses its use for software reliability assessment. Emphasis is on searching all the available data, in its greatest generality, for pattern to exploit in its analysis. As well as more basic techniques, the use of time series analysis and proportional hazards modelling in this context will be discussed. Examples will be presented of the types of results obtained from the application of e.d.a. to software reliability data and, in particular, of the discovery of structure ignored by established models.

1. INTRODUCTION

1.1 Modelling Hardware Reliability

In hardware reliability assessment it is still, unfortunately, the case that much reliability assessment and prediction is carried out on a black-box basis. Methodology is regarded as well-established, and analysis consists of inputing data to standard models and outputing answers, usually without any attempt to check assumptions nor validate the models for the data in

NATO ASI Series, Vol. F22
Software System Design Methods. Edited by J.K. Skwirzynski

hand. As Walls and Bendell (1985) show, such black-box use of models is frequently, if not usually, inappropriate for the particular data structure in hand, and can result in serious errors.

There has, however, been a recent development in hardware reliability analysis towards a less-assumption-based more-exploratory approach. Bendell and Walls (1985a) discuss the general approach to exploratory data analysis (e.d.a.) with reliability data, and simple graphical and analytical techniques that may be applied. Other, partly more advanced, methodologies also share this general exploratory approach. There are three of these of particular importance. First is the application of Time Series methods to reliability work, largely by Nozer Singpurwalla, to identify and model cyclical behaviour etc.; e.g. Singpurwalla (1978, 1980), Crow and Singpurwalla (1984). Secondly, is the use of Proportional Hazards Modelling in the reliability field to identify and model the effects of various potential explanatory factors; e.g. Nagel and Skrivan (1981), Dale (1983), Bendell (1985a), Wightman and Bendell (1985). Finally, there remains a great potential in the use of multivariate methods, such as Principal Component Analysis and Cluster Analysis, in reliability; Buckland (1976), Bendell and Walls (1985b).

The use of models on a black-box basis, where structure is allegedly based upon some "scientific knowledge" of the phenomena in hand, is, naturally, not restricted just to reliability modelling. Bendell (1985b) discusses the general problem of using scientific-knowledge based models, and demonstrates using the case of accident models why such validation as may subsequently be used may not be effective,since the models themselves may squeeze out of the data much of its information content. Common omissions in such models are

(i) insufficient disaggregation;

(ii) ignoring possibility of trend, serial correlation, etc.;

(iii) ignoring possibility of more complex time/order behaviour, particularly cycles;

(iv) ignoring other explanatory variables or factors.

1.2 Modelling Software Reliability

In common with hardware, much of current software reliability prediction is based upon established models which are largely used in a black-box way. The structure of these models reflect supposed scientific observation of the physical process of software failure (i.e. assumptions), together with the conventional desire for modelling brevity. There is little point in presenting here an exhaustive list of the models that the current author would put into this category. Suffice it to say that the models of Jelinski and Moranda (1972), Littlewood and Verrall (1973), Musa (1975) and Littlewood (1981) and their variants would be included. The group is thus a major one.

One very interesting development in software reliability modelling concerns the introduction of adaptive procedures whereby a feedback loop allows the performance of predictions from fitting a model to improve subsequent predictions. See e.g. Keiller and Littlewood (1984), Littlewood (1985). Whilst it is certainly advantageous to use information from the data to improve the model in this way, it also highlights the question as to why not also base the initial structure of the model upon the data? If this is (as usual) not done, then even with adaptive procedures the analyst is unlikely to be using all the information in available data, and certainly not all that in potentially available data which has been discarded a-priori because of the model's structure. This waste of data information is particularly disturbing in the software reliability modelling case because of the recognised shortfalls in performance of the models, e.g. Dale and Harris (1982).

In software modelling terms, there is considerable justification for considering the inadvertent omissions (i), (iii) and (iv) in Section 1.1 as real possibilities. Software reliability models do, of course, typically allow for trend in consecutive inter-failure times (omission (ii)), although of a somewhat restricted kind. However, disaggregation by causes of failure, seriousness of failure, modules, test phases, releases etc. is not typical in the literature, and these complicating explanatory factors effect the application of the models. Similarly, modifications at the end of test phases and changes in operating environment may introduce cycles into the failure data, which are ignored by most models (but see Crow and Singpurwalla 1984). Possible explanatory factors also include the numerous metrics which may assist in explaining and predicting software reliability.

There have, of course, been a number of attempts to include certain metrics, in the explanation of software reliability. These include Akiyama (1972), Boehm, Brown and Lipow (1976), Motley and Brooks (1977), McCall, Richards and Walters (1977), Lipow and Thayer (1977), Walters and McCall (1978),

Thayer, Lipow and Nelson (1978). An excellent review of these and other reliability models is Dale (1982). There is, of course, some variation in these models as to what exactly is being explained. Included are the number of problems, number of operational failures and various definitions of "reliability". Also, various metrics are used for explanation. However, in general these models assume linear relationships (multiple regression techniques), and no time aspect to the definitions of reliability through development or in the field. We do, of course, currently know very little of the true nature of such relationships. If the set of metrics assumed to be important by the models, and/or the form of the assumed relationships are in error, then the descriptive and predictive abilities of the models will be very limited. The report by McCall, Richards and Walters does, for example, provide evidence that this is the case.

The question remains as to how progress is to be made in software reliability assessment and prediction. In the current author's opinion, it seems at this moment of time to be desirable as a general methodology for the analysis of software unreliability to explore any available data for the appropriate structure on which models should be constructed. Such exploration should attempt to identify the appropriate levels of aggregation, explanatory variables, cycles, serial correlations, time structure etc. The structures identified are likely to be specific to various areas of application. Currently there is a great need for individual studies on specific product ranges, in order both to aid reliability predictions, release decisions etc. in those product ranges, and to provide general understanding of the processes involved and help develop a general database.

Whilst good quality execution time data etc. is preferable, the author believes that available data from internal reporting systems still contains valuable information and should not be discarded, despite its poor quality and complexity. Such systems exist to track error clearance and/or to assist field engineers. However, our experience suggests that there is potentially useful information to be obtained from both current and improved versions of such systems, in order to reveal structure for use in reliability predictions, release decisions etc. Such systems contain much auxiliary information compared to that used by most software reliability models. For example, information on problem priority, module, release, phase found, update/clearance, planned/unplanned code etc. may be included. However, the difficulties in using such data whilst not overpowering, are still significant.

In particular, one must expect incomplete records, extensive ties, and inaccuracies in recorded failure/entry dates.

2. EXPLORATORY DATA ANALYSIS

2.1 Literature

Exploratory data analysis techniques have now become standard in statistical methodology. Rather than relying upon formal test procedures, the approach is to apply differing and often conflicting analyses to the data, preferably making few assumptions. The idea is to search the data for unsuspected pattern and abnormalities rather than to just attempt to confirm a-priori assumptions. The seminal book is Tukey (1977).

In the reliability field (whether hardware or software), because of the particular characteristics of the data structure it is the approach rather than the usual techniques which are most appropriate. An introduction to the application of e.d.a. in the reliability area is provided by Bendell and Walls (1985a). In a sense, elements of this approach may also be found in the work of Ascher and Feingold (1984).

Whilst such e.d.a. techniques and their time series, proportional hazards modelling and multivariate method extensions, may be immediately applicable to software reliability assessment, little application can yet be found in the literature. The notable exceptions are Singpurwalla's application of time series methods and the dubious application of Proportional Hazards Modelling by Nagel and Skrivan (1981). See also Bendell and Samson (1985). Since we do not know what is "going-on" in software reliability data, it does seem reasonable to "have a good look at it" in this way before rejecting any of it and inputing the remainder into standard software reliability models.

2.2 Methods

At the simplest level such e.d.a. techniques will consist of simple graphs and simple models and tests applied to the interfailure (or other) data at various levels of disaggregation. For example, cumulative failure against time graphs, fitted Non Homogeneous Poisson Process models with accompanying simulation bands, observed against expected plots, Laplace tests, correlograms etc. For details of these methodologies the reader is referred to Bendell and Walls (1985a).

The time series methods, including Box-Jenkins techniques, recently employed by Nozer Singpurwalla and his co-workers are an important development in the study of software reliability modelling. However, whilst the recognition (and exploration) of the time series structure of software failures is a major step forward, care must be taken particularly with these sort of techniques not to overinterpret the patterns found in software data. Research in this area is currently progressing at Trent Polytechnic.

In contrast, multivariate techniques although discussed, are still largely unused and unvalidated in both hardware and software reliability data studies. Limited work at Trent Polytechnic on hardware applications has shown some potential, but as yet we have not had the opportunity or resources to apply methods such as Principal Component Analysis and Cluster Analysis to software.

The final exploratory method that we discuss has enormous potential in the software reliability, as well as hardware reliability, fields. This is Proportional Hazards Modelling (PHM). At the simplest level, the technique is based upon an assumed decomposition of the hazard function for the time between failures (or alternatives) into the product of a base-line hazard function and an exponential term incorporating the effects of a number of explanatory variables or covariates. In the hardware case, these may correspond to temperature, pressure and other environmental and operational conditions, design changes, etc. In the software case, they may label design teams, characteristics or functions of the software, modules, releases, test phases etc. The proportionality assumption (i.e. multiplicative decomposition of the hazard function) is the only assumption the technique makes, and the validity of this can be verified during the PHM analysis, and where appropriate conveniently liberalised in subsequent analysis. Whilst a few authors, such as Nagel and Skrivan (1981) and Jardine and Anderson (1984) do do so, it is unnecessary to make any distributional assumptions about the underlying process. For more detail see Kalbfleisch and Prentice (1980), Lawless (1982), Bendell (1985a), Wightman and Bendell (1985).

3. EXAMPLES

For illustration, we briefly consider three examples of applying e.d.a. type techniques to explore aspects of software reliability data. These analyses will be treated in more detail elsewhere.

3.1 Data of Crow and Singpurwalla (1984)

The above paper presents three data sets, the first two of which are for identical copies of the same system (A), which they fit, in each case by an empirically developed Fourier Series model. The third data set is fitted very badly by their model, and the second appears to contain some transcribing errors. The paper also indicates that some "fiddling" is necessary to avoid fitted negative times between failures. The assessment of fit in the paper is purely subjective, and in the current author's opinion does not appear good.

The analysis of Crow and Singpurwalla is based upon the use of the spectogram. We considered instead the "complementary" correlation structure approach (Box and Jenkins 1976) as well as other elementary e.d.a. Our results suggest some discrepancies between the two copies of the same system (A); in one case no trend is indicated, whilst in the other there is an increasing trend. Also, Figures 1 and 2, which show the data for each copy together with 95% simulation envelopes, based upon a Non Homogeneous Poisson Process, suggests that the behaviour of the second copy is more variable.

3.2 Data of Musa (1980)

This set of 16 data sets is included here since the first data set, in particular, has received much attention in the software reliability modelling literature, being used to illustrate and compare various models. A proportional hazards modelling analysis of each of these data sets is presented in Wightman and Bendell (1985). This reveals that the information on relative date on which execution took place, which is available in the Musa data but is neglected in conventional software reliability models, is consistently significant for all data sets analysed, either in terms of actual days since start or days since last execution, or both. In contrast, number of previous failures, which is inherent in many software reliability models, is only significant in three cases (including the first often-quoted data set). In all cases, the overall fit of the PHM model is very significant. Based upon which covariates are significant and on the form of the underlying base-line distribution, Figure 3 shows how the 16 data sets are grouped by the PHM approach. Figure 4 also shows the groupings based upon other more basic graphical and formal (trend and serial correlation tests) e.d.a. methods. As one would expect, the various approaches pick up various aspects of the data

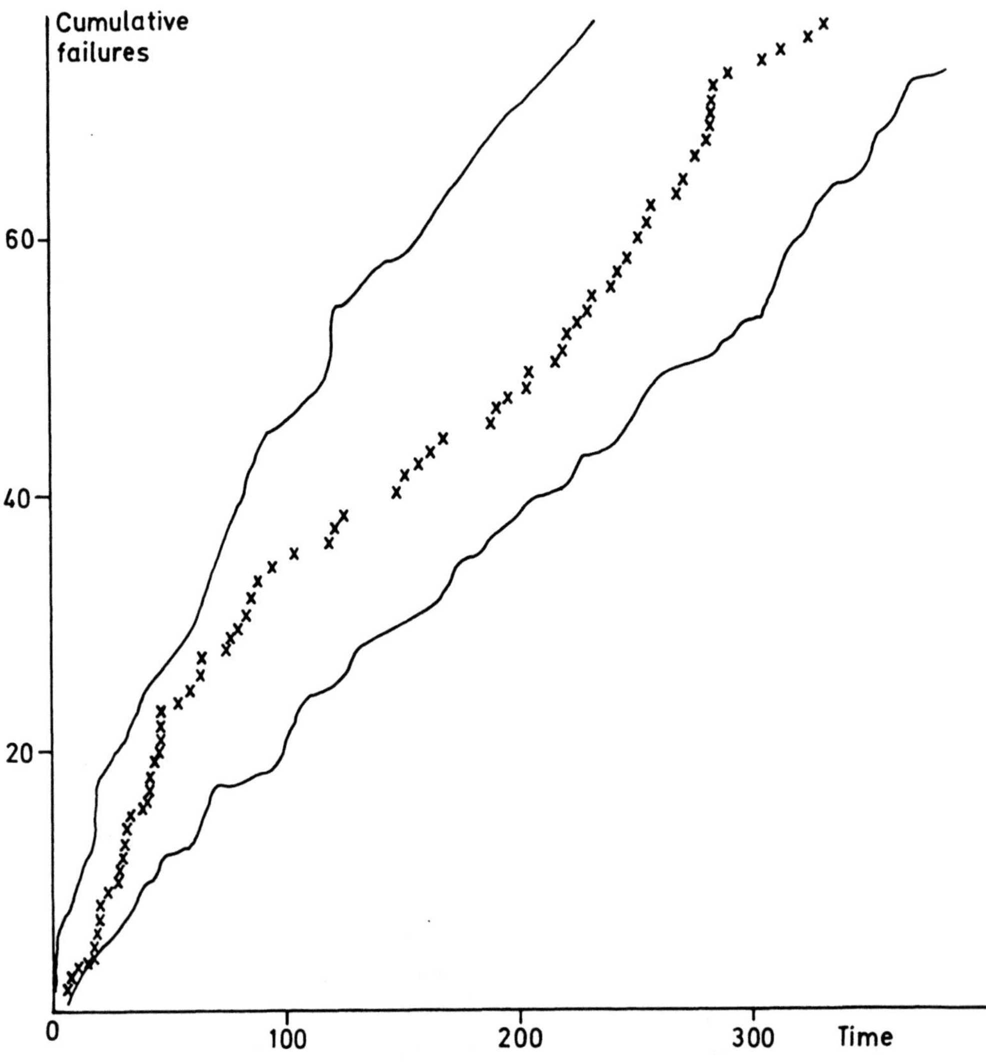

Figure 1. First data set of Crow and Singpurwalla (1984).

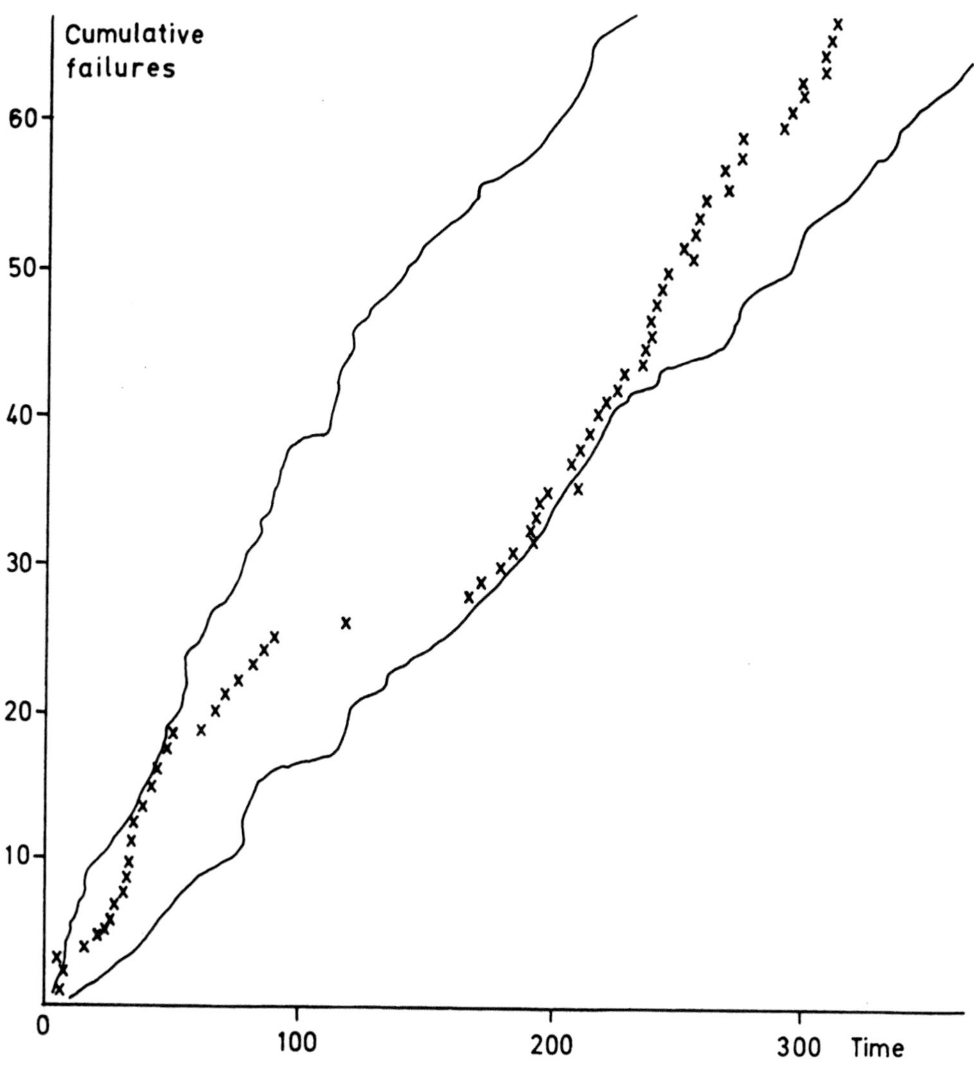

Figure 2. Second data set of Crow and Sinpurwalla (1984).

System Numbers	Nature
1, 2, 3, 4	Real time command and control (Musa project manager)
5	Real time commercial:- <u>Special case</u> - design change and some random time assignment
6	Commercial (subsystem) - on line database used (only one actual CPU time)
14c	Real time
17, 27	Military
40	Military - Musa analysis poor fit - integrated very sequentially
SS1A, SS1B, SS1C	Operating system - same system, different environment
SS4	Operating system
SS2	Time sharing system
SS3	Word processing system

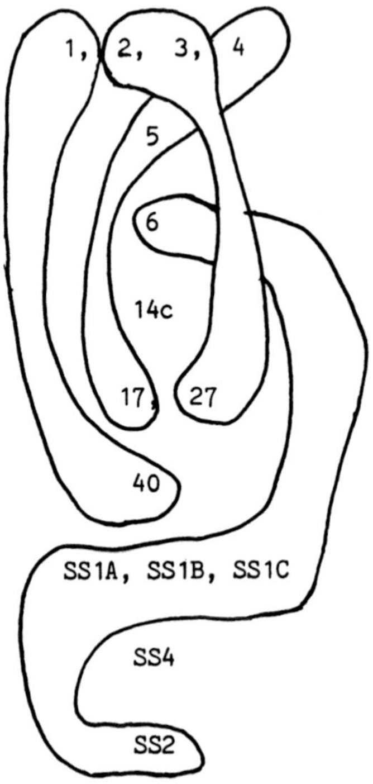

(closed outline) :- groupings from PHM analysis.

Figure 3. Groupings of Systems from Musa (1980) and PHM Analysis

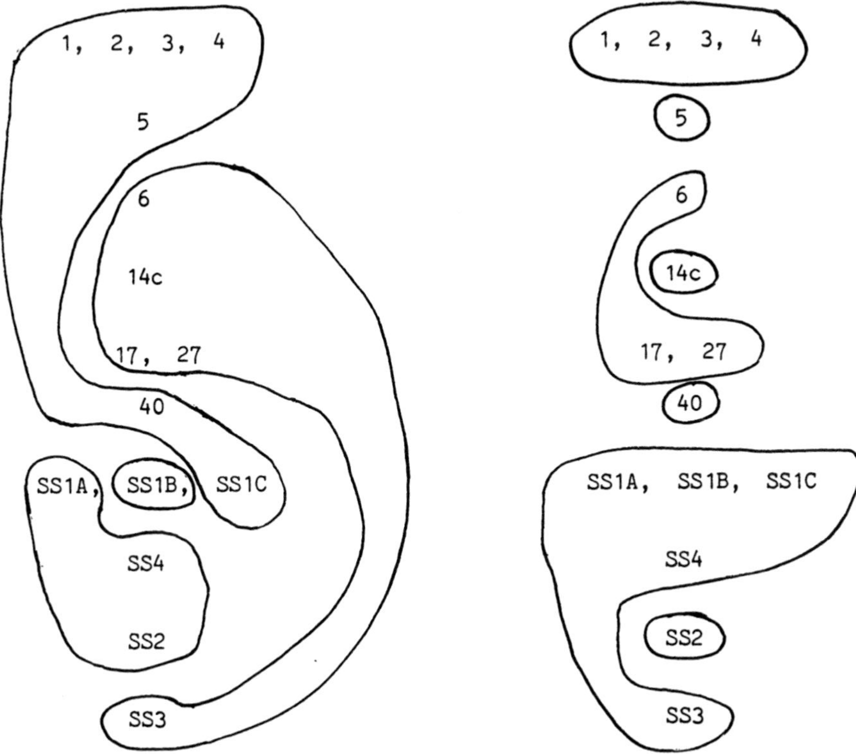

Figure 4. Groupings of Systems from Musa (1980).

structure.

3.3 Software in an Integrated Hardware/Software System

As a final example, Figure 5 shows the results of applying trend and serial correlation tests to various releases in development and various test phases for the software in an integrated hardware/software system. Note that only releases 9 and 14 were actually released to the field. The figure indicates that the reliability growth assumption of the mainstream software reliability models is a simplification which must be used carefully.

4. CONCLUSIONS

(i) More exploration of software data is needed.

(ii) Some useful methods for first analysis exist.

(iii) Product-area-specific models should be developed by more extensive use of the e.d.a. approach.

(iv) E.D.A. methods also allow the identification of important apsects or metrics for summarising software reliability data in future work, data libraries etc.

ACKNOWLEDGEMENTS

The illustrative analyses in Section 3 include joint work with Miss L.A. Walls and Mr. D.W. Wightman of Trent Polytechnic.

REFERENCES

Akiyama, A. (1972). An example of software system debugging, Information Processing 71, North Holland, pp 353-359.

Ascher, H.E. and Feingold, H. (1984). Repairable Systems Reliability: Modelling, Inference, Misconceptions and Their Causes, Marcel Dekker, New York.

Bendell, A. (1985a). Proportional hazards modelling in reliability assessment, Reliability Engineering, 11, 175-183.

Bendell, A. (1985b). Minimising misconceived models. IOS International Conference on Statistical Modelling, Cambridge. To appear in the Statistician.

Bendell, A. and Samson, W.B. (1985). Software quality and reliability, State of the Art Report on the Software Process, Pergamon Infotech.

Bendell, A. and Walls, L.A. (1985a). Exploring reliability data, Qual. and Rel. Eng. Int., 1, 35-51.

Release	Design	Coding	Unit Test	Integration Test
1	+	-	-	-
2			+	+
3				
4				
5				
6				-
7			+	n
8			n	
9			-	
10				
11				
12				
13				
14				
15				e
16				
ALL	+	n	-	-

(No entries where insufficient data)

+ : trend towards longer inter-failure intervals

- : trend towards shorter inter-failure intervals

Figure 5. Integrated Hardware/Software System

Bendell A. and Walls, L.A. (1985b). Multivariate Methods in Reliability - A Case Study concerning Fire Detectors. RSS Multivariate Study Group Workshop.

Boehm, B.W., Brown, B. and Lipow, M. (1976). Quantitative evaluation of software quality, Proc. Int. Conf. on Software Eng., 592-605.

Box, B.J. and Jenkins, G. (1976). Time Series Analysis, Holden Day.

Buckland, W.R. (1976). Reliability of nuclear power plants; statistical techniques for analysis, Task Force on Problems of Rare Events in the Reliability of Nuclear Power Plants, JRC ISPRA 8-10 June 1976; CSNI Report No. 10.

Crow, L.H. and Singpurwalla, N.D. (1984). An empirically derived Fourier series model for describing software failures. IEEE Trans. Rel., R-33, 176-183.

Dale, C.J. (1982). Software Reliability Evaluation Methods, British Aerospace Dynamics Group, Report No. ST26750.

Dale, C.J. (1983). Application of the proportional hazards model in the reliability field. Proc. 4th Nat. Rel. Conf., Birmingham, 5B/1/1-9.

Dale, C.J. and Harris, L.N. (1982). Approaches to software reliability prediction, Proc. Ann. Rel. Maint. Symp.

Jardine, A.K.S. and Anderson, M. (1984). Use of concomitant variables for reliability estimations and setting component replacement policies, Proc. 8th ARTS, B3/2/1-6.

Jelinski, Z. and Moranda, P.B. (1972). Software reliability research, In W. Freiberger (Ed.) Statistical Computer Performance Evaluation, Academic Press, pp 465-484.

Kalbfleisch, J.D. and Prentice, R.L. (1980). The Statistical Analysis of Failure Time Data, Wiley,New York.

Keiller, D.A. and Littlewood, B. (1984). Adaptive software reliability modelling, FTCS-14.

Lawless, J.F. (1982). Statistical Models and Methods for Lifetime Data, Wiley, New York.

Lipow, M. and Thayer, T.A. (1977). Prediction of software failures, Proc. Ann. Rel. Maint. Symp., 489-494.

Littlewood, B. (1981). Stochastic reliability growth: a model for fault removal in computer programs and hardware designs, IEEE Trans. Rel., R-30, 313-320.

Littlewood, B. (1985). Software reliability prediction. Proc. NATO Advanced Study Institute on the Challenge of Advanced Computing Technology to System Design Methods, Springer-Verlag.

Littlewood, B. and Verrall, J.L. (1973). A Bayesian reliability growth model for computer software, Applied Statistics, 22, 332-346.

McCall, J.A., Richards, F.R. and Walters, G.F. (1977). Factors in Software Quality, Report No. RADC-TR-77-369, Rome Air Development Centre (3 vols.)

Motley, R.W. and Brooks, W.D. (1977). Statistical Prediction of Programming Errors, USAF Report RADC-TR-77-175.

Musa, J.D. (1975). A theory of software reliability and its application. IEEE Trans. Software Eng., SE-1, 312-327.

Musa, J.D. (1980). Software Reliability Data Submitted to the DACS, Bell Telephone Labs.

Nagel, P.M. and Skrivan, J.A. (1981). Software Reliability: Repetitive Run Experimentation and Modelling, Boeng Computer Services Co. Report BCS-40366, NASA Report No. CR-165836.

Singpurwalla, N.D. (1978). Time series analysis of failure data, Proc. Ann. Rel. Maint. Symp., 107-112.

Singpurwalla, N.D. (1980). Analysing availability using transfer function models and cross spectral analysis, Nav. Res. Logist. Qtly., 27, 1-16.

Thayer, T.A., Lipow, M. and Nelson, W. (1978). Software Reliability (Vol. No. 2 of TRW Series of Software Technology), North Holland.

Tukey, J.W. (1977). Exploratory Data Analysis, Addison-Wesley, New York.

Walls, L.A. and Bendell, A. (1985). The structure and exploration of reliability field data; what to look for and how to analyse it, Proc. 5th Nat. Rel. Conf., Birmingham, 5B/5/1-18.

Walters, G.F. and McCall, J.A. (1978). The development of metrics for software R & M, Proc. Ann. Rel. Maint. Symp., 79-85.

Wightman, D.W. and Bendell, A. (1985). The practical application of proportional hazards modelling, Proc. 5th Nat. Rel. Conf., Birmingham, 2B/3/1-16.

Failure Patterns and Reliability Growth Potential for Software Systems

Larry H. Crow
AT&T Bell Laboratories
Whippany, NJ 07981

Abstract

In the development of a complex software system the program manager is generally interested in the performance and reliability of the total system, which includes both the hardware and the software. This paper addresses a number of reliability characteristics and concepts for hardware and software which have proven useful in the development of reliable complex systems. These include reliability growth potential, deterministic-state and stochastic state computer systems, and sampling of the input space. The growth potential is the maximum reliability that can be attained with the system design and reliability management strategy. This paper discusses the utilization of the growth potential concept to evaluate the hardware reliability growth during development testing. The state of the computer is the total computer memory together with the logic step of the program, and may depend on the physical environment in which the system operates. Deterministic and stochastic state computer systems are defined and it is noted that the failure patterns for these systems are typically different. In addition, a method for assessing a software reliability parameter based on random sampling of the input space will be discussed and illustrated by example.

Introduction

The development of a complex software intensive system will often include two major phases, a design phase and a testing phase. The testing phase will typically include hardware and software testing to prove out the performance, safety, reliability and other major issues. During the design phase, various reliability activities are generally conducted in the formulation of the basic design. These activities may include reliability predictions, failure mode effects and criticality analysis, fault tree analysis, developing critical parts lists and qualification testing. From the design phase two critical reliability parameters are determined for the system as it enters the development testing phase. These parameters are the inherent reliability and the initial reliability of the system.

The inherent reliability, or growth potential, is the reliability that is determined to be technically achievable for the basic system design within program time and cost constraints. The inherent reliability is the reliability value which is reasonable to expect can be attained by a mature system. It is not unusual for the initial reliability of a complex system at the beginning of development testing to be below the growth potential. If reliability failures are observed during development testing, then this information is generally used to improve the system reliability. The initial reliability is the starting point for reliability growth during development testing.

NATO ASI Series, Vol. F22
Software System Design Methods. Edited by J.K. Skwirzynski

The management strategy toward reliability during development testing determines what problems will receive a corrective action, how effective these corrective actions are, and when the corrective actions are incorporated into the system. Consideration of the management strategy and growth potential can be very useful in evaluating the hardware reliability objectives for the development testing program.

We note in this paper that in some cases software failures may be independent and follow the exponential distribution and in other cases software failures may be dependent and occur in clusters. These concepts are discussed within the framework of deterministic-state and stochastic-state computer systems. The state of the computer is defined as the total computer memory together with logic step of the program. This completely characterizes the computer system at time t. For a deterministic-state computer system, the state of the computer does not depend on the environment in which the system is being used. However, the state of the computer for a stochastic-state system does depend on the physical environment in which the system operates. The failure patterns for these two types of systems are typically different and will be discussed in this paper.

If the software system is operated in a customer use environment, then the test results may be used to directly evaluate the software reliability. An alternative approach to testing the software in an operational use environment is to sample from the software input space. The application of this sampling approach is discussed and illustrated by example.

Hardware and Software Reliability

System reliability is commonly defined as the probability that the total system operates successfully for a stated period of time under specified operational conditions. For a software intensive system, system success implies that both the hardware and software operate without failure. The random nature of both the hardware and software failures is, of course, the basis of the probability statement. This randomness must, however, be viewed differently for hardware and software failures.

The cause of a hardware failure can generally be associated with burn-in, stress or wearout. A stress failure occurs whenever the strength of the failure mode is less than the environmental stress. For a specified operational environment, the randomness of product quality, stress and strength relationships and wearout characteristics induce the stochastic nature of hardware failures. On the other hand, for a particular input condition, the software will either give the correct result according to some definition of software failure or fail to give the correct result. However, under an operational environment, input conditions for a complex software system are typically generated at random. Consequently, the randomness of the input conditions result in the stochastic nature of software failures.

Because of the randomness of software failures in an operational environment it is both meaningful and practical to consider the concept of software reliability. Software reliability is defined as the probability that the software will operate successfully for a stated period of time when subjected to a specified operational environment.

In this paper we assume that hardware and software failures are statistically independent. Let R denote the total system reliability. That is, R equals the probability that the total system, hardware and software, operates successfully for a stated period of time when subjected to a specified operational environment. If R_H, R_S are the corresponding hardware and software reliabilities, then

$$R = R_H \cdot R_S.$$

Reliability Growth Potential

The growth potential for a system design is the maximum system reliability that can be achieved for a particular management strategy. Several elements of the overall management strategy determine the growth potential. First, the management strategy for the system places failure modes into two categories, Type A and Type B. Type A modes are all failure modes such that when seen during test, no corrective action will be taken. This accounts for all modes for which it is determined that it is not economically or otherwise justified to take corrective action. Type B modes are all failure modes such that when seen during test, a corrective action or fix will be attempted.

For the hardware it is assumed that all Type B modes are in series and fail independently according to the exponential distribution. It is also assumed that the occurrence of Type A modes follow the exponential distribution with failure rate λ_A. Fixes for Type B modes found during test may be incorporated into the system during test or incorporated as delayed fixes at the end of the test phase. The management strategy, therefore, partitions the system into an A part and a B part. Each part has a corresponding failure rate and mean time between failure (MTBF).

Let Q denote the number of Type B modes in the system and let λ_i be the failure rate for the i-th Type B mode, $i=1,\ldots,Q$. Then at time 0 the system failure rate r(0) is

$$r(0) = \lambda_A + \lambda_B,$$

where $\lambda_B = \sum_{i=1}^{Q} \lambda_i$.

The actual value of r(0) is determined by the system design effort during the design phase. The partition into the A and B parts is determined by the management strategy.

During development testing, reliability growth is achieved through finding existing problems identified by the test and taking subsequent corrective action. This reliability improvement will result in a decrease in the initial system failure rate. The failure rate λ_A for Type A modes will not change. With the management strategy, reliability growth can only be achieved by decreasing the Type B failure rate λ_B.

It is very important to note that once a Type B failure mode is in the system it is rarely totally eliminated by a corrective action. After a Type B mode is found and fixed, a certain percent of the failure rate will be removed, but a certain percent of the failure rate will generally remain. A fix effectiveness factor (EF) is the percent decrease in a problem mode failure rate after a corrective action has been incorporated into the system.

The initial reliability and growth potential can be related through the failure mode strategy and EF concepts. To see this we note that Type A modes account for all modes for which management determines that it is not economically or otherwise justified to take corrective action. An inherent failure mode is one in which the failure rate cannot be economically reduced further by a corrective action. Ideally, the Type A modes should consist only of inherent failure modes. When all system failure modes are inherent - the failure rate cannot be economically reduced further - then the system has attained its inherent reliability or growth potential.

The growth potential failure rate is the most that the initial failure rate

$$\lambda_I = \lambda_A + \lambda_B$$

can be reduced. The growth potential failure rate will be attained when all Type B failure modes have been seen through testing and fixed by a corrective action. The Type A failure rate λ_A will remain in the system. For an average EF d, d percent of λ_B will be removed and 1-d percent of λ_B will remain in the system when all Type B modes have been seen and fixed. For an average EF d, the hardware growth potential failure rate is given by

$$\lambda_{GP} = \lambda_A + (1-d)\lambda_B.$$

For the software part of the system it is often assumed that a fix for a software error is 100 percent effective. Also, if all software errors are corrected, then the software growth potential failure rate is 0. Consequently, under these assumptions, the growth potential failure for the total system is the hardware growth potential failure rate λ_{GP}. The growth potential MTBF is $1/\lambda_{GP}$.

Growth Potential and Development Testing

Often associated with a development testing program is the attainment of specific reliability objectives. In addition, it is typical for constraints to be placed on the length of testing. For example, it is not unusual for the test length to be restricted by costs and meeting various schedules. Consequently, reliability engineering should address the test time when reliability objectives are to be met when considering the growth potential MTBF and the initial MTBF. Both of these values highly influence the system reliability which is finally achieved during development testing.

The total system may be tested together so that hardware and software problems are found and corrected. A useful parameter for addressing the test time when the hardware reliability objectives will be met during development testing is the growth rate. The concept of growth rate is generally associated with the Duane postulate [2], which is expressed in the following form

$$M(t) = M_I\left(\frac{t}{t_1}\right)^{\alpha}(1-\alpha)^{-1} \quad t>o$$

where

t – cumulative test time
$M(t)$ – system MTBF at time t
t_1 – test time for first test phase
M_I – Initial MTBF
α – growth rate.

It is often of interest to consider the fraction of the initial system failure rate which is addressed by a corrective action. This fraction, U, is given by the ratio of the Type B failure rate to the total initial failure rate. That is,

$$U = \frac{\lambda_B}{\lambda_A + \lambda_B}$$

The parameter U is a measure of the maturity of the design.

The growth potential failure rate is $\lambda_{GP} = \lambda_A + (1-d)\lambda_B$. By the definition of U it follows that the initial failure rate is related to the growth potential by $\lambda_I = \frac{1}{(1-dU)} \lambda_{GP}$. For example, if U = .95 and d = .7, then $\lambda_I = 2.98\, \lambda_{GP}$, or approximately,

$$\text{Initial MTBF} = (1/3) \text{ Growth Potential MTBF.}$$

The growth potential, growth rate, effectiveness factors and U can be very useful in evaluating a development testing program in terms of meeting the hardware reliability objectives.

Example

Suppose we wish to attain a MTBF for an electronic system of 500 hours at the end of T = 5000 hours of a test, analyze and fix (TAAF) program. Suppose also that the current prediction is 600 hours and we wish to evaluate the risk associated with meeting the requirement.

Assume that based on experience with similar systems, representative minimum values for the average effectiveness factor EF (d) is .7 and a minimum value for the ratio U is .95. That is, an average EF of 70 percent is expected and, based on the anticipated level of system maturity, corrective actions will be applied toward at least 95 percent of the initial failure rate.

If we equate the inherent failure rate to the prediction of 1/600, we have

$$1/600 = \lambda_A + (1-d)\lambda_B.$$

From the above assumptions we have approximately, as discussed earlier,

$$M_{GP} = 3M_I,$$

where M_{GP}, M_I denote the growth potential and initial MTBF's.

We next consider the idealized growth curve equation given by the Duane postulate. In this equation suppose that $t_1 = 800$ and we assume a growth rate of $\alpha = .25$. The time t_1 is when fixes are expected to be initially incorporated into the system. Also, a low growth rate of $\alpha = .25$ is not unusual for complex electronic equipment comprised of a large number of components with relatively small failure rates.

We, therefore, have

$$M(t) = M_I \left[\frac{t}{800}\right]^{.25} (.75)^{-1}.$$

If the prediction for the current design is 600 hours, then under the above conditions we estimate the initial MTBF to be approximately 200 hours. Thus,

$$M(t) = 200 \left[\frac{t}{800}\right]^{.25} (.75)^{-1}.$$

Evaluating this equation at T = 5000 hours, the end of the scheduled TAAF, gives

$$M(5000) = 422.$$

As noted earlier, the requirement is 500 hours MTBF, so that under the above conditions a system with an inherent design of 600 hours may not be sufficient to meet this objective in a 5000 hour TAAF program.

If we set M(5000) equal to 500 and solve for M_I, i.e.

$$500 = M_I \left[\frac{5000}{800}\right]^{.25} (.75)^{-1}$$

we have $M_I = 237$. Based on the expected maturity of the system when entering TAAF, we equate the inherent MTBF to three times the initial MTBF. This gives a target of approximately 710 hours MTBF for the inherent design. That is, based on the above assumptions, a system design with an inherent MTBF of 710 will allow us to attain a system MTBF of 500 hours during a 5000 hour TAAF program.

Example

Another strategy may be to further mature the design before system level TAAF by additional component and subsystem testing. Suppose the predicted MTBF is 600 hours and with additional reliability testing at the component and subsystem level, we predict an initial MTBF of 400 hours. In addition, since the design is more mature we should expect a lower growth rate than $\alpha = .25$ in the previous example. Suppose a more conservative growth rate of $\alpha = .15$ is used in the reliability plan.

The total test length is 5000 hours. To apply the Duane postulate, we must determine the time t_1 when fixes will initially be incorporated into the system. To do this we evaluate the Type B mode failure rate λ_B. Corrective actions can only begin whenever a Type B failure mode has been observed. Consequently, t_1 must be long enough so that there is a high probability, say 95 percent, that a Type B mode will be observed in the test time $(0,t_1)$.

The predicted failure rate is 1/600 and the initial failure rate is 1/400. That is

$$\lambda_A + .3\lambda_B = 1/600 \quad \text{and}$$

$$\lambda_A + \lambda_B = 1/400.$$

It follows then that the Type B failure rate is

$$\lambda_B = .00119$$

or the Type B MTBF is approximately 840 hours. Then, $t_1 \doteq 2500$ by

$$1-e^{-\lambda_B t} = .95.$$

Hence, there is a 95 percent probability that a Type B mode will be observed by time t_1.

The Duane postulate evaluated at time 5000 yields

$$M(5000) = 400 \left[\frac{5000}{2500}\right]^{.15} (.85)^{-1} = 522.$$

Therefore with this design strategy and related assumptions, the objective of attaining a 500 hour MTBF at the end of the 5000 hour development testing program would appear to have low risk.

Software Failure Patterns

As discussed in [1], there are basically two types of computer systems. The first type is one in which the operational environment does not influence the performance of the software. This means that if a request is made of the software at time t, it will give a certain response, and if the same request is made at a later time t + s, it will give the same response. The operational environment of the system does not influence the response given by the software. The second type of computer system is one in which the operational environment does influence the performance of the software. If a request is made at time t + s, the software system may give a different response due to the influence of the operational environment between times t and t + s.

We call the first type of computer system deterministic-state and the second type of computer system stochastic-state. The state of the computer at time t is the total computer memory together with the logic step of the program at time t. This completely characterizes the computer system at time t. For a deterministic-state computer system, the state of the computer at the time of a request does not depend on the physical environment in which the system operates.

For a complex stochastic-state computer system, the state of the computer at times t and t + s will generally be similar for small s, and the environment which generates the requests will typically be similar over this time period. A software failure is defined to be the inability of the software to perform a particular request in its current state.

Consequently, if a software failure occurs, there would tend to be an increased chance that another software failure will occur in the near future. One may conclude, therefore, that software failures for stochastic state computer systems will tend to occur in clusters in an operational environment. See [1].

For a deterministic-state computer system, the computer memory does not change with time. In this case the probability of a software failure remains the same as time progresses.

If the hardware and software are operated together in a representative use environment, then the total system reliability can be measured directly from the data. In some cases, however, it may be necessary or desirable to test the software separately, for example, to avoid the expense of hardware testing or to verify with high confidence that the latest software configuration has been sufficiently debugged. We will next consider an approach to testing software based on sampling of the input space.

Let G denote the set of all possible distinct input conditions for a deterministic-state computer system. Let $g \epsilon G$ denote an element in the input set G. For a particular input condition the probability that the software gives the correct response is either 0 or 1. For a specified operational environment, let w_i be the probability or frequency of the software being subjected to the i-th input condition, given that the software is being exercised, where $\sum_{i=1}^{K} w_i = 1$ and K is the total number of input conditions. Let p_i be 1 if the software responds correctly under input condition g_i and o if the software does not respond correctly. The parameter

$$p = \sum_{i=1}^{K} w_i p_i$$

is then the probability that the deterministic-state software will perform correctly when called upon in an operational environment.

For a deterministic-state software system suppose that under the specified operational conditions the requests for the software to perform a task are generated according to the Poisson process with rate λ. Hence, the times between requests are independent and exponentially distributed with mean $1/\lambda$. We denote by $q = 1-p$ the probability that the software will fail to perform the task correctly. Under these assumptions,

$$\sigma = \lambda \cdot q$$

is the rate in which software errors will occur in an operational environment. It also follows that the times of occurrence of software errors follow the Poisson process with mean value function σt, and the times between software errors are independent and exponentially distributed with mean $1/\sigma$.

If T_o is a mission time, then the probability R that the software functions correctly over this period is, according to the exponential distribution,

$$R = e^{-\sigma T_o}.$$

Let r(t) denote the failure rate for the total system and let $r_h(t)$ denote the failure rate for the hardware. In this paper, as noted previously, we assume that hardware and software failures are statistically independent. Hence, for a deterministic-state computer system, we have under the above conditions,

$$r(t) = r_s(t) + \sigma$$

If λ is estimated from data or is a parameter which is assumed known, then we may wish to evaluate q, or p, separately in assessing σ. The number of input conditions K is, of course, generally very large which would prevent testing the software under all possible input conditions to estimate p_i directly. Hence, to estimate p by estimating each p_i is not a viable approach for complex software. However, if the weights w_i are known, then p can be estimated directly by Binomial sampling.

For Binomial sampling, the software will be subjected to testing N times, where N is predetermined. For the j-th trial, the input conditions for the software is determined at random, with the probability that the i-th input condition is selected being w_i, $i=1,2,\ldots,N$. For the j-th trial, the software is then subjected to the selected input condition. The trial is scored a one if the software operates correctly and a zero if the software fails to operate correctly.

The probability that the j-th trial results in a software success is

$$p = w_1p_1 + w_2p_2 + \cdots + w_Kp_K.$$

Let S denote the total number of successes in the N trials. Then, since the trials are independent, S has the Binomial distribution with parameters (p,N). That is

$$\text{prob}(S=s) = \binom{N}{s} p^s(1-p)^{N-s},$$

$s=0,1,\ldots,N$. The maximum likelihood estimate of p is

$$\hat{p} = \frac{S}{N}.$$

Hence,

$$\hat{\sigma} = \lambda \cdot \hat{q}$$

is the rate at which software errors will occur in an operational environment for a deterministic-state system.

If the weights w_i are not known, then Binomial sampling cannot be used to estimate p. However, another useful measure of software effectiveness can be estimated by Binomial sampling which does not require knowledge of the w_i's.

Let

$$p^* = \frac{1}{K}\sum_{i=1}^{K} p_i.$$

Then, p^* represents the proportion of all possible inputs for which the software works correctly. This is a measure of how well the software performs over all possible inputs, where the inputs are given equal weight.

The parameter p^* can also be estimated by Binomial sampling. As before, the software will be subjected to N trials. To estimate p^* the input condition for the i-th trial of the software is selected at random, with equal probability given to each possible input condition. Let S^* denote the total number of successes in the N trials. Then, S^* has the Binomial distribution with parameters (p^*,N) and p^* is estimated by

$$\hat{p}^* = \frac{S^*}{N}.$$

It is noted that the concept of Binomial sampling may be applied to the total software system or to a single software function.

A basic consideration in applying the Binomial sampling approach is how large should the sample size N be. If p is large, that is, the software is highly reliable, then we would expect few failures to occur in the test. In this case a lower confidence bound, instead of an estimate of p, is often of particular interest. A lower confidence bound on p can be determined based on the Poisson approximation to the Binomial. For confidence level γ,

$$p_\gamma = 1-\chi^2_\gamma[2(F+1)]/2N$$

is an approximate lower bound on p, where F is the total number of observed failures in the sample of N trials, and $\chi^2_\gamma[2(F+1)]$ is the γ-th percentile for the Chi-Squared distribution with 2(F+1) degrees of freedom.

Example

Suppose we are interested in evaluating a particular function of a computer system which has been developed for determining the aiming characteristics of a large gun to hit a specific battlefield target. The input vector for the software function consists of the following factors: azimuth of target from gun, quadrant evaluation of gun, altitude of gun above sea levels, latitude of gun, wind direction, wind speed, air temperature and density, propellant temperature, height of target, shell weight, height of burst, shell charge and shell type.

The vectors in the input set G consists of all admissible combinations of the above factors. The set G is clearly very large so that it is not practical to test each possible input vector separately. This function of the computer system is deterministic-state. That is, if the same input vector is entered into the system at different times, the software will always give the same result. For this function the environment does not affect the state of the computer system.

Suppose the software has been developed and boundary conditions and test cases have been checked. Suppose that it is also desired to qualify the fitness of the software over the entire input set G. One approach to this problem would be to estimate or place a lower confidence bound on the parameter.

$$p^* = \frac{1}{K} \sum_{i=1}^{K} p_i.$$

by Binomial sampling.

The determination of the sample size N would generally depend on cost, schedule and the particular objectives of the test. For a sample size N the expected number of failures is

$$\theta = N\, q^*,$$

where $q^* = 1 - p^*$. Also, the probability distribution for the number of failures in N trials is given approximately by the Poisson distribution

$$\text{Prob}(X=x) = \frac{\theta^x e^{-x}}{x!}$$

$x = 0,1,2,\ldots$. If zero failures occurred in a test of N trials, then by the equation given earlier, a lower γ percent confidence bound on p^* is

$$P_\gamma = 1 - \chi^2_\gamma(2)/2N$$

where $\chi^2_\gamma(2)$ is the $\gamma \cdot 100$ percentile for the Chi-Squared distribution with two degrees of freedom. For a 95 percent lower bound,

$$P_\gamma = 1 - 5.99/2N.$$

Suppose that a sample size of N = 1000 is decided on. A computer routine may then be used to randomly select 1000 admissible input vectors to be tested. Each input vector would be entered into the computer software and the resulting aiming characteristics for the gun noted. Each result could then be checked to determine if the software function gave the correct solution. If all results are correct, then $P_\gamma = .997$, and we can state with high confidence that any software problems would be restricted to no more than three-tenths of one percent of all possible input vectors.

References

[1] Crow, L. H., Singpurualla, N. D., "An Empirically Developed Fourier Series Model for Describing Software Failures," IEEE Transactions on Reliability, Vol. 33, No. 2, pp. 176-183, 1984.

[2] Duane, J. J., "Learning Curve Approach to Reliability Monitoring," IEEE Transactions on Aerospace, Vol. 2, pp. 563-566, 1964.

THE USE OF REGRESSION TECHNIQUES FOR MATCHING RELIABILITY MODELS TO THE REAL WORLD

Harold Ascher
Naval Research Laboratory
Washington, D.C. 20375/USA

INTRODUCTION

Similar models are often used in various disciplines. For example, models for time to an event or for times between successive events are needed in biometry and sociology applications, as well as in reliability. The specific circumstances of a particular discipline may suggest a particular family of distribution functions, e.g., the Weibull distribution, when modeling time to an event. Alternatively, a specific point process, e.g. the power law process (a nonhomogeneous Poisson process of specific functional form, see Ascher and Feingold (1984)) may be appropriate in a particular reliability application dealing with times between successive failures of a repairable system. In a biometry application, in which times between successive nonfatal illnesses of a patient are studied, another point process might be suggested. In practice, however, instead of considering that models are *suggested* by circumstances, there is far too much reliance on a priori specification of models. For example, in hardware reliability applications it is usually assumed that the exponential distribution is the appropriate model to use, regardless of the application. If this model is generalized at all, the "generalization" usually is restricted to using a Weibull distribution. In fact, one or the other of these distributions is usually invoked even when *no* distribution whatsoever is the appropriate model! That is, when dealing with a repairable system—and most systems are designed to be repaired rather than replaced after failure—the correct model is a *sequence* of distribution functions, i.e., a point process. Distribution functions and point processes are not equivalent models, even in the most special cases. A homogeneous Poisson process (HPP) can be defined as a nonterminating sequence of independent and identically exponentially distributed times between events. Ascher and Feingold (1979, 1984) show that there are important distinctions between the exponential distribution and HPP models.

Apart from considerations as to exactly which distribution or point process applies in the modeling of times to or between events, respectively, the exact type of event is of no importance in most of the models in use. For example, the event could just as well be the copulation of two fruit flies (Aalen, 1978) as the failure of a transistor. In either case, if explanatory factors (e.g. abstinence period for the fruit flies or number of thermal cycles to which the transistor has been

NATO ASI Series, Vol. F22
Software System Design Methods. Edited by J.K. Skwirzynski

subjected) are not incorporated into the model, the model is the distribution of *time to* an arbitrary *event.* That it is often important to incorporate explanatory factors has been much more widely appreciated in the biometry field than in reliability. It is only in the last few years that the reliability community has begun to pay any attention to a major development, Cox's (1972a) proportional hazards model. This regression model allows for the incorporation of important explanatory factors, such as those mentioned above, in the analysis. A later paper, Prentice, Williams, and Peterson (1981), extended Cox's (1972a) results to the analysis of multiple events, e.g. successive times between infections of a patient or successive times between failures of a repairable system. These models will be discussed, after some additional comments about similarity among sociological, biometrical and reliability modeling and analysis. In particular, it will be shown that the differences between hardware and software modeling and analysis have been overplayed. Certainly some differences exist, but in both cases the basic model is a sequence of times between events, i.e., a point process. The differences between software and hardware can be accommodated, in part, by the choice of specific point process models. In large part, however, the differences should be represented by explanatory factors in regression models.

SOCIOLOGICAL, BIOMETRICAL AND RELIABILITY MODELING AND ANALYSIS

It is sometimes acknowledged that there are considerable connections among the models used in these different disciplines. As one example, Allison (1984), stresses that many of the approaches suited to the analysis of times to, or between, events in sociological applications have been developed by biostatisticians and, as he puts it, engineers. Allison (1984) also points out that, in the past, biometricians concentrated on the distribution of time to an event since, as he emphasizes, the event of primary concern is usually the death of a patient. He does not proffer any explanation for the lack of treatment of times between successive failures of repairable systems in the reliability literature. Instead, he claims that social scientists have concentrated on the study of events such as job changes and marriages which can occur many times during an individual's lifetime. Clearly, even in present society where divorce is common, no one gets married as often as some systems fail!

There also has been some recognition of the interplay between biometry and reliability. For example, a conference was held in 1973 whose Proceedings, Proschan and Serfling (1974), bear the title, "Reliability and Biometry: Statistical Analysis of Lifelength." One of the aims of this conference, as stated in the Proceedings Preface was, "to stimulate the exchange of ideas between biometricians and reliability theoreticians so that the models, concepts and methods of one field would be either applied directly or adapted to the solution of problems in the other field." The Preface also emphasized that "... in looking back over the history of the two subjects, one is struck by the fact that the development of the two fields has proceeded largely independently by separate groups of statisticians." This latter statement is borne out by even casual perusal of the Proceedings. For example, even though only one year had elapsed since the publication of Cox (1972a), two of the biometry papers, Fisher and Kanarek (1974) and Brown, Hollander and Korwar (1974) already were discussing the proportional hazards model. It took the reliability community a decade to begin to respond to Cox's landmark paper.

In my opinion, it would be hard to dispute the contention that the biometry and reliability literatures were far apart in 1973 and have continued to remain so. Since the basic models are identical in both disciplines, this situation should be reversed. Unfortunately, as described above, that was the intention of the 1973 conference.

HARDWARE VS SOFTWARE RELIABILITY

In modeling the reliability of a computer program, one is concerned with the times between successive "bugs" detected during the operation of the program. Similarly, the pattern of successive hardware failures of a single repairable system is also a sequence of times between events. Much has been made of the differences between hardware and software, however, and the literatures of these two fields are far apart. Some differences certainly do exist. If a software fix is properly designed and implemented it will eliminate a problem forever. In contrast, hardware will always be subject to some chance of additional failure, regardless of how well a design fix is implemented. Another example concerns the use of redundancy. Two items in parallel will have higher reliability than one (unless the predominant failure mode is shorting rather than open circuiting). In contrast, the use of duplicate copies of a program will not increase reliability—if one copy contains an error, so will the other.

In spite of substantive differences, such as those described above, there has been some acknowledgement in the literature, e.g. by Littlewood (1981), Meeker (1983) and Shooman (1984) that there should be more commonality in repairable system and software modeling and data analysis. Moreover, some of the differences which "should" exist between software and hardware often do not show up in data sets.

The majority of software reliability models make all of the following assumptions. A program starts with an unknown number of bugs and as testing proceeds, these bugs are detected one by one. Design fixes are then developed and implemented; these fixes are assumed to be perfect, i.e., they totally eliminate the cause of the problem and, in addition, they do not introduce any new errors. These assumptions imply that times between bug detections should tend to become larger and larger as the program approaches perfection. In actuality, many software data sets display considerable—or even great—conflict with these assumptions. In many cases, plots of cumulative bugs detected versus cumulative test time show increasing slope over long periods of time. This corresponds to successive times between bug detections becoming smaller rather than larger.

Results such as these often have been interpreted to show that software modeling is in a less developed state than hardware modeling. Spragins (1984), for example, claims that at the present time, software models are far less successful than those for physical systems. He points to the poor performance of seven software reliability models in fitting data from 51 data sets examined by Angus (1984)—the percentage of good fits obtained with the seven models ranged from 0% to 53%! Part of the problem in obtaining good fits was that the parameter estimation procedures often did not converge or converged to nonsensical estimates, e.g. negative estimates of the total number of bugs in a program. Nevertheless, even when convergence to physically possible estimates was achieved, the models provided good fits only 57-78% of the time. Clearly, there is considerable room for improvement.

Alternative explanations may be proferred, however, for the greater number of demonstrated poor fits of software models. To begin with, there have been very few analyses of real repairable system's failure data in the hardware literature. As discussed in Ascher and Feingold (1984), moreover, the few analyses which have been performed have often been seriously flawed. Perhaps even more importantly, the number of failures of individual system copies are usually very small compared to the sample sizes often encountered in computer programs. For example, the six modules analyzed by Angus (1984) had incurred anywhere from about 210 to 3400 failures at the cutoff time of the analysis. The 51 data sets culled from this large data bank were much smaller, but often contained dozens of failures. Statistical goodness-of-fit tests have notoriously low probability of rejecting whatever model is being tested, when sample sizes are small. The poor goodness-of-fit of software models is probably explicable largely on the basis of much larger sample sizes than are usually available in system reliability studies.

The problems associated with software modeling are formidable. In my opinion, the difficulties in developing accurate models for hardware systems are even greater. Parts can wear out or burn-in. In addition, even before a system suffers its first failure, there are many complex interrelationships among its constituent parts. For example, all parts may meet their specifications but the system may not or conversely, one or more parts may be out of "specs" without the system being in a failed state. Moreover, unlike software, hardware is subject to failure from workmanship errors. Furthermore, as failures accumulate, the effect of damage caused by part failures, as well as by repair actions, is probably beyond the capability of accurate modeling. If the very important long term effects of environmental factors such as on/off cycling, vibration, shock, thermal cycling, humidity, loss of cooling, line voltage variations, etc. are to be added, it becomes clear that accurate modeling simply is not feasible.

Even if a probabilistic model which incorporates at least the most important factors influencing reliability can be developed, the model's parameters are never known a priori. In other words, even with an adequate probabilistic model, statistical analysis is still essential for estimation of the model's parameters. The remainder of this paper is devoted to 1) the development of models which incorporate factors which are likely to have important effects on a system's reliability and 2) techniques for the estimation of those parameters from available data. Since both software and repairable systems data sets involve sequences of times between successive failures, the same basic models are applicable to both. The specific circumstances, e.g. quality and training of programmers for software and number of system on/off cycles for hardware, should be incorporated via explanatory factors, as will be shown. Explanatory factors can—and should—be tailored to each specific situation.

In practice, more and more types of systems are incorporating embedded computers. In other words, it is becoming increasingly important to consider both hardware and software problems when modeling and/or analyzing system reliability.

FORCE OF MORTALITY AND RATE OF OCCURRENCE OF FAILURES

Let X be defined as the random variable, time to some specified event. Then the cumulative distribution function, $F_X(x)$, probability density function $f_X(x)$ and force of mortality $h_X(x)$ are defined as follows:

$$F_X(x) \equiv Pr\{X \leqslant x\} \tag{1}$$

$$f_X(x) \equiv F'_X(x) \tag{2}$$

$$h_X(x) \equiv \frac{f_X(x)}{1 - F_X(x)}. \tag{3}$$

The force of mortality (FOM) $h_X(x)$ is best interpreted in the following terms:

$$h_X(x)\,dx = Pr\{\text{event occurs in}(x,\, x + dx]\,|\,\text{event did not occur in}(0,\, x]\}, \tag{4}$$

i.e., in reliability terms, as the conditional probability of failure in the interval $(x, x + dx]$ given survival to x.

Now assume that a sequence of times between events, e.g., the times between successive failures of a single repairable system, are being observed. In this situation, we are dealing with a point process, rather than a distribution function as above. Let

$$N(t) \equiv \text{Number of failures in}(0,\ t] \tag{5}$$

$$E[N(t)] \equiv \text{Expected number of failures in}(0,\ t] \tag{6}$$

$$\nu(t) \equiv \frac{d}{dt}E[N(t)]. \tag{7}$$

Since $\nu(t)$ is defined as a derivative of an expected number of failures, it will be called the rate of occurrence of failures (ROCOF). In contrast to the interpretation of $h_X(x)dx$, $\nu(t)dt$ is interpreted as

$$\nu(t)dt = Pr\{\text{a failure (not necessarily the first) occurs in}(t,\ t + dt]\}. \tag{8}$$

"Failure rate" is usually defined to be equivalent to $h_X(x)$, Eq. (3), but in practice, "failure rate" is used interchangeably for $h_X(x)$ and $\nu(t)$. See Ascher and Feingold (1984, Chapter 8) for a discussion of the great confusion engendered by the promiscuous use of "failure rate" in the reliability field. The term "failure rate" will not be used again in this paper.

REGRESSION MODELS

Cox (1972a) proposed the following model for incorporating the effects of explanatory factors:

$$h(x;\ \mathbf{z}) = h_0(x)e^{\beta_1 z_1 + \beta_2 z_2 + \ldots + \beta_m z_m} \tag{9}$$

where $h_0(x)$ is a baseline force of mortality common to all items (or patients) under test, the z_i's are the explanatory factors and the β_i's are the corresponding regression coefficients. There is no upper bound on m prescribed by the model itself; practical limits on the maximum value of m are set by the amount of failure data available or if a very large data base exists, by the costs of computation. The baseline force of morality (FOM) can be interpreted as the FOM of an item for which $z_1 = z_2 = \ldots = z_m = 0$. Under Cox's (1972a) formulation, the baseline FOM is totally arbitrary; it can be identically zero at all instants at which failures have not been observed! As Cox pointed out, this is too arbitrary since some smoothness in the baseline FOM is to be expected. By allowing this total arbitrariness, however, Cox was able to totally separate estimation of $h_0(x)$ from estimation of the β_i's; first the β_i's are estimated and then, conditional on $\hat{\beta}_i$, $i = 1, 2, \ldots, m$, $\hat{h}_0(x)$ is obtained.

Estimation of the β_i's can be based on the partial likelihood approach, Cox (1975), or on marginal likelihood, Lawless (1982). In practice, a computer program is required to obtain estimates. Commercially available packages such as BMDP (BMDP2L) and SAS (PHGLM) include routines to perform the calculations. Allison (1984, Appendix C) summarizes the key features of the available programs. Appendix A of the same reference provides a heuristic explanation of maximum likelihood and partial maximum likelihood estimation.

Cox's (1972a) model is applicable to modeling the time to a single event, such as failure of a nonrepairable item or death of a patient. Cox (1972b) extended this approach to repeated events such as successive failures of a repairable system or nonfatal illnesses of a patient. Two generalized versions of Cox (1972b) were developed by Prentice, Williams, and Peterson (1981) (PWP (1981)).

In simplified form, PWP's (1981) models are

$$v_1(t;\, \mathbf{z}) = v_{0s}(t)\, e^{\beta_1 z_1(t)+\ldots+\beta_m z_m(t)} \tag{10}$$

$$v_2(t;\, \mathbf{z}) = h_{0s}(B(t))\, e^{\beta_1 z_1(t)+\ldots+\beta_m z_m(t)} \tag{11}$$

where $B(t)$ is the backward recurrence time to the most recent failure occurring before, or at, t and the notation $z_i(t)$ implies that time varying explanatory factors can be accommodated. For example, $z_i(t)$ might be defined as the number of thermal cycles to which a repairable system has been subjected in the interval $(0,\, t]$. The subscript s refers to the sth stratum. The most straightforward way of defining s is

$$s = N(t) + 1,$$

i.e., a system enters the jth stratum immediately after suffering its $j - 1$st failure, $j = 2, 3, \ldots$, and it enters stratum 1 at $t = 0$.

PWP (1981) applied their models to the analysis of times between successive nonfatal infections and Ascher (1983) used model (11) in the analysis of times between successive failures of marine gas turbines. Dale (1983) has also discussed the use of PWP's (1981) model for the analysis of simulated repairable system failure data.

APPLICATION OF REGRESSION MODELS TO DATA ANALYSIS

The great usefulness of Cox's (1972a) model will be illustrated by applying it to a data set. Ideally, this would be accomplished by using real data. Such data, however, are in very short supply in the reliability field. Moreover, no real data set, in which at least two explanatory factors have important effects, is presently available to me. It is with such data sets that the full power of Cox's approach is manifested. A number of recent papers, Anderson, Jardine and Higgins (1982), Dale (1983), Lawless (1983), Jardine and Anderson (1984), Bendell (1984), Jardine and Buzacott

(1985) and Ascher (1983) have emphasized the application of Cox's model to reliability problems. Perhaps this emphasis on a model which can accommodate the heterogeneous data usually encountered in practice, will help promote the appearance of real data sets for analysis.

The background for the following artificial data set will be phrased in concrete terms for ease of presentation. It is emphasized that the entire problem has sprung from the mind of the writer.

A type of transistor, i.e., 2NXXXX, is produced by a single manufacturer. Some of the transistors have been screened in the factory, whereas others have been shipped after only routine inspection. It is assumed that all transistors are installed in the same type of system and, with a single exception, all system copies are operated under nominally identical conditions. The exception is that some of the transistors have been installed in system copies which have been subjected to a very large number of on/off cycles per unit time whereas the other transistors are in copies which are infrequently cycled on and off. It is assumed that there are no other known differences in testing or operation of these transistors. Note that it is *not* necessary to assume that there are no other factors which affect transistor reliability. What is assumed, is that these factors apply equally to all of the transistors and hence influence only the common baseline force of mortality. (If there were other known sources of heterogeneity, they would be incorporated by defining additional explanatory factors.)

From the way the problem has been formulated, it is clear that there are two explanatory factors, defined as follows, for each transistor under study:

$$z_1 = \begin{cases} 1, & \text{transistor has been screened} \\ 0, & \text{otherwise} \end{cases}$$

and

$$z_2 = \begin{cases} 1, & \text{transistor has been subjected to many on/off cycles} \\ 0, & \text{otherwise.} \end{cases}$$

The model being used, therefore, is

$$h(x; \mathbf{z}) = h_0(x) e^{\beta_1 z_1 + \beta_2 z_2}. \tag{12}$$

For example, for a unscreened, frequently cycled transistor the model is

$$h(x; \mathbf{z}) = h_0(x) e^{\beta_2 z_2}. \tag{13}$$

For an unscreened, infrequently cycled transistor, the model reduces to

$$h(x; \mathbf{z}) = h_0(x), \tag{14}$$

i.e., to the baseline force of mortality.

Table 1 lists the artificial data "collected" at each of the four possible levels (screened and subjected to frequent cycling, screened and not subjected to frequent cycling, etc.). For clarity of exposition, the times to failure have been selected to make it clear that screening has a beneficial effect and on/off cycling decreases transistor reliability. The model would pick up differences in reliability even if considerable overlap in the times to failures existed, provided that sample sizes were adequately large. It is also assumed that each of the 40 transistors has been observed to failure, i.e., that there are no censored data. (A major advantage of Cox's approach, relative to other regression methods, is that it readily accommodates censored data.)

Table 1 — Times to Failure and Associated Explanatory Factors for 40 Transistors

Time to Failure	z_1	z_2
40	1	1
60	1	1
38	1	1
55	1	1
49	1	1
53	1	1
57	1	1
41	1	1
61	1	1
77	1	1
59	1	0
73	1	0
70	1	0
66	1	0
71	1	0
60	1	0
63	1	0
65	1	0
70	1	0
59	1	0
58	0	0
60	0	0
47	0	0
53	0	0
51	0	0
39	0	0
47	0	0
55	0	0
48	0	0
49	0	0
29	0	1
45	0	1
37	0	1
47	0	1
39	0	1
41	0	1
50	0	1
29	0	1
41	0	1
45	0	1

The sample range of the times to failure is 29 (two unscreened, frequently cycled transistors) to 77 (one screened, infrequently cycled transistor). Application of an appropriate computer program (obtained from Mr. Patrick Marek of the University of Washington) yields the Table 2 parameter estimates for β_1 and β_2 as well as other estimates of interest.

Table 2 — Estimates Obtained in Fitting Model

$h(x; \mathbf{z}) = h_0(x) \exp\{\beta_1 z_1 + \beta_2 z_2\}$

to Table 1 Data

$\hat{\beta}_1$	=	−1.97
Std. Error of $\hat{\beta}_1$	=	0.44
$\hat{\beta}_2$	=	1.10
Std. Error of $\hat{\beta}_2$	=	0.35
Maximum Log Partial Likelihood	=	−97.88

Under the null hypothesis that $\beta_i = 0$,

$$\frac{\hat{\beta}_i}{\{\text{Std. Error of } \hat{\beta}_i\}} \sim N(0, 1) \quad , \quad i = 1, 2,$$

i.e., approximately normally distributed with mean zero and standard deviation one. It is clear that both regression coefficients are non-zero, i.e., that each must be retained as having an important effect on transistor reliability. Since $\beta_1 < 0$ and $\beta_2 > 0$, screening and frequent on/off cycling have beneficial and detrimental effects, respectively, on reliability. (Actually, this is clear from "eyeball" analysis of Table 1, but with larger sample sizes and more data overlap one might have to rely on the sign of the regression coefficient. It is also possible that an explanatory factor does not have the desired or anticipated effect, e.g., screening under excessively severe conditions might degrade reliability, rather than improve it.) The estimated model is

$$\hat{h}(x; \mathbf{z}) = \hat{h}_0(x) e^{-1.97z_1 + 1.10z_2} \tag{15}$$

The interpretation of this result in terms of relative risk of failure at any given age x is given in Table 3:

Table 3 — Relative Risk of Failure at any Age x

and Estimated Mean Time to Failure

Expl. Factors of a Transistor	$\hat{h}(x; \mathbf{z})$	$\widehat{\text{MTTF}}$
$z_1 = 0 = z_2$	$\hat{h}_0(x) = \hat{h}_0(x)$	48.5
$z_1 = 0,\ z_2 = 1$	$\hat{h}_0(x) e^{1.10} = 3.0 \hat{h}_0(x)$	41.6
$z_1 = 1,\ z_2 = 0$	$\hat{h}_0(x) e^{-1.97} = 0.14 \hat{h}_0(x)$	63.3
$z_1 = 1,\ z_2 = 1$	$\hat{h}_0(x) e^{-0.87} = 0.42 \hat{h}_0(x)$	54.5

It is clear that the two factors tend to offset each other. In practice, the beneficial and negative effects of different factors might tend to go unnoticed when their combined effects approximately cancel.

It will be instructive to illustrate what happens when one of the explanatory factors is omitted from the model. Assume that the model is specified as

$$h(x; \mathbf{z}) = h_0(x) e^{\beta_1 z_1}, \tag{16}$$

i.e., the possible effect of on/off cycling on reliability is ignored. Fitting this model to the Table 1 data yields $\hat{\beta}_1 = -1.64$ with a standard error of 0.41. Clearly β_1 is again significantly less than 0, even though its magnitude is slightly less than the earlier value of $\hat{\beta}_1 = -1.97$. The adequacy of model (16) in explaining the Table 1 data can be tested by means of the maximum log partial likelihood, which is computed to be -102.7 in this case. Under the assumption that the special case model (16), i.e. with $z_2 \equiv 0$, is an adequate representation of the data

-2[max log partialog likelihood of model (12) - max log partial likelihood of model (16)]

is approximately distributed as χ_1^2, i.e. as Chi-Square with one degree of freedom, Cox (1975). The reason for a single degree of freedom is that, in this case, the models differ by one parameter. Subtraction yields $-2(97.9 - 102.7) = 9.6$. This value is exceeded by χ_1^2 less than 0.5% of the time, which provides very strong evidence for the need to include both explanatory factors in the model. Therefore, model (16) will receive no further consideration.

If we fit a model which includes only z_2, the maximum log partial likelihood is computed to be -108.9. Minus twice the difference in the maximum log partial likelihoods is now 22, thus indicating even more strongly that z_1 is needed in the model. This should come as no surprise since $|\hat{\beta}_1| > \hat{\beta}_2$.

As mentioned previously, it could be argued that with the data of Table 1, eyeball analysis could be substituted for Cox's model. If there were more "noise" in the data, e.g. more overlap in times to failure and/or unequal sample sizes in the different categories, it would become difficult to extract the correct results with "human signal processing." If the sample sizes in specific categories were too small, it would become impossible to perform meaningful eyeball analyses for those categories. On the other hand, as the number of failures becomes very large and especially as additional explanatory factors are incorporated, it also becomes essential to use Cox's model for correct analysis. Moreover, the effect of censored times would also be very difficult to accomodate with eyeball analysis. In any case, obtaining quantitative results requires the use of a quantitative model.

SUMMARY AND CONCLUSIONS

Most of the modeling and data analysis in the reliability field is based on the oversimplified assumption that operating time is the only variable affecting the reliability of either nonrepairable or repairable items. Operating time is not the only important variable—in fact, it is not necessarily even the most important one! Kujawski and Rypka (1978) investigated the effect of on/off cycling on some types of repairable shipboard systems. They found that copies which were turned on and off frequently failed more frequently—by as much as almost an order of magnitude—than copies which were seldom shut down. The conventional wisdom in the reliability field is that reliability over a given calendar period will be maximized by shutting the system off whenever feasible. If this policy results in many on/off cycles the actual effect on reliability may be devastating rather than beneficial. More generally, Ascher and Feingold (1984, Chapter 4) list 18 factors which are usually ignored in probabilistic modeling of repairable systems. The combined effect of all these factors may completely dominate the effect of operating time, even if operating time is measured from the initial system start up, rather than adopting the usual unrealistic approach of measuring it from the most recent repair, cf. Ascher and Feingold (1984).

The use of regression models can help bridge the gap between probabilistic models—which must be oversimplified if they are to be tractable—and the real world. Claims have been made that Cox's (1972) model enables the analyst to estimate reliability as a function of time in the presence of "nuisance factors," i.e., in the presence of heterogeneity. In some situations it may be reasonable to adopt this viewpoint. In others, it will be more appropriate to *exploit* heterogeneity 1) to help determine which factors have major effects on reliability and 2) to quantify those effects. Spragins (1984) quotes Rosanoff (1969) to the effect that rigorous argument from inapplicable assumptions produces the world's most durable nonsense. It is about time that the reliability field began checking its basic assumptions.

Lawless (1983) pointed out that "Cox (1972a) has perhaps influenced the analysis of lifetime data in the biomedical area more than any other paper in the last 25 years ... however, these methods have to date scarcely been used in the reliability area." It is about time that the reliability field began using Cox (1972a) and PWP (1981) to help check its basic assumptions.

REFERENCES

O. Aalen (1978), "Nonparametric Inference for a Family of Counting Processes," Annals of Statistics, **6**, 701-726.

P.D. Allison (1984), *Event History Analysis: Regression for Longitudinal Event Data*, Sage Publications, Beverly Hills.

M. Anderson, A.K. Jardine, and R.T. Higgins (1982), "The Use of Concomitant Variables in Reliability Estimation," Proceedings of the Thirteenth Annual Pittsburgh Modeling and Simulation Conference, Instrument Society of America, pp. 73-81.

J.E. Angus (1984), "The Application of Software Reliability Models to a Major C^3I System," Proceedings Annual Reliability and Maintainability Symposium, IEEE Cat. No. 84CH1992-7, pp. 268-274.

H.E. Ascher (1983), "Regression Analysis of Repairable Systems Reliability," in Electronic Systems Effectiveness and Life Cycle Costing, J.K. Skwirzynski, ed., Springer-Verlag, Berlin, pp. 119-133.

H.E. Ascher and H. Feingold (1979), "The Aircraft Air Conditioner Data Revisited," Proceedings Annual Reliability and Maintainability Symposium, IEEE Cat. No. 79CH1429-OR, pp. 153-159.

H.E. Ascher and H. Feingold (1984), *Repairable Systems Reliability: Modeling, Inference, Misconceptions and Their Causes*, Marcel Dekker, New York and Basel.

A. Bendell (1984), "Proportional Hazards Modelling in Reliability Assessment," to appear in Reliability Engineering.

B.W. Brown, Jr., M. Hollander, and R.M. Korwar (1974), "Nonparameteric Test of Independence for Censored Data, with Application to Heart Transplant Studies," in Reliability and Biometry, F. Proschan and R.F. Serfling, eds., Society for Industrial and Applied Mathematics, Philadelphia, pp. 327-354.

D.R. Cox (1972a), "Regression Models and Life Tables (with Discussion)," Journal of the Royal Statistical Society, Series B, **34**, 187-220.

D.R. Cox (1972b), "The Statistical Analysis of Dependencies in Point Processes" in Stochastic Point Processes, P.A. Lewis, ed., Wiley-Interscience, New York, pp. 55-66.

D.R. Cox (1975), "Partial Likelihood," Biometrika, **62**, 269-276.

C.J. Dale (1983), "Application of the Proportional Hazards Model in the Reliability Field," Proceedings of the Fourth National Reliability Conference—Reliability '83, United Kingdom.

L. Fisher and P. Kanarek (1974), "Presenting Censored Survival Data when Censoring and Survival Times may not be Independent," in Reliability and Biometry, F. Proschan and R.J. Serfling, eds., Society for Industrial and Applied Mathematics, Philadelphia, pp. 303-326.

A.K. Jardine and P.M. Anderson (1984), "Use of Concomitant Variables for Reliability Estimation," Proceedings of the 8th Symposium on Advances in Reliability Technology, Bradford University, United Kingdom.

A.K. Jardine and J.A. Buzacott (1985), "Equipment Reliability and Maintenance," European Journal of Operational Research, **19**, 285-296.

G.J. Kujawski and E.A. Rypka (1978), "Effects of 'On-Off' Cycling on Equipment Reliability," Proceedings Annual Reliability and Maintainability Symposium, IEEE Cat. No. 77CH1308-6R, pp. 225-230.

J.F. Lawless (1982), *Statistical Models and Methods for Lifetime Data*, Wiley-Interscience, New York.

J.F. Lawless (1983), "Statistical Methods in Reliability (with Discussion)," Technometrics, **25**, 305-335.

B. Littlewood (1981), "Stochastic Reliability Growth: A Model for Fault Removal in Computer-Programs and Hardware-Designs," IEEE Reliability Transactions, **R-30**, 313-320.

W.Q. Meeker, Jr. (1983), Discussion of Lawless (1983), pp. 316-320.

R.L. Prentice, B.J. Williams, and A.V. Peterson (1981), "On the Regression Analysis of Multivariate Failure Time Data," Biometrika, **68**, 373-379.

F. Proschan and R.J. Serfling, eds. (1974), *Reliability and Biometry: Statistical Analysis of Lifelength*, Society for Industrial and Applied Mathematics, Philadelphia.

R.A. Rosanoff (1969), "A Survey of Modern Nonsense as Applied to Matrix Computation," Technical Papers for Meeting, AIAA/ASME 10th Structures, Structural Dynamics and Materials Conference, New Orleans.

M.L. Shooman (1984), "Software Reliability: A Historical Perspective," IEEE Reliability Transactions, **R-33**, 48-55.

J. Spragins (1984), "Limitations of Current Telecommunication Network Reliability Models," Proceedings IEEE Global Telecommunications Conference, IEEE Product No. CH 2064-4/84/0000, pp. 836-840.

THE ASSESSMENT OF SOFTWARE RELIABILITY FOR SYSTEMS WITH HIGH RELIABILITY REQUIREMENTS

Chris Dale
National Centre of Systems Reliability
United Kingdom Atomic Energy Authority

ABSTRACT

This paper considers the problems of assessing software reliability when the reliability requirements are high. A number of possible approaches to the problem are discussed and evaluated. These include correctness proofs, software fault tree analysis, software testing, and assessment of the development process. The need for and value of software fault tolerance are also discussed.

INTRODUCTION AND STATEMENT OF THE PROBLEM

Many kinds of systems have associated with them requirements for high levels of reliability. Such systems occur in many branches of human endeavour, including industry (e.g., nuclear power plant control, chemical process control, oil platforms), transportation (e.g., avionics, bridges) and commerce (e.g., banking systems).

The reasons for requiring high reliability are many, and include economic considerations such as availability of process plant, safety considerations such as those associated with avionics or nuclear engineering, and efficiency/effectiveness considerations such as those associated with military systems. It is often the case that reliability requirements are in conflict. For example a protection system in a nuclear reactor is required to shut the reactor down safely when conditions demand, for reasons

NATO ASI Series, Vol. F22
Software System Design Methods. Edited by J.K. Skwirzynski

of safety; it is also required that the spurious trip rate be low, because of the economic consequences of lost power production.

It is increasingly the case that such systems can be expected to contain software. For example, transactions between banks are handled by computer systems, air-traffic control systems depend upon software, and most modern weapons are computer controlled. Even systems which do not contain software may be dependent upon software in some way. For example, if computer programs containing faults are used for designing plant, then the plant when built may be unsafe. An event of this nature led to five US nuclear power reactors being shut down for many months, at a cost of more than a quarter of a billion dollars of lost electricity production, while seismic stress calculations relating to some of the pipework were reworked (Ref. 1).

The fact that software can lead to such hazards implies a need to ensure, when using software in an area where reliability is paramount, that the reliability of the delivered system is indeed adequate, or that any shortfall can be accommodated by other means. This in turn means that it must be possible either to demonstrate that a given piece of software will function reliably in all circumstances, or to quantify the extent of unreliability and establish that this is adequate to the purpose. This paper discusses the extent to which this can currently be done, considering a number of possible approaches to the problem.

CORRECTNESS PROOFS

Consider first whether it is possible to demonstrate that software is correct. Any piece of software is an abstract entity. If the requirements for the software are also specified in an abstract way by means of a formal language representation, then it is at least in theory possible to prove that the software is correct with respect to the specification, by means of mathematical logic. Thus the process of proving software correctness is exactly the same as the process of proving theorems in algebra.

A great deal of work has been done in this area over the past few years (e.g., Refs. 2-4), but capabilities are still very limited. The value in the approach probably lies in the formality of the software development process leading to improved quality of software products, rather than in any hope of being able to give absolute guarantees of correctness. There seems little doubt that added formalism allied with verification throughout development will improve the quality of software production. There is a number of problems with guaranteeing correctness however.

One of the greatest difficulties is the sheer complexity of the tasks software is expected to perform, which leads in turn to very complex software. It is a commonly-held belief that complexity of task leads to human errors in software development; if this is the case, and given that a proof is almost certain to be more complex than the software, it is surely unreasonable to expect the proof to be fault-free. The degree of automation which can currently be achieved in software correctness proving is limited, so the possibility of human error remains.

Even given that for sufficiently small software, a proof is a practical proposition, there still remains the problem that the specification may not be correct. For example, it is unusual for a specification to be complete, in that a great many important areas of functionality are implicit in the (informal) customer requirement but not explicit in the (formal) specification. This problem is exacerbated by the tendency for software to be developed in isolation from any knowledge of the systems requirement.

It seems then that the formal approach does not currently offer the possibility of demonstrating correctness. This is partly because correctness is not an absolute, but is relative to something. Even in cases where it is possible to establish correctness of software with respect to a specification, there is still no guarantee that the specification is correct with respect to the real requirement. Size and complexity of many (real-time) software applications simply exacerbate this basic problem.

SOFTWARE FAULT TREE ANALYSIS

Software fault tree analysis (SFTA) (Ref. 5) is a recently-developed approach which falls some way short of proving correctness, but does enable the possible causes of individual identified events to be investigated. This technique owes a lot to fault tree analysis (FTA) which has been used successfully for many years in the assessment of safety and reliability of many kinds of engineering system. Because of this the technique is particularly useful as one which takes into account the interface between hardware and software aspects of a system, which can often cause problems due to the tendency for hardware and software to be developed separately.

The essence of the technique is to identify some specific (undesirable) event and the conditions which would cause that event to happen. Each of the conditions is then treated as an event, and the conditions which would lead to them are identified in turn. This process continues until a point is reached at which the conditions identified are clearly impossible or clearly possible. If all conditions at the basic level are clearly impossible, and the analysis has been carried out correctly, then it has been demonstrated that the undesirable event at the top of the tree cannot happen. If this is not the case, then the analysis has highlighted a way in which a hazardous situation can occur, and steps can be taken to remedy this.

An attractive feature of the method is that it can readily be used in conjunction with a system FTA. At the point at which a system FTA identifies software as the possible cause of an event, that cause can be expanded by SFTA. Similarly, if some input parameter from system hardware to the software is identified as a possible cause of software malfunction, this can be expanded using FTA techniques. Thus the two methods used hand in hand potentially provide a powerful analysis tool.

There is an important difference between FTA and SFTA. The basic events of a FTA are generally such things as component failures or environmental conditions. In principle, events of this kind occur probabilistically, so a FTA can be used to quantify the probability or frequency with which undesired events can be expected to occur. Thus FTA can be used to quantify system reliability. SFTA cannot be used in this way since basic events are, in general, either true or false, and their importance to the top event is determined by the logic of the SFTA, determining whether or not the top event will happen, and under what conditions.

SFTA is a good complement to more conventional verification and validation techniques for software. These are usually aimed at showing that software does what it is supposed to do, whereas SFTA aims to show that software does not do what it is supposed not to do. This latter aim is very important in safety-related applications of software, but is very difficult to cater for in traditional methods of testing software (Ref. 6).

SFTA is not capable of demonstrating that software is correct. To do this would necessitate the identification of all relevant top events (hazardous and non-hazardous) and the development of a SFTA for each. This task is impracticable for the vast bulk of software applications; even when practicable the complexity of the analysis itself would be too great for complete trust to be placed upon it.

Neither can SFTA be used (as is FTA) to quantify the reliability of a system, for reasons explained above. Nevertheless, it does appear to provide a valuable means of assessing software-based systems from a safety or reliability viewpoint, when it is wished to focus attention on a manageable number of undesirable events.

SOFTWARE TESTING

Consideration now moves to the question of whether it is possible to demonstrate that a given level of reliability has been achieved, on the basis of software testing. The assessment methods reviewed above are based upon analysis of the software; testing offers a way of assessing reliability by studying instead the performance of the software in question. There is a variety of ways in which testing can potentially be used for reliability assessment.

The first question that arises is whether it is possible to submit a piece of software to every conceivable set of inputs, and ascertain that the resulting output is correct in each case. If this can be done, then absolute correctness is guaranteed. It is in fact easy to see that this cannot be achieved, other than for trivial pieces of software. For example, a program which has as input a single 8-bit number will require a total of $2^8 = 256$ tests. If instead there are as few as six such input parameters, then the required number of tests exceeds 10^{14}, which is clearly beyond practicable limits. Thus, the class of software which can be demonstrated to be correct by means of testing can be seen to be extremely restricted.

Software testing is more frequently used as a reliability improvement method than as an assessment method: observation of failure leads to discovery and correction of faults. Since exhaustive testing is not normally possible, as illustrated above, the aim of this kind of testing must be to maximise the efficiency of testing, in terms of the reliability improvement which can be obtained by a given account of testing. A number of testing strategies have been developed in pursuit of this aim, most of which make use of a knowledge of the structure of the software in question (Ref. 6). For example, path testing comprises exercising every possible control path through the software; statement coverage involves ensuring that every statement is executed at least once. Thus it is possible to ensure that all aspects of the software are tested uniformly, in some sense. A rather different approach to testing which is similarly motivated is to attempt to exercise every function of the software, the various functions typically being determined by study of the specification for the software. One problem with this approach is the great difficulty in establishing the various functions of a piece of software.

The use of testing methods of this kind for assessment of reliability is subject to a number of drawbacks. Both of the broad approaches outlined above do of course suffer from the fact that they are compromises: the real desire is to show that the software functions as intended for all possible sets of input; these methods are concerned with ensuring (for example) that each part of the software works for some input, or that each function is correct in some circumstances. The pious hope is that because software works on some occasions, then it will also work in other similar circumstances. These strategies cannot, then, provide guaranteed correctness.

The natural question to ask at this point is whether the degree to which correctness has been demonstrated can be quantified. The answer is a qualified "Yes". It is possible to measure, for example, the proportion of statements which have been executed by given test cases, and thus obtain a number which gives the degree to which the software has been tested (Ref. 7). What it does not give is a measure of reliability. "Testedness" is essentially a static measure of the software and its testing; reliability is a dynamic quantity relating to usage of the software. It seems that it may be possible to relate the two quantities by means of an understanding of the relevance of the testing to the usage environment, but it is hard to see a great deal of progress being made in this area in the near future.

The only possibility which now remains, as far as testing is concerned, is that something can be said about the software reliability on the basis of observing its operation either during use, or during testing which is designed to be representative of use. In principle, statistical methods can be applied to data from this kind of testing to provide reliability measures, but great care must be taken, both in planning and carrying out the testing, and in interpreting the results (Ref. 8).

If several different operating modes are to be experienced, then separate tests should be devised to simulate each, to provide reliability measures for each mode. For example, in the case of a nuclear reactor protection system, the plant can be expected to operate for the vast majority of the time at steady full or near full output with large margins between plant parameters and the values of those parameters which would lead to an emergency shut-down, or trip. The safety role of the protection system only comes into play when trip conditions arise, so that testing the software for safety should concentrate on the inputs to be expected when trip conditions arise. Such a system has another implicit requirement, which is not to trip when trip conditions do not arise (i.e., to reduce false alarms). Reliability testing for this requirement should concentrate on those inputs to be expected during normal operation. It is worth emphasising that a test plan which simply mimics the overall operating conditions of the plant would in this case provide almost no safety assurance.

Choice of test data which simulates the conditions expected to be experienced during the operational life of the program implies a detailed knowledge of plant behaviour. For a complex plant such as an aeroplane or a nuclear reactor it is difficult, if not impossible, to select the appropriate distribution of input conditions manually. Limited groups of inputs for certain expected modes of operation will be identifiable but these will be far from comprehensive. It will often be necessary to engineer a plant model in software (if a simulator already exists then this might be adaptable) incorporating as many behavioural interactions as is practicable, and use this to generate test data. Then all expected normal, abnormal and dangerous circumstances can be simulated, and the corresponding test data applied to the program either immediately or preferably via an intermediate data storage file (to permit repeat testing after fault repair). The representativeness of the test data so generated is clearly determined by the quality of the plant model, but the relationship between infidelity in the plant model and degradation in value of the test data is not known; intuitively it would seem that providing the model did not incorporate gross inaccuracies or errors, then the test results should retain an acceptable level of validity for the real plant.

If quantified software reliability assessment is required, then great care must be taken in calculating and interpreting the reliability figure which is generated. This may seem to be stating the obvious, but it is very easy to generate a number: any set of tests will yield some or no faults in a given number of trials, so by applying whatever statistical confidence level seems reasonable, a failure frequency or unavailability figure can be derived. The danger is that when a number becomes associated with a piece of software it may unduly influence the decision as to whether or not the software is adequate for use, when in fact the number in question may be of low accuracy and based upon assumptions which are unsound.

The basis of quantification should be the results of a reliability testing procedure which applies data from the relevant operational input domain, not a fault detection procedure which uses quite different input domains. If any results other than of reliability testing are used, then the derived figure will be valid only for the particular input domain used during the tests, which might well bear no resemblance at all to the operational input domain.

The bare data from which any reliability figure is derived may well take the form "k failures observed in N trials", the value N being the number of trials that exercise the safety function out of a large sample of input conditions from the operational input domain. It is of course the case that for a safety critical application each of the k failures must be investigated and the corresponding fault removed. However, for the purposes of calculating a reliability figure with an appropriate level of statistical confidence, the k failures must be retained. This is because a further N random trials may well reveal further faults, and the "k failures observed in N trials" may still be the performance level to be expected from those areas of the input domain which were not covered by the original N trials. In this way a suitably pessimistic figure will be generated for the expected number of failures in N demands on the safety function of the program.

There will be occasions when the figure obtained by using "k failures observed in N trials" is inadequate, but it is felt that the removal of the faults leading to those failures has improved the software reliability across the whole input domain. The only sound way of demonstrating this statistically is to carry out a further set of tests to exercise the safety function of the (corrected) software. It may then be possible to base the assessment on data of the form "No failures observed in M trials", where M is the number of inputs used in the new testing, and a much higher level of reliability can be claimed. On the other hand, the additional testing may simply confirm fears that there are further faults which were not exposed by the original reliability demonstration test comprising N input sets.

Any figure so generated should be treated as only one of a number of guides as to the adequacy of the software, others including the development methods and quality assurance procedures used, design philosophy adopted, and performance during the fault removal testing phase. The reason for this is not only the statistical nature of the conclusions drawn and the inevitable uncertainty therefore associated with them, but also the enormous difficulties associated with making the testing as representative of use as possible, and the possible sensitivity of the statistical methods used to the assumption that testing is indeed representative of use.

A rather different approach to the quantification of software reliability on the basis of testing is the use of software reliability growth modelling. This is an area of research which has received a great deal of attention, as a result of which a number of statistical models have been put forward to quantify the growth in reliability of a piece of software as faults are detected and repaired (Refs. 9-13). The times of the occurrence of each failure are recorded and the current and future failure rates derived from these data and the model itself. The value of these models as currently developed lies in making economic decisions such as those related to the best time to release software for commercial purposes, not in predicting the reliability of software for safety critical applications. Work is continuing in this field, however, and may bear fruit for safety applications in due course, especially in cases which have implemented some form of software fault tolerance.

The same comments as made earlier also apply to these techniques, that the data used to quantify the reliability should be taken from testing which is representative of actual operating experience, and not from any of the fault removal testing procedures.

It must therefore be concluded that the quantification of high levels of reliability based upon software testing is in theory possible, but the practical difficulties are enormous and limit the confidence which can be placed in any results generated.

ASSESSMENT OF THE DEVELOPMENT PROCESS

Methods of assessment which make use of failure data from software testing can be applied only very late in the software development. It is therefore useful to be able to carry out assessments of the process of development, for two main reasons. Firstly, the assessment can be applied very early in the development process, and can thus be used to guide the development and to give an early warning of problem areas. Secondly, since the assessment methods which can be applied to the finished product are imperfect (for reasons discussed above), the process assessment can be useful in improving judgement as to whether a given product has reliability of an adequate level. For example if extensive testing leads to no failures, and an assessment of the process indicates many shortcomings, then suspicion is cast on the integrity of the testing; if on the other hand an assessment of the process is favourable, then it is possible to be more confident in the lack of failures during testing, and thus in the level of reliability which this result implies.

Techniques for assessing software reliability based upon the process of development are in their infancy, and are not nearly as advanced as those which make use of testing data.

There is currently no generally applicable technique for quantitatively assessing software reliability based on a knowledge of the process alone - indeed, it is only recently that qualitative methods have become available. It will always be the case that accuracy of predictions of reliability based upon information available early in the life cycle will be limited, due to the very nature of the data which can be used. This does not mean that such methods have no use, as will be seen.

The author's colleagues B K Daniels and R I Wright at the National Centre of Systems Reliability have developed for the Health and Safety Executive a set of guidelines on the safety integrity assessment of programmable electronic systems (Ref. 14). As part of this work a software assessment methodology has been developed based upon a checklist of questions relating to various activities throughout the software development cycle. The purpose of the checklists is to provide a stimulus to critical appraisal of all aspects of the system and its development rather than to lay down specific requirements on the development methodology which should be adopted. The approach can be used to assess the quality of a particular software process from the point of view of the likely reliability of the final product, and can readily be integrated with software quality assurance activities.

The qualitative assessment is carried out by assessing, for each item on the checklist, whether

(a) the question is not applicable,
(b) there is evidence that the requirement is satisfied,
(c) there is evidence that the requirement is not satisfied,
or (d) there is no information available.

In each of the latter two cases, the item is further qualified according to the importance of its safety implications, as either

(a) of low priority from a safety viewpoint,
(b) in need of further investigation,
(c) not practicably satisfiable,
or (d) in need of practicable modifications.

The methodology as it stands is limited in application, both because it is considering safety (as opposed to reliability), and because even within that sphere it does not cater for all types of system. For example, critical applications such as nuclear reactor control are outside the scope of the assessment methodology.

There is a real need further to develop approaches such as this (see also Refs. 15, 16) for wider applicability, and to the point that assessments can be quantified, but before this can be done there must be a much greater knowledge and understanding of the extent to which various development practices have an effect on the resultant product reliability. Current knowledge is little beyond the stage of anecdotal evidence.

However sophisticated such approaches become, the point will never be reached where it can confidently be stated that, because the right methods were used, and properly used, then the resultant software is correct. Thus assessment of the process can never be perfect as a means of ensuring reliability; currently it falls a very long way short of this ideal.

FAULT TOLERANCE

In the absence of methods of accurately assessing high levels of reliability, it is natural to enquire whether gains in reliability can be made and justified by some form of fault tolerance. Thus, although the possibility of residual faults in the software is acknowledged, provision is made to detect failures and take appropriate measures when they are detected.

In hardware, a common fault tolerance technique is simple redundancy. This is where component failure is guarded against by having a second component where only one is necessary for system operation. This tactic is often employed for reasons other than reliability, but the reliability gained can be enormous. Consider, for example, a component with a failure probability (over some defined mission) of 10^{-3}: by employing two identical such components in parallel, the failure probability can be decreased to as little as 10^{-6}. These gains can rarely be justified in full, because of the possibility of common cause failures (Ref. 17). If, for instance, the two components both have the same power supply, then power supply failure will cause both components to fail simultaneously.

With software, simple redundancy provides little protection. Consider the situation where part of a protection system comprising a number of remote sensors feeding into a microprocessor is replicated several times. If all microprocessors use identical software, then all will fail simultaneously if all receive identical input. However, because the various sensors are replicated, it is highly improbable that all microprocessors will receive identical inputs - the least significant few bits of digital inputs corresponding to analogue parameters will differ because of variations in sensor accuracy, resolution and operating characteristics. Thus common software running on replicated hardware provides protection against software faults which are sensitive to the absolute bit patterns of inputs. Faults of this type are felt to be in the minority. It is much more likely that any given fault will be exposed by a range of inputs which have some similarity, and it is also likely that inputs within the necessary range will occur simultaneously from the diverse sensors. Having said that, it is conceivable that the software testing may have been sufficiently thorough to ensure that faults which would be revealed by a range of inputs have been removed, so that only bit-pattern sensitive results remain. If this could be demonstrated (by some means still to be discovered) then reliance could be placed in common software running on replicated hardware. However, the current state of the art in software testing is unable to support claims of this sort, so that it is essential to recognise that for all practical purposes, we should consider that the replicated pieces of software all receive identical inputs. Thus the current position is that no gain in software reliability can be justified simply by running the same software in replicated computers, even if the inputs are obtained from different sensors.

There is then a need to consider more sophisticated approaches, which will collectively be referred to as software diversity. There has been a number of approaches of this kind, including n-version programming and the recovery block. N-version programming (Ref. 18) involves creating a number (n) of versions of the software, all to a common specification. All versions are used in parallel to perform calculations, and some appropriate voting mechanism is invoked to determine what output is accepted for use by the system in question. For example, a system may be shut down in the event that two or more out of four results indicate that the system should be shut down. The recovery block (Ref. 19) on the other hand comprises a single piece of software, with diversity implemented within the software. This is achieved by ascertaining the acceptability of internal results at various stages of computation. If at some point an acceptance test indicates an incorrect value, then all internal values are restored to some previous state, and a different algorithm used to re-calculate the values which were found to be erroneous. If this alternative algorithm gives results which pass the acceptance test, then computation proceeds to the next stage. Otherwise, a second alternative may be available, or a software failure indicated and the system restored to some safe state. Although n-version programming and the recovery block are very different strategies - n-version programming demands execution of all versions, whereas the recovery block invokes alternatives only after detection of failure - both involve diverse implementation of software to a common specification, albeit at different levels.

As with hardware redundancy, common mode failures are important in software diversity, and arise in two principal ways. First, any fault in the specification is likely to permeate through all versions. The exception to this is ambiguities in the specification, which may lead to differing implementations. Though software diversity thus gives little protection against specification errors, the fact that several teams are implementing the specification will mean that there will be an increased chance of certain types of specification error being discovered before it is too late.

The other problem is that of ensuring independence between the various implementations. Recall that with hardware redundancy, if two components each with failure probability p are used in parallel, and independence can be assumed, then the combined reliability is p^2. It is unlikely that full independence will ever be justifiably claimable in the case of software diversity. Even if the respective programming teams are kept apart and communication between them is prevented, two problems remain which may lead to common faults in a number of the implementations. One of these is that software faults come into being as a result of human errors, and that different human beings are prone to making the same sort of errors. The other problem is that due to the general educative process, there is likely to be commonality in the approaches that different software engineers take to the same task.

Thus the gains which can be made by using diverse software are limited, due to the common mode problem. The extent of the gains which can be claimed is hard to quantify at the current time, but they are likely to be substantial.

As with the other techniques which have been examined, then, software fault tolerance does not provide a means of guaranteeing correct operation. Nor, at the current time, is it possible to quantify the extent of the gains which can be made by adopting one of the strategies for software fault tolerance.

CONCLUSIONS

A number of approaches to the problem of producing and assessing software of high reliability have been examined. At the current time there is a tendency in many areas of application towards the increasing use of software in roles which necessitate high reliability. This means the problem of assessing reliability of software takes on added importance.

The current state of the art leaves much to be desired: it is not possible either to guarantee correctness or to obtain accurate assessments of the level of unreliability. Against this background it is necessary, at the current time, to implement one of the strategies for fault tolerance. There is little doubt that this will lead to substantial improvements in reliability, but it is not currently possible to quantify the extent of these enhancements.

There is a very real need to develop methods for the quantification of reliability of fault tolerant systems. This implies a need both for methods of assessing single pieces of software, and for a means of combining such predictions taking account of the structure of the overall fault tolerant system. Assessment methods for single pieces of software do exist, and these may well prove adequate within the context of fault tolerance, with the proviso that operational environments of software need to be very well understood. The area which is currently lacking is in enabling the results of these assessments to be used within a fault tolerant framework, which implies a need to investigate by way of experiment the extent to which independence can be assumed between the various diverse software implementations. Some work has been done in this area; more is needed.

A further area which is ill developed at the moment is assessment of the process of software development. Although it will never be possible to ensure the quality of software simply on the basis of the development methodology which has been used, assessment of the process does provide early warning of problem areas, and also serves to reinforce the results of product assessment techniques. To develop this field further, the need is for collection and analysis of data concerning the efficacy of various development methodologies. This sort of data will not only facilitate assessment, but will also permit the selection of development strategy to be carried out in an intelligent way, based upon hard information rather than informed guesswork.

REFERENCES

1. IE Information Notice No. 79-06, US Nuclear Regulatory Commission, Office of Inspection and Enforcement, 1979.

2. D. Bjorner and C. B. Jones, "Formal specification and software development", Prentice Hall, 1982.

3. C. A. R. Hoare, "An axiomatic basis for computer programming", Comm. ACM. Vol. 12, p576-580, Oct 1969.

4. L. Lamport, "Proving the correctness of multiprocess programs", IEEE Trans. Software Eng., Vol. SE-3, p125-143, March 1977.

5. N. G. Leveson and P. R. Harvey, "Analysing software safety", IEEE Trans. Software Eng., Vol. SE-9, No. 5, Sept 1983.

6. G. J. Myers, "The art of software testing", Wiley, 1979.

7. M. A. Hennell, D. Hedley and I. J. Riddell, "The LDRA software testbeds: their roles and capabilities", Proc. of IEEE Soft Fair '83 Conference, Arlington, Virginia, July 1983.

8. A. Ball, M. H. Butterfield and C. J. Dale, "The achievement and assessment of safety in systems containing software", IAEA Specialists' Meeting on the use of Digital Computing Devices in Systems Important to Safety, Saclay, France, 28-29 Nov 1984.

9. Z. Jelinski and P. B. Moranda. "Software Reliability Research", in Statistical Computer Performance Evaluation. W. Freiberger (Ed), Academic Press, 1972, p465-484.

10. B. Littlewood. "A Bayesian Differential Debugging Model for Software Reliability", Proceedings of Workshop on Quantitative Software Models, 1979, p170-181.

11. B. Littlewood and J. L. Verrall. "A Bayesian Reliability Growth Model for Computer Software", Applied Statistics, 1973, p332-346.

12. J. D. Musa. "A Theory of Software Reliability and its Application", IEEE Transactions on Software Engineering, 1975, p312-327.

13. C. J. Dale. "Software Reliability Evaluation Methods", British Aerospace Dynamics Group Report ST26750, 1982.

14. "Guidance on the safe use of programmable electronic systems", Health and Safety Executive Draft Document for Consultation, 1984.

15. R. W. Motley and W. D. Brooks. "Statistical prediction of programming errors", Rome Air Development Center Report RADC-TR-77-175, Griffiss AFB, New York, 1977.

16. G. F. Walters and J. A. McCall, "Software quality metrics for life-cycle cost-reduction", IEEE Trans. Reliability, August 1979, p212-220.

17. I. A. Watson and G. T. Edwards, "A study of common mode failures", UKAEA report SRD-R146, 1979.

18. A. Avizienis and L. Chen, "On the implementation of n-version programming for software fault-tolerance during program execution", Proceedings of COMPSAC, 1977, p149-155.

19. B. Randell, "System structure for software fault tolerance", IEEE Trans. Software Eng., 1975, p220-232.

PROCESS AND DESIGN CONSIDERATIONS AS THEY AFFECT THE NUMBER, NATURE AND DISCLOSURE OF SOFTWARE FAULTS

By: Gillian Frewin
Standard Telecommunication Laboratories, STC, Harlow

1. INTRODUCTION

A need has been found in several related activities for models of products, processes, and their interactions, especially as these interactions affect fault introduction and fault disclosure. In particular, these models are needed to support work in hand on designing and customising management support systems. Although only informal models (of the factors and mechanisms affecting fault introduction, activation and visibility) have been built up so far, they are proving sufficient to allow useful qualitative treatments for these activities, and frameworks for preliminary work directed towards validating and formalising the models.

The paper will relate the work being done on process and product modelling to its eventual aims of providing useful support for software Product Engineering, Process Engineering and Quality Engineering. This support is expected to develop into the achievement of a range of models, methods and tools, to be used in selecting and supporting efficient processes and in managing 'faultiness' and other qualities during software system design, development, maintenance and use.

2. THE MANAGEMENT OF ERRORS, FAULTS AND FAILURES

2.1 Requirements for manageability

Before going any further, it is necessary to define the terms 'error', 'fault' and 'failure'. An error is an incorrect or inappropriate action, which may be made either by a man or a machine: some errors result in faults, which are wrong or weak areas in a product: a fault which has been activated may result in a failure, which is an observable and unwanted outcome. If we go on to define 'management' as the group of abilities required to predict, control and demonstrate those qualities which are of interest, the specific needs for error, fault, and failure manageability can be derived and stated as follows:-

a) The nature of errors, etc., and the processes in/by which they are made, must be understood.

b) The factors which cause errors, faults and failures, and the interactions between these factors, must be understood.

c) Causative factors must be controllable.

d) Either the errors, faults and failures, OR qualities

NATO ASI Series, Vol. F22
Software System Design Methods. Edited by J.K. Skwirzynski

directly related to them, must be measurable and/or demonstrable.

From informal examinations of errors and faults, it has appeared that errors and faults can be conveniently sub-divided into three groups; roughly related to the three areas of problem analysis, design management, and product development. These have been selected as both covering, and conveniently separating, all the main groups of errors and faults :-

a) Errors in problem analysis,

b) Conceptual discontinuity and inconsistency,

c) Errors in translation,

2.2 Errors in analysis

Problem analysis includes the processes of collecting, identifying (that is, classifying and describing) and evaluating system requirements, and translating the chosen set of requirements through a number of different representations (for example, natural language, graphical languages, pseudo-code, 'formal' mathematical expressions, etc.) - in order both to check their continued validity and to provide appropriate inputs for various users and purposes.

2.2.1 Errors in the collection and analysis of requirements

On investigation, these errors are typically found to have been caused by the presence or application of one or more of the following:-

a) Insufficient science; that is, investigations and records were not made, recorded or reviewed sufficiently thoroughly or systematically to ensure that all doubtful areas were clarified before the collection phase was closed.

b) Insufficient imagination; that is, too narrow a scope was taken, and/or too few people were involved, and/or too few possibilities were raised and taken seriously, and/or too authoritarian views were taken, to ensure that the requirements adequately covered the fields of interest and of influence.

c) Inadequate notations and support systems (equipment, procedures, controls, etc.). Both these problems can be eased, and even partially controlled, by the presence and use of good supporting mechanisms. These include interactive investigations guided and recorded by an 'intelligent' computer system. An 'adequate' notation is one which is understood equally well by its users and by those who need to review the work; which maps well onto the functions and interactions being studied, and which is suitable for translation or transformation into other forms required by the full development process. Reasons for considering a notation "inadequate" are when it is difficult to cross-check, allows variant presentations and interpretations, and is awkward to write, read or transpose.

The most expensive software faults to repair generally arise from an initial failure to understand, or to record and communicate, what was needed: once a wrong concept is included in a design, or a necessary concept is omitted, remedial activities must not only delete or add as required (with the risk of introducing new errors), but must also identify and rectify all the consequences of the original misunderstanding. As the removal of these consequences may necessitate complete re-design, it is clearly worth taking considerable trouble to avoid making errors in system analysis.

During the identification of requirements it is necessary to consider -

a) the input domain,

b) the output domain,

c) the operational domain,

... defining and agreeing for each what is expected, what is possible, and what is certainly excluded. Although precise identification of "impossible" inputs and outputs is often difficult, effort expended on their discovery is highly relevant in selecting the precautions to be taken within the computer system, and in its environment.

The division above reflects a simple model of inputs being transformed into outputs, with all operations occurring in a given functional environment. "Input" must be understood as including complex conditions as well as individual items, and the "environment" as including all aspects of the organisation and supporting equipment and procedures which are capable of affecting the system, as well as those which are directly involved. Inputs are made by one sub-system to another, as well as from the world outside to the system. A "reliable" system is one which consistently achieves the desired transformation from input to output, even allowing for some degree of alteration in the environment as originally captured.

The phrase 'failing to identify' has been used below in a dual capacity - indicating either or both of 'failing to recognise that an item exists' and of 'failing to define the item correctly'. Errors of omission are difficult to control but the attempt must be made. If allowed to remain, they are the prime cause of serious operational failures.

Analytical errors include the following :-

a) Failing to identify all expected inputs.

b) Failing to identify all possible inputs.

c) Failing to identify those inputs which are not possible.

d) Failing to identify (and provide controls for) those inputs which are possible but must be excluded.

e) Failing to define correctly the relationship between each input and its associated output.

f) Failing to identify all expected elements in the interfacing environment.

g) Failing to identify all possible elements in the interfacing environment.

h) Failing to identify those elements which are not possible in the interfacing environment.

2.2.2 Control of analytical errors

Omissions cannot be controlled directly. Indirect methods include parallel analysis by separate teams, with either or both of the results being compared and collated before design OR being used as input to separate design processes and the comparisons being made on the designs and on their associated products. A degree of continuous control is given by regular reviews and animations, using real inputs and outputs (if these are available) together with those generated by a specialist validation team. Involvement of the customer or user has two benefits: it reduces the chances of missing important factors, and it spreads responsibility for both the analysis and the resulting system.

2.2.3 Failing to maintain conceptual continuity and consistency

Once a complete specification exists, there is a risk that items will be added or lost during its several transformations (from specification to design, and design to product). In addition to simple additions or losses, there is the chance that what has been required (or designed) is not possible, or that the existence of one element excludes the existence of another. Logical impossibilities should be identified and removed during the analysis of conceptual requirements. However, decisions made during the development process may so restrict further options as to make features impossible to achieve in practice.

A lack of continuity is seen when items clearly defined in early project documents are not present later, or vice versa. Although similar to the next case (2.2.4 "Errors in translation") it is not identical, since that relates to the detail of low-level technical products and activities while this is more concerned with the overall administrative and technical management of design and development. The low apparent technical content of this class of fault creation should not be allowed to devalue its importance. The uncontrolled addition and subtraction of product functionality can cause exponential instability in a project and its products, and several large projects have reported completion with some planned functions having totally disappeared, and unplanned functions of substantial size having been added, resulting in considerable deviations from expected quality and costs.

2.2.4 Errors in translation

Although an element may be as required at some levels of documentation or development, it can still fail in more detailed embodiments; for example when a "correct" detailed design suffers from mistakes in its computer coding, or code preparation, or added job-control details. These translation failures are usually such that they can be directly ascribed to environmental factors; for example, inconvenient notations and formats which promote errors of transcription, or equipment and services which are not well adapted to the needs and nature of their users.

Many of the technical processes in software development can be regarded as a translation from one notation (or language) into another, with faults arising from:

a) Incompetent translations, where the grammar and vocabulary exist to give an accurate translation but for one reason or another this has not been found. The result is sometimes an awkward translation (with potential for later misunderstanding or inefficiency) rather than an actual error and the whole group could be classified as "mistakes". Causes include lack of experience and understanding, and of adequate exemplars, as well as deficiencies in the content and presentation of the notations themselves.

b) Mistranslations caused by a lack of equivalence between the two systems of description. This might be caused by variant processing (for example, a changed compiler or editor) or by conceptual mismatching.

c) "Accidental" or "mechanical" mistranslations, where an accurate translation has become mangled in transcription between media. While a degree of pure accident will always be present, notations and their handling systems have not always been designed with sufficient attention to the practical requirements of their users. For example, any notation which cannot be verbalised risks errors when being manually transcribed, as does any which cannot be fully represented on a standard key-board and set of display characters. A notation without redundancy is also more liable to transcription and transmission errors.

d) Incomplete, and over-complete, translations. These are either failures to use all the information received when creating the new version, or the insertion of information not present in the original. They are caused by poor documentation, inadequate understanding, and attempts to clarify or augment received statements judged to be unsatisfactory by the translator. They are encouraged by poor control procedures (especially inadequate reviews) in earlier project processes.

2.2.6 General causes of errors

a) Incompetence. This is the situation when a company, department, group or individual, takes a task for which it has not been sufficiently prepared. While previous experience of similar work, in similar conditions, is obviously useful, the content and implications of any new work may be unpredictable. A more manageable and reliable approach to a new area is through a deliberate and early investigation of the differences between this task and those undertaken previously, and the formation of a detailed plan of training, consultancy, acquisition, controls and trials, to fill in any deficiencies and to flag-up any slipping of standards.

b) Stress. Any process can be made more likely to contain errors if it is performed under stress, whether on man or machine. Stressful situations for people include those in which the complexity of the situation is too great, either in general (as with overall time pressure, or frequent changes in requirements and priorities), or in relation to a particular element - such as a design unit with more functions or interfaces than an individual can readily keep in focus.

The affects of stress are individual, and thus difficult to predict and control. However, contributory factors which can be measured and managed include:-

i) The number, severity and timing of changes to whole project schedules, sub-project schedules, product and sub-project requirements, and individual work-packages.

ii) The mode, frequency, clarity, and degree of personal interaction in the agreement and notification of changes.

iii) Changes in the complexity of design elements, and individual work-packages, following changes in schedules and requirements.

iv) Extent to which individuals are supported (technically and socially) by the working environment and by the team and reporting structures of the project.

c) Inappropriate procedures, tools and methods. Particular procedures, tools and methods may be well fitted to one kind of product or process, while being positively harmful when used with others. They may also be more, or less, in conformance with the mental concepts and habitual methods of particular individuals or groups of users. Unless the attempt is made to identify the required concepts and methods and to compare them with those currently used, and then by retraining or by adapting the support mechanisms ensuring that the better ones are used consistently, the resultant product may suffer from serious internal stresses. The errors and faults caused by stresses of this kind typically lead to unnecessary complexity in the design, and to documentation which is difficult to understand or use. These result in a product which is hard to test and to extend or maintain.

d) Inadequate support (professional, personal, services and tools). A simple insufficiency of support can be as bad as being given the wrong kind. If support cannot be obtained as and when it is needed, the results include stress (caused by time pressures and uncertainty), poor quality (caused by the omission of necessary development and checking processes) and low manageability (due to corner-cutting and poor reporting).

3. PRODUCT FAULTINESS, AND THE DESIGN AND IMPLEMENTATION PROCESSES

If products are to contain the least number of faults, it is necessary that they are designed in such a way that the input of faults is minimised, and built by processes which are characterised by both low fault input and high fault disclosure. The previous section discussed the nature and causes of faults: in this section product design and development are examined for their opportunities to attract or to disclose those faults.

It is by testing that potential and actual faults are disclosed, in ways ranging from an individual mentally recognising that elements are in conflict and must be resolved, to the mechanical detection of aberrant behaviour in a computerised system. Thus much of the text below is written in terms of the 'testability' of a design or the product made (or in the process of being made) to that design. It must not be thought that testability is only an important factor when a product is near to delivery: all the ways in which actual or potential faults are disclosed can be classed as testing of one kind or another. Every aspect of a chosen design and development process should allow the current item or representation to be 'tested' against its consistency with the overall requirements, its local requirements, and in terms of its internal validity. Errors in early project concepts and processes, and faults in intermediate products, can be highly influential in reducing the quality of the end products. Thus testing must be a constant and important project activity, with later activities and assessments being based on the records and results of earlier probing and measurements.

3.1 Introduction to the influence of design on fault insertion and fault manifestation

When designs are compared, it is usually clear that some are inherently more error-prone than others. Similarly, some are more testable (both investigation and demonstration testing) than are others. In this context, 'investigation' testing is to be regarded as that which probes the internal details of an item (whether text, graphic or coded for machine animation) to discover its properties; 'demonstration' testing animates or examines a complete item or sub-item to give proof of its abilities and qualities. Lists are given below of the more obvious and general factors leading to high or low testability: in practice local methods, tools, etc., should be examined to locate the factors which are particularly influential in specific circumstances. Note that the factors are not in priority order.

Projects and products may have their initial testability altered as they go along, by the addition or amendment of requirements and conditions. 3.2.3 and 3.2.4 are concerned with this capacity for degeneration and with ways to limit its affects.

3.2 Design Factors leading to high testability (and low faultiness).

a) Retention of initial and intermediate factors in calculations.

b) Provision of alternate routes and routines for high-risk functions.

c) Considerations of traceability, re-start, progress recording and reporting.

d) Simplicity of both design and its documentation, leading to minimum activity strings for the performance of functions, and ease of both access to and understanding of the documentation.

e) Visibility of actions at interfaces.

f) Early and intensive consideration during the design process of error containment, recovery and reporting.

g) Single-purpose use of common routines and storage areas.

h) Highly separated concerns, where activities mainly 'stand-alone', independently of previous or concurrent actions.

i) Early and sufficient studies on loadings, usage, etc.

3.3 Design Factors leading to low testability (and high faultiness).

a) High priority requirements for compactness, efficiency and speed.

b) Multi-purpose usage of common routines and storage areas.

c) Highly 'integrated' activities, in which each action depends on the outcomes of previous activities.

d) "Clever" designs, complex designs, and long activity strings.

e) Low priority put on timely and effective documentation.

f) Concentration at early stages on the 'normal case', with errors and oddities left to the end of the design phase.

g) Lack of sufficient data or design studies on the quality, quantity and interactions to be expected in 'real' use.

3.4 Degeneration of testability during design

An initially acceptable level of testability can degenerate during the development of a design. Some of the causes are:-

a) Unbalancing of the design due to random additions and alterations.

b) Reluctance to consider redefinition of the problem, and redesign, after a certain amount of work has gone into the first attempt.

c) Failure to assign the correct priorities to new requirements ('newest' is not necessarily 'most important').

d) Failure to distinguish between what is vital (for example, maintaining a clean, testable and clearly documented design) from what is currently interesting (possibly contriving to squeeze more functionality or performance out of the design than it can comfortably provide).

3.5 Controlling the testability of designs

The design is the pivot and pilot of the development of a system or product. It marks the transition from theoretical considerations to the series of transformations which will give a tangible outcome. Controlling its testability and other necessary qualities is essential for an acceptable result, and the means available are:-

a) Reviews

b) Simulations

c) Application of metrics

d) Pilot implementations and trials of sections of the design.

The four result in different profiles of revealed faults. Relating the means directly to testability:-

a) Reviews. Demonstration and investigation tests should be developed in parallel with the functional design, and used with relevant scenarios in reviewing whether testing can be undertaken satisfactorily. Estimates of the efficiency and resource costs, as well as requirements for special testing support tools, can be identified with reasonable accuracy at early stages of design, and used with the other elements of the review to assess viability and guide product development strategies.

b) Simulations (whether paper-, person- or machine-based) are a powerful tool for investigating testability since they focus attention on the interfaces between design elements and thus on the data and commands which will cross them and which must be tested. Interface investigations also direct attention to demonstrations of performance, and to considerations of the diagnostic facilities which will be needed both for testing and for in-service support.

c) Application of metrics The particular metrics used, and whether they are extracted mechanically or manually, will depend on the design methods and documentation methods being used. However, although it is not yet possible to prescribe the best metric for every situation, it is clear that there are simple measures related to complexity and cohesion which can be used to guide the decision to accept or reject a design on the grounds of its difficulty to test, to modify and to understand. It is expected that these measures would be used in conjunction with other review criteria.

d) Pilot implementations and trials. Depending on the product and the way in which it is being designed, it may either be possible to implement one or more whole functions, or necessary to create a cut-down version of the entire product. In either case, much useful information on the nature and performance of the design can be obtained, as well as an assessment of its testability in general. The testability should be approached by following normal development standards; creating tests in parallel with the product and applying them as soon as the appropriate structure exists. Pilots and trials should give an accurate answer as to the availability and adequacy of the product's and project's test support requirements, in time for their enhancement if needed before the full development.

3.6 Degeneration of testability during development

Testability can be destroyed during development if :-

a) amendments (whether repairs, additions or deletions) are not controlled, leading to a weakened and/or complicated design,

b) any of the languages or methods (eg. design, pseudo-code, simulation, MMI and Expert systems, assembly code, HLL's, etc.), has constructs which do not fit well with the nature of the function being facilitated - leading to circumlocutions and errors,

c) the design and its documentation are either actually in conflict, or are presented in a confusing way, as a result of amendments made without sufficient care and control,

d) accidents, misunderstandings, and the gradual substitution of the developers' perceptions and assumptions for those of the designer, result in distortions to the design, which may or may not be carried into the developmental testing,

e) insufficient time, training or resources, lead to deviations from the design,

f) insufficient resources and low priority lead to incomplete or shallow testing,

g) unavailability of supporting tools and functions of sufficient quality results in inconclusive or inaccurate testing

h) poor control of testing leads to items being insufficiently tested, not tested at all, or not reported as being tested,

i) an inadequate theory and practice of testing leads to work which cannot be objectively measured or judged.

3.7 Design influences on fault activation and observation

In order to manifest itself, a latent fault must be activated in some way which causes a perceptible and observed result - that is, there must be a failure. If a high level of the embedded faults are to be found, and those as early as possible, it is necessary to design both the system architecture and the detailed software in ways which promote the visibility and traceability of faults.

Some models of SW Reliability assume that faults are evenly (or randomly) distributed in the code, that each element in the code has an equal chance of being activated, and that all failures (that is, activated faults) have an equal chance of being observed. However, this is intuitively unacceptable. SW elements with different functions and designs have their own usage patterns and potential for being observed, as well as having greater or lesser capacities for disturbing the total system in which they exist. Any model of behaviour which ignores these varying characteristics will be of limited use on questions of fault management and product reliability.

3.8 Detailed discussion of design, fault activation and fault observation

This section embodies the assumptions which together constitute an informal model of the elements and relationships involved in the recognition of a SW fault. It is necessary to have such a model if statements about the number, severity, or frequency, of faults found during the active life of a product are to have any meaning.

a) Software products cannot be regarded as being either monolithic or of uniform constitution. Each consists of a number of sub-products (possibly at several levels of dependency) which may be seen as a network of processing strings, activated by inputs and resulting in outputs. An "output" need not be displayed, or passed outside the system: it is any change in state which is caused by a process.

b) A "failure" in a SW item is an unexpected, undefined, and/or undesirable, output. While these may be caused by the arrival of unlooked-for inputs to the item, the existence of such inputs indicates a system failure rather than one of the item affected. Expectations may be justified or not, depending on whether the behaviour observed is in accordance with the product requirements, specification and design. They are formed from product documentation, from the results of demonstrations (or tests), from usage of this or similar products - and, perhaps most importantly (since any disappointment in these expectations is most keenly felt), from the user's personal view of how the system should behave. Ideally, all these sources (documentation, demonstration, usage and personal views) should be entirely equivalent, but in practice demonstrations usually represent only a fraction of the functionality of a product as defined in the documentation, while that documentation is itself only a partial definition of the total possible behaviour of the product. Similarly, training and early styles of usage are usually confined to the simplest and most predictable applications, while with practice users become more ambitious and applications more deviant from the expected norms.

c) Fault activation only occurs as a result of an unexpected input (that is, a system failure), or a wrongly designed or implemented transformation between an input and an output.

d) In use, a software product will exhibit "high profile" areas, in which comparatively large numbers of faults are observed. The three necessary conditions are that faults should exist, should be activated, and that their results are noticed. These high-profile areas are characterised by one or more of the following characteristics:

i) Being in frequent use. Typical areas are those which

manage inputs, outputs, and the higher levels of program logic,

ii) Being complex in their logic or implementation. Any design element with multiple possible conditions risks those conditions being inadequately understood, animated, or demonstrated,

iii) Being poorly protected from unexpected inputs, or under stress because of their functions in the product and system. Because of the inherently low security within a SW item, and between its components, high-risk areas may need protection from stray unexpected inputs - even though they are supposed only to receive data validated by other parts of the system,

iv) Having been implemented poorly. "Poor" implementation includes both actual faults and minor awkwardnesses; in system and program design, translation and documentation. Thus it covers not only actual latent faults, but also that the state of the item encourages the making of further mistakes when it is used or maintained,

v) Having been subject to alteration. Any alteration, whether repairing a previous fault or changing the functionality, adds two risks to the total potential faultiness of a system. The first of these is the possibility that the alteration is actually wrong in itself, and the second is that the original concept is contradicted or weakened, leading to future difficulties in using or supporting the product,

vi) Being system-critical, and/or user-visible. Any fault which affects the whole system will have a high chance of being observed, just as faults of limited local affects might be missed. Faults in the user-interface are almost certain to be noticed, while others of similar "size" but affecting only internal program interfaces may never become visible,

vii) Feeding into poorly protected areas. A fault whose "wrong" output is recognised and dealt with rapidly within the program or system (perhaps by being replaced by a null or default option), may be less visible than those which are allowed to progress.

e) Conversely, in use some product areas will be noticeably low in observed faults. These are characterised by being one or more of the following:-

i) Little used, and thus with minimum opportunities to display any latent faults,

ii) Simple in logic or implementation, and thus with minimum opportunities for wrong implementation or use,

iii) Well protected from unexpected inputs and unusual stresses. For instance, a program element which makes its own checks on the validity of its inputs, and which buffers extreme volumes or timings, is more secure than one which relies on the correctness of other processing in the system,

iv) Well implemented, and thus containing few faults,

v) Coherent (i.e. unchanged from their original conception), and therefore comparatively straightforward to use and to maintain,

vi) Isolated from those parts of the system which are easily observed.

The last point is of special significance, as this is an area where design and development processes have a considerable impact on what can and should be specified. For example, if a system needs to be highly reliable, designs are often highly compartmentalised with the result that much processing has low visibility: if the results of this on testability and traceability are not complemented, the effect of the design aim may eventually be negative.

4. INTERACTIONS BETWEEN PRODUCTS AND PROCESSES

It is intuitively obvious that each item which is affected by a process takes up that affect in a way which is related to both the characteristics of the item and those of the process. Thus the gross affects on composite items (deliverable products and their constituent sub-products) can be regarded as a summation of these elemental changes. In order to study these interactions, and the ways in which they can best be combined, measured and controlled, there must be appropriate vocabularies, classifications, metrics and models. These will be applied to relate aspects of software products - as specified, and as present in the eventual item - to aspects of the development process, in order to achieve the prediction, management and control of significant qualities (both 'good' and 'bad').

Thus it is necessary to have:-

a) a vocabulary (or classification) by which to refer unambiguously to different products, processes, and qualities,

b) means of measuring the qualities of products and processes, and the influences present between them,

c) understanding of the nature of software products; partial, complete, intermediate, and end-product,

d) understanding of the nature of the processes by which products are made,

e) models of ways in which quality management, and production management, might be applied,

f) understanding of the interactions between the quality

management and production management processes, and those processes by which products are made,

g) knowledge of the interactions between processes and products, especially as the nature of partial and intermediate products influences the nature of complete and end-products.

4.1 General Problems in Product and Process Classification

a) No sufficiently general classifications have been found through a literature search: a result which was to be expected since the objectives and requirements of classification of this work is broadly dissimilar to those of the work examined. The main sources of classification elements which seemed to have potential, have been found in work on predictive systems. These typically take a mixture of product and process intentions and expectations, judgements on local effectiveness as compared with some norm, and historical records, and combine them to reach predictions on project resource needs and schedules. The implied classifications, characterisation and metrication are thus idiosyncratic and not ideal as a basis for a rational classification.

b) The classification needed should cover existing, in-production, and future products, as well as being suitable for management and modelling purposes. Thus it must cover factors which only exist within a project (that is, which may not be directly apparent in the final product) and must be extensible to a range of products and development processes which are not currently in existence.

It is more than possible that multiple classifications will be needed to cope with different kinds of product, and for the several different reasons for their being classified. This might lead to either a key-word approach, or to a pre-determined multi-facet description - no decisions can be made on this until more experience has been gained of the areas of application.

c) There is a problem in separating the planned characteristics for a product, from those that actually exist in the completed item. It is also likely that the delivered characteristics will alter with time, and with different circumstances of use. Further, there are several aspects of development and maintenance methodology, and of development and maintenance environments, which will certainly affect the qualities of the product but which might arguably appear in either the product or the process classification.

4.3 Product classifications.

No classification is absolute: each one can only be constructed so as to fulfil the requirements laid upon it by its applications. The product classes briefly discussed below have been selected in the belief that they will be useful in distinguishing and measuring the affects of various processes (and constraints) on the qualities of different kinds of products.

The classes and discussion below represent an intermediate stage between descriptive systems observed or implied in the literature and in common practice, and the specific needs of Quality Management. Candidate groupings for the highest descriptive levels include:-

a) Product Identification. The ultimate, comprehensive, classification of an item is itself. While this may not appear at first sight to constitute either a useful classification or a means of reaching one, in practice all classifications are begun by observing a small number of different instances of similar-seeming items and locating the features in which they either differ or are the same. Where one item has a significant number of aspects which are shared with other items, the characterisation of any other item can be expressed in terms of differences from the chosen class model.

Many estimating methods begin with the concept of a 'normal' product, and progressively amend the picture according to the 'abnormal' features of the item being estimated. Quality engineering, and Quality management, may well be undertaken in a similar way.

b) Gross Product type. Products and partial or intermediate products can be divided as to whether they are executable or not. This could also be stated as a distinction between those which are 'active'(machine interpretable and animatable) and those which are 'passive' (documents, etc., for human use). This two part classification is reflected quite well in the different development methods, controls, required qualities, and testing and measuring techniques appropriate to each of the two groups, and is therefore potentially valuable as a distinction in a system which deals with the interactions of products and processes.

c) Gross Usage (e.g 'application', 'system support', 'control', 'personal', 'weapon', 'life-support', etc.). Although this kind of classification has been used extensively in the past, and may continue to be useful in local situations, it would not appear to condense sufficient information for all our purposes - although we may have to use it when trying to collate data from the literature with that collected specifically for the purposes of the various projects.

d) Size and/or complexity. These are the basic classes used in most schemes for predicting the effort required to create and maintain products, for example, COCOMO, applications of the Rayleigh curve, numbers of functions involved, etc.. However, these methods usually work on calculations or predictions of total finished size (or overall complexity) of the product, and thus must be extended for use in a system used for detailed Quality Management throughout the design and creation periods. The classification must also distinguish between predictions and actuality, remembering that there may be many iterations of 'prediction--actual result' during a complete development, and that both products and processes may be changed between the making of a prediction and the measuring of a result.

e) Physical and conceptual constraints (e.g. "stand-alone", "embedded", "requires [specified] supporting HW or SW systems", "semi-detached"). These factors are included in the COCOMO cost-and-schedule-prediction system, where they are applied across the entire product. This is at best only partly realistic (since the factors cannot be rationally expected to influence every part of a product equally, or every product equally) and would appear likely to become less and less acceptable.

f) Master quality constraints, or quality objectives (e.g safety, security, reliability, size, performance, maintainability, etc.). It has probably been established sufficiently that staff achieve best against the criteria which are known to them [Goals and performance in Computer Programming, Weinberg & Schulman, Human Factors, 16(1), 1974, pp 70-77], and as a consequence of the trade-offs made consciously or unconsciously in meeting known aims, are likely to perform less well against criteria which have not been made specific. Thus the clear communication of objectives and constraints, plus their relative importance-ratings, must be a significant element in the management of quality.

Any selection of classificatory terms should distinguish between required end-product qualities, and those which exist in sub-products and intermediate products. It may also prove useful, if experimental evidence can be obtained and if that evidence indicates significant differences in performance against the classes, to distinguish between technical, social, administrative and stylistic requirements.

g) General, and project specific, training and experience. However clearly quality aims may have been defined, their affects on partial, intermediate and final products will be limited by the ability of staff to identify the processes by which they are affected, and the procedures and/or constructs which can be used in those processes to contribute to the desired result. These abilities will be enhanced by appropriate general training and experience, and by in-project discussions, reviews, reports and seminars, through which the interactions between the constraints and the product and the processes (etc.) are kept in full view.

Training, experience and ability have usually been brought into project and quality modelling only in terms of the nature of staff when they join the project: it seems quite possible that this influence will be at least matched by the more specific training, practice, experience and growth of competence, which occur during the project.

h) Specification methods/notations. A product can be classified by the specification technique used in its

creation. Such classifications have not been strongly represented in the literature so far, although the claims made for various specification techniques (notably 'formal methods' such as SADT, SREM, HOS, VDM, etc.) suggest that indications of the treatment(s) used in specifying and communicating product requirements will soon become part of some of the project descriptions used as the basis of predictions and plans and hence worth investigating for their role in quality definition, creation and measurement. Although a classification could be devised simply by naming available methods, more flexibility and extensibility will be obtained by looking for a set of words related to the similarities and differences between known and envisaged specification methods.

i) Design methods/design support systems. It seems clear that the qualities of a completed product must be affected by those of each stage of development: a good product can only be built on good foundations. Therefore the methods used for design, and their supporting systems (whether manual or machine based - for assessment, validation, verification, animation and presentation), are of great significance to the management of software quality.

Although one kind of classification could be made simply by naming known methods and their associated tools, it seems more useful to seek a classification which identifies the aspects of those methods and tools which most strongly affect quality, or which allow early identification and assessment of probably quality achievements. One approach to a classification of use in the research into quality models would be to identify the facets of products and processes which can be directly linked to aspects of the design method and support. Two examples of this might be the ease, and the accuracy, with which the design is transliterated into the forms used for other purposes.

The following aspects are also potential aspects of products which might prove sufficiently influential to merit inclusion in a product classification scheme -

- Development methods/environments.

- Proving/testing methods/environments.

- Structural types, and structural description.

- Application area.

... they have not been expanded on here, but may be included in later stages of development when there are sufficiently clear concepts and experimental indications to enable more confident selection of descriptors.

4.5 Further work on Product Classification

Action on these schemes needs to be iterative and interactive, gradually refining any chosen classification in terms of both its own validity (that is, its ability to describe present and future products acceptably at several levels of detail) and in terms of its utility as one of the bases of quality management procedures, and of general data collection and characterisation.

A pre-requisite for selection and refinement of product classifications is a clear conceptual model of their nature and anticipated uses. Once this model exists, a possible process for the selection and refinement of a product classification might be:-

a) Draft initial selection and acceptance criteria for the classifications, and then one or more versions of a possible product classification schemes,

b) Obtain products and descriptions of products, such that they cover the classes in the schemes,

c) Look for additional classes, descriptors and measurements, which can be applied to the test set of products and evaluate the performance of these and the initial versions of the classification; extending, amending, replacing, etc., as indicated,

d) Repeat a - c till a reasonably acceptable classification has been built up. Obtain further products for classification in order to support the validity of the work done.

e) Match the product and process classifications to gain an initial impression of whether any items in one are identical or causative with respect to items in the other. Adjust and annotate as required.

4.6 Process Classification, Characterisation and Metrication

The underlying assumptions of the processes described below are that each product is the result of series of transliterations or translations, performed on a formal or informal specification of what is required of that product. The requirements for generality and extensibility in the process classification and characterisation are the same as those for the classification, etc., of software products.

Candidate groupings for the highest levels of breakdown include:-

a) Primary coding, for examples, into natural language, pseudo-code, "formal" languages, and so on.

b) Transliterations (that is, one-to-one transmutations from one representation to another). Each specific transliteration is from one representation into another: necessary supplementary material related to the mechanisms of the present or future transmutation is usually added during such a process.

c) Translations (that is, extraction of the relevant conceptual content of a statement in one representation and its re-statement in another. The two representations are unlikely to map directly onto each other in sequence, content or concept). Each specific translation is from one representation into another: necessary supplementary material related to the mechanisms of the present or future transmutation is usually added during such a process.

d) Verifications (that is, attempts to confirm that the input and output of a transliteration or translation are entirely and only equivalent).

e) Validations (that is, attempts to confirm that the underlying intentions from which the input of a transliteration or translation was constructed, are entirely and only present in the output).

f) Matching (that is, comparing two items in order to be able to state where they are identical and where they are not).

g) Testing, or checking (that is, the performance of a specified course of action, in specified conditions and with defined entry and exit conditions, in order to indicate whether a stated proposition about the product is true or false). Testing can be regarded as the detailed verification or validation of a product.

h) Animation. This is the act of following the rules embodied in a product, and can be regarded as a sub-class of validation, verification or testing. It can be done in any of the following ways:-

- fully automatic (that is, the running of a programme or of the coded interfaces of a design by machine and without human interventions)

- automatic, observable (that is, running by machine and without human intervention, but with added instrumentation and possibly interval adjustment to allow full human understanding of the rules of the product)

- manual/automatic (that is, the product rules are implemented by machine but inputs are made by people with the intention of animating chosen rules or rule systems)

- manual (rules are followed entirely by people, whether eventually intended for manual or for machine operation in the end product).

i) Editing. Active and passive products, once existent in any form, are changed by editing. The main sub-classes of editing are:-

- addition

- deletion

- alteration

j) Measurement. Measurements may be made manually, mechanically, or by a combination of the two.

k) Observation. This is the casual or unspecified reading through of a passive product, or watching of an animated product.

4.7 Further work on Process Classification

The initial steps are to use the candidate classifications in forming and explicating the models and their possible applications. Subsequently, actual and potential processes need to be documented and analysed in order to improve the draft classifications. Once reasonably complete, the classification must be extended to contain equivalent symbols for each entry (for convenience in modelling and recording) and matched with units and methods of measurement for the inputs and outputs of each process. These measures must be both quantitative and qualitative.

5. MAPPING THE INPUT SPACE AND OUTPUT SPACE

Mappings of a product's or sub-product's input and output spaces are needed to enable the planning and management of design and testing, and the making of judgements on the relative qualities of different items. As an example of the need for these mappings, consider trying to extract an indication of relative reliability in service, from the numbers of faults disclosed prior to release, on two separate products. What are the factors which could have contributed to the difference ? Is it reasonable to normalise the fault counts on the gross size of the product, or would a better comparison result from including some assessment of relative difficulty ? Can the assumption be made that the items will be reliable <u>in proportion</u> to the number of faults found (that is, in the belief that the higher fault rate indicates a more thorough testing and thus a more reliable product) ? Could their reliability be <u>inversely</u> related to the faults found (because, given the same processing, if fewer faults were found then perhaps fewer existed to be found) ? Is it realistic to assume (for any purposes) that there is an even distribution of faults in the product, or an even distribution of fault activation during testing ?

This is an area in which much conceptual and practical work

is needed, to enable useful models and analyses of faultiness, fault-prone-ness, maintainability and reliability. For example, the understanding and application of fault data is heavily dependent on the conceptual models of the interpreter, and on the actual forms of the product and its environments of development and testing. Without information on these factors, the effort made to collect and analyse data related to product performance qualities is probably too heavily hampered to be of any practical value.

5.1 Product Models and Representations

For the mapping of input and putput spaces, as well as for the work on interactions between products and processes, it is essential to have appropriate conceptual models of products, and supporting methods of representing these models. These models must cover products at several levels of detail (ideally with consistency between the levels), and at different points in their lives. Additionally, the representations may be required for a variety of purposes and users, and thus there will be a need to use -

a) Mathematical models (manipulation, prediction, comparison, self-checking)

b) Verbal models (discussion, communication, creation of procedures)

c) Static graphical models (high-lighting hot-spots, displaying the distribution of qualities, displaying product history and development progress)

d) Dynamic graphical models (indications of trends, displays of actual and planned progress, distribution and movements of product and sub-product qualities)

e) Data; raw, summarised, edited, fitted, etc.

6. FURTHER WORK

The ideas presented in this paper are currently influencing a variety of Alvey and ESPRIT projects -

a) Consideration of product design and implementation processes, lead naturally to the identification of notations relevant to the planning and managing of software projects. Such work is fundamental to the design of the SPMMS system (Software Production and Maintenance Management Support system) being developed under contract to ESPRIT and in conjunction with Siemens, CIT-Alcatel (TECSI & SESA), Data Management and TRT..

b) Establishment of the mechanisms for characterising design and development processes, permits the processes to be combined to in an optimal fashion; eg to reduce the number of faults created, and increase the proportion of these which are disclosed. The classification and characterisation of interactions between designs, intermediate products, and processes, and their outcomes in terms of the qualities of their delivered products, is essential groundwork for the quality management tools and procedures being investigated in the REQUEST project, under contract to ESPRIT and in conjunction with ICL, Elektronik Centralen, Cisi, NCSR, UKAEA, Thomson, Esacontrol, GRS & AEG.

c) Comparisons between products, in terms of their faultiness, their disposition to reveal faults as failures, and the likelihood that failures will be traceable. Product classification, characterisation and metrication, are vital support topics for the design and implementation of the Software Data Library, which is being investigated and designed under an ALVEY contract; involving ICL, SDL, NCSR, Logica, GEC Software, NCC and the University of Liverpool.

d) Investigations of the appropriateness, effectiveness of different approaches to software testing, given specifed functional and quality requirements, within specified development and operational environments; and identification of their tool support requirements. This work is within the Test Specification and Quality Management project, under an ALVEY contract and in conjunction with ICL, LDRA and the University of Liverpool.

Other areas of work following on from that reported here are as follows:-

a) Improved classifications of products and processes

b) Experimental designs to support investigations of interactions between products, processes, designs and supporting services and tools

c) Automatic and manual data collections, to support validation and characterisation of models

d) As needed and as possible, design and procurement of tool support for collection of data and metrics

e) Consideration of, and (if needed) collection of basic information for, the formation of "Intelligent Query Systems" and "Quality Management Systems", to assist project and product management.

Assessing System Reliability Using Censoring Methodology

by

Hani Doss[1,2], Steven Freitag[1], and Frank Proschan[1]

Florida State University

ABSTRACT

Suppose that we have a sample of iid systems each consisting of independent components. Let F denote the distribution of system lifelength. Each system is continuously observed until it fails. For every component in each system, either a failure time or a censoring time is recorded. A failure time is recorded if the component fails before or at the time of system failure; otherwise a censoring time is recorded. We introduce a method for finding estimates of F(t) based on the mutual censorship of the component lifelengths inherent in this model. We present limit theorems that enable the construction of confidence intervals in large samples. For small samples, we describe and discuss bootstrap schemes that can be used to implement the method.

[1] Research supported by the Air Force Office of Scientific Research Grant AFOSR 85-C-0007.

[2] Research supported by Office of Naval Research Contract N00014-76-C-0475.

NATO ASI Series, Vol. F22
Software System Design Methods. Edited by J.K. Skwirzynski

1. INTRODUCTION

The following problem is of practical and theoretical importance in reliability.

Under study is a coherent structure consisting of n independent components. The structure is observed continuously until it fails. For components failing before or at system failure time, we observe *complete* lifelengths; for components still functioning at system failure time we observe *censored* lifelengths. For the system we observe system lifelength. From a sample of m such structures we wish to estimate the system lifelength distribution.

As far as we know, this problem has not been solved or even treated in the literature.

In this paper we propose an estimator of the system lifelength distribution. As a by-product, we also obtain estimates of the mean and quantiles of the system lifelength and of all the corresponding quantities for component lifelengths. In Section 2 we give several asymptotic results concerning the estimators. In Section 3 we present and discuss two bootstrap schemes that are used in small samples to assess the variability of our estimates and to construct confidence intervals.

NOTATION

We assume that the system and each component are in either a functioning state or a failed state. Thus, we can define the lifelengths of the components and of the system. Let

X_{ij} = the lifelength of component j in system i;

T_i = the lifelength of system i;

$Z_{ij} = \min(X_{ij}, T_i)$;

$\delta_{ij} = I(X_{ij} \le T_i)$;

F_j be the distribution function of X_{ij}, and the component reliability function be $S_j(t) = 1 - F_j(t)$;

F_s be the distribution function of T_i, and the system reliability function be $S_s(t) = 1 - F_s(t)$;

H_j be the distribution function of Z_{ij}, and $\bar{H}_j(t)$ denote $1 - H_j(t)$.

In the definitions above the letter i indexes systems and the letter j indexes components. Throughout the paper i ranges from 1 to m, and j from 1 to n. The random variables X_{ij} are not observed. We observe only the Z_{ij}'s and δ_{ij}'s.

It is helpful to keep in mind a concrete example. Figure 1 below shows diagrammatically a simple structure of 3 components, arranged neither in series nor in parallel. We carry this example throughout the paper. In the example (the subscript i indexing systems has been suppressed) $T = X_1 \wedge (X_2 \vee X_3)$, where $x \wedge y = \min(x, y)$ and $x \vee y = \max(x, y)$.

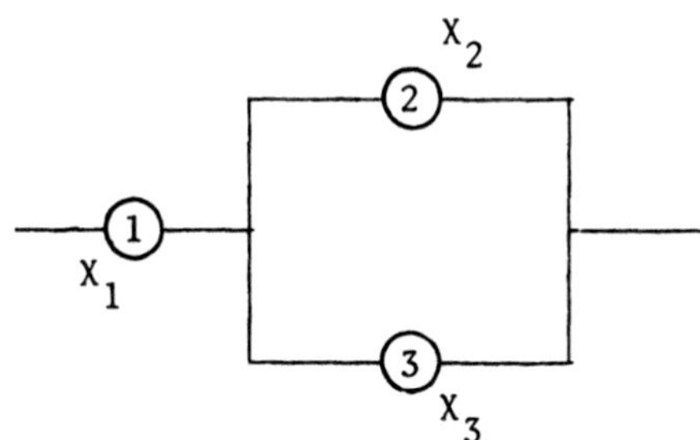

Figure 1 X_i = lifelength of component i, i = 1, 2, 3.

We note that F_s can be estimated naively by the empirical distribution function of the T_i's:

$$\hat{F}_s^{emp}(t) = \frac{1}{m} \sum_{i=1}^{m} I(T_i \le t) \quad \text{for } t \ge 0. \tag{1}$$

However, it is clear that this estimator does not use all the information available in the sample.

THE ESTIMATOR

For any coherent structure of n independent components there corresponds a function $h: [0, 1]^n \to [0, 1]$, such that

$$S_s(t) = h(S_1(t), \ldots, S_n(t)) \quad \text{for } t \geq 0. \tag{2}$$

See Chapter 2 of Barlow and Proschan (1975) for details. In the example given by Figure 1, we have

$$S_s(t) = S_1(t)[1 - (1 - S_2(t))(1 - S_3(t))],$$

so that

$$h(u_1, u_2, u_3) = u_1[1 - (1 - u_2)(1 - u_3)] \quad \text{for } u_1, u_2, u_3 \in [0, 1].$$

To construct our estimator, we first estimate the $S_j(t)$'s by the Kaplan-Meier estimates

$$\hat{S}_j(t) = \prod_{i:\, Z_{(i)j} \leq t} \left(\frac{m - i}{m - i + 1}\right)^{\delta_{(i)j}} \quad \text{for } t \geq 0. \tag{3}$$

($Z_{(1)j} < \ldots < Z_{(m)j}$ denote the ordered values of $Z_{1j}, \ldots, Z_{mj}$, and $\delta_{(1)j}, \ldots, \delta_{(m)j}$ are the δ's corresponding to $Z_{(1)j}, \ldots, Z_{(m)j}$, respectively) and then substitute $\hat{S}_j(t)$ for $S_j(t)$ in (2). The estimator is defined by

$$\hat{S}_s(t) = \begin{cases} h(\hat{S}_1(t), \ldots, \hat{S}_n(t)) & \text{if } t < T_{(m)} \\ 0 & \text{if } t \geq T_{(m)}. \end{cases} \tag{4}$$

Here, $T_{(m)} = \max_i T_i$.

We have shown that the estimate $\hat{F}_s (= 1 - \hat{S}_s)$ is the nonparametric mle of F_s. We do not present a formal proof here, but instead offer the following heuristic argument. It is well known (Kaplan and Meier, 1958; Johansen, 1978) that the Kaplan-Meier estimate is the nonparametric mle of a distribution function when the data is randomly right censored. An extension of this result is that $(\hat{S}_1, \ldots, \hat{S}_n)$ is the nonparametric mle of $(S_1, \ldots, S_n)$; the invariance principle for mle's implies that $h(\hat{S}_1 \ldots, \hat{S}_n)$ is the nonparametric mle of $h(S_1, \ldots, S_n)$.

Equation (4) provides the basis for the estimation of functionals of F_s such as quantiles and the mean. For example, we can estimate $F_s^{-1}(p)$ by $\hat{F}_s^{-1}(p)$, for $p \in (0, 1)$. Similarly we can estimate $\mu_s = \int_0^\infty t dF_s(t)$ by $\hat{\mu}_s = \int_0^\infty t d\hat{F}_s(t)$.

2. ASYMPTOTIC RESULTS

In this section we describe the limiting behavior of the estimates of the system and component reliability functions. As an application, we show how our results can be used to improve the system reliability. The proofs of the theorems stated below will appear elsewhere.

We begin with an important result concerning the simultaneous estimation of the component reliability functions. For $T > 0$, $D[0, T]$ denotes the space of real valued functions on $[0, T]$ that are right continuous and have left limits, with the Skorohod metric topology (see Chapter 3 of Billingsley, 1968), and $D^n[0, T]$ denotes the product metric space.

THEOREM A. Suppose $F_1, \ldots, F_n$ are continuous, and let T be such that $F_j(T) < 1$ for $j = 1, \ldots, n$. Then as $m \to \infty$

$$m^{\frac{1}{2}}(\hat{S}_1 - S_1, \hat{S}_2 - S_2, \ldots, \hat{S}_n - S_n) \to (W_1, W_2, \ldots, W_n)$$

in $D^n[0, T]$, where $W_1, \ldots, W_n$ are *independent* mean 0 Gaussian processes, with covariance structure given by

$$\text{(5)}\qquad \begin{aligned}&\mathrm{Cov}(W_j(t_1),\ W_j(t_2)) = \\ &S_j(t_1)\, S_j(t_2) \int_0^{t_1} \frac{dF_j(u)}{\bar{H}_j(u) S_j(u)} \quad \text{for } 0 \le t_1 \le t_2 \le T.\end{aligned}$$

The weak convergence of the Kaplan-Meier estimator to a Gaussian process has been well-established in the literature (Breslow and Crowley, 1974; Gill, 1983) under the assumption that the lifelengths and the censoring variables are independent. In our situation the component lifelengths are censored by the system lifelength, and the independence condition is clearly violated. We can, however, redefine the censoring variables to bypass this difficulty. This is easiest to explain in terms of the example given by Figure 1. Consider Component 1. Clearly, X_1 is censored by $Y_1 = X_2 \vee X_3$, which *is* independent of X_1. Similarly, X_2 is censored by $Y_2 = X_1$, and X_3 by $Y_3 = X_1$. The construction is general: for an arbitrary system, X_j is censored by Y_j = lifelength of system if X_j is replaced by ∞. One can check that

(i) X_j and Y_j are independent,

(ii) $\min(X_j,\ T) = \min(X_j,\ Y_j)$.

Thus, the known weak convergence results for the Kaplan-Meier estimate apply to the individual $\hat{S}_j$'s.

For fixed m, the $\hat{S}_j$'s are in general dependent. This is easily seen in the example given by Figure 1, in which Components 2 and 3 are both censored by Component 1. For complicated systems the dependence may be complex. Thus, the novel results given by Theorem A are first, the joint asymptotic convergence of the $\hat{S}_j$'s and second, their asymptotic independence.

The asymptotic independence of the $\hat{S}_j$'s is interesting. Before proving Theorem A we conjectured this result by considering the two special cases of parallel and series systems. These are often viewed as extreme cases in reliability theory, and an analysis of these cases may shed light on the dependence structure between the $\hat{S}_j$'s. For parallel systems there is no censoring at all; the $\hat{F}_j$'s are the usual empirical cdf's and are trivially independent for every m. For a series system (say of just two components) we have

$$\text{(6)} \qquad m\,\mathrm{Cov}(\hat{F}_1(t), \hat{F}_2(t)) = m\,E\hat{F}_1(t)\hat{F}_2(t) - m\,E\hat{F}_1(t)E\hat{F}_2(t).$$

Since $\hat{F}_1(t)\hat{F}_2(t) = \hat{F}_s^{\,emp}(t)$ (see (1)), the first term on the right side of (6) is $m\,F_s(t)$. Consider now the second term on the right side of (6). From Efron (1967) we obtain the bounds

$$\text{(7)} \qquad 0 \le F_j(t) - E\hat{F}_j(t) \le S_j(t)e^{-m\bar{H}_j(t)} \quad \text{for } j = 1, 2.$$

Combining (6), (7) and the fact that $F_1(t)F_2(t) = F_s(t)$, we obtain for series systems that

$$\text{(8)} \qquad m\,\mathrm{Cov}(\hat{F}_1(t), \hat{F}_2(t)) \to 0 \quad \text{exponentially fast as } m \to \infty.$$

This proves that $\hat{S}_1(t)$ and $\hat{S}_2(t)$ are asymptotically uncorrelated and hence asymptotically independent, assuming that joint asymptotic normality has been established. Since intuitively the series structures give rise to maximum possible dependence among the $\hat{S}_j$'s, we were led to conjecture the asymptotic independence of the $\hat{S}_j$'s for general structures. Our proof of Theorem A does indeed give the result (8) for arbitrary systems.

To prove Theorem A we show that for each m, the vector of processes

$$\left\{ m^{\frac{1}{2}} \left(\frac{\hat{S}_1(t) - S_1(t)}{S_1(t)}, \ldots, \frac{\hat{S}_n(t) - S_n(t)}{S_n(t)} \right); \ t \in [0, T] \right\}$$

is approximately (as $m \to \infty$) a martingale with respect to the σ-field generated by all uncensored component deaths observable by time t. We then apply an appropriate martingale central limit theorem, via the Cramèr-Wold device, to deduce the result.

The next theorem gives the asymptotic normality of our estimator of system reliability.

THEOREM B. Suppose $F_1, F_2, \ldots, F_n$ are continuous, and suppose T is such that $F_j(T) < 1$ for $j = 1, 2, \ldots, n$. Then as $m \to \infty$

$$m^{\frac{1}{2}}(\hat{S}_s - S_s) \to W \quad \text{weakly in } D[0, T],$$

where W is a mean 0 Gaussian process with covariance structure given by

$$\mathrm{Cov}(W(t_1), W(t_2)) = \sum_{j=1}^{n} \left(\frac{\partial h}{\partial u_j}(u_1, \ldots, u_n) \bigg|_{\substack{(u_1, \ldots, u_n) = \\ (S_1(t_1), \ldots, S_n(t_1))}} \right)$$

$$\left(\frac{\partial h}{\partial u_j}(u_1, \ldots, u_n) \bigg|_{\substack{(u_1, \ldots, u_n) = \\ (S_1(t_2), \ldots, S_n(t_2))}} \right)$$

$$S_j(t_1)S_j(t_2) \int_0^{t_1} \frac{dF_j(u)}{\bar{H}_j(u)S_j(u)} \qquad \text{for } 0 \le t_1 \le t_2 \le T.$$

For fixed $t \in [0, T]$, the asymptotic normality of $m^{\frac{1}{2}}(\hat{S}_s(t) - S_s(t))$ follows from Theorem A and an application of the delta method. Thus, the proof of Theorem B consists of a straightforward generalization of this for the process $\{m^{\frac{1}{2}}(\hat{S}_s(t) - S_s(t));\ t \in [0, T]\}$.

Greenwood's formula can be used to estimate the variance of $\hat{S}_j(t)$.

Since this estimate is well known to be consistent, it is clear that one can consistently estimate the asymptotic variance of $\hat{S}_s(t)$ given by Theorem B. This enables the construction of asymptotic confidence intervals for $S_s(t)$.

We close this section with an application of Theorem A to the joint estimation of the reliability importance of components. The reliability importance $I_j(t)$ of component j at time t is defined by

$$I_j(t) = \frac{\partial}{\partial u_j} h(u_1, \ldots, u_n) \Big|_{(u_1, \ldots, u_n) = (S_1(t), \ldots, S_n(t))} .$$

Let $\varepsilon_1, \ldots, \varepsilon_n$ be small numbers. Note that

$$h(S_1(t) + \varepsilon_1, \ldots, S_n(t) + \varepsilon_n) - h(S_1(t), \ldots, S_n(t)) \doteq \sum_{j=1}^{n} \varepsilon_j I_j(t).$$

Thus, the reliability importance of components may be used to evaluate the effect of an improvement in component reliability on system reliability, and can therefore be very useful in system analysis in determining those components on which additional research can be most profitably expended. For details, see pp. 26-28 of Barlow and Proschan (1975), and the review by Natvig (1984).

Notice that

$$I_j(t) = h_j(S_1(t), \ldots, S_n(t)),$$

where $h_j\colon\ [0, 1]^n \to [0, 1]$ is some smooth function. Thus, to estimate $I_j(t)$, a natural choice is

$$\hat{I}_j(t) = h_j(\hat{S}_1(t), \ldots, \hat{S}_n(t)).$$

THEOREM C. Suppose $F_1, \ldots, F_n$ are continuous and $T > 0$ is such that $\max_{1 \le j \le n} F_j(T) < 1$. Then as $m \to \infty$

$$m^{\frac{1}{2}}(\hat{I}_1 - I_1, \ldots, \hat{I}_n - I_n) \to (Y_1, \ldots, Y_n)$$

weakly on $D^n[0, T]$, where $(Y_1, \ldots, Y_n)$ is a vector of mean 0 Gaussian processes whose covariance structure is given by

$$\mathrm{Cov}(Y_{j_1}(t_1), Y_{j_2}(t_2)) =$$

$$\sum_{\substack{k=1 \\ k \neq j_1, j_2}}^{n} \left(\frac{\partial^2 h}{\partial u_{j_1} \partial u_k} \Bigg|_{(u_1, \ldots, u_n) = (S_1(t_1), \ldots, S_n(t_1))} \right) \left(\frac{\partial^2 h}{\partial u_{j_2} \partial u_k} \Bigg|_{(u_1, \ldots, u_n) = (S_1(t_2), \ldots, S_n(t_2))} \right) .$$

$$S_k(t_1) S_k(t_2) \int_0^{t_1} \frac{dF_k(u)}{\bar{H}_k(u) S_k(u)} ,$$

for $0 \le t_1 \le t_2 \le T$ and $j_1, j_2 = 1, \ldots, n$.

For fixed t, the asymptotic normality of $m^{\frac{1}{2}}(\hat{I}_1(t) - I_1(t), \ldots, \hat{I}_n(t) - I_n(t))$ follows from Theorem A and an application of the delta method. The theorem follows from an easy extension of this argument to the process $\{m^{\frac{1}{2}}(\hat{I}_1(t) - I_1(t), \ldots, \hat{I}_n(t) - I_n(t)); t \in [0, T]\}$.

3. BOOTSTRAPPING SCHEMES

Although the estimates $\hat{F}_s(t)$, $\hat{F}_s^{-1}(p)$, and $\hat{\mu}_s$ are easy to describe and their asymptotic distributions relatively simple, their finite sample distributions (particularly for $\hat{F}_s^{-1}(p)$) are completely intractable. In practice, we will need to supplement any estimate with an estimate of its standard error, and in fact an estimate of its whole distribution. In this section we discuss bootstrapping schemes for estimating the distribution of our statistics and for setting confidence limits.

In what follows, P denotes the true underlying probability model that generates the data

$$(Z,\delta) = \{(Z_{ij}, \delta_{ij});\ j = 1, \ldots n,\ i = 1, \ldots, m\}.$$

Let $\eta = \eta((Z, \delta), P)$ be a given function of the data and of the model. Examples are $\eta = \hat{F}_s^{-1}(p)$ and $\eta = \hat{F}_s^{-1}(p) - F_s^{-1}(p)$, for $p \in (0, 1)$, and $\eta = \sup_{0 \le t \le T} |\hat{F}_s(t) - F_s(t)|$. We wish to estimate G, the distribution of η (or some aspect of G such as its standard deviation). Write $G = G(P)$. The idea of the bootstrap (see Efron, 1982) is to estimate the true model P with an estimated model $\hat{P}$, artificially generate data $\{(Z^{*b}, \delta^{*b});\ b = 1, \ldots, B\}$ from the model $\hat{P}$, where B is some large number, and compute artificial values $\eta^{*b} = \eta((Z^{*b}, \delta^{*b}), \hat{P})$ of η. The empirical cdf of the η^{*b}'s is then used to estimate G.

How to estimate the model is of course a key question, and we now describe two solutions. Let

$$\mathrm{Sys}(i) = \{(Z_{i1}, \delta_{i1}), \ldots, (Z_{in}, \delta_{in})\} \quad \text{for } i = 1, 2, \ldots, m.$$

<u>METHOD 1</u>. Our estimate $\hat{P}$ gives probability $\frac{1}{m}$ to each of the m systems; so we resample m systems from the original m systems.

A formal description of the algorithm follows. For simplicity we assume that η is a statistic, i.e. is observable: $\eta = \eta(Z, \delta)$.

(1) Choose $k_1, k_2, \ldots, k_m$ at random and with replacement from the set $\{1, 2, \ldots, m\}$.

(2) Compute $\eta^* = \eta(\mathrm{Sys}(k_1), \ldots, \mathrm{Sys}(k_m))$.

(3) Repeat Steps 1 and 2 independently B times, obtaining $\eta^{*1}, \eta^{*2}, \ldots, \eta^{*B}$.

METHOD 2. In this estimate of the model P, component j has lifelength distribution $\hat{F}_j$, for $j = 1, \ldots, n$; so we construct artificial systems by resampling component lifelengths from the Kaplan-Meier estimates $\hat{F}_j$.

A formal description of the algorithm is

(1) Generate $X_j^* \sim \hat{F}_j$ for $j = 1, 2, \ldots, n$ independently. This gives one artificial system which we denote by Sys^{*1}.

(2) Repeat Step 1 independently m times giving one sample of artificially constructed systems, denoted $Sys^{*1}, \ldots, Sys^{*m}$.

(3) Compute η^* based on the m systems in Step 2.

(4) Repeat Steps 1, 2 and 3 independently B times, obtaining $\eta^{*1}, \eta^{*2}, \ldots, \eta^{*B}$. Figure 2 schematically describes this method.

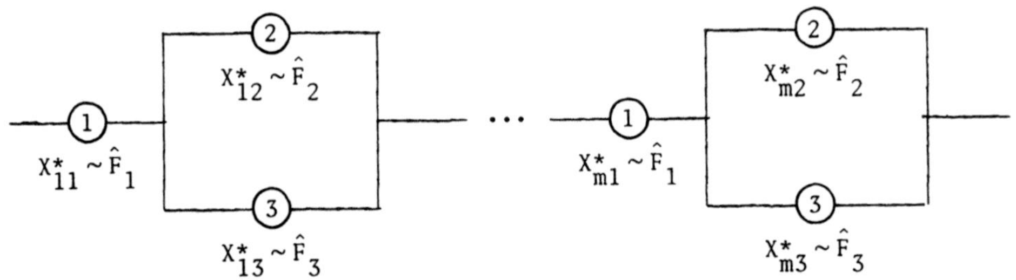

Sys^{*1} has lifelength T_1^* ... Sys^{*m} has lifelength T_m^*

Figure 2. In Method 2, the estimate η^* is based on the data $Z_{ij}^* = \min(X_{ij}^*, T_i^*)$, $\delta_{ij}^* = I(X_{ij}^* \le T_i^*)$.

Note that our version of $\hat{S}_j$ given by (3) is strictly positive for $t \ge \max_i Z_{ij}$ if $\max_i Z_{ij}$ corresponds to a censored observation. In this case, we view $\hat{F}_j$ as giving mass to the point ∞; thus X_j^* is equal to ∞ with positive probability.

In applying either method, the η^{*b}'s are used in the usual way to make inference about G. Let G_m^* equal the empirical cdf of the η^{*b}'s. The standard deviation of G is estimated by

$$\hat{\sigma} = \{\frac{1}{B-1} \sum_{b=1}^{B} (\eta^{*b} - \eta^{*\cdot})^2\}^{\frac{1}{2}} \tag{9}$$

where $\eta^{*\cdot} = \frac{1}{B} \sum_{b=1}^{B} \eta^{*b}$. The standard deviation is not a particularly meaningful quantity if G is asymmetric or far from normal, which may occur when the sample size is small. In that case the intervals $\eta \pm z_\alpha \hat{\sigma}$, where z_α is the $100 \cdot \alpha$ percentile point of a standard normal variate and $\hat{\sigma}$ is given by (9) are essentially useless. As alternatives, we can use the percentile intervals of level α ($\alpha \in (0, 1)$) given by

$$[G_m^{*-1}(\alpha),\ G_m^{*-1}(1-\alpha)], \tag{10}$$

and the more elaborate bias corrected and BC_a intervals (see Efron 1984a, b), all based on G_m^*.

In comparing the two methods of bootstrapping, it is helpful to make an analogy with the regression model in which we observe random pairs (Y_i, X_i), $i = 1, \ldots, m$, where

$$Y_i = X_i'\beta + \varepsilon_i, \tag{11}$$

X_i is a p dimensional vector of covariates, β is a p dimensional vector of unknown coefficients, to be estimated, and ε_i are iid from an unknown distribution F on $\mathbb{R}^1$, centered at 0 in some sense. Let $\hat{\beta}$ be an estimate of β, whose variability we wish to assess.

One way of bootstrapping is to resample the pairs (Y_i, X_i), and construct an artificial value β^* based on the resampled pairs. This corresponds to our Method 1.

Another way to bootstrap is to resample the residuals

$$\hat{\varepsilon}_i = Y_i - X_i'\hat{\beta}.$$

Let F_m be the empirical cdf of $\hat{\varepsilon}_1, \ldots, \hat{\varepsilon}_m$, and let $\varepsilon_1^*, \ldots, \varepsilon_m^*$ be iid $\sim F_m$. We construct $Y_i^* = X_i'\hat{\beta} + \varepsilon_i^*$, $i = 1, \ldots, m$, from which we can obtain an artificial value $\hat{\beta}^*$. This corresponds to our Method 2.

Method 2 makes more use of the structure in our model, in particular the assumption of independence of the component lifelengths. We view this both as a strength and a weakness.

We expect Method 2 to be "preferable", but we have not carried out any studies to assess the two methods. We hope to pursue this problem and report the results in a future paper.

Efron (1981) has discussed use of the bootstrap on censored data. He considered the standard setup for randomly right censored data, which corresponds to two components arranged in series in our model. He showed that for this case, the two methods of bootstrapping are identical. The two methods are not always the same in our situation, as can easily be seen by considering a parallel structure of two components.

It would be of interest to study the asymptotic behavior of the bootstrap in our problem. This would determine whether confidence intervals based on the bootstrap are asymptotically valid. To carry out such a study, it would be necessary to select some relatively simple estimates; $\hat{F}_s(t)$ where t is fixed is a prime choice. Let $\hat{F}_s^*(t)$ denote a bootstrap replication of $\hat{F}_s(t)$, obtained by one of the two methods. Suppose we can show that for almost every sample sequence $\{(Z_{ij}, \delta_{ij});\ j = 1, \ldots, n,\ i = 1, 2, 3, \ldots\}$,

$$m^{\frac{1}{2}}(\hat{F}_s^*(t) - \hat{F}_s(t)) \text{ and } m^{\frac{1}{2}}(\hat{F}_s(t) - F(t)) \quad \text{have the same asymptotic distribution.} \tag{12}$$

It would then follow that the simple percentile intervals (10) are asymptotically correct to the first order, in the terminology of Efron (1984b).

Hjort (1985) has shown that in the standard setup for randomly right censored data, the bootstrap approximation is asymptotically correct to the first order. More specifically, suppose that X_i are iid $\sim F$, Y_i are iid $\sim G$, independently of the X's, and that the data is $(X_i \wedge Y_i,\ I(X_i \le Y_i))$, $i = 1, \ldots, m$. Let $\hat{F}$ be the Kaplan-Meier estimator, and let $\hat{F}^*$ be the empirical cdf of a random sample of size m from $\hat{F}$. Hjort (1985) showed that under certain regularity conditions, for fixed t, with probability one,

(13) $m^{\frac{1}{2}}(\hat{F}^*(t) - \hat{F}(t))$ and $m^{\frac{1}{2}}(\hat{F}(t) - F(t))$ have the same asymptotic distribution.

This result offers hope that (12) is true under some reasonable set of assumptions.

Ackowledgements.

We thank Ian McKeague and Rob Tibshirani for helpful comments.

REFERENCES

Barlow, R. E. and Proschan, F. (1975). Statistical Theory of Reliability and Life Testing. To Begin With, Silver Springs, Maryland.

Billingsley, P. (1968). Convergence of Probability Measures. John Wiley and Sons, Inc., New York.

Breslow, N. and Crowley, J. (1974). A large sample study of the life table and product limit estimators under random censorship. Ann. Statist. 2, 437-453.

Efron, B. (1967). The two sample problem with censored data. Proceedings of the Fifth Berkeley Symposium on Mathematical Statistics and Probability 4, 831-852.

Efron, B. (1981). Censored data and the bootstrap. J. Amer. Statist. Assoc. 76, 312-319.

Efron, B. (1982). The jackknife, the bootstrap, and other resampling plans. SIAM CBMS-NSF Monograph 38.

Efron, B. (1984a). Bootstrap confidence intervals for a class of parametric problems. To appear in Biometrika.

Efron, B. (1984b). Better bootstrap confidence intervals. Department of Statistics, Stanford University Technical Report No. 226.

Gill, R. D. (1983). Large sample behaviour of the product-limit estimator on the whole line. Ann. Statist. 11, 49-58.

Hjort, N. L. (1985). Bootstrapping Cox's regression model. Manuscript in preparation.

Johansen, S. (1978). The product limit estimator as maximum likelihood estimator. Scand. J. Statist. 5, 195-199.

Kaplan, E. L. and Meier, P. (1958). Nonparametric estimation from incomplete observations. J. Amer. Statist. Assoc. 53, 457-481.

Natvig, B. (1984). Reliability importance of components. Statistical Research Report No. 10, Institute of Mathematics, University of Oslo. To appear in Vol. 6 of Encyclopedia of Statistical Sciences, S. Kotz and N. L. Johnson, eds., Wiley: New York.

STATISTICAL DESIGN OF EXPERIMENTS FOR COMPUTER PERFORMANCE EVALUATION

Ali Rıza KAYLAN
Industrial Engineering Department
Boğaziçi University
Bebek, Istanbul, Turkey

ABSTRACT

This study is primarily concerned with the methodology of statistical design of experiments to aid the computer performance analyst. It illustrates the basic principles of design and analysis through case studies. The objective is to find those operating conditions which improve the current system performance.

One must learn by doing the thing; for though you think you know it, you have no certainty until you try.

Sophocles

I. INTRODUCTION

Performance assessment of computer systems is a complex and challenging job. Being composed of multiple resources, the operation of such systems is characterized as a dynamic and stochastic process. The set of resources or servers such as CPU, main and auxiliary memories, I/O channels and various peripheral devices are demanded by user programs

NATO ASI Series, Vol. F22
Software System Design Methods. Edited by J.K. Skwirzynski

running in time-sharing or batch modes. The dynamic allocation of resources within the system to these competing requestors leads into a behaviour which is surprisingly difficult to comprehend.

Once the management objectives are stated in regard to the computer performance, certain indicators reflect the closeness of the real situation to these goals. For a given system configuration and workload, performance measures should be precisely defined in order to have meaningful evaluation. High CPU utilization at the cost of degrading turnaround time may not be appealing to the management. Two commonly used performance measures are response time and throughput. Response time is the difference between completion and arrival times. Throughput is the number of jobs processed per unit time. These measures are highly influenced by the workload, scheduling procedure of assigning resources to workload, how much overlapping is permitted in use of these resources.

The three major approaches to performance evaluation of a computer system are

a) analytical models,

b) simulation models,

c) measurement.

The analytical models consider the system to be a network of queues and jobs circulate among the given set of resources. Central server model and other deterministic and stochastic models are surveyed and presented as the most cost-effective techniques for computer system performance modeling (1,5,10). Due to the inherent validation problems related to assumptions made in analytical models, simulation approach quite often seems very appealing to the analysts. However, simulation models are very expensive to use, and the results are harder to interpret. The third approach, measurement is carried out with special hardware or software monitors which record the busy and idle periods of CPU, peripheral devices and channels.

After this brief review of available tools of performance assessment, this study attempts to emphasize the methodology of design of experiments. Specific cases will be reported to illustrate the basic principles of statistical techniques.

The performance evaluation of a computer system may be carried out with the aim of

a) system selection,

b) system tuning,

c) capacity planning.

At the phase of system selection, it is desired to match the user requirements with the system configuration. Economic benefits are tried to be quantified. The system has to deliver service with a specified minimum level of performance. System tuning is an analysis to balance resources through adjustment of system parameters so that performance is improved for a given workload. In capacity planning, the bottlenecks of the current system is considered and the future workload is tried to be projected. Statistical learning through experimentation is very valuable in all these aspects of performance assessment (2,7).

II. BASIC PRINCIPLES OF EXPERIMENTAL DESIGN

Learning about a real life system is advanced by iterations between theory and practice. An initial hypothesis may be found to be conflicting with the data gathered from the system. The discrepancies between data and initial conjectures lead into refined form of new conjectures. This *information feedback* is an important aspect of scientific research. Statistical design of experiments act as a catalyst in this *iterative process* of learning. G.E.P. Box emphasizes crucial issues of scientific inquiries (3). Analysts should seek an economical description of the system in model construction. They should also worry selectively about the factors under study.

The methodology of designing and analyzing an experiment in regard to computer performance evaluation is outlined as follows:

1. System Description and Problem Formulation : A clear understanding of the system is an essential part of any study. The system configuration and the characteristics of the workload should be fully taken into account. It is also crucial to specify the objectives of the experiments to be performed. A correct formulation of the problem contributes substantially to the overall study and conclusions to be drawn.

2. Selection of Response Variable, Factors and Levels : The investigator has to specify the dependent variable referred as response (performance measure) as well as independent variables or factors. The average turnaround time, throughput or resource utilizations are some candidates for response. The analyst has to choose the factors of the study carefully from the system parameters to investigate their effects on the system performance. The levels of factors at which experimental runs will be performed are also decided at this stage.

3. Choice of Experimental Design : It is always desired to propose a statistically efficient and economical design. The magnitudes of statistical errors to be tolerated determine the amount of experimentation burden. Statistical accuracy and cost of experimentation has to be balanced.

4. Data Collection : In the process of performing experiments, the analyst has to pay attention to measurement accuracy. The conditions of the operational environment should be closely observed. To keep the noise at a low level, special care is necessary to avoid drastic shifts in the workload during experimentation.

5. Data Analysis : Statistical tools are employed in analyzing the data.

6. Drawing Conclusions : Based on the data analysis, statistical inferences are justified. The iterative nature of these investigations may lead into an

earlier stage, and it may be deemed necessary to carry out another set of experiments. Recommendations are made in accordance with the results obtained.

In view of the aforementioned guidelines, performance analysts can suggest an improvement about a computer system. A hypothesized improvement is checked through the design and analysis of the experiments. If the results support the initial conjecture, modification are implemented into the system.

III. AN APPLICATION OF FRACTIONAL FACTORIAL DESIGN

A study to explore what factors significantly affect the response time of a job is a complicated task. The sensitivity of performance relative to the queue and service scheduling parameters for a given system load can be investigated through factorial analysis. Since the workload on the system reflects a stochastic and dynamic behaviour, the analyst has to be very careful in designing and running the experiments.

Job scheduling is the control of flow of jobs in the input, executing and output queues. Scheduling is the input and output queues is based on the priority of the queue entry relative to all queue entries in the system.

The operational environment is governed by numerous parameters related to queue and service limits. First, a typical setting where jobs are processed will be illustrated. When a batch or an interactive job enters the system, it is queued for input and waits for the required system resources to become available or its priority to grow. The scheduling priority of the job is advanced as the job waits. The priority ages to a system-defined limit. The job scheduler periodically scans the queued jobs and active jobs to determine whether action is necessary to ensure that the highest priority jobs are being serviced. This action may include rolling out low priority jobs or rolling in higher priority jobs.

Once a job is scheduled for execution, certain controls are exercised over the job. CPU time limit is checked. Each executing program is allowed to reside in central memory for a certain amount of time before relinquishing its space to another program. When this central memory time slice is exceeded, the program may be rolled out. This means that the information contents related to the program are transfered to mass storage. The program remains on mass storage until it is rolled back into central memory. Execution resumes from the point where rollout occurred.

The relative values of the queue and service parameters, both among service classes (batch, interactive,system) and within a service class, affect system performance. Some of the other job control parameters for each service class are

- initial CPU priority at job initiation
- CPU time slice in milliseconds
- central memory time slice in seconds
- number of jobs per service class.

These parameters are desired to be set at certain values to meet the following objectives

a) to keep system jobs with their high entry priority from monopolizing system resources,

b) to allow most interactive jobs to compile, load and begin execution in one time slice,

c) to give batch jobs a large time slice,

d) to ensure prompt service to all interactive users, without employing an excessive number of rollouts.

The major problem of experimental design is deciding what factors and their corresponding levels will reveal the most information to serve the objectives set at the beginning of the study. As a general rule, the investigation should be viewed as an iterative process. Thus, experimental effort is not to be fully invested in the first design. When the first part of an investigation is completed, the experimenter will usually have a better understanding of the relationship of factors and the response. Thus, this will lead into a better planning of a second set of experiments. It is very common to experience that some of the insignificant variables are studied or some right variables in the inappropriate ranges are investigated.

To comprehend how factorial analysis can aid the practitioners working in the fields of computer performance analysis, an application will be illustrated.

3.1 Description of Design

The computer system where this study is carried out is the CDC CYBER 170/815. The system configuration is portrayed in the Appendix. It is desired to see how certain factors affect the response time of a job. In particular, five factors are selected.

1. Batch: number of batch jobs allowed to reside in the central memory for execution.
2. Terminal: number of terminals active.
3. Scheduler: job scheduler interval in seconds.
4. Recall: CPU recall period in milliseconds.
5. Peripheral: number of available peripheral processors.

The first two variables are the indicators of system workload. The system operator can alter the maximum number of jobs for each service class. If this value is set to 5 for batch jobs, the sixth one has to wait its turn in the input queue until an earlier one is completed. The system delay parameter referred as scheduler is the one which specifies the interval at which the job scheduler and priority evaluation routines are called. The parameter of recall period specifies the amount of time a job remains in recall. The peripheral processors are those devices which process communications between central memory and individual peripheral devices such as mass storage devices, magnetic tape units and line printers. They also perform system control functions. The total number of peripheral processors in the current configuration is equal to 10.

In deciding on a design, a 2^{5-2}_{III} fractional factorial design is employed. The notation 2^{5-2}_{III} tells us that the design accommodates five variables each at two levels requiring $2^3 = 8$ runs altogether. The subscript III is the resolution number which indicates that main effects are not confounded with each other but confounded with two-factor interactions.

The test program to measure the response time is written in BASIC language as

```
10    FOR K=1 TO 20000
20    NEXT K
```

This program counting to 20.000 simply makes an addition, comparison and a transfer operation at each step. The test program is entered from the system console. The batch jobs are synthetically generated and put into the central memory. These jobs which operate continuously are BASIC programs reflecting infinite loops and occupying certain portion of central memory. That is,

```
10    DIM A(30000)
20    GO TO 20
```

The number of available peripheral processors reduces to six from ten since three of them are kept busy by certain system programs and one by the test program. The remaining number of peripheral processors is altered by again introducing fictitious PP programs which keep them continuously busy.

The design matrix displaying the low and high levels of the factors to be used in the experimental runs is given together with the response values obtained in Table 1. A significant amount of variability is expected. Therefore, two replications for each experimental run is obtained in order to estimate the variance.

The full 2^5 factorial requires 32 runs. From these runs, 32 statistics can be calculated which estimate the main as well as the interaction effects. Due to the fact that they are not all expected to be of appreciable size, a 2^{5-2}_{III} fractional factorial design is preferred. The generators of the design are

$$I = 1235 \qquad \text{and} \qquad I = 234$$

where I is the identity column composed of elements of all plus signs.

TABLE 1. The Design Matrix for an Eight Run 2^{5-2}_{III} Fractional Factorial Design for Studying How Response Time is Affected by Five Variables (Generators I = 234, 1235)

Variable	LEVELS Low (-)	High (+)
1. Batch	2	7
2. Terminal	0	25
3. Scheduler (sec)	1	5
4. Recall (millisec)	5	192
5. Peripheral	6	2

Variables 1	2	3	4 23	5 123	Results 1	Results 2	Average Response	Estimated Variance
-	-	-	+	-	2.5	2.4	2.45	0.005
+	-	-	+	+	5.2	3.5	4.35	1.445
-	+	-	-	+	9.7	8.2	8.95	1.125
+	+	-	-	-	11.3	16.1	13.7	11.52
-	-	+	-	+	3.9	3.6	3.75	0.045
+	-	+	-	-	6.6	6.1	6.35	0.125
-	+	+	+	-	4.3	7.5	5.90	5.120
+	+	+	+	+	8.4	6.5	7.45	1.805

Using these generators, the confounding pattern can be obtained which reflects the effects that are revealed in a combined manner in the estimates. These relationships and the estimates are discussed in the data analysis section and portrayed in Table 2.

3.2 Data Analysis

Analysis of data is carried out to obtain

a) Point estimates of the effect,

b) 95% confidence intervals.

TABLE 2. Estimated Effects and Confounding Pattern for the 2_{III}^{5-2} Design

Average Response	Estimated Effect	Confounding Pattern
2.45	6.61	Average
4.35	2.70	1+45+235
8.95	4.78	2+34+135
13.70	.45	3+24+125
3.75	-1.50	12+35
6.35	- .63	13+25
5.90	-3.15	4+23+15
7.45	- .98	5+14+123

Point estimates of the effects are the difference between two averages

$$\bar{Z}_{+} - \bar{Z}_{-}$$

where $\bar{Z}_{+}$ is the average response for the plus level of the variable and $\bar{Z}_{-}$ is the average response for the minus level. Thus, for the batch effect,

$$\hat{B} = \frac{4.35 + 13.70 + 6.35 + 7.45}{4} - \frac{2.45 + 8.95 + 3.75 + 5.90}{4}$$

$$= 7.9625 - 5.2625$$

$$= 2.7$$

It should be noted that the first main effect is confounded with the interaction effect of 45 and 235. All the effect estimates are calculated by means of the algorithm due to Yates (4) and tabulated in Table 2.

To obtain the confidence intervals, it is necessary to compute the variance of effects. The pooled estimate of run variance is

$$s^2 = \sum_{i=1}^{8} \nu_i s_i^2 \Big/ \sum_{i=1}^{8} \nu$$

where s_i^2 is the sample variance at the *ith* experimental run and $\nu_i = n_i - 1 = 1$ is the corresponding degrees of freedom. The pooled variance is computed as

$$s^2 = 2.649$$

and the effect variance is estimated as

$$\hat{v}(\text{effect}) = \hat{v}(\bar{Z}_+ - \bar{Z}_-)$$

$$= s^2/4$$

$$= 0.662$$

The 95% confidence intervals can be drawn as

$$\text{Effect} \pm t_{0.975,\ 7} \cdot \sqrt{\hat{v}(\text{effect})}$$

$$\text{Effect} \pm 2.365 \times 0.814$$

$$\text{Effect} \pm 1.925$$

where the $t_{0.975,\ 7}$ is obtained from the t table with 7 degrees of freedom.

3.3 Interpretation of Results and a Second Design

Assuming three-factor interactions are negligible, the results indicate that

Effects	Estimates
1 + 45	2.70
2 + 34	4.78
4 + 23	-3.15

seem to be significant. The largest increase in the average response time from low to high level is 4.78 in the second case. This can be interpreted as most probably coming from main effect terminals. But it also exists together with two-factor interaction effect of scheduler interval and recall period. Another fractional design in which factor 4 residing with -23 is selected as a second stage. This second design de-alias factor 4 and all its interaction effects.

In the new design, the column corresponding to factor 4 has opposite signs to those in the original design with all other columns kept the same. The results of this second fraction are portrayed in Table 3.

TABLE 3. The Results of the Second Fractional Factorial Design

Replications 1	Replications 2	Average Response	Estimated Effect	Confounding Pattern
4.2	2.8	3.50	6.96	
6.7	7.5	7.10	5.64	1-54+235
4.5	2.9	3.70	4.89	2-34+135
9.0	9.9	9.45	2.66	3-24+125
2.4	2.7	2.55	2.04	12+35
5.2	4.6	4.90	0.96	13+25
7.7	5.9	6.80	3.61	-4+23+15
17.7	17.6	17.65	1.59	5-14+123

The variance estimate of effects is

$$\hat{v}(\text{effect}) = s^2/4$$
$$= 4.835/4$$
$$= 1.209$$

and the 95% confidence intervals are

$$\text{Effect} \pm t_{0.975,\ 7} \sqrt{\hat{v}(\text{effect})}$$

$$\text{Effect} \pm 2.6$$

Combining the data from both fractions yields the estimates given in Table 4.

TABLE 4. Combined Results of the Two Fractions

Effects		Combined Effects			
e_1	e_2	$(e_1+e_2)/2$	Factor	$(e_1-e_2)/2$	Factor
6.61	6.96	6.79			
2.70	5.64	4.17	1	-1.47	54
4.78	4.89	4.84	2	-0.06	34
0.45	2.66	1.56	3	-1.11	24
-1.50	2.04	0.27	12+35		
-0.63	0.96	0.17	13+25		
-3.15	3.61	0.23	23+15	-3.38	4
-0.98	1.59	0.31	5	0.31	14

Conclusions to be drawn after this second design are more certain. The large main effects of factors 1, 2 and 4 are now estimated free of bias from two-factor interactions. All the two-factor interactions of factor 4 are free of aliases assuming all three-factors interactions to be zero. For this particular case, however, none of these interactions seem to be significant.

From the analysis of the two sets of 32 data points, it appears that main effects of variables 1, 2,and 4 explain a good portion of variability in the response value. The remaining variables 3 and 5 are interpreted as inert variables and can be dropped from further study. The data set can be treated essentially as a 2^3 factorial design in variables 1, 2, and 4 with 4 replications at each run. The results are tabulated in Table 5. To comprehend the conclusions better, the results are also displayed geometrically in Figure 1.

The standard error of effects can be estimated as usual:

$$\hat{V}\text{ (effect)} = \left(\frac{1}{16} + \frac{1}{16}\right) \sigma^2$$

$$\hat{V}\text{ (effect)} = 2.33/8$$

$$= 0.29$$

Standard error = 0.54.

The 95% confidence intervals are

$$\text{Effect} \pm 1.28$$

The results suggest that further experimentation is needed to investigate more closely the variables Batch and Recall. A reasonable suggestion is to restrict batch jobs to periods of low system load. Increasing the CPU recall period decreased the response time substantially. Further investigation is deemed necessary especially with higher values of recall period.

This pilot study illustrates how fractional factorial designs may be utilized sequentially by the computer performance analysts. This statistical tool is a vehicle to improve research efficiency in investigating effects of factors on the response value. Some of the variables are screened as the sequential study proceeds. The iterative nature of scientific investigation is reflected in such studies.

TABLE 5. Results of the 32 Trials in Relation to Three Variables (1 = Batch 2 = Terminal 4 = Recall)

Results from Individual Runs				Average Response	Estimated Effect	Identification
3.9	3.6	4.2	2.8	3.63	6.78	
6.6	6.1	6.7	7.5	6.73	4.17	1
9.7	8.2	7.7	5.9	7.88	4.83	2
11.3	16.1	17.7	17.6	15.68	1.56	12
2.5	2.4	2.4	2.7	2.50	-3.38	4
5.2	3.5	5.2	4.6	4.63	-1.28	14
4.3	7.5	4.5	2.9	4.80	-1.77	24
8.4	6.5	9	9.9	8.45	- .79	124

FIGURE 1. Geometric Representation of 2^3 Factorial Design

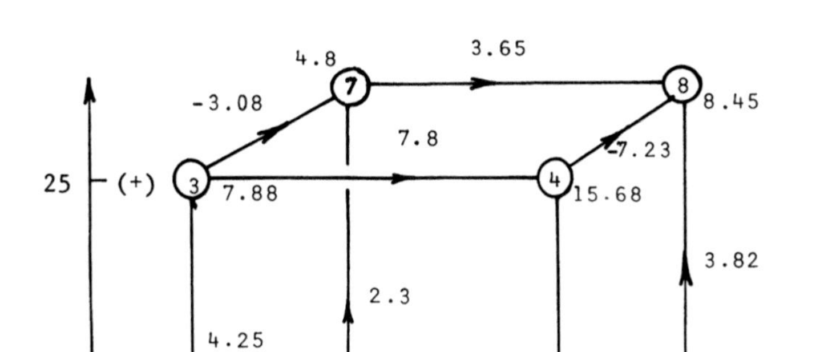

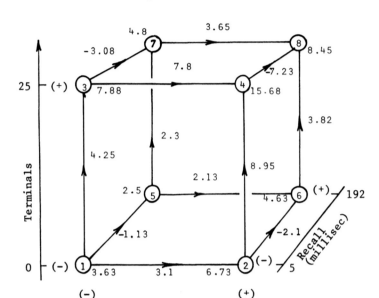

IV. STATISTICAL COMPARISON OF TWO ALTERNATIVES

The CDC CYBER 170/815 Computer System has the feature of partitioning the main memory into two parts and utilizing one portion the same as the disk space. This is found advantageous by some system analysts since the job whose central memory time slice is exceeded does not need to be swapped out onto the disk. By saving the swapping operation, it is conjectured that performance can be improved in terms of response time. Also the burden on the disk channel and peripheral processors are diminished. This feature which is referred as the Unified Extended Memory (UEM) is investigated to see whether it,in fact,improves the system performance.

In order to compare the UEM case and without the UEM case, typical operations such as file getting, full screen editing, test program execution, catalog listing are clearly specified. Two basic programs are selected as the test programs. These are

Program A :

```
10    FOR K=1 TO 20000
20    NEXT K
```

Program B :

```
10    DIM A(100000)
20    FOR K=1 TO 50000
30    NEXT K
```

Response time data is also collected for a 1216 word file on entering and leaving the editing mode. Finally getting a file of 11456 words and catalog listing of 34 files are performed. During data collection, the other significant factors related to workload are observed. The number of batch jobs executing were three in both cases. The number of terminals active were 32 in the UEM case and 28 in the other. The results are tabulated in Table 6. Since a large discrepancy is observed in variances, the equality assumption seems to be invalid. Thus, the degrees of freedom for the t-statistic can be approximated by a formula due to Welch

$$\nu = \frac{(s_1^2/n_1 + s_2^2/n_2)^2}{(s_1^2/n_1)^2/(n_1-1) + (s_2^2/n_2)^2/(n_2-1)}$$

where s_i^2 and n_i denote the sample variance and size of alternative i respectively. The hypothesis testing problem

$$H_o \; : \mu_1 = \mu_2$$

$$H_1 \; : \mu_1 \neq \mu_2$$

questioning the equality of means for the two cases can be solved by computing t-statistic

$$(\bar{X}_1 - \bar{X}_2) \; / \; (s_1^2/n_1 + s_2^2/n_2)^{0.5}$$

and comparing with the critical t-value at a given level of significance. Examining the results, it is concluded that installing UEM does not improve the performance under the current workload. In fact, for the longer program

TABLE 6. Comparison of Response Times for the Two Alternatives
(1 = UEM installed , 2 = No UEM)

	PROGRAMS A		PROGRAMS B		CATLIST		GET		FSE Enter		FSE Leave	
	1	2	1	2	1	2	1	2	1	2	1	2
Mean	8.72	9.79	98	26.74	2.45	2.93	8.27	12.87	13.22	12.04	10.42	7.14
Variance (s^2)	5.24	11.45	118.7	42.13	0.40	1.12	14.22	31.72	11.54	2.57	7.82	1.83
Sample Size (n)	10	10	4	10	4	4	10	10	10	5	10	5
$\bar{X}_1 - \bar{X}_2$	-1.07		71.26		-0.48		-4.6		1.18		3.28	
$\left(\frac{s_1^2}{n_1} + \frac{s_2^2}{n_2}\right)^{0.5}$	1.292		5.821		0.616		2.143		1.292		1.072	
t-statistic	-0.83		12.24		-0.77		-2.15		0.91		3.06	
deg. of freedom (ν)	16		4		5		16		13		13	
$t_{\nu, 0.975}$	2.12		2.78		2.57		2.12		2.16		2.16	
Accept $\mu_1 = \mu_2$ at 95%	YES		NO		YES		NO		YES		NO	

FIGURE 2. Percentage Utilization of the System Resources without UEM

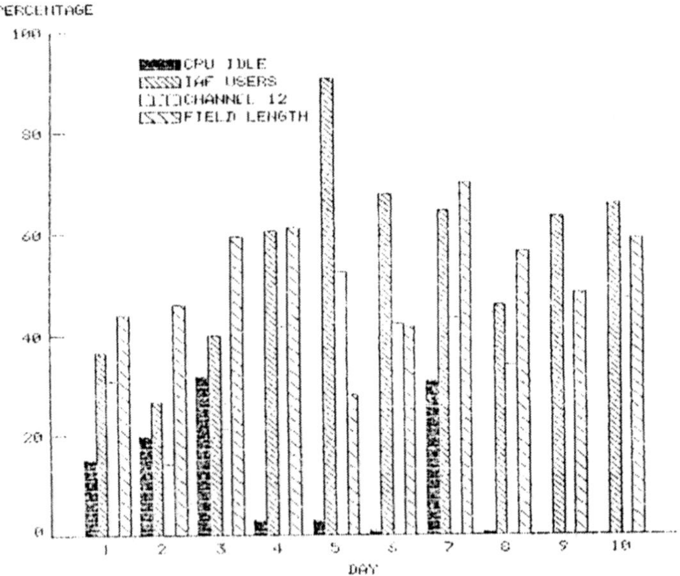

FIGURE 3. Percentage Utilization of the System Resources with UEM

WITH UEM

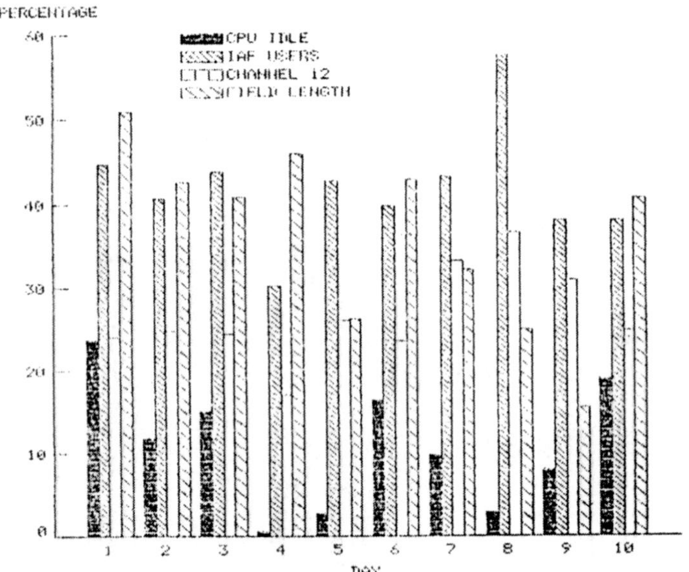

designated as B, the performance has degraded substantially.

Further investigation is carried out with the tracer utility which monitors systems activity and gathers data periodically. Percentages of CPU idle time, available central memory, active time of channel 12 through which disk access is achieved are examined for a considerable amount of time. There is no significant improvement observed and the idea of UEM installation is dropped from further consideration. Some of the graphs on the tracer output results are displayed in Figures 2 and 3.

V. CONCLUDING REMARKS

Computer performance analysts are confronted with complicated systems of stochastic and dynamic nature. The apparent complexity of system configuration and workload makes the process of measuring the system and understanding effects a arduous job. Statistical learning is essentially a valuable asset to the performance analysts. Raw data collected from carefully planned experiments can be turned into useful information and this information can shed light into avenues of system tuning and capacity planning.

This study exposes two statistical investigations. In the first case, the impact of scheduling parameters and other factors on response time are observed through a fractional factorial design. It is desired to achieve the most suitable operating conditions.

Possible conclusions to be drawn are

- response time degrades significantly as the number of batch jobs residing in central memory increases.An effective operating policy should be to restrict the batch jobs during the heavy time-sharing load, that is, to postpone the execution of batch jobs to evening hours of low workload.

- the computer network has the capability of expanding. However, the increase in the number of time-sharing jobs through additional terminals also degrades the response time. Without upgrading the CPU (addition of another CPU or changing the current CPU with a faster one) capacity expansion of the current network with more terminals would hinder the turnaround time severely.
- the number of peripheral processors does not seem to create any bottleneck.
- increasing recall period lessens the response time of the given job. Further experimentation is needed to be performed with other ranges of CPU recall period to search for the best level for the current workload.

This example reflects the iterative characteristic of statistical experimentation. Research efficiency is an advantageous aspect of such designs.

In the second case, a suggestion raised from discussions with system analysts is explored. Two alternative systems are compared based on the performance of various tasks. It turns out that the system performance does not improve significantly in the suggested system.

Reviewing the Figures 2 and 3, the bottleneck appears to be the CPU. The suggestions of upgrading the computational speed of the current CPU or installing an additional CPU should be carefully investigated in the future capacity planning.

Statistical learning is an evolutionary process and a continuing effort which is at its infancy for the aforementioned system. Compiling the information gathered through these studies, one can possibly gain enough insight so that the parameters may be dynamically adjusted depending on the encountered workload. An interface between the current tracer utility and an information based adaptive operating system would aid the performance analyst to achieve the best operation policies.

APPENDIX

The CDC CYBER 170 Model 815 Computer System at Boğaziçi University is a network sytem of 50 interactive terminals. It is an air-cooled, microcoded, single central processor unit providing 524K 60-Bit words of main memory-expandable to 1048K words, 10 peripheral processors, and 12 input/output channels - expandable to 15 or 20 peripheral processors and 24 input/output channels, and a display controller and operator display station.

Each of the peripheral processors (PPs) included with the system has a separate memory and can execute programs independently of each other and of the central processor. Through the exchange jump feature and central memory communication, the PPs control the central processor. The PPs communicate with each other through central memory and the input/output channels. In solving a problem, one or more PPs are used for high-speed information transfer in and out of the system and to provide operator control. A number of problems can be in operation concurrently by time-sharing the central processor. The system configuration is displayed in Figure 4.

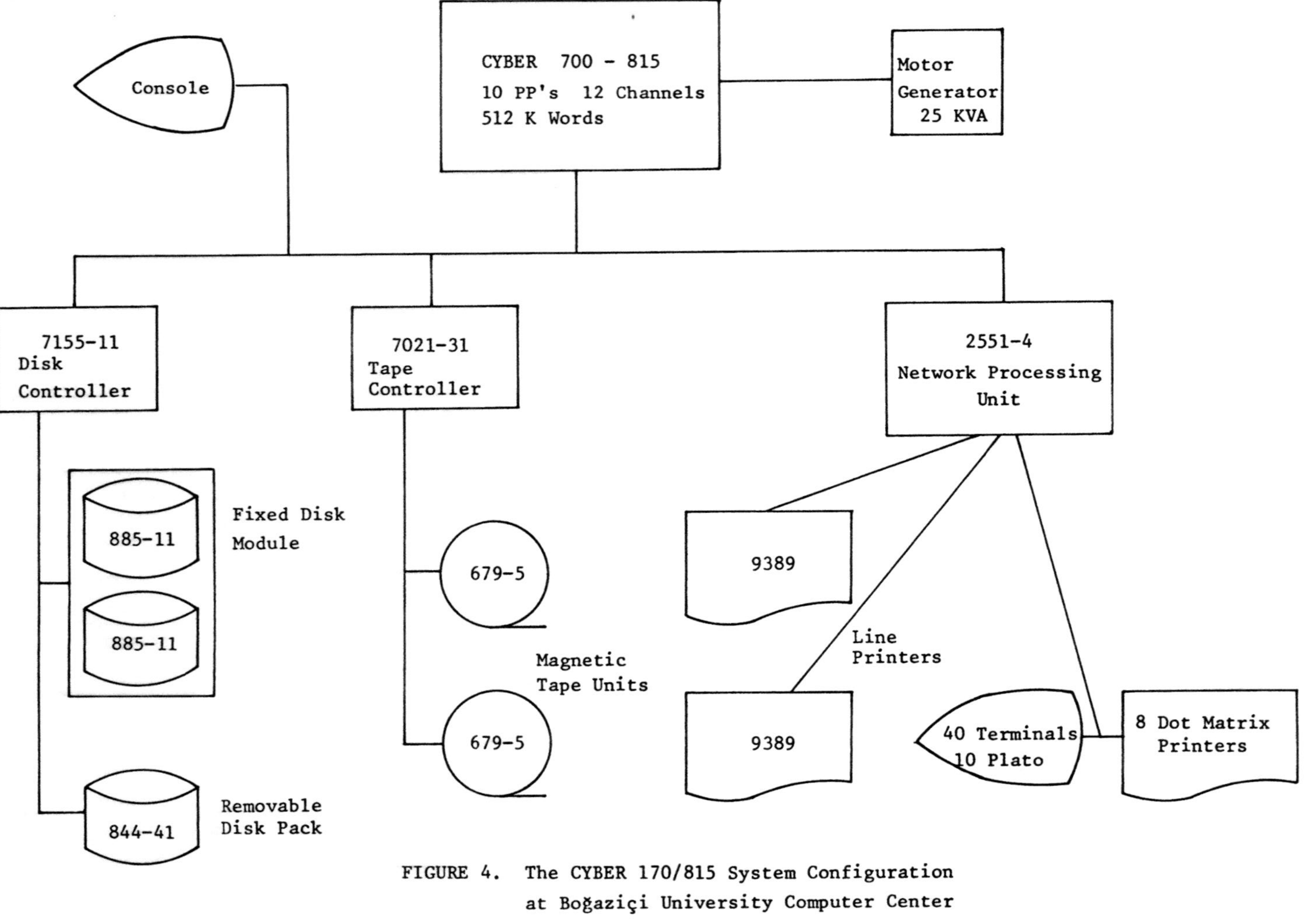

FIGURE 4. The CYBER 170/815 System Configuration at Boğaziçi University Computer Center

REFERENCES

1. Allen, A.O., "Queueing Models of Computer Systems," *Computer*, V. 13, No.4, 1980, pp.13-24.

2. Bard, Yo, "An Experimental Approach to System Tuning," *Proceedings of the International Symposium on Computer Performance Modeling, Measurement and Evaluation,* Edited by P.P.S. Chen, M. Franklin, ACM-Sigmetrics, 1976, pp.296-305.

3. Box, G.E.P., "Science and Statistics," *Journal of American Statistical Association,* V. 71, No.356, 1976, pp.791-799.

4. Box, G.E.P., W.G. Hunter, J.S. Hunter, Statistics for Experimenters, John Wiley and Science, 1978.

5. Kleinrock, L., Queueing Systems, Vol. II: Computer Applications, John Wiley and Sons, N.Y., 1975.

6. Kleinrock, L., A. Nilsson, "On Optimal Scheduling Algorithms for Time-Shared Systems," *Journal of the Association for Computing Machinery,* V. 8, No.3, 1981, pp.477-486.

7. Mamrak, S.A., P.A. Deruyter, "Statistical Methods for Comparing Computer Services," *Computer,* V. 10, No.2, 1977, pp.32-39.

8. Reddy, Y.V., "Experimental Evaluation of a Multiprogrammed Computer System," *ACM Performance Evaluation Review,* V. 4, No.2, 1975, pp.24-32.

9. Svobodova, L., "Computer System Measurability," *Computer,* V. 9, No.6, 1976, pp.9-17.

10. Trivedi, K.S., "Analytic Modeling of Computer Systems," *Computer,* V. 11, No.10, 1978, pp.38-56.

RELIABILITY ANALYSIS FOR INTEGRATED VOICE/DATA NETWORKS

Peter Kubat

GTE Laboratories Inc.,

40 Sylvan Rd., Waltham, MA 02254,

U.S.A.

ABSTRACT

Methodologies to jointly assess reliability and performance for communication and computer networks are discussed. For networks with highly reliable components, a simple and quite general analytic model is proposed. This model is then applied to selected cases.

1. INTRODUCTION

The majority of techniques for predicting reliability and availability of telecommunication networks which are currently available in the literature do not provide satisfactory answers for the practitioner. The most common network reliability measures are related to network connectivity. For instance, one connectivity measure is the probability that the network is connected, given the reliabilities of the individual commponents. Theoretically, the connectivity problem is well treated; in practice, however, it is somewhat difficult to find algorithms which will solve this problem in a reasonable time. This and some other major difficulties of current network reliability models were recently discussed by Spragins (1984).

Yet, from a practical point of view, it seems that connectivity is not the major issue in judging the quality of a commercial network. The main reason

NATO ASI Series, Vol. F22
Software System Design Methods. Edited by J.K. Skwirzynski

for this claim is that typically the network components are quite reliable -- nodes have multiple connections to allow possible rerouting of messages in the event of a network failure, and the failed components are quickly repaired. Thus, it is not surprising to find that the connectivity failures are rare (i.e., the probability that the network is disconnected is very low). However, the network can fail because of other causes. For example, the failure of certain components directly or indirectly may lead to increased traffic intensities and slower transmission speeds, which, in turn, cause unacceptable delays, congestion, buffer overflow, high call-blocking probabilities, and other performance degradation. Therefore there is a clear need to quantify the reliability of the network in terms other then network connectivity.

In another approach recently advocated by some researchers [Beaudry (1978), Li & Silvester (1984), Meyer (1980,1982), Kubat (1984a,b)], it has been suggested that combining reliability and a performance measure into one quantity may overcome some of the drawbacks of the connectivity models. This approach seems to be promising becouse it integrates some of the important factors related to the general performance of telecommunications and computer networks.

A brief survey of the network reliability models in the current literature and a theoretical basis for a joint assesment of reliability and performance for highly reliable networks were considered by Kubat (1984a.). Namely, in the underlying model it had been assumed that at most a small number of components can be "down" at a time and that the average repair/replacement time of a failed commponent is small when compared with the average failure time of network components. At the steady state, the network is assumed to follow a regenerative stochastic process. This methodology was then applied to evaluate highly distributed voice/data integrated networks. In a particular example, motivated by burst switching [Amstutz (1983)], "traffic loss rate" was the measure of performance combined with reliability.

In a subsequent paper [Kubat (1984b.)], the network performance was measured in terms of network throughput for steady-state operation. For the single type of traffic, the throughput and availability were then jointly assessed.

The major advantages of the reliability and performance model considered by Kubat (1984a.) are:

* Acceptance of general measures of performance
* Assumption of general distributions for maintenance/repair times
* Intuitiveness and ease of implementation

The joint assessment of reliability/availability and performance measures produces a single figure of merit and may be a valuable tool for network designers and managers to use in evaluating alternative architectures, identifying bottlenecks, evaluating potential measures for improvements, suggesting routing alternatives and estimate important parameters for both new and existing networks.

Another intricate problem of the integrated voice/data environment is the presence of multiple performance measures (some for voice, some for data). In addition, the fact that the voice traffic may have priority over the data traffic further complicates the performance analysis of the network.

2. DEFINITION OF RELIABILITY/AVAILABILITY FOR A COMMUNICATION NETWORK

In the most general scenario, the performance of a communication network at the time t can be described by a vector valued stochastic process $Y(t) = (y_1(t), \ldots, y_m(t))$. The individual components represent important performance measures taken at the time t: for instance, an average delay for data, average set-up call time, quality of the signal, call blocking probability, and fraction of voice clipping. The state space Ω of the process Y(t) can be partitioned into two subsets: a set of "good" states $\mathbf{S}$, where the performance of the network is judged acceptable and a set of "bad" states $\mathbf{F} = \Omega - \mathbf{S}$, where the network performance is unacceptable. The process alternatively wanders over states in $\mathbf{S}$, then over states in $\mathbf{F}$, and again back to $\mathbf{S}$, etc. We can then define the reliability of the network as

$$R = \frac{E[T_S(t)]}{E[T_S(t)] + E[T_F(t)]}$$

where $E[T_S(t)]$ is the time the network will spend in $\mathbf{S}$ during the time interval (0,t] and $E[T_F(t)]$ is the time the network will spend in $\mathbf{F}$ in (0,t]. Unfortunately, even at steady state the expectations $E[T_S(t)]$ and $E[T_F(t)]$ may be very difficult to obtain.

To overcome this drawback, let us describe the stochastic behavior of the network in two stages and make some simplifying assumptions. First, define a stochastic process $\mathbf{X}(t) = (X_1(t), \ldots, X_n(t))$ which describes the working status of the network components. Namely,

$$X_k(t) = \begin{cases} 1, & \text{if the component } k \text{ is "up" at the time } t; \\ 0, & \text{if the component } k \text{ is "down" at the time } t. \end{cases}$$

The state space $\Omega_{\mathbf{X}}$ of $\mathbf{X}(t)$ contains $N = 2^n$ states. In steady state, when a failure (or a change in a global network state) occurs, the traffic flow in remaining working components is assumed to reach equilibrium quickly. Let $p(\mathbf{x})$ be the steady state probability that the network's global state is $\mathbf{x}$. When the network is in the state $\mathbf{x}$, its performance is described by a process $\mathbf{Y}(\mathbf{x}) = (Y_1(\mathbf{x}), \ldots, Y_m(\mathbf{x}))$. This process is considered to be also at equilibrium. We assume that when the network state changes from $\mathbf{x}$ to $\mathbf{x}'$, the performance process jumps from equilibrium process $\mathbf{Y}(\mathbf{x})$ to the process $\mathbf{Y}(\mathbf{x}')$, neglecting any transient behavior which might occur during this transition.

One possible reliability measure in this case may be defined as

$$\sum_{\mathbf{x} \in \Omega_{\mathbf{x}}} P[\, \mathbf{Y}(\mathbf{x}) \in \mathbf{S} \,] \,.\, p(\mathbf{x}) \tag{2.1}$$

The average performance (sometimes called performability) of the i-th component of the vector performance measure $\mathbf{Y}(\mathbf{x})$ is then

$$\sum_{\mathbf{x} \in \Omega} E[Y_i(\mathbf{x})]\, p(\mathbf{x}) \quad , i=1, \ldots m. \tag{2.2}$$

Yet , the set $\Omega_{\mathbf{x}}$ (and Ω) may still contain too many states, making the summations too extensive and thus impossible to complete in a reasonable amount of time. Therefore this definition in its full extent can be used for only very small problems. Li and Silvester (1984) proposed to evaluate the sum over the points $\mathbf{x}$, such that $p(\mathbf{x}) > \varepsilon$, where ε is a very small number. Thus (2.2) becomes

$$\sum_{\mathbf{x} \in \Omega(\varepsilon)} E[Y_i(\mathbf{x})]\, p(\mathbf{x}) \quad , i=1, \ldots m. \tag{2.3}$$

where $\Omega(\varepsilon) = \{\, x: p(\mathbf{x}) > \varepsilon \,\}$. For systems with highly reliable components [i.e. $P(x_k = 0)$ is very small for most k], the set $\Omega(\varepsilon)$ will have only a few members.

3. ASSESSING PERFORMANCE AND RELIABILITY FOR NETWORKS WITH HIGHLY RELIABLE COMPONENTS

For the sake of tractable analysis, we will make the following assumptions:

* The network components are highly reliable; i.e., component uptimes are large (order of magnitude : years or months, say).
* The repair times (downtimes) are much shorter then uptimes (order of magnitude : days or hours).
* The call/packet/message interarrival times and processing times are much shorter then the downtimes (order of magnitude : seconds or milliseconds).
* The network is in a steady state; when a failure occurs, the traffic flow in the remaining components reaches equilibrium quickly (in comparison with the downtimes), and thus we can neglect any transient behavior.

These assumtions are not very restrictive and fit a large number of real networks. In light of the above, we can proceed to formulate the model.

Consider a network having N components (i.e., I nodes and L links, N=I+L). The components are highly reliable; however, from time to time they fail. Sometimes even a group of components can fail simultaneously. When a component fails, a repair/replacement procedure is initiated. After repair, the component is back to full function and is assumed to be "as good as new." Since the downtimes are assumed to be relatively short when compared with uptimes, we will assume for simplicity that the probability of another component failure during the downtime is zero. More precisely, we assume that a component failure (or simultaneous failure of a group of components) censors any future failures until the completion of the repair. There are M distinct failure types (states), each having a positive probability of occurrence.

The stochastic behavior of the network can be then modeled by the following process X(t): Initially, the process X(t) spends an exponential amount of time (with the mean Λ) at state 0, the state in which all the network components are "up". When a failure occurs, with probability λ_i/Λ it is of the type i, i=1, . . .M; ($\Lambda = \Sigma^M_{i=1}\lambda_i$, $\lambda_i > 0$). The downtime due to the failure type i has a general distribution with the mean $E[D_i]$. After the repair completion the process always returns to the state 0. The process will oscillate between the "up" state , 0, and some "down" state, i, as shown in Figure 1.

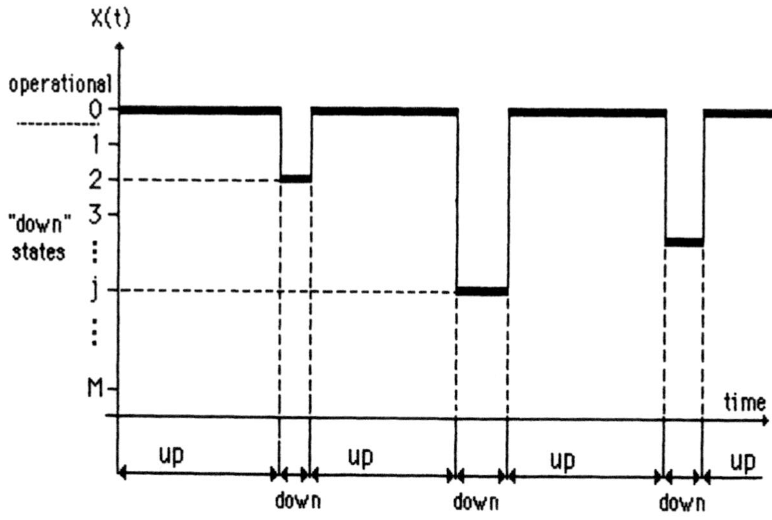

Figure 1. A typical realization of the process X(t).

Equivalently, we can say that when the system returns to the state 0, M independent Poisson processes start simultaneously. The process i corresponds to failure type i and has a failure rate λ_i. Clearly, when the first failure occurs, with probability λ_i/Λ, it is of the type i and the system enters the i-th repair stage during which no new failures can be generated.

The times in which X(t) changes from the state i to the state 0 can be regarded as regeneration points of the process. It follows from the theory of alternating regenerative processes [Ross (1983)] that the steady state probabilities $p_j = \lim_{t\to\infty} P\{X(t)=j\}$, j=0,1,...,M, are :

$$p_0 = 1/(1 + \Sigma^M{}_{j=1}\rho_j), \tag{3.1}$$

$$p_j = \rho_j p_0, \quad j = 1,\ldots,M; \tag{3.2}$$

where

$$\rho_j = \lambda_j \, E[D_j], \quad j = 1,\ldots,M. \tag{3.3}$$

Moreover, utilizing the Theorem 3.6.1 [Ross (1983,p.78)], we get the average network performance:

$$AP = \frac{E[\text{ performance during one cycle}]}{E[\text{cycle time}]}$$

$$= \frac{r(0) + \Sigma^M{}_{k=1} r(k)\,\rho_k}{1 + \Sigma^M{}_{k=1}\rho_k} = \Sigma^M{}_{k=1} r(k)\, p_k \tag{3.4}$$

Here, by the cycle time we mean the time between two successive regeneration points, and r(k) is the equilibrium performance of the network while the network state is k.

For instance, let r(k) be the fraction of the time/per unit time where the performance of the network is acceptable, i.e., $r(k) = P\{Y(k) \in \mathbf{S}\}$. In this case AP measures the overall availability of the network. In another simple example we will define r(k) as an indicator function, namely:

$$r(k) = \begin{cases} 1, & \text{if the network is in state k and is connected;} \\ 0, & \text{otherwise.} \end{cases}$$

In this case, AP measures the steady state probability that the network is connected.

5. AN EXAMPLE

To illustrate the method mentioned above, let us consider a packet-switched ISDN communication network in which only nodes can fail. Both voice and data are transmitted through the network in packets and we will assume, for simplicity, that we cannot distinguish between voice and data packets (i.e., no priorities). The measure of performance selected here will be a traffic loss rate in units of packets/second or in equivalent units. Define:

state 0 - fully operational state, all nodes are "up

state i - node i is "down" and being repaired, ($i = 1, \ldots, n$)

λ_i - failure rate for the node i

$E[D_i]$ - mean downtime of the node i

W_i - input traffic rate in the node i

f_{ij} - fraction of the traffic originated in i which will terminate in j

$$I_{kij} - \begin{cases} 1, & \text{if all the traffic originated in k must go to j via failed node i,} \\ 0, & \text{otherwise} \end{cases}$$

In addition, let us assume that the network is capable of handling all the traffic at any given time; and thus losses due to voice clipping, buffer overflow, and call blocking are negligible. In the case of a node failure, the traffic is rerouted and packets are only lost due to the inability of the failed node to transmit, retransmit, and accept packets.

Using formula (3.4), the average network performance AP can then be written as:

$$AP = \sum_{i=1}^{n} \Big(W_i + \sum_{\substack{j \\ j \neq i}} W_j f_{ji} + \sum_{k} \sum_{\substack{j \\ k \neq j \neq i}} W_k f_{kj} I_{kij} \Big) p_i, \qquad (4.1)$$

where the steady-state probabilities p_i, $i = 1, \ldots, n$ are given by (3.1) -(3.3).

More specifically, let us consider a simple six-node network, as shown in Figure 2.

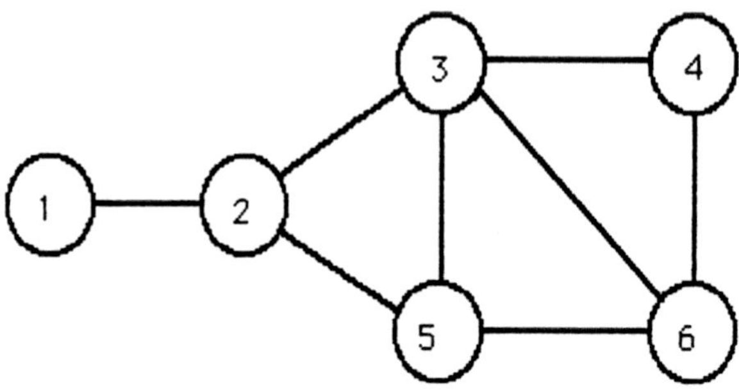

Figure 2. An example of a six-node network.

When node 1 fails, the corresponding loss of traffic will be:

$$W_1 + \sum_{i=2}^{6} W_i f_{i1},$$

since $I_{i1k} = 0$ for all $i,k \neq 1$.

On the other hand, if node 2 fails, the corresponding loss of traffic will be:

$$W_2 + \Big(\sum_{j \neq 2} W_j f_{j2} \Big) + W_1 \Big(\sum_{j=3}^{6} f_{1j} \Big) + \sum_{k=3}^{6} W_k f_{k1},$$

since $I_{i2j} = 1$, for all k, $j \neq 2$; i.e., the failure of node 2 separates node 1 from the rest of the network.

5. CONCLUSIONS

In this paper we discussed some issues pertaining to evaluation of reliability and/or performance of communication and computer networks. For networks with highly reliable components, we have proposed a simple yet quite general analytical model that jointly assesses reliability and performance.

The joint assessment of reliability/availability and performance measures produces a single figure of merit and may be a valuable tool for network designers and managers, helping them to evaluate alternative architectures, identify bottlenecks, evaluate potential measures for improvements, suggest routing alternatives, and estimate important parameters for both new and existing networks. The methodology for jointly assessing reliability and performance provides an important practical approach to the reliability of communication and/or computer networks. However, it is only one of many building blocks which form the overall decision support system.

Apart from the study of more detailed models motivated by particular examples, it would be appropriate to consider the broader question of overall network support strategy and its synthesis from components such as reliability, redundancies, preventive maintenance, network layout, and parts supply.

REFERENCES

Amstutz, S. R. (1983). "Burst Switching - An Introduction," *IEEE Communication Magazine, Vol.21*, 36-42.

Beaudry, M. D. (1978). "Performance-Related Reliability Measures for Computing Systems," *IEEE Trans. on Computers, Vol. C-27*, 540-547

Kubat, P. (1984a). "Reliability Analysis for Burst Switching Networks", TN 84-262.1, GTE Laboratories Inc., Waltham, MA 02254, U.S.A.

Kubat, P. (1984b). "Assessing Throughput and Reliability in Communication and Computer Networks," TN 84-262.2, GTE Laboratories Inc., Waltham, MA 02254, U.S.A.

Li, V. O. K. & Silvester, J. A. (1984). "Performance Analysis of Networks with Unreliable Components," *IEEE Trans. on Communication, Vol. COM-32*, 1105-1110.

Meyer, J. F. (1980). "On Evaluating the Performability of Degradable Computing Systems", *IEEE Trans. on Computers, Vol. C-29*, 720-731.

Meyer, J. F. (1982). "Closed-Form Solutions of Performability", *IEEE Trans. on Computers, Vol. C-31*, 648-657.

Ross, S. M. (1983). *Stochastic Processes*. J. Wiley & Sons, New York.

Spragins, J. (1984). "Limitation of Current Telecommunication Network Reliability Models," GLOBECOM'84, Atlanta, Conference Record.

COMPUTERS OF THE FIFTH GENERATION AND THEIR ROLE IN COMMUNICATIONS

F.L.H.M.Stumpers
Philips Research Laboratories (ret.)
Elzentlaan 11,Eindhoven,5611 LG
the Netherlands

Introduction.

Around 1950 the first generation of computers had just started(ENIAC 1946,20000 vacuum tubes),but two books had just appeared,that were going to have a major influence on the development of science in the following years:Shannon's: "Mathematical Theory of Communications." and Wiener's:"Cybernetics."In the early years of what soon was called "information theory",the fact,that it was possible to measure information,made a great impression on a wide range of scientists, who had to work with some form of information processing.In September 1950 the first international symposium on Information Theory was organised in London by professor Sir Willis Jackson and dr.Colin Cherry.It was attended by an intriguing mixture of mathematicians,statisticians,physicists,biologists, physiologists and communication engineers.Processes,by which living organisms conveyed information were of interest,as well as the thinking of a chess,aster,and its potential duplication by computer.The purpose of the Symposium was to afford opportunity for a discussion of the nature and potentialities of Shannon and Wiener's work among diverse interests and there were stimulating discussions.
During a stay at M.I.T.(Cambridge,Mass.)I had the opportunity of discussing aspects of information theory with many of the leading people of that time,such as Wiener,Wiesner,Fano,Mc Culloch,and to complete a bibliography of Information Theory, on which I had started earlier in my function of secretary of the Information Theory Group of U.R.S.I.,of which prof.dr. Balth.van der Pol was president.Supplements appeared in 1955, 1957 and 1960.Looking back on it,the first London Symposium and some analogous symposia,organised by the Macy Foundation

NATO ASI Series, Vol. F22
Software System Design Methods. Edited by J.K. Skwirzynski

in the United States,had given us a feeling,that a unity of science was approaching,an era,in which again we would be able to understand the work of people in different domains.It is intriguing,that in those early years,it looked likely,that some problems,we have not even solved today,were ready for an early solution.I might mention:Speech analysis,synthesis and recognition(Fry,Denes),Phonetic typewriters('Olsen,Dreyfus Graf) Learning machines,Machines that think and speak,Biological Computers(Mc Culloch),Automatic Programmimg(Grace Hopper,Backus) Automatic medical diagnosis(Paycha),Artificial Intelligence (Minsky,Rosenblatt),Automatic translation(Bar-Hillel).A Symposium on the Mechanization of Thought Processing in Teddington, Middlesex,England,November 1958,remains in my mind,because of many interesting papers and personalities in this field.[2)]
Although I remained interested in Information Theory,and chaired Symposia on it in Brussels,1962,and Noordwijk,1970,it became clear,that the general trend was more in the direction of making it a branch of applied mathematics.
In 1971 I organized for the first Eurocon(European Conference on Electrotechnics),a symposium on Information Processing in Large Systems,in Lausanne,where people from many different disciplines talked on the possibilities the computer gave them.We had sessions on:Information Processing in Radio Astronomy and Meteorology, Computers in Communications(EMC,planning,speech recognition), Information Processing in Living Systems(nervous system,visual recognition),Information Processing in Real Time Systems(structural analysis,traffic and air traffic control),Information Processing in Physics(high energy physics,Erasme-CERN),Information Processing in Space Systems(Computers in the NASA Space Flight Programme),Information Processing in Industry.Already at that time several authors expressed the need for larger and more powerful computers(e.g.in meteorology and high energy physics). [3)]
During the 1975 World Telecommunication,Technical Symposium, several authors stressed the importance of the computer for telecommunications.At that time Stored Program Control(introduced by the Bell System in 1965 in ESS No 1) was getting wide acceptance (Fuhrmann[4)]) Schramel stressed,that the much greater logical power of the computer,as compared with classical control principles,

enables the telecommunication engineer to realize new functions in a more economic way.[5] With the introduction of electronic components and computers in the switching part of the telephone network, a new era in the development of switching systems has started. For the first time,switching systems are no longer designed around a number of sometimes very ingenious electromechnanical components dedicated more or less to certain specific functions,but they are conceived from an architectural point of view.The superior logic of the computer is being used to improve the service to the subscribers,ease and economizemaintenance,operation and supervision,evolve a better network architecture and over-all network economy.On the same occasion the french described their E 10 system with a central Mitra 15 computer for 40000 subscribers in max. 16 centres(Mereur [6]).Haughton[7] described the Datapac packet switching technology and the Infoswitch system with circuit and packet switching techniques,both with network node computers. At the 1979 World Telecommunications Forum Y.Kitahara treated the INS(Information Network System),he had introduced in 1978,and he proposed: the rapid development and introduction of non-telephone services,the digitalization of the telecommunications network and its integration with information processing,the establishment of a new bit-based tariff structure.His book[8] gave many examples of new services,already introduced in Japan.In 1979 the british introduced their System X,a family of computer controlled(SPC) digital switching systems,the french had a time-switching solution for their E 10 system,and ITT introduced the 1240 Digital Switching System with modern software techniques.1979 was also a year with many contributions on optical fibres,and the introduction of new services(Viewdata,Teletext,Videotex) possibly to be integrated in ISDN,studied at that time by C.C.I.T.T..In 1983 the Chairman of the Forum,Secretary-General of I.T.U. gave the following message:"In 1983 we are on the eve of what is perhaps the single most important current development in world telecommunications: the application of the merging computer and communication technologies,its impact on national and international policy development.It will lead to the accelerated introduction of Integrated Services Digital Networks which will greatly expand the number,quality and variety of signals and services available to subscribers all over the world."[9]

The first plenary sessionon "Technology today and tomorrow"showed,that many of the leading authorities present there,agreed on the importance of ISDN.In the special session on ISDN,the ten authors selected could treat the subject in much more detail.It was the session,that drew the largest audience of all parallel sessions.

The Exhibition,that accompanies the World Telecommunication Forum is always interesting,and when one of the exhibitors,the japanese company N.E.C. announced a demonstration of machine translation,there was a lot of interest.In a filmed telephone conversation of an english businessman in London with a spanish colleague in Madrid,it was shown,how,with a suitable computer,each of them could speak his own language and be heard at the other side in the language of his partner.There was also a film of a british lady in difficulties at a japanese station and unfortunately the japanese conductor does not speak english.Again a computer terminal comes to the rescue.We also heard,how fluent english was translated in fluent japanese,and many of us,who had just heard from mr.Ian Ross, the president of Bell Labs,how far out the recognition of fluent discourse still is,were amazed.About half a year later I read in a paper by dr.K.Kobayashi:"In order to cope with the language barrier in international communications,I proposed the development of an automatic interpretation telephone system in 1982 and 1983.When this is achieved,the language spoken by you will reach me in japanese,and my own thoughts will be interpreted and transmitted to you in your own language.As this system will be comparatively large and expensive in the beginning,it will initially be installed at a centralized information centre near the international gateway station,and will be shared by users.However,with reductions in size and price,it will gradually come to be used beside the terminal,and will be installed as a part of office processors. Eventually,it might even be incorporated into all telephone sets. I am confident,that automatic interpretation systems be realized before the coming of the year 2000.This marvellous technology will be the greatest gift,that C and C can bring mankind."Now,since dr. Kobayashi is Chairman of the Board of NEC,there was sufficient interest to show us his vision of the future,even it had to be only by simulation.We shall return to this subject later.[10)]

2. Computers of the future.

In 1981 the Japanese Ministry of International Trade and Industry announced two projects:1)The Very High Speed Scientific Computing Systems(1981-1990).2)The Fifth Generation Computer Systems,1982-1991. The japanese realized,that to reach the present level of U.S.technology,might take the first three years of the projects.

2.1.Supercomputers .

By 1989 the 100 to 200 million dollar supercomputer project plans to produce a computer,that is a thousand times faster than any currently available design.The research issues in this project are divided into two major areas.One is concerned with very high speed devices and the project staff is studying three candidate technologies:gallium arsenide,high electron mobility transistors and Josephson junctions.The other area concerns ultra-parallel processing.It was thought,that such computers would be needed for scientific calculations,processing of image information from satellites,structural analysis of three-dimensional systems,search for energy sources a.s.o..[11]
In the European Economic Community the Council adopted the first European Strategic Programme for Research and Development in Information Technologies (ESPRIT)on February 28,1984.[12]For its research in the computer architecture area it specified:1 Ultracomputer, multiprocessor machines;2 Non-von Neumann architectures:highly parallel computer architecture(constructing machines with very large numbers(over 1000)of interconnected computing elements,capable of concurrent operations),dataflow machines(In this case data can be considered the active agents,moving through the "code graph",as they are transformed into the final result),reduction machines(A reduction machine takes the view,that the source-and-input,and output are merely two different forms of the same object,the output being the reduced form of the original program and input),inference machines.In the microelectronics area submicron MOS,submicron bipolar, an integrated design system,capable of handling VLSI circuits,containing several million components(C.A.D.)are mentioned.
In the U.S.A. there were a few institutes,e.g.in defense research, that had a supercomputer,but many universities missed an entry to it in their specialized research.However,in 1984 the National Science Foundation made available 200 million dollars to create four new supercomputer centres to universities and to establish a unified computer network,that ultimately would connect every scientist to

every other scientist in the United States.[14)]
With regard to advanced technology the US Defense Dept Advanced Research Project Agency asked industry to produce chips with a million gates,and only 0,5 micron spacing between elements:The Very High Speed Integrated Circuit.Such microscopic devices will be working on the molecular level,permitting electron movement close to the speed of light.It is said,that 17 firms made available such circuits,early this year.A commercial 1 micron chip CMOS was introduced by TRW Inc.last October.A high electron mobility transistor switches from off to on(or vice versa) in slightly more than 10^{-12} sec.,consuming only little more than 10^{-15}joules is made in Ga As-Al Ga As by several firms.The Josephson junction may be faster,but it is not practical now.[15)]
The Microelectronics and Computer Technology Corporation,MCC,began operations in Austin ,Texas,September 1983.It has 13 shareholder companies and is focussed on long term research and development.One of the goals in CAD/CAM is,laying out a chip with 10^7transistors in less than a month.The Semiconductor Research Corporation at the Microelectronics Centre of North Carolina reached 3 micron in 1984,aims at 1 micron this year.On the hardware side the limits of miniaturization are in sight,and further quantum leaps involve fundamental changes in computer design,e.g.thousands or millions of processors operating in parallel.
Already in 1978 Cray Research constructed a "vector" machine Cray 1, capable of 20 million operations per second(at that time 10 times faster than any other machine on the market)."Vector" refers to the machine's ability to process several streams of data simultaneously. Control Data Corp.introduced its Cyber 205 in 1981,machines of this class allow researchers to simulate systems,whose complexity approaches that of the real world.In aerodynamics a new airfoil design can be "flown" in a supercomputer,modified and flown again,until it is optimized.In particle theory supercomputers test the theory of strong interactions.In astrophysics they model,what happens,when gas and dust spiral into a black hole.
The Universities of Illinois,Cornell,Princeton and San Diego will each get 7 to 13 million dollars a year during 5 years.San Diego's Cray X-MP-48 will be the most powerful computer,a multiprocessor capable of two types of operations:simultaneous scalar/vector processing of independent job streams and simultaneous scalar/vector

processing of independent tasks within one job.Princeton's Cyber 205 will be followed by ETA 10,a multiprocessor machine to be developed by Control Data for 1987.Cornell and Illinois will have a top of the line IBM machine with eight auxiliary processors from Floating Point Systems.In the summer of 1982 Fujitsu and Hitachi announced supercomputers,that on paper seemed cosiderably faster than current supercomputers.The Fujitsu VP 200,also available as Amdahl 1200,should outperform Cray X-MP with three alternative vector instruction modes,multiple pipelines,interactive help request.The Hitachi S 810/20 has a one to five pipeline extension of Hitachi's integrated array processor.In April 1983 NEC displayed the powerful supercomputers SX 1 and SX 2,capable of complicated large scale simulation and structural analysis at super high speed. The Lawrence Livermore Laboratory needs supercomputing because of nuclear weapons design,laser fusion and magnetic fusion.They want an MIMD(multiple input,multiple data)10Gflop machine in the near future.Goodyear Aerospace builds for NASA the Massively Parallel Processor,a single instructor,multiple data parallel computer with 16K processors,that can perform 6.10^{9} eight bit adds and $1.8\ 10^{9}$ eight bit multiplies per second.An exciting new tool for all types of pattern recognition and image processing applications.
The principle ways of introducing parallelism in computers are:[16)]
1)Pipelining(the application of assembly line techniques to improve the performance of an arithmetic or control unit.)
2)Functional(providing several independent units for performing different functions,such as logic,addition or multiplication,and allowing these to operate simultaneously on different data)
3)Array(providing an array of identical processing elements under common control,all performing the same operation simultaneously but on different data stored in their private memories)
4)Multiprocessing(the provision of several processors,each obeying its own instructions,and usually communicating via a common memory).
Fault tolerant computing was a necessity even in the early days of computers.It gives the correct execution of a specified algorithm in the presence of defects.Faults can be avoided by the use of high reliability components.If they still arise,duplication and error correction may help.Various techniques have been devised by AT&T, Bell Labs for use in its family of ESS computers.Computers incorporated in switching complexes must provide very high availability (no more than two hours outage in 40 years).Details differ in each

ESS implementation,but in general all critical components/such as the control unit and memory system,are duplicated.The running system utilizes one set of subsystems,while a duplicate is either in a"hot back-up" mode or executing synchronously with the on-line set. The system detects errors,either by matching the results produced by both sets or by constructing each set from self-checking modules, which are themselves duplicates,that match one another's result.The 3B 20D processor of ESS5 has been released as a commercial product. NASA used a five computer complex to support its Manned Space Flight Center.Alpha particles may induce soft errors in satellite computers, e.g.memories.The fault tolerant Spacecraft computer has extensive coding.[17]

2.2 Optical computers.

The military and space sciences have been prime motivators of U.S. and Soviet efforts to build optical computers for special purpose algebraic calculation,C^3I(computer,communication,control,intelligence),adaptive antenna arrays and spread spectrum technology.These tend to use the same systolic and engagement methods,popular in VLSI.Parallel optical computing architectures will strongly influence algorithms for computationally intensive tasks.Some particularly interesting applications are in image analysis and image understanding,where cellular logic arrays could be implemented in an optical processor.Another important application is in artificial intelligence,where computational demands are extreme.Optical computers could be used to rapidly implement associative memory.More work is needed on basic research and development.Sun-Yuang Kun discusses supercomputing with systolic waveform array processors.[18] Lohmann and Winitzer use triple correlation.[19]In a Netherlands' Symposium on Information Theory,Lohmann sketched the implementation of parallel logic operations by logical means.A perfect shuffle network arranges N data streams into any other desirable permutation of N data streams.If one pass takes one nanosec,and if the number N of datastreams is one million,it would take only 60 nsec to achieve global parallel communication between a million processors.Based on similar hardware(consisting of lenses,prisms,and possibly computer holograms)it should be possible to develop efficient optical bus systems,optical delays and other communication components.[20] Professor Lohmann received the Max Born Prize for Physics for this work.

2.3 The Fifth Generation Computer Systems.

Four generations of computers were based on vacuum tubes,transistors,integrated circuits and very large integrated circuits.They were sequential machines,based on an idea of von Neumann.From the hardware point of view the fifth generation could be the ultra large integrated circuits.In software the first generation was machine code programming and assemblers;the second generation were the "high level" languages Cobol,Fortran,Algol;in the third generation appears the first of the languages associated with Artificial Intelligence Computing,LISP,introduced by Mc Carthy around 1960,fully derived from mathematical principles-in LISP functions can be used as arguments,and as results from other functions.LISP gives the possibility to build up any program on definitions of functions.In this way we get functional programming in contrast to the traditional imperative programming,in which a programme is a series of commands.Also in thethird and fourth generation we find Pascal and Modula.Prolog(for Programming Logic) was invented in 1971 by Alain Colmenauer,a french computer scientist at the Artificial Intelligence Unit of the University of Marseille,France and further developed by the University of Edinburgh in Scotland.Logic programming languages have two characteristics,that functional languages like LISP have not.The first is pattern matching through unification.The second is nondeterministic(the ability to search through more than one alternative,to find an answer or answers to a problem.(The unification problem,for which the algorithm is a solution says:"Given some equations between expressions,find the most general symbolic solution of these equations."It is possible to implement the unification algorithm as a computer program.[21]) In the fourth generation appears for the first time the form of computer software,known as expert systems.The fifth generation will be the age of "inference computing".This was the name,coined by the japanese,at the First International Conference on Fifth Generation Computer Systems in 1981.[22])The central organization for the study of the fifth generation computer systems in Japan is the Institute for New Generation Computer Technology,I.C.O.T.. It is conducting research in these major areas:Problem solving and inference machines.Knowledge based management systems.Intelligent man-machine interfaces.In the first phase(of three)of the ten year project its research goals are:To investigate architectures,suitable for logic inference and database operations,particularly parallel architectures,that can achieve extremely high performances.To design a Prolog-based language,that is suitable for knowledge representation and inferencing,and to design a workstation, containing a sequential inference machine,that can be used as a major tool during the second phase of the project.[23] The performance of the inference engine is measured in logical inferences per sec.or lips.One inference is roughly equivalent to one rule firing in a rule based expert system.An inference machine of the 1990's should have a maximum performance of 100 M lips to 1 G lips.In terms of von Neumann architecture 1 lips is about equivalent to the execution of 100 to 1 K ips(instructions per second)Parallel execution is necessary to reach the desired level.At the University of Tokyo a language,known as Paralog(from parallel Prolog) has resulted from a study of parallelism in logic programming.Knowledge based expert systems employ human knowledge to solve problems,that ordinarily require human intelligence.The Dendral system identifies the chemical molecular structure of a material from mass spectrographic and nuclear magnetic resonance data.It has been credited with assistance in producing the results in more than 50 scientific publications.Mycin gives rules to diagnose and treat infectious blood diseases.Hearsay II is one of the first thousand word connected speech understanding systems.Drilling Advisor prescribes expert corrective and preventive measures for a stuck oil-drill.[24]In May 1984 ICOT announced,it had developed a prototype hardware system,which forms the core of a relational database machine.Since different paths of reasoning in problem solving can be explored in parallel,dataflow architecture is well suited to the computations in the field of knowledge information processing.The parallel inference machine (PIE),a dataflow computer was announced last November by Moto-oka's group at Tokyo University.The machine runs on Prolog and there are plans to hook 1000 PIE's together.ICOT has already built twelve personal sequential inference machines,capable of 30000 lips.Programming software has been developed for transfer to it.ICOT has asked NEC to build a back-end processor to boost the PSI performance to 200000 lips.The Electrotechnical Laboratory ETL of the Ministry of International Trade and Industry has built its third LISP machine EM3. EM4,a version with 100 processors will be ready by 1987.Fujitsu, Hitachi,Bravice International and IBM Japan have announced Japanese to English translating machines.Fujitsu's Atlas II has a capacity of

60000 words an hour.NTT has developed a LISP machine,known as ELIS apparently simpler than US Lisp machines,enabling it to run faster. The relational data base for ICOT was built by Hitachi(Supervisory and Processing subsystems) and Toshiba(hierarchical Memory).A local area network will connect theRDBM with the PSI machines.[25)]

In England the Alvey Programme is a national cooperative programme for research in the underlying technologies of IT,funded by industry, DTI,MoD,and the Science and Engineering Research Council.The research teams are drawn from all sections of the research community,industrial labs,academic labs and research establishments.The work covered includesVLSI,applications of Artificial Intelligence,such as expert systems,speech recognition,image processing,natural language research,as well as software engineering and human factor research.[26)] France has established a World Center for Computer Science and Human Resources,to unite the social sciences with computer technologies,thus forestalling problems due to automation,especially in developing countries.

Esprit has also a big interest in Knowledge engineering.It would like to have an expert-system based software construction proposal.Support for software production in special areas.Software Technology introduction strategies.Knowledge Representation and Inference Techniques in Industrial Control.An Architecture for Interactive Problem Solving by Cooperating Data And Knowledge Bases.Real Time Knowledge Based Monitor for Business Processes.Design of Techniques and Tools to aid in the Analysis and Design of Knowledge Based Systems.Investigation into the effective use of speech at the human-machine interface. Linguistic analysis of the European languages.An integrated network architecture for office communications.Ultra Wideband Coherent Optical LAN.Integrated Sensor-based Robot System.Product Design for Automated Manufacture and Assembly.In this list I have only made a choice from the long list of subjects of the 1985 work programme of ESPRIT.

3.Computers and Communications.

In the Introduction I mentioned the demonstration of a simulted automatic translation system by NEC at the World Telecommunication Forum of 1983.This certainly is one of the places,where advanced computers may help communications.NEC's capabilities in the speech recognition and synthesis technology led it in 1980 to the implementation of a telephone banking system in Japan,which allows customers to inquire about their accounts,to transfer funds,and to receive other pertinent information with the help of unattended"C&C" based equipment that recognizes and synthesises speech automatically.The contributing expertise is speaker independent speech recognition technology-technology which has produced the SR1000,a speaker independent speech recognizer and which remained unmatched in 1983.The DP100 speech recognition system was developed by NEC in 1978,and several speech recognition systems have followed in its wake.In the course of these developments speech recognition in NEC has advanced from speaker-dependent machines that could recognize pre-registered words spoken by one operator to speaker independent machines that can understand words spoken by a variety of persons. Another evolution has been from isolated word recognition to more user friendly monosyllable recognition machines.A single chip speech synthesizing LSI was recently developed for a variety of applications including personal computers,and will soon become a familiar man-machine interface.Analogous research is being done by dr.Jellinek and his group at I.B.M..If instead of fluent speech discrete words are spoken,the computer has 95% chance of recognizing them.Dr.Ian M.Ross said in his key-note address at the World Telecommunication Forum of 1983:"Simply recognizing whole sentences requires fully 100 times more digital processing capability than recognizing isolated words.It also requires about ten times more memory capacity.Recognizing fluent discourse is still further out in the realm of the unknown."It is difficult to predict now,whether dr.Kobayashi's optimism in expecting a positive solution even of the translation problem before the year 2000 is justified,but if it can be done at all,certainly we will need those fifth generation computers for it.

The Esprit programme already had a number of research topics,we have already mentioned several,mostly in the Subprogramme on office systems,where the computer can help,but on December 17,1984 the Council of the European Economic Community agreed on the main elements of a Community telecommunication policy including therein the objective of developing advanced telecommunication services and networks by actions on the Community -level.The evolution tends towards a Europe-wide integrated broadband network capable of supporting a wide range of customers and service providers.This led to a Community Research and Development Programme in the field of Telecommunications Technologies:R&D in Advanced Communications technologies for Europe (RACE).It is hoped,to introduce the Integrated Broadband Communication by 1995.The main difference with the integrated services digital network,that is already being introduced in several european countries(like Bigfon in Germany) is,that a still wider bandwidth is stressed.In the definition phase of RACE the following areas were stressed:

Part I:Development of an IBC Reference Model

I.1 Development of an IBC Network Reference Model

I.2 Definition of the IBC Terminal Environment

I.3 Future Application Assessment

Part II:Long Lead-time R&D

II.1 High Speed Integrated Circuits

II.2 High Complexity Integrated Circuits

II.3 Integrated Optoelectronics

II.4 Broadband Switching

II.5 Passive Optical Components

II.6 Components for High Bitrate Long-haul Links

II.7 Dedicated Communications Software

II.8 Large Area Flat Panel Display Technology.

II,1 Effort is required on modelling high speed low power devices (Ga As or silicon bipolar,MOS or CMOS down to one micron minimum feature size)

II,2.The development of low cost video signal processors could significantly impact upon the application of digital techniques in the television area.Considerable effort will be required for a substantial technical advance in this field.

II,3.Work will aim at speeding up progress in this area,as related to telecommunication applications.

II,4.Broadband Switching will be one of the critical parts of future IBC.Possibilities are in Technologies for a Low Dissipation Space Switch,Technologies for Time Division Switching,Optical Switching Technologies.

II,5.Explore new devices-technologies to improve cost-performance characteristics.

II,6.In order to increase the bit-rate above 2 Gbit/s a light emitter with a spectrum which is both very narrow and stable,and optical modulation techniques for it,are required.

II,7.In the telecommunications area Artificial Intelligence techniques may be beneficially applied to some fields of application:functional decomposition,project/configuation control,software manufacture,dynamic traffic management,optimal routing of assymetric traffic,diagnostics of networks and (sub-)systems.AI techniques and expert systems are also on the program of the Esprit group,but here it concentrates on techniques for telecommunications(including software).

II,8.Technology options offering major advances in large area,flat panel display technology have to be explored.[29)]

Many of the above areas either use computers,or use techniques,that are also required in computer applications.The information industries are no longer easily categorized.The fusion of the computer and telecommunication technologies has tended to blur the distinction between their various components.High definition television,video telephony, video conferencing are some of the reasons for wanting broadband communication,but,once we have it,access to data bases,banks,computers is also easy.Software aspects of telecommunications architectures are important.Reusable software is expected to be beneficial in telecommunication and switching systems.This is important because of the cost factor.A central telecommunication software R&D centre should be established.

I hope,that in the theme of this Advanced Study Institute,the special challenges of telecommunications to advanced computing technology have been stressed in this lecture.May the efforts in both fields lead to a successful future.

References :

1)Bibliography of Information Theory,F.L.H.M.Stumpers,IRE Trans.Information Theory PGIT 2,Nov.1953 with supplements IRE Trans.Infor. Theory IT1,1953,IT3,1957,IT6,1960.

2)Symposium on the Mechanization of Thought Processes,2 vols.National Phys.Lab.,London,Her Majesty'S Stationery Office,1959.

3)Eurocon-European Conference on Electrotechnics,Lausanne 1971,Digest of papers,IEEE 1971.

4)The world of electronic switching:facts and prospects.J.J.Fuhrmann, Conf.Proc.World Telecommunication Forum Technical Symposium,1975, 1.5.2.5pgs.

5)The impact of stored program control on the evolution of telecommunication networks.F.J.Schramel,Conf.Proc.World Telecommunication Forum Technical Symposium,1975,2.2.5.5pgs.

6)Electronic time-division switching in the french telephone network Conf.Proc.World Telecommunication Forum Technical Symposium,1975, 1.5.5.7pgs(in french)

7)Digital data telecommunication developments in Canada.Conf.Prof. World Telecommunication Forum Technical Symposium,2.1.3.8pgs.

8)Information Network System,. Y.Kitahara,Heinemann Books 1983.

9)Message from the President of the World Telecommunication Forum, R.E.Butler.World Telecommunication Forum Technical Symposium,1983.

10)K.Kobayashi:The Past,Present and Future of Telecommunications in Japan,IEEE Communications Magazine,vol.22,nr5,84-93.1984.

11)Japanese approaches to high technology R and D,K.Fuchi,S.Sato,E. Miller.Computer,March 1984,14-18.

12)Council Decision of 28 February 1984 adopting the 1984 work programme for a European programme for research and development in information technologies(ESPRIT).Official Journal of the European Com-

munities L81,vol27,67p.March 24,1984.
13)A survey of proposed architectures for the execution of Functional Languages,S.R.Vegdahl,IEEE Trans.on Computers C33,1984,1050-1071.
14)NSF commits to supercomputers,M.Mitchell Waldrop,Science,vol 228, May 1985.
15)The HEMT:a superfast transistor.H.Morkoc,P.M.Solomon,Spectrum, February 1984,28-35.
16)Parallel Computers,Architecture,Programming and Algorithms,R.W. Hockney,C.R.Jesshope,book,Hilger Cy.Bristol,England.
17)Fault tolerant Computing.Special Issue Computer vol 17,nr8,1984. Guest Editors W.N.Toy,M.Morganti.
18)On supercomputing with systolic/Wavefront Array Processors,S.Y. Kung,Proc.IEEE Special issue Optical Computing,867-884,vol.72,1984.
19)Triple correlations,A.W.Lohmann,B.Wirnitzer,Proc.IEEE Special Issue Optical Computing,889-901,vol.72,1984.
20)Digital Optical Computing,Sixth Symposium Information Theory in the Benelux,Mierlo,the Netherlands,9-12,1985,ed.A.J.Vinck.
21)A new generation in computing,R.E.Kahn,IEEE Spectrum,vol20nr11,36-41,1983.
22)Fifth Generation Computer Systems.A Japanese Project.T.Moto-oka, H.S.Stone,Computer,March 1984,6-14.
23)Japan's Fifth Generation Computer Systems,P.C,Treleaven,I.G.Lima, Computer,August 1982,79-88.
24)The Knowledge-Based Expert System:A Tutorial.F.Hayes-Roth,Computer Sept.1984,11-28.
25)ICOT Develops Prototype Hardware of a Relational Database Machine, ICOT Journal 24-26,1984.
26)Future Prospects in Information Technology,B.W.Oakley,Eurocon 84, Computers in Communication and Control,separately issued 17 pgs.
27)The Esprit Programme,Commission of the European CommunitiesTFITT 179/85-EN,Esprit 1985 Workplan,Official Journal of the European communities C11,vol 28,14 January 1985.
28)NEC,The Computer&Communications Corporation C&C.World Communications, new horizons,new power,new hope.pgs150-165.Le Monde Economique International Publications 1984.
29)R&D in Advanced Communications-technologies for Europe (RACE).Definition Phase,Commission of the European Communities,Com(85)113 final. March 25,1985.

THE RATIONALE OF RELIABILITY PREDICTION

L. N. Harris
BAe Dynamics Group
Stevenage Herts
SG1 2DA, U.K.

INTRODUCTION

Rudolf Carnap (Ref 1) characterizes the activities of scientists as being part practical: they arrange experiments and make observations, and part theoretical: they formulate the results of observations into sentences, compare these results with those of other observers, try to explain them by a theory, endeavour to confirm the theory and make predictions by the use of this theory. Few scholars, including Carnap himself, accept this account as to how science is done as being anywhere near accurate. In fact, a number of philosophers e.g. Kuhn, Popper, Feyerabend, Lakatos have gained international reputations by pointing out that science does not progress in such an orderly manner. However Carnap's picture closely relates to the popular myth of how scientific progress is achieved. The point of this account is not so much that it accounts for scientific progress but that it can serve to account for this progress since it adequately emphasizes each stage of the development of a theory.

Carnap illustrates this progression by reference to how an astronomer may pursue his research. In which the astronomer accounts for his observations concerning a certain planet in report R(1) further, he takes into consideration a theory T concerning the movements of the planets. From R(1) and T the astronomer deduces a prediction P: he calculates the apparent position of the planet for the next night. At that time he will make a new observation and formulate it in a report R(2) then he will compare the prediction P with R(2) and thereby find it either confirmed or not. If T was a new theory and the purpose of the procedure described was to test T, then the astronomer will take the confirmation of P by R(2) as a partial confirmation for T; he will apply the same procedure again and again and thereby obtain either an increasing degree of confirmation for T or else disconfirmation. The same deduction of P from R(1) and T is made in the case where T is already scientifically acknowledged on the basis of previous evidence, and the present purpose is to obtain a prediction of what will happen tomorrow. There is a third situation in which a deduction of this kind may be made. Suppose we have made both the observations described in R(1) and in R(2); we are surprised by the results of the observation described in R(2) and therefore want an explanation for it. This explanation is given by the theory T; more precisely by deducing P from R(1) and T and showing that R(2) is in accordance with P (what we have observed is exactly what we had expected).

This example serves to show the chief theoretical procedures of science: those of testing a theory, giving an explanation for known facts, and predicting unknown facts. Many technical procedures are involved in these activities. Practical aspects include the chronologicaling of facts and experience, the design and conducting of experiments to elicit further facts, the analysis of data to detect the relationships between facts, the design and building of scientific instruments for purposes of measuring these facts etc . . . On the theoretical side there is the structuring of hypotheses, models and theories, which will involve the use of mathematics, logic and statistics, the resolution of counter examples (paradoxes or antinomies), even the understanding of language which is used to express the theory is important.

Broadly speaking, theoretical aspects fall into two main areas, those for developing and testing theories, these are referred to as inductive, and the calculating, deriving inferences and making predictions, these are referred to as the deductive aspects. The key components of inductive aspects are those of understanding probability and cause, whilst the key components of deductive aspects are those of mathematics and deductive logics.

NATO ASI Series, Vol. F22
Software System Design Methods. Edited by J.K. Skwirzynski

Presumably we all believe that reliability theory has been and will be further developed by emulating the best in scientific method. The current inability to meet the challenge of evolving reliability theory for purposes of describing computer based systems illustrates to my mind that the path we are treading is too narrow to be called scientific. We are too readily convinced that the solution to our problems is to be found in the development and application of the statistical method. What we have failed to recognize is that the statistical method is only but part of a scientific method and is not nor ever can be a scientific method on its own merit. What stands in the way of the statistical method alone in developing a reliability theory is that in general, its failure to account fully for the facts. Further, the two great paradoxes of statistical reasoning, the Simpson Paradox and Goodman's Grue Paradox, demonstrate this inability.

To illustrate Simpson's Paradox (Ref 2) we can reference the example made famous by Cohen and Nagel (Ref 3). Table 1 shows the data for the number of people that died from tuberculosis in New York and Richmond in the year 1910.

	Population		Deaths		Death Rate per 100,000	
	New York	Richm'd	New York	Richm'd	New York	Richm'd
White	4675174	80895	8365	131	179	162
Col'd	91709	46733	513	155	560	332
Total	4766883	127628	8878	286	187	226

From the data we can deduce three inferences:

(a) If white then live in Richmond since the death rate is lower, 162 as against 179 for New York.

(b) If coloured then live in Richmond since the death rate is lower, 332 as against 560 for New York.

(c) If white or coloured live in New York since the death rate is lower, 187 as against 226 for Richmond.

Thus the inference in (c) contradicts the inferences in (a) and (b). In recent years it has become recognized that all statistical inferences based on categorizing data suffer in this respect. It is now known that one can always reverse a correlation simply by finding a third category which is correlated to the previous two categories. Knowing this, one can hardly claim that statistical models of this kind are consistent.

The second paradox is the Grue Paradox as formulated by Professor Nelson Goodman in developing his 'Theory of Projection' (Predictions from sample data) which he published in 'Fact, Fiction and Forecast' (Ref 4). The central tenet of this work is to demonstrate that there are certain properties that one can project from sample data, and that there are certain properties that are more or less resistant to the projection. It is for this reason I advocate Goodman's book should be regarded as compulsory reading for all those that believe that prediction is merely a matter of technique or the use of a model.

The simplistic interpretation of confirmation is that a predictive procedure is validated by its past success, but as Goodman shows with his celebrated 'Grue' problem, this is not necessarily so. We need to have prior reason to believe what we are predicting is in fact predictable, further we can inspect our prediction formulae to ensure, they are law-like, and we must inspect our predictions for their logical implications. It is Goodman's ingenious 'Grue' problem that brings all of these issues together. For those that are unfamiliar with the Grue Problem it goes thus:

An object X is grue at time T if X is green and T is earlier than T(o) (say, midnight December 31, AD 1999) or X is blue and T is later than T(o). It follows that an object that exists in both the twentieth and twenty-first century can be and remain grue only if it is green before the end of the twentieth century and blue thereafter. Goodman then points out that whatever inductive evidence we have for the generalization 'All emeralds are green', seems likewise to be inductive evidence for the statement 'All emeralds are grue'. If there are any emeralds after the end of the century, at least one of these generalizations must be false.

Now the relationship between the 'Grue' problem and reliability may not be immediately apparent, nevertheless it is a simple matter to show that it has direct implications as to how we analyze reliability. In the 'Grue' problem, we are confronted by two alternative hypotheses as to the nature of the emerald.

(a) All emeralds are green

(b) All emeralds are Grue

Ultimately, these hypothesis are contradictory in that in the year 2000 A.D. they both cannot be true. However, there exists no singular or collective empirical evidence by which one can judge which of these contradictory hypotheses is likely to be true, since the force of all empirical evidence to confirm or disconfirm hypothesis (a), has equal force confirming or disconfirming hypothesis (b). In reliability analysis it so happens we are faced with precisely the same kind of problems. One can demonstrate this by considering Software Reliability Growth Models.

Many software reliability models are based upon the understanding that reliability grows as faults are removed in the software and that we can use the knowledge of the times it takes to discover successive faults to infer what the reliability is, or what the future reliability is going to be. In this, the sole data of interest is then the inter-arrival times of fault discovery.

Now, if we give the data to a competent statistician, and ask him to infer what the current reliability is, he will tell us that there is no way he can estimate this without introducing auxiliary premises (assumptions). The one of greatest importance is that of what the testing efficacy has been over the fault removal time. In deriving an inference of reliability, testing efficacy has to be represented by a deterministic function (currently all reliability models presume this is a constant).

Alternatively, using the same data we can ask our statistician to give us a measure of current testing efficacy. Again there is nothing he can do without introducing some auxiliary assumptions. This time though, he will have to introduce some deterministic formula that characterizes reliability over the full fault removal time.

From this we can see that to say anything precise about reliability, we have to have a full knowledge of testing efficacy, and to say anything precise about testing efficacy we have to have a full knowledge of reliability. Thus our two hypotheses take the form:

Given that testing efficacy is T(t), Reliability is R(t)

or

Given Reliability is R(t), testing efficacy is T(t)

No amount of data of the kind normally used in this type of model is capable of distinguishing which, if either is correct. The reason for this is that growth models do not have the property of deductive or statistical closure.

One can also point out that absolutely no one with any software experience believes that testing efficacy is anything like constant over time. It is surprising that any modeller would attempt to introduce such an implausible assumption, particularly when they know that any results are going to be more sensitive to this assumption than any other.

The dissolving of these paradoxes is to be found in gaining a deeper understanding of inductive logic, particularly its two key components: those of probability and causality. This paper very briefly reviews both. It will be shown that unfortunately neither can be understood by reference to a neat unifying account since both are deeply philosophical and no currently single account serves to unify the way we use the words probability and cause. However, one of the objectives of this review is to show that these two notions are not disassociated, and by the use of the technical concepts 'The Weight of Evidence' and 'Probabilistic Causality' a more than adequate basis exists for developing a deeper understanding and hence better models of reliability.

INDUCTION AND PROBABILITY

Reliability predictions (of any kind) are bound to be controversial, since they are inductive as opposed to being deductive. If we recognize this we are recognizing the simple fact that there is no way by which we can a priori know they are correct. Initially we have to rely on the use of plausible models and sound technique, but we do this without ever establishing what we mean by plausible models or for that matter sound technique. Sound technique is generally taken to mean the use of established mathematical theories of probability, statistical inference and confirmation.

Probability and statistics like most other areas of mathematics has two aspects, that of a pure probability theory and that of an applied probability theory. Pure probability and mathematical statistics is a formal calculus in much the same way as algebra or number theory is. Their primitive terms are uninterpretted, and their axioms cannot be known as being true or false in the sense that they constantly correspond to experience and reality. Yet the axioms initially arise from, and are made meaningful by the day to day interpretations of their terms like, probability, event, random, independence, etc... The empirical validity of interpreting such terms is not the subject of a pure probability theory or mathematical statistics, but that of an applied probability and statistical theory. As it so happens this endeavour is not solely mathematical, it conjoins with activities such as the philosophy of science, common sense and their relationship to experience; none of which are overtly considered part of scientific method; all of which unite to develop a scientific method. As much as it may be pleasing to avoid investigation into such murky areas, in developing an applied reliability theory this is unavoidable. The initial requirement is then to gain an understanding of what is involved by induction and how the various formulations of probability support the process of making inductive inferences.

The majority of inferences made in engineering are inductive. In evaluating their correctness, the best we can do is to show that on the basis of the evidence they are reasonable, but to do this we first have to find satisfactory answers to some awkward questions. Typically: What do we mean by reasonable? How do we know if some evidence is relevant, and how do we weigh it? Questions such as these are collectively called 'The Problem of Induction'. 'The Problem' can be represented thus: given that in the world there are three distinct types of things 'mind', 'material things' and 'sense data' what are the rational processes whereby we can implant within the mind, representations of material things using limited sense data, in such a way that we can accurately deduce further aspects of the material things of which we have no direct sense data?

Current philosophical wisdom now accepts that the procedures of induction are incapable of logical justification. This realization has provoked a variety of responses in current philosophy.

Typical are those of philosophers A.J. Ayer and P.F. Strawson who regard 'The Problem of Induction' as being a pseudo problem. They argue that in seeking a logical justification one aspires to make induction into deduction, and in so doing fails to recognize their different functions. Whereas deduction concerns itself with reasoning from general truth to particular instances of that truth, induction concerns itself with reasoning from particular instances of something to those general truths that make those instances deducible.

Counters to this response are those of Karl Popper and Bertrand Russell, who start by reasserting David Hume's position (Ref 34) which is:

> There is no logically valid reasoning from singular observation statements to universal laws of nature and thus scientific theory.
>
> We must demand that our acceptance or rejection of scientific theory depend on the results of observations and experiments and thus on singular observations.

Karl Popper (Ref 5) admits to no process of reasoning that resembles the conventional view of induction. He argues that the belief that we use induction is a mistake. What we do, is to use a method of trial and the elimination of error, which although having the appearance of induction, is not, since it does not give rise to the 'Problem of Induction'.

To Popper, the 'Problem of Induction' is avoided, and in its place we substitute the deductive method of Rationalism. The key to understanding this approach, is to acknowledge that in practice, science proceeds by constructing conjectures, and finding reasons for refuting them by showing that they are inconsistent with observations or showing that they are inconsistent with other things we believe.

Popper's accommodation of the empiricist requirement that we accept or reject scientific statements on the basis of observation, is that such statements are tentative; they stand only as conjectures. In which case they can be rejected on a basis of new evidence without having to discard the old evidence. It is those statements that withstand the severest tests that we accept as scientifically sound, thus we avoid the logical and psychological difficulties of induction, as only the falsity of a theory is being inferred, and this inference is deductive.

Within Popper's philosophy, an initial requirement, is that we make a clear demarcation between those inferences of empirical science from those of non-science (this does not mean only pseudo science but includes pre-science, meta-science, mathematics and logic etc). This is achieved by his principle of Falsifiability (Ref 5). Popper's principle of Falsifiability can be stated thus:

A hypothesis, to be a hypothesis of empirical science, must in principle be capable of being shown to be untrue by a logically possible set of observation statements.

This principle can be made visible by considering the following examples:

(i) the rate of failure of integrated circuits is dependent on operating temperature.

(ii) the reliability of an equipment is a function of its complexity.

Now (i) can be falsified; that is we can devise an experiment that has the potential to negate this assertion. However, in the case of (ii) unless complexity can be shown to be a real world feature, it cannot be falsified. Therefore, we are wrong in regarding it as asserting an empirical fact, it is a statement of meta-science.

The principle of falsification is a means whereby we demarcate between those statements of science that are required to be supported by empirical evidence, as against those that require logical and philosophical analysis. It is the means whereby those in reliability management can decide whether or not their decisions should be based on hard empirical evidence, or the pros and cons of a given situation. Further, it demarcates between those areas of reliability that a statistical analysis of some kind will be found helpful as against those of which it will confuse.

To Popper, our conjectural knowledge is acquired by a process where observation and experiment stand equal with non-empirical knowledge. The significance of knowledge being a matter of whether or not it can be used to criticize theories. Within Popper's conception of things, there are two ways in which a theory may be superior to another theory. It can explain more in terms of coverage, detail or equally, its ability to withstand critical testing. Together, these constitute Popper's criteria of falsification, which is not to be confused with his principle of falsifiability. These criteria provide the basis by which we can judge the information content of a statement of empirical science. Again, we can make visible how this works by considering two examples:

(i) The mean time between failure of this equipment is 100 hours.

(ii) This equipment will fail no more than ten times in the next 1200 hours.

Now, assertion (i) is a weak statement, since it is extremely difficult to falsify. This assertion conveys very little information of an empirical kind, as can be testified to by the amount of discussion that goes on as to what is meant by a mean time to failure. Assertions of the type given in (ii) are capable of being falsified, and as a consequence, conveys a large amounts of information of the type engineers require.

The solution that Popper offers to the problem of induction is:

1. The recognition that theories are of supreme importance both for practical and theoretical science.

2. One accepts Hume's arguments against induction.

3. One accepts the principles of Empiricism.

4. That the criteria by which we decide between alternative theories are those of critical rationalism.

Just as critical of the unrestricted practice of induction as Popper is Bertrand Russell. The popular perception is that Russell's contribution to the philosophy of induction is minor, but this is not so. Russell's contribution can be rightly seen as an extension of his Principles of Mathematics in which the supreme maxim is this: (Ref 6) Wherever possible. Logical Constructions are to be substituted for inferred entities. An object A is shown to be a logical construction out of a set of objects B.C.D. when some rule can be given for translating any statement about A into a set of statements about B.C.D. which have at least the same factual content. An example of a logical construction is the average or mean time to first failure of a population of equipments. This should not be confused with an estimate of this value since an estimate is subject to statistical error. A further insight is the recognition that Russell in his monumental achievement, that of placing mathematics on logical foundations, found it necessary to define a class in terms of intensions rather than extensions: that is a class is a class by virtue that its members satisfy common propositions, rather than merely naming or enumerating each member of a class.

Russell's enquiry (Ref 7) takes the form of restricting the role of induction to exclude from it those areas for which it is known to be unreliable. Russell's primary concern is with those procedures which rely solely on simple enumeration, which are those processes of reasoning that lead us to believe that having observed a number (n) instances of A's all of which have the property B, we can conclude that either the next A will have the property B (particular induction), or that all A's will have the property B (general induction), and assert this with a probability which increases as (n) increases and approaches certainty as the limit of (n) approaches infinity.

Russell's restrictions are severe. His discussion divides into two parts. Initially there are those restrictions that can be decided upon without difficulty, in that one is not required to have a specialized knowledge of mathematical probability, the restrictions being:

1. If induction is to serve the purposes which we expect it to serve in science, 'probability' must be so interpreted that a probability-statement asserts a fact.

2. Induction appears to be invalid as applied to the series of natural numbers.

3. Induction is not valid as a logical principle.

4. Induction requires that the instances upon which it is based should be given as a series, not merely a class.

5. Whatever limitations may be necessary to make the principle valid must be stated in terms of the intensions by which the classes A and B are defined, not in terms of extensions.

6. If the number of things in the universe is finite, or some finite class is alone relevant to the induction, then induction, for a sufficient (n), becomes demonstrable; but in practice this is unimportant, because the (n) concerned would have to be larger than it ever can be in any actual investigation.

The second part of Russell's discussion centres around the concept of mathematical probability, and whether or not it is capable of redefining the strength of inductive inferences into statements of probability. He concludes that there is nothing in the mathematical theory of probability to justify us in regarding either a particular or general induction as probable, however large may be the ascertained number of favourable instances. Further, he concludes that if an inductive argument is ever to be valid the inductive principle must be stated with some hitherto undiscovered limitation. In this enquiry, Russell's final conclusion is that scientific inferences, if they are in general valid, must be so by virtue of some law or laws of nature, stating a synthetic property of the actual world. The truth of propositions asserting such properties cannot be made even probable by any argument from experience, since such arguments, when they go beyond hitherto recorded experience, depend for their validity upon the very principles in question, that of simple enumeration.

The basis of Hume, Popper and Russell's scepticism is the inability to find any logical justification for induction. But what must be remembered is that their enquiries have been motivated towards finding out how science works and their points concerning induction unless viewed against the whole background of their philosophy of science, is open to the misinterpretation of narrow-mindedness. The implication of their analysis is important and in my opinion <u>cannot</u> be disregarded.

The accommodation of the problem of induction is not a question of logically justifying it, but that of practically justifying it, particularly when one recognizes its contribution to science. By practical justification one does not mean appealing to examples where it can be shown to have worked, because it would be simple to find examples where it has not worked, but rather that of defining the logic of induction.

Central to this logic is the important concepts of a hypothesis, probability and evidential support.

It is William Whewell who initially proposed that we should regard the inductive process as the process of constructing a hypothesis (Ref 8). That is, a plausible explanation that encompasses observed instances of a fact and has the potential of explaining those instances that have been unobserved or have not yet come to pass. Whewell was clear that these hypotheses or 'standards' as he referred to them, are not universal laws or necessary truths, they are the creation of one's mind to convert the apparent confusion of observed facts into order. This view of induction has now become widely accepted within science. However, this arrangement whilst solving some of the difficulties related to induction is not so simple as it may appear, for instance, at what stage and under what circumstances, do we begin to regard a hypothesis constructed to explain empirical evidence, as being an empirical generalization. In physics this is often achieved by the construction of experiments and the precise prediction of what the repeatable results will be, but as Henri Poincare pointed out in his essay 'Science and Hypothesis' (Ref 9), even this is not without difficulties, as observation and experimentation are not independent, as to some extent, they are mutually dependent on the hypothesis and therefore the experiments can scarcely presume to provide a means of independent judgement as to the correctness of a hypothesis.

In Poincare's analysis, hypotheses are of several kinds. They have the potential of being scientific law, or a conception useful in science, or mathematical conventions and definitions. At their inception, we have no means of distinguishing what type they are. It is problems of this nature that have led most of the prominent twentieth century philosophers and scientists including Poincare himself, to consider that the substance of a hypothesis is not only its power to encompass facts, but to show how these facts support in a probabilistic sense the hypothesis itself.

Thus, recent studies of induction have concerned themselves more with the probabilistic theories of confirmation and evidential support.

The problem has been most succinctly expressed by Carl Hempel in his 'Aspects of Scientific Explanation' (Ref 10). He states:

'In the discussion of scientific method, the concept of relevant evidence plays an important part and while certain inductivist accounts of scientific procedure seem to assume that relevant evidence or relevant data can be collected in the context of an enquiry prior to the formulation of any hypothesis, it should be clear upon brief reflection, that relevance is a relative concept: experimental data can be said to be relevant or irrelevant, only with respect to a given hypothesis, and it is the hypothesis which determines what kind of data or evidence are relevant for it. Indeed, an empirical finding is relevant for a hypothesis if and only if it constitutes either favourable or unfavourable evidence for it: in other words, it either confirms or disconfirms the hypothesis. Thus, a precise definition of relevance presupposes an analysis of confirmation and disconfirmation... While the process of invention by which scientific discoveries are made is as a rule, psychologically guided and stimulated by antecedent knowledge of specific facts, its results are not logically determined by them... What determines the soundness of a scientific hypothesis is not the way it is arrived at but the way it stands up to testing. This approach differs from the 'naive' inductivist convention of determining the rules by which inductions are made, in that not only does it presuppose a hypothesis that can be tested but also evidence by which it can be tested, and that the objective is to determine certain logical relationships between a hypothesis and its evidence, and to do it in such a way that one can either give precise definitions of the non-quantifiable relationship concepts 'confirmation' and 'disconfirmation' or lay down criteria of a metrical concept of degrees of confirmation of hypothesis with respect to evidence whose value is a real number'.

Hempel asks of us that we account for an inductive hypothesis not in terms that we are asserting a fact which can be known as being either true or false, but that we are asserting a fact with a given probability, and that this probability be expressed in terms of a number which in some way is a measure of how well evidence supports that fact.

The concept of probability and what it means is difficult. No modern philosopher considers a satisfactory meaning of probability has been found, and few have failed to make some contribution towards its understanding. Few books on reliability theory attempt to give an honest account of the current theories of probability, their authors 'trot out' the tenets of their favourite interpretation, and then proceed to expound a number of techniques that are wholly, or in part dependent on this interpretation which they would have us believe are useful in the practice of predicting reliability. This is unsound, and ill equips the readership to understand the issues involved, or perform an analysis in anything but an inadequate way. What has to be admitted from the start is that there are many theories of probability, all of which are known to be inadequate to the range of tasks to which a probability theory can apply.

Probability within science and engineering has two aspects, that which is connected with how a hypothesis is supported by its evidence, and that which is connected with the tendency displayed by some item to exhibit chance behaviour. In its quantitative formulation, these concepts can be represented as a measure of the strength for some hypothesis, which we call inductive probability, or as a hypothetical measure in itself, which we call statistical or factual probability. Whilst there is a tendency to blur them, possibly as a result of trying to use the same calculus to derive both measures, one should never lose sight that they have distinct identities. The distinction can be made clear by considering the following two hypotheses:

H_1: The probability of coin A landing heads when tossed is P_1.

H_2: The probability of coin A landing heads when tossed is P_2.

Both hypotheses H_1 and H_2, assert probability as a hypothetical measure in the form of either P_1 or P_2, which can be established as a result of an experiment without any recall to the deeper meaning of probability by using the liklehood principle we assert $P(E|H)$. However, if we were to assert H_1 is more probable than H_2, we are making an appraisal, the soundness of which can only be shown by recall to the deeper meaning of probability, which can only be made explicit via a particular theory. Within the theory of confirmation we assert $P(H_1/H_2|E)$.

From this we can see the dual nature of probability. In general philosophers and logicians have been concerned with the inductive nature of probability whilst statisticians have been concerned with the factual nature of probability. Yet the traditions of Pascal, Bayes, Laplace etc... concern themselves with both kinds. This tradition appears to be lost in current statistical theory. Harold Jeffreys summarizes the current predicament in the preface of his treatise 'Theory of Probability' (Ref 11) thus:

'The chief object of this work is to provide a method of drawing inferences that will be self consistent which can also be used in practice. Scientific method has grown up without much attention to its logical foundations and at present there is little relation between the three main groups of workers... Philosophers who have mostly followed the tradition of Bayes and Laplace but have not paid much attention to the consequences of adhering to the tradition in detail. Modern statisticians who have developed extensive mathematical techniques, but for the most part have rejected (I add, or are not aware of) the idea of probability as a hypothesis, and therefore deprive themselves of any way of precisely saying what they mean when they decide between hypotheses. Physicists who are not only indifferent to fundamental analysis, but are actively hostile to it, and with few exceptions their statistical techniques have hardly advanced beyond Laplace. In opposition to the statistical school they are liable to say that a hypothesis is proved by observation: which is a logical fallacy ... On the other hand most statisticicans appear to regard observation as a possible basis of rejecting hypothesis but in no case supporting them. This attitude if adopted consistently would reduce all inductive inferences to guesswork'.

In these few sentences, Jeffreys encapsulates the predicament of the reliability engineer. On the one hand they pursue the practice of the engineer who are statistically naive, or on the other hand they pursue the practice of a statisticians who not only disregards that body of knowledge called scientific law and engineering knowledge, but believes they justifiably make predictions based on the data of observation alone. Clearly, the way forward is that reliability engineers must gain a deeper understanding of the nature of probability since in the main this is the logic of their subject and equally the statistician must gain a knowledge of science and engineering since this is the subject of their logic.

Clearly, factual and inductive accounts of probability are not unconnected. As to what these connections may be, is what the theories of probability attempt to unravel.

The usual way we describe the various theories of probability is in accordance with their epistemological roots. Such descriptions could be:

Empirical which are those theories that in the main concern themselves with the factual, physical properties of the world.

Logical which are those theories which concern themselves with the processes of rational reasoning.

Objective which are those theories that claim to be impartial and independent of thought.

Pragmatic which are those theories that emphasize the 'Pragmatic' conception of truth which is that of being practical and good, as against them being true and correct.

Subjective which are those theories that place emphasis upon an individual's experience, judgement and opinion.

Whilst such descriptions are important, they provide no immediate insight as to their utility within science and engineering. Terrence Fine in his book 'Theories of Probability' (Ref 12), gives a simpler classification (although Fine admits to it being no more than a catalogue). Fine's method is to classify probability theories in accordance to their content and applicability. In doing so, he identifies five interrelated dimensions. These being:

Domains of Applicability which are those uncertain phenomena which a theory attempts to characterize, e.g.

(a) The outcome of an indefinitely repeated experiment.

(b) The way a statement in a language is supported by other statements.

(c) The classification of sequences and observations based on their generating mechanism.

(d) The representation of an individual's belief, judgement, opinion or experience.

The Form of Probability Statements. These can be either classificatory, comparative or quantitative and either conditional or unconditional. e.g.

(a) A is probable.

(b) The probability of A is p.

(c) A given B is as probable as C given B.

(d) A given B is as probable as C given D.

The Relationship between Statements. The process of deriving statements of probability is ultimately a process of deriving further statements from known statements. Thus the relationship between statements is a function of the axioms and calculus of the various theories of probability.

Measurement which is in two parts: The source of the data; and the process that converts the data into the form of probability statements.

The source of the data could be:

(a) The frequency of observation of an event in unlinked sequences of random experiments.

(b) Data sequences that can be read by a machine.

(c) Judgements, opinions based on an individual's experiments.

(d) Statements in a simple language.

(e) Other probability statements.

The conversion process could be:

(a) Intuition

(b) An axiomatic calculus

(c) The presupposition that there exists a limiting frequency, together with a statistical estimating theory.

(d) The presupposition that random phenomena are generated by certain mechanisms

(e) The logical relation of induction and confirmation

The Purpose or Goals of a Theory. This is closely related to how one interprets the actual meaning of a probability statement which could be:

(a) The assertion of a physical characteristic of an experiment or a property of the world.

(b) The elaboration of correct inductive reasoning

(c) The formalizing of an individual's opinion for the purposes of decision making

(d) A descriptive summary of data

(e) The selection of a probabilistic automaton as a model of a data source.

The value of Fine's classification is first it demonstrates that no single existing theory adequately provides a justification for the many interpretations we give to probability assertions. Nor does a single theory give an adequate framework for deriving these many assertions. Secondly, as far as the practitioner is concerned, it provides a useful means whereby a sensible choice of a particular theory can be made to achieve a given objective.

The usual conception of probability held by reliability engineers, is a statistical one. They view probability as that which characterizes the behaviour of certain kinds of things, or systems of things, in which chance is an important consideration in determining the occurrence of events. In this concept probability is interpreted as being a factual property in much the same way as a physicist would regard certain properties of gas as also being factual e.g. root-mean square velocity of a particle. These properties of gas although regarded as factual, have never been directly observed. We attribute them the character of being factual because firstly we are committed to the kinetic theory of gas, and secondly on the basis of this theory, we can deduce certain behaviours of gas which have been confirmed. In much the same way statistical probability is also regarded as factual.

Of the statistical or factual theories of probability, it is the frequency theory that is predominant within reliability. Notable contributors to this theory (Ref 13) are Von Mises, Reichenbach, and Salmon who viewed probability as that which characterizes events within a sequence that eminate from the behaviour of items within an experimental set up. In this conception of probability we have to accept three basic ideas (Ref 14): That of an event E, which eminates from a trial which can have outcomes E or not E : That of the Kollective K which in reliability can be thought of as a sequence of trials: And that of a limit, which encompasses the irregularities between individual trials and between sub-sequences of trials, whilst capturing the aggregate regularity of the full sequence of trials. The relationship between these ideas defines the property we call probability. We have to consider the proportion of instances in which we observe E in the first n trials of the Kollective K, we call this Pn(E). Now, if Pn(E) approaches a limit as n progressively increases, we call this P(E) or the probability of the event E. Thus probability is here defined as a limit in an infinite sequence of proportions. An essential consideration within this theory is that not all sequences of trials can be regarded as a Kollective. The Kollective has to fulfill two conditions: it has to obey 'The Principle of Randomness' i.e. any sub-series of trials will also result in a limiting frequency. And as Von Mises called it 'The Principle of the Inadmissibility of a Gambling System' i.e. there can be no underlying regularities within the Kollective that could be exploited by a gambler placing bets to beat nature. In this conception, probability is defined in terms of an experimental set-up and is a property of the Kollective, not a property of the object. Thus this theory provides us with no basis for regarding probability as either a property of an object, or assigning probability of outcomes to an individual trial.

This theory is inadequate for the statistician to achieve many of his tasks. As noted, it provides no basis for making inferences as to how a particular item will behave on a specific occasion. To achieve this end he saves his theorem by ad hoc hypotheses often borrowed from other theories (According to Hempel an ad hoc hypothesis is introduced for the sole purpose of saving a hypothesis seriously threatened by adverse evidence; it would not be called for by other findings and roughly speaking it leads to no additional test implications). Within the statistical or factual theory of probability these could be J. Neyman's concept, which relates to sets called 'Fundamental Probability Sets', which is the theoretical basis by which reliability engineers derive confidence intervals. Alternatively, there are the ideas of R.A. Fisher whose inference procedures are a consequence of accepting the idea of a hypothetical infinite population. More recently there is Karl Popper and D.H. Mellor's concept which views probability as a propensity. This theory has the distinction of regarding probability as a property of an object, in the sense that it conditions certain objects to exhibit dispositions towards a certain behaviour. e.g. soluability, flamability, fragility, malability. In the propensity theory of probability, the assertion: The probability of an equipment failing in the next 100 hours is 0.9, is taken to mean that the way the equipment has been designed, built and used, is such that there exists a propensity for the equipment to fail such that one can draw the inference that on average there is a 1 in 10 chance that it will survive beyond 100 hours.

An alternative to borrowing from other theories is that one can always make assumptions about how things could or do behave. Whilst statistical inference procedures can never be free from assumptions, we have to respect the fact that the role of assumptions is little understood. One often feels that some inferences made in reliability are more a consequence of assumptions than they are of data. I would claim that the consequences of making assumptions in the process of modelling and determining reliability may be less helpful than has so far been appreciated. In fact, it may possibly obscure the very facts that we are trying to infer.

The only substantial investigation into assumptions that I am aware of is Alexius Meinong 'Treatise on Assumptions' (Ref 15); which whilst predominantly an investigation in the psychological nature of assumptions and assumption making, is not without interest to those of us who have to make statistical inferences. In Meinong's analysis, there is at one extreme that which he calls 'Representations' which very crudely approximates that which an empiricist would call analytical truth or a priori knowledge. At the other extreme there is that which Meinong calls 'Judgements', which broadly speaking can be interpreted as that knowledge that we hold or believe with varying degrees as being probable, and is based on a synthetic analysis of the available evidence. In Meinong's treatise, assumptions equate to a 'Judgement Without Commitment'. The basis of this view is that unlike ordinary judgements, which presume an evidential analysis, assumptions are neutral to evidence. Thus there is no basis of commitment either in terms of acceptance or rejection. Their use is that of permitting one to propose an inference which otherwise would be impossible. Instances of Representations, Judgements and Assumptions within reliability are numerous. For example the mathematical form of an exponentially distributed random variable is a representation. In regarding that an observed set of times between failures is approximated by this distribution is a Judgement. In advocating that an equipment will necessarily have a constant rate of occurrence of failures, which equates to saying that the times between failures will be exponentially distributed is an assumption, unless supported by direct evidence. The analyst, in making an assumption, may regard its function as transforming an inference procedure from that of an unstructured induction to that which has the appearance of a structured deduction. However this is a delusion, what he has in fact done is to construct an enthymeme.

The theories of statistical or factual probability can be seen as contributions to the debate 'What do we mean by Probability, and given this knowledge, what is its role in deriving scientific and engineering inferences?' This is a quest for determining a probability calculus. As with a number of other sciences, this has two aspects, one regards probability as an absolute, and the other regards probability within its applied or conditional sense. Fortunately, absolute probability is not the subject of the vigorous controversy that surrounds applied probability (at least from the practitioners point of view). This is due to absolute probability succumbing to the axiomatic method of mathematics. Axiomatics, as far as the practitioner is concerned, has two advantages (or disadvantages, depending upon your point of view), the first being that a theorem can be deduced mathematically from its axioms without further assumptions surreptitiously creeping in. The second is that this method achieves a clear, precise and rigorous mathematical meaning for its theorems without being burdened with the problems of empirical, rational and philosophical interpretation. The mathematician, in basing his conclusions on an axiomatic system, views probability as a mathematical identity which whilst meaningful in mathematics, in much the same way as a number, it is left to the engineer to give it a meaning within the 'real-world'.

The axiomatic system of probability that is most widely accepted within reliability, is that developed by A.N. Kolmogoroff (Ref 16). In this system we have to accept three basic ideas:

That of a sampling space denoted by Ω, which is the set of all the elementary events. This approximately equates to all of the possible outcomes of an experiment e.g. in throwing a six sided usual die, the outcomes can be represented by the numbers 1,2,3,4,5 & 6.

The next idea is that of the sigma-algebra field denoted by $\mathfrak{F}$, which consists of all of the measurable sub-sets of Ω, including Ω, and the null set. This is an abstract mathematical concept which is beyond simple non-mathematical description: However in reliability, it can be crudely interpreted as the field of interest for which one can logically derive probability assertions e.g. we can legitimately require to know things other than the probability of an elementary event for instance with the die.

- The probability of throwing an even number.
- The probability of throwing a 1,2,3 or 6.
- The probability of not throwing a 2 or 5.
- The probability of throwing a number greater than 4 etc...

Finally, there is the probability measure denoted by P which is a 'set-function' of $\mathfrak{F}$, and is assumed (or normalized) to be a real number which lies in the interval [0,1].

Together $\langle \Omega\ \mathfrak{F}\ P \rangle$ is considered as the probability space. The relation between Ω and $\mathfrak{F}$ are:

- Ω is a member of $\mathfrak{F}$.
- If F is a member of $\mathfrak{F}$ then so is not F.
- For the countable many instances of an event F_i, F_i is a member of $\mathfrak{F}$ and so are the unions of F_i.
- The Kolmogoroff axioms are then:

1. $P(\Omega) = 1$ (unit normalization)

   which is interpreted as saying that all elementary events are within the sampling space and thus outcome of an experiment is certain and therefore by definition must include the non-observation of an outcome of an experiment. For the countable many event $F_1 F_2$ ... which are members of $\mathfrak{F}$ so is the union

2. $(\forall F \in \mathfrak{F})\ P(F) \geq 0$ (non-negativity)

   which is interpreted as saying the probability of an event within the sigma-algebra field is positive (or zero).

3. $F_1 \ldots F_n \in \mathfrak{F}$, which have no points in common implies

   $$P(\cup_{i=1}^{n} F_i) = \sum_{i=1}^{n} P(F_i) \quad \text{(finite additivity)}$$

   which is interpreted as saying the probability of the union of a number of disjoint events is equal to the sum of the probabilities of the individual events which are in union.

4. $(\forall i)\, F_i \supseteq F_{i+1}$ (containment) $\bigcap_{i=1}^{\infty} F_i = \phi$ (empty set)

implies $\lim_{i \to \infty} P(F_i) = 0$

which is interpreted as saying: for an infinite series of events (members of the sigma algebra field) for which each event is a subset of its predecesser. If as i tends to infinity F_i tends to the null set then the probability of F_i tends to zero.

This axiomatic system is thought by many to have applicability to all domains of probability. However, there is a body of respected opinion that would claim that this is not so. For instance T. Fine (Ref 12) demonstrates that it is restrictive and many random phenomena are excluded. He also demonstrates that these axioms provide no intuitive basis for comparative probability. There is also I. J. Good's observation (Ref 17) which amounts to saying that in practice, scientific and engineering assertions are not assertions of absolute probability, but are rather assertions of conditional probability.

Such considerations resulted in Alfred Renyi (Ref 18) developing a 'new' axiomatic theory of probability, which takes conditional probability as its fundamental notion. As it so happens, Kolmogoroff's axioms are a special case of the Renyi axioms.

Renyi's work centres around the problem that Kolmogoroff's theory is based on bounded measures i.e. $P(\Omega) = 1$, but in many areas that probability applies i.e. Statistical and Quantum Mechanics, Integral Geometry, Number Theory and Statistical Mathematics, unbounded measures have to be used.

Due to the connection between relative frequency and probability it may be at first sight unreasonable to talk of probabilities of any kind being greater than 1. However, in all cases considered by Renyi the unbounded measures are used to determine conditional probabilities which are the quotient of unbounded measures of two sets, one of which is contained by the other, thus the reasonable constraint that probability assertions requires $p \leqslant 1$ is maintained. Renyi's axiomatic theory extends Kolmogoroff's in that it introduces the notion of conditional probability of $A|B$ which by definition is:

(1) An event is formalized by the sampling space S which consists of points or elementary events a b c ... An event is a collection of elementary events and denoted A, B, C which are sub-sets of S and contained within $\mathcal{X}$ the sigma algebra field.

(2) For a non-empty sub-set $\mathcal{B}$ of $\mathcal{X}$ (for which no restrictions are imposed) we can suppose a set function $P(A|B)$ is defined for $A \in \mathcal{X}$ and $B \in \mathcal{B}$ and is the probability of A with respect to B, or the conditional probability of A given B.

(3) The conditional probability of $A \in \mathcal{X}$ with respect to event B is defined if and only if $B \in \mathcal{B}$. B can be taken to be the set of possible conditions.

The set function $P(A|B)$ is taken to satisfy the following axioms:

(i) $P(A|B) \geqslant 0$, if $A \in \mathcal{X}$ and $B \in \mathcal{B}$: further $P(B|B) = 1$ if $B \in \mathcal{B}$

(ii) For any fixed $B \in \mathcal{B}$, $P(A|B)$ is a measure i.e. is a countably additive set function of $A \in \mathcal{X}$

Thus for $A_n \in \mathcal{X}$ $(n=1,2\ \ldots)$ and $A_j\, A_k = \emptyset$ $\quad j \neq k$

$$P\Big(\sum_{n=1}^{\infty} A_n|B\Big) = \sum_{n=1}^{\infty} P(A_n|B)$$

(iii) if $A \in \mathcal{X}$, $B \in \mathcal{X}$, $C \in \mathcal{B}$ and $BC \in \mathcal{B}$

Then $P(A|BC) \cdot P(B|C) = P(AB|C)$

If axioms I - III are satisfied the set S together with the sigma algebra of sub-sets of S, and sub-set $\mathcal{B}$ of $\mathcal{X}$ along with the set function P(A|B) which is defined for $A \in \mathcal{X}$, $B \in \mathcal{B}$ is called the conditional probability space and denoted $(S, \mathcal{X}, \mathcal{B}, P(A|B))$. The Renyi axioms reduce to the Kolmogoroff axioms when $\mathcal{B} \equiv \mathcal{X}$

Both Kolmogoroff's and Renyi's mathematical theories of probability are Set Theoretic definitions. Although most reliability texts introduce the axioms (generally Kolmogoroff's) it appears to me they are included merely for completeness. In practice the mathematics of reliability is based on the less rigorous and less formal presupposition that there exists a limiting frequency together with a plausible statistical estimating theory, neither of which are developed explicitly from axioms.

I have referred to the statistical and mathematical conceptions of probability. But in many philosophers' view, this is not only inadequate, but may be so restrictive as to require us to believe certain things, which when viewed against the more general background of science, are clearly implausible, or the general background of science itself may be the source of making more substantial claims. Consider for instance the example of why we believe that in the natural course of events, water will always flow downhill. We can certainly arrive at this conclusion by using statistical inference, since presumably all observed instances of water flow on a hillside confirms this hypothesis. However, observations are not the only source of this belief. One can for instance consider the consequence to science of not believing it. This belief is directly deducible from Newton's Laws of Motion and Gravitation plus the empirically determined properties of water, and to hold views that contradict this belief is the same as denying either Newtonian Law, or the properties of water. Against this background, the implication of one unexplained observation of water flowing uphill would be very serious for all of science. However if our belief was solely based on simple enumeration, the effect on our general beliefs of science would be profoundly negligible.

The point is, that in normal science, laws (universal propositions) cannot be regarded in isolation of one another, together they will form a system of laws with each law fitting within the system such that it mutually reinforces each other law. Thus an observation that directly confirms one law indirectly confirms the others, and the abandonment of one law requires the abandonment or alteration of a large number of other laws.

It is in light of considerations such as this one that have lead many philosophers to think of probability in two senses, a factual one, and a logical one. Logical probability has been variously called, degrees of confirmation and credibility.

Notable contributions to the logical theories of probability are those of Keynes (Ref 19), Jeffreys (Ref 11), Koopman (Ref 12 & 13) and Carnap (Ref 20). It is possibly Carnap's theory that is the most highly developed, which is a quasi-logical interpretation of probability, using the formal apparatus of a constructed language system. A constructed language consists of giving a proper name to each individual or particular of the theory, a predicate for each basic property, truth functional connectives and precise rules of punctuation. In his theory, logical probability is a logical relation somewhat similar to logical implication: and thus can be regarded as partial implication. The measures of probability can be interpreted as the degrees of belief of a hypothetically perfectly rational being.

Therefore, if the evidence is overwhelming that a hypothesis logically follows from it i.e. is logically implied by it, the logical probability value is equal to 1. On the other hand, if the evidence is such that the negation of the hypothesis is implied by the evidence, the logical probability value is 0. In between these two extremes there is a continuum of cases about which deductive logic tells us nothing beyond the negative assertion that neither the hypothesis nor its negation can be deduced from the evidence. On this continuum inductive logic takes over, but inductive logic is like deductive logic in being concerned solely with the statements involved, not with the facts of nature. By a logical analysis of a stated hypothesis (h) and stated evidence (e) we conclude that (h) is not logically implied but is so to speak partially implied by (e) to the degree of so-and-so much. It is Carnap's view then that there are two kinds of probability, that of logical probability and factual probability which he happens to consider the frequency interpretation of Von Mises and Reichenbach as more acceptable. He also considered that in some circumstances, logical probability could be seen as a coarse estimate of factual probability.

It this is so there are two coexisting theories of probability one factual and one logical. As D. C. Stove has pointed out (Ref 21), in such an arrangement there will be four kinds of propositions about probability. The principles and statements of 'factual probability' and the principles and statements of 'logical probability'. If there is to be compatibility, the principles of factual and logical probability do not involve contradictions. Thus it will only be in the statements of probability that the differences will be apparent.

A statement of factual probability is being made when we combine two propositions of which we regard one as being completely known and the other as being completely unknown e.g. the likelihood of an event measured by the ratio of the favourable chances to the whole number of chances.

A statement of logical probability is being made when we assess the probability of one proposition in relation to a second proposition, which picks out possible evidence for or against the first and, according to Carnap, is the degree of confirmation of the hypothesis (h) by the evidence (e).

The distinction between these two kinds of statements may not be apparent, unless the context in which they are made is considered, for example, a manufacturer may claim for his devices a probability of failure of .04 per 1000 hours operating at 100 C, he may also claim a probability of failure of .09 per 1000 hours at 200 C. Now if the first claim is based simply on subjecting a sample of his product to life tests at 100 C, he is making a statement of factual probability. We regard this as being so as one of his primary propositions is in the form of data which has a degree of rational credibility in its own account. If he has derived the probability of failure at 200 C using the Arrhenius relationship, he is now making a statement of logical probability. This is apparent if one restructures the statement thus: The hypothesis that a device will fail within 1000 hours when operating at 200 C has .09 degrees of confirmation (probability) and my evidence for making this claim is the measurements made at 100 C and the Arrhenius relationship.

The importance of the distinction is now apparent. In spite of the reasoning being valid the conclusion may be false. For instance, in this example the Arrhenius relationship may not hold. Even if it is a reasonable approximation, we cannot regard both statements as having the same authority. The accuracy of the first statement is a matter of statistical error, whereas the accuracy of the second statement is a matter not only of statistical measurement error but also the relevancy of the Arrhenius relationship.

It is my contention that the major cause of inaccuracy in reliability predictions is not the inappropriate use of mathematical and statistical probability, but rather, that the models used cannot be shown to relate to the system that is being modelled. Whilst the statistical conception of probability can be further refined to provide more meaningful measures of factual behaviour, this of itself will only bring about minor improvements. The concepts of logical probability permit one to assess in a systematic manner further consequences of using a particular model.

In more recent times a new conception of probability has become important, that of the Subjectivist-Bayesian view. Few important current philosophers of inductive logic (there are some) do not consider in one form or another the tenets of Bayesian probability as central to both understanding and determining the logic of inductive inferences. Yet at the level of the professional statistician, it still remains controversial. Whether this be based on misunderstanding, or the solipsism of some of its less thoughtful early advocates, or the distaste for philosophizing by practical people, I do not know, but what is clear is that in spite of the populist view that it is ill considered, it is the product of some of the most thoughtful and technically competent mathematicians, statisticians and philosophers that have operated in the field of statistics. It is gratifying to see current trends in fundamental research are more directed towards synthesizing the alternative interpretations of probability. The coalescent paradigm is the Bayesian paradigm, the controversial and, to many, unacceptable view of the 1960s and 1970s is becoming the central and unifying view of the 1980s and possibly the 1990s.

Its major proponents are Savage (Ref 22), De Finetti (Ref 23), Good (Ref 24), DeGroot (Ref 25) and Lindley (Ref 26). One should also note the influential Treatise on Probability by Jeffreys, which whilst its aspirations and foundational issues are clearly aimed at introducing the logical method into statistical and probabilistic inference making, the techniques expounded have only a passing relationship to those of the logical probabilist such as Keynes and Carnap. They are more closely identified with the current Bayesian position.

The Subjectivist theory of probability identifies probability as the actual degree of belief in a given assertion held by some individual at some specific time. This degree of belief has to conform to specific requirements. Firstly, to be meaningful, it has to be the subject of a rational measuring process, and secondly that of coherence in which any degree of belief in an assertion must agree with or conform to other beliefs in a certain way. In satisfying these criteria it is easy to demonstrate that they have to conform to a mathematical axiomatic theory of probability such as Kolmogoroff's or Renyi's, and thus at the mathematical level in this respect, they do not differ from other theories.

The essential difference is that of whether one considers probability as an objective entity or a subjective entity. It has long been held by popular accounts of science that science is objective and thus its entities to be real, must be capable of measurement either by direct observation or by scientific instruments. Unfortunately things are not so simple as this. A traditional viewpoint dating back to Locke recognizes that the entities or qualities of science consist of primary qualities and secondary qualities. The primary qualities are those such as shape, size, weight, motion etc... they exist independent of human perception. The secondary qualities are those such as texture, smell, colour, sound etc... It is thought that for these qualities to exist they have to be experienced. The primary qualities are the objective qualities of science, whilst the secondary qualities are subjective. Now, to say that a car is travelling at 30 m.p.h. references the primary qualities and thus is an objective statement, but to say the car is red references the secondary qualities since the claim to be red is to claim that it consists of looking red. The nature of the primary objective qualities in an object is that in disposition they produce functional experience, whilst those of the secondary subjective qualities in disposition produce sensory experience in a perceiver of a phenomeno-logical kind. The subjectivist view of probability is to say that probability is a secondary quality, whilst those that oppose this position would claim that probability is a quality of a primary kind. The debate between primary and secondary qualities has become increasingly important in science since the advent of Quantum Theory where it is known that the act of perceiving a phenomena is an influential aspect of how that phenomena appears. The opening statement to Heisenberg's Autobiographical memoirs (Ref 27) is: 'Science is made by men, a self-evident fact that is far too often forgotten'. If this be true and for Quantum physicists it is considered true, then the whole of science has a subjective element. If modern physicists have had to come to terms with this problem and as a result and through the Copenhagen Interpretation of Quantum Mechanics has developed theories that have proved the most powerful in prediction yet devised by man, one would have thought that the statisticians task was easier since he can cite previous success in the most respected area of all science. Yet to some statisticians, subjectivism still remains unacceptable in the area of probability and statistical inference, but they are inconsistent because on the basis of the arguments they expound against it, they are not prepared to extend them into physics.

The proponents of the Bayesian theory claim that it facilitates inferences to be made whereby one can combine knowledge of the logical kind (that which logical probability aspires to do) with that which the frequencist theory aspires to do, and do it such that it is consistent with an axiomatic theory of probability. Its structure bridges the gap between the a priori and the a posteriori.

As with the logical probabilists, Subjectivist-Bayesians claim their inferences are those of how a completely rational man would fix betting odds. However it differs in one fundamental respect from the frequencist interpretation, in that the evidence is not restricted to being objective. The reason for this is that Bayesians deny that probability in a frequency interpretation necessarily or exclusively manifests itself as a physical property. To them, probability is a belief function. According to the Bayesian view (Ref 28), all quantities are of two kinds: those known to the person making the inference, and those unknown to the person: the former are described by their known values, the uncertainty surrounding the latter being described by joint probability distributions. The analyst then has to progressively combine these two sources of information by using Bayes Theorem to derive precise inferences. Within the Bayesian framework all calculations are performed by the probability calculus using probabilities for the unknown quantities. An important but much overlooked aspect of the Bayesian thesis is that an analysis is progressive, and thus the influence of the original priors on an inference rapidly decreases as further evidence (data) is incorporated. The whole direction of a Bayesian analysis is that of updating one belief about something as further evidence is considered; a process called conditionalization. The consequence of this approach is threefold, initially, priors can be determined by background information, engineering judgement or some scientific theory. Secondly given two independent analysis each of which starts with differing priors if the process of conditionalization is rational (or even simply coherent) as each progressively considers further evidence rapid convergence takes place between the inferences of the alternative analysis. And finally this working implies that the Bayesian approach is at least in principle an extremely efficient means of analyzing data.

Bayesians claim there are two fundamental reasons for adopting their viewpoint, the first is once having made the basic step of describing uncertainty through probability, we have a formal procedure, that of Bayes Theorem, for solving all inference problems. The second reason is that of coherence, that is the basic properties of statistical procedures not only have to be reasonable properties, but they must fit together in a sensible way and be devoid of contradictory aspects. It is easy to show that all other statistical theories lead to incoherencies.

As to which concept of probability an individual uses this is likely to be a result of an accident of education. He will use the system of which he has been taught or is best informed. As to the open-minded, they will find themselves in the position of having to judge between the different viewpoints and if they read the right books, each view will be presented in a sufficiently clever way so that they will find themselves being swayed by each in turn. The fact remains that all theories of probability are incomplete. However, given an appropriate grasp of the points at issue (it is only in the detail that they are incommensurate), some form of compromise is attainable. This can no longer be regarded as a side issue, the advent of the computer and information technology has put paid to that. My advocacy is that we adopt the compromise espoused by I. J. Good in which he takes the Subjective-Bayesian interpretation of probability as the most operational in that it is the closest to action, and permits one to extend ordinary logic into a general purpose system of reasoning. In Good's philosophy this is not inconsistent with the Frequency or Propensity interpretation of probability, since in measuring physical probabilities on a reasonably consistent basis subjective probabilities are necessary. Nor is it inconsistent with the logical theories of probability (except in detail) since the logical theory is the subjective theory held by a completely rational person. It recognizes the notion of a hierarchy of different types, orders, levels, or stages of probability is natural, and in so doing accepts that probability is not necessarily completely ordered but may be a partial ordering. Further, Good's theory is compatible with the notion of The Weight of Evidence, and with Probabilistic Causality each of which will become recognized as being fundamental to the problem of evaluating complex systems reliability. This having been said, as a matter of taste I think engineers prefer the words of Bruno De Finetti in describing these various notions in which he calls Logical Probability - Credence; Factual or Physical Probability - Chance; Subjective Probability - Probability; and Weight of Evidence - Support (Ref 29).

Until recent times a synthesis of Good's views required reference to an extensive number of his papers. It is fortunate for us that he has now published his synthesis in his book 'The Foundations of Probability and its Application' (Ref 24). Clearly I am of the opinion that this volume constitutes a foundational work on the rationale of reliability inferences.

CAUSE

In most respects causal analysis and statistical analysis are antithesis. At the one extreme we consider phenomena to be causally directed, which in the limit results in causal determination. At the other extreme, we consider the realization of phenomena to result from randomness or chance which in the limit are statistically determined. Traditional procedures of causal analysis exclude any perceptive means of assessing the impact of chance on observed behaviours. In like manner statistical analysis excludes any perceptive means of assessing causal influences. The generating mechanism of reliability data is neither fully causally determined nor solely due to chance behaviour, the truth lies somewhere in between.

Kendall and Stuart in their 'Advanced Theory of Statistics' (Ref 30) say 'A statistical relationship, however strong and however suggestive, can never establish a causal connection. Our ideas on causation must come from outside of statistics, ultimately from some theory or another'. They continue, 'We need not enter into the philosophical implications of this: for our purposes we need only reiterate, that a statistical relationship of whatever kind, cannot logically imply causation'.

Comments such as these occur in most good books on statistical theory, and clearly no informed person would disagree. But in my opinion such comments are not entirely adequate for a statistical education, since they place upon the reader two prior requirements. The first being that there exists a clear and agreed understanding of what is meant by cause, and that this is known by the reader. Unfortunately this is not the case. There is no agreement as to what is meant by cause, and in certain areas of science (e.g. quantum mechanics), all of the traditional interpretations appear to breakdown. Further, in standard statistical education the student is not exposed to any of the refined theories of cause. The concept of cause that he or she adopts is the concept that he or she presumes.

The second is also in the nature of a presumption, and that is, that the reader knows, at least in principle what is implied by a statistical relationship. This in turn suggests the existence of a Modal Theory of Statistical Relationships, and to my knowledge there has never even been an attempt to structure such a theory.

Within reliability, there is on the one hand the presumption held by engineers that all failures have a cause, and thus they are the subject of a causal analysis, and if predictions are to be believed, they must be based on the concept of 'Causality'. On the other hand there is that view which is in the main held by reliability theoreticians that the occurrence of a failure is as much due to chance as due to any other factor. Thus the occurrence of failures has to be analysed by statistical theory. The truth lies somewhere in between. Within reliability I do not believe that even a complete knowledge of causal factors would permit accurate predictions to be derived, but equally neither will a prediction scheme that ignores cause altogether. The function of statistics in principle is that of finding quantitative or qualitative relationships between the properties of concern from which hopefully, models of explanation and prediction can be built. The two underlying metaphysical concepts that order these observations are those of chance and cause, and thus each is going to have a major influence in observed relationships. If statistics is to be useful in engineering, it must acknowledge this.

This requirement is important for reliability, since it is only on the basis of a knowledge of causal relationships that one can justify, even on a common sense basis, reliability predictions. This does not mean that causal relationships alone are an adequate basis for making precise predictions, for to do this requires a knowledge of all the relevant facts and all the relevant laws of science. In situations where this information is known, predictions are a consequence of the facts and laws, and one could precisely specify an event prior to it happening. Such events are viewed as being antecedent and causal, in other words deterministic. But even with partial information, given an insight into the causal relations, predictions of a kind are possible, but they are of a weaker type, in that they are expectations, and one can never be surprised at them being wrong.

This leads me to believe that a statistical theory of reliability, whilst it may be adequate for some tasks such as component and simple non-repairable systems, will prove inadequate for repairable and advanced systems incorporating for example, VLSI, Software and Artificial Intelligence technologies. To deal with these, the statistical theory will have to be superseded by a more general theory based on concepts of cause and probability. In other words 'A Probabilistic-Causal Theory of Reliability'. The reason for this is that not only will prediction be more plausible, but it will also be more suitable to a task of explaining unreliability, and thus provide a means of controlling unreliability.

An initial step in this direction is for reliability theorists to gain a greater understanding of the current philosophies of Cause and Effect. The usual philosophy argues that if we have a class of events A, which is always followed by an event B, we term A as 'cause' and B as 'effect'. In such a scheme, a knowledge of 'cause' permits inference to be made about 'effect'. Although less reliable, if precautions are taken, reverse inferences from B to A can be made. In this philosophy, there need be no connection between 'cause' and 'effect' other than their order, in which case, they are merely limiting areas of statistical regularities. However, this is not the usual concept of cause in science as it is implicit in all science that there is connection. These connections one can refer to as Causal Laws.

Such primitive concepts have intuitive meaning in classical physics, because this is our common experience, and in most cases science has explained the connections involved, which are not necessarily direct. The connections are often tenuous or complex, and beyond a general perception. In such cases scientists usually resort to other principles to describe connection. Typically, the use of Differential Equations, the Law of Quasi-Permanence (which argues that in a certain sense things will continue much as before unless interfered with), and the concepts of Statistical Regularity (which view the fundamental regularities of physics as statistical, and not such as to tell us what, for instance an individual atom will do).

This conception of causality gives causality a status of being law-like. It is closely related to two concepts of logic, those of 'necessary' and 'sufficient' conditions (Ref 31, 32 & 33).

A necessary condition for something is a condition in which the absence of a thing or event could not exist or occur. e.g. a necessary condition for human life is the presence of oxygen.

A sufficient condition for something is a condition in which the presence of a thing or event will always exist or occur. e.g. a sufficient condition for human death is the absence of oxygen.

Closely allied with these concepts are those of contingent 'necessary' and 'sufficient' conditions. A contingent necessary condition for something implies that you cannot have that something without also having this thing. e.g. a contingent necessary condition for being alive (in the sense that it is normally understood) is the fact that one is breathing. A contingent sufficient condition for something implies you cannot have that something and also have this thing. e.g. a contingent sufficient condition for a person to be dead (in the sense that it is normally understood) is the fact that he or she is not breathing.

To specify fully the contingent necessary and sufficient conditions of something is to make what logicians call a 'material implication', which is a statement of the kind

If this (conditions A, B, C,...)

Then that (condition x)

There are those who believe that all scientific inferences are, or should be, of this form and that the difference between a strong prediction (deterministic) and a weak prediction (statistical inference) is that in the former the 'If' conditions are completely specified and certain, whereas in the latter they are either incomplete and/or uncertain. Reliability assessment techniques such as Failure Modes and Effects Analysis and Fault Tree Analysis are based on specifying the contingent conditions of system failure.

Contingent necessary and sufficient conditions are weaker interpretations of the order and relationship between things than those of necessary and sufficient conditions, since they are indifferent to time. Thus Cause is usually specified in terms of the former. On this basis one can construct three law-like relationships between cause and effect that, taken together, go a long way towards defining a logic of cause, namely:

1. Necessary Condition
   An event C is a cause of an event E if and only if, C and E are actual and all other things being equal C is necessary for E.

2. Sufficient Condition
   An event C is a cause of an event E if and only if, C and E are actual and all other things being equal C is a sufficient condition of E.

3. Insufficient but none redundant parts of unnecessary but sufficient conditions (INUS)
   If an event C is a cause of an event E (on certain occasions) C is a condition which un-usually combines with other conditions to cause E, C is itself unnecessary but exclusively sufficient for E (on that occasion).

If one now considers the effect to be either a component, equipment, or system failure we have now defined three law-like relationships whereby we can link failures with those conditions which we call cause. An example of (1) a necessary condition for system function is that the power supply works. An example of (2) is the failure of the power supply due to a sudden voltage transient which causes a transistor to fail. An example of (3) is a surge in the voltage supply to a system that in combination with the point in time of maximum loading, causes the system to fail due to overloading.

The acceptance of these law-like definitions of cause, although substantial, are not without philosophical difficulties. It is the treatment of these difficulties that is one of the major aspects that separate the Rationalist from the Empiricist. Whereas the Rationalist (of the Descarte tradition) argues that it is possible to obtain by reason alone a knowledge of the nature of what exists and thus the condition of existence, which in turn demands a law-like structure between cause and effect, the Empiricists refute this, demanding objective evidence in the form of sense data. They argue that acceptance of these law-like definitions of cause, makes the substance of science purely a matter of logical implication. Further, it strongly suggests that cause is an essential property of the universe and is thus an object of Empirical science. Yet cause as it is nearly always used in discourse is not a property, nor is it a basic metric of the universe, it is a subject of metaphysics being a concept that permits us to order our data and knowledge of circumstances in such a way that certain deductions of the forms of explanations and predictions can be made.

It is this view that led Hume in his 'Treatise' (Ref 34) to form a different analysis as to what is understood by cause and effect. Hume's view of cause is that it is that identity that proceeds in time, is contiguous with (such that one can view it as touching in space or time) and is constantly conjoined with that identity termed effect: and is such that in all instances of a particular identity termed cause is placed in a like relation to another particular identity termed effect.

A second concept of cause is also given by Hume and in that it does not contradict any aspect of his other concept and is also identically structured, one presumes his intention was that they should be combined. In this concept, cause is that identity that proceeds in time, is contiguous with and is constantly conjoined with that identity termed effect: and is such that within the imagination the idea of one invokes a vivid mental picture of the other.

It is clear from Hume's discussion on causality that what he had in mind is a substitution of a logical relation between cause and effect for that of a psychological relation. In other words, the relationship is not that of the way the universe is, but is that of the way we perceive the universe of being.

On this basis others were able to build substantial systems by which scientific inferences can be made. The most notable being John Stuart Mill, who being aware of the limitations of Induction by simple enumeration, built on the early traditions of Duns Scotus and Sir Francis Bacon an inductive system of casual canons, which have become to be called 'Mill's Methods of Causal Connection' (Ref 32 & 33) of which there are five:

(i) The Method of Agreement
(ii) The Method of Difference
(iii) The Joint Method of Agreement and Difference
(iv) The Method of Residue
(v) The Method of Concomitant Variation

The basis of Mill's method is to specify the cause (the whole cause) which is the set of conditions sufficient to produce the event termed effect.

One can best describe these methods by reference to some simple examples

Consider the situation where we believe that an equipment failure may be due to either: (A) high ambient temperature, (B) excessive humidity, (C) excessive vibration, or (D) mechanical shock. In determining the cause of failure by the 'Method of Agreement' we can construct an experiment where each of these conditions (antecedent circumstances) are presented in various combinations. To determine the cause effect relationship using the Method of Agreement we structure a series of experiments of the following format.

Instance	:	Antecedent Circumstances				:	Effect
1	:	A	B	C	D	:	f
2	:		B	C	D	:	f
3	:	A		C	D	:	f
4	:	A	B		D	:	f
5	:	A			D	:	f
6	:		B		D	:	f
7	:			C	D	:	f

From which we observe that it is only in the presence of condition D that the effect, failure is observed, we thus infer (D) mechanical shock, is the cause of failure.

The Method of Agreement is represented by the following schema.

Given that Capital Letters denote circumstances, and lower case letters denote effect

A B C D occur together with a b c d
A E F G occur together with a e f g

Therefore A is the cause (or effect) or
an indispensable part of the cause of a

To determine the cause effect relation by The Method of Difference one constructs an experiment similar to that of The Method of Agreement.

Instance	:	Antecedent Circumstances				:	Effect
1	:	A	B	C	D	:	f
n	:	A	B	C		:	

From this new arrangement we can observe that once again it is only in the presence of (D) that failure occurs, and thus infer that (D) mechanical shock, is the cause of failure.

The Method of Difference is represented by the following schema:

A B C D occur together with a b c d
A B C occur together with a b c

Therefore D is the cause (or effect) or an
indispensable part of the cause of d.

The Method of Agreement and Difference is represented by combining the schemata of The Methods of Agreement and The Method of Difference, thus:

A B C -- a b c   A B C -- a b c
A D E -- a d e   B C -- b c

Therefore A is the cause (or effect) or an
indispensable part of the cause of a.

The Method of Residues differs in some important respects from the other methods. It is the only method that requires a single experience of like observations. Another difference is that it is the only method in which one is required to have knowledge of other causal relations. This has led many to regard its schema as a deductive rather than an inductive method. Whilst on many occasions it does reduce to a deductive schema, in general it is incorrect to view it as such, primarily for two reasons. The first is that the evidence cannot be shown to be complete or for that matter even relevant, which leads to the second which is that its conclusions can only be regarded as probable.

The Method of Residues is represented by the following schema.

A B C	occur together with	a b c
A	is known to cause	a
B	is known to cause	b

Therefore C is the cause (or effect) or an indispensable part of the cause of c.

It is relatively easy to show how this schema can be reduced to a deduction. Consider the example of a vessel containing two objects, which has a total weight of 4lbs. If we know that the vessel weighs 2lbs and one of the objects weighs 1lb we can deduce that the other also weighs 1lb, but such examples are deceptive in such simple applications. In the hands of a sophisticated researcher, this method is extremely powerful. Copi (Ref 32) gives the example of how the use of this method led to the discovery of the planet Neptune, one of the greatest achievements of mathematical astronomy.

In 1821 Bouvard published tables of planetary motion. In deriving these tables he had considerable difficulties with the planet Uranus. The observational data obtained after 1800 was incompatible with that data obtained immediately after the discovery of Uranus. Thus he disregarded both sources of data preferring to make his own observations. However, only after a few years, predictions of the position of Uranus based on Bouvard tables were in error. By 1841, this error was substantial, yet the predictions for other planets were essentially correct. In 1845 Leverrier considered the problem and after completely re-checking Bouvard's calculations, in which he found no error, formulated an explanatory hypothesis: that of an undiscovered planet which disturbed the orbit of Uranus. On this hypothesis Leverrier did certain recalculations, which he completed in June 1846. He wrote to Galle in Berlin suggesting he looked for this yet undiscovered planet, which he did. Within one hour Galle had discovered Neptune within 1 degree of the prediction made by Leverrier.

This example illustrates a very important point. Whilst the schemata of Mill's Method are simple they are by no means naive. In the hands of the perceptive and sophisticated researcher, who understands their implications they are one of the most powerful and successful tools of modern scientific enquiry.

The Method of Concomitant Variation is directed towards those situations where a causal circumstance cannot be completely eliminated. For example, if we consider the mechanical strength of soldered joints, in that solder is a low melting point binary alloy, which is known to have certain undesirable properties such as creep and room annealing, which are both dependant on temperature: and solder in particular has further undesirable properties at about room temperature namely; tin transformation (tin pest) which takes place at about 14 degrees centigrade, and that the soldered joint has to function within its arbitrary defined plastic region (for low melting point alloys, the arbitrarily defined plastic region is that region below its melting point and above the mid-point between absolute zero and its melting point). One may be lead to believe that a cause of soldered joint failure is a high operating temperature. However, there are also other possible causal influences that need to be considered, typically vibration, corrosion, shock, low cycle thermal fatigue (which as it turns out is the major cause of soldered joint failure). One cannot construct any experiment in which temperature is eliminated. Thus the experiment has to proceed using the Method of Concomitant Variation, the schema of which is shown below.

A	B C	occur together with	a b c
A+	B C	occur together with	a+ b c
A++	B C	occur together with	a++ b c

Therefore A is causally connected with a

Simply interpreted, one infers that if an effect sympathetically varies with a particular circumstance, that circumstance is causally connected with that effect.

This method differs from other methods in that it is a quantitative method of inductive inference, whereas the others are qualitative. Also it was the first quantitative method to be formulated which presupposed the existence of a refined means of measurement and estimating the degrees to which the phenomena vary. Its importance to the development of statistics is thus obvious.

The preceding description of the schemata are related to experimental conditions. This is purely for simplicity of description. Observations are not only those of experimental conditions but those of actual real world behaviour.

Mill's Method of Causal Connection is an inductive method, but unlike ampliative methods such as simple enumeration, which attempts to widen one's knowledge beyond that of experience, Mill's methods are eliminative. They are directed towards eliminating hypotheses to those and only those that can be demonstrated. This requires of the analyst that he accepts that initially there is an extensive number of either causal or statistical hypotheses that have the potential for explaining the relationship between the antecedent circumstances and the effect they lead to. The direction of the investigation is that of systematically eliminating those hypotheses for which the evidence fails in a probabilistic sense to support. The ampliative method is directed to solving a different kind of problem: that of prediction of how things could be either at some other place or at some other time. This task is not eliminative: it is constructive. The direction of the exercise is to structure a plausible hypothesis as to how things may behave in the future based on the evidence of the past and the present. It is not solely an exercise in applied statistics and probability theory, as some Reliability Theorists have presumed. The tenets that give us the authority to presume we can do this, are not the techniques of statistics or the axioms of some probability theory, they are deeply held philosophical positions and thus are the subject of a philosophical logic.

Those areas of statistics that have been built on Mill's Method are extremely successful in engineering. There can be no dispute about the success of the techniques such as 'Design of Experiments', 'Evolutionary Processes', 'Analysis of Variance', 'Statistical Quality Control', etc... However those that rely on ampliative methods such as simple enumeration seem to me to be 'flabby' and are more successful in seeding dispute than providing insight. The explanation for this is simple, firstly the failure to recognize the philosophical nature of the task, and secondly the failure to recognize that ultimately predictions are not based on countable discrete chunks of evidence, but the weight that a chunk of evidence gives to supporting a predictive hypothesis, and this is a matter of the relevancy of the evidence to the hypothesis. It is the information content of evidence and not the evidence itself that make prediction a possibility. The failure of simple enumeration is the failure to acknowledge this fact. The Mill's Method of causal connection has relevancy to this point in that it is a qualitative method and as such each case is a limiting case of quantitative evaluation. Each of the five canons are entailed by the Laplace - Bayes - Turing - Good paradigm of the Weight of Evidence (for a full mathematical survey see Ref 35, for an approachable less technical account see Ref 24).

The notions of cause invoked by Mill's Causal canons is that of strict cause in that given the cause, the effect will always follow. It has long been realized that strict cause succumbs to a logical notation, and in so doing its calculus has much in common with the calculus of symbolic logic. The achievement of expressing strict causal relationships in logical notation is that great clarity can be brought into the process of deriving causal inferences, and in much the same way that establishing the validity of an argument using symbolic logic is mechanical, so is the determining of the soundness of causal inferences mechanical. However the relationship of causal logic to experience and reality is also that of symbolic logic to reality, whilst it can establish that the structure of one's inference procedure has desirable properties, e.g. do not lead to contradictory claims. To have usefulness in engineering it has to be interpreted, and that is not the subject of logic it is the the subject of science.

The problem with the traditional causal logics is that in interpretation, they present an oversimplified approach, in which the direction of the analogies is that of looking for a single argument that accounts for the facts. The truth is a little more sophisticated, in that events do not arise from a single cause or even a regiment of causes. They usually arise from a complexity of causes, which unfortunately are not so graphic, but nevertheless are more realistic. The problem appears to be that in developing causal arguments which are usually related to highly complex situations, we are forced to resort to a simplification. Merely by qualifying an event called cause as a necessary, or sufficient, or contingently necessary, or contingently sufficient condition for an effect, conveys no true impression as to the influence that a causal event has in producing an effect. Equally, we recognize that there are causal influences that do not submit to such qualifications. For example, in the much advocated activity of 'burning-in' components, it seems reasonable to qualify a system's failure as due to the components not being 'burned-in'. But it seems arbitrary to argue that 'burn-in' is a necessary condition for system reliability, or that the absence of 'burn-in' is a sufficient condition for system failure. Causal logic based on necessary and sufficient conditions references strict regularity and thus what is referred to as 'Strict Cause'. Strict Cause is inadequate to the task of explaining the causal influences of many events, yet there are many circumstances where causal logic seems totally adequate to this task. An intuitively attractive explanation for this is given by Mario Bunge (Ref 36). He refers to it as a process of causal isolation.

In this derivation, strict cause is viewed as a simplification between the linking and cross linking of events in the real world. Explanation and logical methodical activities in science and engineering require this, as they are not prepared to operate merely on the chronologicalling of events called cause with apparently disconnected events called effect. Thus we proceed by invoking connectivity by appealing to causal chains. A causal chain is a mechanism for establishing order between events by denoting an effect as a further cause e.g.

> The car failed <u>because</u> of the bearing failure, which was <u>caused</u> by the bearing running dry, which in turn was <u>caused</u> by it not being adequately greased at its regular maintenance activity, <u>because</u> the mechanic did not rigorously follow the maintenance procedure, <u>because</u> he was not clearly instructed as to what they were, <u>because</u> etc etc...

Whilst this connectivity has obvious descriptive advantages, it more often than not represents an extreme oversimplification of the circumstances; at best it is a rough-and-ready approximation for a short period of time as to the true connection between a large number of interconnecting contributing events, all of which within a full analysis may need to be taken into consideration. It is evident upon reflection that every event is produced and accompanied by an extensive number of factors, all of which are interconnected. This labyrinth of interconnections is referred to as 'A Causal Net'. It is not difficult to show that however apparently disconnected two events appear, they can be connected by a Causal Chain drawn from a Causal Net. But mere connectivity is not the property of concern, it is the influence of one event on the other that is of interest. If this influence is significant, proceeds in time, and is constantly conjoined with another event, we refer to that event as strict cause, and the event that is being influenced as the effect.

Now, what Causal Chains presume is that those events in the Net that are not directly in the chain have negligible influence. Thus a Causal Chain is a mechanism of isolating one path of the Causal Net from the many possible paths. In physics this is often a realistic way of looking at things. For example; if we are considering the path of a falling body, given that the body has a high mass to surface ratio (say a lead ball), we can isolate if from the influences of air resistance, temperature, humidity etc... since these will have a very minor effect on the results of any calculation. Given that a body has a low mass to surface ratio (say a feather), to adequately describe its path many more causal influences have to be considered in calculation in deriving even grossly approximate results.

One needs to stress that whilst causal chains are fictitious in the sense that they isolate those events that are chained, from those that proceed and accompany them, nevertheless they are necessary structures for scientists to gain an understanding and develop methods of scientific inference. What the scientist achieves in structuring a chain is that in singling out and connecting those few entities that are germane to understanding phenomena, from which he can construct an idealized mathematical model that can be used for deriving further inferences. In cases where no single simple causal chain consistently dominates, he finds it necessary to consider behaviour as to some degree or other, random. This is the nature of those events called 'System Failure'.

Unfortunately as the causal nets are evolving in time, for reliability analysis this becomes even more complex. To understand why, we have to recognize one further important fact, that is: that a system (in the sense of an equipment) never exists in isolation, it is conjoined with another system; that of its environment. Reliability (that which deals with the rates of occurrence of failure) is a characterization of how these two systems (equipment and environment) interact in the time domain. Thus three causal scenarios are relevant, each of which will result in a somewhat different causal chain. We can refer to these scenarios as:

The Equipment Scenario

The Environment Scenario

The Time Scenario

The Equipment Scenario prescribes for a given equipment state which will vary in time, its susceptibility to failure from environmental influences where one can consider the environment as having a constant average effect. It is a matter of convenience that in reliability modelling we more often than not treat the equipment state as invariate in time (that is given that we exclude infant mortality and the wearout phase depicted by the 'bath-tub' curve). Engineers know better, they recognize the importance of many influences that can lead to changes in the equipment state and thus make it more prone to failure. Typically,

•The effect of cumulative damage such as metal fatigue and embrittlement.

•The proneness of failure based on varying demands put on system components.

•The effect of operating temperature particularly that of internal generated heat.

•The effect of atomic and molecular activity within components e.g. corrosion, metal migration, room annealing, work hardening etc...

•The effect of degenerative processes in materials such as plastic.

•Even maintenance activities have considerable effect in determining the proneness of equipment to fail.

In the main, such phenomena are the result of natural physical processes. The only influence the environment has is in deciding the rate at which the phenomena become manifest. The traditional way of dealing with these is that of giving advice in terms of design rules. More recently techniques such as Sensitivity Analysis have been developed which attempt to quantify and minimize these influences. These techniques invariably rely on very simple causal chains.

Unlike the equipment scenario which presumes an average environment and develops causal chains for equipment behaviour, the environment scenario reverses this viewpoint. Here we presume an average state for the equipment and evaluate its susceptibility to failure due to environmental changes.

The process of singling out and connecting events in a causal chain, leads one to presume that the joint influences of these events is someway additive. This is not true in all circumstances, the perceptiveness of the eliminative method of statistical analysis is the recognition of this. Statistical techniques recognize the importance of interactions, by which one means that in the interplay between a large number of causal influences irrespective of their similarity, may result in characterizations of the environment that are not merely characteristics of the individual aspects of the causal influences. Thus a causal influence, say an increase in ambient temperature, which can often be ignored in calculation, when accompanied by another causal influence which in isolation can also be considered unimportant, say a rise in humidity, can produce an undesirable effect out of proportion to their individual additive influences. Even forces of the same kind in combination can produce surprisingly different intensities in their effect than one may be lead to believe from simple additive models. It is well known that the cumulative effect of vibration made up of two fundamental frequencies each of which in isolation can be considered low level, can combine to react with an equipment with catastrophic results. If this is true of vibration, how much more complex is the picture when we combine essentially different influences such as shock, temperature, vibration, human involvement, chemical aggression etc etc...

The fact that we model these linearly is not that we presume this is the way of nature. It is both the poverty of our understanding, which is reflected in the models we use, plus the fact that we just do not know how to represent these interacting influences mathematically in anything but the most simple of cases.

In the time scenario we concede the difficulty of realistically characterizing dynamic causal chains, and we revert to exploiting the statistical nature of causal influences. If both equipment and environment state were time invariate we could presume that the influences interconnect in such way that opposites tend to cancel producing a harmonious state of equilibrium. Thus no particular influence would prevail, and nothing new or surprising would happen. As far as reliability is concerned, this is not a state we recognize. Each influence is under a constant process of change. The complexity entailed in grasping the interactions between these influences is such that for all practical purposes we consider it impossible. However given the none-additivity of the interplay of presumably independent influences, in terms of observation and measurement their gross effect can be represented by a statistical model. A series of independent measurements of this gross effect more often than not shows it can be characterized by some well know statistical distribution. Equally as it unfolds in time, it can be represented as a stochastic influence. Thus we regard such measurements as characterizing a whole rather than a mere heap of disconnected influences. Statistical measures used in reliability thus represent the collective properties of the effect of a large number of varying influences. The fact that the number of influences may be large and are constantly varying and interact with each other is not an obstacle to a successful statistical representation. Such conditions are actually quite important for the success of this approach since statistical measures such as means, variancies, correlations etc... depend on a large number of interacting entities for cancelling out small deviations and thus producing stable measures.

This grossly simplified account of the relationship between causal chains and causal nets and the consequential causal isolation involved, presumes that chance, probabilistic and statistical phenomena are merely mechanisms of characterizing concealed cause. Which is the line that Bruno De Finetti follows in developing his subjective theory of probability, hence its surprising opening statement 'Probability does not exist'. 20th Century physics and social science have done much to question this premise. There is now a growing authoritative body of opinion that regards statistical laws as being as fundamental as causal laws in ordering phenomena. However, Causal Chains and Nets provide an important unifying frame between engineering reasoning (based on strict causality) and statistical reasoning (based on the laws of chance). It has the virtue of dissolving many of the antagonisms that exist between these modes reasoning. If on the one hand the process of causalization does not in any meaningful way distort the facts and the influences involved are few, genuinely useful functional relationships can be formulated from which deductions and predictions can be made. These for practical purposes, can be regarded as deterministic rather than probabilistic. On the other hand, if no chain can be found that consistently dominates, we have to be prepared to accept a statistical representation for the gross effect.

The advantage of the former is that engineering actions can be taken on the sound understanding of what has caused the phenomena, its disadvantage is that as far as reliability calculus is concerned, it presents a gross oversimplification as causal isolation is a process of idealization, hence providing no basis of measuring or calculating reliability except in idealized conditions. The advantage of the latter is that given an understanding of the statistical processes involved, realistic measurements along with their uncertainties, can be ascertained. Its disadvantage is that it rarely provides a basis from which engineers can decide upon specific actions for eliminating unreliability.

PROBABILISTIC CAUSALITY

The resolving of the dissonance between causality and probability in ordering facts, is a central objective if one is to develop a reliability theory of practical importance. A key aspect of practical theories is the recognition that to be practical they must be capable of handling counter-to-fact conditionals (counterfactuals). A 'conditional' is a sentence expressing a proposition which whilst being a function of two or more premises, is not a truth functional e.g.:-

> The reliability of System X will be improved if we replace the components of type A with components of type B since components of type A appear to account for the majority of failures and our experience of components type B has shown fewer instances of being associated with failure.

Whilst maybe being true, the conclusion of this argument does not logically follow from the premises.

The subjunctive form of a conditional (or simply counterfactual) is of particular importance in reliability, as it introduces the quality of being a prediction. Most decisions made by engineers for purposes of achieving reliability are more or less based upon counterfactual reasoning. A counterfactual is a sentence expressing a proposition of the kind:

> If we had done M instead of N, then the consequence would have been P instead of Q

e.g. If we had used components of type B instead of A, then the rate of occurrence of failure would have been lower.

By weakening the consequent conditions from 'would' to 'probably would', results in a probabilistic subjunctive.

It should be evident that conditional reasoning involves an understanding of inductive logic. However in counterfactual reasoning the quality of prediction and the invoking of the counter-to-fact conditions (Condition M) add extra dimensions of complexity. A considerable literature exists on the logic of counterfactuals, the majority of which argues that counterfactual inferences can only be shown to be sound if they invoke law-like sentences, by which is meant to invoke the condition 'it must be so' rather than the weaker condition 'it is so'. In other words, sound counterfactual reasoning is thought to require at its basis scientific law, most usually based on causality rather than mere empirical generalizations since they extend the law beyond the immediate knowable facts. Further, many who have made a point of studying this logic argue that by their very nature the logic of counterfactuals is that of Modal Logic since it involves both logical necessity and possibility as well as causal necessity and possibility. (Ref 37).

There is little doubt in my mind that counterfactual logic, hence modal logic, is important to the problem of reliability prediction of new designs, but this will not be pursued. Those that are interested should refer to A. W. Burks' treatise (Ref 38) for a full treatment of the logic of chance, cause and dispositions (propensity), he is one of the most respected computer scientist/philosophers of modern times.

For our purposes one will exploit a remarkably simple, yet perceptive analysis of counterfactuals, that of J. L. Mackie (Ref 39). To Mackie, counterfactuals are merely condensed arguments for which we get into difficulties when we try to characterize them as being either true or false. Such difficulties can be avoided if we concentrate on the circumstances in which we can legitimately use them. Mackie concedes that the notion of cause is relevant since in his analysis, empirical generalizations or accidental universal propositions do not sustain counterfactuals in the same way as causal laws. An accidental universal is a proposition of the kind: no polar bears live at the south pole - which whilst being true (is so), there appears no particular causal reason as to why this should be (thus must remain so).

Having demonstated that counterfactuals are condensed arguments, and recognized that one cannot determine how such arguments may be completed so that the conclusions logically follow from the premises, we have to concede that they are merely <u>sustained</u> by the premises. Unlike most logicians, whose enquiries concern themselves with the special nature of causal laws, Mackie concentrates on the deficiencies of accidental laws. He points out that the essential difference between these is that in general, accidental laws are thought of as being true by virtue of their enumerations (citing of examples) within a localized set of circumstances, whereas causal laws are true by virtue of them expressing some universal natural order amongst things. In reliability, an example of a universal law is that of:

The distribution of a random variable, which is the sum of numerous independently distributed random variables, in which no individual dominates is normal.

An example of an accidental law is:

That the distribution of maintenance times of some complex equipment can be represented by the log-normal distribution.

Mackie concludes that ultimately counterfactuals are supported by full inductive evidence not simply enumerative evidence. This analysis identifies the importance of developing methods by which one can decide if the support for a counterfactual is based simply upon enumeration or more substantial inductive evidence. We must know if the patterns in data are due to local circumstances at some particular point in time, or are due to more general causal influences. This cannot be totally determined by statistical analysis since statistical measures such as correlation and goodness of fit statistics can result from either causal influences at one extreme, or be totally spurious at the other. The problem reduces to that of formulating and giving definition to the relevant notions, thereby permitting the problem to be treated rigorously.

A notion of particular importance of providing this unifying synthesis for probability and cause is that of Causal Propensity, or as it is more usually referred to: Probabilistic Causality. It is the subject that deals with the probabilistic measure of one event to cause another event. However, as both cause and probability are entrenched within our language so as to be an antithesis of each other, an explanation of what one means by probabilistic causality requires it to be defined.

It is often presumed that to remove misunderstandings all we need to do is to define our terms. There are many circumstances when the demand for definition cannot be legitimately made, and also there are many circumstances when the act of defining is a major source of confusion, so an important starting point in a discussion of defining an unfamiliar notion is to gain an understanding of the process of definition itself.

Definition is one of the most complicated aspects of scientific discourse. Much of the controversy that surrounds reliability has arisen from the fact that the subtleties of definition are not recognized. Thompson in his excellent paper 'Foundations of Reliability' (Ref 40) shows how the term 'Failure Rate' has come to be used in an extensive number of different ways, which as far as the engineer is concerned, none of which mean the same thing, and each of which is likely to have a different numerical value. The present situation is crazy, currently reliability engineers use 'intensity functions of stochastic processes', 'renewal rates', 'hazard rates', 'measures of central tendency', 'averages of failure observations' etc... as if they all mean the same thing. The sad thing about this situation, is that it has been propagated by an eagerness to become mathematically sophisticated without the necessary care needed in determining one's reference boundaries and defining what is meant by the elemental terms used.

The task of defining a term can be difficult, and if one is required to avoid confusion some insight into these difficulties is required. P.A.Angeles in his Dictionary (Ref 41), lists twenty different types of definition, none of which are synonymous and many of which can be combined to produce yet another type. He points out that his list is not exhaustive, which is as well, since he does not include an explication; one of the most important types of definition in science, and particularly in reliability.

Whilst it is inappropriate to discuss in full the ramifications of the role of definition, it is important that some insight of what is involved is given. The following discussion is an extremely brief precis of the relevant part of Carl G. Hempel's monograph 'Fundamentals of Concept Formulation in Empirical Science' (Ref 42).

As far as Hempel is concerned, definitions are capable of being categorized as either:

Nominal Definition

Real Definition

Explication

A 'Nominal Definition' is a convention which merely introduces an alternative (and usually abbreviated) notation for a given linguistic expression. For example, we may define

> The conditional probability that a part from a population with a distribution F, put into service at Time t = 0 and known to have survived until Time = tx, fails during the time interval (tx, tx + dtx)/dtx as dtx tends to zero: as the Hazard Rate at time tx.

The form of a 'Nominal Definition' has the form

> Let the expression E2 be synonymous with the expression E1

Here Nominal definition is the process whereby one introduces or defines a new expression. Usually in science it is the process of singling out and naming a particular concept, which may be a property, a class, a relation, a function etc... The majority of Nominal Definitions in physics and reliability are those that specify a particular relation and are usually in the form of a mathematical function.

There is only one requirement of a nominal definition of a term, and this is, that it must enable us to eliminate that term from any context in which it can grammatically occur in favour of the other expression. An essential property of this class of definition, is that since it is merely a substitute for another linguistic arrangement, it brings with it no new knowledge whatsoever. In consequence, its inferences are already logically implied and any results of mathematical manipulation are considered to have been latent within the original formulation.

Hempel points out, in traditional logic, a real definition is not a stipulation determining a meaning of an expression, but a statement of the essential nature or essential attributes of some entity, but the concept of what is essential, is so vague as to render this characterization as useless. However in the Empiricist thesis, one can re-interpret this as: The quest for a real definition as being a search for either an Empirical explanation of some phenomena, or as a 'meaning analysis'.

Thus a Real definition has the form

(x) is an x if and only if it satisfies conditions C

Thus one may define an equipment as being reliable if and only if it satisfies conditions (A.B.C...)

Where A for instance may be the condition that the equipment conforms to its performance specification.

Where B may be the condition that under a specified condition it will operate for T time.

Where C for instance may be that should a component fail, the equipment will still satisfy some performance criteria.

These conditions may take the form of either an Empirical assertion, or an Analytical assertion.

An Empirical assertion is an assertion that characterizes that which is a matter of empirical fact, in that they are necessary and sufficient for the realization of the phenomena of interest. They are most likely to be expressed as mathematical formulae which have the character of being a scientific law.

An Analytical assertion is an assertion whose meaning has already been understood. This understanding is derived from the analytical process called a 'Meaning Analysis'. Suffice to say, that this procedure is a highly technical one that presupposes the existence of a language whose expressions have a precisely determined meaning.

Belatedly, we are now in the position of making known what is meant by an explication. An Explication is Rudolf Carnap's term and is broadly synonymous with what is termed a 'logical analysis' or a 'rational reconstruction'. It is concerned with those expressions whose meaning in normal communication are more or less vague (such as truth, probability, number, cause, law). The aim of an explication is to give to these vague terms, a new and precisely defined meaning, to render them more suitable for a clear and rigorous discourse on the subject matter in hand.

Explications have the nature of being proposals and thus cannot be qualified as being either true or false. However their formation is not an ad hoc procedure. They must satisfy two requirements, namely; that the explicated term must permit us to reformulate precisely a large part of what is customarily understood by that term, and it should be possible to develop in using the explicated term a comprehensive sound theoretical system.

An important form of explication that is a basis of constructing models, is that of an axiom, and its counterpart, an axiomatic system or axiomatic model.

Until recently, it was reasonably clear what was meant by an axiom (Ref 43). An axiom, maxim, or postulate was regarded as a principle of a science in the form of a proposition, whose appearance of being true was so compelling, that it was accepted as such without proof: It was regarded as being self-evidently true. Axiomization then consisted of organizing a body of axioms or propositions into a fully coherent system, such that the principles of the system appear indubitable by virtue of their own self-evidence. The result is a logico-mathematical deductive apparatus from which implications could be deduced that embodied the certainty of its formulating axioms.

The 19th Century saw the transformation of this logico-mathematical structure into a formal and semi-rigorous procedure by which scientific theories could be constructed and inferences made. In general, its development progressed in three stages.

From A categorical deductive system which demonstrated the truth of its consequences by the truth of its principles which were laid down dogmatically.

To A system of hypothetical deductions which prove the a posteriori truth of its provisional hypothesis by demonstrating the truth of their consequences.

To A system of pure hypothetical deductions whose principles are introduced as a plausible fiction removed from the domain from what is true and what is false, so that the concepts of truth only comes into play at the level of logical and mathematical consequences.

A point of importance is to distinguish how definitions differ within axiomatic systems of mathematics as against axiomatic systems of physics. Whereas definitions within mathematics are conceptual in that it clarifies the meaning of a concept by means of other concepts. Within physics (and for that matter science and engineering) the physical definitions take the meaning for granted and co-ordinates it to the physical thing. In Reichenbacks terminology physical definition is a co-ordinative definition. They are in the nature of 'real definition' since they co-ordinate mathematical definitions to a piece of reality.

In terms of explaining the notion of probabilistic causality, a survey of the literature identifies two outstanding contributions both of which are developments of the axiomatic method, those of Patrick Suppes (Ref 44) and I.J. Good (Ref 45).

Suppes' contribution is intended to have a wide coverage of issues to which causation can be addressed. Suppes' whilst acknowledging that causal analysis is restricted to those areas where causation is intuitively meaningful e.g. innoculation against cholera, as against examples where it has no possible meanings e.g. the familiar coin tossing experiment, Suppes identifies at least three conceptual frameworks in which it is meaningful to make causal claims, these being:

A conceptual framework that arises in respect to a particular scientific theory.

The framework that arises in connection with a particular experiment or class of experiments.

The framework of expressing beliefs with respect to the evidence available.

In developing his theory of causal relations, Suppes initially proposes a number of definitions of causal connection in terms of a probabilistic relationship that exists between an event called cause and an event called effect, these being:

Prima facie

The event Bt′ is a prima facie cause of the event At if and only if

(i) $t' < t$
(ii) $P(Bt') > 0$
(iii) $P(At|Bt') > P(At)$

Spurious Cause

Intuitively the idea of a spurious cause is that of an early event called cause denoted Ct″ which accounts for the conditional probability of the event called effect denoted At and is such that a provisional definition of a spurious cause is

Let Bt′ be a prima facie cause of At. Then Bt′ is a spurious cause of At if and only if there is a $t'' < t'$ and an event Ct″ such that $P(Bt'\ Ct'')>0$ and:

$$P(At|Bt'\ Ct'') = P(At|Ct'')$$

By Suppes' account, this intuitive definition is inadequate and thus further refined definitions of spurious cause type 1, type 2 and ε type are given

Spurious Cause Type 1

An event Bt′ is a spurious cause in sense one of At if and only if Bt′ is a prima facie cause of At and there is a $t'' < t'$ and an event Ct″ such that

(i) $P(Bt'|Ct'') > 0,$
(ii) $P(At|Bt'\ Ct'') = P(At|Ct''),$
(iii) $P(At|Bt'\ Ct'') > P(At|Bt').$

Spurious Cause Type 2

An event Bt′ is a spurious cause of At in sense two if and only if Bt′ is a prima facie cause of At and there is a $t'' < t'$ and a partition $\pi t''$ such that for all elements Ct″ of $\pi t''$

(i) $P(Bt'\ Ct'') > 0$
(ii) $P(At|Bt'\ Ct'') = P(At|Ct'')$

Spurious Cause Type

An event Bt′ is an ε-spurious cause of At if and only if there is a $t'' < t'$ and a partition $\pi t''$ such that for all elements Ct″ of $\pi t''$

(i) $t' < t,$
(ii) $P(Bt') > 0,$

(iii) $P(At\ Bt') > P(At)$,
(iv) $P(Bt'\ Ct'') > 0$,
(v) $\| P(At|Bt'\ Ct'') - P(At|Ct'') \| < \varepsilon$

In Suppes' monograph each of these definitions is supported by explanations, theorems and examples.

In like manner Suppes continues to define other classes of causal relationships e.g.

- Direct cause: ε direct cause.
- Supplementary cause: ε supplementary cause.
- Sufficient cause.
- Negative cause.

These definitions require no commitment to any particular theory of probability. However, in formulating a qualitative theory of causal relationships, the commitment is to the subjective theory of probability in that Suppes extends Di Finetti's axioms to the introduction of the notion of qualitative conditional probability. He then proceeds to define the qualitative relationships between cause and effects e.g.

The event Bt' is a qualitative prima facie cause of At if and only if

(i) $t' < t$
(ii) Bt' is non-null
(iii) $At \mid Bt' \succ At$ ($\succ$ reads more probable)

In like manner various other definitions of Qualitative causal connection are given.

As Suppes points out, his theory is likely to be of little interest to the objectivist who holds a frequencist view of probability.

It should be stressed that in no way have I intended to give an account of these elaborate theories, since to give even a reasonable account demands a monograph treatment.

In terms of reliability analysis, possibly Good's explication is of more immediate interest as it is quantitative. To understand the derivation of Good's theory, one must introduce his notion of the 'Weight of Evidence'.

The 'Weight of Evidence' was formulated by Alan Turing and its mathematical development is due to I. J. Good (Ref 35). In standard statistical reasoning, we often imply a probable effect of a cause. If this is a legitimate pre-occupation, so is determining the probable cause of an effect. In principle it should be an easier task as cause always proceeds an effect, thus the concept of prediction is surplanted by the concept of retrodiction. Thomas Bayes (the 17th Century logician) formalized how this may be logically achieved. It is the well known Bayes' theorem. Its logical frame is now known as 'Inverse Probability'. At its simplest, it is nothing more than the common-sense notion of the likeliness of a cause.

We can describe how it works by reference to a simple experiment. Say we have 2 boxes each of which contain 3 balls. We know that in one of the boxes there are two white balls and one black, whilst in the other there are two black balls and one white. We now have to guess which box contains which set of balls. The only information that we can go on is that we can select at random one ball from one box. Now, say we select a white ball from box (A), common sense tells us that it is twice as likely that this is the box that contains the two white balls. Instead of talking about what is likely, we can talk in terms of betting odds. We could say that the odds are 2:1 that box (A) contains the white balls. Equally we could say that the probability is twice as high that box (A) contains the white balls (in this instance these statements are logically equivalent).

It was Alan Turing the eminent mathematician, that saw that within this concept there was a means of deciding between alternative hypotheses. Turing's insight was to consider what would happen within a series of such experiments. He reasoned that if the hypothesis: box (A) contains the white balls, is true, the odds in favour of this would accumulate to a very large number as the experiments continued. For purposes of mathematical ease, Turing preferred the idea of summing the logarithms of the odds rather than multiplying them. In our example, the discovery of a white ball from box (A) then added a weight of evidence of log 2 that it was box (A) that contained the two white balls. A consequence of this reasoning is that we can explicitly state a mathematical theory that gives us a measure in favour of a hypothesis as the evidence accumulates.

The bringing of this idea into mathematics was achieved by I. J. Good (Ref 35) and is relatively easy to understand. It follows three stages: that of showing that it relates in an obvious way to the probability calculus, secondly that it relates to the intuitive concepts of information and finally, that the information can be shown to support a hypothesis in a probabilistic manner.

To remain consistent with the usual axioms of probability a measure of the gain in information denoted I(A) about an event A, when A occurs has to satisfy two simple conditions.

(i) I(A) has to be a decreasing function of P(A), since the larger the value of P(A) the less information about A will be gained on observing A.
e.g. Given tha Ohm's Law completely specifies the relation between voltage, current and resistance in a DC network: The observation of 1 amp flow in a network whose resistance is 1 Ohm when 1 Volt is applied elicits no gain in information.

(ii) It is desirable that the gain in information about a sequence of independent events $A_1\ A_2 \ldots A_n$ should be equal to the sum of the individual $I(A_i)$'s.

The function

$I(A) = -\text{Log}\, P(A)$ (or some other function which is proportional to this)

satisfies both these conditions. From this we can deduce some of the properties of I(A) which are

(i) $I(\Omega) = 0$, since there is no gain of information about the events when the outcome of an experiment is known with absolute certainty.

(ii) $I(A) \geqslant 0$, for all A in $\mathfrak{F}$, the sigma algebra field of the probability space.

(iii) $I(A) = \infty$ if $P(A) = 0$ so I is unbounded

Good developed the simple notion of the gain in information I(A) to that of the conditional information I(A|B) which is defined as the gain in information when the event A occurs given that the event B has occurred, that is given that P(B) > 0, For this

$$I(A|B) = -\text{Log}\, P(A|B) = -\text{Log}(P(AB)/P(B))$$

$$= \text{Log}\, P(B) - \text{Log}\, P(AB) = I(AB) - I(B)$$

Where AB stands for the intersection of A and B ie $A \cap B$

Some of the properties of conditional information are

(i) if $B \subseteq A$ then $I(A|B) = 0$ which is reasonable since the occurrence of B provides the full information about the occurrence of A

(ii) if $A \subseteq B$ then $I(A|B) = I(A) - I(B)$

(iii) if A and B are independent then $I(A|B) = I(A)$, thus B gives us no information concerning A

(iv) if $P(AB) = 0$ then $I(A|B) = \infty$ providing $P(B) > 0$

In like manner the concept of Mutual information between events A and B is formulated

$$I(A{:}B) = I(A) - I(A|B) = I(A) + I(B) - I(AB)$$

$$= I(B) - I(B|A) = I(B{:}A)$$

which can also be expressed

$$I(A{:}B) = \operatorname{Log} \frac{P(A|B)}{P(A)} = \operatorname{Log} \frac{P(A\,B)}{P(A)P(B)} = \operatorname{Log} \frac{P(B|A)}{P(B)}$$

$I(A{:}B)$ can be thought of as the measure of the positive or negative information concerning the occurrence of A (or B) provided by the occurrence of B.

Some of the properties of $I(A{:}B)$ are

(i) if A and B are independent then $I(A{:}B) = 0$ since the occurrence of B gives us no information about the occurrence of A

(ii) if $B \subseteq A$ then $I(A{:}B) = I(A)$ since the occurrence of B provides all the information about the occurrence of A

(iii) if $P(A) > 0$, $P(B) > 0$, and $P(AB) = 0$ then $I(A{:}B) = -\infty$ which would be the case if A and B were mutually exclusive.

The important notion 'The Weight of Evidence' can be interpreted as the difference in information about competing hypothesis H_1 compared to H_2 provided by the event B. It is defined

$$W(H_1/H_2{:}B) = \operatorname{Log} \left[\frac{O(H_1./H_2.\,B)}{O(H_1/H_2)} \right]$$

$$= I(H_1{:}B) - I(H_2{:}B)$$

where $O(H_1/H_2\ B)$ is the odds in favour of H_1 as opposed to H_2 given B.

It should be noted that although treated without much attention in this paper the Weight of Evidence is one of the most important concepts of modern statistical thinking. It, for instance, provides a basis for developing many of the important criteria of science e.g. measures of corroboration, explanation, simplicity etc... and in particular I believe, has great applicability in the development of reliability theory as applied to computer systems. At least 40 of I. J. Good's papers make reference to it. A suitably complete account is to be found in (Ref 46).

A similar formulation was developed by Abraham Wald (Ref 47) that of the Sequential Probability Ratio test, which has recieved wide applicability in Quality Control and Reliability testing, it is the mathematical basis of the testing plans in MIL HNB 781-Testing for Reliability. However in Walds formulation only objective evidence within a testing sequence is permitted to be considered.

It is well known that a statistical association between various events does not provide a basis of formal inference since this may arise for a variety of reasons. Firstly, it may be purely spurious in which case a knowledge of one event implies nothing about the other. Alternatively one event may be statistically relevant but not causally relevant to the other e.g. the sale of soft drinks in Australia is statistically relevant to the sale of Umbrella's in Britain (when it is summer in Australia, it is winter in Britain). Within the Concealed Cause Thesis statistical relevance implies a common causal ancestry. Whilst statistical relevance as such will not be further persued in this paper, for those interested the work of Wesley Salmon is important (Ref 48 and 49). Finally a statistical association may be a result of a causal connection in which case, all things being equal the occurrence of one event can be regarded as making the other event more probable. One should note the condition - all things being equal - since there are many situation where one event can be legitimately referred to as a cause, makes its effect less likely e.g. the taking of some birth control pills is considered a probablistic cause of thrombosis, yet to some people the onset of thrombosis will be less likely since pregnancy is a greater cause of thrombosis.

It is the statistical associations that characterize causal connections which is the subject of I.J. Good's Probabilistic Causal Calculus (Ref 24 and 45). Good explicates the causal propensity of an event F to cause an event E as the Weight of Evidence against F if E does not occur.

The formula for Causal Propensity Q is

$$Q(E:F) = W(\bar{F}:\bar{E}) = W(\bar{F}:\bar{E}|U \,\&\, H) \qquad \text{(: denotes provided by)}$$

which reads:

The Causal Propensity Q of the event F to cause E is equal to the Weight of Evidence against F if the event E does not occur, which is equal to the Weight of Evidence against F if the event of E does not occur given the physical circumstances denoted U and the true laws of nature denoted H.

The conditions U & H are often taken for granted and hence in notation are dropped but always presumed.

By introducing the formulation of the Weight of Evidence as previously outlined:

$$Q(E|F) = \text{Log} \left[\frac{P(\bar{E}|\bar{F} \,\&\, U \,\&\, H)}{P(\bar{E}|F \,\&\, U \,\&\, H)} \right]$$

which reads:

Causal Propensity Q of the event F to cause E is equal to the Logarithm of the ratio of probability of the event E not occuring given the event F does not occur to the probability of the event E not occuring given the event F does occur.

This formulation of Probablistic Cause is already (albeit informally) part of reliability engineering methodology. For example in a reliability growth exercise of the Test - Analyse - Fix type, we subject a new design to various stresses, the purpose of which is to induce failures.

From the circumstances that resulted in failures we construct an explanation that accounts for the failure mode and then introduce a design change in the equipment under test that inhibits the relevant failure mode thus increasing reliability. If we denote F (the probablistic cause) as the circumstances that lead to equipment failure, and E (the effect) as the equipment failure, the form of our inference is that of Good's explication.

Implied within this account of reliability growth testing is an important working heuristic that distinguishes between causal explanation which is an explanation invoking the concept of cause that accounts for the facts but of itself is an inadequate basis for suggesting corrective actions, and that of an implied causal relationship which strongly suggests that if the cause can be suppressed, improved reliability will be achieved. The heuristic is that if a logically possible design change exists that would improve reliability we can designate unreliability as being caused, in which case the cause once formulated, constitutes a prima facia cause of the unreliability.

Examples of causal explanations for unreliability are:

Poorly defined requirements

Badly written specifications

Badly structured designs

Inadequate Quality Control

Inadequate Testing

Etc ...

Examples of obvious causal relations are:

Inability to withstand stress

Inadequate protection against radiation

Breakdown in insulation

Timing Faults

Inadequate lubrication

Etc ...

The distinction is now apparent in that causal explanations provide the means of justifying how failures could have been avoided in the first place, but unfortunately suggest no obvious mechanism for improvement, whereas causal relationships suggest how improvement may be achieved but may well fail to provide as adequate account for the circumstances that lead to the incorporation of a particular failure mode.

The virtue of Good's explication of Probablistic Cause is that given a sufficiently detailed analysis, the potential exists for combining the causal explanatory variables and the direct causal relations within a common frame, that of the causal net. However, this must be a topic of further research for which I suspect Good's calculus provides the foundational work.

Goods quantitative explication of probablistic causality, is in terms of what is referred to as statistical or factual probability. Whilst Good claims that it is independent of a commitment to a particular theory of probability e.g. Von Mises frequency theory or De Finettis subjective theory Good states, in the opening of his paper, that he is committed to the subjectivist interpretation of probability, and thus his theory is possibly more meaningful within this frame. It is clear that Good saw his theory as initially having its first clear cut application in terms of providing a foundation to modern statistics. However, it is worthy of note that so far the statistical fraternity are in the main unaware of it. A possible explanation for this is given by Wesley Salmon (Ref 50) in which he attributes the forbidding mathematical style of Good which is highly formal, as a possible reason as to it not having the impact it deserves.

In spite of the highly formal presentation of Good's theory, stripped of its axioms and theorems, the basic concept is not difficult to grasp. Good himself suggests how this may be done by drawing attention to the fact that a resistive network can be viewed as an analogy of the connections between a variety of causes and a variety of effects in which a number of causes participate. At the heart of Good's explication is the 'Causal Net': Which is an arrangement of events (an event can at one and the same time be a cause and an effect). The physical analogy given by Good is to describe this net as a resistive network, where each resistor is an event, and each junction between resistors in a network is that point where one event conjoins with another. Of course, within each link of the network a diode is placed to ensure that time only travels in one direction.

The 'causal chain' is a special case of a causal net consisting in the analogy as an isolated series path of resistors. To complete the analogy any event called cause which is antecedent to its related event called effect, is mapped or pathed to the event called effect which a consequence of the events called cause: This can loosely be thought of as being a part of a resistive network in which the degree of causality between input and output of the causal net is the effective resistance. It should be stressed that Good intends the resistive network to be an analogy of the causal net and not a functional model of it. To support the causal net, and to provide a means of quantifying degrees of causality, Good gives 24 axioms and 18 theorems. The general plan of Good's theory is to suggest explicta for:

(i) Q(E:F), or Q for short, the 'causal support for E provided by F, or the tendency for F to cause E'.

(ii) The strength of a causal chain joining F to E.

(iii) The strength of a causal net joining F to E.

(iv) χ (E|F), or χ for short, the contribution of the causation of E provided by F, i.e. the degree to which F caused E. Which is defined as the strength of a causal net joining F to E when the details of the net are completely filled in so there is no relevant events omitted.

Further important discussions on probabilistic causality and related subject matter are to be found in references (49 and 50).

In recent times an increasing interest in probabilistic causality is being shown within various scientific circles normally considered to be statistical. These include Medical, Insurance, Risk Analysis, Economics and Physics. It is my belief that currently Suppes' and Good's account will be shown to be inadequate, but within reliability they are vastly superior to any currently alternative available account for thinking about causality.

In conclusion, I am conscious that to the reliability engineer this paper has touched upon many unfamiliar topics. The brevity of the discussion is such that it does not provide an adequate account of its subject matter. For this reason an extensive Bibliography is included.

REFERENCES

1. Foundations of Logic and Mathematics
Rudolf Carnap
Volume 1 Number 3 Foundations of the Unity of Science
The University of Chicago Press Third Impression 1971

2. The Interpretation of Interactions in Contingency Tables
E. H. Simpson
Journal of Royal Statistical Society
Series B No:2 (1961) 238 - 241

3. An Introduction to Logic and Scientific Method
M. R. Cohen. E. Nagel
Routledge & Kegan Paul. Reprinted 1978

4. Fact, Fiction and Forecast.
N. Goodman
Harvard University Press 4th Edition 1983

5. On Induction Chapter 1.
On Demarcation (Falsifiability) Introduction.
On Verification (Falsification) Chapter 2 Section 22.
Objective Knowledge.
Karl R. Popper.
Oxford & Clarendon Press Revised Edition 1983

6. Sense Data and Physics Published in Mysticism and Logic (Page 155)
Bertrand Russell
George Allen & Unwin 1918

7. Chapter vii - Probability and Induction.
Human Knowledge Its Scope and Limits
Bertrand Russell
George Allen & Unwin

8. Induction as Hypothesis
The Philosophy of the Inductive Sciences (1840) Volume II
William Whewell
Quoted in Readings on Logic
Edited by Irving M. Copi & James A. Gould
MacMillan Publishing Co. Inc. 1972

9. Science and Hypothesis
Henri Poincare
Dover Books 1952

10. Page 6
Aspects of Scientific Explanation
Carl G. Hempel
The Free Press
Collier Macmillan 1970

11. Preface to First Edition
Theory of Probability
Harold Jeffreys
Clarendon Press
Third Edition 1983

12. Theories of Probability
Terrence L. Fine
Academic Press 1973

13. Logic of Statistical Inference
Ian Hacking
Cambridge University Press reprinted 1979

14. Probability, Statistics and Truth
Richard Von Mises
Dover 1981

15. On Assumptions
Alexius Meinong
Edited and translated and Introduction by James Heanue
University of California Press 1976

16. Foundations of Probability
A.N. Kolmogoroff
English Translation Edited by Nathan Morrison
Chelsea Publishing Co. 2nd Edition 1956

17. See entry - Axioms of Probability
Contribution by I. J. Good
Encyclopedia of Statistical Sciences
John Wiley & Son Vol 1 - 1982

18. On a New Axiomatic Theory of Probability
Alfred Renyi
ACTA Mathematics ACAD
SCI Hungary 1955 Volume 6

19. Treatise on Probability
John Maynard Keynes
MacMillan Press Ltd
Royal Economic Society Edition 1973

20. Logical Foundations of Probability
Rudolph Carnap
University of Chicago Press 2nd edition 1962

21. Probability and Hume's Inductive Scepticism
D. C. Stove
Oxford University Press 1973

22. The Foundations of Statistics
Leonard J. Savage
Dover 2nd Edition 1972

23. Theory of Probability. A Critical Introductory Treatment
Bruno De Finetti
John Wiley 1974 & 1975 (2 Vols)

24. Good Thinking: The Foundations of Probability and its Applications
I. J. Good
University of Minnesota Press 1983

25. Optimal Statistical Decisions
Morris H. DeGroot
McGraw Hill 1970

26. Bayesian Statistics: A Review
D. V. Lindley
SIAM 1971

27. Physics and Beyond
Werner Heisenberg
George Allen & Unwin 1971

28. See entry Bayesian Inference Contribution by D.V. Lindley
Encyclopedia of Statistical Sciences
John Wiley & Son Volume I 1982

29. Initial Probabilities: A Prerequisite For Any Valid Induction
Bruno De Finetti
Induction, Physics and Ethics
(Proceedings and Discussions of the 1968 Salzburg Coloquium in the Philosophy of Science)
Edited by Paul Weingartner & Gerhard Zecha
Humanities Press 1970

30. Advanced Theory of Statistics (Vol II page 299 Section 26.4)
Sir Maurice Kendall and A. Stuart
Griffiths 1979

31. Causation and Conditionals
Ernest Sosa - Editor
Oxford reading in Philosophy
Oxford University Press re-printed 1980

32. Introduction to Logic
Irving M. Copi
Collier MacMillan 6th edition 1982
(For conditions of Cause see Pages 409 - 415, On Mill's Method see pages 415 - 461)

33. The Cement of the Universe: A Study of Causation
J. L. Mackie
Clarendon Library of Logic and Philosophy
Oxford at the Clarendon Press reprinted in Paperback 1980
(On Mill's Method see particularly the Appendix on Eliminative Methods of Induction)

34. A Treatise of Human Nature
David Hume Edited by D.G.C. MacNabb
Fontana/Collins P/B 5th Impression 1978 (2 vols)

35. Information, Weight of Evidence, The Singularity between Probability Measures and Signal Detection
I. J. Good & D. B. Osteyee
Springer, Verlag 1974

36. Causality and Modern Science
Mario Bunge
Dover Publications Inc 1979

37. Laws Modalities and Counterfacturals
Hans Reichenbach
University of California Press 1976
see also Ref 4

38. Chance, Cause, Reason
Arthur W. Burks
The University of Chicago Press 1977

39. Counterfactuals and Causal Laws
J. L. Mackie
Published in: Analytical Philosophy
Edited by R. J. Butler
Basil Blackwell Oxford 1966

40. Foundations of Reliability
W. A. Thompson
Technometrics Vol 23 No:1 1981

41. Dictionary of Philosophy
Peter A. Angeles
Barnes & Noble Books 1981

42. Fundamentals of Concept Formation in Empirical Science
Carl G. Hempel
Published in: Vol 2 Foundation of the Unity of Science
Edited: Otto Neurall, Rudolph Carnap & Charles Morris
University of Chicago Press 1970

43. Dictionary of the History of Ideas Vol 1
Philip P. Weiner Chief Editor
Charles Scribner & Son 1973
Entry on Axiomization contributed by Robert Blanche

44. A Probabilistic Theory of Causality
Patrick Suppes
North-Holland 1972

45. A Causal Calculus (see also Ref 24)
I. J. Good
The British Journal for the Philosophy of Science
Part 1 Pages 305 - 318 Volume 11 1961
Part 2 Pages 43 - 51 Volume 12 1962

46. Corroboration, Explanation, Evolving Probability, Simplicity and a Sharpened Razor
I. J. Good
British Journal of Philosophy of Science No: 19 1968

47. Sequential Analysis
Abraham Wald
Dover Publications Inc 1947

48. Statistical Explanation and Statistical Relevance
Wesley C. Salmon
with contributions by Richard C. Jeffrey & James G. Green
University of Pittsburgh Press 1971

49. Scientific Explanation and the Causal Structure of the World
Wesley C. Salmon
Princeton University Press 1984

50. Probablistic Causality
Wesley C. Salmon
Pacific Philosophical Quarterly
Vol 1 1980 (pages 50 - 74)

Part 4

The Economics of Computing and Methods of Cost Assessment

Organised by Gerry McNichols

NEEDS ASSESSMENT: THE FIRST STEP IN A COST-EFFECTIVE DESIGN OF A COMPUTER-BASED SYSTEM

By

Gerald R. McNichols
Gary L. Sorrell

MANAGEMENT CONSULTING & RESEARCH, INC.
Four Skyline Place
5113 Leesburg Pike, Suite 509
Falls Church, Virginia 22041
(703) 820-4600

NATO ASI Series, Vol. F22
Software System Design Methods. Edited by J.K. Skwirzynski

ABSTRACT

Needs assessment is one of the initial steps of an operations research study, preliminary even to the start of a software engineering effort. This presentation discusses the "needs assessment" process, as related to cost-effective design of computer-based, decision support systems. The flow from identification of need through feasibility analysis will be traced. The philosophy is to be not only _efficient_ ("doing things right"), but to be _effective_ ("doing right things").

Whether generated internally or by a user group within the client's organization, a proposed system need _must_ be analyzed to determine if the justification for a need is complete and accurate. The analysis performed during a needs identification study can be minor or it can be very involved depending on the magnitude of the proposed need. MCR has conducted this type of analysis for the U.S. Army and U.S. Navy and specific examples will be cited.

The result of a Needs Identification Study will indicate one of two things. Either:

- the need is not great enough to consider automation further, or
- a feasibility study should be conducted.

The scope of a feasibility study, if required, depends on whether the questions to be answered involve replacement of manual systems, conversions or modifications of existing systems, or combinations of operational systems. The study itself should be structured so that meaningful decision points can be established during the course of the study. For example, if a requirements analysis is completed and it indicated there is no need to automate the particular processes involved, then obviously the study should be terminated. This decision may not be possible until after a cost-benefit analysis is performed. The key point is that <u>not all feasibility studies result in a decision to automate</u>. The "Needs Assessment" is thus a critical input to the economics of computing and methods of cost assessment.

INTRODUCTION

How many times have you heard of an automated system being more cumbersome than the old manual method, or so complex/complicated that the intended users could not or would not use it? Too often (even if your answer is one)! How can this happen? Isn't automation always the best way? The answer is a qualified "maybe". The current slump in the computer industry, in addition to being tied to economic conditions and the strength of the dollar, may also be reflecting the failure of users of personal computers to conduct a proper/valid needs assessment. Numerous owners of computers rushed out to buy equipment before knowing what they wanted and for what they would use the new capability. Other potential owners became so confused by the computer industry advertising that they simply gave up on trying to understand, did not buy and probably will not buy a computer. How can we avoid false starts or automation where it is not warranted? A thorough needs assessment should permit the proper decision.

In the automated system life cycle process, the first or conceptual phase is where the needs assessment is conducted. The purpose is to determine whether to proceed with the software development process. The needs assessment usually consists of five major efforts:

- Needs Identification Study,
- Feasibility Study,
- Cost-Benefit Analysis,
- Recommended System Summary, and

- Functional and Data Requirements Documentation.

The points covered here will concern only the first three of these efforts, since the last two occur after the decision to automate has been made. Unfortunately for many automated systems, the first three efforts are too often ignored, and a system is developed starting with the system summary effort. With existing automated decision support systems, which we will discuss later, there is no reason why the first three efforts can not be accomplished quickly and easily. Once these three have been completed, we should feel comfortable in proceeding to the development process, if it is justified by the needs assessment process.

NEEDS IDENTIFICATION STUDY

During the needs identification study, the following information is usually gathered and analyzed:

- a description of what generated the requirement (e.g., need for an accounting system because checkbook is never balanced, need for legislative actions, need for program changes);
- the objective of a system proposed to satisfy the perceived need;
- the time-frame in which the need is to be satisfied; and
- particular requirements such as:
  - purpose/scope of the proposed system,
  - data requirements,
  - generic outputs, and
  - proposed general plan/schedule.

The process may come to a conclusion as a result of this study if it does not appear that the need is strong enough to continue. The analysis here is basically the same, whether you are deciding on a simple automation tool or whether you are considering a multi-million dollar system. For example, if our checkbook balance is never off by more than a few cents (or few pence), then why should we automate? On the other hand, if we can save on our income taxes by using an automated accounting system, then the automation might be cost-effective. Sometimes it is not possible to conclude the needs assessment with the needs identification study. Often there is a need to carry the assessment into the second (feasibility study), or third (cost-benefit analysis) steps.

FEASIBILITY STUDY

The feasibility study should be conducted to the point where a meaningful decision can be made to proceed with automation, proceed to the cost-benefit analysis, or stop the automation process. Obviously, for some needs assessments, there will be a concurrent cost-benefit analysis during the feasibility study. The study should be conducted in an unbiased atmosphere (meaning an outside party might be better to perform the study) and be as comprehensive as possible. Sometimes it is good to use the "red team" approach to ensure the study is being objective. The major steps of the feasibility study are:

- problem description;
- study approach;

- analysis which translates current processes into "system" parameters (e.g., functions, users, information flows, existing processes, existing deficiencies, existing difficulties); and

- alternative systems identification and comparisons.

What must be kept in mind is that it is not necessary to "automate for automation's sake." We must try to retain any parts of the existing process that make sense (i.e., are cost-effective). We must also try to discover alternatives that are the most cost-effective from a life-cycle standpoint and not just an initial cost standpoint. Use of off-the-shelf software products (e.g., Lotus 1-2-3, dBASE III, relational DBMS) may be far better than starting from scratch, even if the existing software needs to be modified or integrated properly.

COST-BENEFIT ANALYSIS

Once the feasible alternatives have been identified and described, a cost-benefit analysis should be performed to select the "best" alternative. Remember, the current system, even if it is totally manual, should always be considered as a feasible alternative. MCR is in the business of resource analysis - including cost analysis and development of resource management systems. Based on our experience, there are three steps in the cost-benefit analysis:

- identify all costs to develop, implement and operate each system,

- identify all economic and other benefits resulting from the use of each system, and

- develop a method of weighing the costs and benefits to obtain a cost-benefit relationship.

The costs will include:

- initial costs (analysis, programming, documenting, conversion, hardware/spares, site prep, supplies, training); and
- recurring costs (labor, parts, supplies, updates, maintenance).

The economic benefits include:

- labor displacement (savings from direct and indirect salaries and fringes);
- eliminated materials and supplies;
- equipment displaced (salvage and/or operating costs); and
- floor space reduced (rent, utilities).

The non-economic benefits include:

- efficiency of operation,
- management requirements satisfaction,
- improved accuracy and timeliness, and
- future potential operations.

If the economic benefits are substantial, then the non-economic benefits may not be considered important. It is often difficult to place financial value on benefits like accuracy, so usually the non-economic are considered in alternative selection. There are several ways to construct a cost-benefit relationship, such as:

- a pure economic benefit to cost ratio,
- a return on investment calculation, or
- a subjective assessment of the non-financial benefits.

The cost-benefit analysis is very straight-forward if the decision is to be made on the basis of the first two relationships shown above (i.e., purely financial or cost to benefit ratio). What if two or more alternatives were found to be feasible, but no clear cut objective measure of cost benefit could be found. How then would one proceed with an analysis and select the most cost-effective system? When this occurs, it occurs because the analyst has placed a premium on some characteristics which are difficult to cost in economic terms. These characteristics are factors like:

- user-friendliness,
- idiot-proofed,
- simple operation,
- modular design, and
- flexibility.

How does one deal with these types of "subjective" characteristics of cost-benefit analyses? How also can one deal with so many (seemingly endless) combinations of decisions which are not quantifiable? The analyst could and should use a special decision support system to help in this decision process.

SPECIAL DECISION SUPPORT SYSTEMS

There are several special, automated _decision support systems_ on the market which are available on personal computers and thus readily available for this problem. Some of the most commonly used are:

- Decision Aide,

- Lightyear,
- Expert Choice, and
- Brainstorm.

Bruce Golden at the University of Maryland (with others) has done an evaluation of special decision support systems for microcomputers, including those systems listed above. We are not here to recommend any one of these over the others, but we have used Expert Choice[1/] successfully and will illustrate how one can improve the needs assessment and cost-benefit processes when non-economic factors are involved.

The use of the Analytic Hierarchy Process (AHP) to help with a needs assessment requires subjective judgments on the part of the user. Expert Choice permits the decision process to be structured in a hierarchical fashion, allows for pair-wise decision making and analytical aggregation/synthesis of results of these decisions into an overall goal-oriented conclusion. Figure 1 is an example of a basic hierarchy consisting of an overall goal, criteria, and alternatives. The goal is to decide whether automation is appropriate or not. The criteria suggested are as follows:

- low cost,
- high dollar benefits,
- accurate,

1/ Expert Choice is a product of Decision Support Software of McLean, Virginia. It is based on Dr. Tom Saaty's Analytic Hierarchy Process and was developed by Dr. Ernie Forman of The George Washington University. See the Appendix for more details.

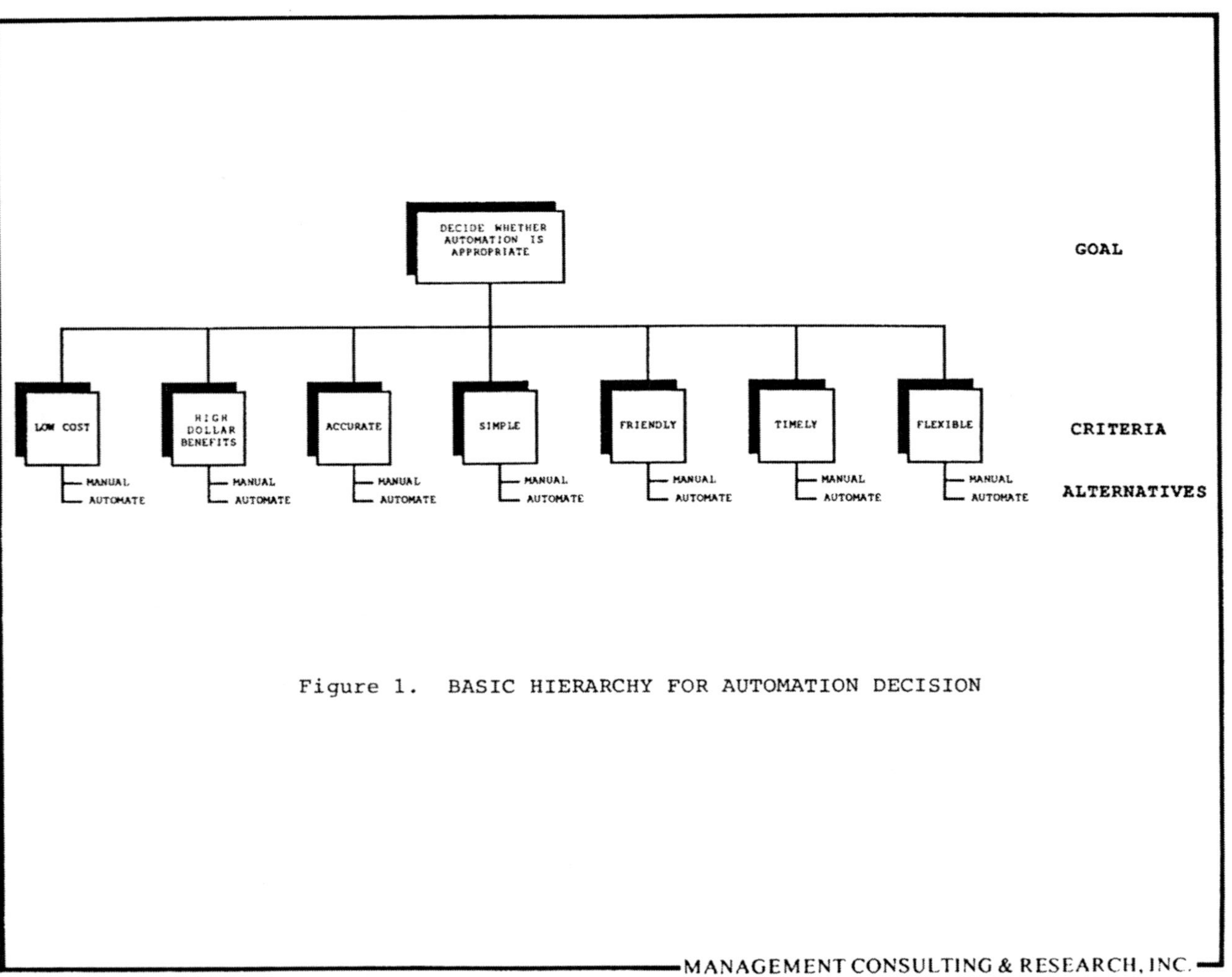

Figure 1. BASIC HIERARCHY FOR AUTOMATION DECISION

- simple,
- friendly,
- timely, and
- flexible.

The alternatives are to retain the manual system or automate. By making decisions about the relative importance of each of the criteria, and then by deciding of how each of the criteria impacts on the decision to automate or remain manual, we can obtain an overall conclusion about automation. Remember, the examples here are just that - examples. Using a special purpose decision support system is a personal (or a group) operation. There are no right answers - the inputs must be tailored to the specific problem at hand and the decision makers use all their collective knowledge to arrive at their conclusion.

Figure 2 illustrates what the automation decision would be if cost were the key criterion. Figure 3 shows the result if cost were overshadowed by other criteria. The outputs are graphical representations of standard Expert Choice formats.

The authors have been involved in numerous large and small automated system developments. Numerous needs assessments have been conducted. Among the conclusions we have reached, based on our past analyses, are the following:

- It is better to automate to the point of significant payoff than to automate to reach a complete solution. This is illustrated by a U.S. Army cost project in which we were required to process every requisition for spare parts on a worldwide basis and match the cost of these parts to all hardware systems which used the parts. To do this completely would have taken an enormous amount of processing time (for hundreds of thousands of part types and thousands of systems). We used

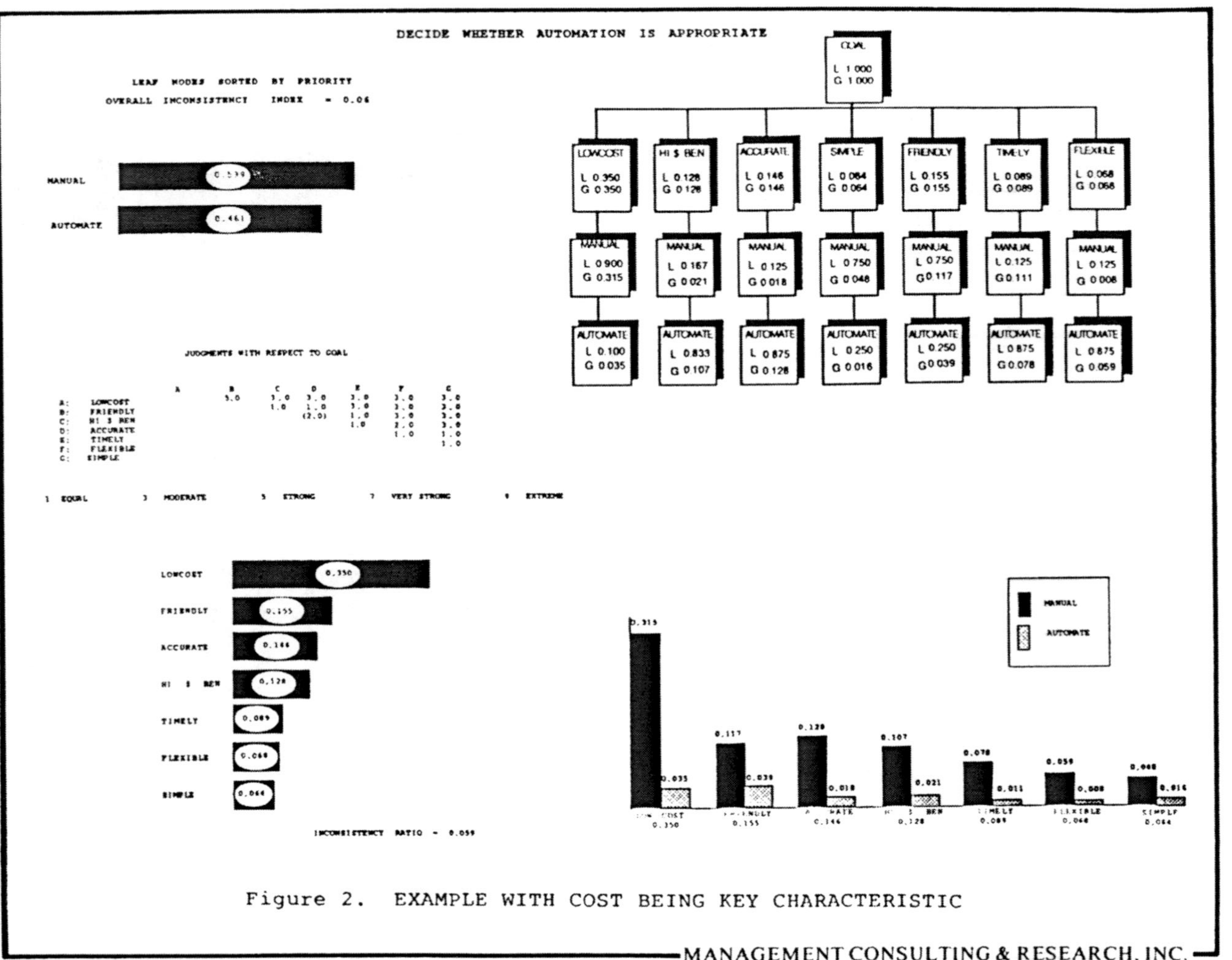

Figure 2. EXAMPLE WITH COST BEING KEY CHARACTERISTIC

MANAGEMENT CONSULTING & RESEARCH, INC.

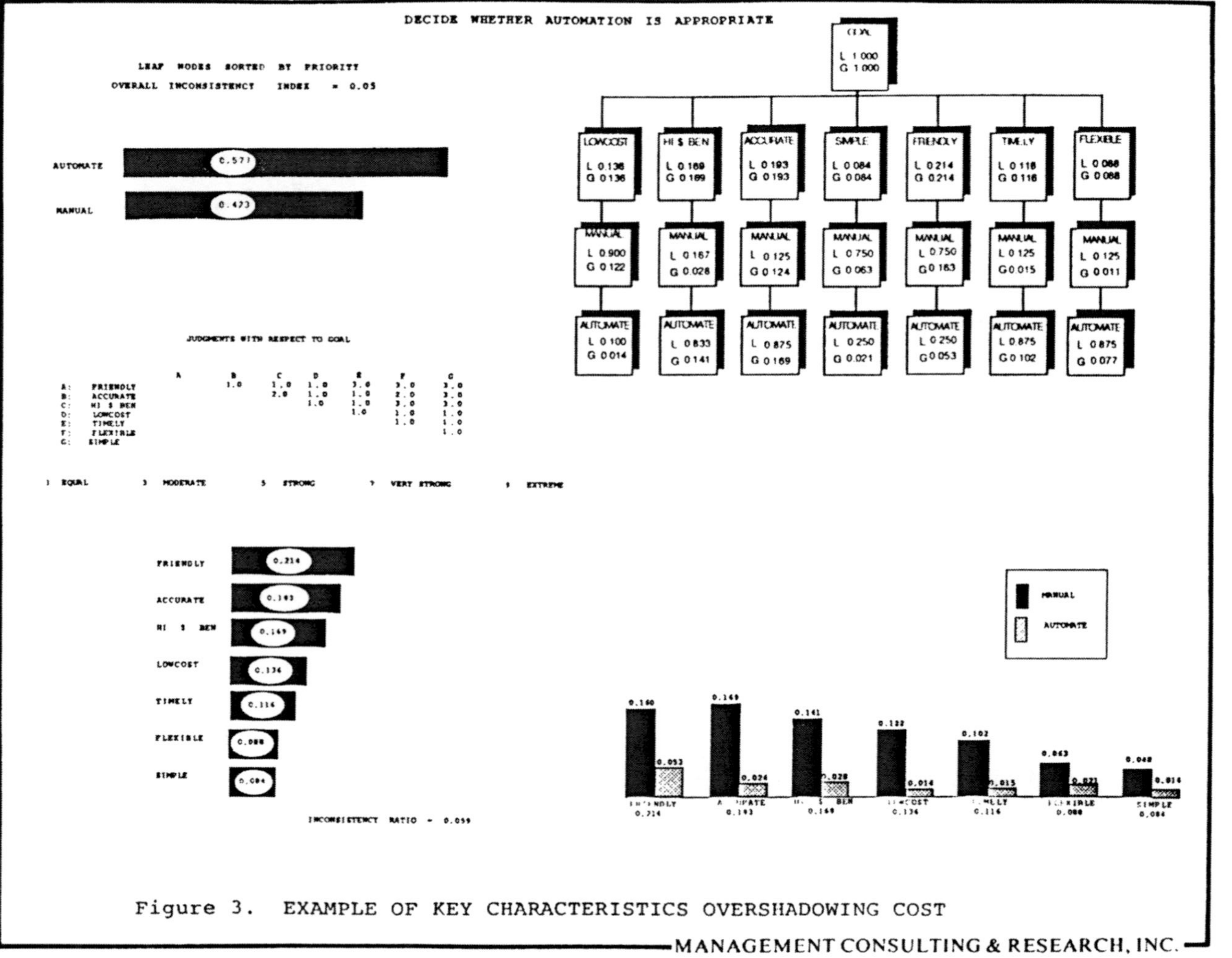

	A	B	C	D	E	F	G
A: FRIENDLY		1.0	1.0	1.0	3.0	3.0	3.0
B: ACCURATE			2.0	1.0	1.0	2.0	3.0
C: HI $ BEN				1.0	1.0	3.0	3.0
D: LOWCOST					1.0	1.0	1.0
E: TIMELY						1.0	1.0
F: FLEXIBLE							1.0
G: SIMPLE							

Figure 3. EXAMPLE OF KEY CHARACTERISTICS OVERSHADOWING COST

the so called "80/20" approach and were able to collect 97% of the costs by processing only 13% of the part types. The results were accomplished using minimal processing time.

- When there is sufficient resistance to or fear of automation, the prudent thing to do is either remain in a manual mode or ease into automation. The approach we have taken several times is to install a rather simplistic, crude automated system which may do little more than avoid multiple inputs of data (and maybe some arithmetic). Once the users have become accustomed to the newness of the automated approach and have gotten over their fear of the machine, then more sophisticated features can be added.

- The use of existing software will speed the process of converting to an automated system, or the process of converting from one automated system to another. The use of spreadsheet software (e.g., Lotus 1-2-3, Jazz, SuperCalc), data base systems (e.g., dBASE III, ORACLE, INFO), and integrated packages (e.g., SYMPHONY, ORACALC, ORAGRAPH) can shorten development and implementation time. The needs assessment should consider the use of such available software. We are currently planning to use Lotus 1-2-3 to automate the entire U.S. Army programming, planning, budgeting and execution system. In doing this, we will get inputs from current users of the manual system.

These are but a few examples of the numerous uses of the needs assessment process.

CONCLUSIONS

We would like to leave you with the following points:

- do not short-change the needs assessment phase - it could save you a lot of headaches if done properly;

- be efficient (do things right) but also be effective (do right things) - do not rush out and solve the wrong problem;

- do not automate for automation's sake - remember the current (perhaps manual) system is one alternative;

- keep the users in mind - do not create an overly-complicated system which users can not or will not use;

- do not overautomate - there may be some parts of the system which should always remain manual;

- do not lock yourself in to an automated monster - keep it flexible and test it thoroughly before full implementation;

- make sure your system can grow with future changes (e.g., we worked with an existing system which failed to operate once one cost item got above $999);

- make sure you get the inputs from and win the cooperation of potential users of the automated system being considered; and

- do not reinvent the wheel - use off-the-shelf software where available.

One of the largest challenges of advanced computing technology is deciding <u>when</u> to automate a system. Automated tools themselves help in this decision paper.

REFERENCES

Forman, Ernest H., Expert Choice software package, Decision Support Software, McLean, Virginia, 1983-1984.

Forman, Ernest H., "Decision Support for the Evaluation of the Strategic Defense Initiative (Starwars)", presented at The Impacts of Microcomputers on Operations Research Conference, Denver, Colorado, 20-22 March 1985.

Golden, Bruce L., et al, "Decision Insight Systems for Microcomputers: A Critical Evaluation", presented at The Impacts of Microcomputers on Operations Research Conferences held in Denver, Colorado, 20-22 March 1985.

Saaty, Thomas L., The Analytic Hierarchy Process, McGraw-Hill, New York, 1980 and Decision Making for Leaders, Wadsworth Publishers (Van Nostrand Reinhart Division), 1982.

Saaty, Thomas L., "An Eigenvalue Allocation Model for Prioritization and Planning", Energy Management and Policy Center, University of Pennsylvania, 1972.

Appendix A.

EXPERT CHOICE INFORMATION

Expert Choice is a unique and powerful decision support system that helps you make informed, logical decisions. It is as revolutionary today as electronic speadsheets were when they were first inroduced. Spreadsheets let you manipulate numbers to answer "What if" questions. Expert Choice lets you manipulate values and judgements. In the real world, successful decision makers must exercise judgement that is, to a large degree, subjective. Few decisions are made on numbers alone.

If we had to write an equation for decision making, perhaps it would look something like this:

DECISION MAKING (PROBLEM SOLVING) = NUMBERS + JUDGEMENT

Expert Choice's ability to accomodate both quantitative data and subjective judgements provides you with the decision support required for high level decisions.

Two factors make Expert Choice especially powerful. The first is flexibility. You define the problem which needs solving, and you decide what factors ought to be considered in the decision-making process. Expert Choice easily handles both objective and subjective criteria. Expert Choice doesn't just allow you to evaluate employees...it doesn't just help you decide which suppliers your company should deal with...it doesn't just help you decide whether to extend credit to a customer. It does all these things and more.

Suppose you want ot evaluate your employees. How important are the employee's years of experience? How important are supervisor evaluations? How much weight do you give to individual initiative? Ability to follow others? Education? Punctuality? Productivity? Ability to work with others? An ideal employee in one company may be a misfit in another. Expert Choice enables you to consider all the elements you deem relevant, and balance them, examine trade-offs and clarify your evaluation and decision-making process.

Suppose you're the purchasing manager for Widgit Industries. Your production line needs a constant supply of widgits. One manufacturer offers well-machined but costly widgits. A second offers lower-quality widgits at bargain prices. A third offer low-quality, expensive widgits...but with excellent delivery times and outstanding credit terms. Whom do you purchase from?

The second important element of Expert Choice is that it contains no built-in biases...no "right" answers. Once you have defined all the elements of a problem which you consider important Expert Choice helps you prioritize them, and it does this in a remarkably innovative and effective way - on the basis of your verbal judgements, not arbitrary guesses from an arbitrary numerical scale.

In the widgit example, is price more important than quality? Is delivery time more important than price? Are credit terms more important than widgit quality? Your needs may well differ from a competitor's. Thus, you and your competitor - each relying on your own expertise and judgement - may well decide to purchase from different widgit manufacturers. Expert Choice does not make your decision-making conform to a pre-established value system, but rather, assist you in making decisions according to your own set of values.

EXPERT CHOICE will help you:

* Structure a complex problem into a manageable form.

* Establish priorities based on your judgements.

* Measure the consistency of judgements.

* Integrate or synthesize judgements and priorities.

* Conduct cost/benefit analysis.

* Transform group decision-making into an efficient, informative, and productive process.

There is no practical limit to the number of factors you can consider, or to the amount of refinement you may apply.

Suppose you are evaluating possible sites for corporate relocation. In evaluating towns and cities, you may consider the wage levels, the quality of the work force, tax levels, availability of sites, and quality of life.

You may separate "quality of life" into such elements as the crime rate, quality of schools, recreation, and fine arts.

You may separate "fine arts" into quality and/or number of museums, art galleries, orchestras, and theaters.

You may separate "theaters" into Broadway-quality, community, and experimental.

And so on.

And once separated into these components, Expert Choice lets you decide their relative importance to you, helping you make the best decision.

Expert Choice is ideally suited to both individual and group decision-making. Group decision-making is an everyday occurence at almost all levels of management. Varying personalities, emotions, and inequalities of power exist within groups. Expert Choice can accomodate these factors in group-decision making by establishing an appropriate forum for discussion. Expert Choice can help highlight the full range of considerations to be taken into account through its use in decision-making models. If a model needs to be changed to explore new options and choices, it can be done immediately, in the conference room.

Expert Choice is now being used by a leading bank to evaluate leading risks and opportunities in foreign countries. This bank had previously used studies to weigh ecenomic, financial, and political considerations. While the bank was satisfied with the quality of the reports, both the bank and the consultant preparing the reports felt the information was not being put to best use. The complex data and decision-making process resulted in "too much" or "too little" weight being placed on various aspects of the decision process. The bank's credit committee also had difficulty integrating the "expert information" into the deliberation process. Consequently, the bank's consultant prepared an Expert Choice model, enabling the credit committee to use the most recent information in making comparisons among factors. Without any prior exposure to microcomputers or Expert Choice, the bankers began using the software and evaluating the subject country within a matter of minutes.

Expert Choice is so flexible, it can even be used for personal decision-making.

Suppose you're considering where to go on a vacation. Perhaps you like big cities, excitement, entertainment. Your spouse may prefer a quiet, tranquil setting. Is cost a factor? Will you bring your children along? Do you like to drive, or would you prefer flying? Expert Choice allows you to balance all these considerations, letting you arrive at the best choice for you and your family.

The logic of Expert Choice acknowledges the important role of experience and intuition in decision-making. Expert Choice is a vital tool for today's decision makers.

WHO NEEDS EXPERT CHOICE?

Managers, purchasing agents, finanacial planners, retail computer stores, real estate agents, lending institutions, small business owners, human resource managers, portfolio managers, chairmen and members of standing and ad hoc committees, strategic planners, advertising agencies and markets, lawyers, management consultants, chief executive officers, and more. In short, anyone who is called upon to make complex decisions needs Expert Choice.

EXPERT CHOICE'S THEORETICAL FOUNDATIONS

Expert Choice is based on the analytical hierarchy process theory developed by Dr. Thomas L. Saaty and described in two of his books. "The Analytical Hierarchy Process" and "Decision Making for Leaders". The theory has been integrated into a sophisticated, yet easy to use, computerised decision support system by Dr. Ernest H. Forman. Expert choice can graphically display the structure of a complex problem for decision makers. It then calculates priorities using a mathematical technique of finding the "eigenvalues" and "eigenvectors" of a matrix. The procedure is far too complex and time-consuming to be done manually. Expert Choice performs it quickly, enabling you to apply this powerful and coherent theory to important real-world decision-making problems.

SYSTEM REQUIREMENTS

* IBM PC, PC/XT, or 100% compatible

* 128K

* IBM DOS 1.1, 2.0, or higher

* Will support a hard disc, color graphics or monochrome adapter; printer not required but highly recommended.

Expert Choice 495 dollars.

Decision Support Software, Inc.,
1300 Vincent Place
McLean, VA 22101, USA.

Tel. (703) 442-7900.

APPENDIX B

INTUITIVE JUSTIFICATION OF THE ANALYTIC HIERARCHY PROCESS *

* Saaty, T., The Analytic Hierarchy Process, (McGraw-Hill, New York), 1980

NATO ASI Series, Vol. F22
Software System Design Methods. Edited by J.K. Skwirzynski

INTUITIVE JUSTIFICATION OF THE METHOD

Assume that n activities are being considered by a group of interested people. We assume that the group's goals are:

(1) to provide judgments on the relative importance of these activities;
(2) to insure that the judgments are quantified to an extent which also permits a quantitative interpretation of the judgments among all activities.

Clearly, goal (2) will require appropriate technical assistance.

Our goal is to describe a method of deriving, from the group's quantified judgments (i.e., from the relative values associated with *pairs* of activities), a set of weights to be associated with *individual* activities; in a sense defined below, these weights should reflect the group's quantified judgments. What this approach achieves is to put the information resulting from (1) and (2) into usable form without deleting information residing in the qualitative judgments.

Let $C_1, C_2, \ldots, C_n$ be the set of activities. The quantified judgments on pairs of activities C_i, C_j are represented by an n-by-n matrix

$$A = (a_{ij}), \qquad (i, j = 1, 2, \ldots, n)$$

The entries a_{ij} are defined by the following entry rules.

Rule 1. If $a_{ij} = \alpha$, then $a_{ji} = 1/\alpha$, $\alpha \neq 0$.

Rule 2. If C_i is judged to be of equal relative importance as C_j, then $a_{ij} = 1$, $a_{ji} = 1$; in particular, $a_{ii} = 1$ for all i.

Thus the matrix A has the form

$$A = \begin{bmatrix} 1 & a_{12} & \cdots & a_{1n} \\ 1/a_{12} & 1 & \cdots & a_{2n} \\ \vdots & \vdots & \vdots\vdots\vdots & \vdots \\ 1/a_{1n} & 1/a_{2n} & \cdots & 1 \end{bmatrix}$$

Having recorded the quantified judgments on pairs (C_i, C_j) as numerical entries a_{ij} in the matrix A, the problem now is to assign to the n contingencies $C_1, C_2, \ldots, C_n$ a set of numerical weights $w_1, w_2, \ldots, w_n$ that would "reflect the recorded judgments."

In order to do so, the vaguely formulated problem must first be transformed into a precise mathematical one. This essential, and apparently harmless, step is the most crucial one in any problem that requires the representation of a real-life situation in terms of an abstract mathematical structure. It is particularly crucial in the present problem where the representation involves a number of transitions that are not immediately discernible. It appears, therefore, desirable in the present problem to identify the major steps in the process of representation and to make each step as explicit as possible in order to enable the potential user to form his own judgment on the *meaning and value* of the method in relation to *his* problem and *his* goal.

The major question is the one concerned with the meaning of the vaguely formulated condition in the statement of our goal: "these weights should reflect the group's quantified judgments." This presents the need to describe in precise, arithmetic terms, how the weights w_i should relate to the judgments a_{ij}; or, in other words, the problem of specifying the conditions we wish to impose on the weights we seek in relation to the judgments obtained. The desired description is developed in three steps, proceeding from the simplest special case to the general one.

Step 1 Assume first that the "judgments" are merely the result of precise physical measurements. Say the judges are given a set of pebbles, $C_1, C_2, \ldots, C_n$ and a precision scale. To compare C_1 with C_2, they put C_1 on a scale and read off its weight—say, w_1—305 grams. They weigh C_2 and find $w_2 = 244$ grams. They divide w_1 by w_2, which is 1.25. They pronounce their judgment, "C_1 is 1.25 times as heavy as C_2" and record it as $a_{12} = 1.25$. Thus, in this ideal case of *exact measurement*, the relations between the weights w_i and the judgments a_{ij} are simply given by

$$\frac{w_i}{w_j} = a_{ij} \qquad (\text{for } i, j = 1, 2, \ldots, n) \tag{1-1}$$

and

$$A = \begin{bmatrix} w_1/w_1 & w_1/w_2 & \cdots & w_1/w_n \\ w_2/w_1 & w_2/w_2 & \cdots & w_2/w_n \\ \vdots & \vdots & & \vdots \\ w_n/w_1 & w_n/w_2 & \cdots & w_n/w_n \end{bmatrix}$$

However, it would be unrealistic to require these relations to hold in the general case. Imposing these stringent relations would, in most practical cases, make the problem of finding the w_i (when a_{ij} are given) unsolvable. First, even physical measurements are never exact in a mathematical sense; and, hence, allowance *must* be made for deviations; and second, because in human judgments, these deviations are considerably larger.

Step 2 In order to see how to make allowance for deviations, consider the ith row in the matrix A. The entries in that row are

$$a_{i1}, a_{i2}, \ldots, a_{ij}, \ldots, a_{in}$$

In the ideal (exact) case these values are the same as the ratios

$$\frac{w_i}{w_1}, \frac{w_i}{w_2}, \ldots, \frac{w_i}{w_j}, \ldots, \frac{w_i}{w_n}$$

Hence, in the ideal case, if we multiply the first entry in that row by w_1, the second entry by w_2, and so on, we would obtain

$$\frac{w_i}{w_1} w_1 = w_i, \qquad \frac{w_i}{w_2} w_2 = w_i, \ldots, \frac{w_j}{w_j} w_j = w_i, \ldots, \frac{w_i}{w_n} w_n = w_i$$

The result is a row of identical entries

$$w_i, w_i, \ldots, w_i$$

whereas, in the general case, we would obtain a row of entries that represent a statistical scattering of values around w_i. It appears, therefore, reasonable to require that w_i should equal the average of these values. Consequently, instead of the ideal case relations (1-1)

$$w_i = a_{ij}w_j \qquad (i, j = 1, 2, \ldots, n)$$

the more realistic relations for the general case take the form (for each fixed i)

$$w_i = \text{the average of } (a_{i1}w_1, a_{i2}w_2, \ldots, a_{in}w_n)$$

More explicitly we have

$$w_i = \frac{1}{n}\sum_{j=1}^{n} a_{ij}w_j \qquad (i = 1, 2, \ldots, n) \tag{1-2}$$

While the relations in (1-2) represent a substantial relaxation of the more stringent relations (1-1), there still remains the question: is the relaxation *sufficient* to insure the existence of solutions; that is, to insure that the problem of finding unique weights w_i when the a_{ij} are given is a solvable one?

Step 3 To seek the answer to the above essentially mathematical question, it is necessary to express the relations in (1-2) in still another, more familiar form. For this purpose we need to summarize the line of reasoning to this point. In seeking a set of conditions to describe how the weight vector w should relate to the quantified judgments, we first considered the ideal (exact) case in Step 1, which suggested the relations (1-1). Next, realizing that the real case will require allowances for deviations, we provided for such allowances in Step 2, leading to the formulation (1-2). Now, this is still not realistic enough; that is, that (1-2) which works for the ideal case is still too stringent to secure the existence of a weight vector w that should satisfy (1-2). We note that for good estimates a_{ij} tends to be close to w_i/w_j and hence is a small perturbation of this ratio. Now as a_{ij} changes it turns out that there would be a corresponding solution of (1-2), (i.e., w_i and w_j can change to accommodate this change in a_{ij} from the ideal case), if n were also to change. We denote this value of n by λ_{max}. Thus the problem

$$w_i = \frac{1}{\lambda_{max}}\sum_{j=1}^{n} a_{ij}w_j \qquad i = 1, \ldots, n \tag{1-3}$$

has a solution that also turns out to be unique. This is the well-known eigenvalue problem with which we will be dealing.

In general, deviations in the a_{ij} can lead to large deviations both in λ_{max} and in w_i, $i = 1, \ldots, n$. However, this is not the case for a reciprocal matrix which satisfies rules 1 and 2. In this case we have a stable solution.

Recall that we have given an intuitive justification of our approach. There is an elegant way of framing this in mathematical notation. It is given in detail in later chapters. Briefly stated in matrix notation, we start with what we call the paradigm case $Aw = nw$, where A is a consistent matrix and consider a reciprocal matrix A'

which is a perturbation of A, elicited from pairwise comparison judgments, and solve the problem $A'w' = \lambda_{max}w'$ where λ_{max} is the largest eigenvalue of A'.

We have sometimes been interested in the opposite question to dominance with respect to a given property. We have called it recessiveness of one activity when compared with another with respect to that property. In that case we solve for the left eigenvector v in $vA = \lambda_{max}v$. Only when A is consistent are the elements of v and w reciprocals. Without consistency they are reciprocals for $n = 2$ and $n = 3$. In general one need not expect them to have a definite relationship. The two vectors correspond to the two sides of the Janus face of reality—the bright and the dark.

STEPS TOWARD ESTABLISHING NORMAL RULES FOR SOFTWARE COST, SCHEDULE, AND PRODUCTIVITY ESTIMATING

Capers Jones
Software Productivity Research, Inc.
Acton, Massachusetts

ABSTRACT

Software economics and software estimating have been subject to wide variations and large errors. One of the fundamental reasons for these problems has been the lack of standard definitions for dealing with source code, lack of standard definitions for the scope of activities to be included in the estimate, and lack of standard definitions for the tools and methodologies applied to software projects. This paper describes the source code conventions, chart of accounts, and standard methodology definitions used by the Software Productivity, Quality, and Reliability [SPQR] estimating models.

INTRODUCTION

Software has achieved the dubious reputation of being the most difficult major occupation in terms of management, measurement, and understanding of economic factors. While there are many reasons for this situation, a basic factor has been the ambiguity of the terms and activities that are involved with software development and maintenance.

Basic terms such as "lines of source code," "productivity," "development," and "maintenance" either have no agreed-to definitions at all, or are used unconsciously with varying meanings by different authors and estimators. The net result of this ambiguity can be two papers or speakers describing the same program and the same activities, yet differing by as much as 1000% in apparent results because the two authors had different concepts in mind when they discussed "lines of code" or "development productivity."

To cite but a single example, the IBM Corporation has a standard definition for lines of source code which differs significantly from the definition used in Barry Boehm's "Software Engineering Economics." It is easily possible for the size of the same program to differ by several hundred percent, depending upon whether the IBM rules or the Boehm rules are invoked:

NATO ASI Series, Vol. F22
Software System Design Methods. Edited by J.K. Skwirzynski

	IBM CONVENTION	BOEHM CONVENTION
COMMENTARY LINES	Not Counted	Counted
DELIMITERS	Counted	Not Counted
PHYSICAL LINES	Not Counted	Counted

When a program with many comments is counted, the Boehm method will give larger sizes by 15% to 25%. But when a multi-statement language such as BASIC is counted, the IBM technique will yield sizes that appear 200% to 500% larger than the same program counted via the Boehm conventions.

Neither method is intrinsically good or bad: what is needed by the industry is to select any single method and then adopt it widely, so that software engineers begin to deal with standard concepts and definitions, rather than today's ambiguous and loosely defined terminology and nebulous concepts.

DEFINING SOURCE CODE

There are 12 common variations in defining what is meant by "a line of source code" which can yield apparent size differences of about an order of magnitude depending upon which variations are selected:

1] Count only executable lines
2] Count executable lines and data definitions
3] Count executable lines, data definitions, and comments

4] Count lines as physical lines
5] Count lines as terminated by delimiters

6] Count only new lines
7] Count new lines and changed lines
8] Count new lines, changed lines, and unchanged base lines

9] Count macros or included code once
10] Count macros or included code at each occurrence

11] Count code only in the delivered software
12] Count both the delivered code and temporary code

Without considering the relative merits of the variations, the line-counting conventions in the SPQR estimating models are normalized as closely as possible to the IBM techniques, i.e.:

-- Executable lines and data definitions are counted
-- Lines are terminated by delimiters
-- New lines and changed lines are counted
-- Macros or included code are counted at every occurrence
-- Delivered code only is counted

-- Commentary lines are not counted
-- Physical lines are not counted
-- Base code is not counted
-- Temporary code is not counted

Commentary lines are excluded because they are considered "easy" and tend to dilute productivity measurements. Delimiters are counted, rather than physical lines, because a programmer's mental effort is proportional to the number of actual instructions rather than to physical lines. Once the ambiguity of line counting is realized, it is possible to see the value of several SPQR functions: 1) The SPQR models can predict source code size for any of 30 different languages; 2) The SPQR models can automatically change line counting rules to match local assumptions.

MEASURING SCOPE OF ACTIVITIES

As of 1985, there are more than 50 United States companies offering productivity tools whose advertisements feature phrases such as "10 to 1 improvement in productivity" or "order of magnitude productivity gains."

Unfortunately, none of the advertisements define either the baseline against which the improvements are made or the scope of activities included in the projects that the advertisements purportedly cite.

From discussions with some of these vendors to find out what they really meant, it was found that the vendor measured a programmer for a short period of perhaps an hour to a day while carrying out some task such as coding. Then the observation was converted to an annual rate. The annual rate was then contrasted with normative data gathered from full lifecycle studies, which of course included many other tasks, many other employees, breaks between assignments, vacations, and so forth.

There are some 20 major job categories that are often part of software development and maintenance, and it is desirable to specify which of these were actually used on the project:

1] Managers or supervisors
2] User or client personnel assigned to project
3] Systems Analysts
4] Programmer/Analysts
5] Application Programmers
6] System Programmers
7] Database Specialists
8] Integration Specialists
9] Test Specialists
10] Network Specialists
11] Quality Assurance Specialists
12] Technical Writers
13] Technical Editors
14] Document Production Specialists
15] Program Librarians
16] Secretarial Support
17] Administrative Support
18] Customer Support Specialists
19] Field Service Specialists
20] Maintenance Programmers

The SPQR models assume that any or all of these 20 job categories [plus 20 other less common categories] may be utilized.

DEFINING DEVELOPMENT PHASES AND ACTIVITIES

In addition to a lack of standard definitions for the skills and job categories applied to software, there is considerable ambiguity in defining what is meant by "life cycle," "phase," "development," and "maintenance."

The number of phases in typical software life cycles vary from a low of four to a high of 15, depending upon author and project preferences. For the purposes of aggregating costs, a relatively small number of phases which contain relatively major activities seems preferable to a larger number of phases containing minor activities. The SPQR models adopt a four-phase structure for cost aggregation purposes:

1] Requirements
2] Design
3] Development
4] Integration and Test

The SPQR models also aggregate development costs to two other key activities: management and documentation. These activities are not phase-specific, and are spread more or less evenly throughout a typical development cycle.

The general SPQR rationale is to allow a very detailed, granular set of activities to be used for planning and work-breakdown purposes, but to aggregate costs and effort against a small set of major accounts for financial control and management reporting purposes.

For example, the under the general SPQR account of documentation there can be more than 80 different kinds of plans, manuals, tutorials, and user's guides. Under the general account of integration and test there can be more than 15 kinds of testing included.

DEFINING MAINTENANCE ACTIVITIES

The word "maintenance" is the most troublesome single term in all of software engineering. The most common definition is also the most ambiguous, i.e.: "Any enhancement or defect repair performed on a program or system after it has been delivered to users." This definition lumps together the disparate activities of enhancement and defect repairs, and leads to notable ambiguity and confusion.

The normal SPQR definitions of what goes on after delivery are somewhat less troublesome:

"Maintenance" is defined to mean defect repairs made to correct errors or omissions.

"Delivery Support" is defined to mean on-site assistance at customer premises when installing software [or hardware].

"Field Service" is defined to mean maintenance carried out on the customer's premises.

"Enhancements" are defined to mean new functions or new capabilities added to satisfy new user requests or to allow the software to run with new hardware types.

"Mandatory Updates" are defined to mean changes made because of a change in law or enterprise policy, such as changes in tax rates and the like.

"Conversion" is defined to mean reprogramming an application so that it operates on a new computer or on new hardware types.

"Restoration" is defined to mean restructuring and redocumenting aging programs or systems without degrading or changing their functional capabilities.

Since the cost factors and productivity rates in real life are notably different for maintenance, field service, enhancements, mandatory updates, conversions, and restoration most estimating tools that handle post-development activities utilize a fairly granular definition of terms. The SPQR models handle all post-development activities on a year-by-year basis, and accumulate all costs by year, accumulating annual costs from the sum of a finer structure that includes maintenance, field service, enhancements, etc.

THE CONSOLIDATED SPQR CHART OF ACCOUNTS

The normal SPQR chart of accounts for a software project looks like this:

DEVELOPMENT
Requirements
Design
Development
Integration and Test
Documentation
Management
Total Development

POST-DEVELOPMENT
Year 19NN
Delivery Support
Maintenance
Field Service
Enhancements
Mandatory Updates
Conversion (Optional)
Restoration (Optional)
Total Post-Development

The post-development costs are accumulated on a year-by-year basis for up to 15 years.
These development and post-development activities are used merely to accumulate cost and effort data into convenient "buckets." There is of course a much more detailed fine structure in real life than the development activities and post-development activities just shown. Over 200 key development tasks and 300 maintenance tasks could be identified, but at that level any kind of consistency would be difficult to achieve.

When the starting point for an estimate is itself an enhancement of maintenance project, it is necessary to consider aspects of the base code that is being updated as well as the type and structure of the update itself.

Estimating enhancements and maintenance changes are much more difficult to do than estimating new development, since many of the productivity rates and algorithms derived from new software are inappropriate for quantifying modifications to existing software.

The SPQR models, in common with other expert-system estimating tools, have separate algorithms and productivity tables for enhancement and maintenance estimates that are quite different from the ones used for new development.

DEFINING SKILLS, TOOLS, AND METHODOLOGIES USED FOR SOFTWARE

Not only is there ambiguity in defining source code and scope of activities for estimating purposes, but there is equal ambiguity in trying to define exactly how to quantify the specific skills, tools, and methods used for software development.

As of 1985, there are approximately 220 known programming languages, 150 specification and design methods, 2000 possible productivity aids, and 1500 different computer and workstation combinations. The permutations of all possible combinations is for practical purposes, infinite.

The SPQR models deal with this situation essentially by limiting the choices that can be dealt with. There are three plateaus of granularity, as follows:

SPQR/20 is a "quick sizing" model that contains only those parameters known to have a net productivity impact of as much as plus or minus 15%. There are approximately 30 such parameters.

SPQR/50 contains all parameters known to have a productivity impact of plus or minus 5%. There are approximately 80 such parameters.

SPQR/100 contains all parameters known to have a productivity impact of plus or minus 1%. There are approximately 350 such parameters.

Automated estimating models usually are associated with a data base of both actual and estimated project cost, schedule, and productivity information. A challenge for estimators is to capture the essential factors that impact a project in a way that lends itself to statistical analysis across many projects. Straight text inputs, due to the possiblity of errors and ambiguity, are not desirable.

The SPQR methodology for capturing tool and methodology information is to use multiple-choice questions, with each question having a spectrum of possible answers. This technique couples relatively good granularity with a reduced probability of error.

To illustrate this technique, here are several sample questions from the SPQR/20 model:

PROJECT NOVELTY?: ________

1] Conversion of an existing well-known program
2] Conversion, but some new features will be added
3] Even mixture of repeated and new features
4] Novel program, but with some well-known features
5] Novel program, of a type never before attempted

RESPONSE TIME ENVIRONMENT?: ________

1] Response time is not a factor on this project
2] Subsecond response time is the norm
3] One to two second response time is the norm
4] Two to 10 second response time is the norm
5] More than 10 second response time is the norm

PROGRAMMING OFFICE ENVIRONMENT?: ________

1] Private offices and adequate facilities
2] Doubled offices and adequate facilities
3] Multi-employee shared offices and facilities
4] Cramped offices and inadequate facilities
5] Open offices and inadequate facilities

As can be seen, this multiple-choice technique is very easy to use, but at the cost of absolute precision. Nonetheless, in some 15 years of usage the technique has proven to be useful and surprisingly accurate.

To allow fine-tuning of the user inputs, decimal answers are permitted. For example, a response of "2.5" is an acceptable answer on SPQR multiple-choice question.

As used in the SPQR models, the scaling is similar in concept to the Richter scale: low numbers of 1 and 2 are better than average; 3 approximates the United States averages for the parameter, and the higher numbers of 4 and 5 are worse than average. This technique allows very rapid analysis of projects, and very interesting combinations of data can be explored.

One might expect wide variations in responses due to individual human opinions, but in practise this has seldom been a problem.

SUMMARY AND CONCLUSIONS

As of 1985, there are approximately 25 automated software estimating models and more than 100 manual estimating techniques available for software engineering projects.

So far as can be determined, all of them use unique assumptions and definitions regarding source code counting methods, scopes of activities included in the estimates, phases, definitions of maintenance tasks, and assumptions about tools and methodologies.

The lack of standard terms and definitions means that it is very difficult to perform side-by-side comparisions of estimating tools and algorithms, since variances often reflect merely the different assumptions of the tools rather than actual cost or productivity differences.

As the software industry matures, it will eventually be necessary to adopt standard methods for describing both software and the environment surrounding it.

Since both estimating and productivity analysis need reliable data, some form of standardization is a critical step toward true software engineering.

THE ECONOMICS OF SOFTWARE

Bernard de Neumann
GEC Research
Marconi Research Centre
Chelmsford CM2 8HN U.K.

SUMMARY

The Software Engineering Industry seems set to become an important sector of "High Technology" Economies. However, unlike other sectors, the software engineering industry uses negligible material resources directly, using mainly intellectual resources, to produce a product which cannot wear out and is thus, in principle at least, capable of having an infinite life. Such products are radically different from convential products, and require careful analysis if rational decisions are to be taken regarding the software products' and enterprises' development. This paper will discuss and contrast the impingement of economic considerations on the Life Cycle Costing/Decision Analysis of software reliant products, including VLSI, VHPIC etc.

INTRODUCTION

The availability of cheap computing power has led systems engineers to propose systems where more and more function is implemented on digital computers by means of software. The general purpose digital computer implemented in VLSI, VHSIC or VHPIC has become a possible component in many control situations. And of course, naturally, systems with very many of these components are being considered now as a means of realizing our future systems needs. Of course this has also meant that it has been possible to incorporate "smart functionality" into systems as a replacement for the often, in comparison, crude functionality of existing and past systems.

NATO ASI Series, Vol. F22
Software System Design Methods. Edited by J.K. Skwirzynski

Thus there has been a considerable pressure towards reliance upon software in systems design. Indeed since the design of computer software is no more than the design of a subsystem with perfect components (perfect that is in the reliability sense) and other system design by necessity has to choose from less-than-perfect components we can consider all aspects of design to be a software process. Now the development of software is notoriously expensive and it is common for software development costs to exceed quite alarmingly the original allocation, if they are completed at all. Thus software cost estimation and Life Cycle Costing are important, as is good project management, and as an obvious prerequisite, a proper understanding of these areas by both project management and customers. Also cost estimation/LCC analysis is but half the story, we must have some yardsticks to evaluate them and make decisions.

As a retrospective example, suppose that a Neanderthal Entrepeneur (or perhaps Technical Director) was approached by a contemporary transportation engineer who had some ideas which could, if feasible, and, if developed, lead to a revolutionary new mode of transport, thereby changing and challenging the entire culture of the known world. How could the value of the proposed product be estimated and how could a realistic budget be set to ensure that the invention, if feasible, could be developed and used? What is value? And to whom?

Time also plays a crucial role in value judgements. The Fast Fourier Transform, the fast algorithmic implementation of the Discrete Fourier Transform, has a history which extends back to Runge in the Nineteenth Century. However, the technique only became practically viable after the advent of the digital computer. It is now extremely useful in real time spectral analysis etc.

A third example of a valuable design, which had been a goal for many years, and which facilitated the Software Industry is of course the logical design (architecture) of the general purpose digital computer. This design has stood the test of time, and appears to be a fundamental component of many so-called "Fifth Generation" Computers. Note also that this design was not inhibited by technology when it was first implemented electronically - history shows that the electronics necessary had already been available for some years.

That software can have high value is unquestionable since such vast sums have been spent on some developments, and equally the software-pirates can make such large illegal profits from their activities. The crux of the problem is that the process of developing software uses virtually no material resources directly using intellectual resources and information processing devices in often large quantities, yet the output, the software, once completed can be copied using very few resources. This applies also to audio and video material, and in particular to VLSI. Thus there exists a strong potential to encourage the pirates. The high cost of producing (valuable) software deters the producers and spurs the pirate - the producers being concerned with not recovering their investment. This is a difficult situation for a free-market economy to sustain since the market would collapse without the producers. We are thus led to several possible courses of action:

1) Legal protection of software
2) Technological protection of software
3) Reducing development costs of software

All of which act by lowering the potential for piracy.

A tacit assumption of the above is that the software is marketable, which implies that it is implementable and has useful functions, and is reliable and safe. We thus need to verify that software does indeed match its requirements, and to do this we need to both map the requirements efficiently into code, and also to test the code both to debug it, and to attempt to measure the products] reliability. All of these stages are expensive and a great deal of research is directed towards improving these phases.

Software Engineering seems set to become an important sector of many "High Technology" Economies, indeed it is seen governmentally as being of strategic importance. However the present free market environment is a dangerous one for this nascent industry and steps must be taken at national/international level in order to ensure its continuation. The collaborative ventures such as Alvey and ESPRIT are a step in the right direction, but much more needs to be done to protect the industry from looming anarchy. It is unreasonable to expect the software producers to act altruistically and risk financial collapse in a climate which does not offer adequate protection for its products.

It is not possible to consider in detail all of these possibilities here, and so we intend to concentrate upon mainly Reliability and Maintainability, and Cost and Value in an Economic Context.

SOFTWARE AS AN ECONOMIC PRODUCT

Software is an unusual product insofar as it is non-material; however it is a product rather than a service. The stock of software is increasing, and will continue to do so, since software has a potentially infinite life - it does not wear out, and we will continually look for new uses for our programmable machines which will thus require new software.

It can be shown quite simply that a standard Net Present Value analysis of the value of "reusable software" is possibly infinite (see B de Neumann ref 1). This of course is a useless result, other than it serves to demonstrate that we need new concepts in order to make meaningful cost-benefit analyses. Similarly the production function of micro-economics does not seem appropriate in the case of software products.

The existing economic theory of value which is based upon utility functions is contained in ref 3. This analysis, whilst being based upon an intuitively appealing axiom-based procedure, gives subjective results which are consistent but nevertheless based upon personal preferences. Samuelson (reference 2) in his discussion of the Paradox of Value as applied to water and diamonds resolves it by stating:

"The more there is of a commodity, the less the relative desirability of its last little unit becomes, even though its total usefulness grows as we get more of the commodity. So, it is obvious why a large amount of water has a low price. Or why air is actually a free good despite its vast usefulness. The many later units pull down the market value of all units".

This argument cannot apply to particular software products since the cost of producing more than one copy is essentially the same as the cost of producing the first i.e the marginal cost of producing copies is essentially zero.

The current high development costs of software make it imperative that we reexamine our techniques for producing and analysing software products. For example, because of these high development costs, and the fact that much software is machine and job specific, it seems intuitively obvious that we should endeavour to utilise existing software as much as possible, and indeed to attempt to set up a process whereby this will become much easier. The vogue name for these endeavours is reusable software. It is quite possible that this work will lead to "reusable hardware" whereby specific software compatible processors will be incorporated into a multiprocessor architecture so that existing software can indeed to reused. Thus computer architecture could become software dependent.

Thus these economic problems must be solved if we are to design cost effective system in the future.

NEED FOR AND VALUE OF REUSABLE SOFTWARE

The costs of producing well tested complex software packages is increasing rapidly, and the costs of failure to perform in service are becoming critical as more systems become critically dependent upon software.

Reusable software as a concept is one of many techniques which may be expected to improve "in-service" reliability and reduce overall costs. The real success of reliability theory to date has stemmed from its ability to analyse the reliability of structured systems in terms of the reliability of their constituents and their structures. This has resulted in the identification of good structures, and hence engineering techniques, and more cost effective products. The extension of this analysis to software would be desirable, and would reap similar benefits. However, many difficulties have to be overcome.

THE ECONOMIC BENEFIT OF IMPROVED RELIABILITY MODELLING

There are both direct and "knock-on" benefits which can accrue from improvements in measuring and modelling reliability. The direct benefits are associated with maintenance costs arising from failure and will be considered quantitately in an approximate model to be described later. The more important "knock-on" effect is to enable reliability targets to be set and demonstrated thus making it possible to produce assuredly reliable products: This is dealt with elsewhere in this ASI (See for example refs 4 and 5).

An approximate software maintenance cost model follows.

The purpose of this model is to facilitate the calculation of software maintenance costs due to "in-service" failure, given that the failure rate, λ ,is approximately known, and also that the distribution of the consequential maintenance costs associated with failures is also known.

Let λ be the "in-service" failure rate of one copy of the software. Let there be n copies of the software in service, and let failures from copy to copy occur independently. Let c_i be the cost of consequential maintenance incurred as a result of failure i .

Define $\lambda \varepsilon U[\bar{\lambda}-\varepsilon, \bar{\lambda}+\varepsilon]$ where U is uniform distribution

$$c_i \varepsilon U[\bar{c}-\Delta, \bar{c}+\Delta]$$

and N_{ob} = random variable - the counting process of failures in time interval $[0, T]$

We assume that "times of failure" are exponentially distributed with constant, but unknown, failure rate λ . It can be shown that the counting process of failures in $[0,T]$ is asymptotically Normal ($T \to \infty$), with

$$\text{mean} = \text{variance} = n\lambda T$$

Let C^* be the total maintenance cost in $[0,T]$

then $C^* = \sum_{i=1}^{N_{ob}} c_i$ (Note: C^* is a random variable)

Then by the well known Random Sum Theorem (see for example Feller ref 6) will also be asymptotically Normal with

$$E\{c^*\} = E\{N_{ob}\}E\{c_i\}$$

$$\text{and } Var\{c^*\} = E\{N_{ob}\}Var\{c_i\} + Var\{N_{ob}\}E^2\{c_i\}$$

$$\text{Now } E\{N_{ob}|\lambda\} = Var\{N_{ob}|\lambda\} = n\lambda T$$

$$\therefore E\{N_{ob}\} = nT\,E\{\lambda\}$$

$$\text{and } Var\{N_{ob}\} = n^2T^2 Var\{\lambda\} + nT\,E\{\lambda\}$$

$$\text{Thus } E\{c^*\} = nT\,E\{\lambda\}E\{c_i\}$$

$$Var\{c^*\} = nT\,E\{\lambda\}Var\{c_i\} + \left[n^2T^2 Var\{\lambda\} + nT\,E\{\lambda\}\right]E^2\{c_i\}$$

Now, in accordance with our original definition

$$E\{\lambda\} = \bar{\lambda} \text{ and } E\{c_i\} = \bar{c}$$

$$Var\{\lambda\} = \varepsilon^3/3 \text{ and } Var\{c_i\} = \Delta^2/3$$

Hence

$$E\{c^*\} = n\bar{\lambda}T\bar{c}$$

$$Var\{c^*\} = \frac{n^2\bar{\lambda}^2T^2\bar{c}^2}{3}\left[\frac{1}{n\bar{\lambda}T}\left(1+\left(\frac{\Delta}{\bar{c}}\right)^2\right)+\left(\frac{\varepsilon}{\bar{\lambda}}\right)^2\right]$$

In practice the estimate of $\bar{\lambda}$ will improve with time, thus driving ε towards 0. Therefore for sufficiently large T

$$Var\{c^*\} = \frac{n\bar{\lambda}T}{3}\left(\bar{c}^2 + \Delta^2\right)$$

If n, the number of copies of the software in service and being maintained, is varying with time, independently of the failure rate then n in the above formulae should be replaced by

$$\int_0^T n'(t)\,dt = n$$

A maintenance organisation would need to set aside (or charge) a quantity of money C_0 say to attempt to cover the maintenance costs arising from field failures. Furthermore let be the probability that $c^* \leq C_0$

$$\text{ie } \alpha_0 = P\{c^* \leq C_0\}$$

Define

$$\Phi(z) = \frac{1}{\sqrt{2\pi}}\int_{-\infty}^{z} e^{-z^2/2}\,dz$$

Now if

$$\beta_0 = \Phi^{-1}(\alpha_0)$$

Then

$$c_0 = n\bar{\lambda}T\bar{c} + \frac{\beta_0 n\bar{\lambda}T\bar{c}}{\sqrt{3}}\left[\frac{1}{n\bar{\lambda}T}\left(1+\left(\frac{\Delta}{\bar{c}}\right)^2\right)+\left(\frac{\varepsilon}{\bar{\lambda}}\right)^2\right]^{1/2}$$

For sufficiently large T the second term in the square brackets will dominate, and thus the contingency due to uncertainty about the reliability will be approximately

$$\beta_0\frac{E\{c^*\}}{\sqrt{3}}\left(\frac{\varepsilon}{\bar{\lambda}}\right)$$

and hence an increase in reliability measurement accuracy reduces this contingency proportionately (e.g. an 80% improvement in accuracy reduces the contingency by 80%). It does not, of course, effect in any way the actual costs incurred directly. However in terms of opportunity costs for the tied-up capital it is still a significant saving.

For example for a product which requires \$1,000,000 / annum for maintenance and a maintainer needing to be 95% certain of meeting its consequental maintenance costs, the contingency would be

$$\doteq \frac{3.10^6}{\sqrt{3}}\left(\frac{\varepsilon}{\bar{\lambda}}\right) \doteq 1.7.10^6\left(\frac{\varepsilon}{\bar{\lambda}}\right) \$/\text{annum}$$

An 80% improvement in reliability estimation would reduce this by $1.4.10^6$ dollars/annum (if $\varepsilon/\bar{\lambda} = 1$).

Now assuming interest rates of 10% /annum this represents an opportunity costs of $1.4.10^5$ dollars/annum, which for a product with a 20 year life is approximately 3.10^6 dollars.

CONCLUSIONS

The importance of software to the survival of high technology Economies is very great, and it is anticipated that large sectors of these Economies will become dependent, in one way or another, upon the availability of "quality-software". Software production is also seen as a possible saviour of our Economies by various of our government. It is essential therefore that means of analysing the benefits that can accrue from the existance of useful software can be evaluated and weighed against development costs. Some problems in this area have been aired in this paper, but it is necessary to address them more thoroughly if we are to see a stable and successful software industry.

REFERENCES

1. Life Cycle Cost Models. B de Neumann in "Electronic System Effectiveness and Life Cycle Costing" edited by J.K. Skwirzynski, Springer-Verlag, 1983
2. Economics. P. Samuelson. McGraw-Hill
3. The Theory of Value. G. Debreu. Yale U.P.
4. Evaluation of Competing Software Reliability Predictions B. Littlewood, A.A. Abdel Ghaly and P.Y. Chan (this issue)
5. Application of Basic and Logarithmic Poisson Execution Time Models in Software Reliability Measurement. J. Musa & K. Okumoto. (this issue)
6. An Introduction to Probability Theory and its Applications Vol I & II. W. Feller, Wiley.

PANEL DISCUSSION

ON

COMPARISON OF EVALUATION METHODS OF COST ASSESSMENT IN COMPUTING

Thursday, 8th of August, 1985 at 15.00 hours.

Chairman and Organiser: Dr. G.R. McNichols, President, MC&R Inc., U.S.A.

Panel Members:

Mr. E.R.Branyan, General Electric Co., U.S.A.
Mr. A.B. Ovens, Naval Research Laboratories, U.S.A.

Contributors:

Ms. G.D. Frewin, STL, Harlow, U.K.
Dr. I. Or, Bogazici Univ., Turkey
Dr. B. Curtis, MCC, Austin, U.S.A.
Mr. T.C. Jones, SPR Inc., U.S.A.
Mr. A.A. Wingrove, RAE, Farnborough, U.K.
Mr. M. Woodman, Open Univ., U.K.
Mr. J. Musa, AT&T Bell Laboratories, U.S.A.
Mr. J. Bromell, Cambridge Cons., U.K.

Dr. McNichols. This particular panel discussion will mainly consist of two important presentations, and you will be welcome to ask any questions during these. The proper discussion on relative merits of various cost estimate methods will take place during the panel chaired by Mr. T.C. Jones.

The first speaker today is Mr. Elmer Branyan of the Space Systems Division of the General Electric Company in the U.S.A. I have stressed the location of this Company, since we also have the General Electric Company in the U.K., whose part is the Marconi Company, where our Director works. Operations Research/Management Science as applied to cost estimating is now my subject, and talking on the subject of this discussion, my main problem is to assess the viability of a cost prediction model, and of its utility. It is my belief that the latter is inversly proportional to the number of variables involved. This was reported in the journal Management Science, 1971, as "McNichols Law". In the U.S., we call it the KISS principle, and the KISS stands for: "Keep it simple, stupid". That is what I believe in as a practicing analyst. It is much better to be approximately right, than precisely wrong, and in practice it is difficult to find out whether you are precisely wrong.

NATO ASI Series, Vol. F22
Software System Design Methods. Edited by J.K. Skwirzynski

The problem of cost estimation is predicting one realisation of a random experiment, (i.e., the cost of a system). This is all that we are trying to do. A manager would ask: 'Give me the cost of your system'. He wants a number and then says: 'Do not worry whether it is 1983 or 1994 dollars, or pounds, just give me the cost'.

The problem we have when we deal with software costing is that we do not quite know how to select the basic statistical distribution, and how to convince a manager that this is a difficult problem.

It is a practical, not a theoretical problem. That is why this panel consists of practical men, the peple who are doing and who are assessing cost estimates. We want to go over several topics that were discussed at this Institute, (e.g., namely the productivity, human factors, reliability, etc.) all those are inputs to a cost model, that is the generation of a number to which we have to budget.

Software is particularly important here, for many people believe that it is going to dominate the hardware, at least in terms of cost. Software is becoming an ever increasing percentage of cost of a system being produced, particularly in defense contracts. For instance, the U.S. Air Force Electronics Systems Division believes that about 70% of the cost of a system is that of the software, whereas the U.S. Navy believes that it is only 30%. Dr. Boehm uses a chart for this and it is shown here.

Now there is another problem. Generally, we do not talk about the reliability of a system, when we do a cost estimate, and this shows that the cost would mean different things to different people. When we look at the feasibility of a project, the question which we are really asking, when we say: 'What is the cost of this project?', is truly: 'Can we really afford it ?' Whenever anybody asks me what will be the cost of a hardware or a software, I will say: 'What are you going to do with that number ?' This is a very real,

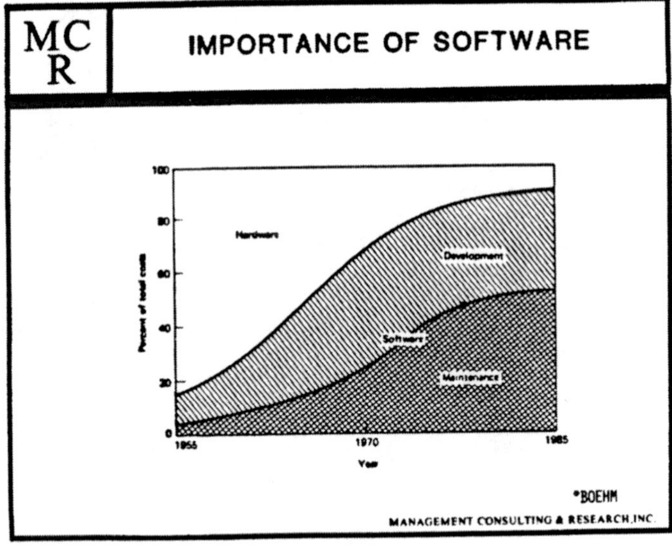

practical problem. Software cost estimates are being used for:

* project feasibility,
* trade-off analyses,
* funding requirements,
* schedules, and
* progress measurement.

Now let us consider the problem of estimating uncertainty in cost prediction. During the course of development of software, the point to consider, as you get on with the system, is the relative cost range and associated errors. Why is this problem so difficult? What I have found four or five years ago is that software has only recently become a main component in a system cost. Maybe it has become so fifteen years ago, but managers are just now starting to believe that this is a major component. This is what causes difficulties. Mr. Jones (1) understands the relationship of cost factors to project costs, so does Dr. Boehm, but their understanding is quite different. Good quality historical cost data are many - say 3000 points. I do not have these, but to me they are just data, and not information. This is the problem with software data costs - we may have data, but until you have translated these to something that is useable, it is not information.

When we look at the productivity of programmers, as Dr. Curtis has shown us in his lecture (2), we see a tremendous variance, although they may be solving the same problem. He has shown us many examples, but I have one here which supports what he was saying. This was a case in 1974. Each of several groups of software students, of equal level of capability, were asked to solve a problem of computer modelling. Each team has a different objective. These were:

* to minimize the required core memory;
* to minimize the required number of statements;
* to minimize the execution time;
* to maximize the program clarity;
* to minimize the programmer's man-hours; and
* to maximize the output clarity.

They all solved the problem, but each of their programs had a different number of statements, and each had a different number of man-hours to produce the same specification. So, if you look for productivity, you would find there a factor of eight, or ten, in the number of statements per man-hour. The results are shown here.

This leads us to the fixed cost environment, or rather to the fixed price environment. This is the way the U.S.A. has gone at the end of last year with competitive contracts, and more recently also the U.K. has adopted this attitude. What do you think a contracting officer and a client would make of these variable man-hours? Would they accept this? If your estimate is more than 30 man-hours, then certainly you would not win the contract. And yet this all depends on what a bidder is trying to optimise, and this again depends on what he thinks is the objective of software. That is why I believe we have to understand the purpose of data bases, because different objectives will imply different results from raw data, and you cannot just use one set of data to solve different problems.

MCR

EFFECT OF OBJECTIVES ON PRODUCTIVITY

TEAM OBJECTIVE: OPTIMIZE	NUMBER OF STATEMENTS	MAN-HOURS	PRODUCTIVITY (STATE/M-H)
CORE MEMORY	52	74	0.7
NUMBER OF STATEMENTS	33	30	1.1
EXECUTION TIME	100	50	2.0
PROGRAM CLARITY	90	40	2.2
PROGRAMMING MAN-HOURS	126	28	4.5
OUTPUT CLARITY	166	30	5.5

*WEINBERG-SCHULMAN

MANAGEMENT CONSULTING & RESEARCH,INC.

We keep talking about efficiency, which means doing things right. We want a computer to be efficient, that is to do things faster, and to do them correctly. The problem is that we are effective if we do the right things, and it is here that fortunately the human being enters the loop. We, the cost estimators, believe that you do not just make models to get results out of them. We have to employ an analyst in the loop, who will use the model as a tool, or perhaps several of these models as tools, and employ them as inputs to a loop where a decision is made. Then possibly a good result might come. We are estimators and we do not necessarily believe in models. We can only use them to put inputs to our decisions, then we might be able to be sure that we are making right decisions.

Our pannelists will talk to you on definitions of cost models, most of which contain the number of lines of code as input parameters. Mr. T.C. Jones has mentioned this in his lecture (1). What do we mean by this ? Are they source line code (DSLOC), or delivered source instructions (DSI)? Do we mean that they delivered executable machine instructions (DEMI), and do we include comments, or not ? So this measure may mean different things.

In the problem of life cycle cost, at least in the U.S.A., the life cycle costs are quite different in software, when compared with hardware. This causes us a great problem. We have 'milestones' for hardware phases of development. Each of these 'milestones' are review stages by the Defense Systems Acquisition Review Council (DSARC). They decide whether a system development is progressing or not, and accordingly they agree on the budget estimate, or a founding prophile. But we do not have such a DSARC for software, so we do not know whether we can go ahead. So what you do is to slip-in a decision at a 'milestone'. However, if we have a hardware-software dependency in a system, our decision might go the wrong way. That indeed is our difficulty.

Some of the estimating methods currently used for software cost assessment include:

* analogy,
* expert judgement,
* Parkinson,
* price to win,
* algorithmic:
  - regression,
  - heuristic, and
  - phenomenological.

When we compare the list of parameters for inputing them into a cost prediction, as produced by Mr. T.C. Jones (1), we have other lists, as also have other model designers. I put this as an estimating method, and I believe that this method is used most widely by anybody, except possibly by the members of this panel, so their presentations will be very interesting. It seems to me that that software cost estimations obey the Parkinson's Law, so that, given how much money you have, it will cost you that much for your software project!

In the algorithmic area we have started the regression analysis of actual data to form cost estimations in most models, though some of them are heuristic. We are now beginning to go into the phenomenological state, where we try to predict the cost at a functional level. Yet we still have not solved the firmware-hardware-software problem to know what is the cost of doing a function. The problem here is the degree of knowledge of a system; does an analyst need to be an expert, or a novice, to be able to make a cost prediction in these cases ? And secondly, does he have enough technical knowledge or the data bases available to him or her ?

The reliability prediction 'model war' is now in disarray, but the software cost prediction 'model war' has just begun. Now we are going to start this battle by asking Mr. Branyan to continue.

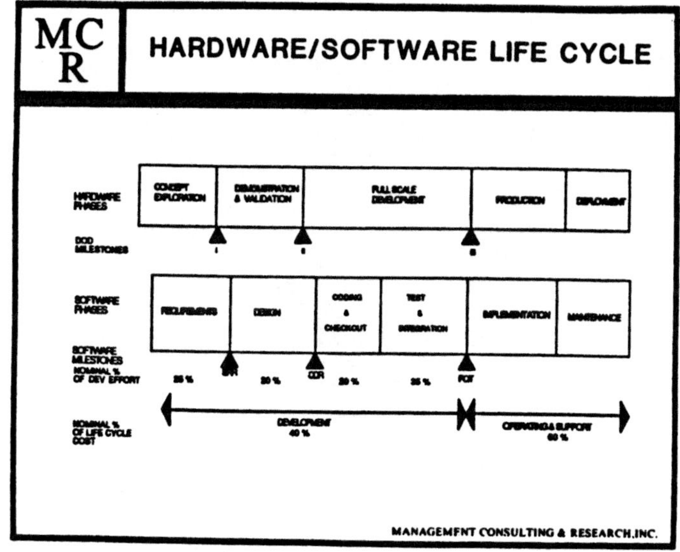

Mr. Branyan. My General Electric Company is very large, and I have nothing to do with building refrigerators and such like. I am working in the Space Systems Division, Data Systems Resource Management, and we have hundreds of customers. We built systems that appear in one place, because generally there is one copy of it. If there is an avionics package, it goes into one aircraft, on its board, and we call it a support to that aircraft. If you change it, then you change the aircraft. In all these cases there is software involved. That is the problem we wish to solve, and where we want ot be successfull. We have started this about 15 years ago. Then we had no idea what we were doing, so we had a lot of difficulties. After a loss of few general managers, we now think that we can tackle the software problem.

The point that I now want to stress is that THE ART (SCIENCE?) OF SOFTWARE ESTIMATION is now coming from three sources of expertise:

1. Myself, in the General Electric Company, we have the viewpoint of a contractor for building software.

2. Thomas F. Masters, President of the International Society of Parametric Analysts (McLean, Virginia, U.S.A.) was also engaged in the National Security Agency of the U.S.A. He is the buyer of software.

3. Marilee J. Wheaton, The Aerospace Corporation, Mission Information Systems Division (Los Angeles, California, U.S.A.) has a different approach, for she wants to make sure that the Air Force gets its money's worth.

Thus all of us have a common task, common approach and opinions.

We consider that the art (science?) of software estimation has the following six tasks:

I. SOFTWARE ESTIMATION BACKGROUND, where we have to trace the buyer's opinion, and once we settle the background of what we want, we can start to built the software.

II. SOFTWARE MANAGEMENT METHODOLOGY, which hopefully will allow us to be successful in cost estimation, and that follows:

III. OVERVIEW OF SOFTWARE ESTIMATION, which we have to establish.

IV. SOFTWARE RISK ANALYSIS. We refer to this as management's reserve; how to prevent the so-called over-runs and mis-schedules. The other two aspects which I will discuss later, are:

V. SOFTWARE METRICS

VI. PERSPECTIVES

There was a study performed at the Electronics Industry Association in 1979. It concerned the embedded computer systems (in avionics, space, defence etc.). It was then agreed that by 1990 we shall require about 30 billion dollars for the software in these systems (Fig.1), while hardware will go from 1.2 to 4.6 billion. I was very sceptical of this in 1979. Then in 1983 I participated at a meeting in Orlando, Florida, where the four Services met at a Commanders' Meeting; they looked at this estimate and were still sceptical. But by 1984 we have got some information from the Pentagon which made us less sceptical, for by 1984 we had already nearly 10 billion dollars of software cost.

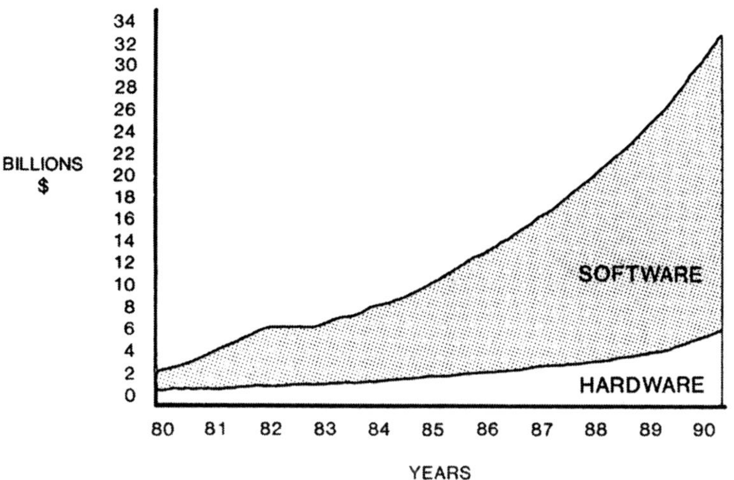

Fig 1: DOD EMBEDDED COMPUTER MARKET
SOFTWARE/HARDWARE

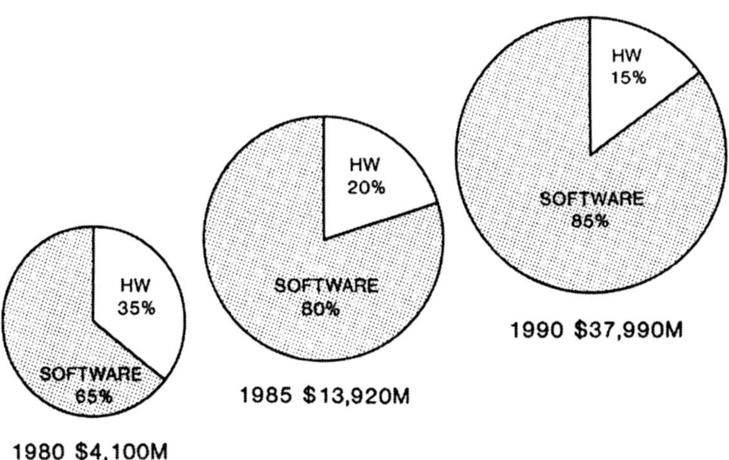

Mr. Ovens. Is this the actual cost of acquisition, or does it include orders, and other stages of life cycle ?

Mr. Branyan. It is very difficult to establish this, for a lot of money is passing on at different stages of a contract. When we receive the acquisition money from an operational establishment, this implies that the whole package is ready, but then follows the support and maintenance money. Thus, I cannot answer your question beyond that.

What we are now concerned with is, that if you project the cost growth until 1990, and if we are going to develop and to support that much of software, then this implies that we shall be short of about 100,000 people in being able to perform that work.

Another way of looking at this in terms of growth is to show that there is a representation of hardware cost versus that of software (Fig.2). Here we see that for embeded computers there is going to be about 85% of software cost out of the total cost. In 1981 we started to work on this problem by developing standards, and these standards have now been approved. They are referred to as the Military Standard No.165 in our numbering system. In that system we insisted that we are going to deal with things as unique packages, so we well understand what we are dealing with. Thus, in this concept of software cost estimation we want somewhat to break it into packets, to be able to ensure that we understand what we are going to replace if need arises.

The stages of software life cycle phases are illustrated in Fig.3. Now let us concentrate on the chart in Fig.4, to which Dr. McNichols has already referred. This is the result of us trying to understand how do the cost estimation models fit into the real situation. We break it down into pieces of work to be performed. We have schedules which we have to meet, and budgets, that we must meet. There are several models here: of Jensen, Boehm and Putman, and that of RCA. There are stages here which each of them calls by different names, such as C/A (Contract Award), or P&R (Plans & Requirements), or SRR (System Requirement Review), or PDR (Preliminary Design Review), etc. etc. These stages have their names, but they also mean that you have to accomplish in each case very specific things; in each case we have to know where we have got to. I might ask the modellers if there is something in their models that matches my present situation. Then Jensen will say that I am in SDR, and Boehm that I am in A&C. Other question is what happens between the SDR and the FOT ? This may mean to me that this stage represents another 23% of work. Whether the additional 23% is realistic or not, has really nothing to do with the problem, because every contract turns out to be different. As Dr. McNichols has told us, each thing has a different problem.

What we should really try to do with these studies on cost estimation is to match the models to real world. For instance, in the NSA model they do not have any SDR (System Design Review); they do not even mention this thing. They just have the design phase, the code phase and the test & integration phase, and if you try to price these things, you will find that they have quite a lot of overlap.

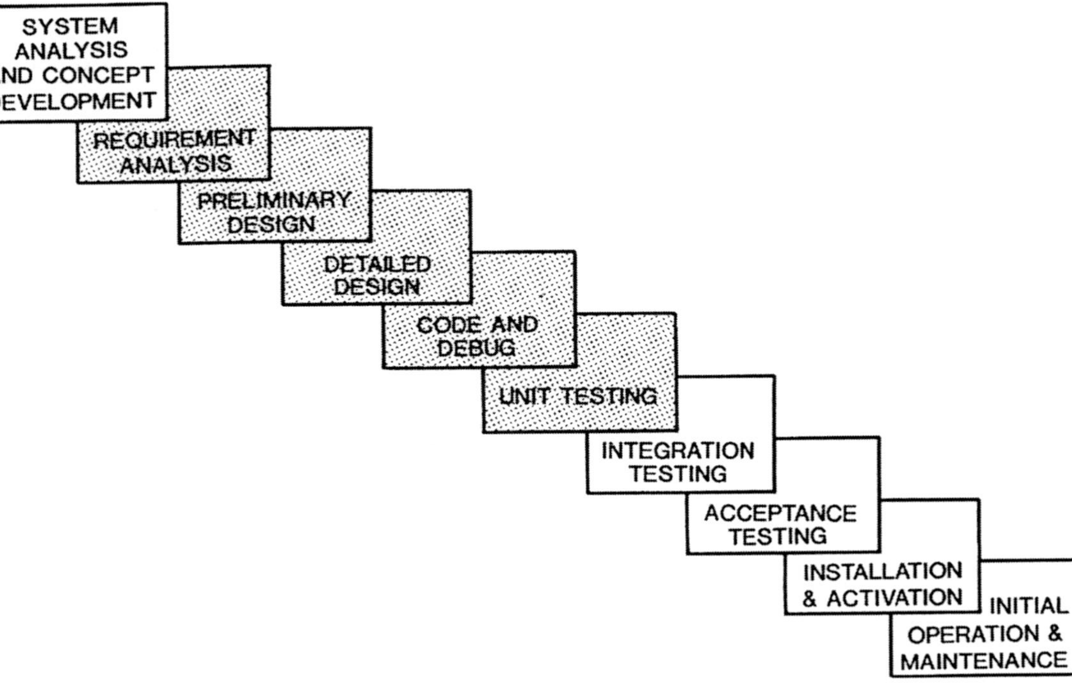

Fig 3: SOFTWARE LIFE CYCLE PHASES

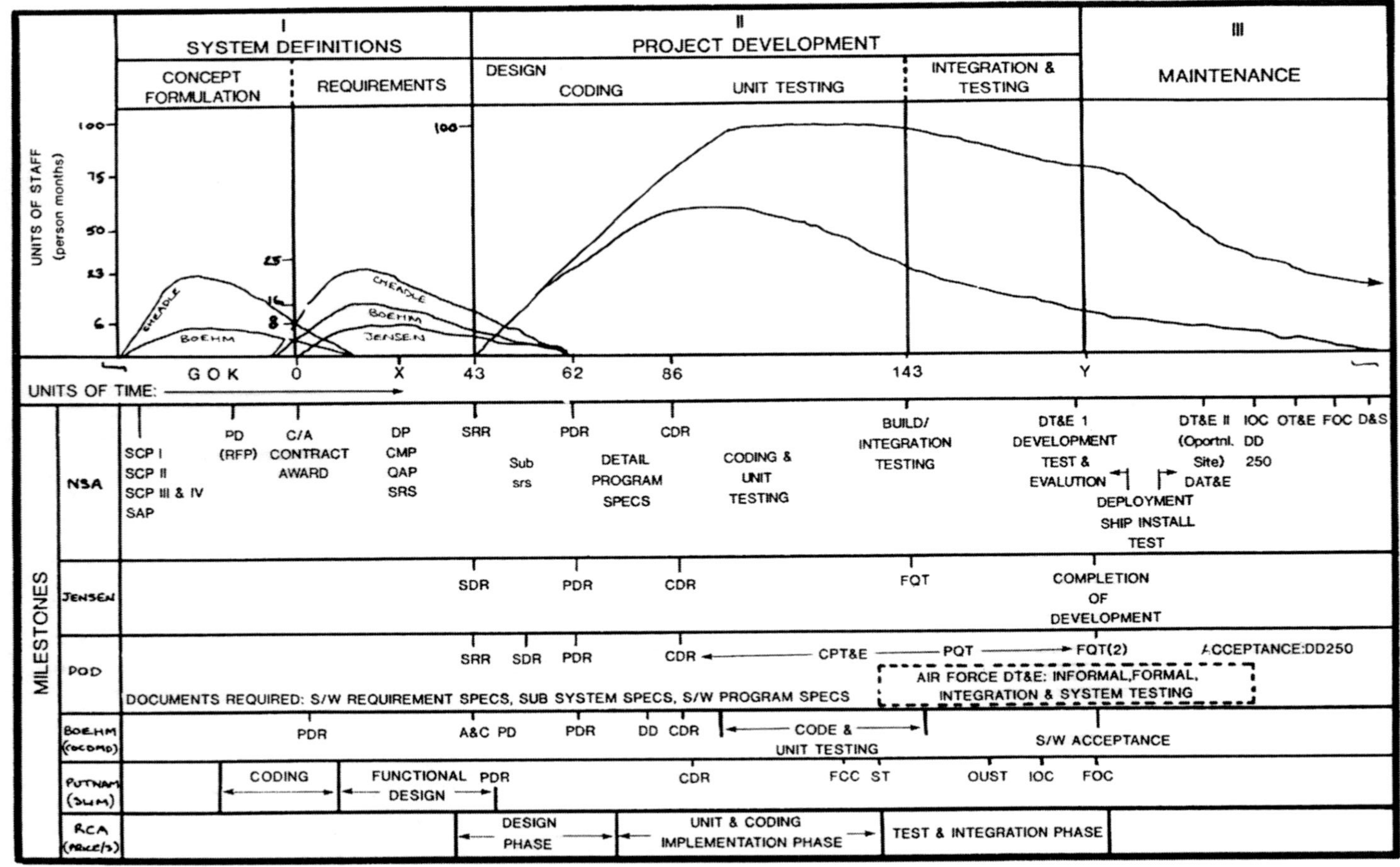

Fig 4: SOFTWARE LIFE CYCLE

LEGEND TO ABBREAVIATIONS IN FIG.4.

∞	Infinite
A&C	Approval & Completion
CDR	Critical Design Review
CMP	Configuration Management Plan
DD	Detailed Design
DD250	Final Acceptance
DT&E-II	Operational DT&E
FCC	First Code Completed
FOC	Full Operational Capability
FOT	Final Qualification Test
FOT(2)	Formal Qualification Test
GOK	Government only knows
IDC	Initial Operational Capability
NSAPD	Purchased Description
OAT&E	Operation Acceptance Test and Evaluation
O&S	Operational & Support
OTE	Operational Test and Evaluation
PD	Product Design
PDR	Preliminary Design Review
PQT	Preliminary Qualification Test
P&R	Plans & Requirements
QAP	Quality Assurance Plan
SPCI	System Requirements Specifications
SPCII	Requirements Approval
SPCIII	System Concepts
SPCIV	Alternative (Concept) Solutions
SAP	System Acquisition Plan
SIT	System Integration Test
SDR	System Design Review
SRS	S/W Requirements Specifications
SRR	System Requirements Review
S/W	Software
UOST	User Oriented System Test

Thus, if I am in the real world and want to deal with this situation, then using these models I have to relate them back to the things that I am doing, and to what my customers are expecting me to accompish. We have spent a lot of time on this chart in Fig.4. When I published my paper with this chart and the modellers read it, they still are coming back to me and say that I have not got it right. So no matter how much work we are trying to do in talking to them, we still do not understand their models. That is a major problem for people who are trying to use these models, and try to establish some real world situation. I am supporting here Dr. McNichols.

Lot of people argue about this and I still have no idea what the real number is that I input to a model. In any case it takes some time and effort to produce a software and if this software has some life-time, say 7 years (typically in systems that I deal with), then over that period there is a lot of work going on, as you can see in Fig. 5. Here we are trying to get rid of the word maintenance; we refer to it as cost of development support. This is because the phase called maintenance does not consist of correction of errors. It has to do with lots of enhancement, adaption, perfection, system changes, mission changes etc. Lots of things get changed, and that means a lot of work. So we do not call it maintenance.

In the development phase (see Fig. 5) there is another work that goes on. This is the requirements development, coding & debugging and testing. In my organisation testing ranges in the area of 50% of the total development work. This is the area that Mr. T.C. Jones (1) called 'removing the defects'. We are trying very hard to establish requirements so that we remove defects from a design. Then in the debugging phase we are trying to get rid of syntax errors.

We have to establish that before a system comes out, it will perform a mission. A tremenderous amount of work goes into this. We have to take into account various scenarios in which a system must fulfill its requirements, so that, if a system is in operation, it will in no way cause to stop a mission. You may be able to degrade a mission, but you cannot afford to stop it.

The next item to discuss is how are we going to do it. What we have recognised about 15 years ago, is that in software, if we cannot measure an effect, we cannot manage it. We have to come out with some policies how to go about this job. Here are the goals of software management planning:

- Minimum Development Schedule at Lowest Possible Cost.
- Accuracy of Estimate.
- Guidance:
  Project Development and Support Plan;
  Contingency Plan (in case of crisis).
- Progress Evaluation.

People often talk of minimum development schedule at lowest cost; this is not really what we are after. We are after solving a problem. So we do not want minimum cost if all that you are producing are program lists.

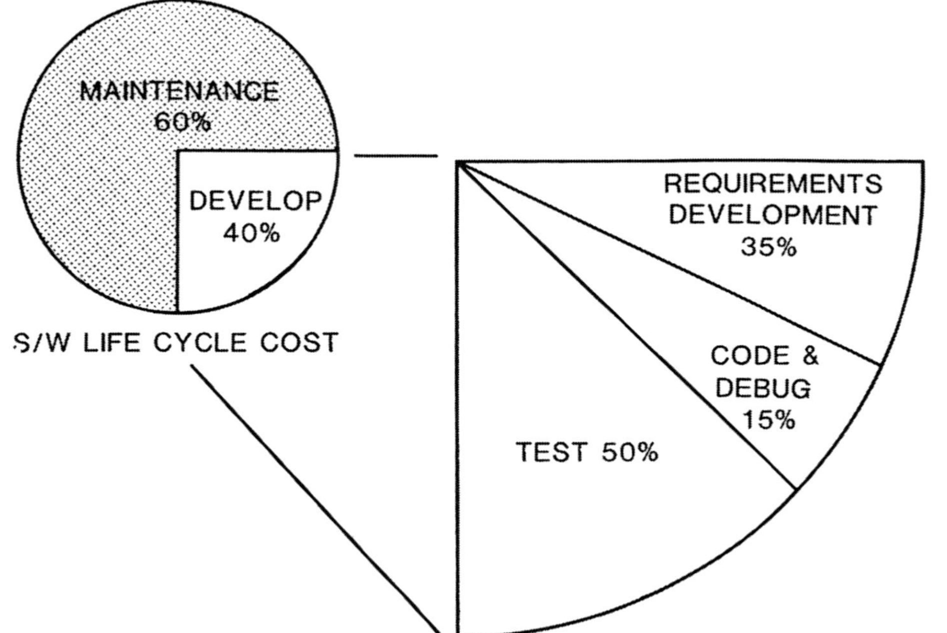

Fig 5: TYPICAL SOFTWARE COST DISTRIBUTION

We are worried about the accuracy of estimates; it really does not matter that we should know exactly what is the cost; what matters is whether we can manage it, and can we understand what we are trying to do.

Once we get certain guidance, we can start to develop a project as planned. One of the risks we have to face is how to manage the project if wrong things happen. We have also to uderstand all the time at what point of the project plan we are; whatever is the system cost this is important, and our systems costs are 50 to 100 million dollars which take 3 to 5 years to complete. Thus the progress evaluation is an important part of our task.

To accomplish this we have to consider the software cost estimation process (Fig. 6). I have no time frame here, but what I do have is the information we must deal with. The first issue is to find out whether a system is feasible, for this impinges on the 'growth factor'. Mr. T.C. Jones (1) has mentioned that this factor is about 44%. We have done some study of it with Marilee J. Wheaton, and have found that in systems we deliver to the Air Force, we deliver 75% more code than we have initially estimated before we have started a project; this is our 'growth factor', and this concerns the resources.

We have very preliminary information and very preliminary requirements, and from that we have to begin to consider what the cost is. To get this cost we have to consider what kind of resources we are going to deal with. On an average project you will need about 200 people, and they are not just sitting on the wing, trying to jump in the next day. There is always the problem of hiring them and of training them. The resources also include computer facilities. The question arises, do I have enough computer power ? The system that exists today will not be necessarily sufficient in five years' time, for technology changes. You start with a machine with 32 Kb memory, and by the time you have finished, you might need millions of Kb. You have to face all these problems, and this is why we need a continuous feedback of information.

The cost models are not something you work with at the very beginning and decide then on the cost value and schedule, just like that. Models have to be dynamic and you have to adjust then frequently.

To summarise, this is our idea of

SOFTWARE MANAGEMENT PROJECT PLANS:

- Development Schedule
- Development Effort (Cost)
- Milestone Schedules
- Staff Requirements
- Resource (Staff) Allocation over Development Cycle
- Risk Estimates (Schedule and Effort)
- Trade-off Analysis Support
- Design-to-Cost Estimate
- Cost-to-Complete Estimates
- Disaster Planning Data

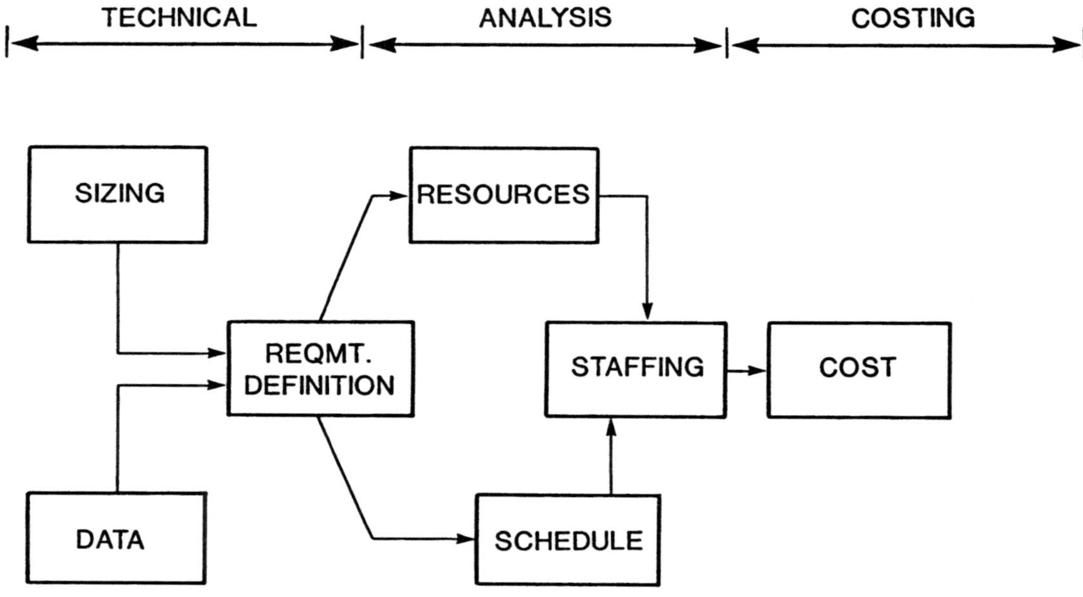

Fig 6: SOFTWARE COST ESTIMATION PROCESS

Thus, when I am developing a project plan, I have to know what our estimates really are. This is very important. I start with a development schedule, then I plan the development effort and I separate out the cost. I would like to make a point about this. I am not really interested in dollar values when I try to manage a project. I am really interested in resources: people, computer facilities, building space. The things I want to manage the job with are the things that I need to have the job done, and money is not the one of them. Money is for the accountants to work with; they think of overheads and salaries. I deal frequently without this. When I use a cost model like the one from the RCA, it does not work in hours, so I have to spend a long time to make it work in hours. As a software developer, I need to work with effort. If I wish to put 200 people on a job, I have to deal with the management stress factor - you just cannot employ 200 people in a short period of time.

I am also very interested in risk estimates in order to isolate elements that are going to bring me difficulties. I want to be able to do trade-offs. Is it really worth doing an extra chunk of work, or will I get enough extra effort to built up that additional capability of software? As we proceed with a project, we continously go back and re-visit the past, to do either a design-to-cost estimate or a cost-to-complete estimate. We do it at least every six months in a three year project. If the project time is shorter, we do it more frequently.

Now we are coming to the overview of software estimation. This is a management tool and we claim that:

SOFTWARE ESTIMATE IS THE MOST KNOWLEGEABLE STATEMENT THAT CAN BE MADE ABOUT THE RESOURCES REQUIRED TO DEVELOP A PROGRAMMING SYSTEM PRODUCT.

This estimate contains:
- Estimated Cost
- Schedule
- End Products
- Assumptions
- Risks
- Definitions

When we are trying to accomplish this on the contract side, this allows us to plan the work on the project, and on the acquisition side, it allows them to measure us; it allows them to do it in a very educated way to decide how we can do this job in the best way.

To accomplish this work the organisation has to be quite serious in developing software, for it has to consider:

COSTING SOFTWARE AS AN ENGINEERING DISCIPLINE

Here are ideas for this concept:

- RESPONSIBILITIES: Each software producing department is responsible for collecting data on project cost and quality.
- POLICY: Data concerning the effectiveness of each project's software engineering and management processes shall be collected and analysed.
- GOALS: Develop guidelines for collection of software development information - Develop capabilities for producing quantitative cost estimation and calibration parameter values - Develop capabilities for bidding and managing software projects by producing reports based on collected data.

Ms. Frewin. Everybody in every organisation has people more senior than him- or her-self. Then how are you going to accept these data by your seniors, and how are you going to convince them that you need time to perform this data collection ?

Mr. Branyan. Personally, in my experience, this is a situation where I have to establish this activity little by little over a year, and to claim that this has a lot of value. I have also been able to establish that this does not cost a great deal. If we do it in a right way, this becomes an important part of the business. We have people filling up time-sheets every day. We structure various tasks in such a way that the numbers are put in a coordinated way with the job we are doing. It is easy to collect the hours worked. If we break this structure down in any detail, we also know how to amend this.

Ms. Frewin. How do you deal with this data collection and how do you persuade people to do it ? This happens also in many companies here in the U.K.. Yet it also happens that they occasionally sneekingly collect the data, as if this was a vice (Laughter).

Mr. Branyan. In our organisation this has a complete management's attention, and although I hate to admit this, you might be right on some occasions. My own personal experience is not unlike that. I have created a disaster, where I wrote a report and presented it to customers. Then the managers nearly fired me, but fortunately next day they accepted me (Laughter).

Now I am going to the research area., namely to the models of cost estimate. First let us consider

THE COMPONENTS OF A COMPLETE ESTIMATE

these components are:

DEFINITIONS (What the estimate includes (WBS items) - quantification of terms)

ASSUMPTIONS (major assumptions within the estimate)

RISKS (what risks are accounted for - what contingency plans exist)

SOFTWARE END PRODUCTS (what will be developed, e.g. code specifications, documentation, etc.)
REQUIRED RESOURCES
ESTMATED SCHEDULE
ESTMATED COSTS

Now we come to test the definitions:

IMPORTANCE OF CLEAR DEFINITIONS

SCOPE (include conversion - training - documentation)
END POINTS (include requirements - system test)
INSTRUCTIONS (source - object - executable - comments)
PRODUCT (applications - support software - test drivers)
DEVELOPMENT (include resused software - furnished utility software)
MAN-MONTHS (include clerical and support personnel - vacation)

It is important ot observe that these can bias results by factor of 2 - 10. If I worry about model, I tried to begin with systematic approach, particularly relating to the cost. Thus we have to consider:

SOFTWARE COST ESTIMATION MODEL CHARACTERISTICS

SOFTWARE COST MODEL (systematic procedure that relates cost to certain variables or cost factors)
COST FACTORS (describe the product under development - describe the manner in which it is built)
RELIABILITY OF COST FACTORS (affected by relatively new discipline - explosive development of technology - recently became major cost and accepted cost factors not established - historical data almost nonexistent)

Now let us look at the models that we have to use to do this cost estimation. I will first attempt to characterise them:

SOFTWARE COST ESTIMATION MODELS

1. CLASSICAL METHODS (The basic methods of estimation whic attempt to use all existing information and experience to forecast software costs. Fundamental techniques which form the foundations for all models)

2. PHENOMENOLGICAL MODELS (Models characterised by hypothesised fundamental laws governing basic phenomena. Models incorporating concepts explainable in terms of basic phenomena, not dependent on the mechanics of software development. Models which combine basic phenomena to explain more complex phenomena)
Examples: SLIM, HALSTEAD, WOLVERTON-SCHICK, JENSEN.

3. REGRESSION MODELS (Estimation of future relationships among project parameter metrics using best-fit techniques for a given population of measured (past) data)
Examples: RADC, ARON, IBM

4. HEURISTIC MODELS (Estimation models characterised by freedom from any particular mathematical formulation, but combining a number of different estimating strategies, usually following through a series of adjustments and refinements as time progresses, and generally intersperses observation and interpretation with supposition)

Examples: PRICE/S, DoD MICRO-ESTIMATION, BOEING, COCOMO

Here I want to have a somewhat systematic approach to cost relationship and cost factors, so I will list the following:

CHARACTERISTICS OF A GOOD MODEL

CALIBRATION (allows the user to calibrate to his/her data base)
DEFINITION (terms unambigously defined)
FIDELITY (predictions represent reality plus-or-minus)
STABILITY (model can handle singularities and side effects)
USABILITY (easier to use than not to use)
WHAT-IF PROCESSING (handles real world variations in parameters)

It is known tht cost factors can be used to describe a project that one wants to develop. I had to agree strongly with Mr. T.C. Jones (1) when he came up with his 300 factors. I do not have 300 of them, but in some sense there are still a lot of them, and you have to pay a lot of attention to them. In our models we use much fewer factors than 300. In dealing with these cost factors, we have to try to reproduce reliably the actual situations, but this does not happen too well, because the whole idea of doing cost estimation is relatively new. It is changing quite rapidly and at the moment we are trying to use the artificial intelligence, for instance linking this with the EXPERT system. Yet this has to be fitted with some sort of executive programme. At present the models do not seem to fit that kind of work. The other problem is the constant change of technology. The idea that software has became only recently a major cost factor causes us to be not as good in this estimation business as the hardware people are.

We are constantly looking at realtionships between models. Some people say that such exist, but we find that they are different. For instance, people say that everything looks like a Rayleigh curve, and that with this curve I can predict how long it is going to take errors out of software. We have plotted all the errors in several major projects and it turned out that this was not the Rayleigh curve. The distribution was rather like a Beta skewed the other way. These things are just hard to establish. Maybe we should have flattened the data, or maybe we have not cathegorised them properly. In any case, historical data are very difficult to come by.

There are many models. People play with them, but I have not learned how to use most of them. My experience has been with SS, Putman and Slim models, and I have done some work with the Halstead model. Mr. R. Rambo, who works with me and has joined us at this Institute, has been looking at the problem of software size metrics and their relation to the complexity measure.

Dr. Or. I do not think that I understand your terminology. How do you differentiate between simulation models and mathematical models ?

Mr. Branyan. This differentiation cannot be done very clearly. Jensen, for instance, does simulation, but he does not like the Monte Carlo method. He has a set of curves and they are very similar; this is almost a combination of COCOMO and Putman put together. But in his next step he notices that in every input element there is uncertainty. So he selects a random number from every one of these input probability distributions, and then he says, that if you do a Monte Carlo simulation on it, you will have a thousand of solutions. Then if you plot the probability of success, based on this simulation, you may get a model which gives an answer. If you want to do a sensitivity analysis on this, you subtract a 10% of the end of his range, and add 10% to the beginning of his range, and you have it. This would indicate the sensitivity of the result with respect to one input value.

Dr. Or. So in fact these are not mathematical models.

Mr. Branyan. COCOMO is a mathematical model; GE is not really so; some of Putman's work is of mathematical type.

Dr. McNichols. The COCOMO, RCA and Price models are mathematical, but some people try to classify them further into phenomological versus regression, but basically they have a mathematical approach. They are models indeed, for they are available, and you can get your hands on them, and actually run them or use them. Is this clear ?

Dr. Or. I was just interested about mathematical models and about the way you differentiate them.

Mr. Branyan. Mathematical models are all published - you can see the equations. Putman and RCA are computer models - they are black-box models, if you will. You can provide inputs to them, get outputs from them, but you do not know what is the mathematical model inside. I do not think that the RCA model is mathematical, because they have not published anything about it; it is probably a purely heuristic model.

Dr. Curtis. So all this information is a black art, or possibly witchcraft ? (Laughter)

Mr. Branyan. I will try to show you the strengths and weaknesses of these models, as we see them (Fig. 7).

STRENGTHS AND WEAKNESSES OF
SOFTWARE COST-ESTIMATION METHODS

METHOD	STRENGTHS	WEAKNESSES
Algorithmic Model	Objective, repeatable analysable formula. Efficient, good for sensitivity analysis. Objectively calibrated to experience.	Subjective inputs. Assessment of exceptional circumstances. Calibrated to past, not future.
Expert Judgement	Assessment of representativeness, interactions, exceptional circumstances.	No better than participants. Biases, incomplete recall.
Analogy	Based on representative experience.	Representativeness of experience.
Parkinson price to win	Correlates with some experience. Often wins.	Reinforces poor practice. Generally produces large overruns.
Top-down	System level focus. Efficient.	Less detailed basis. Less stable.
Bottom-up	More detailed basis. More stable. Fosters individual commitment.	May overlook system level costs. Requires more effort.

Figure 7.

The characteristic of a good model, if you are going to use one, is whether or not you can calibrate it. I have to keep historical data bases, and by calibration I can find what I am doing with a model. Otherwise I get garbage in and garbage out. I have to find the meaning of ambigous terms in a model, at least in some fashion, so that I can understand them; then I do not need an expert everytime I run a model. In most cases they will not let you touch a model, unless you take two or three weeks of instructions from the model builder. Otherwise he will not let you run it. I have a lot of trouble, for instance, with the term 'fidelity'. This is because in my opinion, models do not make estimates; it is an estimator that does it. A friend of mine has made a study of models few years ago. He took about eight models and three data bases, one from the Air Force Software Engineering Laboratory, one from NASA, and one from an unnamed commercial organisation. He then proceeded to find out whether he can match the results. He normalised the data, and hence the projects where they came from. The net result was that, if you normalise the data, then in a historical sense you cannot confirm the past work by better than by 50% in the cost figure; sometimes it reaches 100% off the value of the true cost. So I got into several organisations and got 42 projects, and used the Slim model to project the cost. In his model Slim has a term which he calls 'technology concept'. In my 42 projects that 'technology concept' ranged from 600 to 30,000. Would that imply that I should take a mean and accept this as a normalisation factor ? That would be an utter nonsense. What is really the truth, is that for any single project I can fit a model to it, This does not mean however that I can do the same with every project. I can predict the cost only if I deal with something that is analogous. Let me summarise this:

COST ESTIMATION METHODS ARE BASED
UPON ANALOGY TO PAST PROJECTS

Organisations which exhibit best record for reasonable estimates tend to have the following:

1. Access to detailed history of past experience.
2. Use of experienced estimators.
3. Use of more than one cost estimation method concurrently.
4. Use of estimates derived independent of budgets and required schedules.
5. Frequent updates of the estimate during the course of a project.

Thus we have to be very careful with the concept of fidelity. Estimators have to learn how to use it, for estimators make estimates, and not the model.

Mr. Jones. Can I make a point here ? In January 1986, at a conference in Hawaii, all important cost estimation models will be given the same case study. The idea is to compare results from individual models.

Mr. Branyan. So you say that they will deal with a single project. I have historical data for about 100 projects and I could characterise all of them. In the case of a single project various models come with cost numbers within few percent of each other.

Mr. Jones. They do not.

Mr. Branyan. Maybe this is also possible, but I can take one of my projects and results will indeed come within few percent. I can take the Jensen model and my own cost comes within 9% of that of Jensen's model. Here are my ideas on this:

WHY DO SOFTWARE COSTS DIFFER ?

Product Characteristics:
- Size Instructions
- Type of Software Application
- Specifications/Operation Environment
- Processor Loading Utilisation
- Interface (software/hardware) Integration

Project Constraints:
- Schedule
- Manpower
- Inventory (Design/Code) New Design/New Code
- Changing Requirements
- Multi-team Coordination

Technical Capability:
- Personnel (skills/experience)
- Product Familiarity
- Development Aids/Facilities

Management Factors:
- Rates (labour/overheads)
- Procedures/Habits
- Economics/Inflation

I have to deal with all these things to allow me to make proper estimates. With this we proceed as folows:

COLLECTING DATA -
WHAT, WHEN AND HOW ?

Data collection is needed to calibrate your models and metrics to your environment.

What data do you collect ?
1. Product data is the easiest to collect.
2. Process data is the most useful.
3. People data is almost impossible to gather.

When do you collect it ?
1. The sooner, the better.
2. Realize that the most valuable data is also the hardest and most expensive to gather.

How do you collect it?
1. Forms and interviews
2. Automated data collection
3. Automated data analysis.

At the same time you have to define your work:

DEFINE THE WORK ELEMENTS

1. What activities are to be included within this estimate and what are not ? (Use software work breakdown structure)
2. What programs are to be included within this estimate and what are not ? (Analyse needs statement and requirements)
3. What are the documentation requirements ? (Identify customer standards or use your own)
4. How volatile are the operational and performance requirements (if they exist) ? (Analyse the situation and make an assessment)
5. Do I understand enough about the nature of the job to come up with a rough order of magnitude estimate ? (If not, do your homework)

One thing that has come up, and I spent a lot of time on it, is trying to estimate the size. Lot of people talk about this, but what we have to do is to estimate the effective size, and apply this to every work package. I have to be very careful what I count - so we have rules how to count very carefully. And we also make sure that we account for all the work which we do. This is a thing that Jensen calls 'reverse engineering'. He understands that if I am going to change something at one stage, I canot do it without knowing whether I am affecting anything that I have already worked on. So in terms of design activities this is called 'reverse engineering'. If I test one of these things, I have also to test all of them. If I change 30% or 60% of software, I will have to test the whole 100% of it. In fact, I have to test it at the same rate as I did built it from the scratch.

One last thing I want to say is about the maintenance. This is very poorly understood. Hopefully next year I might be able to deal with this, for I am collecting a lot of data for it. We are aware that a lot of things are happening beside improvements and additions. How do we cost this ? We do not know at the moment. Some people are queering as to what we should do about this, and how are we going to proceed to budget this. I do not think that models cater for this very well.

To summarise, I propose what you should do:

STEPS IN SOFTWARE COST ESTIMATION

1. Establish Objectives (Rough Sizing - Make-or-Buy - Detailed Planning)
2. Allocate enough time, dollars, talent
3. Pin down software requirements (Document Definitions - Assumptions)
4. Work out as much detail, as objectives permit.
5. Use several independent techniques + sources (Top-down versus Bottom-up - Algorithm versus Expert Judgement)
6. Compare and Iterate Estimates (Pin down and resolve inconsistencies - Be conservative)
7. Follow-up

The algorithmic procedures are quick and easy to use, but there is a lot of subjectiveness in them. In every one of them I have to choose one particular answer. Someone has asked me what is the percentage of programmers' efort in a cost price. They might spend 95%, or 60%, or even 25%, it all depends how you measure programmers' effort. All these things deal with people, and to say how good or how poor they are is not measurable. In an algorithmic method you cannot deal with these things.

I do believe in top-down and bottom-up techniques. My approach is to have a combination of these two approaches. Then I can be successful and prepare a good cost estimate, provided I have an access to data and if I have experienced estimators. I do not trust any other models or methods beside these two.

Mr. Ovens. How do you know how to fit together the top-down and bottom-up procedures ?

Mr. Branyan. By trial and error. We develop an estimate and then go to the customer. He may say that he wants it for less. We then tell him to get somebody else to do it. You probably do not believe that we do it (Laughter), but it does happen that we turn down jobs. It could be that occasionally we do not understand the problem and we walk away from it, but we do not take jobs that we think we cannot do.

I will give you now our ideas on:

GUIDELINES FOR ESTIMATING SOFTWARE SIZE

1. Understand the system requirements
2. Develop your own design and work breakdown structure
3. Employ as much detail as possible
4. Compare to similar functions on other projects
5. Compare to other similar projects

Here it is important to consider details and top-down and bottom-up designs come into this. We are trying here to take into account everything that Mr. T.C. Jones has mentioned (1). We cost everybody exactly on the job he or she are doing. So we do believe in the 300 items Mr. T.C. Jones has mentioned. We try to cost them all individually. Then we compare and try to do analogy if we have the ability to do this, in order to find where we are.

In our work we break down the structure of a project; all the activities are broken down by organisations that are involved, be this system engineers, or programmers, no matter who it is. We also break it down into phases to determie how long it takes to do a phase, taking into account all the activities and all the people, and what is included in terms of documentation. We have the Engineering Review Board (ERB) who pay special attention to requirements. Nothing changes in the software or in requirements unless this is decided by the ERB. All these activities help us to understand the project and thus to make a good cost estimate.

In order to do this, all the objectives are allocated time to make sure that we have sufficient number of people to do this work. All this is already computerised, since we have been doing this for the last 15 years, and we can deal with this no matter how many people are involved. We take the top-down and bottom-up methods in this work construction and the algorithm which we use most frequently is the Jensen model, but we are also using the RCA model and the EXPERT judgement. We try to compare results so obtained, and if we have inconsistency, we look back to find reasons for it.

Ms. Frewin. Concerning the time allocation, how much time does it take to do it all? For surely, in most cases you have to do this before you make your bid.

Mr. Branyan. Indeed this is the case. On a major project, say of 50 million dollars, this usually takes about three months: to read the job description, to go over all the details and then to cost the project.

Ms. Frewin. What resources are you using in that time ?

Mr. Branyan. In terms of the number of people, on a 50 million dollars project we put for this a team of 20 to 25 people over a three months' period. We have set aside certain funds to be able to do this properly. This is a part of our business. We estimate each year how much money we shall need for this. The actual size of a team naturally depends on the size of job we are trying to attack. All this is done just for the software part of a project.

Dr. McNichols. In this preliminary work surely you are doing more than just cost estimation; you are also working on the technical project proposal, are you not ?

Mr. Branyan. It is as result of this work that we are writing technical proposals. For each task teams write down what they know about it and then they cost that task. We start up with one team leader who breaks the project into packages.

Mr. Wingrove. How do you manage for a project to do a software proposal with cost and all, without intermingling this with the hardware part ?

Mr. Branyan. People with whom we are dealing understand this problem. They usually have some persons called System Integrators, say of an Aerospace Organisation. Their job is to state what in a system hardware is supposed to do, and what software is supposed to do. They write the so called 'Segment Specifications'. Suppose the job is a 2 billion dollar satellite communications system. Then software in it may cost 2 million. Then a ground station would be a segment in that system. This segment has to interface with the lot.

System Integrators are also responsible to write the so called 'Interface Control Documents' (ICD), which tell me exactly how to communicate with the world outside, that is the world outside software. The other thing we have is the 'Mission Description' (MD). This tells me precisely what I am supposed to do.

Mr. Wingrove. What interests me is how do you decide the apportionment of software and hardware before you actually finalise the design.

Mr. Branyan. What software will do and what hardware will do is known before I start to make the cost estimations. If that changes, then the contract will also change. There are sometimes proposals to change things, but once we get a contract award, we freeze the requirements and anything that happens to that system thereafter has to happen by agreement of all the people involved.

Mr. Wingrove. Requirements should tell you what a customer wants and how you are to do it. However, how do you integrate the software team with the hardware team ? It sounds to me that you just have separate teams.

Mr. Branyan. We still use the same process to break a project down. When we deal with a software interface for an antenna, then we talk to the antenna people, and with them we break down the work structure. We know what the antenna people want to do, and they know what interface we are producing.

I have discussed here many things, yet now let me consider the development of cost estimation. It looks like this (see Fig.8), in a somewhat theoretical sense. On the left side is the customer and I try to analyse all these things like complexity and choice of cost model. From that information I develop a package which tells me and him what this is going to cost. Then I do compare all the inputs for reasonabless. If it all matches pretty well, then I am ready to go with my estimate. If it does not, then I go back and look at these documents again and I reiterate. My objective is that the agreement is within 15% when compared on the same basis. In other words, if all the models I have been using give cost results within 15%, then I give the estimate, though a model I am using may only represent 60% of the job., for this may not cover the development of new mathematical algorithms. This may be the Jensen model or the Slim model. If I am over 15%, I start looking for the differences and try to find reasons for them. The differences of 25% to 30%, or more, that cannot be explained, will cause us to go back and re-do some steps in cost allocation.

Mr. Woodman. How do you measure the complexity ?

Mr. Branyan. What we have done, in a historical sense, is to look at many things in connection with this. In the case of many models, several of them do not calibrate this, but if you can get smart enough with a model, you can do it.

SOFTWARE DEVELOPMENT
COST ESTIMATING

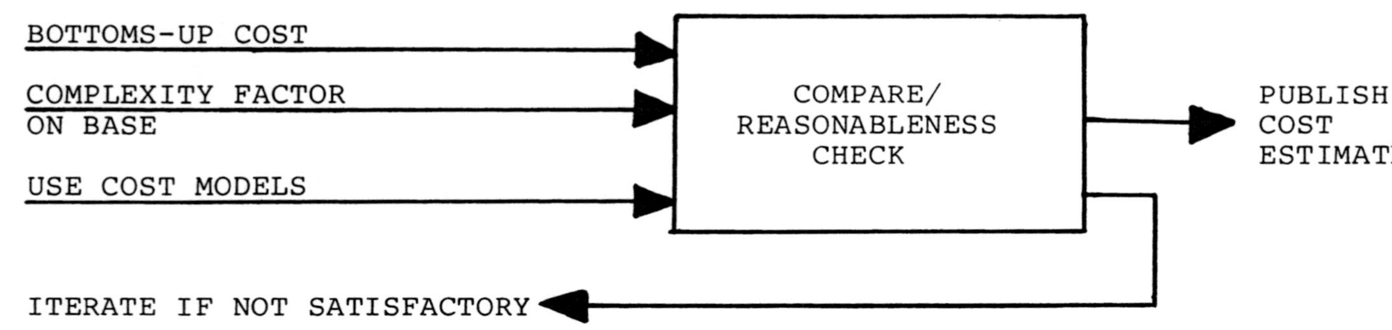

* OBJECTIVE IS AGREEMENT WITHIN 15% WHEN COMPARED ON THE SAME BASIS

* DIFFERENCES OF 25 - 30% OR MORE THAT CANNOT BE EXPLAINED IS CAUSE TO GO BACK AND RE-DO SOME STEPS

Fig. 8.

You can actually keep everything fixed and then look what the complexity comes out to be. I have done this with several models. In terms of experience we just use the fact, that if two projects you are working on are identical, like in telemetry programs, then we say that the complexity ratio between them is one. But if the new project is more difficult, then I try to find an expert judgement, and ask how much more difficult the new job is compared to the previous one. I play games in that situation. No matter what I do and how hard I try, The estimating techniques still allow one to fall into traps, and then I cannot come with a perfect answer. The estimating techniques are imperfect, and anyhow, every project is different - each one is unique in itself and has its own characteristics. The software itself is a very evolving thing, constantly changing.

In the rest of this field there are a lot more of things, like the risk analysis and software metrics, but there is no time to carry on like this and our chairman is already winking at me that I should stop, so I thank you for your attention and your questions.

Dr. McNichols. Professor Leveson has said in her lecture (3) that things in plain English sound trivial, and several people here have asked me whether our panel discussion is trivial or not. I consider that both our discussion and that chaired by Mr. T.C. Jones (4) are not trivial. Now let me introduce our next speaker, Mr. Alvin Ovens.

Mr. Ovens. I am with the Naval Research Laboratory in the U.S.A. and my viewpoint is a little bit different. We often have to evaluate Mr. Branyan's proposals to figure out exactly what is going on. Recently on one project we had 14 respondees and had to spend two-and-half weeks to evaluate these 14 different cost estimates, looking at all the documents and trying to make sense of them. We cannot do it in the top-down or bottom-up fashion, since there is not enough man-power in the Government. So we are forced to rely on parametric models.

We like to think of cost estimation like something resembling shooting ducks in a mist. It is a very dangerous occupation and you might shoot yourself, or be shot by others, doing this. There are several estimates in front of you and you have to pick one. Then you are lucky, even if you have used some heuristics in doing this. I am using this duck analogy, because everybody says to me that there is no such thing as the true cost. As requirements change, and environment changes, costs also change from day-to-day. When we do this job we get a lot of failed shots.

We now have up to 36 cost estimation models, but for a given project we tend to use no more than four of them. Even so, we do not know what is in them. Some people seem to be worried about this, but myself, I do not use anything that I do not know what is in it.

For how can you use a model without knowing what is its main equation? They tell us what their model is based on, but generally that is all that we know about commercial models. We also know that they produce different answers for the same project. Part of this difference is supposed to be due to variations in design philosophy.

Mr. Musa. I am not sure whether you are stating a fact concerning this problem, or whether you are just taking a stand. I know that if I take a stand, I will have problems with any model, particularly if it is not quite understandable.

Mr. Ovens. My answer is yes and no. I have the obvious problem in not understanding the basis of some models. The nice thing is that there are many other people who are using these models, and it helps when you communicate with them. This has now become a separate language. A lot of government estimators use the same models; then they communicate and talk on their own estimations.

Mr. Musa. You have a good point here, so let me modify my statement. I am concerned about a model which nobody has an opportunity to examine. Thus, I do not care how my car works, but hopefully my mechanic does.

Dr. Heimbinger. Can you tell us which model you like to use?

Mr. Ovens. There is now available an Air Force form S169. Once you enter the contract data in the input sheets of that form, it tells you how good a given model is for that particular contract. They seem to know it in the Air Force. Once we had response for a project from 14 contractors. They all filled that form differently, and half of them did it so that it became apparent that they did not understand it. You could hope that there is some consistency in this, but there is none. The only model on which we have a lot of information is the SLIM one.

There are many problems here. One is to do a syntactic analysis of estimates. So here is a challenge to people dealing with Artificial Intelligence (AI). Here is an area: Can you use AI to do a syntactic analysis of software requirements? The requirement document is the thing that is going to drive your cost: it is a thing that government wants, and ultimately everything comes out of the requirement document.

Mr. Jones. The IBM have a standard format for specifications. it is very detailed and rigorous. As long as you use this format correctly, you can get the direct estimate of the project cost. Here the function specifications have eight pages per 1000 lines of code.

Mr. Ovens. So by measuring the thickness of the document, and assuming that there are two sides to each page, you can make your estimate (Laughter).

The Air Force have just released a specification to all the parametric model builders, asking them to submit a proposal to provide their models on an hourly usable basis. This is a true challenge for competition among fast modellers.

Here are some factors that a cost model should have. They should handle the size of a project, and this would be one of the inputs. They should also be involved with engineering change effects and with economic trends; these are just a part of the large table of escalation fctors which you build into a model. Contractors are also allowed to put their own escalation factors.

Organisational efficiency and training of personnel comes under the heading of "Resource Value" and is also one of the inputs to a model. Other inputs to such a model are machine executable instructions and applications of the software (e.g. radar control systems, real-time interactive systems, etc). Then comes the utilisation, i.e. how much of computer memory you need, and what computer speed you are going to utilise. Finally comes the complexity. This tells you whether the project is going to be a multi-site development, whether the type of work is familiar to a contractor, etc. This could be registered as say 0.1 or 0.2 of the standard value of 1.0, though you might also have weights like -0.1!

Mr. Bromell. Is it reasonable for a user of such a model to provide a guess on the number of machine-executable instructions?

Mr. Ovens. This is a real problem. Quite often, given a computer language, some people will tell you that they need 9000 statements, while others might need to have 20,000 of them. In both cases there might be the same number of source instructions, but they use different degrees of expansion. That expansion ratio is again a factor that should be inputed into a model.

Mr. Bromell. There is even the problem to guess the number of source statements.

Mr. Ovens. Yes, this is so. some models use function points, as mentioned by Mr. T.C. Jones. This is also used in the SLIM model.

Dr. McNichols. Unfortunately now we have to finish this interesting discussion, for time for dinner is approaching and our director tells me so. Thank you all for yor contributions, and we shall meet again at the panel organised by Mr. T.C. Jones (4).

REFERENCES

(1) CAPERS JONES: Steps towards establishing normal rules for software cost, schedule and productivity estimating (in this volume).

(2) BILL CURTIS: Psychological research on software development (in this volume).
(3) NANCY LEVESON: Software hazards analysis techniques (in this volume).
(4) Panel discussion on: SOFTWARE COST ESTIMATING, chaired and organised by Mr. T.C. Jones (in this volume).

PANEL DISCUSSION

ON

SOFTWARE COST ESTIMATING

Friday, 9th of August, 1985 at 16.00 hours.

Chairman and Organiser: Mr. T.C. Jones, SPR Inc., U.S.A.

Panel Members:

Dr. B. Curtis, MCC, U.S.A.
Mr. A.B. Ovens, Naval Research Laboratory, U.S.A.
Mr. J. Musa, AT & T Bell Laboratories, U.S.A.
Dr. G.R. McNichols, MC&R Inc., U.S.A.
Dr. B. Boehm, TRW, U.S.A.

Contributors:

Major A.L. Lake, Royal Artillery, U.K.
Mr. N. Harris, British Aerospace, U.K.
Ms. G. Frewin, STL Ltd., U.K.
Mr. P. Mellor, City Univ., U.K.
Mr. A.A. Wingrove, RAE, Farnborough, U.K.
Prof. B. Littlewood, City Univ., U.K.
Prof. G. Fischer, Univ. of Colorado, U.S.A.
Mr. M. Dyer, IBM, U.S.A.
Ms. J. Clapp, The MITRE Corp., U.S.A.
Dr. B. Bedrosian, The Rand Corp., U.S.A.

Mr. Jones. We shall continue here considering the status of cost estimation, following the panel discussion chaired by Dr. McNichols. This panel is on methods of cost estimation and on their theory. We shall continue with residue issues of things which were not finished during that panel. In this panel we have Mr. Musa and Dr. Curtis, who will first give us short remarks on topics which they feel were significant during this Institute, particularly in software reliability fields, and in software engineering life cycle considerations. So we begin with Mr. Musa.

Mr. Musa. I have few random remarks. By random, I do not

NATO ASI Series, Vol. F22
Software System Design Methods. Edited by J.K. Skwirzynski

necessarily mean uniform! There are points that tie up loose ends, and some observations on the whole Institute.

One of them relates to technology transfer. We had exchanges here between people working in different fields. It is possible that the variety of these topics have confused some people at some times. I do hope that those of you who might be confused will forgive us for this, recognising the creative values of conflict and diversity. The aim here was to use technology transfer between different fields to enhance technology creation.

I would like to say something on the issue of software reliability models, but this might touch other areas as well. Those of you who are here to learn something have probably witnessed a lot of critique, many arguments, and many disputes between various parties. You might come out with idea that all we ever do is to disagree, and that there is nothing we agree on. I would like to correct this impression, because I think that in this field there is a large proportion, perhaps even majority, of things that we agree on. Disagreements have been blown out of proportion. I ask that you keep this in mind.

Another general comment is that disagreements and critiques are a very healthy thing. Although it is not very comfortable sometimes at the receiving end of a critique, it does take a certain amount of courage on the part of a 'critquer' to get up and say something. Critques should be properly appreciated, as they do help to sharpen one's thinking. Contrariwise, I think that you should be a little suspicious of areas in which there is no critique or differences of opinion. I consider that it is absolutely necessary to have then to bring out the facts. If you hear absolutely smooth and unchallenged presentations, I would be very suspicious.

It is my opinion that selecting software reliability models is like selecting a restaurant on your holiday in a strange place. The guides might disagree, but this does not stop you from eating. Thus I hope that disagreements will not discourage you from using these models. They <u>are</u> useful.

There is one comment that I have picked up from someone in the audience on software reliability models. This participant said that since he does not understand them, he is not going to use them. I also heard another comment concerning some cost estimation models, where this person did not want to understand them, and therefore he claimed that he had no problems with the secrecy of these models (Laughter). I find this just a little bit "closed". We can accept a legitimate comment and critcism that perhaps not all the lecturers have clarified everything properly. But you are not going to understand everything completely the first time you hear it. In most cases it will be necessary to read the papers, and I hope that you will approach them with an open mind.

One final comment, regarding again software reliability measurement. At the present time most of the measurements are based on data that are developer-oriented. A great deal of these data, perhaps the majority, relate to faults, and faults are the sort of things that developers look for. I do not mean to criticise this approach, but I think that we need to go beyond that, because what is really important is the user-oriented viewpoint. Therefore we need user-oriented measurements such as those related to "failures".

There was a discussion during the panel chaired by Dr. McNichols on the impact and severity of failures. I certainly agree that this is a very important concern. This concludes my random comments.

Dr. Curtis. My offer still goes for any of you who make it to Austin, Texas. I will take you to a Mexican restaurant for the hottest chili in the western hemisphere and you can experience the restaurant selection phenomena Mr. Musa just described. In honour to Dr. Marilyn Musa, a clinical psychologist who is present here, I want to make a few remarks on the clinical prediction of software costs.

I ran an experiment last night to develop a predictive model of software costs. I took the following measures prior to knowing the costs. Thus, in keeping with the methodology of a rigorous predictive study, I was blind to the criteria I wanted to predict. I got the project managers from each of 45 projects and collected the following data from them:

- the educational level of manager's wife,
- the number of days from the 1st January to the manager's birthday,
- the number of kids in the manager's family,
- the manager's performance scores in each of the 5 subsets of the Watson/Glaser Test of Critical Reasoning,
- their scores on each of the 10 factors of the Minnesota Multiphasic Personality Inventory,
- their scores on the 3 subsets of the Embedded Figures Test,
- their scores on each of the 10 traits measured by the Guilford/Zimmerman Personality Inventory,
- their scores on the 11 tasks of the Wechsler Adult Intelligence Scale,
- their speed in the hudred meter dash,
- the number of credit cards they own, and
- the age at which they first tasted beer.

This gives me 45 variables with which to predict software costs. Now there is a strong way and a weak way in which I am able to predict software costs from these measures. The weak model will not predict the costs perfectly, but the strong one will. The weak model works as follows.

The most important impact on productivity, and thus ultimately on cost, lies, as I argued in my lecture at this Institute, in the individual differences among the people assigned to the project. Managers, because of their broad influence on projects, will be the individuals whose talents and decisions will have the greatest impact on project outcomes and costs. The weak model of predicting software costs says that with all this information about the manager, I will be able to describe quite accurately what will one of the most important factors determining costs. Thus, I will be able to develop a good predictive model based on knowledge about the source of cost decisions. But the weak model acknowledges that we can never describe people with complete accuracy and that there are many important influences on project performance and costs other than the manager. Therefore, we do not expect prediction to be perfect.

The strong model of predicting software costs says that I can now develop a model for use in predicting software costs without error. It really does not matter what the nature of my predictive variables is so long as they are not linear combinations of each other. I will always be able to develop multiple regression equations that have a perfect correlation with the criterion, so long as I have as many predictors as criterion data points. Thus, I had perfect prediction in my little study last night. It could not have happened otherwise, it was a matter of mathematics and matrix algebra.

So the question is this: when we talk of modelling, to what extent are we taking care of statistical and methodological issues that determine the rigor with which we are offering our models of various phenomena? I do not want to imply that these problems are a trademark of software cost research. I see them more pronounced in research on software complexity. The level of methodology in that field is horrible. I do not want to blame individual researchers themselves, I would rather blame their training. They simply have not been trained in the statistical, analytic, and methodological techniques for collecting exploratory or experimental data.

There are several important methodological issues in using any estimating model. If I have 45 predictors and 45 projects, I will be able to get a perfect multiple correlation between my predictors and the actual costs as a matter of statistics. The important question is whether there is a small subset of predictors that will account for most of the variance in project costs. For instance, can I account for 90% of the variation in costs with only 5 predictors? If I could, these five would provide most of the power in my prediction, and the predictive equation developed from this reduced set will be more likely to remain stable when validated on other data sets. If I am able to find a reduced set of predictor veriables, then I must ask questions about multiple-collinearity, homogeneity of variance, and non-normality of underlying distributions. If I do not investigate these isssues, then the weights used in my predictive equation might not remain stable over different sets of data.

I may find in data from another programming environment that the processes which drive costs are completely different from the cost drivers in my original set of projects. If so, then I should not expect my original set of predictive variables to predict as well against a new set of projects. Even if the overall level of prediction stays the same, then the weights for the various predictors might not remain stable. The possibility of experiencing instability accross different sets of projects argues that I should calibrate any predictive cost equation to the process occuring in my programming environment.

This problem brings me to the issue of clinical prediction, which is much like how doctors and clinical psychologists work. They have a set of measures they collect for diagnosing problems and predicting future health. They do not always understand the processes that undelie these measures, but they use these measures so many times (often 500 to 1000 before they truly master their use) that they understand how these measures are related with various problems and outcomes. Through lengthy experience, they understand important cues in the data they collect that yield a wealth of information about the patient's current and future condition. Through experience they have developed a set of expectations (naive correlations) about how their measures relate to problems and symptoms, and they are adroit in ientifying the cues in the data that trigger one or more of these expectations.

Thus, predictive models require calibration beyond purely statistical and methodological issues. This calibration involves identifying, in a clinical sense, which indicators are capturing the processes that drive drive costs in a given programming environment. One valuable source of information available to other professionals who must diagnose or predict future behaviour is a large set of data for comparing the outcomes of predictions. Most software managers have data from 5 or 10 projects at their location, but they do not have what other areas of business have: case studies. It is difficult to trace the history of decisions accross a software project, but it is these decisions that will ultimately drive performance and costs. The most popular book in computer science, The Mythical Man-Month by Fred Brooks, is just that, an extended case study from which much of our popular wisdom about software projects is derived.

My argument is that having a predictive model is not enough. We have to learn how to use models clinically. This means learning how to calibrate them and which cues to attend to in which circumstances. Also, we need to infuse software engineering research with much stronger statistical and methodological techniques. These techniques need to be trained in universities, but there is little currently offered to computer scientists in these areas. Thank you.

Major Lake. Fig. 1 shows a model which we have developed, but I don't know if we have reinvented the wheel. What I like to do is to find out how valid you think this model is for a system software life-cycle. We have the normal

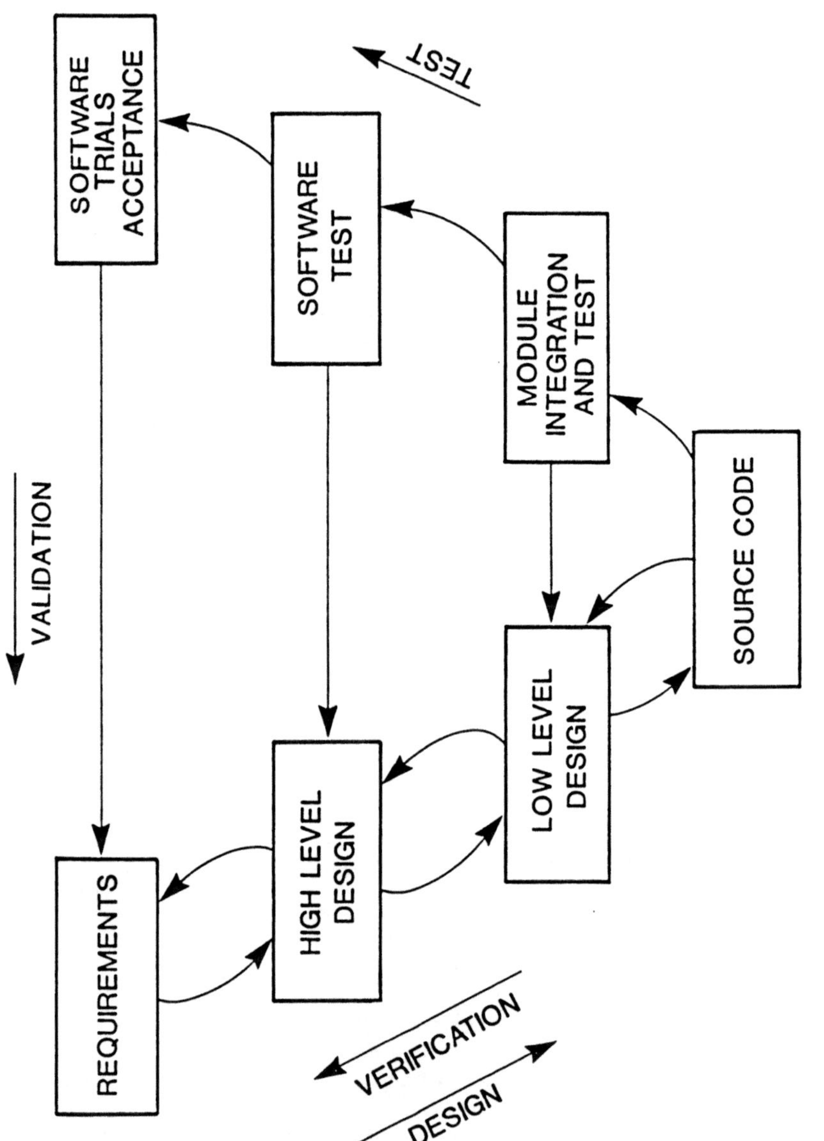

Fig. 1 SOFTWARE LIFE CYCLE

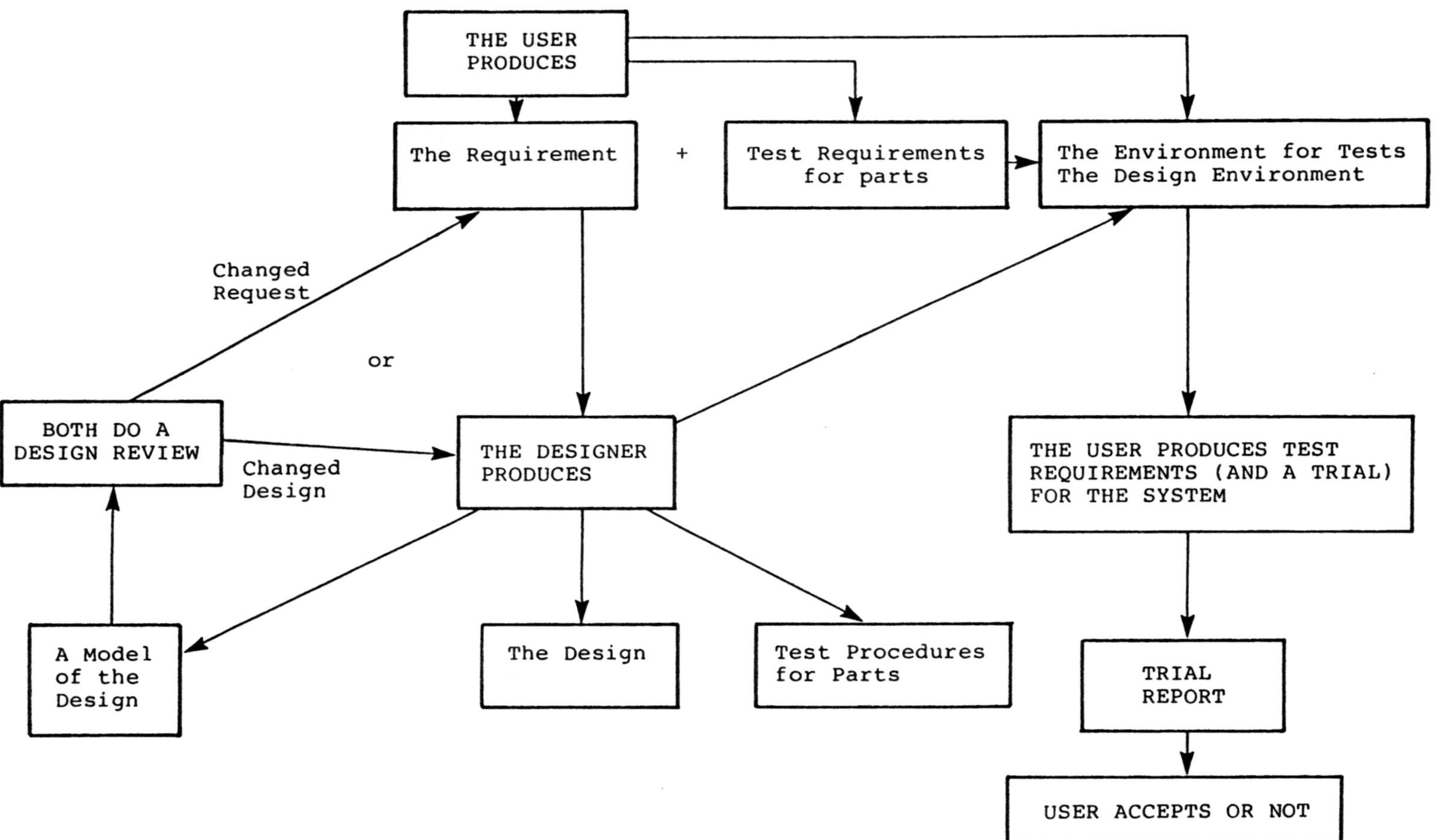

Fig. 2. The Recurrent Cycle in Development

waterfall concept with the turning point at the source code stage. We come from the REQUIREMENTS via HIGH and LOW LEVEL DESIGN to SOURCE CODE and then back up through TEST AND INTEGRATION. This model allows me to rationalise the use of words like USER, REQUIREMENTS and SPECIFICATIONS. People do not make it clear how they are using the words REQUIREMENTS and USER. One man's design specification becomes another man's requirement specification, e.g. the system design becomes the software requirement.

Fig. 2 shows another model related to Fig. 1. The major purpose is to show that the cost of faults in high level design is very high, and how to avoid this cost. All levels of design have the same functions which are shown in Fig. 2, i.e. the one design model is repeated at each level of design decomposition from system design to source code design. The 'User' here does not therefore mean the 'End User' except in the case of the highest level of system design. If there are four levels of design, there are four 'Users', each being a designer of the level above. Looking at the model in detail, design must produce not only an idea but also a model. The design model is important because it is a tool for design review. This is the driving force for prototyping and simulation, because one can only do the design review if one has good visibility of the design. Of course, the prototype has to be appropriate to the level in which it is used.

At all stages of the design review there are three possible outcomes:

first, the design is correct;

second, the design is wrong but can be corrected without affecting the requirements;

third, the design is wrong and requirements have to be changed.

Last, the model shows that the tests cannot be designed until the next level of design has been completed.

<u>Mr. Harris</u>. You have identified that even design has elements of recursive structuring, and in this you make a good point. A considerable number of models, or so called models, are developed with scant regard to what is actually being done. In this they provide no insight and hence provide a poor basis for future planning. Who actually produces software along the lines of the Waterfall model?

I believe the structure you have just described does provide insight. I therefore hope you pursue this, perhaps even to the extent of developing a system model that can be used in actual system design.

<u>Major Lake</u>. We have people (i.e. human activities), products, and documents. I have found that it is a good thing to track down the documentation by the method in Fig. 2. There is a tremendous amount of paper that comes out from a computer project, and here is a nice way of tracking it down.

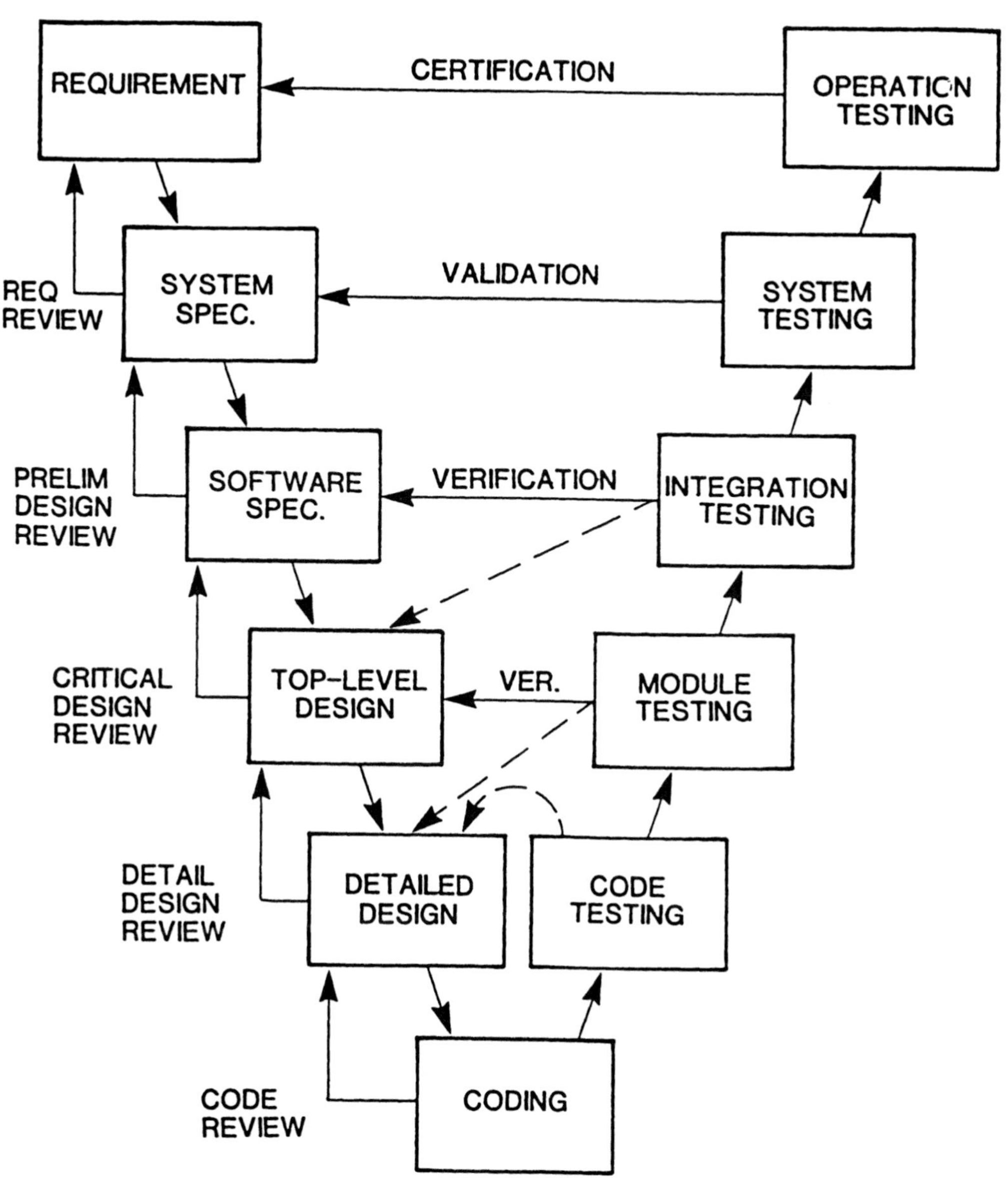

Fig 3: SOFTWARE DEVELOPMENT

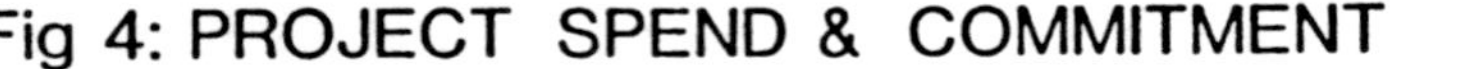

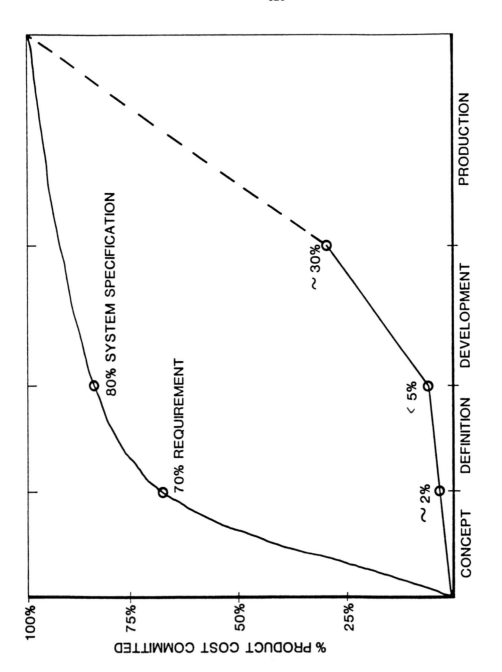

Fig 4: PROJECT SPEND & COMMITMENT

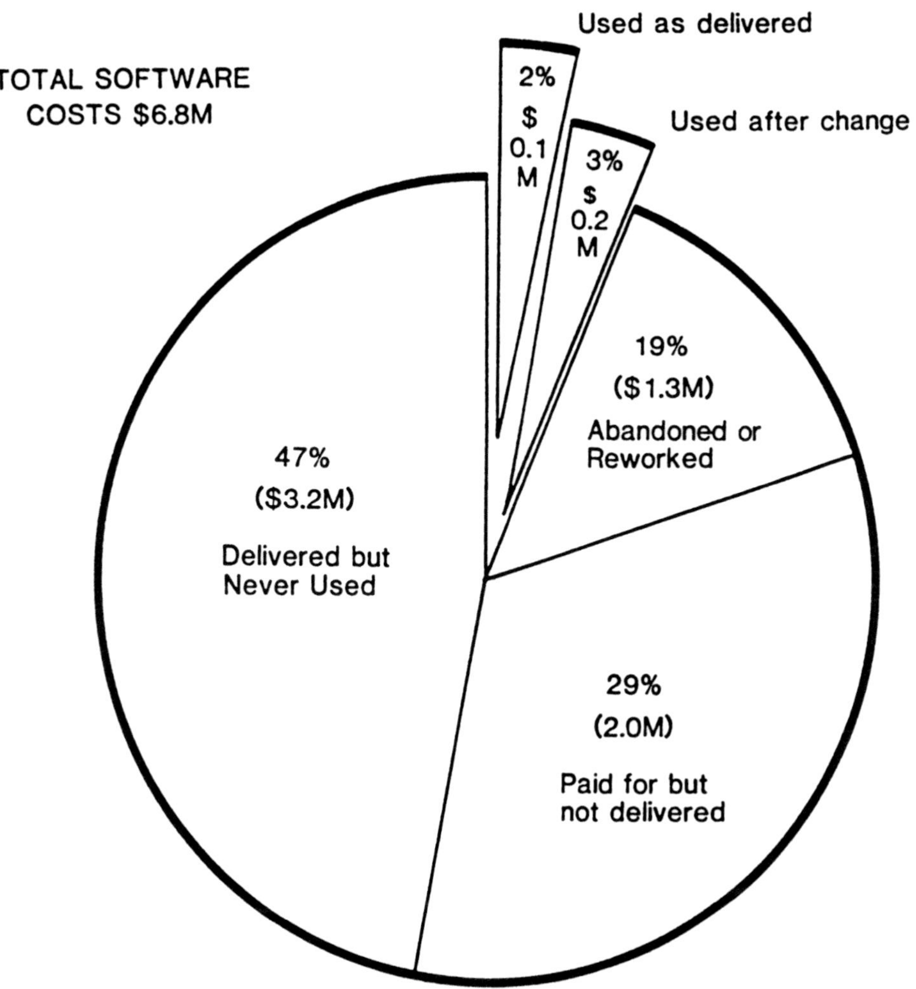

Fig 5: NINE US FEDERAL PROJECTS

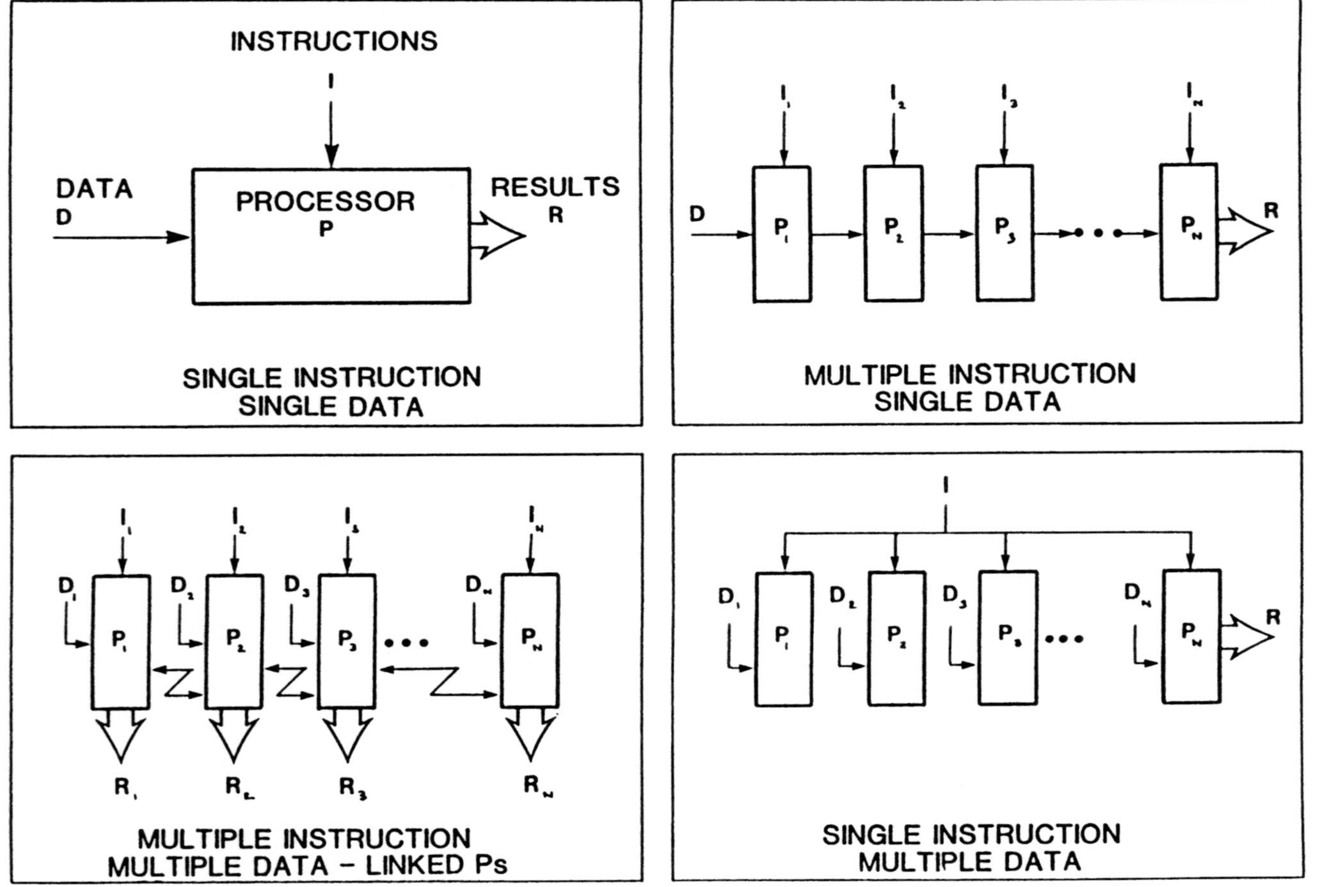

Fig 6: SYSTEM ARCHITECTURES

Ms. Frewin. We are working in a multi-company and in multi-country projects. So we have to draw data diagrams and communication diagrams in order to keep our ideas and our work in line with one another. We use diagrams similar to those you have been showing us, in order to coordinate our activities and to keep up with changes.

Major Lake. I have dealt with many firms, and yet I have never seen anything in their specifications structures in the orderly way I have proposed here. What models do you have to construct software systems specifications?

Ms. Frewin. We have diagrams similar to yours and they describe the way we model designs.

Mr. Wingrove. Can we first consider the problem of management? Management is about reaching CLEAR OBJECTIVES with AVAILABLE RESOURCES in a SET TIME. This presumes that we have an availability to PLAN, MEASURE and CONTROL, the three parameters of PERFORMANCE, SCHEDULE and COST. I am concerned about these abilities (to plan, measure and control) when we talk about models.

I use software development life-cycle (Fig.3) not unlike Major Lake's Figure 1, but with a bit more detail of the reviews and checks used as the system is developed. But models like these still do not give a project manager guidance on how to plan specific items. For instance, how does one approportion hardware and software, and when? During early design or later, as the design evolves? Fig.4 illustrates the significance of this point - where it can be seen that early low level spending commitments of a substantial proportion of the total project budget, which means that during development funds are limited for major design changes.

Another question is how to cost software. Should the cost relate to the number of lines of code written, or the number of lines used? Fig.5 shows an analysis of software costs from nine US Federal projects reported by the US GAO in 1979. If only 3% (or 5%) was actually used (or needed?) it would seem to be difficult for a model, even with 300 parameters, to predict the cost. While these USA data, I have a feeling that UK data (which we do not have!) might reveal a similar story.

Finally, a question for reliability modellers. Fig.6 shows a number of common computer architectures. Fig.6A is the simplest configuration which is commonly modelled - data into a processor, acted on by instructions with results coming out. But how are you going to model the reliability of a distributed system such as in Fig.6C, with multiple streams of data, instructions and results, all interacting through linked processors? Our problem is that this has become a very common system configuration today, yet we have no reliability or cost models which cover it.

Mr. Jones. There is now work going on on a reliability model for a number of parallel processing environments. there is also some work going on this for cost modelling.

Perhaps now we should go to the next topic of this

Mr. Harris. Maybe I will be permitted to tell you an old "Music Hall" joke. A woman goes to her doctor and such conversation ensues:

WOMAN: My husband thinks he is a hen.
DOCTOR: How long has he thought that he is a hen?
WOMAN: About ten years.
DOCTOR: Then why did you not bring him to me sooner ?
WOMAN: Because I need the eggs.
DOCTOR: So do I.

The relationship between management and modellers is analogous. Just change the subject and roles and the joke would be:

MANAGER: One of my personnel thinks he is a modeller.
MANAGEMENT CONSULTANT: How long has thought like this?
MANAGER: About ten years.
MANAGEMENT CONSULTANT: Why did you not tell me sooner?
MANAGER: I needed the models.
MANAGEMENT CONSULTANT: So do I.

A management needs modellers, and modellers should provide a service to management, but scepticism exists between them. I hope I have illustrated that the relationship betweeen them is often obscure.

Mr. Jones. This is a very good point. I have been a modeller for a very long time and I find that it has been for me much more important to be believable, than to be accurate.

Dr. Boehm. I would like to clarify the diagram shown to us by Mr. Wingrove in his Fig. 5. This is a very misleading set of data; it has a lot of observational bias in it. If you notice the total number of dollars in this project is 6.8 million., but the actual number of dollars spent by the US Government in that year was nearer 6 to 10 billion. Therefore this is not a full sample, nor is it a representative sample. You are looking at a project that was introuble; yet they did a rather straighforward reporting, and then some statistician at the end of it produced this pie chart, which indeed looks very troublesome. This is not really a characterisation of Goverment acquisition at large. It is certainly not true that 97% of what the Government buys is not used.

Dr. Littlewood. What percentage you think this is then ?

Dr. Boehm. I think it is about 10% to 20%.

Dr. McNichols. We should look at the definition of what we mean by 'not used'. Was it not used for its initial purpose ? This could give us an even higher percentage. As things change and circumstances change, the government beaurocracy is very slow. By the time you get some software developed that the government has requested, you may find that you have to operate on the next generation computer system. This is how slow is the government.

Professor Fischer. When you read in the newspapers that the U.S. government pays 700 dollars for a toilet set - why should we assume that similar things do not happen in the software business?

Dr. McNichols. There are some simple cost estimating 'rules of thumb' which are used for allocating overhead costs. The press does not seem to understand these, nor does the public. It makes a very good headline to say that we have paid 600 dollars for a toilet seat which we envision as a little roud thing, flat at the top. There was however a case of a 'toilet chair', which had a lot of formal specifications to hang things on it, and indeed it did cost more with overheads.

Mr. Ovens. It is easy to criticise governments, for most of them are inept, otherwise they would not change from time to time. I have a consultant friend who did a similar study in private industry; in this case it was a large oil company. He was doing a small study on the use of productivity tools for software, and he discovered that while in such a large company there are about 300 programmers, each one of them required about 400 productivity tools, whereas the actual number in daily use was about 11. The company has obviously a tendency to buy many more things than in fact they really ever use. The same kind of study was carried on in banks, who are famous in the U.S.A. for buying anything that you can stop and buy yourself, whether they needed them or not. So this is not just governments that spend money foolishly. It is large, and sometimes even small companies, who do the same thing. I suspect that the same thing would be found in the U.K. and in other European countries.

There is a large amount of software delivered to the U.S. Department of Defence that we frankly hope will never be used.

Dr. Curtis. You are looking at software pieces; there are many functions there. If you look at a 'frequency of use' chart, it will look like a power curve. There are many functions and someone will want to use each of them at some time. However, some functions will be used quite often and other rarely. The issue with that chart is not cost modelling; it is the matter of requirements' analysis. Given a set of requirements, you identify a system to develop; then the cost model is used to tell you how much developing is going to cost. This is not the same issue as whether you are going to use it or not.

Mr. Jones. These indeed are separate issues. Modelling of the user community, i.e. what are they actually using, once they have acquired the product, is a much sparser field than modelling the cost of development. The only study I have seen myself was the study of large IBM customers, to which I have alluded in my lecture (5). This indicated that about 80% of their entire machine capacity was spent running packets they have acquired from vendors; only 20% was spent on programs which they themselves have developed. There was another study of the same thing in a production library with about 2000 programs in it. This indicated that the average life expectancy of programs, before they disappear, and are never seen again, was only 16 months.

There is a small number of 'bread and butter' systems, like payroll systems, benefit systems, investors' management systems, that may last for ever. But the surprising thing in this inventory was that for more than 2000 programs in a large corporation the life expectancy, before they disappear completely, is only 16 months. What this means is that there is a lot of valuable software being written, that may live for a while, and then it will go away and you may never see it again.

That is not a cost developemnt problem, but it is a very interesting area which we have not yet fully explored in the software engineering domain: what are the patterns and the characteristics of users of our products once they have been installed; how long do they last; when do they deacy and are removed from service ? This is a very interesting topic that we have not covered at this Institute, but one day in future we may get down to it.

Now we shall turn the panel to some perhaps intriguing business, where we can get an exercise in direct democracy. Here is a list of 28 different items that can be measured and estimated. What we want here are your views on the ease of collecting data about these items, the accuracy of such data once they have been collected, and then the importance of these data to the general technique of cost estimating. Here are the items:

SIZE IN LINES OF CODE
SIZE IN FUNCTION POINTS

COMPLEXITY OF THE PROBLEM
COMPLEXITY OF CODE
COMPLEXITY OF DATA

SCHEDULES OF ACTIVITY
EFFORT BY ACTIVITY
COSTS BY ACTIVITY
UNPAID OVERTIME
STAFF SIZE BY ACTIVITY
STAFF JOB CATHEGORIES

DOCUMENT TYPES
DOCUMENT SIZES
DOCUMENT COSTS

DEFECT ORIGINS
DEFECT QUANTITIES
DEFECT REMOVAL EFFICIENCY
DEFECT REMOVAL COSTS
USER REPORTED DEFECTS
RELIABILITY
STABILIZATION PERIOD

TOOLS USED
METHODOLOGIES USED
PHYSICAL ENVIRONMENT

HIRINGS
ATTRITION
TRAINING

To get you a litle preview on what kinds of things these items are, I have arranged them in sets. The first two items are on the size of a product in terms of lines of code, and the size of a product in terms of function points.

I would like the pannelists to discuss the ease, accuracy and importance of these items. Then we will have an exercise to see what all of you think about it.

It is my hope that the audience will vote on the scale: easy, medium to hard; then on your feeling that the collecting of this information is a true requirement, you should vote on the scale: good, medium or bad, considering the accuracy of these data coming out in your environment; then, regarding the importance of this item in your experience, you should vote on the scale: high, medium and low.

Mr. Dyer. Do you have an actual scale of the size of a project in terms of function points ?

Mr. Jones. I have not defined this, but this is a special way of measuring software developed by the IBM Corporation and put into public domain. It is a measure of the inputs, outputs, interfaces, enquiries and data files that the program uses, rather than in terms of lines of code. It produces a dimensionless number which, like the Dow Jones stock number, is a unit of relative value, but it is totally independent from the number of lines in the source code. It is used in the U.S.A. as a unit of measure by probably hundred largest corporations, and a number of multi client productivity studies have been published using that unit, instead of the other measure of size. This is because it does not conceal or penalise the productivity, as the line of code metrics sometimes do.

The first issue on which I want to get comments from the panel, and then may be also from the audience, is: 'What are your perceptions on the ease of collecting data on size in terms of lines of code, on the accuracy of this data when it is collected, and on the importance of even collecting that parameter in the first place'.

Mr. Musa. Importance with regard to what and whom?

Mr. Jones. Well, what definition of importance would you like to adopt for this exercise ?

Mr. Musa. I would suggest that the importance should refer to you and to your idea for using this metric.

Mr. Jones. Here we are an estimating panel, and the sense of what I am trying to get at is that in order to estimate anything, you need to have certain realistic information from real projects. Concerning the importance, what I mean is that having collected this particular kind of information, do you reagard this as an important potential vehicle for improving estimates and for using this to understand software engineering and estimating aspects. Looking to the future, it is important if it is considered as a part of estimating vehicle.

Mr. Musa. Based on your definition, size could certainly be an important thing, and you would want its accuracy to be high.

Mr. Jones. My experience with accuracy is that it is often very low. I would like it to be high, but it hardly ever is. So I would like to have your opinion on the pragmatics: Do you in your day to day operations regard the accuracy of data, that you actually see, as high, medium or low ?

Mr. Musa. If we have these three categories, I would say that the importance of accuracy is medium, because otherwise I could not differentiate this from the number of other things that I see clearly as being low. As far as the ease of collection is concerned, I would also say medium.

Mr. Ovens. Concerning first our environment, we actually have two of them. One of then is looking at the rest of the world, and trying to figure out what goes on; the second is looking at our own internal things and come out with projects. In the first case, this is the most important parameter; its accuracy is medium and its ease of collection is generally easy for us in the first of our environments, for we give out contracts and ask companies to provide us with this information; so we have a real easy time, for we do not have to do anything. In the second environment, when we have to come out ourselves with the size of a software project, it is considerably more difficult to collect data.

The accuracy however goes up high in that situation, and its importance stays the same, very high.

Dr. McNichols. I begin by hiring design experiment experts to help us to construct these things, and to provide us with data in a dictionnary fashion, that is to put together definitions of these terms. Collecting data is always hard; we have to pay for this; it is a cost driver (Laughter). Accuracy is always fair. There is no such thing as good data; if you say that you know the size and your accuracy is good, someone will give you a counter example. So we never admit that anything is good. The question of importance in understanding software development I cannot answer, except relative to other parameters, unless I say it is medium. It depends on what else you have. If you have nothing else but size, then that is going to be the most important item. It is clearly highly correlated with most other cost drivers that you can think of.

Dr. Curtis.Size measures such as lines of code and function points are not independent. They are both driven by the volume and largeness of a project. In fact, Albrecht has published a study in 1983, where he found that the correlation between these two is about 0.9. In essence, they are giving you the same thing, i.e. volume. Volume is also going to drive most of the factors listed by Mr. Jones, no matter how you define them. Lines of code and function points in COBOL, when used in real time systems, can be counted in different ways. You can get them, but no data is accurate until you verify it.

When Mr. Jones and I worked at the ITT, we collected a lot of data from all over the world on productivity and quality. We then called the people back and challenged the accuracy of at least 50% of data they sent us on defects, costs and other things. And typically, 30% of data submitted to us had to be changed.

In fact, there was one particularly interesting case we received from one of our international associates. In developing 22,000 lines of APL they reported an incredible productivity rate. We called them back and said that this thing seems strange, because we can simulate all known functions in the universe with only 15,000 lines of APL. Yet they insisted that they wrote 22,000 lines of APL. On the day we published our report which went to the Chief Executive of ITT, they called us back and said that their number was in fact a token count! They had actually written only 4000 lines of APL. So the counting is only as accurate as you verify it, and verifying is a very time consuming process. You can get lines of code from many compilers, but still it matters how you define them.

Most variables dicussed here will be driven by volume. Lines of code is going to be the easiest thing to get. If you enter several of these size metrics into a factor analysis, they are going to define that factor very well.

Therefore this measure is important because it frequently accounts for 80% of the variance in your other cost drivers. Therefore, it is usually the most important cost driver and the most important to collect.

Dr. Boehm. It is our experience that we can estimate function points, but in early requirements phase we were lucky if we could estimate these with a factor of four, on either side of the nominal size of lines of code. After you finish your program, it is relatively easy to estimate the number of lines of code. However, there have been situations when we had seven people building the Cocomo cost model (7), and in this model we are required to define precisely this number; these people were supposed to build a user friendly interface for a single user file system. Of these seven projects, one of them took 1400 instructions, and another had 4500 of them. So there was a range of factors of three among seven people who were building exactly the same product. This was because at that initial point you could not define exact features of the project. The ease and accuracy of estimating the number of lines of code depends where you are. you can always add an additional line. This also depends on the vendor and things like that. In terms of importance, the lines of code in our environment are extremely high in terms of importance. This factor is what everybody relates to; if you ask anybody to estimate some size parameter, he will think of lines of code, and then he may relate the functionality in terms of lines of code, rather than relating it to something else.

Mr. Jones. Do any of you, and how many of you are using function points as a factor in size estimation.

Ms. Frewin. In our projects we are looking at several measures of size, including function points.

Mr. Dyer. Before we begin to count function points, we allways first count the number of lines of code.

Dr. Curtis. If you look at the commercial market, then you will find that banks and insurance companies are devoted to function points; they use them widely, particularly in commercial COBOL data processing.

Mr. Mellor I was interested in what Dr. Boehm was saying on the variations of the three code estimates. I also have an example of a project in which there were different parts, for each of which were responsible for separate development teams. Each of these was asked to estimate the size of their own contribution to the total project. Their estimates varied by a factor of three from what was eventually written.

Dr. Boehm. The variance of estimation I was talking about

referred to the number of lines of code. The seven project teams used all the Cocomo estimate model. One of them took 1400 instructions, another team took 2400, and still another 4500, yet every team finished their job in ten weeks.

Mr. Jones. There is still a problem of data definitions in an executable protion of an estimate. These data may have comments, and also physical lines may have delimiters on the same line. You can include semicolons and temporary delimiters if you like, so the actual number of lines may never get to a user. You can also include codes for test cases, as is often done, parts of BASIC code, and parameter lines.

The range of apparent size will then vary by factor up to fifteen. One of the basic issues that we have in industry is that there are no standard definitions used by any single corporation, so we can obtain various sizes of lines of code.

Professor Fischer. If I take this inference to be valid for any program, then how does one determine the quality of a code ? Would it not be better to take part of a code and then to count the portions it is made of; this then could be considered as a measure of the quality of code, when it is misleading to count the number of lines.

Dr. Boehm. If, for the same program, you count the lines, and I do, we can still present quite different counts by several magnitude factors; this particularly depends on the nature of our count; is it done for a high level language or for executable instructions ? Most people are aware of this when they do a count.

Mr. Jones. In my work I read a lot of publications on software productivity, and I have to say that in the last hundred articles that I have read, probably half of the authors have not defined in any serious way what their definition of the lines of code was, although they expressed the productivity in that unit. Whenever I see an article of paper which states productivity without defining the meaning of lines of code, I give a low mark to the potential accuracy of this estimate.

This is because I do not know if the author is dealing with the lines of code the same way as I do.

How many of you in the audience have sensed the same problem, that is the lack of general understanding of what is a line of code in your company or enterprise ?

I see that there is a significant number of raised hands.

Mr. Bromell. Dr. Boehm's example of seven projects indicates how useless is the measure in terms of lines of code. Assuming that all the teams implemented the same function, you cannot say that the team which produced 4500 lines is less productive than the one which produced 2400 lines of code, even though they did this in the same time. They took the same amount of time to produce the same function, so were they not all equally productive ?

Dr. Boehm. They took the same amount of calendar time, but we do not know how long they have actually worked on it.

Dr. Curtis. In fact, we know little about their productivity, for we have no data on how amny man hours of personnel it took them to create this thing. It is difficult to estimate early in life cycle what you are going to create in terms of lines of code. Thus, to estimate the cost at that stage is a very difficult problem. That is what function points are meant to solve in COBOL environments, namely what can be done and how long will it take. I am not aware of too many good cost estimattes available right now for real time or distributed systems. That is the real problem.

Mr. Jones. There was an experiment of Jerry Weinberg with six project teams, each asked to optimise a particular parameter, such as execution time. For producing the same function they were given different directives what to optimise, and the number of statements they produced varied greatly. One of the teams was asked to optimise function points. The interesting thing about function points is that their number should presumably be the same. Yet even here there was a factor of 2.5 between the lowest and highest man hours. so function points seem not to be a good correlator in terms of man hours. Hoever, assuming the same inputs, outputs, enquiries, data files and interfaces, the number of function points ought to be the same, and randomness will only appear in the number of lines of code. In a study of high languages there was a great deal of variation in COBOL sizes per function point, partly because of ambiguity in specifications. When some teams were rigorous in their specifications they varied only in 10% on the average of 105 lines per function point, and for 61 lines in PL1 per function point the variation was also only 10%.

Dr. Curtis. It is important in any study that one should give a person or a team a clearly stated objective, for they will not optimise all factors. Here we had six teams and six separate objectives. There were many important factors in these data other than those measured. The teams were not assigned randomly to objectives, so this study makes a point, but it should not be overinterpreted.

Dr. McNichols. A point well taken, but in some studies we have made we wanted to be sure that when we had experts versus novice programmers, we wanted to minimise the number of lines of code; yet the experts rather tried to minimise the execution time. So this was a problem with an intrinsic objective function. What is it ? It cannot be measured.

When you get senior people and experts, they have a lot of funny things running around their heads, things that they want to do. I know two of them, working for me. When they come up with a mathematical algorithm, that no one else will understand, they will be ready to do it, even if it takes them an inordinately long time, because they feel good about it. It usually results in a completely unstructured code that nobody else would understand.

Mr. Jones. Let us now try this direct democracy I have mentioned earlier. My question to the audience is: How do you rate collecting data on lines of code, in terms of easy, medium and hard ?

The answer is: EASY 8
MEDIUM 16
HARD 7

Mr. Harris. Could you also count the abstentions ?

Mr. Jones. Those who have abstained have disenfranchised themselves.

Now the next question to the audience:

How about the accuracy of data, once it is collected, on the scale good, fair and bad.

The answer is: GOOD 6
FAIR 4
BAD 8

Here it seems that the abstainers outnumber the 'bad' voters by a substantial number.

Now the final question: How about the importance of this metric, when used in general for estimating cost and for understanding software, on the scale high, medium and low.

The answer is: HIGH 6
MEDIUM 14
LOW 8

Therefore, according to my records, the size of lines of code was considered as medium in terms of ease of gathering such data, it was bad in terms of accuracy, and medium in terms of importance.

The next set of parameters deals with complexity, and there are three complexity issues that I thought would be significant: complexity of a problem itself, complexity of a code, and complexity of data. Complexity is of course an ambigous term on its own right and I do not really have a proper definition of it, but let me start with the panel memebers and I invite Mr. Musa to get his views on attempts to measure the complexity of a problem which will eventually be programmed.

Mr. Musa. As far as the problem is concerned, I think that the importance of it is medium, and ease and accuracy are low, mainly because we have no good measure.

Mr. Ovens. I am not sure what the complexity of a code is.

The complexity of a problem will turn directly into that. I would say that its importance is medium.

Dr. Boehm. Whatever definition you are using for complexity, within the TRW and Cocomo model we have come with a definition of complexity which has turned up to be reasonably easy to use, and to be reasonably consistent accross groups defined as various classes of software such as computational operations, data dependent control operations, display operations, and things like that. There are things with typically low complexity, and with typically high complexity. If you do a string of assignement statements, then this is very low; if you are reinventing algorithms for real time signal filtering, then this is extra high. If you are doing device dependent things, then this is low, but if you do micro code synchronisation, then it is extra high. We have found these scales fairly easy for people to relate to, and they give fairly consistent answers when put on cost estimating forms. The importance of that is quite high. If you look at Mr. Jones' list of cost drivers, then complexity is the second important one, with a factor of two between really hard things and really simple things.

Dr. Curtis' comment drives me to say a little bit about what we have done in TRW to modify the Cocomo model. This was to combine together personnel capability and complexity ratings. This resulted in a single rating, called complexity relative to the personnel. This modification does two good things.Firstly it normalises things properly, and secondly it eliminates political problems, e.g. if one department looks much more stupid than the other. If you are going to put in your form that you are working with a dumb programmer, this might occasionally give you extra resources (Laughter).

Professor Fischer. I would like to know what is more important, the complexity of a problem or the complexity of code. For instance, in certain computational problems, if you are using APL, you can readily do matrix multiplication, but if you have less structure in your language, then it is not so easy. Therefore, in some cases you have to consider the matching of your problem with your tool. That says very little about the complexity of the original problem as such. So all you can measure is the degree of matching the complexity of your problem to your tool.

Mr. Musa. One aspect that should be mentioned here is that there have been many studies which indicated that size and current metrics for complexity are very highly correlated. Thus at present any separate complexity metric for problem or code would add only slight additional information to your cost estimate. That is why I do not value the role of complexity very highly for this purpose.

Professor Fischer. It may also be useful to differentiate

between syntactic complexity and semantic complexity. In the syntactic case you can use a type of Shannon method of measurement (8) of the complexity of your code. The semantic case is much more relevant, yet much harder to define; it relates to our memory structure, e.g. how many chunks of short memory can a human have. Therefore the two measurements are unlike each other.

Mr. Jones. This is a very good point. I feel that psychologists and computer engineers need cooperative studies. Then they may come to grips with the complexity issue, since this problem goes beyond any individual domain.

Ms. Clapp. May I return to the general theme of this discussion. One interesting part of US Government practice is to recognize that by standard regulations we should accept bids with lower cost values. In the US Department of Defence, there is a cost range that is considered acceptable by the Government, which establishes these limits by its own independent cost estimate. You just cannot buy below that. Also, there are several steps in negotiations. After the technical part has been accepted, then we have separate cost negotiations. Industry has to to explain their cost estimates in terms of cost models. This helps in the communication process.

Mr. Jones. This is a very good point. I seat myself near the lower cost boundary, below which you may be faking your bid.

Ms. Clapp. This may be due to misunderstanding of the project requirements, or even for some valid reasons. Anyhow, that puts people in position, where they have to explain how they got their cost estimate. There is clearly a great need of data. One of the things that has been pointed out here many times, is the inconsistency of data.They have actually contracted to define that easy-to-collect and minimal set of data. Anyhow, there is now a movement in the USA, and I do not know how strong this is, to try and come up with a standard set of reasonable items that could be collected accross programs, and that could serve different purposes. One aim is to feed a common data base, which anybody can use, while preserving the anonimity of the contributors. It would not cost too much to assess by means of these data your own performance against others, and to get some average cost value. That is an action that a collective group can take and it has been advocated for at least last three years.

Mr. Jones. Who is trying to esablish that data base?

Ms. Clapp. I do not think that there is anybody particular who is trying to do it. It tends to be local, like in my organization, and we work for the Air Force. They are trying to come out with something that they can use universally accross their programs. They have actually contracted to define that easy-to-collect and minimal set of data. They have also started researching how they can put it into contracts to collect the data. We would see this as a historical data set that can be used in models, and also as a way of measuring status. This database could help you as the program goes on; you can go back and see how you are doing compared to the original estimate. Do not forget this at the start of a program; see how you are doing and see how correct are these parameters. This may also give people insight into the efficiency of their own methods of developing software and their cost estimating techniques.

Dr. McNichols. In the U.S. Department of Defense there is a Cost Improvement Group, set up in 1972, which is very cost conscious. There are three elements of concern. One is the Cost Data Collection, the second is Cost Estimating, and the third is Cost Modelling. We have tended to confuse all three together. The Cost Data Collection element involves a data reporting system called the Contractor Cost Data Reporting (CCDR) system, which was intitially established for hardware systems, but now is extended to include software data elements. This involves a cost breakdown structure. The U.S. defense industry is well familiar with CCDR. Detailed data elements are required to be collected for all major weapon systems acquisitions under DoD contract. All military services are also developing support and maintenance costs.

In the Navy, the title is VAMOSC (Visibility and Management of Support Cost); there is one for aircraft and one for ships. The Air Force has the same name for aircraft systems. In the Army it is called OSCMIS (Operating and Support Cost Management Information System), which is a decision support system with five commodities in it. The military services have made massive efforts for data collection. This naturally results in lots of data and all of them are proprietary.

In the software world there are also software databases which you can collect from aerospace corporations, of from other organizations (i.e., from their cost analysis groups). They all use "lines of code" measures.

Cost modelling is a separate area. These models use different databases, for example Dr. Boehm (2) uses 63 data points. Other people talk of 200 data points, or 100 data points. However, data for avionics systems are not the same as for those that build tanks, or control systems, for different functions are being performed. The same happens if you mix reliability data of such differing systems, and necessarily you then get into the same trouble with cost data.

Cost data are collected independently of cost models. The U.S. Department of Defense has Army, Air Force and Navy Cost Groups at the Pentagon level and they try to do independent cost estimates. Most of these people do not believe in using cost models. They believe in using expert judgement and analogies; they are questioning, rather than making raw estimates. The cost realism is another name given to the upper and lower bounds of acceptable bid costs, mentioned by Ms. Clapp. In general, they throw off the highest and the lowest bidders and pick out someone in the middle. In their minds this is the cost realism.

A lot is being done in this cost area, but this is not an academic subject, in the sense that it is not rigorous for the most part. Some of us have tried to move it into the operational research area. There are some analytical models developed, but others, like "SLIM", are using simulation and some linear programming. Some of us are hoping that basic research will be done on cost estimating and that universities will get funds to do that.

Ms. Clapp. You have been saying here that reliability data are much simpler to collect than data for cost models. Is it really true ?

Mr. Musa. This is certainly true for failure data; to collect these is relatively simple. It is also desirable to have some information on the type and size of a project, number of people involved, etc. If you want to estimate the system test completion date, you need to have information on resource and resource usage. But there is a small quantity of data, which is less complex overall than the most of cost data we are now talking about.

Mr. Ovens. For data of this kind the U.S. Navy uses the same form as does the Air Force; its number is 169. There is also the corresponding hardware form. Both are used primarily for price models. There is another form, prepared by the Navy, in which various cost models, like Slim and Cocomo, can be used. It sets how many questions you are likely to ask a contactor. You could ask up to 300 questions, and the same canonical questions are to be asked each of the contractors. Once these data are collected, each of the models can be run several times.

But data is a strange thing. I have collected data two years ago on a space system, and I was told that this was a very complex system in terms of software. You had to use 85% of the memory available in the computer. Today we have a bigger chip, and the same piece od software would today be considered elementary. We need only 5% of the space available for the same function in the computer memory. So, what is happening with data, is that as time goes on, it does not stay stationary; what was complex yesterday, is elementary today, simply because of changing technology. It is important, when you define your technology, not to think of it as a point. The same applies to the complexity issue; it is a range, not a point.

Dr. McNichols. It is for that reason that some believe that past data are worthless because of technology advances.

Hopefully this is not true.

Mr. Mellor. I have tried to apply reliability models in real life to real data. So I have some insight why they are not used here as much as in cost models. There are two basic reasons:

One is that the computational difficulty in constructing a reliability model, and of implementing one, is very high compared with cost models. You can implement the basic Cocomo model with 30 lines of BASIC. If you are faced with one of the reliability models, you require quite a lot of advanced numerical computations, such as maximum likelihood searches to do your parameter estimation. Thus getting started with that is very difficult. Also, there are no proprietory reliability models on the market.

The other point is that getting data to put into a model is diabolically difficult for the reliability case. Even if you have a large data base of faults and failure rates, they have most likely been kept for different purposes than reliability estimation. Such data bases have been set up initially to drive the software correction process and for progress chasing of customers' bug reports.

Actually, pulling the different strands together and getting the necessary failure statistics is very time consuming. To make any kind of reliability statement requires records of run time, and there are often simply non-existant.

I can recall trying to do a study of a high volume product. I went to the marketing team responsible for it and asked them how many copies of this system are in the field. The answered that they do not know. Until we get people to record their data properly, we are not going to get good predictions through any reliability model, model wars apart. We cannot apply these models realistically until we can persuade manufacturers that reliability is worth going for, and therefore essential to measure. To get that data they ought to start looking at automatic means of recording. This is the only way you can get a decent record of events.

Mr. Musa. I certainly agree with you that there is a lot of data now in existence collected without any particular aim in mind. But one can generalise this a bit, saying that this is not just the case with reliability modelling. If you try to use data produced in any past realm, when it was collected without any particular regard to any particular objective, you will have a problem.

As far as the computational difficulty is concerned, it certainly differs among the models that have been developed; some of them look very complex to me, more complex than cost models.

I would like to mention that the program for the model we have developed is reasonably simple and is available to people interested in it; all you need do is to contact me.

Mr. Jones. One more point I wish to raise is the problem of code complexity. We shall not be able in time provided for this discussion to consider the rest of my list, but we have some time left for this issue. So what do you think of measuring the code complexity ?

Mr. Musa. I still take the stand I did before, that size is about as useful as most code complexity measure. Most metrics that have been proposed are highly correlated to size, so we do not seem to be getting much more information from them.

Mr. Ovens. Complexity of code depends on many factors, most important being the application and the utilisation. By application I mean whether you are going to use your program as an operating system, or just feed it in as another chunk to your existing program. Utilisation deals with the size and speed of your computer. There is always a trade off there. You can throw off a bigger machine and thus lower down the complexity. but you have to be very carefull here, because something that is complex in one machine need not be so in another.

Dr. McNichols. There is a point mentioned here already by Professor Fischer concerning the type of complexity. If you have a LISP processing function, and you are not using the LISP language for it, then your code will be very difficult and complex. If you use for this FORTRAN or BASIC, then your complexity will be really tough.

What metric are we to use for the code complexity ? Everyone that answers this has a subjective notion, and he answers this differently.

Dr. Curtis. Given two users, the complexity of code will be different for each of them; it is as simple as that. Measuring the code complexity does not measure the psychological complexity of the software. There have been some Japanese studies showing that if you measure the control flow and measure the volume, you can get a reasonable correlation with defects in the software.

Mr. Jones. There is another aspect of the IBM study just mentioned. Half of the complexity issues seemed to be accidental, either because people were pressurised to do something rapidly, or that they have not used the proper language for the problem, or that they had no sufficient training, or that there were other factors outside the essence of what they were trying to program. The cause of complexity, as was concluded in that study, was random and could be avoided. It was not due to some basic problems, but due to some extraennous factors.

Dr. Boehm. My definition of code complexity is similar to that I gave earlier, namely that complexity is reciprocal to the understanding of what we are doing.

Mr. Musa. One more coment on what I have said already. Professor Fischer has mentioned the mismatch between the problem domain and the domain where a human being understands this problem. This is really a translation process, and it seems to me that perhaps the complexity is a measure of the amount of translation that has to be made.

Dr. Curtis. Complexity is the measure of how much resource a system will have to expend in interacting with the software. Computational complexity is related to the amount of machine processing. Psychological complexity represents the understanding, creating, debugging, or modifying a piece of software. It is an intervening variable that is difficult to define.

Professor Fischer. New formalisms should be developed in directions that they absorb complexity. To understand a problem represented in assembly language may be very difficult, but if the programming formalism contains abstractions which are tailored for a specific problem domain, the same problem may be very easy to understand. After we have understood recursion, many problems of a recursive nature can be represented in a much clearer way.

Mr. Jones. We are now ending this discussion; there is time just for one more question.

Dr. Bedrosian. I am not an expert on computer technology, but I am interested in information theory. Thus I would like to ask the panel to tell me what do they think of input/output flow of information; can this be measured ?

Dr. Curtis. 30 years ago, shortly after the publication of Shannon's article, psycholgists considered his idea very powerful. Psycholgists have tried to use the information theory measure to predict human information processing. But, up to now, this has largely failed, because of our inability to find out what the measure of human information is. This concept changes continously and that is the essence of the problem. People chunk information into higher level concepts that can then be handled as a single chunk, but then it is difficult to establish what a single information bit is in a human brain. We know that a human can change his/her capacity and accept higher level information chunks. Nevertheless, it is very difficult to relate this to the psychological complexity of software or other things. If you want to use the information theoretic mathematics to describe human information processing, you have to define the nature and size of individual information chunks.

Mr. Jones. Indeed, in high level languages it is difficult to measure the lines of code, never mind the information bits. Each chunk has a lot of functionality in each line of code, so the information measure changes continously.

This is the end of the last session of this Institute. I thank you for your interest and contributions to this interesting panel.

Part 5

Security, Safety, Privacy and Integrity in Developing and in Using Computer Communication and Computer Data Storage and Retrieval

Organised by Rein Turn

SECURITY, PRIVACY, SAFETY AND RESILIENCY IN COMPUTATION

Rein Turn
California State University, Northridge
Northridge, CA 91330, USA

INTRODUCTION

Recent advances in computer technology are making available, at acceptable cost, computer systems with virtually unlimited processing power, storage capacity, and capability for data communication. The very large scale integration (VLSI) technology permits placing on single chips tens of thousands of logic circuits or millions of bits of memory, and to mass-produce these for near-negligible cost [1]. It is economical, therefore, to maximize the use of computer technology in any system. Such use produces old products and services in new, digital form, and engenders new services or products. The digital telephone, electronic funds transfer systems (EFTS), and the "fifth generation" knowledge-based information systems [2] are examples of such new developments.

In other application areas, a microprocessor and memory can be embedded in a plastic card to produce the "smart card" now being tested extensively in France, the United States, and elsewhere for electronic payment systems or for use as a portable medical information file [3]. Likewise, special-purpose microprocessors for signal processing can be coupled to digital video scanners to search for specified objects in areas under surveillance [4], such as the faces of wanted persons. In many systems, ranging from sewing machines to jumbo jets, microcomputers are used for their operational control.

The new computer technology and its applications are profoundly affecting and changing the functioning of societies worldwide. Dependence on computer systems is increasing, and they are becoming critical components in systems that will af-

NATO ASI Series, Vol. F22
Software System Design Methods. Edited by J.K. Skwirzynski

fect our future as well as daily life. This means that the traditional computer system design requirements, such as high performance and reliability, software portability, system interoperability, and easy maintainability must be strengthened and augmented by new requirements such as system safety, system and data security, privacy protection for personal information, and preservation of societal resiliency. The purpose of this paper is to provide an overview and a rationale for these new requirements, and to discuss approaches taken for their implementation.

SAFETY REQUIREMENTS

A general concern of the users of any system, or of people directly affected by the operation of a system, is its trustworthiness: Is it available when needed? Will it function correctly and reliably? Is it safe to use? Is it protected against misuse or tampering? For a simple system such as a chain saw, it may be possible to answer these questions by inspection at the time of use. For complex systems, such as an air traffic control system, the designers and operators must be trusted to have implemented the appropriate safeguards and requirements.

The safety of computer-controlled real-time systems is also receiving increased attention. The principal goal is to prevent physical harm to the users of the system, to anyone or any property within the system's domain of operation, or to the system itself and its operators. Concerns here go beyond the reliability of the controlling computer system alone -- while the latter is recovering, the controlled system must not be unsafe. Thus, system safety encompasses the total system, including its human operators and users, and even other systems that may be encountered. As discussed in a companion paper in this volume [5], safety techniques must be developed and integrated into all phases of the system's life cycle, especially the life cycles of the system's software, data bases, and interfaces with users or other systems.

COMPUTER SYSTEM SECURITY

Computer security is usually defined as the: "protection of the system and the data stored therein against unauthorized access, modification, destruction or use, and against actions or situations that deny authorized access or use of the system." While accidental events that threaten security are included, the emphasis is on deliberate attempts to weaken security.

Security Requirements.

The need for access controls in a computer system should be self-evident from the large body of evidence that attacks against computer systems have occurred [6,7], even though the degree to which such controls should be implemented in a given system may not be simple to determine. In general, the following are among the principal reasons for providing access control and security [8]:

Protection of resources: The computer system and, more importantly, the data stored and processed therein tend to be critically valuable to an organization's functioning. Some data (e.g., financial accounts) in the system directly represent tangible value and must be protected against unauthorized alterations.

Mandated by law: Several countries have enacted laws that require protection of certain categories of information, such as national defense information or personal information; other laws may require that the integrity of financial data be ensured.

Maintain management control: A goal for any organization is to be in full control of the computer resources and their use.

Ensure safety and integrity: Security is an essential prerequisite for the system safety and for the integrity of the data bases and processes being used (e.g., in computer-aided design or in computer-based modeling).

Operational advantages or economies: A secure computer system is important in organizations whose business depends on their customers' trust, such as in financial institutions. It can increase the organization's advantage over competitors with less secure systems. It can also reduce operating costs such as insurance premiums.

Additional material on the need for security can be found in [9]. However, despite of the convincing rationale, many systems employ only a minimal set of security safeguards. The principal reason is that the operating systems software provided by computer systems vendors is intrinsically not capable of preventing unauthorized access -- security was not a design objective. While these operating systems generally do perform their intended functions correctly, they contain many design or implementation flaws and shortcuts that permit any existing access control mechanisms to be bypassed and, thus, cannot prevent unauthorized access and use [10].

The theory of designing truly secure operating systems is now well in hand and design criteria exist [11], but applying these in practice is a different matter. Secure operating systems will require radical changes in the currently used hardware and software architectures, and it will be very difficult to maintain compatibility with the existing systems and software. Vendors and their customers are reluctant to develop new systems which, even if they provide much better security, require expensive conversions of the existing software and data bases. Many users would accept the uncertainty of suffering large losses in the future due to lack of security rather than making modest expenditures for security now.

Those managers who do want to improve security find a very sparse market place: a few access control software packages for managing passwords [12], some devices for controlling dial-up access to thwart hackers, and various anchoring devices for personal computers. With very few exceptions (e.g., MULTICS or SCOMP for Honeywell's Level 6 minicomputer [13]), there are no secure operating systems on the market.

Security Risk Management.

Not all systems require a high level of security, and different approaches can be taken to achieving a desired degree of secureness. The determination of security requirements for a given system, and the selection of appropriate security mechanisms are a part of the risk management activity. The basic steps are [14]: value and criticality analysis, vulnerability analysis, threat identification, risk analysis, risk assessment, security safeguards selection and implementation, development of contingency plans, and effectiveness reviews. Again, these steps may be difficult to apply in practice. For example, it is difficult to place value on information, discover all vulnerabilities, or develop threat scenarios for exploiting these vulnerabilities.

Risk analysis requires determining for each threat its probability of occurrence over a specified time period (e.g. a year) and the amount of loss that would be incurred. These quantities can be multiplied to obtain the annual loss expectancy (ALE), as described in [15]. However, since very little actuarial information is available about threats to computer systems, computations of the ALE's is usually based on the analyst's subjective judgement.

The operational environment is also taken into account. Thus, in general, security risks are higher in systems where:

The "distance" is large between the highest information sensitivity or processing criticality level in the system, and the lowest trustworthiness level of the users.

User capabilities in the system include assembly language programming rather than being restricted to higher-level language (HOL) programming only. Systems where users are limited to predefined transactions are even less risky.

System architecture is complex, such as in the case of multiprocessors or in distributed data processing systems; The risk is even higher in computer networks.

There is considerable uncertainty over the trustworthiness of the system software developers. The situation worsens when hardware developers' trustworthiness is also in doubt.

The result of risk analysis is a list of threats ordered by some severeness measure (such as ALE). In the risk assesment step, decisions are made about each threat: either to accept the risk due to that threat or to reduce the risk by selecting and implementing a set of additional security mechanisms. However, in practice the granularity of strengthening security is much more coarse and, correspondingly, security cost increases are also in much larger increments that might be expected. In addition, tradeoffs may need to be made with system design objectives or requirements other than cost, such as functionality, performance, resource sharing, and user-friendliness.

Security Policies.

The conceptual elements of a security system are: (1) a security policy which establishes the security framework for the system; (2) prevention mechanisms which provide isolation, identification and authentication, and access control; (3) active protection mechanisms which perform monitoring and response functions, (4) integrity assurance procedures for the security mechanisms, (5) backup and recovery mechanisms, and (6) deterrence provisions.

In general, a security policy of an organization or a system defines the data protection requirements, establishes the information sensitivity levels and access categories, defines access criteria and protection requirements, and establishes authorization and accountability systems. A formal model of the access control rules defined by the policy is developed to permit formal proofs of the correctness of the design, implementation, and enforcement of the policy in the computer system software [16]. This model is called the "reference monitor", and it is implemented in the operating system as the "security kernel" [17].

The security policy model of the U.S. Department of Defense (DoD) for protecting national defense information can be used as an illustration [18]. The model is stated as follows:

> The system contains protected entities, called "objects",O, and active entities that seek access to the objects, called "subjects", S.
>
> Each object is assigned a "security level", SL(O), and membership in a set of access control categories, CAT(O). Each subject is granted a "clearance level", CL(S), and it may have access to a set of categories CAT(S). The security and clearance levels form a hierarchical system. Beginning with the most sensitive, they are designated "top secret", "secret", "confidential", and "unclassified" (i.e., TS, S, C, and U, respectively). The categories are unordered and may exist at any security level. Together, the levels and categories form a lattice structure.
>
> Two main access modes of subjects to objects are defined: read (observation but no modification), and write (no observation, appending of new information only).

The DoD security policy has a mandatory (nondiscretionary) part, and a discretionary part. The latter is a need-to-know access control policy enforcement which applies after the mandatory policy requirements have been satisfied. A model of discretionary access control is based on the access control matrix and on access rules [18] which may be implemented by using "capabilities" or "access control lists". The mandatory (non-discretionary) security policy rules for granting access are:

Simple security condition: A subject is granted "read" access to an object if and only if

CL(S) >= SL(O) and CAT(S) >= CAT(O)

Star-property (*-property): A subject is granted "write" access (without being able to read) if and only if

CL(S) <= SL(O) and CAT(S) <= CAT(O)

The purpose of the *-property is to prevent copying of information from objects at a higher SL into objects at a lower SL by untrusted software or users.

The mandatory access rules must be invoked by the reference monitor mechanism in the system each and every time access is sought to an object. In order to compare the security and clearance levels, every object and subject in the system must be labelled. Labels must be unforgeable and the labelling and label transfer mechanisms must be proven correct -- they must be trusted.

An additional security requirement not explicit in the above model is "confinement" -- prevention of information leakage to unauthorized subjects via unconventional, "covert" information flow channels. Two types of covert channels must be considered:

Covert storage channels -- direct or indirect writing into a storage location by one process, and the direct or indirect reading of this location by another process, such that the security policy is violated.

Covert timing channels -- a process in the system signals information to another process by modulating the information about or the use of some global resource of the system which is accessible or observable by the receiving process. For example, signalling may be by locking or unlocking of a shared file. An important consideration is the bandwidth of the covert channel -- the maximum signalling rate.

Security policies in the private sector are less precisely defined and tend to emphasize data integrity and denial of services rather than data disclosure. However, the DoD security policy and systems that implement it are also suitable for use in commercial applications [8,19].

Secure Operating Modes

Security policies can be implemented in several ways, using combinations of physical isolation, logical isolation in operating system design and in hardware architecture, or administrative procedures. This yields a hierarchy of systems that provide different levels of security at different levels of confidence as specified, for example, in the DoD trusted systems evaluation criteria [11]. Several standard modes of operation are in use:

Dedicated security mode -- the system is totally reserved for the particular application involving sensitive processing or data. Only the users with appropriate clearances and need-to-know are permitted access to the system. All other users and devices (e.g., terminals) are physically isolated from the system. The system's software can be untrusted since it has no security role in this mode. The cost here is an inefficient use of the system and no resource sharing with other applications or users.

System-high security mode - all users are cleared to the highest security level of data or processing in the system, but may not necessarily have the need-to-know. Thus, many applications could be processed concurrently.

Any security lapse that may occur due to untrusted software will be only an inadvertent need-to-know violation which can be handled with appropriate debriefing. This mode is less restrictive in the use of the system, but requires clearing some users to a higher security level than necessary.

Multilevel secure (MLS) mode -- the system permits concurrent storage and processing of information with different security levels and categories, and permits concurrent access by users with different clearances and categories, but prevents unauthorized accesses. Full resource sharing is possible and the system is efficiently used. The cost is in developing a trusted operating system.

In a MLS system, the operating system software is proven to be correctly designed and implemented to handle security and clearance level labels correctly and reliably, and to perform the reference monitor function correctly and reliably, such that no unauthorized accesses, overt or covert, can occur. The state of the art of operating system security, especially verification of design and implementation correctness, has not yet progressed to the point where general purpose MLS operating systems are available [20].

Security Evaluation Criteria

In 1983, the U.S. DoD Computer Security Center published the Trusted Computer System Evaluation criteria which have become a de facto framework for evaluating system security, especially the operating system software security. The criteria emphasize policy enforcement, users' accountability, correctness assurance, and system documentation. Based on these, the following system of security divsions is defined:

Division D -- minimal protection: Systems in this class have been evaluated, but fail to meet the requirements for a higher evaluation division.

Division C -- discretionary protection: Systems in division provide discretionary protection and accountability of the subjects for their actions.

Division B -- mandatory protection: In this division, all systems contain a Trusted Computer Base (TCB) that preserves the integrity of security labels and uses them to enforce the mandatory access control policy. The implementation of the reference monitor concept must be demonstrated.

Division A -- verified design: Systems in this division have been subjected to formal verification to assure that the mandatory and discretionary security controls in the system can effectively protect sensitive information.

The concept of a "trusted computing base" is defined in the criteria document [11] as follows: "TCB is the totality of protection mechanisms within a computer system -- including hardware, firmware, and software -- the combination of which is responsible for enforcing a security policy. It creates a basic protection environment and provides additional user services required for a trusted computer system. The ability of a TCB to correctly enforce the security policy depends solely on the mechanisms within the TCB and on the correct input by the system administrative personnel of parameters (e.g., a user's clearance level) related to the security policy."

Security Mechanisms.

Security mechanisms are hardware or software features which implement the trusted computing base by providing isolation, identification and authentication, and access controls. In conventional operating systems they provide password validation, memory protection, memory management, and user/supervisor domains separation. In the future trusted operating systems they will provide the following features (see also [21]):

Labels -- designations of security/clearance levels and categories for each object/subject. They must be indelibly attached to the objects/subjects in their internal representations, and externally (such as on hard copy, on the screen, or on demountable storage devices).

Mandatory access control -- implementation of the reference monitor function and the associated access authorizations; enforcement is based on labels. In software implementation, the reference monitor is in the kernel. In hardware/firmware implementation, special-purpose processors can be used.

TCB protection -- TCB self-protection is an important architectural requirement. It requires the isolation of the TCB from subjects by use of privileged operating modes of the processor hardware. It is enhanced by virtualizing all the resources, especially the memory.

Storage object reuse -- upon reallocation of a storage object (e.g., a memory segment) previous information in it is erased, or other techniques are used to prevent scavenging.

Identification and authentication -- TCB will require users to identify themselves, and verify the identity by providing authentication information. The latter will be protected against user access (e.g., by applying one-way transformations). The identity will be associated with all auditable actions of the user in the system. A trusted path will be provided for the initial log-in of a user.

Discretionary access control -- The access control matrix and access rules are implemented in the system. Architecturally, either the "capability" model or the "access control list" model is implemented. Both may require additional hardware features, such as data word tagging or more storage space.

Confinement -- measures to prevent covert channels or to reduce their bandwidth. This requires thorough analyses of the system architecture and operation.

Security auditing -- maintenance of a secure log of users' actions in the system, and access in real time to audit information on events that have security implications. This can support real-time detection of security violations, or after-the-fact analyses of possible security compromises.

While the above are not all the architectural features necessary for the implementation secure operating systems, as per DoD security evaluation criteria, they do form an important set of design requirements that must be incorporated. In more complex architectures such as distributed systems, there are additional concerns regarding the security of interprocessor communications (typically using a local area network or LAN). Applicable security mechanisms include encryption [22], and architectural approaches for achieving MLS operation based on the use of a secure LAN and processors dedicated to specific security levels [23]. Security measures for computer networks are also based on the use of encryption [24] and secure protocols for the various communications functions [25].

Finally, one must not overlook the interactions of security requirements and mechanisms with the other system design requirements. Of special interest is fault-tolerance [26], where certain software-based techniques for "corrective" may be incompatible with security requirements. In using corrective redundancy errors in computation due to a hardware fault are corrected by repeating the computation. However, it may not be possible to correct a security violation in this manner.

PRIVACY PROTECTION

Privacy is a concept with many meanings. In this paper it is defined as the rights of individuals regarding the collection, storage, processing and use in decision making of personal information about themselves. It beccomes an issue in computer applications in the context of computerized personal information record-keeping systems. While privacy was also a problem in manual systems, modern computer-communication technology makes it economical to store and process large volumes of data, permits complex correlations at high speed, allows high-speed access from distant locations and, thus, makes technically feasible for physically decentralized systems to become centralized "logically". This lays the groundwork for integration of data records and assembly of personal information dossiers on individuals. And this is viewed by the public as a threat to their liberties. There are other problems, too. Since information in computers is not directly readable by humans, they cannot determine without the services of the record keeper what information about them is stored. Further, in the computer system, undetected hardware and software errors can cause information distortions, and information can be altered without detection by accident or deliberately.

Privacy Protection Principles

Privacy protection is as a societal policy and value which must be balanced with other policies and values and, in system design, with other requirements. It is clear that record-keeping on individuals is necessary when privileges are granted (such as the driver's license) or qualification for some benefits is determined. In these cases, the individual voluntariliy foregoes some of his privacy in order to receive the privilege or benefit. This is in the best interest of the society. On the other hand, the society must also protect the individual against excesses of the record keepers and against unfair decisions.

Since the government at its various levels from national to

local is a major record-keeping entity, much of the concern about privacy protection centers on its activities. However, in the private sector, too, are large collections of personal information on education, health, employment, financial status, purchases, and life style [27, 28]. On the international scale, operations of multinational corporations and international data processing service bureaus has resulted in transborder data flows (TDF) of personal information [29, 30].

The principal mechanisms for ensuring privacy protection to individual data subjects are legislative and administrative, rather than technical. Often this distinction is misunderstood -- threats to individual privacy arise mainly from authorized users of the system, rather than from unauthorized users. National level legislation to provide privacy protection (or data protection, as it is commonly called in Europe) legislation is now in force in a dozen countries: Austria, Canada, Denmark, Federal Republic of Germany, France, Israel, Luxenbourg, New Zealand, Norway, Sweden, United Kingdom, and the United States. Legislation is pending in several other countries (e.g., Australia, Belgium, Finland, Italy, Japan, the Netherlands, Portugal, Spain and Switzerland). Although the implementation approaches and protection scope tend to vary from country to country reflecting different cultural environments and legal traditions, the privacy rights granted are remarkably similar.

The principles for privacy protection have evolved over the last decade, beginning with several national studies, advancing with the early national privacy or data protection legislation (as in West German province Hessen and in Sweden), and arriving to the current form in the OECD Guidelines [31]. The Code of Fair Information Practices formulated by a U.S. Government advisory committee on privacy [32] was the initial foundation for these principles:

Openness -- no secret record-keeping systems, uses, or record-keeping practices.

Individual access -- the right of individuals to know what data are kept about them, and how these data are used.

Individual participation -- the right to correct or amend erroneous records.

Collection limitation -- restrictions on data types that may be collected, and on the collection methods.

Use limitation -- restrictions on the use of data for unannounced purposes.

Disclosure limitation -- restrictions on any external circulation of personal data.

Information management -- requirements to maintain data quality and confidentiality.

Accountability -- clearly fixed responsibility for compliance with privacy protection requirements.

Privacy protection efforts in the United States have developed along three lines: the federal government, state and local governments, and the private sector. Federal-level privacy laws, especially the Privacy Act of 1974, apply to the federal government agencies, but with law enforcement and intelligence communities exempted. They also apply to the private sector in financial credit reporting, to educational institutions that receive federal support, and to government access to individuals' banking transaction records. The states have enacted numerous privacy protection laws that cover government agencies and also some private sector business, addressing one or more of the following: employment records, financial credit reporting, insurance and medical records, law enforcement and criminal justice records, EFTS and cable television, and the use of polygraphs.

The future trend in the U.S. is for more extensive protection, even though it is not likely that any new federal-level privacy protection law will be enacted soon; states are likely to be more active. Thus, the private sector record-keeping systems are likely to remain unregulated on the federal level for some time, despite the Privacy Protection Study Commission's recommendations [33], and the general perception of the U.S. public that the threat to privacy is increasing [34].

The Impact of New Technologies.

The public concern over threats to privacy is further supported by the emergence of so-called "new technologies" based on the use of computers: computer networks, electronic mail, office automation, electronic funds transfer systems (EFTS), smart cards, interactive home services, and embedded microprocessors as controllers in other systems. Collectively, these applications tend to have a set of common attributes or modes of operations which may increase their potential for adverse impacts on privacy protection, since they potentially support:

Automated services that generate large volumes of transactions involving individuals, and keep records on them.

Automated techniques and systems for collecting and transmitting computer readable personal information.

Direct or indirect integration of systems which handle personal information.

Applications and services that allow inferring personal information.

Automated decision-making based on personal information about individuals.

Physical or information surveillance of individuals.

Overt or covert markets for personal information.

The above features of the new computer technology applications set the stage for potential privacy protection problems. For example, connecting computers into networks, and networks into super-networks, is progressing rapidly. The benefits for data communication are obvious, even though the resulting systems contain multitudes of complex, hard-to-trace communication paths which contribute to problems in providing security, access control, and message intrgrity and authenticity. From privacy protection point of view, computer networks where personal information data bases are on-line can support de facto integration of record-keeping systems and, thus, the capability for "virtual dossiers" and extralegal exchanges of personal information. Networking will also enhance matching of personal information files in different systems for investigative purposes [35,36], increase the difficulty in monitoring compliance with privacy protection requirements, and render more difficult to detect misuse of personal data bases. Similar privacy protection problems arise in other applications of the new technology.

Privacy protection and TDF.

Privacy protection is also an important transborder data flow (TDF) issue. Some countries with data protection laws are concerned that less privacy protection will be given to personal infomation about their citizens when transmitted abroad, especially to countries with less comprehensive data protection laws than their own. Howevr, some countries that provide international data processing services or operate private networks tend to view these concerns as of little merit and, instead, promote the principle of "free flow of information". These countries, mainly the United States, are also aginst the concept of providing privacy protection to information about legal persons, such as corporations. Standardization of privacy protection requirements, such as acceptance and implementation of the OECD privacy protection guidelines, is one approach to resolving these differences. The Council of Europe convention on privacy [37] is another such effort.

Technical Implications of Privacy Protection.

A technical consequence of the privacy protection requirements in the design and operation of computerized record-keeping systems is the incorporation of new functions not normally needed. These include:

Preparing notifications of the system's functions and procedures in using personal information;

Providing facilities and procedures for inspections, challenges, reviews, and submission of corrections or rebuttals by individuals;

Accounting for, and auditing of the collection, use, and disclosure of personal information, and interactions with the data subjects;

Maintaining data quality, confidentiality and security;

Demonstrating compliance with protection requirements.

Collectively, these technical requirements imply more computational tasks to be performed, and more data storage resources to be used. For example, the Privacy Act of 1974 requires that "...agencies shall maintain all records with such accuracy, relevance, timeliness, and completeness as is reasonably required to assure fairness to individuals in determinations". This calls for the following policy decisions: selection of data items to be used (relevance), the level of detail of information items (precision), the retention time (timeliness), and criteria for verifying accuracy of factual and evaluative information. In addition, mechanisms must be provided for assuring authenticity of the data items, for access authorization, and for revalidation or purging of data items.

The above, in turn, call for error control in data collection and entry, reliable identification of individuals, maintaining data integrity in the system, providing additional data fields in records for privacy protection purpose, operating privacy protection related audit trails, implementing in the systems data security safeguards and access control mechanisms, and adequate provisions for system backup and recovery.

Data security requirements in national data protection laws, and in international agreements, provide another example. The Council of Europe convention provides that: Appropriate security measures shall be taken " ... against accidental or unauthorized destruction or accidental loss, as well as against unauthorized access, alteration or dissemination". In addition, the convention requires that specific security measures be provided for every file; that the degree of vulnerability, need to restrict access, and requirement for long-term storage be considered; and that the current state-of-the-art security measures, methods, techniques be used.

Concluding this section, it may be observed that privacy protection continues as a concern in many countries, and that privacy protection principles are well-formulated and implementable. Since the technical aspects of privacy protection requirements are substantial, they must be considered early in the system's design phase and maintained throughout its life cycle.

SOCIETAL RESILIENCY

In an information society, production and distribution of information is central to the economic, political, and social life. The benefits that accrue through the availability of information drive the society to obtain even more information. This leads to extensive automation of the information collection, processing, and dissemination functions. Examples are the decision support systems, in business firms, computer-aided design and manufacturing systems, automated process control, office automation, electronic funds transfers, military command and control systems, and many others. It would be very difficult to operate a in modern society without computerized information systems.

As early as in the mid-1960s when the total computer population of the world was a few tens of thousands, concerns were voiced over the increasing dependence on computers (e.g., [38]). Now, when the computer population of world is in tens of millions, and extensive computer networks exist, they are beginning to be regarded as a new, potentially serious technological vulnerability of the society.

In 1979, Sweden released a report of its Committee on the Vulnerability of Computer Systems (SARK) [39], which concluded that "vulnerability is unacceptably high in today's computerized society". Responding to this, the OECD held a workshop in 1981 on computer vulnerability [40]. Its conclusion was that there are sufficient reasons to justify concerns. In the United States, the American Federation of Information Processing Societies (AFIPS), reacted to the Swedish by establishing a panel to examine the applicability of SARK conclusions to the United States. The panel observed that the SARK findings were not representative of the situation in the U.S., and that this country still appears to be adequately resilient [41].

An analysis of societal vulnerabilities and potential hazards due to massive use of computers is similar to performing a technology assessment or a risk analysis. Vulnerabilities and threats are identified and their effects are postulated. Among the effects identified by the AFIPS panel as sufficiently severe to cause society-wide problems were:

A severe disruption of the national economy, and large losses which are only partially recoverable, especially in the national financial system.

A large decline in the productive capability of an important industrial sector, or massive wasting of scarce resources.

A drastic decline of the standard of living of the entire population, or of a large subpopulation of the country.

Erosion of citizens' rights and freedoms.

Increased dependence on foreign powers in economy, finance, or politics.

Coup d'etat, conventional war, or a nuclear conflict.

If it is not possible for computer systems in a given country to directly cause, or to contribute to the occurrence of such harmful effects as listed above, then it would appear that there are no serious computer-related vulnerabilities in that country. On the other hand, some computer application may contribute indirectly by creating potential vulnerabilities which then may cause harmful societal effects. Examples are command and control systems, real time process control systems, systems for distributing goods and services, personal information record-keeping systems, electronic funds transfer systems, and management information systems.

Through a sudden unavailability of a sufficient number of computer systems a societally paralyzing chain of events may be triggered. For example, a coordinated attack on computer systems may be launched by terrorists, anti-social elements may embark on a long-term effort of subversion or sabotage, or computers may be damaged through some natural or man-made event (e.g., radiation or electromagnetic pulse from a nuclear accident in earth orbit [42]). A paralyzing situation may also develop gradually, such as the accumulation in data bases of erroneous information which results in wrong decisions and, over time, renders important computer systems unusable. Deliberate contamination of data bases or software could result in similar problems.

Resiliency is the ability to absorb disruptions and damages

without suffering long-lasting or irreversible ill effects. In the present context, it is the ability to recover from computer system failures or from their misuse without society-wide harms. Resiliency may be due to certain intrinsic attributes of the society in question, or it may be achieved by deliberate actions of the users, the system designers, and the governmental agencies which may be involved. The following factors appear to affect resiliency:

The geographic and demographic aspects of the society. Large countries are likely to be more resilient.

The degree of multiplicity and redundancy in providing critical services to the society. The existence of multiple, overlapping, competing, and decentralized service providers increases resiliency.

The amount of service-level and society-level preparedness, contingency planning, and backup provisions.

The extent of preservation of the "corporate memory" of how functions were performed and supported prior to automation. Deliberate maintenance of adequate manual backup capability enhances resiliency.

The level of technical sophistication of the population. People who are used to working with technical devices tend to be innovative in overcoming disruptions or crises and contribute importantly to resiliency.

The existence of legal safeguards against misuses of computer systems (e.g., such as privacy violations or computer crime).

Requirements to perform societal resiliency impact analyses for all new applications are necessary.

Some of the factors listed above are depend on the size, location, culture, history, and the geopolitical situation of a country. Others are controllable and achievable by appropriate policies. Thus, a computerized country is not necessarily a vulnerable one. On the other hand, resiliency cannot be expected to be a permanent condition. Deliberate efforts are required by all sectors of the society to preseve it. For example, public awareness of the capabilities as well as limitations of computer technology must be increased, industry associations must assume a role in maintaining resiliency in their specific functional areas, and the government must promote resiliency as a part of its national information policy. Individual organizations that are dependent on automated systems must plan for quality control in their data processing operations, provide for adequate security, establish and test contingency plans, and take steps to maintain the corporate memory of how to perform critical functions without computer support.

REFERENCES

1. Christiansen, D. (Ed.), " Technology '85", IEEE Spectrum, January 1985, pp. 34-95.
2. Feigenbaum, E.A. and P. McCorduck, " The Fifth Generation: Artificial Intelligence and Japan's Computer Challenge to the World", Addison-Wesley, Reading, MA, 1982.
3. Weinstein, S.B., "Smart Credit Cards: The Answer to Cashless Shopping", IEEE Spectrum, February 1984, pp. 43-49.
4. Fu, K.-S. and A. Rosenfeld, "Pattern Recognition and Computer Vision", IEEE Computer, October 1984, pp. 274-282.
5. Leveson, N., "Software System Safety", (this volume).
6. Parker, D.B., "Fighting Computer Crime", Charles Scribner Sons, New York, 1983.
7. Norman, A.R.D., "Computer Insecurity", Chapman and Hall, London, 1983.
8. Turn, R., "Private Sector Needs for Trusted/Secure Computer Systems". AFIPS Conference Proceedings, Vol. 51: 1982 National Computer Conference. AFIPS Press, Reston, VA, 1982, pp. 449-460.
9. Davies, D.W., "The Neeed for Data Security", (this volume).

10. Linde, R.R., "Operating System penetration", AFIPS Conference Proceedings, Vol. 44: 1975 National Computer Conf., AFIPS Press, Reston, VA, June 1975, pp. 361-368.
11. Department of Defense Trusted Computer System Evaluation Criteria, CSC-STD-001-83, DoD Computer Security Center, Ft. Meade, MD, 15 August 1983.
12. Eloff, J.H.P., "Selection Process for Security Packages", Computers & Security, November 1983, pp. 256-260.
13. Fraim, L.J., "SCOMP: A Solution to the Multilevel Security Problem", IEEE Computer, July 1983, pp. 26-34.
14. Campbell, R.P., and G.A. Sands, "A Modular Approach to Computer Security Risk Assessment", AFIPS Conference Proceedings, Vol. 48: 1979 National Computer Conference, AFIPS Press, Reston, VA, June 1979, pp. 293-303.
15. Guidelines for Automatic Data processing Risk Analysis, FIPSPUB 65, U.S. National Bureau of Standards, Washington, DC, August 1979.
16. Cheheyl, M.H., et al., "Verifying Security", ACM Computing Surveys, September 1981, pp. 279-339.
17. Ames, S.R., Jr., M. Gasser, and R.R. Schell, "Security Kernel Design and Implementation: An Introduction", IEEE Computer, July 1983, pp. 14-22.
18. Landwehr, C.E., "Formal Models for Computer Security", ACM Computing Surveys, September 1981, pp. 247-278.
19. Lipner, S.B., "Non-Discretionary Controls for Commercial Applications", Proceedings, 1982 Symposium on Security and Privacy, IEEE Computer Society.
20. Landwehr, C.E., "The Best Available Technologies for Computer Security", IEEE Computer, July 1983, pp. 89-100.
21. Landwehr, C.E., and J.M. Carroll, "Hardware Requirements for Secure Computer Systems: A Framework", Proceedings, 1984 Symposium on Security and Privacy, IEEE Computer Society, pp. 34-40.
22. Meyer, C.H., and S.M. Matyas, Cryptography -- A New Dimension in Computer Data Security, John Wiley & Sons, New York, NY, 1982.
23. Rushby, J., and B. Randell, "A Distributed Secure System", IEEE Computer, July 1983. 55-67.

24. Davies, D.W., and W.L. Price, Security for Computer Networks, John Wiley & Sons, New York, NY, 1984.

25. Voydock, V.L., and S.T. Kent, "Security Mechanisms in High-Level Network Protocols", ACM Computing Surveys, June 1983, pp. 135-171.

26. Avizienis, A.A., "Fault-Tolerance: The Survival Attribute of Digital Systems", Proceedings of the IEEE, Oct. 1978.

27. Westin, A.F., Computers, Health Records, and Citizens' Rights, NBS Monograph 157, Government Printing Office, Washington, DC, December 1976.

28. Westin, A.F., Computers, Personnel Administration, and Citizen Rights. NBS SP 500-50, Government Printing Office, Washington, DC, July 1979.

29. Turn, R. (Ed.), "Transborder Data Flows: Concerns in Privacy Protection and Free Flow of Information", AFIPS Press, Reston, VA, 1979.

30. "Transborder Data Flows and the Protection of Privacy", ICCP-1, OECD, Paris, 1979.

31. Guidelines on the Protection of Privacy and Transborder Flows of Personal Data, OECD, Paris, 1981.

32. Records, Computers, and the Rights of Citizens, Government Printing Office, Washington, DC, July 1973.

33. Personal Privacy in an Information Society -- The Report of the U.S. Privacy Protection Study Commission, Government Printing Office, Washington, DC, July 1977.

34. The Dimensions of Privacy: A National Opinion Research Survey of Attitudes Toward Privacy, Sentry Insurance Co., Stevens Point, WI, 1983.

35. Shattuck, J., "Computer Matching Is Serious Threat to Individual Rights", Comm. of the ACM, June 1984, pp. 538-541.

36. Kusserow, R.P., "The Government Needs Computer Matching to Root Out Waste and Fraud", Communications of the ACM, June 1984, pp. 542-545.

37. Convention on Protection of Individuals with Regard to Automatic Processing of Personal Data, Council of Europe, Strasbourg, France, 1981.

38. "Is the Computer Running Wild?", U.S. News and World Report, February 24, 1964.

39. The Vulnerability of Computerized Society: Considerations and Proposals, Ministry of Defense, Stockholm, Sweden, December 1979 (Translation).
40. "Workshop Stresses Dependence on Computers", Transnational Data Report, July/August 1981.
41. Turn, R., and E. Novotny, "Resiliency of the Computerized Society", AFIPS Proc. Vol. 53, 1983 National Computer Confer., AFIPS Press, Reston, VA, June 1983, pp. 341-349.
42. Lerner, E.J., "Electromagnetic Pulses: Potential Crippler", IEEE Spectrum, May 1981.

SOFTWARE HAZARD ANALYSIS TECHNIQUES

Nancy G. Leveson
Computer Science Department
University of California, Irvine
Irvine, California 92717

As computers are increasingly being used to monitor and/or control systems where software faults or deficiencies could lead to serious consequences such as loss of life, injury, or loss of property, concern is mounting about how to ensure that these computer systems are safe. If it were possible to guarantee that large software systems are correct[†], there would be no problem. However, the state of the art for building large software systems does not allow us to achieve this degree of perfection. In fact, we may be orders of magnitude away from the reliability requirements (e.g. 10^{-7} to 10^{-9}) for such safety-critical systems as aircraft, nuclear power plants, military systems, aerospace systems [Dunham and Knight (1981)].

In many countries, a formal validation and demonstration of the safety of the computers controlling safety-critical applications is required by an official licensing authority. Many system purchasers are including requirements for software safety analysis and verification in their contracts. Unfortunately, there are few techniques available to satisfy these analysis and validation requirements. Much more work is needed in this area.

This paper describes two methods of safety analysis and verification which have been proposed. The first is software fault tree analysis. Fault Tree Analysis is a safety analysis technique which was developed in the early 60's and applied originally to anti-ballistic missile systems [Vesely et.al. (1981)]. Since that time it has been applied to hardware analysis in aerospace, defense, nuclear, and other

[†]By "correct" we mean that not only does the software completely satisfy the requirements, but that there are no errors in the requirements. That is, the correct implementation of the requirements will guarantee that the software will operate as desired by the purchasers or ultimate users.

NATO ASI Series, Vol. F22
Software System Design Methods. Edited by J.K. Skwirzynski

been applied to hardware analysis in aerospace, defense, nuclear, and other systems. Although several people have suggested that it would be useful to apply it to software [Ramamoorthy et.al (1977), Hecht and Hecht (1982)], it was not until 1982 that two research groups working independently and unaware of each other showed how this could be accomplished [Leveson and Harvey (1983), Taylor (1982)].

The second technique which is briefly described in this paper involves the use of Petri net models. This approach is newer than software fault tree analysis and so far has less real application experience. Tools are currently being developed and the theory extended to allow more realistic testing of the technique. The paper concludes some of the open questions which still need to be answered.

SOFTWARE SYSTEM SAFETY

There are many possible failures of differing consequences in any complex system. The consequences of these failures may vary from minor annoyance up to death or injury. System safety engineering focuses on those failures which have the most drastic consequences and either attempts to eliminate them, or if that is not possible, to lower the probability of their occurrence to within acceptable limits.

Safety analysis techniques are based on the following assumptions: (1) not all failures are of equal cost and (2) there are a relatively small number of failures which can lead to catastrophic results. Under these circumstances, it is possible to augment traditional reliability techniques which attempt to eliminate all failures with techniques which concentrate on the high-cost failures. These techniques often involve a "backward" approach which starts with determining what are the unacceptable or "high-cost" failures (called *mishaps*) and then ensures that these particular failures do not occur or at least minimizes the probability of their occurrence. Another way of looking at this is that a "forward" approach would ensure that all possible reachable states of the system are safe whereas a backward approach would ensure that unsafe states are not reachable. This is only practical under the above assumptions that there are a relatively small number of failures which are unacceptable and that these can be determined. In practice, this is usually the case even in complex systems. For example, this type of analysis has been applied to nuclear power plants and missile defense systems.

Note that safety analysis has a much more limited goal than ensuring complete correctness. The aim is to minimize the risk that the system will cause harm. In fact, the system may do nothing -- this is considered safe as long as no harm is caused in the process.

A *hazard* is a condition or set of conditions which can lead to a mishap. The system safety engineer usually determines the potential hazards in a system and classifies them as to severity and probability (*risk*) in a process called *Preliminary Hazard Analysis* (PHA). The software hazards are derived from the PHA in order to determine the software safety requirements. This is the first aspect of software hazard analysis. The second is to verify that the software satisfies these requirements. One important feature of software safety verification is the need to extend verification and validation of software beyond showing consistency between the software specification and the implementation to verifying that the software correctly implements the total system safety requirements.

In general, a system can get into an unsafe state in several ways including:

- hardware component failure
- interfacing (communication and timing) problems between components of the system)
- human error in operation or maintenance where a human error is defined as a human action producing an unintended result
- environmental stress
- software control errors.

The safety requirements and design for a particular system under construction would need to consider all of these possible safety problems. In particular, in determining software requirements, it is necessary to look not only at software control errors, but also to examine the interaction of the software with other components of the system. For example, a control action of the software may only be unsafe in the event of a separate failure of another component of the system or unusual environmental stress. Many (if not most) serious accidents are caused by complex, unplanned (and unfortunate) interactions between components of the system and by multiple failures. That is, most accidents originate in subsystem interfaces [Frola and Miller (1984)]. Therefore, any software safety techniques, especially analysis and verification, are going to have to consider the system as a whole (especially the interactions between the components of the system) and not just the software alone.

SOFTWARE SAFETY REQUIREMENTS ANALYSIS

The problem of determining the requirements for software systems has proved very difficult to solve. However, in terms of safety (and probably most other software qualities), this may be one of the most important sources of problems. Consider the following examples of mishaps or near mishaps:

- In a fly-by-wire flight control system, a mechanical malfunction set up an accelerated environment for which the flight control computer was not programmed. The aircraft went out of control and crashed [Frola and Miller (1984)].
- A computer issued a close door command on an aircraft after maintenance personnel removed a mechanical inhibit but two hours after the command had been given by the pilot -- luckily nobody was standing there at the time [Frola and Miller (1984)].
- Industrial robots have killed or injured humans who entered restricted areas to trouble-shoot or perform maintenance [Fuller (1984)].
- A wing-mounted missile failed to separate from the launcher after ignition because a computer program signalled the missile-retaining mechanism to close before the rocket had built up sufficient thrust to clear the missile from the wing. The aircraft went violently out of control [Frola and Miller (1984)].
- In a computer-controlled batch reactor, the programmers were told that if a fault occurred in the plant, all control variables should be left as they were and an alarm sounded. The computer received a signal that there was a low oil level in a gearbox when it had already added catalyst to the reactor but just as the computer had started to increase the cooling-water flow to the reflux condenser. The computer program did as specified -- the controls were left as they were and an alarm sounded. By the time the operators had responded to the alarm, the reactor had overheated [Kletz (1983)].

One common feature of the above is that the problems can be traced back to a fundamental misunderstanding about the desired operation of the software. These examples are not unusual. Several studies have shown that a majority of production software problems can be traced back to faults in the requirements or design [Boehm et.al (1975), Endres (1975), Lipow (1979)]. After studying actual mishaps where computers were involved, safety engineers have concluded that inadequate design foresight and specification errors are the greatest cause of software safety problems [Ericson (1981), Griggs (1981)]. These problems arise from many possible causes including the difficulty of the problem intrinsically, a lack of emphasis on it in software engineering research (which has tended to concentrate on avoiding or removing implementation faults), and a certain cubbyhole attitude which has led computer scientists to concentrate on the computer aspects of the system and engineers to concentrate on the physical and mechanical parts of the system with few people dealing with the interaction between the two [Ericson (1981)].

Given that requirements errors account for a large number of safety problems, then emphasis needs to be placed on this problem. The software requirements specification usually includes the functional or mission requirements of the system where the *mission* of a system is the culminating operation and fundamental reason for which the system is built and operated. In safety critical applications it must also include the safety requirements, and one of the goals of software hazard analysis is to determine what these are. There are some applications such as pacemakers where the sole purpose of the system is to maintain safety and thus the safety requirements are identical to the mission requirements. However, these systems are in the minority. Most complex, real-time safety-critical software systems have both mission and safety requirements although there may be some overlaps.

While functional requirements often focus on what the system shall do, safety requirements must also include what the system shall *not* do -- including means for eliminating and controlling hazards and for limiting damage in case of a mishap. An important part of the safety requirements is the specification of the ways in which a system can fail safely and to what extent failure is tolerable. One technique which may be helpful with this problem is Fault Tree Analysis.

Fault Tree Analysis (FTA) is an analytical technique used in the safety analysis of electromechanical systems whereby an undesired system state is specified and the system is then analyzed in the context of its environment and operation to find all credible sequences of events which can lead to the undesired state [Vesely et. al. (1981)]. The fault tree is a graphic model of the various parallel and sequential combinations of faults (or system states) that will result in the occurrence of the predefined undesired event. The faults can be events that are associated with component hardware failures, human errors, or any other pertinent events which can lead to the undesired event. A fault tree thus depicts the logical interrelationships of basic events that lead to the undesired event.

One advantage in using this technique is that all the different types of system components (including humans) can be considered. This is extremely important since, for example, a particular software fault may cause a mishap only if there is a simultaneous human and/or hardware failure. Alternatively, the environmental failure may cause the software fault to manifest itself. In many previous mishaps, e.g. the nuclear power plant accident at Three Mile Island, the mishap actually was the result of a sequence of interrelated failures in different parts of the system [Perrow (1984)].

The analysis process starts with the categorized list of system hazards which have been identified by the PHA. The basic procedure involves assuming that the hazard has occurred and then working backward to determine the set of possible causes for the condition to occur. The root of the fault tree is the hazardous event to be analyzed called the "loss event." Necessary preconditions are described at the next level of the tree with either an AND or an OR relationship. Each subnode is expanded in a similar fashion until all leaves describe events of calculable probability or are unable to be analyzed for some reason. Figure 1 shows part of a fault tree for a hospital patient monitoring system.

Once the fault tree has been built down to the software interface (as in figure 1), the high level requirements for software safety have been delineated in terms of software faults and failures which could adversely affect the safety of the system. Software control faults may involve:

- failure to perform a required function, i.e. the function is never executed or no answer is produced
- performing a function not required, i.e. getting the wrong answer or issuing the wrong control instruction or doing the right thing but under inappropriate conditions, for example, activating an actuator inadvertently, too early, too late, or failing to cease an operation at a prescribed time.
- timing or sequencing problems, e.g. it may be necessary to ensure that two things happen at the same time, at different times, or in a particular order.
- failure to recognize a hazardous condition requiring corrective action
- producing the wrong response to a hazardous condition.

As the development of the software proceeds, fault tree analysis can be performed on the design and finally the actual code.

SOFTWARE FAULT TREE ANALYSIS

Once the detailed design or code is completed, software fault tree analysis

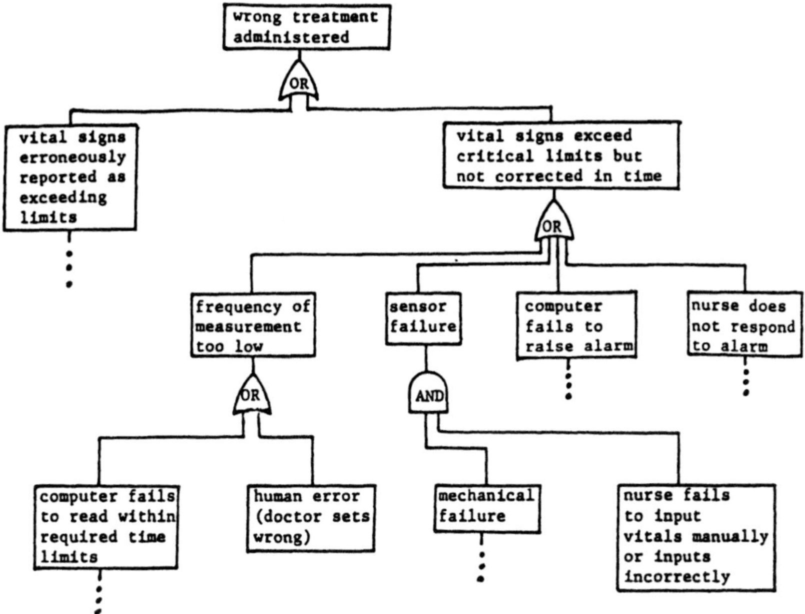

Figure 1. Top Levels of Patient Monitoring System Fault Tree

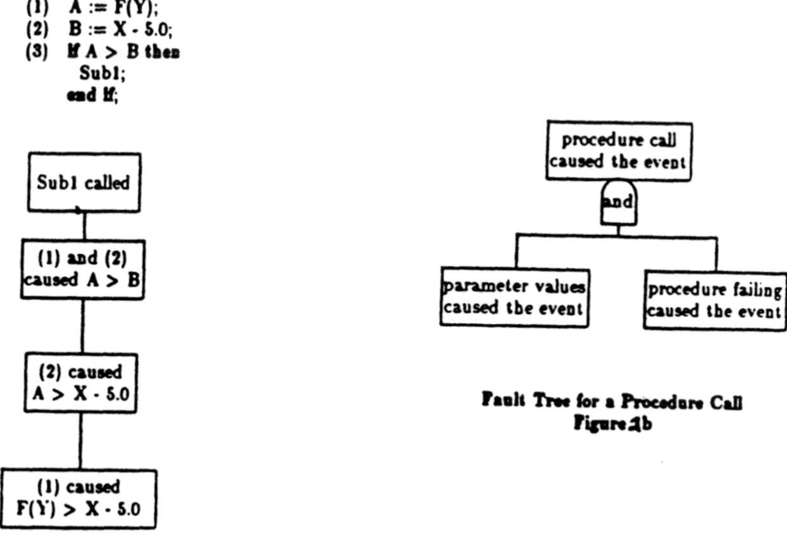

Fault Tree for a Procedure Call
Figure 2b

Fault Tree for Several Assignment Statements
Figure 2a

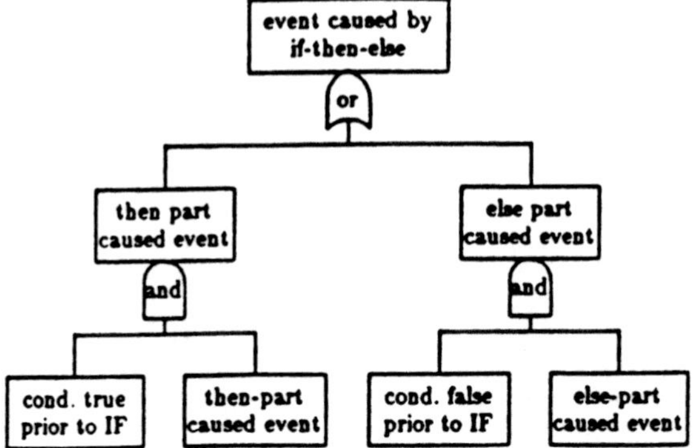

Fault Tree for an If-Then-Else Statement
Figure 2c

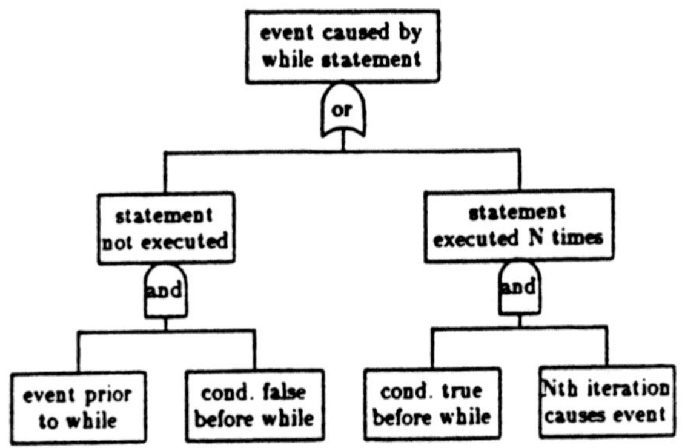

Fault Tree for a While Statement
Figure 2d

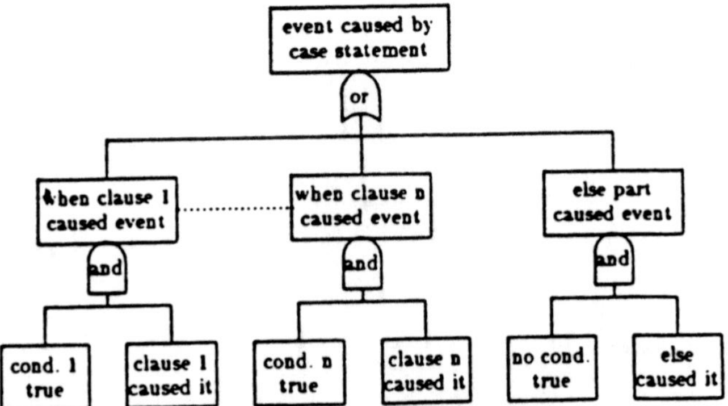

Fault Tree for a Case Statement
Figure 2e

procedures can be used to work backward from the critical control faults determined by the top levels of the fault tree through the program to verify whether the program can cause the top-level event or mishap. The basic technique used is the same backward reasoning (weakest precondition) approach which has been used in formal axiomatic verification [Hoare (1969), Dijkstra (1976)], but applied slightly differently than is common in "proofs of correctness." The set of states or results from a software system can be divided into correct and incorrect. Formal proofs of correctness strive to verify that given a precondition which is true for the state before the program begins to execute, then the program will halt and a postcondition always will be true of the state once the program halts. For continuous, purposely non-halting programs, intermediate states may be considered. That is, the program results in all and only correct states. The basic goal of safety verification is more limited. Given that the incorrect states are divided into two sets -- those which are considered safe and those which are considered unsafe -- proofs of safety attempt to verify that the program will never allow an unsafe state to be reached (although they say nothing about incorrect but safe states).

Since the goal in safety verification is to prove that something will not happen, it is useful to use proof by contradiction. That is, it is assumed that the software has produced an unsafe control action, and it is shown that this could not happen since it leads to a logical contradiction. Although a proof of correctness should theoretically be able to show that software is safe, it is often impractical to do this because of the sheer magnitude of the proof effort involved and because of the difficulty of completely specifying correct behavior. In the few safety proofs which have performed, the proof appears to involve much less work than proof of correctness (especially since the proof procedure can stop as soon as a contradiction is reached on a software path). It is often also easier to specify safety, especially since the requirements may be actually mandated by law or government authority as with nuclear weapon safety requirements in the U.S.

Details on how to construct the trees may be found in Leveson and Harvey (1983) and Taylor (1982). Constructs for some structured programming statements are shown in figure 2. In each, it is assumed that the statement caused the critical event. Then the tree is constructed considering how this might have occurred.

An example of the procedure (taken from Leveson and Stolzy (1983)) is shown in figure 3. An Ada program segment is shown which iteratively solves a fixed point equation. One possible top-level (loss event) for the segment is that no answer is produced in the required time period (and the answer is critical at this point). This loss event corresponds to the **while** loop executing too long (shown in

```
get (X, Eps);

Err := Eps;
I := 0;

while Err ≥ Eps loop

   NewX := F(X);
   Err := abs(X - NewX);
   I := I + 1;
   X := NewX;

end loop;
```

Example of Ada code
Figure 3a

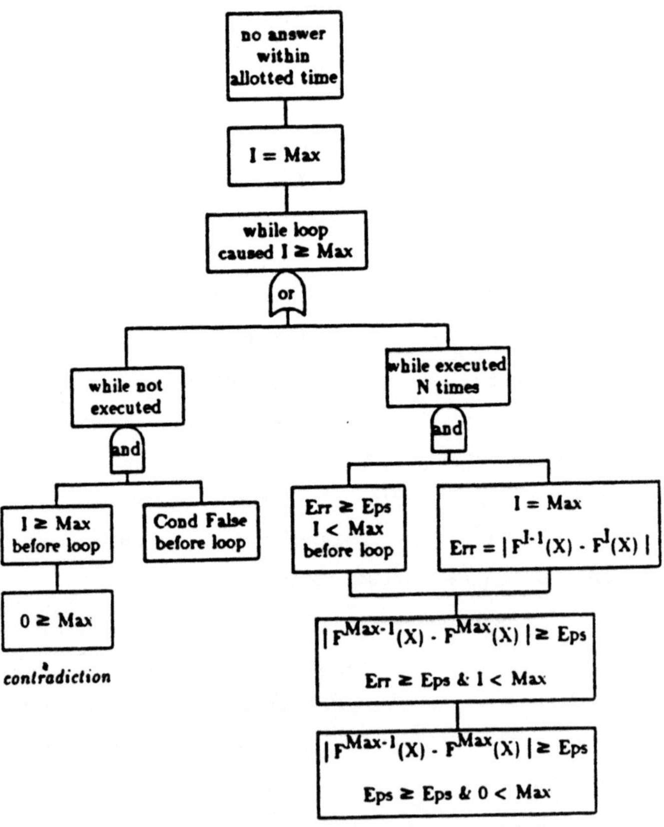

Fault Tree For Example in Figure 3a
Figure 3b

figure 3b as "Max" iterations).

In general, the software fault tree has one or both of the following patterns:

[1] A contradiction is found as shown in the left branch of figure 3b. The building of the software fault tree (at least for this path) can stop at this point since the logic of the software cannot cause the event. This example does not deal with the problem of failures in the underlying implementation of the software, but this is possible. There is of course a practical limit to how much analysis can and need be done depending on individual factors associated with each project. It is always possible to insert assertions in the code to catch critical implementation errors at run-time. This is especially desirable if run-time software-initiated or software-controlled fail-safe procedures are possible. Note that the software fault tree provides the information necessary to determine just what assertions and run-time checks are the most critical and where they should be placed. Since checks at run-time are expensive in terms of time and other resources, this information is extremely useful.

[2] The fault tree runs through the code and out to the controlled system or its environment. In the example of figure 3b, the fault tree shows one possible path to the loss event, and changes are necessary to eliminate the hazard. One appropriate action in this case may be to use run-time assertions to detect such conditions and to simply reject incorrect input or to initiate recovery techniques. Another possibility is to add redundant hardware, e.g. sensors, to eliminate incorrect input before it occurs.

Process control software often contains complex features such as concurrency and real-time constraints. Software fault tree procedures for analyzing concurrency and synchronization are described in [Leveson and Stolzy (1983)]. Introducing timing information into the fault tree causes serious problems. Fault tree analysis is essentially a static analysis technique while timing analysis involves dynamic aspects of the program. For example, analyzing the effects of an Ada **delay** statement requires knowledge of the range of execution times of the code which in turn involves knowledge of the underlying hardware and software systems. Similar problems occur with multi-tasking since the programmer usually is not allowed to make any assumptions about the behavior of the scheduler except that the task will eventually be run (and will have a particular priority if a priority specification is allowed in the programming language).

Taylor [1982] has added timing information to fault trees by making the assumption that information about the minimum and maximum execution time for sections of code is known. Each node in the fault tree then has an added component of execution time for the node. In view of the nondeterminism inherent in a multitasking environment, it may not be practical to verify that timing problems cannot occur in all cases. However, information gained from the fault tree can be used to insert run-time checks including deadline mechanisms into the application program and the scheduler [Leveson and Shimeall (1983)].

The above high-level language fault tree examples have focused on software logic problems. Fault trees can also be applied at the assembly language level to identify computer hardware fault modes (such as erroneous bits in the program counter, registers, or memory) which will cause the software to act in an undesired manner.

In summary, software fault tree analysis can be used to determine software safety requirements, to detect software logic errors, to determine multiple failure sequences involving different parts of the system (hardware, human, and software faults) which can lead to hazards, and to guide in the selection of critical run-time checks. It can also be used to guide testing. This latter is especially useful if used in conjunction with a system simulator. The interfaces of the software parts of the fault tree can be examined to determine appropriate test input data and appropriate simulation states and events.

Experimental evidence of the practicality of SFTA is lacking. Examples of two small systems can be found in the literature [Leveson and Harvey (1983), McIntee (1983)]. But even if the software system is so large that complete generation of the software trees is not possible, partial trees may still be useful. For example, partially complete software fault trees may be used to identify critical modules and critical functions which can then be augmented with software fault tolerance procedures [Hecht and Hecht (1982)]. They may also be used to determine appropriate run-time acceptance and safety tests. Although checking for complete correctness may not be practical, SFTA can provide information on minimal checks necessary to at least provide safe (if not totally correct) operation.

SAFETY ANALYSIS USING PETRI NETS

Another technique which has been proposed for hazard analysis involves the use of Petri nets. Petri nets [Peterson (1981)] allow mathematical modeling of discrete-event systems in which a system is modeled in terms of conditions and events and the relationship between them. Analysis and simulation procedures have been developed to determine desirable and undesirable properties of the design especially with respect to concurrent or parallel events. Leveson and Stolzy (1985a, 1985b) have developed analysis procedures to determine software safety requirements (including timing requirements) directly from the system design, to analyze a design for safety, recoverability, and fault tolerance, and to guide in the use of failure detection and recovery procedures. Procedures are also being developed to measure the risk of individual hazards.

Some of the potential advantages of using Petri net models include:

- They can be used early in the development cycle so that changes may be made while still relatively inexpensive.
- A system approach is possible with Petri nets since hardware, software, and human behavior can be modeled using the same language.
- Petri nets can be used at various levels of abstraction.
- Petri nets provide a modeling language which can be used for both formal analysis and simulation.
- Adding time and probabilities to basic Petri nets allows incorporation of timing and probabilistic information into the analysis.
- The model may be used to analyze the system for other features besides safety.

In a Petri net, the system is modelled in terms of conditions and events. If certain conditions hold, then an event or "state transition" will take place. After the transition, other (or the same) conditions will hold. A condition (called a "place" in Petri net terminology) is represented by a circle "O" and an event or transition by a bar. An arrow from a condition (or place) to a transition indicates that the condition is an input (or pre-condition) to the transition. Similarly, a post-condition is indicated by an arrow from the transition to the condition. Figure 4 shows a simple example. It says that if conditions A and B hold, then the transition can "fire." After it fires, then conditions B and C will hold.

The Petri net model can be "executed" to see how the design will actually work. "Tokens" represented by a dot "●" are used to indicate that a condition is currently true. Thus if a condition holds, it will contain a token. In the example in figure 5, transition t_1 cannot fire because P_1 does not have a token. But all the pre-conditions for t_2 are currently true (i.e. P_2 and P_3), so t_2 can fire. Figure 6 shows the next state of the Petri net. When t_2 fires, the tokens are removed from the pre-conditions and a token is deposited in each of the post-conditions. In the

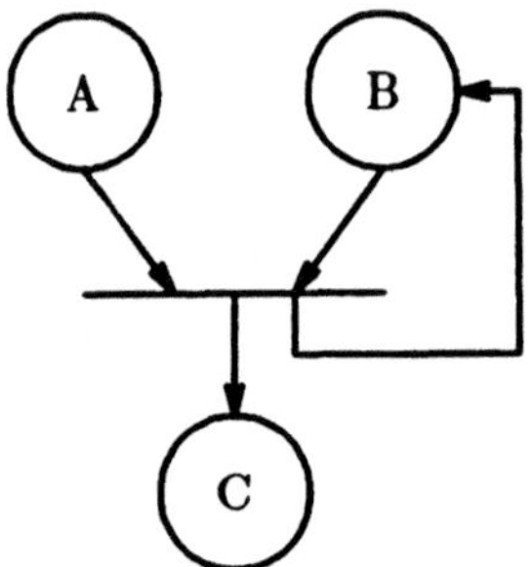

Figure 4.

example, the only post-condition is P_5. Note that it is possible for the same condition to be both a pre-condition and a post-condition for a transition. If a transition has no pre-conditions, then it can fire at will.

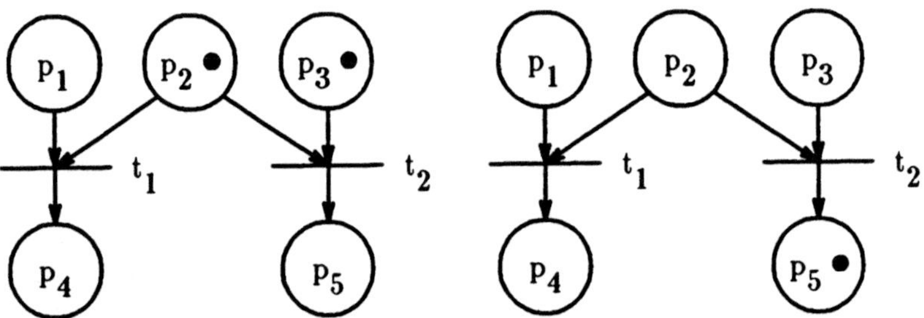

Figure 5. Example Petri Net Figure 6. The Next State

During the execution of the Petri net, the "state" of the system at any time consists of the set of conditions which contain tokens. Starting from some initial state, the Petri net model can be executed showing all the legal states (sets of conditions) that the system can "reach." This information can be depicted graphically in a "reachability graph," i.e. a graph that shows the possible state sequences from a given initial state. If the design is non-deterministic (i.e. the order of the transitions or events is not constrained by the design), then the graph will have branches for the different possible orderings of events. Figures 7 and 8 show a Petri net and the corresponding reachability graph for a simple model of a railroad crossing where the left part of the model represents the train, and the middle part represents the actions of the computer which is controlling the crossing guard gate (which is on the right). The reachability graph shows that the design is flawed (from a safety standpoint) since it is possible for the train to be at the crossing and the crossing guard gate to be up at the same time. That is, there are two reachable states where both P_3 and P_{11} hold. Note that it also shows the sequence of events which can lead to this hazard so that appropriate measures can be taken to avoid it.

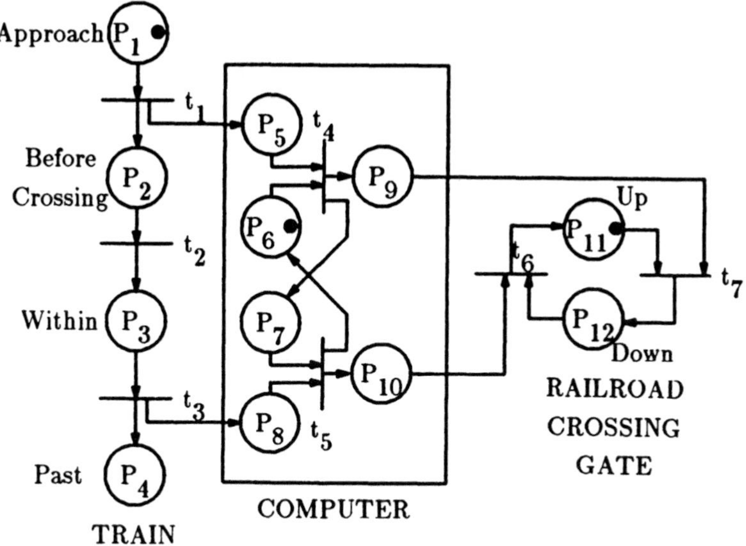

Figure 7. A Petri Net Graph

Although creating the entire reachability graph will show whether the system as designed can reach any hazardous states, in practice the graph is often too large to generate completely. However, it is possible to use the same type of backward analysis used in fault trees. Details of an algorithm to do this can be found in Leveson and Stolzy (1985a).

Briefly, the algorithm starts with the set of unsafe conditions. For each member of this set, the immediately prior state or states are generated from the inverse Petri net. Each of these "one-step-backward" states is then examined to see if it is potentially a *critical state* (a state from which there is both a path or paths from which it is possible to reach unsafe and possibly also safe states and a path or paths from which it is possible to reach only low-risk states). This can be used to eliminate one path to the high-risk state. Note that we start not with complete states but only with partial states. That is, some conditions in the state are unimportant as far as safety is concerned, and therefore it is not known at the beginning of the algorithm the complete composition of the reachable unsafe states (the complete states from which to start the backward analysis). The "don't-care" places in each state are "filled in" with those conditions which are possible in the process of executing the algorithm. Note that it is necessary only to look forward

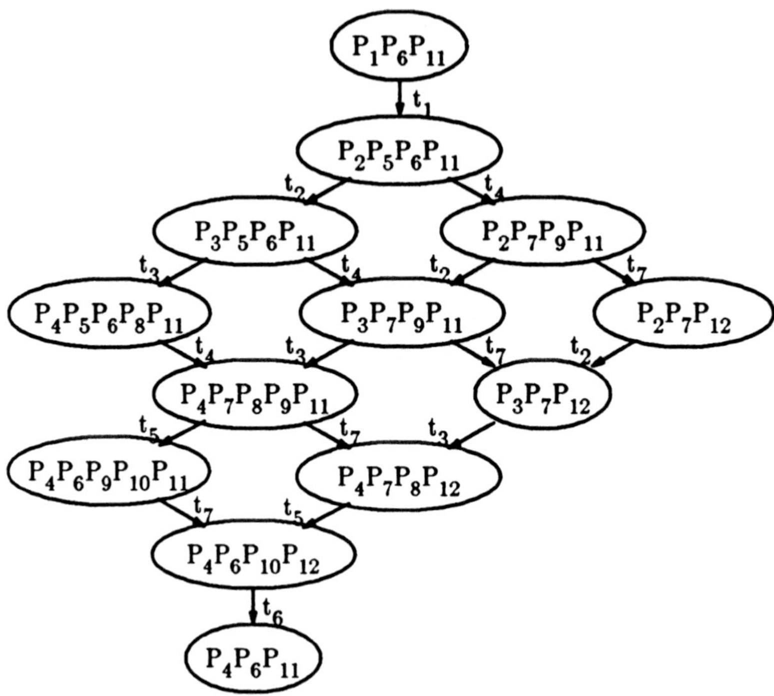

Figure 8. Reachability Graph for Figure 7

one step from each potentially critical state in order to label it as critical (i.e. there exists a next-state which is safe). This is true because if this path also leads to an unsafe state, then it will be eliminated by the algorithm in a later step.

The technique is conservative, i.e. in order to reduce the large amount of computing to produce the complete graph, a larger number of critical states may be identified than actually exist. But it does no harm to eliminate the possibility of a mishap which would not have occurred. Also, eliminating a non-existent path may have the effect of eliminating or lessening the possibility of mishaps caused by run-time faults and failures.

Hazards which have been determined by the analysis to be plausible can be eliminated by appropriately altering the design to ensure that paths (sequences of events) which will lead to the hazard are not taken. For example, an interlock to ensure that one transition or event always precedes another is shown in figure 9. Figure 10 shows the Petri net equivalent of a lockout (i.e. a design feature that ensures that two conditions, in this case conditions P_3 and P_4, do not hold at the same time).

Faults and failures can be incorporated into the model to determine their

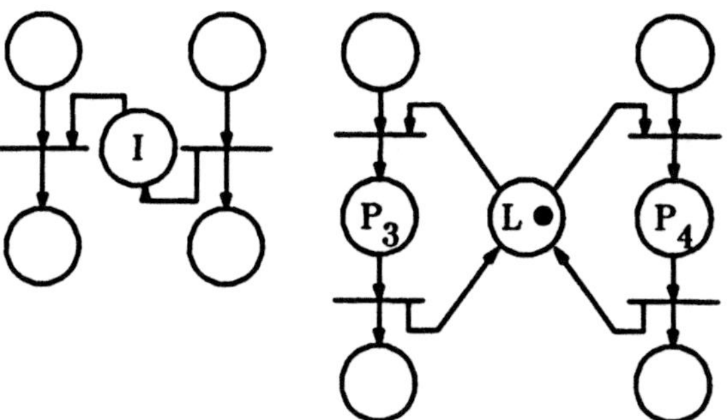

Figure 9. Interlock Figure 10. Locking Place

effect on the system [Leveson and Stolzy (1985b)]. Backward analysis procedures can be used to determine which failures and faults are potentially the most costly and therefore which parts of the system need to be augmented with fault-tolerance and fail-safe mechanisms. Early in the design of the system, it is possible to treat the software parts of the design at a very high level of abstraction, i.e. only failures at the interfaces of the software and non-software components may be considered. By working backward to this software interface, it is possible to determine the software safety requirements and to determine which functions are most critical.

Timing has been added to Petri net models by putting minimum and maximum time limits on transitions or by putting times on conditions. Either way, it is possible to determine worst case timing requirements so that, for example, watchdog timers can be incorporated into the design if necessary.

Finally, when probabilities are included in the model, minimal cut sets and other probabilistic information is obtainable.

CONCLUSIONS

There is much more to be learned about how to build safe computer-controlled systems. This chapter has tried to outline some of what is known or has been suggested to date. Some of these approaches have been tested and used extensively while others are still in the development stage.

There are still many open questions such as:

- Are these techniques useful and practical for real systems (not just the toy examples in research papers)?

- For systems of what size and level of complexity are they useful?
- How can they be extended to provide more information?
- How can they most effectively be used in software development projects?
- What other approaches to software hazard analysis are possible?

Much important work remains to be done in extending and testing these proposed techniques and in developing new ones.

REFERENCES

[1] Boehm, B.W., McClean, R.L. and Urfig, D.B. Some Experiments with Automated Aids to the Design of Large-Scale Reliable Software. *IEEE Transactions on Software Engineering*, SE-1, no. 2, 1975, pp. 125-133.

[2] Dijkstra, E. *A Discipline of Programming*. Prentice Hall, 1976.

[3] Dunham, J.R. and J.C. Knight (editors). Production of Reliable flight-crucial software. *Proc. of Validation Methods Research for Fault-Tolerant Avionics and Control Systems Sub-Working-Group Meeting*, Research Triangle Park, North Carolina, Nov. 2-4, 1981, NASA Conference Publication 2222.

[4] Endres, A.B. An Analysis of Errors and Their Causes in Software Systems. *IEEE Transactions on Software Engineering*, SE-1, no. 2, 1975, pp. 140-149.

[5] Ericson, C.A. Software and System Safety. Proc. 5th Int. System Safety Conf., Denver, 1981, vol. 1, part 1, pp. III-B-1 to III-B-11.

[6] Frola, F.R. and Miller, C.O. System Safety in Aircraft Management. Logistics Management Institute, Washington D.C., January 1984.

[7] Fuller, J.G. Death by Robot. *Omni*, vol. 6, no. 6, March 1984, pp. 45-46, 97-102.

[8] Griggs, J.G. A Method of Software Safety Analysis. Proc. 5th Int. System Safety Conf., vol. 1, part 1, Denver, 1981, pp. III-D-1 to III-D-18.

[9] Hecht, H. and Hecht, M. Use of Fault Trees for the Design of Recovery Blocks. *Proceeding of 12th Symposium on Fault Tolerant Computing*, Santa Monica, June 1982, pp. 134-139.

[10] Hoare, C.A.R. An Axiomatic Basis for Computer Programming. *Communications of the ACM*, vol. 12, October 1969, pp. 576-580

[11] Kletz, T. Human problems with computer control, *Hazard Prevention* (The Journal of the System Safety Society, MarchApril 1983, pp. 24-26.

[12] Leveson, N.G. and Harvey, P.R. Analyzing Software Safety. *IEEE Transactions on Software Engineering*, vol. SE-9, no. 5, September 1983, pp. 569-579.

[13] Leveson, N.G. and Shimeall, T.J. Safety Assertions for Process Control Systems. *Proc. 13th International Conference on Fault-Tolerant Computing*, Milan, June 1983.

[14] Leveson, N.G. and Stolzy, J.L. Analyzing Ada Programs using Fault Trees, *IEEE Transactions on Reliability*, December 1983.

[15] Leveson, N.G. and Stolzy, J.L. Analyzing Safety and Fault Tolerance using Time Petri Nets. *TAPSOFT: Joint Conference on Theory and Practice of Software Development*, Berlin, March 1985a.

[16] Leveson, N.G. and Stolzy, J.L. Safety Analysis using Petri Nets, *Proc. 15th Int. Symposium on Fault Tolerant Computing*, June 1985b.

[17] Lipow, M. Prediction of Software Errors. *Journal of Systems and Software*, vol. 1, 1979, pp. 71-75.

[18] McIntee, J.W. Fault Tree Technique as Applied to Software (SOFT TREE), BMO/AWS, Norton Air Force Base, CA. 92409.

[19] Perrow, C. *Normal Accidents*. New York: Basic Books, Inc., 1984.

[20] Peterson, J.L. *Petri Net Theory and the Modeling of Systems*. New York: Prentice Hall, 1981.

[21] Ramamoorthy, C.V., G.S. Ho, and Y.W. Han. Fault Tree Analysis of Computer Systems. *Proc. of NCC*, 1977, pp. 13-17.

[22] Taylor, J.R. Fault Tree and Cause Consequence Analysis for Control Software Validation. RISO-M-2326, Riso National Laboratory, DK-4000 Roskilde, Denmark, January 1982.

[23] Vesely, W.E., F.F. Goldberg, N.H. Roberts, and D.F. Haasl. *Fault Tree Handbook*, *NUREG-0492, U.S. Nuclear Regulatory Commission, January* 1981.

DATA SECURITY

by

D.W. Davies, C.B.E.

Data Security Consultant
Fair Winds
15 Hawkewood Road,
Sudbury-on-Thames
Middlesex TW16 6HL. U.K.

Threats to Information Systems

Now that digital information processing, storage and transmission are an essential part of all our activities, the threats to these systems from unwanted or illegal activity are growing.

Data bases now hold valuable commercial information which could be stolen by a competitor. Some companies exist to provide information services (such as financial or travel information) and their livelihood could be threatened by stealing and re-selling this information. Even entertainment can be threatened because broadcast television programmes are sold to subscribers and must be protected from non-subscribers.

Another kind of attack is the production of fraudulent records or transactions. It is obvious that high value payments need to be protected, as they are in the SWIFT and CHAPS networks. A recent example was an attempted jail break carried out by a trusted inmate of a US prison who was able to alter the date recorded for his release. He tried to change this from January 1985 to before Christmas 1984, a modest and worthy ambition which failed when he was overheard talking about it. He later claimed to have secured the early release of some of his friends and this was still being investigated at the time of the newspaper report.

Another type of attack is to threaten the destruction of a system. Important computer systems are protected against physical attack but a logical attack could be difficult to diagnose and prevent, and the threat would enable money to be obtained by extortion. In one example, vital tapes were stolen but the extortionist gave up before being paid. Note that all published examples seem to fail, which is because the successful ones are either undetected or the victim does not want to let them be known.

Vunerabilities of Information Systems

Information sytems are very complex with many components and almost every component can be used by the attacker. A communication network is difficult to protect physically and is therefore the most vunerable target. The protection of communications by encipherment and related techniques will be the main theme of this paper.

NATO ASI Series, Vol. F22
Software System Design Methods. Edited by J.K. Skwirzynski

Where an attack only reveals information but does not change any of the messages in the network it is called a "passive" attack. Usually, this is technically quite easy to do, trivially so where radio is used, as in business satellite systems. The more difficult form of attack attempts to change the data while it travels though the network and this "active" attack can be worth the extra trouble if valuable data or transactions can be altered for the benefit of the attacker.

Local networks are particularly vunerable because they employ a form of broadcast technique. An Ethernet sends its messages through all parts of the network and the ring or loop network, in its commonest form, makes each message travel round the whole ring.

Attacks on information storage can be classified in the same way and most of the techniques for safeguarding information on communication network apply equally, or in a corresponding way to stored information.

Terminals and storage media are another vulnerable component. In particular, the bugging of terminals or the use of their natural radiation can be a potent method of stealing information.

Every part of an information system is controlled by software and the integrity of this software is an essential part of its protection mechanism. Changes to the software can remove protection, for example by changing a table which records access rights. The possibilities for attack via the software are limitless but even crude measures can be a dangerous threat. Software "bombs" can be arranged to trigger at a particular date, in response to a special stimulous given as part of a normal transaction.

The security of a system depends on its people and therefore on i dentifying the person who is transacting with it at a terminal. The verification of personal identity is perhaps the least understood aspect of data security and lack of space prevents us from treating it here except for the warning that passwords are not the whole answer.

Attacks on Communication Systems

A "passive" attack could consist of tapping a line, listening to a radio signal, stealing or copying a floppy disk or looking over the shoulder of someone as he logs in. The aim is to obtain information for which access is normally denied.

"Passive" attacks can be frustrated, in many cases, by cryptography. Reading an enciphered message in a communication system cannot be prevented but the value to the attacker is lost. Nevertheless, in some cases the mere existence of a message from a particular source to a particular destination, with perhaps a knowledge of the approximate size of the message, could be valuable information. It seems uncertain how much this 'traffic information' matters in commercial systems. A more extreme example of concealment is to prevent an attacker knowing that a communication channel exists. The significance for us is that concealment of a channel is always possible and security measures must reckon with this fact. For example, sensitive encryption functions could be carried out in a highly secure environment but if the software has been tampered with it

could read out important key variables, at a low rate, by using redundant bits in messages or timing or any other inconspicuous features.
In experiments on military systems, clandestine channels of about 300 bit/s were produced by interaction through the timing of calls on the operating system.

Protection against "active" attacks proves to be quite subtle because of the variety of attack method. The obvious attacks consist of inserting messages, changing message content or deleting messages. Other attacks which have to be considered are the replaying of old messages or changing message sequence. These can be effective, even though the messages concerned are in cipher. Finally, the origin of a message can be falsified or a false acknowledgement produced. A message deletion can sometimes be concealed if the acknowledgement is falsified.

Cryptography - Frustration of Passive Attacks

We shall be considering the kind of cryptography known as a "cipher" which is the employment of an algorithm to transform data into unreadable form and a corresponding inverse algorithm to restore it to its plaintext form. In considering the strength of a cipher we always assume that the algorithm is known to the enemy. Many commercial systems employ a standard algorithm which certainly is known but even confidential algorithms, when they have been in use a long time, cannot be regarded as secret any more. The secrecy of data is preserved by making both the encipherment and the decipherment function depend on a secret key. The key must be known to sender and receiver. The need for secrecy in transmitting a stream of messages has been transformed into a requirement for the secret transfer of just one key.

Historically the most common form of cipher is a stream cipher, an example of which is shown in Figure 1. P is a stream of plaintext bits or characters which is transformed by modulo 2 addition (XOR) using a Key Stream, which is generated in a special way. At the receiving end, a similar function restores the plain text. This will be a perfect cipher if the Key Stream were entirely random but since it must be generated by an algorithm, we can only hope for a psuedo-random sequence and design it so that repetition of an earlier part of the sequence is impossible or very improbable. Both key sequence generators employ the secret key in order that they are not compromised merely by a knowledge of the algorithm. If transmission using the same key always began in the same way, generating the same bit sequence, an easy attack would be possible, given a moderate amount of redundancy in the plaintext message. For this reason, each transmission begins with an initialising variable (IV) which sets the internal state of the key sequence generator and, with high probability, does not allow its key sequence to repeat. Usually, the initialising variable can be transmitted in clear form across the network and a random value is generated for this purpose at the beginning of each session. There must be a limitation on the number and length of sessions allowable with a given key.

Figure 1

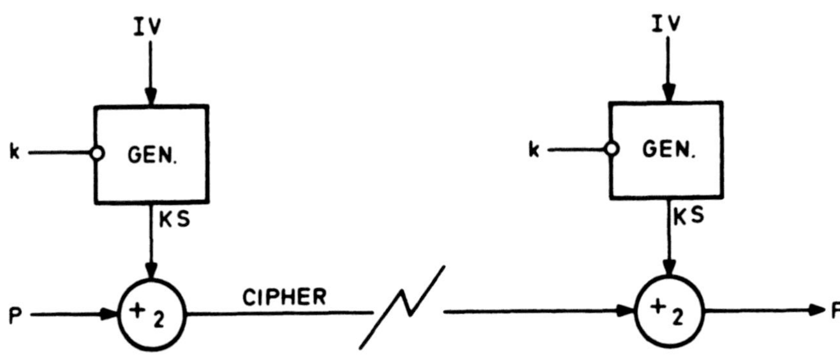

A Stream Cipher

Stream ciphers have been much used, but much of the modern development of commercial cryptography has centred around block ciphers typified by the Data Encryption Standard algorithm introduced first for non-classified US Government operations and subsequently adopted as an ANSI standard and a de facto standard for banking. It is now being considered as an ISO standard under the title "Data Encipherment Algorithm No. 1".

The DES or DEA 1 employs a 56 bit key (with 8 parity bits added) and enciphers a 64 bit block. Figure 2 shows, with some simplifications, the principle of its design. The 64 bit block is divided into two sections of 32 bits denoted by L and R in the Figure. Each is enciphered by a sequence of modulo 2 additions using a complex function F and a sequence of "subkeys" derived in a simple way from the 56 bit key. Each operation employing F is called a "round" and there are 16 rounds using subkeys k1 to k16. Finally, the two sections of data are interchanged to form the L and R content of the result. It will easily be seen that this method of computation produces an exact inverse if the sequence of sub-keys k1 to k16 is reversed.

The DES has been the subject of very careful study by many experts without revealing any serious weaknesses in its basic structure. Of the many critical comments which have been made, there are two significant ones.

Assuming there are no other weaknesses in the cipher, an attack is possible when corresponding plain and cipher text is known by searching through all possible values of the key to find which one matches this result. A search of 2^{56} possibilities, even with a very fast implementation, would take a very long time but as semi-conductor logic improves its performance or reduces its cost, the feasibility of this direct attack by searching increases, particularly if the time available

Figure 2

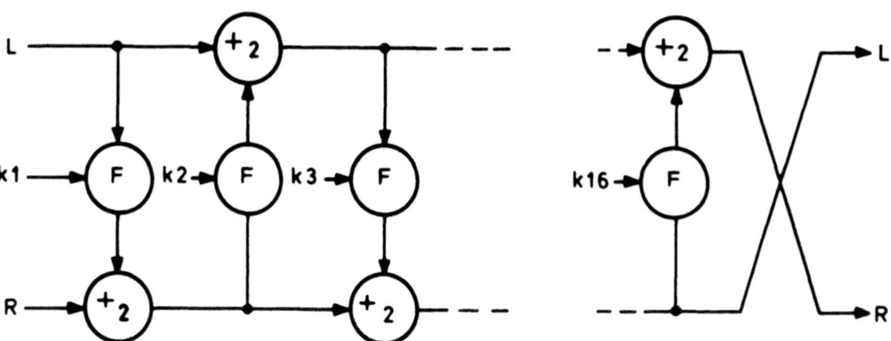

Simplified Form of the DES

for finding a solution is measured in months or years other than hours or days. As technology progresses, the DES, like all ciphers, must become weaker in this respect. The key size of 56 bits, it is said, leaves little margin.

A second criticism concerns the very simple way in which the subkeys are derived from the given 56-bit key. Because of this simplicity, there are 4 key values, called weak keys which give the same values for all the sub-keys and therefore make encipherment and decipherment the same function. Additionally, there are 6 pairs of keys called "semi-weak" keys in which encipherment by one key of the pair equals decipherment by the other. Other regularities have been observed in the structure of the cipher which were, apparently, not observed by its designers but these seem to have no functional effect.

The weak and semi-weak key phenomenon can be avoided by key selection if it is considered significant. Therefore the only inescapable disadvantage of the DES, according to its critics, is its key size.

To avoid this problem it has been suggested that double encipherment, using two different keys, should be used. This might be thought to give the effect of a cipher of key size 112 bits. Unfortunately, this is not quite the case as Figure 3 illustrates. This shows a known plain text enciphered by key k1 then by key k2 to produce a known ciphertext C.

Give the values of P and C, the attacker can apply all possible values of k1 to the encipherment of P and produce a table 2^{56} entries shown. He can also apply decipherment to C with all possible values of k2 to produce another table of 2^{56} entries. Any possible set of key values k1 and k2 whic match the plaintext - ciphertext pair will be shown by the equality of two values, one from each table. Such equality is easy to determine without an expensive search, by sorting the tables into order. In order

Figure 3

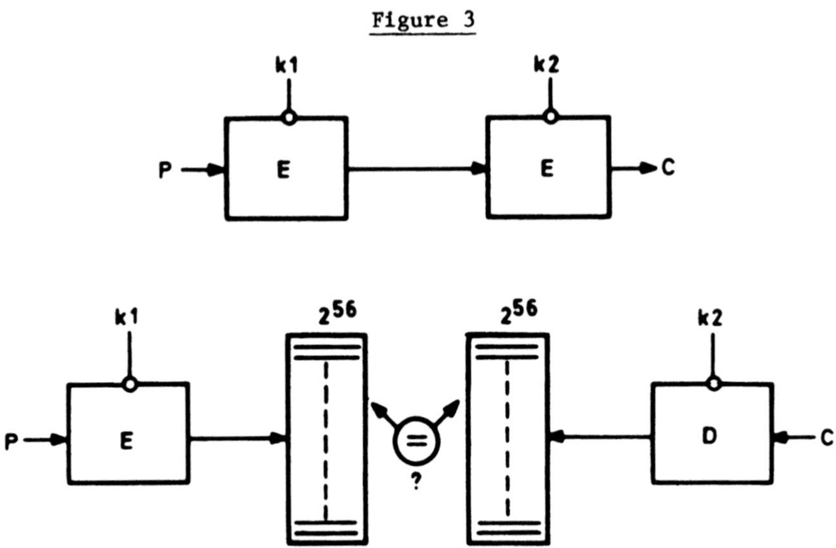

Meet-in-the-Middle Attack

to interpret the result, each entry in the table must be be labelled with its key value. The result of the calculation we have described will not be unique because only 64 bits of data are being used to determine 112 bits of key. There will be approximately 2^{48} solutions for the key pair. In order to obtain a unique key, these must be tested again with a second pair of matching plaintext and ciphertext blocks.

The calculation we have described is not enormously greater in processing requirements than the search for a single key but it does involve the storage in fast access memory of very large tables. Therefore, double encipherment is considerably stronger than single encipherment, but not equivalent to the use of a 112 bit key.

To produce an encipherment by a double key which is closer to what is required, the treble encipherment method shown in Figure 4 has been devised and is now incorporated in a draft key management standard. This employs encipherment followed by decipherment followed by encipherment with the keys kl, k2, kl respectively. Decipherment uses the same keys with the EDE sequence replaced by DED. There are theoretical methods for attacking this cipher in the way shown in Figure 3, but they depend on being able to exercise the treble encryption for each entry in the tables so they cannot be regarded as practical. Though nothing is certain in cryptography, it seems that this treble encryption with a double key will give the Data Encryption Standard the extra strength it needs where keys are employed for a long period, as in the higher levels of key management. It would not normally be used for encipherment of data or even for lower level keys.

We have emphasised the Data Encryption Standard because of its wide use in banking and because it is the only published standard. Many dislike the whole concept of an encryption standard, because the algorithm is so exposed, and they use private algorithms instead. Many encryption

Figure 4

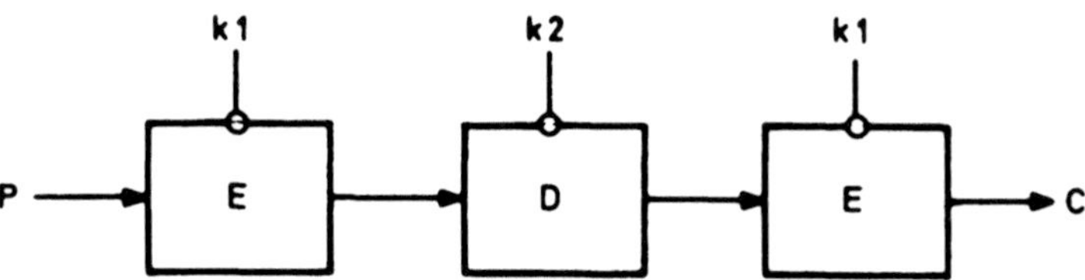

A Proposed Encipherment with 2 Keys

equipments use proprietary ciphers which are held as commercial secrets. With cheap and fast micro-computers it is possible to devise reasonably effective ciphers that can be implemented as a program. The use of programmed ciphers has been criticised because the stored keys are not as physically secure as those held in an encryption chip. Where a micro-processor is dedicated to the encryption functions and held in a physically secure enclosure, the loss of security in this respect is minimised.

The message which requires encipherment may be longer than 64 bits, perhaps many times longer, yet the DES enciphers only 64 bits at a time. Breaking the message into 64 bit blocks and enciphering them individually is not a satisfactory method. All messages have redundancy, for example they may consist of streams of ASCII characters and then any eight consecutive characters which recurred in the message within discrete 64 bit blocks would show as equal cipher text blocks. Examples of commonly recurring sequences are strings of zeros or spaces. This is sometimes described as the "dictionary" attack on a cipher. With this method of encipherment, the sequence of enciphered blocks could be changed with an easily predictable effect on plain text. If the message format if known, pieces of one message could be extracted and substituted in another.

To overcome these problems, a method of using the DES called "Cipher Block Chaining" has been standardised. This is shown in Figure 5. When enciphering a string of blocks, the ciphertext resulting from each block is modulo 2 added to the next plaintext block before that one is enciphered. The 64 bit register shown in the figure simply illustrates that the block employed comes from the previous operation. In the decipherment of the message at the receiving end, cipher text blocks are delayed by one block and added into the resulting plain text. It is obvious from the symmetry of the diagram that, provided that no errors occur in transmission, plaintext will be restored in this manner. The cipher text now depends on all the preceeding plaintext blocks, because of the feedback path in encipherment. A dictionary attack fails because plain text is changed in a "psuedo-random" way before entering encipherment. Also, the blocks are linked or "chained" in a way which prevents a juggling with their sequence or taking them out of context.

Figure 5

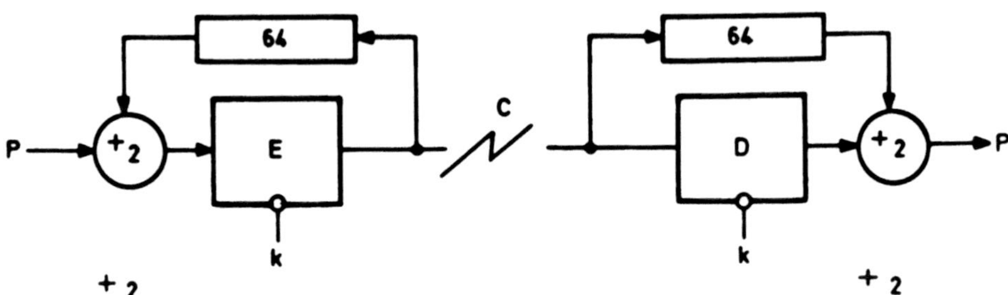

Cipher Block Chaining

If the first block of plain text were to enter the encipherment unchanged (that is to say the initial value in the register was zero) then a dictionary attack would be possible on the first block. This is the part of messages which tends to be repetitive. Furthermore, if the first block tends to repeat, then for its commonest values a dictionary attack on the second block becomes possible, and so forth. To avoid this, the first block in a message should be designed to contain variable data, such as a sequence number. It would also be possible to use a variation in the initial value in the register but this value would have to be communicated in secret at the beginning of the message. In practice, a secret initialising value (IV) is used but, by convention, this is held constant during the life of a given key and is transmitted in cipher at the time that the new key is established.

The cipher block chaining method is "self synchronizing" in the sense that ciphertext errors, though they affect two consecutive blocks, do not produce a permanent effect on the system. Most systems which use this method of operation would reject any sequence of blocks which contained an error, therefore the self-synchronizing property is not used in practice.

There are two other methods of operation used for different purposes, called Cipher Feedback and Output Feedback which are not described here. Reference 1 contains more details about the structure of the DES, the modes of operation proposed in standards and the application of the cipher in networks.

Authentication - Detection of Active Attacks

By means of authentication we hope to preserve the integrity of messages. This has two aspects, ensuring that the message received has not been altered (or detecting if an alteration has taken place) and verifying the identity of the sender. Either of these precautions, by itself, is little use and they have to go together. Authentication can be extended further to the whole of the transaction, defending the integrity of the messages and their sequence and ensuring that each party correctly identifies the other.

Sometimes we require both authentication and encipherment and this will be considered later but a very frequent requirement is to authenticate messages or transactions without encipherment. When messages are enciphered, no part of the system can act on them without a knowledge of the secret key. Installing this key in too many places reduces its security. When messages have to be handled by several parties, but finally acted upon by only one that is vitally concerned with their integrity, authentication of cleartext messages has the advantage. It is the commonest approach for payment messages generally. An authenticator is calculated and travels with the message to be checked at the receiving end. Figure 6 shows the arrangement. An algorithm A is provided, and is known to both parties, together with a secret key k which only they know. At the sending end, the authentication function is applied with the secret key to the whole text of the message and generates a number A, typically of 32 bits, which is transmitted. At the receiving end, the same algorithm and key are applied to the message and the message is accepted if the received value of A agrees with the locally computed one.

Figure 6

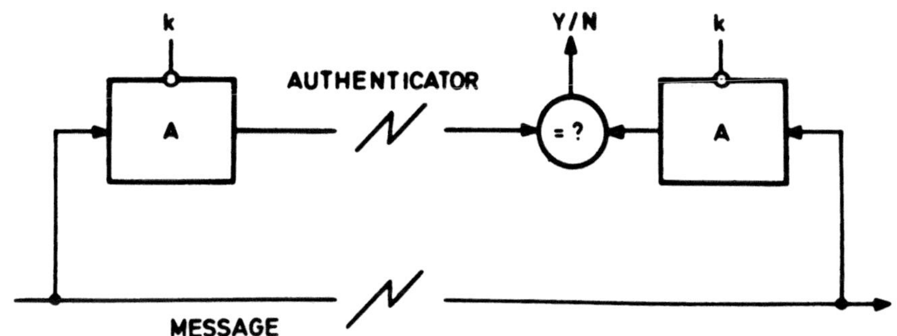

Principle of Authentication

The algorithm A should be such that the key cannot be discovered even though a number of examples of the message M and the authenticator A are available to the attacker. Indeed, a good algorithm should be safe even if the attacker can choose any messages and be given the corresponding authenticator. The second requirement is that it should not be possible to find different messages which correspond to a given authenticator, without knowledge of the key. A name which is often used for the authenticator is "message authentication code" or MAC. It is not strictly a code but is more like a cipher in its operation, except that no inverse is required.

An example of an authentication algorithm is provided by the cipher block chaining mode mentioned above. An initialising variable of zero can be used and the whole message run through the CBC encipherment operation. The ciphertext in the last complete block is then a cryptographic function of the whole message, due to the feedback, and this or part of it can be employed as an authenticator. A number of other authenticator algorithms are in use; some, like that of SWIFT are not public knowledge, some like the 'Data Seal' are commercially exploited and there are a few algorithms which are candidates for standardisation and therefore public knowledge. One of these is called "Decimal Shift and Add" (DSA) and is designed for a programmed decimal calculator. Its purpose is to operate in small, hand-held calculators where other machinery for calculating authenticators is not available. One version of it will be employed in home banking in Germany. Based on the same principle as DSA, an algorithm was designed for a 32 bit computer exploiting the multiplication function. This is called the Message Authenticator Algorithm (MAA) and has received some independent testing.

Checking the authenticator verifies whether the message has been altered in the communication network. The secret key employed can identify the origin of a message if it assumed that the key is available only to the authorised sender. Protection against replay and re-sequencing attacks can be obtained by including in every message a sequence number and checking the regularity of the sequence at the receiving point. A full understanding of authentication in a given context requires analysis of the whole protocol, key management and user identification. What we have described is a typical set of precautions which, in certain circumstances, are sufficient.

Where both authentication and encipherment are required, one approach is to employ two secret keys and append an authenticator to the message before it is enciphered. Given the right kind of cipher, authentication can be obtained as a by-product of encipherment, with less computation. Some kinds of stream cipher are not suitable. For example, a stream cipher as shown in Figure 1 allows controlled changes to be made to the plain text simply by modifying the appropriate bits of the cipher text. If the entire format is known, useful changes can often be made to the plain text message, for example, a payment amount can be increased by changing a high order bit from zero to one. Cipher block chaining prevents this kind of attack, so any change made to the cipher text will produce an apparently random change to the resultant plain text. Therefore, if a suitable redundancy check is made in the plain text, this should authenticate the message.

Acting on this principle, the NBS proposed redundancy check which was a modulo 2 sum of 16 bit words. This proved to be unsuitable for the CBC mode of operation, since there were a number of modifications to cipher text which could be designed to prevent detection. For example, two 64 bit blocks (other than the last block) can be interchanged and the effect on the plain text sum cancels out. This is because each ciphertext block contributes two parts to the plain text sum, one from the deciphered block and one from the feed forward path. When the blocks are interchanged in the cipher text, their contributions to the plaintext simply arrive in a different order and the sum is unchanged. This is an unfortunate mistake which illustrates the care needed in the design of secure systems. No decision has been made on a replacement for the NBS proposal, but in a recent draft standard the sum check is formed as a CBC authenticator using a standard key which is, in hex characters, the increasing sequence 0 1 2 3 . . . E F, which has the odd parity required for a DES key. This method of authentication requires, in effect, two encryption processes for the entire message.

As with authentication alone, the use of encryption combined with authentication requires other precautions such as a sequence number, proper key management, authentication of acknowledgements etc. and good authentication is a property of the entire protocol, not just the method of treating the messages.

Public Key Cryptography

A classical or symmetric cipher employs the same secret key in both the encipherment and the decipherment algorithm. A public key cipher, illustrated in Figure 7 employs two different keys of which the encipherment key is generally called a Public Key while the decipherment key must be a secret key. In order that the encipherment and decipherment shall be mutually inverse, the public key pk and the secret key sk must be related and they are derived by a known algorithm from a random seed value. The three parts of the algorithm, the key generation, encipherment and decipherment are all public and the secrecy depends on the secrecy of the seed value and the secret key. A remarkable property of public ciphers is that the encipherment key need not be kept secret. In the best known example, the RSA cipher it happens that the encipherment and decipherment algorithms are identical.

All aspects of the encipherment process, including its key, are public yet a knowledge of the cipher text should not enable the plain text to be discovered. It follows that the algorithm, with its known key constitute a one-way function - a function which is easy to compute in one direction (plain to cipher) hard to compute in the other (cipher to plain). On the other hand, when the secret key is known, the inverse transformation is easy, as the decipherment operation illustrates. Therefore this is often called a one-way function with a trap door. When the trap door is sprung by a knowledge of sk, it becomes a two-way function. Clearly the key generation process must prevent the knowledge of pk from giving sk, except with an unacceptably large amount of computation.

One-way functions are essential to the study of public key cryptosystems, most of which are based on number theoretic properties. Given a large prime p we can easily define arithmetic operations on the residues modulo p (a Galois field). Modular addition and subtraction are well known and multiplication can be defined as repeated addition. In the same way, the exponential operation is easily defined so, given numbers a and x, both less than p, a quantity a^x can be computed, all the calculations being residues modulo p. With large values of p, the calculations are quite heavy but nevertheless feasible. We shall discuss their practical aspects later.

Figure 7

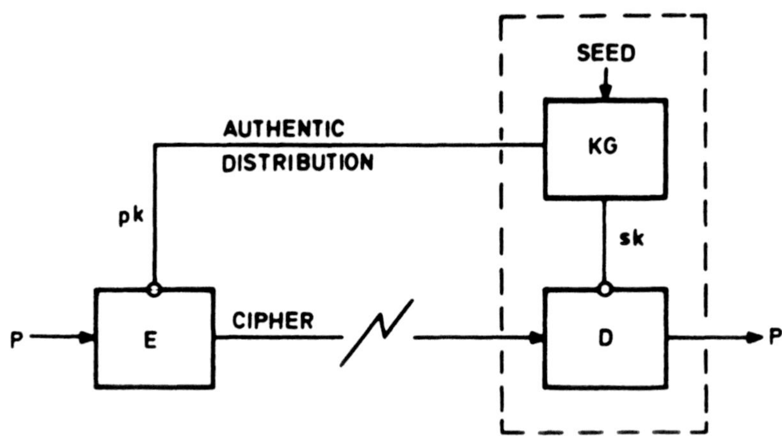

Public Key Cryptosystem

Very many of the possible values of a are "generators" sometimes called "primitive roots" in the sense that as x takes all the values 0, 1, 2, ..., p - 2 the function a^x takes on, in some scrambled sequence, all the values 1, 2, 3 ..., p - 1. Thus a, using only the multiplication function, generates all the members of the multiplication group. In general, a large proportion of the possible values of a are generators.

The inverse function, finding the value of x which corresponds to a given value of a^x, is extremely hard to compute and is generally regarded as infeasible when the modulus p has 300 bits or more. This is the so-called 'discrete logarithm problem' and it requires that p - 1 should not be entirely made of small factors. The difficulty of the calculation depends on the largest factor of p - 1.

Using only the obvious properties of the discrete exponential, Diffie and Helmann showed that a secret value could be generated by two persons using public messages. Figure 8 illustrates the process. First the players choose a suitable large prime p and a generator a. Then each chooses a secret number, x and y respectively, and sends to the other party the quantities a^x and a^y respectively. Because of the one-way property of the exponential, knowledge of these quantities by third parties does not enable them to determine x or y.

When the person who selected secret quantity x receives a^y, he then raises this to the power x thus generating the quantity a^{xy}. Similarly, the other party receives a^x and raises this to the power y generating the same quantity. Thus both parties now have the secret value a^{xy} which cannot be determined by any third parties who merely receive the public information which is a, p, a^x and a^y. As far as we know (though this has not been proved) the only method of breaking this method is by calculating a discrete logarithm.

This method can be used by two parties to generate secret data in common which can then be used as a key in a symmetric cipher algorithm. Neither party has complete control over the result produced, therefore it is not itself a cipher. It was some time before El Gamal of Stamford University showed that it could be the basis of a public key cipher. The method is very similar to the expedential key exchange method.

Figure 8

PARTICIPANT	PUBLIC	PARTICIPANT
x	a, p	y
a^x →	a^x, a^y	← a^y
$(a^y)^x$ ←		→ $(a^x)^y$

ALL MODULO P

Key Distribution by Public Messages

A prime p and a generator a are discovered and are public knowledge. All subsequent calculations are made with modulous p. The one which is to receive the message (like the right hand side in Figure 7) chooses a secret key x and publishes $z = a^x$ where x should be prime to $p - 1$. z is made public and is known to the sender of the message M. The sender chooses a value y at random and must choose a new value for each message sent. He calculates the quantity $r = a^y$ and the cipher text which is $M.z^y$. This cipher text, together with r is sent to the other party who knows the secret value x. Only this person can recover the value M by dividing the cipher text by the quantity r^x. Note that this is the same quantity that was established in the exponential key exchange and that $a^{xy} = r^x = z^y$.

The public key cipher appears to solve the problem of key distribution by removing any requirement for secrecy in the public key. It does, however, leave a strict requirement for authenticity, because an enemy could generate and promulgate a public key masquerading as a friend's public key. If accepted, encipherment with this key would give secrets to the enemy. While it solves one problem, the public key system leaves another problem behind, that of authenticity. We shall see later how another application of the same mathematical devices can provide a particularly strong form of authentication.

The RSA Cipher

Two years after the first publication of the principle of public key cryptosystems, Rivest, Shamir and Adleman proposed a number theoretic cipher which has proved to be the most dependable public key system. Other proposals have been shown to be weak or have required continual modification to overcome crypanalytic methods. Yet others are inconvenient in use. Only the RSA cipher has shown long-term stability. The El Gamal cipher is also based on sound principles but gives a cipher text which is twice the length of the plain text.

The RSA cipher is based on the exponential in the form $y = x^e$ where x is the plain text, y the cipher text and e is part of the public key. This also employs arithmetic computations with a modulus m but in this case the modulus is not a prime.

To begin with, assume that the modulus is prime and let us look for a decryption exponent d such that x is equal to y^d. A consequence would be that x is equal to x^{de} and this will always follow, because of Fermat's theorem, if de is congruent to 1 modulo p - 1, where p is the chosen modulus. In this case, it is very easy to find e given d and vice-versa. Consequently, this cannot be a public key cipher though it is a useful cipher if both exponents are kept secret. The value of p must be public so that encipherment calculations can be made using this as modulus.

Even in this simple form, the algorithm can be used as a method of avoiding the secret transmission of keys. The principle is shown in Figure 9. The sender of message x, knowing the chosen modulus p, finds two exponents e and d with the property described above. The receiver independently finds two similar exponents f and g and both keep their exponents secret. The sender calculates x^e and sends it to the receiver who raises this quantity to the power f and returns x^{ef} to the sender. The sender raises this quantity to the power d and the result is x^f which he returns to the receiver who raises this to the power g and restores the plain text message x. In this scheme none of the keys (the exponents) has to be distributed but the problem of authentication cannot be avoided, because the sender needs some way of discovering who returned the response to his first message.

The only change required to this simple cipher to make it into a public key cipher is that the modulus m should be composite, the product of two large primes p and q. These must be chosen with some care, for example p - 1 must have a large factor, and some other conditions must be met. Now corresponding exponents can be found for encipherment and decipherment with this modulus but the condition to be met is that de is congruent to 1 modulo λ where λ is the least common multiple of p - 1 and q - 1. This relationship between d and e cannot be exploited by an enemy since he does not know p and q, the factors of m and therefore cannot calculate the modulus λ.

Figure 9

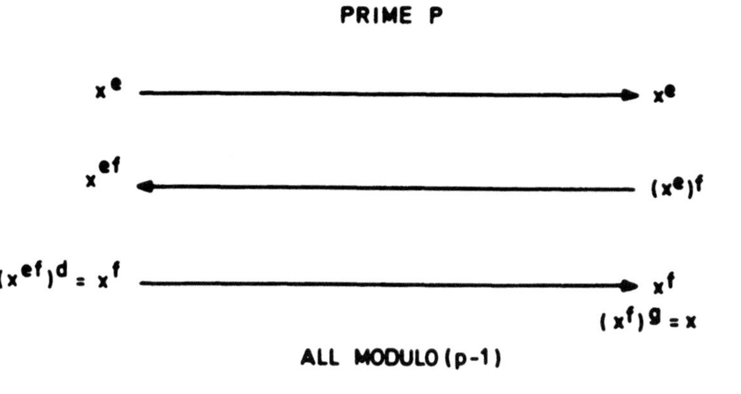

Secret Transmission with Local Keys

The strength of the RSA cipher depends on the difficulty of factorizing m, though there is no proof that this is the only way to break the cipher. The difficulty of factorization depends on number size in rather the same way that the discrete logarithm depends on number size, so the size of numbers required for a secure algorithm is similar in both cases.

The present day limit for factorisation is in the region of 250 bits. To allow for improved technology and better factorisation methods, a good margin of safety is needed, partly because the difficulty of factorisation increases rather slowly with number size. It is often considered that numbers of the order of 512 bits represent a reasonable safety margin. With such numbers, a single RSA exponential in a simple 8 bit micro-processor takes in the region of 500 seconds. An advanced 16 bit micro-processor reduces this to about 50 seconds and a state-of-the-art micro-processor to 5 seconds. To achieve any reasonable encipherment rate requires a special purpose chip, and the simplest of these would typically require 500 milli-seconds while in a more advanced form, 50 milli-second RSA operations should be possible. It is doubtful that high speeds of RSA encipherment will ever be available but this does not detract from its use as a tool in key management, where the object is to transmit keys that will be used in more efficient, symmetric ciphers. The use of RSA operations for digital signature, described below, does not depend on very fast operation.

Although public key cryptosystems do not themselves provide authentication (because a received message could have been generated by anyone knowing the public key) it is easy to build authentication into a dialogue where both parties have published a public key.

The party who begins the conversation includes in his message a random number which, under the assumptions of the public key system, can only be received and deciphered by the party to which it is sent. According to the protocol, this random number is returned with every message coming back from that party and its presence in the messages authenticates their origin. Similarly, the second party includes his own random number in the first reply and this is returned by the first party with every subsequent message he sends. After the first two messages, all subsequent messages have their origin authenticated. In order to prevent a replay, sequence numbers are also needed. Therefore, the loss of authentication in individual messages sent by public key crypto systems may not present a great problem if the protocol is handled correctly.

Digital Signature

Authentication is an effective method for verifying the origin and integrity of a message, but it cannot be used in the place of a signature to sign a contract. It is unfortunate that the word signature is sometimes used for an authenticator but we use the term 'digital signature' only in a stronger sense, based on public key crypto systems.

The problem with authentication by means of a secret key is that both parties have the same knowledge and therefore neither can be protected against dishonesty by the other. For example, an authenticator used to "sign" a cheque would not prevent the receiver of the cheque from increasing the value of the payment and changing the authenticator to match. Authentication protects the two parties against any third party but not against each other's dishonesty. Similarly, an authenticated message which commits a person to a course of action can later be denied on the ground that the receiver could have forged it. The type of dispute due to this dishonesty is not resolvable by using the evidence in the authenticator.

Figure 10 illustrates the principle of the digital signature based on a public key system. Here the sender of the message transforms it using his secret key in an algorithm called S (for sign). At the receiving end, the public key is used in an algorithm called V (for verify) to transform the message back to its original form. Note that the transformed message is not in any sense enciphered, because anyone with the public key can determine its content. The receiver, observing that the transformation generates the clear text message, can be sure that the inverse transformation must have been performed by someone possessing the secret key, therefore the origin is verified as that of the owner of the public key. Once again, the security depends on the authenticity of the public key which must be guaranteed in some way. The algorithms S and V are no more than the public key algorithms D and E respectively, used in a different way. The nature of the RSA algorithm easily shows that the transformations are inverse in which ever sequence they are used.

Figure 10

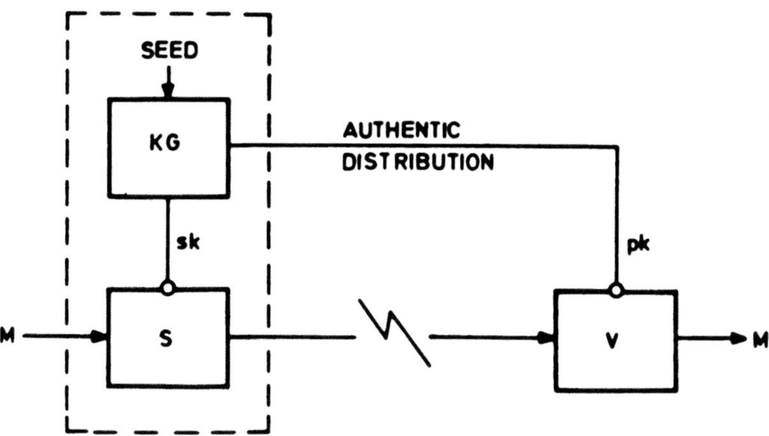

Public Key Signature

This method of signature provides evidence for a third party so that disputes could be taken to independent arbitration. The evidence consists of the transformed message, a public key, which can be verified as to its origin, and the message which results from the publicly known algorithm which contains the content of the agreement which is under dispute. The existence of a simple algorithm for verifying authenticity should avoid the need for taking disputes to arbitration.

In the literature, a lot has been made of the possibility that the owner of the secret key could make this key public and then claim that many of the documents that he signed were forgeries. Though there are legal ways in which this could be made an unprofitable trick, the simplest precaution is to lock up the secret key in a tamper-resistant module which prevents its owner from discovering it as well as defending it against third parties.

The arrangement shown in Figure 10 is inconvenient because the whole transformed message must be stored as a "signature" and the clear text message is required on which to take action, for filing systems etc. In practice, a better method is shown in Figure 11 in which a condensed one-way function of the message is subjected to the signature and verification process, the result being compared with the same one-way function at the receiving end. There are also good security reasons for this arrangement and in Rabin's signature method, which is a variant of RSA, the one-way function is essential. In this arrangement, a single block of data serves as the signature for the clear text document and it provides the necessary message redundancy for verification purposes.

Figure 11

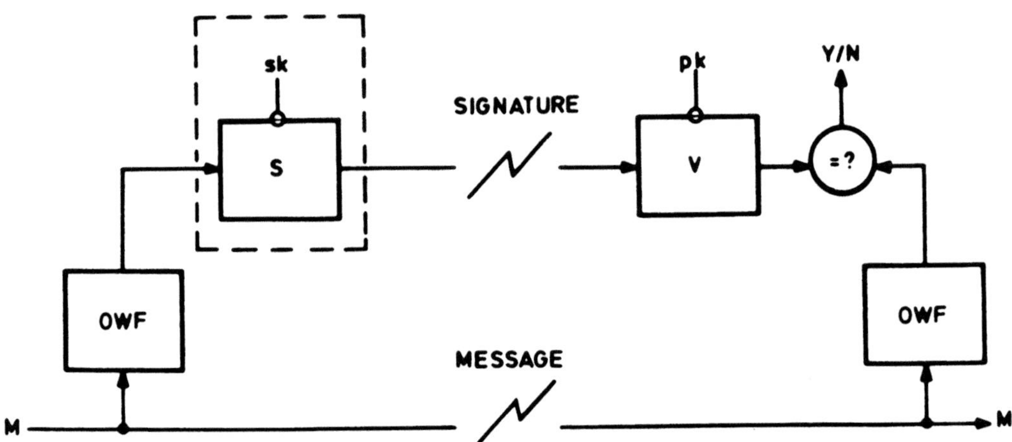

Alternative Signature Method

Proposals for suitable one-way functions have been published, based either on the DES cipher or on number theoretic calculations similar to those of RSA. These are described in Reference 2. When the DES method is used, the one-way function generates a 64 bit result and this gives a possible attack on the system by a "birthday paradox". This is described in Reference 1 and can be avoided if a field is left in the message format where the signing process can insert a random number, for example of 64 bits, just before signature.

El Gamal has proposed a signature method using the exponential function and having a similar principle to his cipher, described above. As before, a prime p and generator a are made public and the signer has a secret key x and makes public the value $z = a^x$. When he wishes to sign a message M, he chooses a value y at random and sends the two quantities r and s, where r is equal to a^y and the signature s is a solution of the conguence

$$M = xr + ys, \text{ modulo } p - 1.$$

Verification uses the relationship

$$a^M = a^{xr}.a^{ys} = z^r.r^s$$

Depending, as it does, on the difficulty of the discrete logarithm, this signature method would not be weakened if a more efficient method of factorization were discovered. Though the problem of factorization and that of the discrete logarithm are closely related, it is thought that the logarithm is the harder problem, in other words it can safely be used with a rather smaller modulus than that needed for RSA. The El Gamal signature has the disadvantage of occupying two words of the size determined by the modulus.

The computational cost of the RSA and El Gamal methods is due to their use of a modular exponential calculation. A method was proposed by Schnorr which uses only multiplications and divisions and is therefore much faster in operation. Like RSA it requires a modulus m which is the product of two primes p and q but unlike RSA these primes are not required again after the value m has been formed. The secret key u is used to generate the public key $k = -1/u^2$, modulo m. The inverse operation is infeasible because of the composite modulus.

The signature of a message z uses a random number r which must be a new random number for each signature. The signature consists of two values s and t given by

$$s = \frac{z + r^2}{2r} \qquad t = \frac{u(z - r^2)}{2r} \qquad \text{modulo } m.$$

The testing of a signature uses the identity

$$z = s^2 + kt^2 \qquad \text{modulo } m.$$

This method was developed from the original one by Schnorr, in collaboration with Ong and Shamir and is sometimes known as the Ong, Schnorr and Shamir method (OSS). When first published Pollard discovered that it could be broken by a method which generated values of s and t to match the message z, in other words a forgery. Schnorr proposed a cubic version which, unfortunately, could be broken by a similar method. However, the Schnorr quadratic method we have described appears, at present, to be secure against attack if the numbers employed are algebraic numbers of the form $a + b\sqrt{d}$ where d is a suitable integer making this number field non-Euclidean. The security of the OSS method with algebraic integers cannot be trusted until it has withstood the investigation of number theorists for some time.

Conclusions

We have described some of the tools which can be used to make systems more secure. No one can guarantee the security of any system because it is impossible to enumerate all possible attacks. Each system requires its own analysis of vunerability and levels of risk and standard solutions seem only to be possible in very limited applications. It has not been possible in the scope of this paper to cover more than a representative selection of topics or to give a real impression of the task of examining the security of a complex system. We hope to have shown that a useful set of techniques now exists which, put together in an intelligent manner, will make the task of the attacker very difficult indeed.

References

(1) D.W. Davies and W.L. Price,
Security for Computer Networks, Wiley, Chichester 1984.

(2) D.W. Davies and W.L. Price, Digital Signatures - An Update,
Proc. ICCC, Sydney, Australia, 1984.

PANEL DISCUSSION

ON

HUMAN BEINGS AS THE SOURCE OF PROBLEMS, CONCERNS AND PROTECTION NEEDS, E.G. COMPUTER CRIME

Thursday 1st of August, 1985 at 15.30 hours.

Chairman and organiser:	Professor R.Turn	California State Univ., Northridge, U.S.A.
Panel Members:		
	Major A.L.Lake	Royal Artillery, U.K.
	Mr.G.A.Karpel	Software Sciences Ltd., U.K.
	Ms.S.L.Brand	Dept. of Defense, U.S.A.
	Dr.D.Heimbigner	Univ. of Colorado, U.S.A.
Contributors:		
	Dr.I.Or	Bogazici Univ., Turkey.
	Mr.N.Harris	British Aerospace, U.K.
	Dr.R.W.Selby, Jr.	Univ. of Maryland, U.S.A.
	Mr.A.M.Gordon	GEC Avionics, U.K.
	Mr.D.W.Davies, CBE	Security Consultant, U.K.
	Mr.A.Wingmore	R.A.E.,Farnborough, U.K.
	Dr.H.Trzaska	Univ. of Wroclaw, Poland.
	Mr.G.L.Sorrell	M.C.& R. Inc., U.S.A.
	Mr.P.Mellor	City Univ., London, U.K.
	Ms.J.Clapp	MITRE Corp., U.S.A.
	Dr.J.Milewski	Warsaw Univ., Poland.

Professor Turn. The way we intend to operate this panel discussion is that first of all our panel members will make each a statement for 10 or 15 minutes, giving their views on this particular subject. They will try to respond to your questions, but all this questioning will have to be well disciplined. One person only speaks at a time, and only after he or she has been recognised by me, to make sure that we are properly recorded. You can address your questions to specific panel members. We ourselves might get into a debate, though ours is not such a controversial subject.

The human factor in software does exist. We say 'yes' to the question posed in the title of our discussion. We have tried to organise this panel to show in which fashion the humans cause problems as system designers, implementers, requirement interpreters, as well as users, both authorised and unauthorised. We shall look at the question how, and how much and why they are the problem, and we shall try to suggest what to do about it.

The first speaker is Major Tony Lake of the Royal Artillery in the U.K.

NATO ASI Series, Vol. F22
Software System Design Methods. Edited by J.K. Skwirzynski

Major Lake. I am going to give you a soldier's view, not an academic view. This should be quite relevant however to those among you who are not soldiers, and certainly to those who are developing military systems.

First I would like to talk on two things which I call 'indirect human problems'.

The first is project management which consists of activities like listening, consulting, thinking and deciding, and while military project managers might be able to think and to decide, they are not always that good at listening and consulting. The particular problem here is listening which means not only hearing but also understanding. Not all the military project managers have the background knowledge to understand the things that you, as a design manager, or a designer are saying. You might say to them that a thing is not at all possible for some reasons that are clear to you. Because they do not understand the language that you are using, they do not hear you and we have problems.

The second problem is the system testing. Mr. Dale (1) has covered this topic very well, and I am not going to talk about this for very long. The problem we have is not the analysis of data, the creation of data or the running of a program. The problem is the specification of the scenario in which the test data are generated. We have not fought a war for some time. Thus any scenario is generated by conjecture, and you can easily get many opinions on what the next war is likely to be. This presents quite a problem for system testers, for if they do not know what the war is going to look like, they cannot test a computer in the realistic scenario, and we have no valid tests, nor valid test results.

Now we shall pass to direct human problems and I will consider three of them.

First is the problem of 'design to user constraints'. This is something which the Japanese taught the British in car making, in their use of ergonomically designed cars. Their cars sold, and ours did not. This refers to physical attributes of humans. The problems I see here are the mental attributes of humans. In particular, it is now generally regarded that people understand and assimilate information quicker with pictures. So we need pictures. In a military environment this is not always feasible. We have not yet found a computer system which works with a graphic display in a tank on the move. So we ask the question: 'Is such an information system possible and feasible?' Professor Leveson's (2) first point was the advice that the first option is not to try to build such systems. Are we too early?

Now we come to specification errors. These have been covered already in many lectures here. I am not going to talk about normal errors. I would like to suggest that there may be deliberate errors. One computer system had been working very well for about nine months. Then on the 25th of December it said 'Happy Christmass', and produced Christmass trees on its screen. That computer had gone through extensive testing, and yet that fault had not been found.

Let us next consider specifications with exploitable weaknesses. We can relate this to the hardware problem. If specifications for a tank lead to weaknesses in that tank, then somebody who gets hold of these specifications might be able to exploit these weaknesses. In a large command and control system there are tons, not just pages, of specifications. They float around and are very difficult to control; there is quite a chance that some of them might float into wrong hands, so that someone studying them might find these weaknesses.

The second consideration arises when a system starts operating. We have managed to test it and it looks reasonably usefull. Operators might start playing with it and there is a chance that this playing will turn into ´hacking´, or maybe worse. If his happens somebody might find by accident a very nasty fault in the computer, and sell this knowledge to the enemy. There is a good hardware analogy here. Consider a chain saw. When it comes from a shop, it is a fairly safe device. If you take away the safety devices, that saw is not quite so safe.

Lastly let us consider the third type of problem, namely the maintenance problem. Humans tend to relax their guard after completing the higher prophile business of getting a system up and running. Then the problem of maintaining it remains. It is difficult to keep up our guard in this period and remember the security.

Professor Turn. Now I ask Mr. Karpel to discuss one particular problem that we need to concentrate on, namely the software integrity testing.

Mr. Karpel. My presentation will be constrained to a ´high level overview´ of the field I am currently working in. This is concerned with the undesirable effects that ´soft machines´ cause in ´software machines´. Such concerns, as Major Lake has already mentioned, cause many problems.

My viewpoint is that it is the human that causes the problem, not the machine. Consider a situation that there were ´software machines´ around long before there were any humans! A couple of primitive examples might be a bacterium or a protozoan. They both execute a code to produce desirable (at least to them!) effects, namely growth and reproduction. Such code is of course the genetic code, which obeys precise rules. The basic JCL (Job Control Language) is provided by particular combinations of ´codons´. Each codon has a word size of 3. This allows 64 possible ´words´, and this is very interesting, because organisms need only 20 of these words for the production of 20 amino acids. Thus, in this particular case there are 44 ´spare´ words, and these are not just discarded. In fact, they are use to provide redundancy for the production of ´system critical´ amino acids. For example, some amino acids have 2, 3 or 4 different words, each coding for their production. Others have as many as 6 words! There are still a few spare words left after all that.

Fig: 1a User's conception of "A Single User River Transport System"

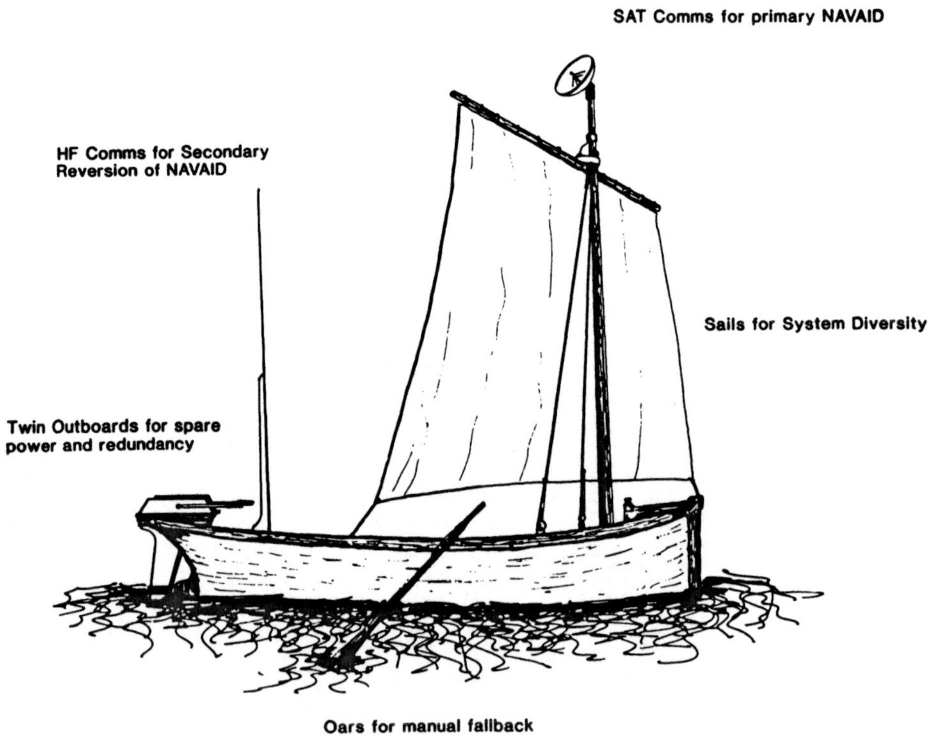

Fig: 1b Advising Consultants' Conception of such a System

Fig: 1c Revised Requirement Specification After Cost Benefit Analysis

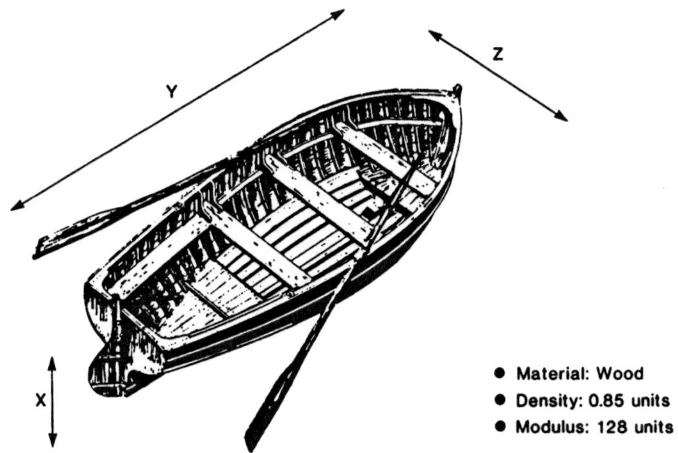

Fig: 1d Design Concept (System Level)

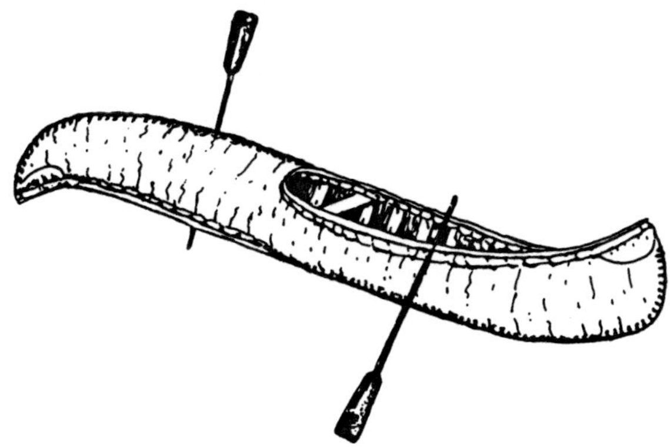

Fig: 1e The Product !

In fact there are 3 like that, all coding for the ´stop command´; a very ´safety conscious´ feature. Maybe Biocomputing will be the thing of the future.

But back to the present. Humans can greatly affect the system performance, and might do so in the following three ways:

Reqirements Expression

This is typically a very verbose and probably conflicting description of what a ´user´ wants from a system he is ordering. As an example, consider Fig. 1A. At least some users might know precisely what they want. However, these hypothetical users are also worried about going out to tender on their own requirements specification. They therefore decide to retain a firm of ´Advisory Consultants´, who, after detailed analysis and expert considerations, completely rewrite the original specification, which now of course incorporates redundancy, diversity and manual ´fall back´ operation. The net result might look like that in Fig.1B. A vigorous and frank exchange of views then ensues between the users and the ´Advising Consultants´; the net result of this could be like that shown in Fig.1C. Now the users are quite impressed by the remarkable cost savings, so they promptly go out to tender with it. A highly respected, but not too expensive Systems House is retained. This promptly produces the item we next consider:

Design Specification

This too is typically elaborate and probably inconsistent; not only with the requirements specification, but also between its own various design levels. However, the final design is written, which will specify a feasible product that will meet the user´s requirements and be produced within the necessary time scale and expected budget. Again the result might look like that in Fig.1D. Lastly we consider the final stage:

Implementation

This is obviously concerned with producing a real system that will meet the possibly ambiguous and probably conficting design criteria. You see the typical result in Fig.1E.

These five pictures illustrate an old theme, known in different versions by many project engineers and designers. Hovever, it is a fact that such incidents of misunderstanding and misinterpretation still occur.

How do we tackle this problem? By ensuring ´System Integrity´ and by increasing the quality of significant components. ´Sofware Integrity´, or ´S.I.´ is not to be confused with System Integrity. S.I. can be defined as: ´The freedom of software from errors that may cause a system to deviate from its intended function´. There are various ways to ensure such a goal, all coming under the title of ´Software Integrity Testing´, or SIT for short.

Now SIT involves the validation and verification (V+V) of the requirements, down to the resultant code and subsequent test specifications, and in practice, this might be facilitated by the following analysis (see Fig.2).

Here Completeness is the attribute which indicates how much each specification level matches the working environment established by the preceding higher level.

Typically this is concerned with the inputs and outputs perceived at each level, and how close these are to the 'actual situation' in the real environment.

Correctness is that attribute which indicates how 'technically valid' each specification is, notwithstanding any lack of completeness.

Specification Level	Attribute		
	Completeness	Correctness	Consistency
Requirements			
Design			
Code			
Test			

Fig.2. SIT Analysis (or the "three C's").

The Correctness attribute is 'loosely coupled' to the next attribute, which is the Consistency. This is an indication of trouble! However, it has not yet been determined whether it indicates more trouble when applied to one particular specification level, or across two of them. As we have already heard today, there exists a little controversy over some techniques and formal methods in software engineering. This is particularly true when we attempt to analyse and to determine such attributes as the "Three C's".

Thus perhaps this is a good point at which to hand over to this forum for discussion.

Professor Turn.- Since we have as yet no questions from the audience, we shall now invite Ms. Sheila Brand, the Chief of Standards in the National Computer Security Center of the Department of Defense in the U.S.A., to tell us something on legislation against computer crime.

Ms. Brand. This panel is concerned with computer crime, and about 'hacking'. My belief is that people are the problem here and that legislation will not help to alleviate this problem, in spite of the fact that in the USA we have legislation in a number of States and one in Federal Law. Thus the only way to solve this problem is to approach it systematically. I will mention what I think about hackers and about the nature of computer crime.

I have worked for many years in the computer security field and most of that time I have been involved in the Federal Government with the problem of computer crime. While working for the Inspector General of HHS I conducted a survey of the U.S. Government on computer related crime.

I was asked to go to other Law Enforcement offices in the Government, known as the Inspector Generals, to ask them what they thought the problem was in terms of computer crime. Basically I got the same answer every where I went: 'We do not know that there is a problem; we cannot solve this problem, even if there is one, because we have no trained poeple to do this job'. This was a typical 'Catch-22' reasoning. So I went to the Inspector General and said to him that nobody seems to know what the problem is.

Then we conducted a large survey of the 26 Federal Agencies by sending them a very involved questionnaire. This was one of the series of surveys that have been done in the last five years in the USA on computer crime. The bottom-line answer to our questions was that it is people that are the problem. They are greedy. If there are funds to be got through the system, they will get them. They are not very sophisticated in the methods they are using. They do not use 'Trojan horses', i.e. they do not use sophisticated means of penetrating systems. They either become computer operators, claim adjusters or input clerks, or they bribe input clerks and thus get lots and lots of money. This is not only the conclusion of the Federal Government survey; I have with me five different surveys and they show the same thing, whether in the banking, or in manufacturing industries. The main reason for penetrating a system is greed.

The second major reason is revenge. Many people are disgrunted and they try to get back at their company or agency by tampering with their computer system. As I said before, the modus operandi that they are using is not very sophisticated. The amounts of money they managed to get ranges from nothing (when they just abuse a computer system), to up to 500 million or to a billion dollars in the banking industry.

The third, least likely reason, for penetrating a system is the intellectual curiosity, which is the 'hacker' problem. I am always amazed at how much publicity the hackers have gotten in the USA. Being a computer security person, I feel that this is a good aspect, for it increases the amount of awareness of the problem, and one of the results of our survey is that there is no awareness. The American Bar Association did a survey similar to the one I have conducted. The overwhelming response they received was that there is a lack of awareness among company managers that there is a problem. The answer was similar to the one I have got. The hackers are receiving lots of publicity, but they are not the main reason that we need more computer security, or integrity, or resilience in our systems. The hackers are only a very 'high noise level' problem.

I have said already that I do not think that legislation is the answer. I say this because:

1. No one knows how to go after computer criminals. The law enforcement men who have law at their disposal and use, are not computer people and they do not know how to solve computer crimes. Thus they end up trying these cases under non-computer oriented statutes. When I was doing the survey I asked the FBI how they deal with this crime.

I found that they do not recognise computer criminals; they catagorise computer crimes under communication statutes.

2. An interesting thing that we have found is that many times computer criminals do not care whether they are caught. They are not sent to jail and our statistics bear this out. Either the are dismissed from their jobs, or they are not dismissed, but get a bonus! This is because they are such an embarrassment to their organisation. Victimized companies do not want the public to know the security status of their computer systems.

3. In order to have an effective statute, that statute should be rather crisp, and to date we have not defined computer crime crisply. Until we can define our problem precisely and formulate it in legal terms, legislation will act as a large loop-hole. In conclusion, people are the problem and technology is the solution. Technology can better be used to secure our computer systems and applications. The need for data confidentiality, data integrity, and resource availability must be addressed to lessen the occurance and impact of computer crime. We now have a loss from 100 million dollars annually to several billions. This is because systems are so lax, and indeed it is now impossible to estimate accurately what the actual losses are. Only with improvemments in technical security can we lower these estimates.

This is all I wish to say now. Any questions?

Dr. Or. You have said that management does not want to pay for data protection. I am rather surprised at this. Is it that the actual losses are small, or is it that the management does not understand the nature of these losses?

Ms. Brand. The losses are enormous, but few of them are reported. If some loss is reported, say of 20 million dollars or so, a company will react, but most crimes go unmentioned. There are no detection devices in most systems, nor is there any accountability. The real losses are caused by alteration of data. If you can get to data bases relatively easily, and there is no mechanism in the system that will record who does what to what files, then the management cannot detect problems and they do not think that they have been ripped off. Why should they then take any measures to secure that are so expensive to put on? The answer is that they do not know how much loss they have, so they spend no time or effort to do anything about it. All the studies done by us have shown that this is a real and a significant problem. However, it is not so endemic that all managers will start implementing the necessary security in computer systems.

Mr. Harris. I recall the time when I was first made aware of the problem of computer crime. It relates to a British Broadcasting Corporation television programme, which was in depth review of the problem of computer crime.

The programme set out to demonstrate the problem by allowing a U.S.A. expert in crime, a reasonably free rein to convince a panel of representative business experts (industrialists, lawyers, accountants, etc.) of the problem. The highlight of this broadcast was when the U.S.A. expert who has previously invited some members of the panel to bring with them relevant computer "print-outs" of their organisations accounts, reviewed these print-outs showing how a considerable number of the payments made to contracting companies were in actual fact, payments made to bogus organisations set up by himself for purposes of demonstrating how easy it is to defraud using the computer. This demonstration was completely successful to the extent that even the B.B.C. accounting system had been infiltrated, and they above all others could have anticipated this since they had set the programme up.

At the time this T.V. programme impressed me primarily for two reasons. Firstly, the ease by which the U.S.A. expert achieved his objectives: he set the whole operation up in a period of a few weeks prior to the programme and secondly the scepticism of the panel to which the U.S.A. expert was attempting to demonstrate the nature of the problem. They tended to view it as a high technology "trick" rather than a potential problem. A further point of considerable interest is that this broadcast (if my memory serves me correctly) took place some 15 years ago. At that time the opportunity of detecting such frauds was easier as the administration of accounts still involved a lot of human activity which thereby ensured checks and balances that invigilated the computerised accounting procedures. Now, some 15 years later, this human involvement is at a minimum. As is demonstrated by this discussion even the basic lessons have still not been learned. The business community are still loathe to accept that computer crime is a large and increasing problem; they still regard it as a high technology "trick" and not a major threat to normal business activity.

Ms. Brand. Another difficulty is indeed that they do not understand the problem. The computer is still a mystique to the managers. It is a psychic 'black box'.

Dr. Selby. Do you see a future for loss insurance in this problem? The losses are large, but are isolated, so what is your opinion?

Ms. Brand. Right now there is a big push for insurance for physical protection, but this is only after there have been some damaging fires, or burst pipes that ruined the whole computer setup. However, to ensure software is not so easy. Lloyds of London have an insurance policy just for that. I do not know enough about this to speak here. I just know that it exists, and that they started it two years ago.

Professor Turn. Getting an insurance policy like this would be a familiar activity for management to handle, but since there is very little actuarial data (your reports might contribute more to this), the insurance companies are in doubt, and their premiums are quite large.

This makes it unattractive for management. Therefore they just wish the whole thing away, like we wish away the potential threat of bulglary in our houses. We rather think that we shall not be victims, though there are cases of thefts in the neighborhood.

We will now proceed with our last panel memeber, Dr. Dennis Heimbigner of the University of Colorado, who will tell us about hackers and hacking.

Dr. Heimbigner. Though this is not my profession, I will try to relate to you few things about hacking. First, I should possibly say what my qualifications are. At the university of Colorado I became intimately aware of the activities of hackers. There was a situation where a group of students first learned how to crash a system, and then proceeded to take it over completely. Ms. Brand has mentioned 'Trojan horses'; these students have in fact used such techniques. In general there was open warfare between managers of our Computing Centre and student hackers.

I suppose that the first question is: where do hackers come from? My belief is that, originally, they came from academic environments. Indeed, for a long time, university computing centres had to deal with hackers, who tried to take over the computer systems. I suspect that this still remains the main arena for this phenomenon.

Then something happened in the middle of seventies, which gave hackers a wider scope for their activity. Many commercial systems provided hook ups to the telephone network, so you could dial in via a modem and get into a system. Suddenly everybody, students included, had access to computer systems. It was the bright students in high schools and up who tried to break into computer systems. High schools began to buy computers and students had access to modems. It was at this point that public attention began to focus on hacking. It would be interesting to establish why hackers attracted such sudden attention, and yet earlier bank thefts had not.

What did they need to do to perform a hacking? They could access a computer system via a modem without any need of approaching such a system directly. One should note that if there is no path, there is no problem of access. Thus, military establishments which use only physical connections and do not use phone lines are secure from outside penetration, though not necessarily from an internal one.

Another aspect worth noting is the community of peers, some of whom like to show off. There are two things that happen: one is the ability to show your peers how clever you are; the other is, as was already mentioned by Professor Turn (3), that they began to use computer systems to enlarge their community. There are bulletin boards all over the USA where hackers can exchange information.

Ms. Brand has already mentioned the problem of motivation in hacking. There are essentially two of them: there is the issue of power; adolescents have this much in common. They like to have power either to destroy systems, or to take over the control of them.

The other aspect is the notion of competition. This is a form of intellectual curiosity. This aspect can be used in two ways. First groups of hackers like to compete against each other. In one university there was a situation where one group of hackers was in control, and another began to grow up trying to penetrate the system. They competed against each other, and the first group tried to prevent the penetration by the other. Now it is more common to try gaining such control over an institution by two or more cooperating groups. This is a more serious problem, for two heads are better than one.

There is one more problem I should mention, namely the computer versus non-computer hacking. There have been several cases of what news media call hacking, but which do not really involve computers: stealing telephone codes and things like that.

What can we do about this? I agree with Ms. Brand that criminal sanctions are of no use, probably because hackers are juveniles. The law for them is less restrictive, as it must be. Another important thing is the notion of ethics: how do we convince those who have access to machines that there are activities that are right, and activities that are wrong. The rules should be 'black and white', with no greys in between.

Another thing I have not heard mentioned here is that an important way to tackle this problem is to give hackers some place to play. Give them an arena: a computer of their own; bring them into an organisation by making them responsible for protecting the system. This might sound like a very nonproductive thing to do, but this would give them the responsibility for keeping others out. This in my opinion is the best solution of the hacking problem.

I would like to ask Ms. Brand where she thinks the problem lies. She has mentioned people who steal money. this is likely to be the high probability problem. They steal money, but such thefts are not likely to destroy an institution. The danger of hackers is that they are not motivated by money; they are motivated by other things like power. Here we have a low but finite probability that they could destroy the total computer system. Thus we have a question. Which is the more dangerous problem: Small loss with high probability that will not destroy a company, or a low probability loss that will destroy a company?

Ms. Brand. Let us consider your suggestion of giving hackers a safe place to play. It has been found that most people who perpetrate a computer crime have studied the subject before. Hacking is a relatively new phenomenon. It has arrived with the large number of minicomputers which are now available to a large segment of population, particularly that of young age, where there is much curiosity. Our studies have shown that computer crimes have been carried out by people who have had a criminal past, even those serving in government agencies. So should we give them a safe place to play? In our Computer Security Service we had interviewed young hackers and thought of giving them jobs, for they seemed to be very smart.

This raises however a question: can you give them a safe place? I am not sure that you can do that. Maybe you can find for them an intellectual place like a university?

Professor Turn. It is clear that you should not give them too much power.

Dr. Heimbigner. Please tell me which is more dangerous, the high probability low loss case, or the low probability and total loss.

Ms. Brand. In a survey we did recently it was found that a lot of computer abuse was committed by hackers. I do not think that these people will stop at non malicious activities. They start by dialling phone numbers, then they get into data bases. There was a case recently where they penetrated the data base of a cancer patient treatment establishment. Then they tempered with these data. This is no longer a casual play. They start small and grow big.

Mr. Gordon. Computers are always alert; they do not go to sleep, and they have no emotions, nor are they corruptable. Thus any problem in defence occurs either when the man responsible did not think hard enough on what could happen, or when he did not design a program well enough to be secure or well behaved. I do not see any real reason why we should not get the computer to recognise that a person is testing logically all combinations of passwords, in order to break in. We could then block that input port.

Ms. Brand. I would like to comment on this password problem. After the film "War Games" was first shown, a lot of hacking penetrated password systems. Because of these events our Center has decided to develop password guidelines. We have published a gide on the subject. We have suggested that before you can login again, a few seconds should elapse before the computer tries the next password. This would to some extent defray the zeal of a hacker. We had a lot of resistance when we sent these guidelines around, because people had to spend longer times logginig into a system. You can build more secure passwords and integrity checks, but this is expensive and it is a 'pain in the neck'. It is a question in which priorities are going to prevail, those of the management, or those of the security minded people.

Mr. Gordon. I was not thinking of time diversity. If someone tries to break into a system logically, then a pattern will be developed very quickly that he is trying and having detected an attempt, we block it.

Professor Turn. Before we proceed with further questions, I would like to ask Mr. Donald Davies from U.K., a very prominent computer security expert, to make some comments on this security problem in his country.

Mr. Davies. I would like to make some comments from the point of view of someone who advises on data security to banks and similar institutions. They have a lot to lose and hence are very concerned with security problems. Here we are talking about human factors, and there are two of them which I would like to mention.

We are concerned with motivation, the driving force of these attacks. We have heard a lot about the motivation of hackers. The essential point is the intensive intellectual activity of the very large number of people, and the extent to which they can collaborate together.

Thus, they are a formidable ennemy. So far, as far as I am aware, hackers have mostly attacked systems that are quite simple. That does not mean however that we should remain complacent, for reasons that have already been listed out, namely that this is just the first generation of hackers. Historically we can go back to phone freaking which was mentioned earlier. This did not concern computers particularly, but it did show the same characteristics. It was an intellectual exercise to break into control signals of a telephone service, with virtually no financial reward, yet with power over a large organisation. Phone freaking developed from a very simple technique to a very sophisticated one. For example, in Britain, where the system was rather more carefully protected by means of filters from ordinary voice signals, it was rather hard to break in. This was overcome by sending signals rather loudly, so they broke through the filters. The other way was to rearrange the equipment in the telephone exchange, as was done by two engineers in the Bristol telephone exchange. The same is likely to happen with hacking; their techniques will become more clever.

Another thing that worries me is that out of thousands of hackers one may have a real criminal intent. If hacking gets combined with a large scale crime, the level of threat to banking might become formidable. So we should try to understand not only who the enemy is now, but also what it might become in future.

Still another aspect of human factor concerns systems that we are building to ensure that banking systems are secure. In my lecture (4) I spoke about cryptography and its applications. There is a lot of technology available here. The effect of applying these techniques tends however to concentrate the need of security in one or two places. You can protect the channels, but then you have the problem of distributing the keys. You may find that the vulnerability is actually greater with such an arrangement. Further, when you finish building such a system, you have then to arrange a management structure around it to make it work and to make sure that it continues to work. This is actually the hardest part in the design of a secure system.

Professor Turn. It seems that a consensus is emerging that solution for security of computer systems should be a technical one. We have heard that law will not work effectively with juveniles, or when a crime is hidden or ignored.

There is also the need to instill some ethics into the new crop of potential hackers, namely those coming out of schools right now. Next question please.

Mr. Wingmore. I will take just one issue in Dr. Heimbigner's presentation. He used the phrase: 'No path, no problem'. Was he serious?

Dr. Heimbigner. This was probably an overstatement. It is difficult to stop all paths into a computer system.

Mr. Wingmore. Of course. People often do not realise that any computer installation has EM (electromagnetic) emission. With a very small amount of money you can construct a circuitry with which you can listen in from fair distances to a computer installation, if it is not specially protected. You might think that you will just hear dynamic movement of data, but most computer installations have security back up dumps. Then a remote listener can connect his phone to a sizeable computer and can listen to a data dump, and transfer all the files to his computer memory. This does not allow to alter the files dynamically, so this is rather a surveillance technique, rather than a criminal activity. This is however something people should be aware of.

Professor Turn. You refer to a radiation pickup from computer systems. Can anyone else comment on this?

Dr. Trzaska. This problem in my opinion has two aspects. A very good paper has been recently presented by members of the Phillips Company this Spring at the EMC Symposium in Zurich, Switzerland (5).They stated that using standard selective radio receiver, at a distance 200 to 300 meters, you can reconstruct data displayed on a video display unit (VDU) screen. In my activity, as a ham radio, I have met a lot of interference from VDU sets. This radiation picks up over a narrow frequency band which works similarly to SSTV (Slow Scanning TV). To reconstruct a full display from a VDU to your VDU is easy, for you have direct data, not encrypted ones. These data can be picked up without direct connection to a computer system. Inverse bahaviour seems to be possible as well. It is a well know susceptibility of computer devices and of systems to external electromagnetic (EM) field; big effort is done in the field of protection against this. Wireless interference or intended change in computers is conceptually simple. However, it is practically difficult, as it needs among others quite a high electromanetic (EM) field intensity. Usually professional computing systems are well protected against such external EM interferece.

The second aspect of EM radiation from a VDU concerns the problem of human body reaction to EM radiation, which started, being considered seriously, from early sixties (6). Thus these days some people working with VDU's are worried that this work could be dangerous to their health.

We have measured the radiation from a VDU and concluded that, from the point of view of being in power work safety standards, such worries look rather as a result of a phobia. Taking into account hypothetical low level interactions, as well as a psychological role of phobia, the Polish Ministry of Health and Social Welfare decided that pregnant women must no be allowed to work with VDU's.

Mr. Sorrell. I have a question to Dr. Heimbigner, concerning the hacker problem. I do not think we can compete with the criminals by paying these hackers to do a police work. Eventually they will turn into criminals, for this way they will get more money.

Dr. Heimbigner. Only a small percentage of these hackers are in some sense criminally minded. Some time ago I heard that computer people seem to go through several phases. They start as naive computer users, then they start abusing the system in one way or another, and eventually they go for protecting the system and become socially responsible. Most of them become well adjusted citizens. I do not know what we can do about these few that become criminals; possibly you should place them in jail.

Mr. Sorrell. I suggest that the criminal element would seek these hackers out as a means of getting what they want. My second point is that if you give them facilities to play with the system harmlessly, this will be not as exciting as abusing this system.

Dr. Heimbigner. My experience has been that this is not the case.

Mr. Mellor. The hackers had a playground for a long time; this was called the adventure games. Concerning your statement on motivation, you seem to be saying that 'boys will be boys'. What motivation can you give them to feel that what they are doing is wrong? Are there not women hackers?

Ms. Brand. Yes there are!

Ms. Clapp. But they are too smart to get caught! That's why you never heard of them.

The situation concerning access to computers is changing so dramatically now. In the early days the only people who got access to computers were the people who worked in the computer field. Now, for a very low entry cost, people can get a computer at a young age and learn how to use it. People would find other outlets for their intellectual activity, but a computer is very tantalizing one. So you cannot compare the situation of few years ago to the present one. Too many people view a system as impersonal, and are capable of abuse when quite young.

Dr. Milewski. I have heard here that some software systems managers are not enough interested in maintaining the system security. Maybe the professionals should try and make the software sufficiently secure? On the other hand, maybe this is a misleading direction, because protection against a human attack is not precisely the same as is the protection against internal software faults. Thus, to improve the protection of our systems is not the same as improving the quality of software as such, but is simply a way to make it more secret.

Mr. Karpel. This is a very good point. Monitoring all the activities of a computer system facilitates the securing of its software environment. This naturally includes monitoring the system related activities of software personnel as well. However, without first ensuring that the computer system has 'System Integrity', the activity monitoring will certainly not secure the software environment. I would therefore state that improving the quality of software is the first step in improving the protection of computer systems.

Dr. Or. I am quite a layman in the area of software security, so please allow me to ask a naive question to Ms. Brand and to Dr. Heimbigner. It seems to me that any computer system should have some kind of security code or a password. Assuming that this is true, an unauthorised intruder would either have a knowledge of that password, or he would have to find that password either by trial and error, or by some enumeration process. As Mr. Gordon has already suggested, if he uses an enumeration, or a trial and error process, then the computer or the program should be so programmed as to catch him. On the other hand, if he knows that password, he must have stolen it, which is a simple theft, and is equivalent to a theft of a sensitive document.Thus the only problem would then be that of hiding and keeping secret other sensitive documents. If this is not possible, why not arrange the software so that it would catch him, or her?

Ms. Brand. This is one of the solutions that we are considering and using already; we have passwords and we monitor people who attempt to use our passwords and who fail. When someone has a password, he or she will have the access to that system, or rather a limited access. However, not all systems have passwords; when they have them, they also can have a good login accountability system. If all systems had passwords, then each password system should require access on an individual basis; in other words, each of us should have his or her individual password. Secondly, that password should be a key to certain specific authorisations. Once you you have a good password system, you also need a good detection method for detecting illegal access attempts. Very few systems have a good detection method. There is a question of priorities and the question of where companies wish to put their money.

The people who develop password systems are not application programmers; they are usually engineers who develop such systems and offer them as a part of the operating system. In the USA there is a growing awareness among computer vendors of the need for good password systems. We only need to convince people where their priorities should lie.

Mr. Davies. I am rather surprised at the emphasis on passwords as the method of access control. In my work for financial institutions, who need to protect payments at billions of pounds per day, the system may use passwords, but they are a minor part of the protection scheme. Any secure system must have some part which is physically protected, or 'tamper resistant'.

Even for retail banking, as in ATM's, banks use passwords (PIN's) combined with magnetic striped cards. For higher level of access control the best solution seems to lie with the 'smart card', which protects its stored data and also requires a password to actuate it. Passwords alone are too vulnerable for most purposes.

Major Lake. How is that thing promulgated throughout the UK? Presumably you have to inspect all establishments to check what security level they have got?

Mr. Davies. It is the inspection departments and the auditors who are responsible for this in individual banks in the UK. I am surprised at the many companies in the UK, who take big risks in security without realising what they are doing.

Professor Turn. Thank you for participating in this discussion, the first one at this Institute. It was very interesting.

References.

(1) C. Dale: 'The Assessment of Software Reliability for Systems with High Reliability Requirements' (in this volume)
(2) N.G. Leveson: 'Software Hazard Analysis Techniques' (in this volume)
(3) R. Turn: 'Security, Safety and Resiliency in Computation' (in this volume)
(4) D.W. Davies: 'The Need for Data Security' (in this volume)
(5) W. van Eck, J. Neissen, P. Rijsdick: 'On the Characteristics of Electromagnetic Field Generated by Video Display Units', Proc. 1985 International EMC Symposium, Zurich, Switzerland, pp. 623 to 628.
(6) J.K. Skwirzynski (ed.) 'Theoretical Methods for Determining the Interaction of Electromagnetic Waves with Structures', NATO ASI Series, No.E.40. Sijthoff & Noordhoff 1981. (Part III. The Mechanisms of Biological Interaction and Microwave Bioeffects)

PANEL DISCUSSION

ON

WOMEN IN INFORMATION SCIENCE

Tuesday, 6th of August, 1985 at 15.00 hours.

Chairman and organiser: Mrs. Eileen Jones, Software Productive Research Inc., U.S.A.

Panel Members: Ms. S. Brand, US Dept. of Defense.
Dr. B. Curtis, MCC, U.S.A.
Prof. N. Leveson, Univ. of California, U.S.A.
Mr. J. Musa, Bell Labs. U.S.A.

It became quite clear from discussions on this topic that occured prior to the panel that the topic can become somewhat an emotional one. So although all panels are taped and the transcripts are then published, it was requested no tape be made and a paper be submitted instead, outlining the general discussion. In this way less inhibited and more poignant discussion could take place. And it did, indeed.

The more interesting questions raised were:

- Are women really discriminated against?
- Should there be different motivation/incentive considerations for women in the labor force?
- Do women offer unique or special contributions to computing?
- Who will mind the children?
- Why wasn't there a greater enrollment of females in computer science and engineering curriculum and therefore more prospective females in that labor force?
- Why do females excell in mathematics from grades 1 to 12 but not afterward?

Observations and statements generated by the above questions were as follows:

Yes, discrimination does, indeed, exist. (The person posing the question was male). Panel members and the chairperson cited personal experiences of outright discrimination due to the fact that they were female. The chairperson also held a series of private interviews with women in the computing industry who have experienced blatant discrimination. It was also noted that discrimination does not only occur within the hierarchy of an organization (mostly females at lower levels versus mostly males in upper

NATO ASI Series, Vol. F22
Software System Design Methods. Edited by J.K. Skwirzynski

levels), but it also occurs within each level itself (e.g. females not being considered as serious, loyal memebers who are able to make substantial contributions to a team). This more than likely stems from the fact that women tend to leave the work force to bear and sometimes rear children. To this fact, a very poignant view was raised: yes, there is no guarantee a woman will not leave to have a child; but by the same token, there is no guarantee ANY emploee (male or female) will not leave for another position either. (Quite well stated by a male in the audience).

There were some very interesting comments on whether women should be motivated/treated differently in the labor force. A male pannelist felt that ".. positively, women should be treated differently ..". Once the outcries subsided he was allowed to explain that he doesn't treat any of his staff the same. He treats them all according to their needs, and any female (or male) working for him would be treated accordingly. It was generally agreed that motivation and incentive should not have a gender but a purpose to suit the individual.

There was serious doubt professed by a male pannelist that focussing on unique or special contributions of individuals due to their sex had any merit. He also felt that in the extreme, this would probably do more harm than good. It was noted that although women could sooner use intuition and nurturing abilities (supposedly exclusive female characteristics) to perform well, this would offset rather than discount male abilities.

We had the good fortune of having husband and wife teams present, as well as many working parents and female heads of households present to discuss just who will or is supposed to mind the children. After explanations of child care services in different countries (the U.S. shown to be far behind), it was a general feeling that quality child care is a basic need and that government and industry should be a part of its support. Working parents in the audience felt they spent more "quality" time with their children as opposed to time "just being available". When the issue of physical energy was raised, parents assured all that it never lacked; when needed it was simply found.

The previous question helped us to consider why there are fewer females in the labor force. Right now it is chiefly the women's role to bear and rear children. It was felt that with the availability of quality (and with abuse so prevalent, quality is certainly an issue), child care lacking, it becomes very difficult for women not only to obtain the desired education, but also to enter the workforce. This last issue is also related. If females do not excell in mathematics after grade 12, then education in mathematics-intensive topics (such as computer science and engineering) would not obviously appeal to them. But let's step back to the cause, and the discussion will end in a query: Is there a discrimination in the upper-level education system against females learning mathematics?

A general wrap-up cited that discrimination is a problem, and obviously by the first question posed, we must create an awareness of it. If a problem is recognised, it can be solved.

Solutions as evidenced by the panel discussion were as follows:

- We must bring about a conditioning (social, educational and mental) that accomodates individualness rather than discrimination by sex.
- We as individuals can affect change by:
    - our parenting
    - our educating
    - our choice of education for our children and involvement in its administration
    - obtaining and proliferating ope-mindedness in the workforce
    - actively seeking quality child care from the government and industry.

LIST OF DELEGATES

Dr. Nilsen Altintas, Chemical Engineering Dept., Marmara Scientific and Industrial Research Institute, P.O.Box 21, Gebze Kocaeli, Turkey.

Dr. Sabri Altintas, Mechanical Engineering Dept., Bogazici University, Istanbul, Turkey.

Dr. Jorge C. Alves, Universidade de Aveiro, Dept. de Electronica e Telecomunicacoes, 3800 Aveiro, Portugal.

Mr. B.G. Anderson, British Aerospace Dynamics Group plc., Six Hills Way, Stevenage, Herts SG1 2DA, U.K.

Mr. Harun Artuner Hacettepe University, Dept. of Computer Science and Engineering, Beytepe, Ankara, Turkey.

Dr. Harry Ascher, Naval Research Laboratory, Code 1206, Washington, D.C. 20375, U.S.A.

Dr. Edward Bedrosian, The Rand Corporation, 1700 Main Street, Santa Monica, CA 90406, U.S.A.

Dr. Anthony Bendell, Head of Dept. of Mathematics, Statistics and Operational Research, Trent Polytechnics, Burton Street, Nottingham, NG1 4BU, U.K.

Mr. Julio J. Berrocal, ETSI Telecomunicacion, Dpto. Comunicacion de Datos, Ciudad Universitaria S/N, 28040 Madrid, Spain.

Dr. Bharat Bhargava, Detp. of Computer Sciences, Purdue University, Computer Science Building, West Lafayette, IN 47907, U.S.A.

Ms. Alev Bingol, Neyzen Tevfik Sok No. 22/2, Maltepe-Ankara, Turkey.

Dr. Barry Boehm, TRW-DSG, 02-2304, 1 Space Park, Redondo Beach, CA 90278, U.S.A.

Mr. R.E. Booth, British Telecom, Scottish Mutual House, Lower Brook Street, Ipswich, Suffolk IP4 1AQ, U.K.

Ms, Sheila L. Brand, U.S. Dept. of Defence, Computer Security Center, 9800 Savage Road, Ft. George G. Meade, MD 20755-5000, U.S.A.

Mr. Elmer R. Branyan, General Electric Co., Space Systems Division, Ground Systems Programs Dept., P.O.Box 8048, Philadelphia, PA 19101, U.S.A.

Mr. John Bromell, Cambridge Consultants Ltd., Science Park, Milton Road, Cambridge CB4 4DW, U.K.

Mr. P.Y. Chan, Centre for Software Reliability, The City University, Northampton Square, London EC1V 0HB, U.K.

Mr. B. Chatlers, International Computers Ltd., Wenlock Way, West Gorton, Manchester M12 5DR, U.K.

Mr. Wei Chen, Dept. of Electrical Engineering, University of Edinburgh, The King's Building, Mayfield Road, Edinburgh EH9 3JL, U.K.

Ms. Judith Clapp, The MITRE Corporation, Bedford, MA 01730, U.S.A.

Mr. F.P. Coakley, Dept. of Electronic & Electrical Engineering, University of Surrey, Guildford, Surrey GU2 5HX, U.K.

Ms. Donna Cohen, 11/9 Piyade Sokak, Cankaya, Ankara, Turkey.

Mr. T. Cozens, Borroughs Machines Ltd., Hunslow Road, Feltham, TW14 9AE, U.K.

Dr. Larry H. Crow, AT&T Bell Laboratories, Undersea Systems Developemnt Laboratory, Whippany Road, Whippany, N.J. 07981, U.S.A.

Dr. Bill Curtis, B644 Ranch Creek, Austin, Texas 78732, U.S.A.

Mr. Chris Dale, National Centre of Systems Reliability, UKAEA, Wigshaw Lane, Culcheth, Warrington WA3 4NE, U.K.

Mr. Donald W. Davies, 15 Hawkewood Road, Sudbury-on-Thames, Middlesex TW16 6HL. U.K.

Mr. Bernard De Neumann, GEC Research Laboratories, West Hanningfield Road, Great Baddow, Chelmsford, Essex CM2 8HN, U.K.

Prof. Hani J. Doss, Dept. of Statistics, Florida State University, Tallahassee, florida 32306, U.S.A.

Mr. Mike Drury, ICL (Group Quality), Cavendish Road, Stevenage, Herts SG1 2DY, U.K.

Mr. Michael Dyer, IBM Federal Systems Division, 6600 Rocledge Drive, Bethesda, MD 20718, U.S.A.

Prof. Dr. E.-H.T. El-Shirbeeny, School of Electrical Engineering, University of Technology, Baghdad, Iraq.

Prof. Dr. Bahri Ercan, Dept. of Electrical and Electronic Engineering, Hacettepe University, Beytepe-Ankara, Turkey.

Prof. Dr. Ahmet N. Eskicioglu, Computer Engineering Dept., Middle East Technical University, Ankara, Turkey.

Dr. Antonio Ferrari, Dept. Electronica, Universidade de Aveiro, 3800 Aveiro, Portugal.

Mr. John W. Finnegan, School of Engineering, University College, Galway, Ireland.

Prof. Gerhard Fischer, Dept. of Computer Science, Campus Box 430, University of Colorado, Boulder, CO 80309, U.S.A.

Ms. Gillian D. Frewin, Software Developemnt Support Systems Dept., Standard Telecommunication Laboratories Ltd., London Road, Harlow, Essex CM17 9NA, U.K.

Dr. James W. Gault, U.S. Army European Research Office, "Edison House", 223 Old Marelybone Road, London NW1 5TH, U.K.

Mr. M. Gibson, GEC Avionics, Airport Works, Rochester, Kent ME1 2XX, U.K.

Mr. Don Gill, GEC Research Laboratories, West Hanningfield Road, Great Baddow, Chelmsford, Essex CM2 8HN, U.K.

Mr. A.M. Gordon, Head of Software Quality Assurance, GEC Avionics, Basildon, Essex SS14 3EL, U.K.

Dr. Thomas R.G. Green, MRC Applied Psychology Unit, 15 Chaucer Road, Cambridge CB2 2EF, U.K.

Mr. H.R. Gumrukcu, Dept. of Computer Engineering, Middle East Technical University, Ankara, Turkey.

Mr. Mustafa Gunduzalp, Dokuz Eylul Universitesi, Elektrik-Elektronik Muhendisligi Bolumu, Bornova-Izmir, Turkey.

Mr. Norman Harris, British Aerospace plc., Dynamics Group, P.O.Box 19, Six Hills Way, Stevenage, Herts SG1 2DA, U.K.

Dr. Paul K. Harter, Dept. of Computer Science, University of Colorado, Boulder, CO 80303, U.S.A.

Dr. Dennis Heimbinger, Dept. of Computer Science, University of Colorado, Boulder, CO 80309, U.S.A.
Dr. D.J. Holding, 44 Midgley Drive, Four Oaks, Sutton Coalfield, West Midlands B74 2TW, U.K.
Mrs. Jan Honey, EASAMS Ltd., Lyon Way, Frimley Road, Camberley, Surrey GU16 5EX, U.K.
Dr. David Hutchens, Dept. of Computer Science, Clemson University, Nursing Building, Clemson, S.C. 29631, U.S.A.
Mrs. Eileen H.P. Jones, Software Productivity Research Inc., 34 Squirrel Hill Road, Acton, MA 01720, U.S.A.
Mr. T. Capers Jones, Software Productivity Research Inc., 34 Squirrel Hill Road, Acton, MA 01720, U.S.A.
Mr. Glenn A. Karpel, Software Sciences Ltd., Abbey House, 282/292 Farnborough Road, Farnborough, Hamps GU14 7NB, U.K.
Prof. Ali R. Kaylan, Dept. of Industrial Engineering, Bogazici University, Bebek-Istanbul, Turkey.
Dr. M.K. Khan, Dept. of Mathematical Science, Kent State University, Kent, Ohio 44242, U.S.A.
Prof. Dr. Ayse Kiper, Dept. of Computer Science, Middle East Technical University, Ankara, Turkey.
Dr. Peter Kubat, GTE Laboratories Inc., 40 Sylvan Road, Waltham, MA 02254, U.S.A.
Major Anthony L. Lake, 21 Stainswick Lane, Shrivenham, Swindon, Wilts. SN6 8DU, U.K.
Prof. Nancy G. Leveson, Information and Computer Science Dept., University of California, Irvine, CA 92717, U.S.A.
Prof. Bev Littlewood, Centre for Software Reliability, The City University, Northampton Square, London EC1V 0HB, U.K.
Mr. B.E. Luke, GEC Avionics, Basildon, Essex SS14 3EL, U.K.
Dr. Gerald R. McNichols, President, Management Consulting & Research Inc., 5113 Leesburg Pike, Suite 509, Falls Church, VA 22041, U.S.A.
Mr. Peter Mellor, Centre for Software Reliability, The City University, Northampton Square, London EC1V 0HB, U.K.
Dr. Jaroslaw Milewski, Institute of Informatics, Warsaw University, P.O.Box 1210, PL-00-901 Warsaw, Poland.
Mr. John Musa, Room 3A332, AT&T Bell Laboratories, Whippany, N.J. 07981, U.S.A.
Dr. R. Nagendra, School of Computer Science, 350 Victoria Street, Ryerson Polytechnical Institute, Toronto-Ontario, Canada M5B 2K3.
Dr. Ilham Or, Industrial Engineering Dept., Bogazici University, Bebek, Istanbul, Turkey.
Mr. Alvin B. Owens, Naval Research Laboratory, Code 2311, 435 Overlook Avenue, Washington, D.C. 20375, U.S.A.
Prof. L.F. Pau, Battelle Institute, 7 route Drize, CH-1227 Carouge, Switzerland.
Mr. Rob Rambo, General Electric Co., Space Systems Division, P.O.Box 8048/10C52, Philadelphia, PA 19101, U.S.A.

Prof. Brian Randell, Computing Laboratory, University of Newcastle upon Tyne, Claremont Tower, Claremont Road, Newcastle upon Tyne, NE1 7RU, U.K.
Dr. Ditlef Rauer, MBB/ERNO Raumfahrttechnik GmbH, Huenefelstrasse 1-5, Abt. RB 022, D-2800 Bremen, Federal Republic of Germany.

Major J.W. Rawlings, Chief, Information Sciences & Manufacturing Technologies, European Office of Aerospace Research & Development, 223/231 Old Marelybone Road, London NW1 5TH, U.K.
Mr. Baruch Revsin, Armament Development Authority, Dept. 66, P.O.B. 2250, Haifa 31021, Israel.
Mr. Juan A. Saras, ETSI Telecomunicacion, Dpto. Comunicacion de Datas, Ciudad Universitaria S/N, 28040 Madrid, Spain.
Mr. Patrick Saunier, CISMA, 10-12 avenue de l'Europe, BP 44, 78140 Velizy, France.
Mr. M. Taylan Sekerci, Electronics Dept., Hacettepe University, Beytepe-Ankara, Turkey.
Dr. Richard W. Selby Jr., Dept. of Computer Science, University of Maryland, College Park, MD 20442, U.S.A.
Ms. Bilgehan Sendal, Turkish Airlines, Electronic Data Processing Center, Yesilkoy-Havaalani, Istanbul, Turkey.
Mr. J.K. Skwirzynski, GEC Research Laboratory, West Hanningfield Road, Great Baddow, Chelmsford, Essex CM2 8HN, U.K.
Dr. Gary L. Sorrell, Management Consulting & Research Inc., 5113 Leesburg Pike, Suite 509, Falls Church, VA 22041, U.S.A.
Mr. Bolek I. Stuart, 56 Gloucester Avenue, Chelmsford, Essex CM2 9LE, U.K.
Prof. Dr. F.L. Stumpers, Elzentlaan 11, Eindhoven 5611 LG, The Netherlands.
Prof. Alvin Surkan, Dept. of Computer Science, Ferguson 115, University of Nebraska, Lincoln, NE 68588, U.S.A.
Mr. G.E. Thomas, Dept. of Mathematical Sciences, University of Dundee, Dundee DD1 4HN, U.K.
Dr. Hubert Trzaska, Institute of Telecommunications and Accoustics, University of Wroclaw, Wyspianskiego 27, 50370 Wroclaw, Poland.
Prof. Rein Turn, Dept. of Computer Science, California State University, Northridge, 18111 Nordhoff Street, Northridge, CA 91330, U.S.A.
Dr. Mazhar Unsal, Dept. of Mechanical Engineering, METU Gazantep Campus, Box: 300, Gazantep, Turkey.
Dr. Pedro Veiga, Rua Alves Redol 9-3, 1000 Lisboa, Portugal.
Prof. Claude Vibet, Laboratoire de Robotique Industrielle, 22 Allee J. Rostand, 91011 Evry Cedex, France.
Mr. M.I. Wardlaw, SES 9.1, British Telecom, St. Vincent House, 1 Cutler Street, Ipswich, Suffolk, U.K.
Mr. Ian A. Watson, Systems Reliability Service, National Centre for Systems Reliability, UKAEA, Wigshaw Lane, Culcheth, Warrington WA3 4NE, U.K.

Dr. G.G. Weber, Kernforschungszentrum Karlsruhe, P.O. Box 3640, D-7500 Karlsruhe, Federal Republic of Germany.
Mr. Alan A. Wingrove, MOD(PE), AW Dept., T 70 Building, Royal Aircraft Establishment, Farnborough, Hants GU14 6TD, U.K.
Mr. M. Woodman, Computing Discipline, Faculty of Mathematics, The Open University, Walton Hall, Milton Keynes, MK7 6AA, U.K.
Dr. Erdem Yazgan, Electric & Electronic Engineering Dept., Hacettepe University, Beytepe-Ankara, Turkey.
Mr. Ersin Yigiter, Biomedical Engineering Dept., University of Miami, Box 248294, Coral Gables, Florida 33124, U.S.A.

NATO ASI Series F

Vol. 1: Issues in Acoustic Signal – Image Processing and Recognition. Edited by C. H. Chen. VIII, 333 pages. 1983.

Vol. 2: Image Sequence Processing and Dynamic Scene Analysis. Edited by T. S. Huang. IX, 749 pages. 1983.

Vol. 3: Electronic Systems Effectiveness and Life Cycle Costing. Edited by J. K. Skwirzynski. XVII, 732 pages. 1983.

Vol. 4: Pictorial Data Analysis. Edited by R. M. Haralick. VIII, 468 pages. 1983.

Vol. 5: International Calibration Study of Traffic Conflict Techniques. Edited by E. Asmussen. VII, 229 pages. 1984.

Vol. 6: Information Technology and the Computer Network. Edited by K. G. Beauchamp. VIII, 271 pages. 1984.

Vol. 7: High-Speed Computation. Edited by J. S. Kowalik. IX, 441 pages. 1984.

Vol. 8: Program Transformation and Programming Environments. Report on an Workshop directed by F. L. Bauer and H. Remus. Edited by P. Pepper. XIV, 378 pages. 1984.

Vol. 9: Computer Aided Analysis and Optimization of Mechanical System Dynamics. Edited by E. J. Haug. XXII, 700 pages. 1984.

Vol. 10: Simulation and Model-Based Methodologies: An Integrative View. Edited by T. I. Ören, B. P. Zeigler, M. S. Elzas. XIII, 651 pages. 1984.

Vol. 11: Robotics and Artificial Intelligence. Edited by M. Brady, L. A. Gerhardt, H. F. Davidson. XVII, 693 pages. 1984.

Vol. 12: Combinatorial Algorithms on Words. Edited by A. Apostolico, Z. Galil. VIII, 361 pages. 1985.

Vol. 13: Logics and Models of Concurrent Systems. Edited by K. R. Apt. VIII, 498 pages. 1985.

Vol. 14: Control Flow and Data Flow: Concepts of Distributed Programming. Edited by M. Broy. VIII, 525 pages. 1985.

Vol. 15: Computational Mathematical Programming. Edited by K. Schittkowski. VIII, 451 pages. 1985.

Vol. 16: New Systems and Architectures for Automatic Speech Recognition and Synthesis. Edited by R. De Mori, C.Y. Suen. XIII, 630 pages. 1985.

Vol. 17: Fundamental Algorithms for Computer Graphics. Edited by R.A. Earnshaw. XVI, 1042 pages. 1985.

Vol. 18: Computer Architectures for Spatially Distributed Data. Edited by H. Freeman and G. G. Pieroni. VIII, 391 pages. 1985.

Vol. 19: Pictorial Information Systems in Medicine. Edited by K. H. Höhne. XII, 525 pages. 1986.

Vol. 20: Disordered Systems and Biological Organization. Edited by E. Bienenstock, F. Fogelman Soulié, G. Weisbuch. XXI, 405 pages. 1986.

Vol. 21: Intelligent Decision Support in Process Environments. Edited by E. Hollnagel, G. Mancini, D.D. Woods. XV, 524 pages. 1986.

Vol. 22: Software System Design Methods. The Challenge of Advanced Computing Technology. Edited by J.K. Skwirzynski. XIII, 747 pages. 1986.

CPSIA information can be obtained at www.ICGtesting.com
Printed in the USA
LVOW11s0831040813

346172LV00009B/379/P

9 783642 828485